U.S. Forces
Travel & Transfer Guide U.S.A.
& Caribbean Areas

L. Ann Crawford
Publisher, Military Living Publications, and
Vice-President, Military Marketing Services, Inc.

William Roy Crawford, Sr., Ph.D.
President, Military Living Publications, and
Military Marketing Services, Inc.

Editor: Donna L. Russell

Cover Design: L. Ann Crawford

Vice President - Marketing: R.J. Crawford
Chief of Staff - Nigel Fellers

Office Staff:
Timothy Brown, TSgt, USAF (Ret.), Eula Mae Brownlee, Maureen Fleegal, Irene Kearney, Lourdes Medina, Chris Tschantz, Joel Thomas, MSG, USA (Ret), Larry Williamson.

Military Living Publications
P. O. Box 2347
Falls Church, Virginia 22042-0347
TEL: (703) 237-0203
FAX: (703) 237-2233

NOTICE

The information in this book has been compiled and edited either from the activity/installation listed, its superior headquarters, or from other sources that may or may not be noted by the authors. Information about the facilities listed, including contact phone numbers and rate structures, could change. This book should be used as a guide to the listed facilities with this understanding. Please forward any corrections or additions to: **Military Living Publications, P. O. Box 2347, Falls Church, Virginia 22042-0347.**

This directory is published by Military Marketing Services, Inc., a private business in no way connected with the U.S. Federal or any other government. This book is copyrighted by L. Ann and William Roy Crawford, Sr. Opinions expressed by the publisher and authors of this book are their own and are not to be considered an official expression by any government agency or official.

The information and statements contained in this directory have been compiled from sources believed to be reliable and to represent the best current opinion on the subject. No warranty, guarantee, or representation is made by Military Marketing Services, Inc., as to the absolute correctness or sufficiency of any representation contained in this or other publications and we can assume no responsibility.

Copyright 1996
L. Ann and William "Roy" Crawford
MILITARY MARKETING SERVICES, INC.,
(T/A MILITARY LIVING PUBLICATIONS)
First Printing - January 1996

All rights reserved under International and Pan-American copyright conventions. No part of this book may be reproduced in any form without permission in writing from the publisher, except by a reviewer who wishes to quote briefly from listings in connection with a review written for inclusion in a magazine or newspaper, with source credit to **MILITARY LIVING'S** *US FORCES TRAVEL & TRANSFER GUIDE U.S.A. AND CARIBBEAN AREAS*. A copy of the review, when published, should be sent to Military Living Publications, P. O. Box 2347, Falls Church, Virginia 22042-0347.

Library of Congress Cataloging-in-Publication Data

Crawford, Ann Caddell.
    U.S. forces travel & transfer guide. U.S.A. & Caribbean areas / L. Ann Crawford, William Roy Crawford, Sr. ; editors, Leon G. Russ & Donna L. Russell.
    p. cm.
  ISBN 0-914862-60X
  1. Military bases, American--Directories. 2. Soldiers--United States--Recreation. 3. Military dependents--United States--Recreation. I. Crawford, William Roy, 1932- . II. Russ, Leon G. III. Russell, Donna L. Title.
UA26.A2C73   1996
355.7'0973--dc20   95-63
                                                               CIP

ISBN 0-914862-60-X

HOW TO USE THIS DIRECTORY

Each listing has similar information, listed in the following order:

Name of Installation (AL01R2)
Street/PO Box (if required)
City/APO/FPO, State, ZIP Code

LOCATION IDENTIFIER: Example (AL01R2). The first two characters (letters) are Country/State abbreviations used in Military Living's books (Appendix A). The next two characters are random numbers (00-99) assigned to a specific location. The fifth character is an R indicating region and the sixth character is the region number.

TELEPHONE NUMBER INFORMATION: C- This is the commercial telephone service for the installation's main or information/operator assistance number, the designation has also been used for other commercial numbers in this directory. Within the U.S. Area Code System, the first three digits are the area code. For foreign country locations, we have provided full telephone numbers from the U.S. and in-country. The first two digits, after direct dial long distance, are the Country Code (consult your local directory or operator for specific dialing instructions). The next three digits are the area telephone exchange/switch number. For foreign countries, the exchange number can be either fewer or more digits than in the U.S. system. The last four digits are usually the information or operator assistance number.

D- This is the Department of Defense, worldwide, Defense Switched Network (DSN). We have, at the request of our readers, included the DSN prefix with most numbers in each listing. In most cases, the number given is for information/operator assistance. *Note: The 312 area code on defense number is for calls from outside North America. When calling within North America the 312 is not needed.*

FTS: This is the Federal Telephone System. The number given is for information/operator assistance. On smaller installations the information/operator assistance number may be the contact number for Temporary Military Lodging.

LOCATION: Specific driving instructions to the installation from local major cities, interstate highways and routes are given. More than one routing may be provided. **USMRA:** is **MILITARY LIVING'S "United States Military Road Atlas"** reference to the location. **NMC:** is the nearest major city. The distance and direction from the installation to the NMC are given.

GENERAL: Major activities, organizations, military units and special information concerning the installation, if any, are provided in this section.

TEMPORARY MILITARY LODGING: The billeting/lodging office or check-in point, location and complete telephone contact/reservation numbers are provided. Hours of operation are noted. Category of persons accommodated is specified and special contact numbers for DV/VIP (Distinguished Visitor/Very Important Person, both officer and enlisted grades) are provided. **Detailed information at over 425 installations worldwide is contained in Military**

Living's all-time best-selling title, *Temporary Military Lodging Around the World*. See coupons in this book for ordering information.

LOGISTICAL SUPPORT: The scope of support facilities available at the installation is specified and the telephone for the facility is provided. Space limitations preclude listing all support numbers; however, the telephone numbers for facilities not listed are available through the information operator number in each listing.

HEALTH & WELFARE: The installation or nearest medical emergency information and/or appointment service numbers are listed. The installation or servicing medical inpatient numbers are provided as well. Chaplain support and chapel service contact numbers are specified.

RECREATION: The contact telephone number for most rest, recreation, athletic facilities, and opportunities are given for each installation. Information about camping and recreation areas on the installation, controlled by the installation, or near the installation is provided. **Complete camping and recreation area details are contained in** *Military Living's Military RV, Camping and Rec Areas Around the World*. **See coupons in this book for ordering information.**

SPACE-A: The location, hours of operation, contact telephone numbers and flight-location opportunities are specified for departure locations on each installation. The numbers provided are the Space-A information numbers at specified departure locations. If no Space-A is available at the given installation, the name of the nearest installation with Space-A opportunities is provided. **Full Space-A information such as arrival locations, aircraft used, schedules, terminal facilities, eligibility, rules, travel documents needed and more, are all contained in Military Living's best-selling book,** *Military Space-A Air Opportunities Around the World*. **See coupons in this book for ordering information.**

ATTRACTIONS: This section provides information to the traveler about attractions on the installation or in the surrounding area.

Please review the appendices for abbreviations used in this book and for other helpful information. **Address your questions regarding this title or other Military Living books to: Military Living Publications, P.O. Box 2347, Falls Church, Virginia 22042-0347. ATTN: Ann or Roy Crawford. You may telephone us at 703-237-0203, FAX 703-237-2233. No collect calls accepted.**

UNITED STATES

LOCATION IDENTIFIER	INSTALLATION	PAGE

NOTE: Bases scheduled for closure are designated by a date in parenthesis.

ALABAMA

AL13R2	Anniston Army Depot	1
AL15R2	Birmingham Air National Guard Base	1
AL01R2	Fort McClellan	2
AL02R2	Fort Rucker	3
AL04R2	Gunter Annex to Maxwell Air Force Base	4
AL03R2	Maxwell Air Force Base	5
AL08R2	Mobile Coast Guard Aviation Training Center	6
AL16R2	Mobile Coast Guard Group	6
AL06R2	Redstone Arsenal	7

ALASKA

AK04R5	Adak Naval Air Facility	9
AK18R5	Clear Air Station	9
AK15R5	Eielson Air Force Base	10
AK09R5	Elmendorf Air Force Base	11
AK10R5	Fort Greely	12
AK03R5	Fort Richardson	13
AK07R5	Fort Wainwright	14
AK19R5	Juneau Coast Guard Air Station	15
AK21R5	Ketchikan Coast Guard Base	15
AK08R5	Kodiak Coast Guard Support Center	16
AK24R5	Kulis Air National Guard Base	16
AK25R5	Sitka Coast Guard Air Station	17

ARIZONA

AZ01R4	Davis-Monthan Air Force Base	19
AZ02R4	Fort Huachuca	19
AZ16R4	Gila Bend Air Force Auxiliary Field	20
AZ03R4	Luke Air Force Base	21
AZ05R4	Yuma Army Proving Ground	22
AZ04R4	Yuma Marine Corps Air Station	23

Other Installations in Arizona

AZ17R4	Holbrook Radar Bomb Scoring Site	23
AZ18R4	Sky Harbor Air National Guard Base	23

v

ARKANSAS

AR07R2	Camp Joseph T. Robinson	24
AR04R2	Fort Chaffee (October 1997)	24
AR02R2	Little Rock Air Force Base	25
AR03R2	Pine Bluff Arsenal	26

CALIFORNIA

CA28R4	Alameda Coast Guard Support Center	27
CA33R4	Alameda Naval Air Station (March 1997)	27
CA39R4	Armed Forces Reserve Center Los Alamitos/CA ARNG	28
CA13R4	Barstow Marine Corps Logistics Base	29
CA47R4	Beale Air Force Base	30
CA97R4	Camp Parks/Parks Reserve Forces Training Area	30
CA30R4	Camp Pendleton Marine Corps Base	31
CA98R4	Camp Roberts	32
CA83R4	Camp San Luis Obispo	32
CA34R4	China Lake Naval Air Warfare Systems Center, Weapons Division	33
CA58R4	Concord Naval Weapons Station	34
CA38R4	Coronado Naval Amphibious Base	35
CA52R4	Defense Distribution Region West-Sharpe Site	35
CA48R4	Edwards Air Force Base	36
CA09R4	El Centro Naval Air Facility	37
CA22R4	El Toro Marine Corps Air Station (December 1999)	38
CA37R4	Fort Hunter Liggett	39
CA01R4	Fort Irwin National Training Center	39
CA46R4	Fort MacArthur	40
CA100R4	Imperial Beach Outlying Landing Field	41
CA06R4	Lemoore Naval Air Station	41
CA55R4	Long Beach Naval Shipyard (September 1997)	42
CA75R4	Los Angeles Air Force Base	43
CA20R4	Marines' Memorial Club	43
CA35R4	McClellan Air Force Base	44
CA14R4	Miramar Naval Air Station	45
CA15R4	Moffett Federal Airfield NASA/AMES	46
CA16R4	Monterey Naval Postgraduate School	47
CA43R4	North Island Naval Air Station	48
CA89R4	Novato-Department of Defense Housing Facility (Hamilton NS)	49
CA18R4	Oakland Army Base	49
CA42R4	Oakland Fleet & Industrial Supply Center (February 1998)	50
CA96R4	Onizuka Air Station	51
CA23R4	Petaluma Coast Guard Training Center	52
CA40R4	Point Mugu Naval Air Warfare Center, Weapons Division	52
CA32R4	Port Hueneme Naval Construction Battalion Center	53
CA74R4	Presidio of Monterey	54
CA36R4	Presidio of Monterey Annex	55
CA53R4	San Clemente Island Naval Auxiliary Landing Field	55
CA77R4	San Diego Coast Guard Air Station	56

CALIFORNIA, continued

CA57R4	San Diego Marine Corps Recruit Depot	56
CA59R4	San Diego Naval Medical Center	57
CA26R4	San Diego Naval Station	58
CA79R4	San Diego Naval Submarine Base	58
CA54R4	San Diego Naval Training Center (April 1997)	59
CA25R4	San Pedro Coast Guard Support Center	60
CA17R4	Santa Clara Naval Air Reserve Station	61
CA80R4	Seal Beach Naval Weapons Station	61
CA44R4	Sierra Army Depot	62
CA51R4	Stockton Naval Communications Station	63
CA50R4	Travis Air Force Base	63
CA21R4	Treasure Island Naval Station (September 1997)	64
CA86R4	Tustin Marine Corps Air Station (December 1997)	65
CA27R4	Twentynine Palms Marine Corps Air/Ground Combat Center	65
CA29R4	Vandenberg Air Force Base	66

Other Installations in California

CA93R4	Channel Islands Air National Guard Station	67
CA02R4	Humboldt Bay Coast Guard Group	67
CA24R4	Lake Tahoe Coast Guard Station	67
CA19R4	Presidio of San Francisco	67
CA08R4	March Air Force Base	67
CA90R4	San Diego Fleet Combat Training Center Pacific	67
CA92R4	Tracy Defense Depot Activity	67

COLORADO

CO11R3	Buckley Air National Guard Base	68
CO13R3	Falcon Air Force Base	68
CO10R3	Fitzsimons Army Medical Center	69
CO02R3	Fort Carson	70
CO06R3	Peterson Air Force Base	71
CO03R3	Pueblo Depot Activity	71
CO07R3	United States Air Force Academy	72

Other Installations in Colorado

CO12R3	Cheyenne Mountain Air Force Base	73
CO14R3	La Junta Air Force Station (July 1996)	73

CONNECTICUT

CT03R1	Bradley Air National Guard Base	74
CT04R1	Long Island Sound Coast Guard Group	74
CT01R1	New London Naval Submarine Base	75
CT02R1	United States Coast Guard Academy	76

Other Installations in Connecticut

CT05R1	Camp Rowland Exchange	76
CT06R1	West Hartford U.S. Army Reserve	76

DELAWARE

DE01R1	Dover Air Force Base	77
DE02R1	New Castle County Airport/Delaware Air National Guard	78

DISTRICT OF COLUMBIA

DC02R1	Anacostia Naval Station	79
DC01R1	Bolling Air Force Base	79
DC05R1	Fort Lesley J. McNair	80
DC09R1	Marine Barracks	81
DC06R1	USO World Headquarters	82
DC03R1	Walter Reed Army Medical Center	82
DC07R1	Washington Naval Security Station	83
DC04R1	Washington Navy Yard	84

Other Installations in District of Columbia

DC11R1	Armed Forces Hostess Association	84
DC08R1	U.S. Coast Guard Headquarters	84
DC10R1	U.S. Soldiers' and Airmen's Home	84

FLORIDA

FL42R1	Camp Blanding	85
FL06R1	Cecil Field Naval Air Station (September 1998)	85
FL32R1	Clearwater Coast Guard Air Station	86
FL19R1	Corry Station Naval Technical Training Center	87
FL27R1	Eglin Air Force Base	88
FL17R1	Homestead Air Reserve Base	88
FL18R1	Hurlburt Field	89
FL08R1	Jacksonville Naval Air Station	90
FL15R1	Key West Naval Air Station	91
FL02R1	MacDill Air Force Base	91
FL13R1	Mayport Naval Station	92
FL31R1	Miami Coast Guard Air Station	93
FL30R1	Miami Coast Guard Base	94
FL11R1	Orlando Naval Training Center (December 1998)	94
FL35R1	Panama City Coastal Systems Station, NSWC	95
FL03R1	Patrick Air Force Base/Cape Canaveral Air Station	96
FL14R1	Pensacola Naval Air Station	97
FL20R1	Pensacola Naval Hospital	98
FL33R1	St. Petersburg Coast Guard Group/Station	98
FL34R1	Saufley Field	99

viii

FLORIDA, continued

FL49R1	Shades of Green on Walt Disney World Resort	100
FL04R1	Tyndall Air Force Base	101
FL05R1	Whiting Field Naval Air Station	101

Other Installations in Florida

FL45R1	Canaveral Air Force Station	102
FL46R1	Cortez U.S. Coast Guard Station	102
FL47R1	Fort Myers Beach Coast Guard Station	102
FL48R1	Jupiter U.S. Coast Guard Station	102
FL44R1	Mayport Coast Guard Base	102
FL50R1	New Smyrna Beach Coast Guard Station	102
FL43R1	Panama City Coast Guard Station	102

GEORGIA

GA17R1	Albany Marine Corps Logistics Base	103
GA12R1	Athens Naval Supply Corps School	103
GA16R1	Atlanta Naval Air Station	104
GA23R1	Camp Frank D. Merrill	105
GA13R1	Dobbins Air Reserve Base	105
GA11R1	Fort Benning	106
GA21R1	Fort Gillem	107
GA09R1	Fort Gordon, Headquarters U.S. Army Signal Center	108
GA08R1	Fort McPherson	109
GA15R1	Fort Stewart	109
GA10R1	Hunter Army Airfield	110
GA03R1	Kings Bay Naval Submarine Base	111
GA02R1	Moody Air Force Base	112
GA14R1	Robins Air Force Base	113

HAWAII

HI01R6	Barbers Point Naval Air Station (July 1997)	115
HI22R6	Barking Sands Pacific Missile Range Facility	116
HI18R6	Bellows Air Force Station	116
HI15R6	Camp H.M. Smith Marine Corps Base	117
HI08R6	Fort DeRussy Hale Koa Hotel AFRC	118
HI09R6	Fort Shafter	119
HI11R6	Hickam Air Force Base	119
HI21R6	Honolulu Coast Guard Base and Coast Guard Housing Red Hill	120
HI12R6	Kaneohe Marine Corps Base	121
HI17R6	Kilauea Military Camp AFRC	122
HI23R6	Lualualei Naval Magazine	122
HI19R6	Pearl Harbor Naval Base	123
HI20R6	Pearl Harbor Naval Station	124
HI13R6	Schofield Barracks	125

HAWAII, continued

HI03R6	Tripler Medical Center	125
HI16R6	Wahiawa NCTAMS EASTPAC	126
HI05R6	Waianae Army Recreation Center	127
HI14R6	Wheeler Army Airfield	128

Other Installations in Hawaii

HI04R6	Aliamanu Military Reservation	128
HI24R6	Barbers Point Coast Guard Air Station	128
HI02R6	Fort Ruger, Cannon Club	128
HI06R6	Hilo Big Island Exchange	128
HI07R6	Maui Exchange	128

IDAHO

ID04R4	Gowen Field	129
ID01R4	Mountain Home Air Force Base	129

ILLINOIS

IL04R2	Charles Melvin Price Support Center	131
IL07R2	Great Lakes Naval Training Center	131
IL11R2	O'Hare Air Reserve Station (July 1997)	132
IL08R2	Rock Island Arsenal	133
IL02R2	Scott Air Force Base	134

Other Installations in Illinois

IL12R2	Capital Airport Air National Guard Base	134

INDIANA

IN05R2	Camp Atterbury	135
IN03R2	Crane Division Naval Surface Warfare Center	135

Other Installations in Indiana

IN02R2	Fort Benjamin Harrison	136
IN01R2	Grissom Air Reserve Base	136
IN08R2	Stout Field	136

IOWA

IA02R2	Camp Dodge	137

Other Installations in Iowa

IA01R2	Des Moines Exchange	137

Other Installations in Iowa, continued

IA03R2	Sioux City Gateway Airport	137

KANSAS

KS01R3	Forbes Field	138
KS04R3	Fort Leavenworth	138
KS02R3	Fort Riley	139
KS03R3	McConnell Air Force Base	140

KENTUCKY

KY02R2	Fort Campbell	142
KY01R2	Fort Knox	143

Other Installations in Kentucky

KY05R2	Standiford Field Air National Guard Base	143

LOUISIANA

LA01R2	Barksdale Air Force Base	144
LA12R2	Camp Beauregard	145
LA07R2	Fort Polk/Joint Readiness Training Center	145
LA13R2	Jackson Barracks	146
LA10R2	New Orleans Coast Guard Support Center	146
LA11R2	New Orleans Naval Air Station/Joint Reserve Base	147
LA06R2	New Orleans Naval Support Activity	148

MAINE

ME10R1	Bangor Air National Guard Base/Bangor IAP	149
ME07R1	Brunswick Naval Air Station	149
ME08R1	Cutler Naval Computer and Telecommunications Station	150
ME11R1	South Portland Coast Guard Base	151
ME09R1	Winter Harbor Naval Security Group Activity	151

Other Installations in Maine

ME12R1	Camp Keyes	152
ME14R1	Rockland Coast Guard Station	152
ME15R1	Southwest Harbor Coast Guard Group	152

MARYLAND

MD11R1	Aberdeen Proving Ground	153
MD02R1	Andrews Air Force Base	154
MD01R1	Curtis Bay Coast Guard Yard	155

MARYLAND, continued

MD07R1	Fort Detrick	155
MD08R1	Fort George G. Meade	156
MD13R1	Fort Ritchie	158
MD04R1	Indian Head Naval Surface Warfare Center	159
MD06R1	National Naval Medical Center	159
MD09R1	Patuxent River Naval Air Station	160
MD05R1	Solomons Navy Recreation Center	161
MD10R1	United States Naval Academy Annapolis Naval Station	162

Other Installations in Maryland

MD15R1	Cheltenham Naval Communications Station	163
MD21R1	Martin State Airport/Warfield Air National Guard	163

MASSACHUSETTS

MA12R1	Boston Coast Guard Support Center	164
MA06R1	Hanscom Air Force Base	164
MA11R1	Natick Soldier Systems Command	165
MA07R1	Otis Air National Guard Base	166
MA05R1	South Weymouth Naval Air Station (September 1996)	167
MA03R1	Westover Air Reserve Base	168

Other Installations in Massachusetts

MA14R1	Camp Edwards	168
MA15R1	Nantucket Coast Guard LORAIN Station	168

MICHIGAN

MI16R2	Alpena Combat Readiness Training Center	169
MI10R2	Camp Grayling Training Site	169
MI13R2	Detroit Coast Guard Group	170
MI06R2	Grand Haven Coast Guard Group	170
MI15R2	Sault Ste. Marie Coast Guard Group	171
MI01R2	Selfridge Air National Guard Base	172
MI07R2	Traverse City Coast Guard Air Station	172

Other Installations in Michigan

MI11R2	Battlecreek Air National Guard Base	173
MI09R2	Detroit Arsenal	173

MINNESOTA

MN02R2	Camp Ripley	174
MN01R2	Minneapolis-St. Paul International Airport ARS	174

Other Installations in Minnesota

MN03R2	Duluth Air National Guard Base	175

MISSISSIPPI

MS07R2	Camp Shelby Training Site	176
MS01R2	Columbus Air Force Base	176
MS03R2	Gulfport Naval Construction Battalion Center	177
MS09R2	Jackson International Airport/Thompson Field	178
MS02R2	Keesler Air Force Base	179
MS05R2	Key Field Air National Guard Base	179
MS04R2	Meridian Naval Air Station	180
MS06R2	Pascagoula Naval Station	181
MS10R2	Waterways Experiment Station	181

Other Installations in Mississippi

MS08R2	Armed Forces Retirement Home (U.S. Naval Home Facility)	182
MS11R2	Gulfport-Biloxi Regional Airport/ANGB	182
MS12R2	Vicksburg Municipal Airport	182

MISSOURI

MO03R2	Fort Leonard Wood	183
MO02R2	Marine Corps Activities at Richards-Gebaur Airport	184
MO05R2	St. Louis Coast Guard Base	184
MO04R2	Whiteman Air Force Base	185

Other Installations in Missouri

MO06R2	Lambert-St Louis International Airport	186
MO07R2	Rosecrans Memorial Airport/ANG	186
MO10R2	Scott-Page Exchange	186
MO08R2	St Louis Post Exchange	186

MONTANA

MT03R3	Malmstrom Air Force Base	187
MT06R3	Montana Air National Guard Base	188

Other Installations in Montana

MT07R3	Fort Harrison Site	188

NEBRASKA

NE05R3	Nebraska Air National Guard Base	189
NE02R3	Offutt Air Force Base	189

xiii

NEBRASKA, continued

Other Installations in Nebraska

NE03R3	Camp Ashland	190

NEVADA

NV02R4	Fallon Naval Air Station	191
NV03R4	Indian Springs Air Force Auxiliary Field	191
NV01R4	Nellis Air Force Base	192
NV06R4	Nevada Air National Guard Base	193

NEW HAMPSHIRE

NH04R1	New Boston Air Station	194
NH01R1	Pease Air National Guard Base	194
NH02R1	Portsmouth Naval Shipyard	195

NEW JERSEY

NJ10R1	Bayonne Military Ocean Terminal	196
NJ13R1	Cape May Coast Guard Training Center	196
NJ11R1	Earle Naval Weapons Station	197
NJ03R1	Fort Dix Army Garrison	198
NJ05R1	Fort Monmouth	199
NJ08R1	Lakehurst Naval Air Warfare Center	200
NJ09R1	McGuire Air Force Base	200
NJ01R1	Picatinny Arsenal (ARDEC)	201

Other Installations in New Jersey

NJ16R1	Atlantic City International Airport	202
NJ19R1	Camp Pedricktown Support Installation Exchange	202
NJ18R1	Sea Girt National Guard Exchange	202

NEW MEXICO

NM02R3	Cannon Air Force Base	203
NM05R3	Holloman Air Force Base	203
NM03R3	Kirtland Air Force Base	204
NM04R3	White Sands Missile Range	205

NEW YORK

NY18R1	Brooklyn Coast Guard Air Station	207
NY06R1	Fort Drum	207
NY02R1	Fort Hamilton	208
NY20R1	Fort Totten	209

NEW YORK, continued

NY21R1	Mitchell Complex	210
NY01R1	New York Coast Guard Support Center	210
NY12R1	Niagara Falls Air Reserve Station	211
NY03R1	Seneca Army Depot Activity	212
NY17R1	Soldiers', Sailors', and Airmen's Club	212
NY25R1	Suffolk County Air National Guard Base/Francis Gabreski ANGS	213
NY09R1	Stewart Army Subpost	214
NY16R1	United States Military Academy, West Point	214
NY19R1	Watervliet Arsenal	215

Other Installations in New York

NY27R1	Buffalo Coast Guard Group	216
NY26R1	Camp Smith	216
NY07R1	Gateway National Park	216
NY11R1	Griffiss Airfield	216
NY10R1	Hancock Field ANGB	216
NY31R1	Roslyn Air National Guard Station	216
NY23R1	Schenectady County Airport/NGB/Scotia NAU	216
NY30R1	Shinnecock Coast Guard Station	216
NY22R1	United States Merchant Marine Academy	216

NORTH CAROLINA

NC10R1	Camp Lejeune Marine Corps Base	217
NC09R1	Cape Hatteras Coast Guard Group	218
NC20R1	Charlotte Douglas IAP/NCANGB	218
NC02R1	Cherry Point Marine Corps Air Station	219
NC03R1	Elizabeth City Coast Guard Support Center	220
NC05R1	Fort Bragg	220
NC18R1	Fort Macon Coast Guard Group	221
NC06R1	New River Marine Corps Air Station	222
NC01R1	Pope Air Force Base	223
NC11R1	Seymour Johnson Air Force Base	223

NORTH DAKOTA

ND03R3	Camp Gilbert C. Grafton Army National Guard Training Site	225
ND08R3	Cavalier Air Station	225
ND04R3	Grand Forks Air Force Base	226
ND02R3	Minot Air Force Base	227

Other Installations in North Dakota

ND06R3	Fraine Barracks NGHQ	228
ND07R3	Hector Field ANGB	228
ND09R3	Raymond J. Bohn Armory (ND Army National Guard Headquarters)	228

xv

NORTH DAKOTA, continued

ND02R3   Rickenbacker Air National Guard Base 228

OHIO

OH07R2	Cleveland Coast Guard Marine Safety Office	229
OH05R2	Defense Construction Supply Center	229
OH04R2	Newark Air Force Base (September 1996)	230
OH03R2	Toledo Air National Guard	231
OH01R2	Wright-Patterson Air Force Base	231
OH11R2	Youngstown Air Reserve Base	232

Other Installations in Ohio

OH06R2	Camp Perry Training Site	233
OH08R2	Cleveland North Coast Guard Exchange	233
OH10R2	Mansfield-Lahm Airport	233
OH12R2	Toledo Coast Guard Station	233

OKLAHOMA

OK02R3	Altus Air Force Base	234
OK03R3	Camp Gruber	234
OK01R3	Fort Sill	235
OK09R3	McAlester Army Ammunition Plant	236
OK04R3	Tinker Air Force Base	237
OK05R3	Vance Air Force Base	237

Other Installations in Oklahoma

OK10R3   Will Rogers Air National Guard Base 238

OREGON

OR05R4	Astoria Coast Guard Group/Air Station	239
OR03R4	Kingsley Field	239
OR02R4	North Bend Coast Guard Group	240
OR01R4	Portland Air National Guard Base	240

Other Installations in Oregon

OR06R4	Coos Bay Coast Guard Exchange	241
OR04R4	Portland Coast Guard Marine Safety Office/Group	241

PENNSYLVANIA

PA08R1   Carlisle Barracks 242

PENNSYLVANIA, continued

PA12R1	Charles E. Kelly Support Facility	242
PA06R1	Defense Distribution Region East	243
PA02R1	Defense Personnel Support Center (June 1999)	244
PA04R1	Fort Indiantown Gap	245
PA03R1	Letterkenny Army Depot	245
PA07R1	Mechanicsburg Naval Inventory Control Point	246
PA19R1	Philadelphia Coast Guard Group	247
PA15R1	Pittsburgh International Airport/Air Force Reserve Installation	247
PA05R1	Tobyhanna Army Depot	248
PA17R1	Warminster Naval Air Warfare Center (July 1996)	249
PA01R1	Willow Grove Naval Air Station/Joint Reserve Base	249

Other Installations in Pennsylvania

PA13R1	Chambersburg Municipal Airport	250
PA14R1	Harrisburg International Airport	250

RHODE ISLAND

RI01R1	Newport Naval Education and Training Center	251

Other Installations in Rhode Island

RI03R1	Quonset Point State Airport	251

SOUTH CAROLINA

SC01R1	Beaufort Marine Corps Air Station	252
SC06R1	Charleston Air Force Base	252
SC16R1	Charleston Coast Guard Base	253
SC11R1	Charleston Naval Weapons Station	254
SC09R1	Fort Jackson	255
SC18R1	McEntire Air National Guard Base	256
SC08R1	Parris Island Marine Corps Recruit Depot	256
SC10R1	Shaw Air Force Base	257

Other Installations in South Carolina

SC07R1	Beaufort Naval Hospital	258
SC15R1	Charleston International Airport	258

SOUTH DAKOTA

SD03R3	Belle Fourche Air Force Station	259
SD01R3	Ellsworth Air Force Base	259

TENNESSEE

TN02R2	Arnold Air Force Base	261
TN07R2	McGhee Tyson Air National Guard Base	262
TN01R2	Memphis Naval Support Activity	262
TN09R2	Tennessee National Guard Armory, Houston Barracks	263

Other Installations in Tennessee

TN11R2	Chattanooga Armory Exchange	263
TN08R2	Defense Distribution Region Central	263
TN12R2	Kingsport Site Exchange	263
TN06R2	Nashville International Airport/Tennessee Air National Guard Base	263
TN10R2	Smyrna Exchange	263

TEXAS

TX26R3	Brooks Air Force Base	264
TX39R3	Camp Mabry	264
TX10R3	Corpus Christi Naval Air Station	265
TX12R3	Dallas Naval Air Station (Scheduled to relocate in 1996)	266
TX14R3	Dyess Air Force Base	267
TX06R3	Fort Bliss	267
TX02R3	Fort Hood	268
TX18R3	Fort Sam Houston	269
TX21R3	Fort Worth Naval Air Station/Joint Reserve Base	270
TX24R3	Goodfellow Air Force Base	271
TX30R3	Ingelside Naval Station	272
TX03R3	Kelly Air Force Base	272
TX22R3	Kingsville Naval Air Station	273
TX25R3	Lackland Air Force Base	274
TX05R3	Laughlin Air Force Base	274
TX19R3	Randolph Air Force Base	275
TX09R3	Red River Army Depot	276
TX20R3	Reese Air Force Base (September 1997)	277
TX37R3	Sheppard Air Force Base	278

Other Installations in Texas

TX45R3	Biggs Field	279
TX40R3	Camp Bullis	279
TX41R3	Ellington Field ANGB/Houston Coast Guard Air Station	279
TX47R3	Galveston Coast Guard Base	279
TX11R3	Headquarters Army & Air Force Exchange Service	279
TX48R3	Houston Coast Guard Marine Safety Office	279
TX46R3	Waco Shoppette	279

xviii

UTAH

UT11R4	Camp W.G. Williams	280
UT04R4	Dugway Proving Ground	280
UT02R4	Hill Air Force Base	281
UT09R4	Ogden Defense Depot	282
UT05R4	Tooele Army Depot	282

Other Installations in Utah

| UT10R4 | Salt Lake City IAP | 283 |

VERMONT

Installations in Vermont

| VT01R1 | Camp Johnson | 284 |
| VT02R1 | Ethan Allen Firing Range | 284 |

VIRGINIA

VA44R1	Alexandria CG Telecommunication & Information Systems Command	285
VA48R1	Armed Forces Staff College	285
VA02R1	Cheatham Annex Fleet & Industrial Supply Center	286
VA42R1	Chesapeake Naval Security Group Activity Northwest	287
VA06R1	Dahlgren Naval Surface Warfare Center	287
VA25R1	Dam Neck Fleet Combat Training Center Atlantic	288
VA30R1	Defense General Supply Center	289
VA17R1	Fort A. P. Hill	290
VA12R1	Fort Belvoir	290
VA10R1	Fort Eustis	291
VA15R1	Fort Lee	292
VA13R1	Fort Monroe	293
VA24R1	Fort Myer	294
VA16R1	Fort Pickett (September 1996)	295
VA08R1	Fort Story	296
VA21R1	Henderson Hall USMC	297
VA01R1	Judge Advocate General's School	297
VA07R1	Langley Air Force Base	298
VA19R1	Little Creek Naval Amphibious Base	299
VA18R1	Norfolk Naval Base	300
VA26R1	Norfolk Naval Shipyard	301
VA09R1	Oceana Naval Air Station	301
VA41R1	Pentagon	302
VA43R1	Portsmouth Coast Guard Support Center	303
VA27R1	Portsmouth Naval Medical Center	304
VA11R1	Quantico Marine Corps Base	304
VA03R1	Vint Hill Farms Station (September 1997)	305
VA46R1	Wallops Island AEGIS Combat Systems Center	306

VIRGINIA, continued

VA28R1   Yorktown Coast Guard Reserve Training Center 307
VA14R1   Yorktown Naval Weapons Station 307

Other Installations in Virginia

VA49R1   Chesapeake Coast Guard Exchange 308
VA47R1   Chincoteague Coast Guard Group-Eastern Shore 308
VA23R1   Davison Aviation Command 308

WASHINGTON

WA08R4   Bangor Naval Submarine Base 309
WA10R4   Everett Naval Station 310
WA02R4   Fairchild Air Force Base 310
WA09R4   Fort Lewis 311
WA07R4   Jim Creek Naval Radio Station 312
WA05R4   McChord Air Force Base 313
WA19R4   Port Angeles Coast Guard Group 313
WA11R4   Puget Sound Naval Shipyard 314
WA20R4   Seattle Coast Guard Support Center 315
WA06R4   Whidbey Island Naval Air Station 315

Other Installations in Washington

WA18R4   Fort Lawton 124th Regional Support Command 316
WA17R4   USAF Survival School 316
WA23R4   Vancouver Barracks 316
WA24R4   Yakima Training Center 316

WEST VIRGINIA

WV02R1   Eastern West Virginia Regional Airport 317
WV04R1   Sugar Grove Naval Security Group Activity 317
WV05R1   Yeager Airport 318

Other Installations in West Virginia

WV03R1   Camp Dawson Army Training Site 318
WV01R1   Charleston Armory 318

WISCONSIN

WI02R2   Fort McCoy 319
WI05R2   General Mitchell International Airport/Air Reserve Station 320
WI06R2   Milwaukee Coast Guard Group 320

WISCONSIN, continued

Other Installations in Wisconsin

WI10R2	Milwaukee Post Exchange	321
WI07R2	Truax Field	321
WI08R2	Volk Field Air National Guard Base	321

WYOMING

WY01R4	Francis E. Warren Air Force Base	322

Other Installations in Wyoming

WY04R4	Cheyenne Municipal Airport/ANGB	323
WY05R4	Powell Air Force Station	323

UNITED STATES POSSESSIONS

GUAM

GU01R8	Andersen Air Force Base	324
GU02R8	Guam Naval Activities	325

PUERTO RICO

PR03R1	Borinquen Coast Guard Air Station	326
PR07R1	Camp Santiago Training Site	326
PR01R1	Fort Buchanan	327
PR02R1	Roosevelt Roads Naval Station	328
PR04R1	Sabana Seca Naval Security Group Activity	329

Other Installations in Puerto Rico

PR05R1	San Juan Coast Guard Base	329

VIRGIN ISLANDS

Installations in US Virgin Islands

VI01R1	Virgin Islands National Guard Base	330

WAKE ISLAND

WK01R8	Wake Island Air Force Base	331

FOREIGN COUNTRIES

CANADA

CN04R1   Trenton Canadian Forces Base .... .332

CUBA

CU01R1   Guantanamo Bay Naval Station .... .333

DENMARK (GREENLAND)

DN02R7   Thule Air Base .... .334

PANAMA

PN08R3	Albrook Air Force Station	.335
PN02R3	Fort Clayton	.335
PN07R3	Fort Kobbe	.336
PN06R3	Fort Sherman	.337
PN01R3	Howard Air Force Base	.337
PN09R3	Panama Canal Naval Station (December 1999)	.338
PN03R3	Quarry Heights Post	.339

APPENDICES

APPENDIX A - Country & State Abbreviations .... .340
APPENDIX B - General Abbreviations .... .341
APPENDIX C - Defense Base Closure and Realignment Status .... .344
APPENDIX D - United Services Organization (USO) listing .... .347

Roy, Ann & R.J. Crawford, Publishers, thank you for buying our book. We hope it will save you many, many dollars on your travel and bring more fun into your life. Please see a description of our current publications on Page 360, which can also help you *travel on less per day....the military way*!

xxii

PHOTO CREDITS

FRONT COVER:

Top Left - Fishing is great at the Waianae Recreation Area, Hawaii. Photo by John Kay.

Top Center - Enjoy the sunsets at Fort Gordon Recreation Area, Georgia. Photo courtesy of the US Army.

Top Right - Check out the all new beach-side hotel, the Cape Henry Inn, at Fort Story, Virginia. Photo courtesy of the US Army.

Center - Have a small family reunion at Fort A.P. Hill, Virginia. Photo by Ann Crawford.

Bottom Left - US Coast Guard Marathon Recreation Cottages in Florida welcomes you. Photo courtesy of the US Coast Guard.

Bottom Right - Enjoy the Thayer Hotel at West Point, New York. Photo courtesy of the Thayer Hotel.

BACK COVER:

Top Left - Fish at Seward Military Recreation Camp in Alaska. Photo courtesy of Fort Wainwright.

Top Right - The enlisted club overlooks the ocean at Dam Neck, Virginia. Photo by Ann Crawford.

Center left - Fly Space-A in a C-5 or other military aircraft with your family to Hawaii, ALaska, and other U.S. areas outside the continental U.S.A. Photo by Roy Crawford Sr.

Center Right - Bronson Field Naval Recreation Area in Pensacola, Florida has gentle waters for fun. Photo courtesy of the US Navy.

Lower right - You'll love the beauty of the beach cottages at Bellows Recreation Area in Hawaii. Photo courtesy of US Air Force.

RENT A CAR

Call 1-800-800-4000. Get a military rate by using your Military Living ID # ML3009. Retirees/Active Duty/Reserve/Guard.

The Value Of A Dollar Is Even Greater with Dollar Rent A Car:

Call Us Anytime, Anywhere.

Through our state-of-the-art automated computer reservation center, you can reserve a Dollar Rent A Car. Just contact our 24 hour toll-free worldwide reservation center at 1-800-800-4000 and give your Military Living ID #ML3009.

U.S. FORCES TRAVEL & TRANSFER GUIDE U.S.A. - 1

UNITED STATES

ALABAMA

 Call 1-800-800-4000. Get a military rate by using your Military Living ID # ML3009. Retirees/Active Duty/Reserve/Guard.

ANNISTON ARMY DEPOT (AL13R2)
7 Frankford Avenue
Anniston, AL 36201-5000

TELEPHONE NUMBER INFORMATION: Main installation numbers: C-205-235-7501, D-312-571-7501.

LOCATION: From I-20 take Oxford exit onto Highway US-78 and follow signs to the depot. USMRA: Page 36 (F-3). NMC: Anniston, 10 miles east.

GENERAL INFORMATION: Units at the Depot include the Defense Reutilization and Marketing Office, the TMDE Support Center, and the CECOM Liaison Office and Defense Logistics Agency.

TEMPORARY MILITARY LODGING: None. See Fort McClellan listing, C-205-848-4338, D-312-865-4338.

LOGISTICAL SUPPORT: Limited support facilities available.

Exchange-237-9159
Locator-235-7501
Public Affairs-235-6281
SATO-235-6367
Fire Department-235-6171
Medical-235-7521
Recreation-235-6385
Legal-235-6334
MWR-235-7170
RV/Camping-235-7170

HEALTH & WELFARE: US Army Health Clinic C-312-571-7521. Inpatient, see Fort McClellan listing, C-205-848-4671.

RECREATION: Camping Equipment EX-7170, Fitness Center EX-6385.

SPACE-A: None. Try 117th TRW (ANG), Birmingham Municipal Airport, 5401 East Lake Blvd., Birmingham, AL 35217-3595. C-205-841-9408, D-312-778-2441, Fax: C-205-841-9219. Also see Maxwell AFB listing.

ATTRACTIONS: Anniston Museum of Natural History.

BIRMINGHAM AIR NATIONAL GUARD BASE (AL15R2)
5401 Eastlake Boulevard
Birmingham, AL 35217-3595

TELEPHONE NUMBER INFORMATION: Main Installation Numbers: C-205-841-9200, D-312-778-2210.

LOCATION: Exit I-59/20 at Tallapoosa St., north for one-half mile to a right on Eastlake Blvd. to installation. USMRA: Page 36 (D,E-4). NMC: located in the northeast section of Birmingham.

2 - U.S. FORCES TRAVEL & TRANSFER GUIDE U.S.A

ALABAMA
Birmingham Air National Guard Base, continued

GENERAL INFORMATION: Headquarters 117th Recon Wing.

TEMPORARY MILITARY LODGING: None. See Fort McClellan listing, C-205-848-4338, D-312-865-4338.

LOGISTICAL SUPPORT: Limited support facilities available.

Exchange-841-9348   Gas Station-841-9294   Medical-841-9213
Police-841-9240

HEALTH & WELFARE: Outpatient clinic C-205-841-9213.

SPACE-A: Pax Terminal C-205-841-9441, D-312-778-2441, Fax 205-841-9219. Some unscheduled flights available on MEDEVAC and KC-135's.

ATTRACTIONS: Vulcan (Iron Man Statue) on Red Mountain. The largest shopping mall in the Southeast is located in Birmingham.

FORT McCLELLAN (AL01R2)
Fort McClellan, AL 36205-5000

This base is scheduled to close under the 1995 BRAC.
No closure date has been established.

TELEPHONE NUMBER INFORMATION: Main installation numbers: C-205-848-4611, D-312-865-1110.

LOCATION: From I-20 take AL-21 north nine miles to fort. From I-59 take US-431 25 miles southeast to fort. USMRA: Page 36 (F-3). NMC: Anniston, three miles southeast.

GENERAL INFORMATION: US Army Chemical and Military Police Centers and Fort McClellan.

TEMPORARY MILITARY LODGING: Lodging office, Bldg. 3295, 14th St. and Summerall Rd., 24 hours, C-205-848-4338, D-312-865-4338. All ranks. DV/VIP C-205-848-3808/5616.

LOGISTICAL SUPPORT: Complete support facilities available.

ACS-848-4525   Cafeteria-820-2000   CHAMPUS-848-2126
Chaplain-848-5351   Child Care-848-4857   Commissary-848-3130
Conv Store-848-9280   Exchange-820-9400   Fire Dept-848-5936
Gas Station-820-9250   Golf Course-820-7299   ITT Office-820-6372
Legal-848-5435   Locator-848-3281   McClellan Club-848-5301
Medical-848-2126   MWR-848-3526   Package Store-820-9280
Police-848-5555   Public Affairs-848-3743   Recreation-848-3526/3536
Retiree Services-820-5300 SATO-820-6372   SDO/NCO-848-3821
Snack Bar-820-2000   Theater-848-3861   Visitor Center-848-4338

HEALTH & WELFARE: Noble Army Community Hospital, Emergency C-205-848-2152, Appointments C-205-848-4671, 48 beds. Chapels serving all faiths C-205-848-5311.

U.S. FORCES TRAVEL & TRANSFER GUIDE U.S.A. - 3

ALABAMA
Fort McClellan, continued

RECREATION: Rec Services EX-4323, Bowling, EX-5149, Swimming EX-4656, Gym EX-4160/5249/4656, Sports Arena EX-4802, Skeet/Trap EX-3700, Auto Craft EX-5146, Library EX-3715, Bingo 820-6699, Youth Activities EX-3607, Golf 820-7299. McClellan Recreation Area & Campground located on post, year round, C-205-848-5663, D-312-5649, eight camping spaces w/W&E hookups, four camping spaces without hookups.

SPACE-A: None. Try 117 TRW (ANG), Base Ops, Birmingham Municipal Airport, C-205-841-9408. Also see Maxwell AFB listing, C-205-953-6454, D-312-493-6454, Fax 205-953-4564.

ATTRACTIONS: Military Police, Chemical Corps and WAC Museums on post. Natural History Museum located nearby. Fort adjacent to Talladega National Forest. Atlanta, home of the 1996 Summer Olympics, is only a one-and-a-half hour drive away.

FORT RUCKER (AL02R2)
Fort Rucker, AL 36362-5033

TELEPHONE NUMBER INFORMATION: Main installation numbers: C-334-255-3156, D-312-558-1110.

LOCATION: Ninety miles southeast of Montgomery, midway between the capital city and the Florida Gulf Coast, and seven miles south of Ozark, off US-231 on AL-249. Clearly marked. USMRA: Page 36 (F,G-8). NMC: Dothan, 26 miles southeast.

GENERAL INFORMATION: US Army Aviation Center & School.

TEMPORARY MILITARY LODGING: Lodging office, Bldg. 308, 6th Ave, 24 hours daily, C-334-255-3780, D-312-558-3780. All ranks. DV/VIP, Bldg. 114, C-344-255-3100/3400.

LOGISTICAL SUPPORT: Complete support facilities available.

ACS-255-2887
Child Care-255-3564
Family Services-255-2341
Legal-255-3482
NCO Club-598-2491/2/3
Police-255-2222
SATO-598-9034
Vet Clinic-255-2159

CHAMPUS-255-7233
Commissary-255-3610
Gas Station-598-0276
Locator-255-3156
O'Club-598-2426/7
Recycling-255-9505
SDO/NCO-255-3100

Chaplain-255-2989
Exchange-598-0221
ITR Office-255-9517
Medical-255-7900
Package Store-598-0283
Retiree Services-255-9124
Theater-255-2408

HEALTH & WELFARE: Lyster Army Community Hospital, Emergency C-334-255-7900, 72 beds. Chapels serving all faiths C-334-255-2989.

RECREATION: Arts/Crafts 255-9131, Bowling 255-9503, Golf 255-9539, Auto Hobby 255-9725, Equestrian Center 598-3384, Gym 255-9567, Library 255-9772, Outdoor Rec 255-4305, Swimming EX-3998, Youth Services 255-9108. On-post recreation area at Lake Tholocco, year round (camping area closed Nov-Feb), Outdoor Rec C-334-255-4305, D-312-558-4305, 18 camper spaces w/W&E hookups.

SPACE-A: Cairns Army Airfield, Bldg. 30501, C-334-255-8564, D-312-558-8564, flights via executive aircraft to CONUS locations.

ALABAMA
Fort Rucker, continued

ATTRACTIONS: National Peanut Festival, first week of Nov in Dothan. Monument to the Boll Weevil, Enterprise, AL, seven miles west. US Army Aviation Museum on post, 0900-1600 daily; group tours and library usage, C-334-255-3036.

GUNTER ANNEX TO MAXWELL AIR FORCE BASE (AL04R2)
60 West Maxwell Boulevard
Maxwell AFB, AL 36112-6307

TELEPHONE NUMBER INFORMATION: Main installation numbers: C-334-953-7100, D-312-493-5496.

LOCATION: Take I-65 to Northern Bypass, six miles to exit on AL-231, continue west one mile to AFB. Coming from the opposite direction, from I-85, follow signs and take Eastern Bypass north one mile to AL-231. Then west one mile to AFB. USMRA: Page 36 (E,F-6). NMC: Montgomery, two miles southwest.

GENERAL INFORMATION: Standard Systems Group, Extension Course Institute, USAF Senior NCO Academy, and educational activities.

TEMPORARY MILITARY LODGING: Lodging office, Bldg. 826. 24 hours daily, C-334-416-3360, D-312-596-3360. Extensive facilities. DV/VIP call Maxwell AFB, C-334-293-2095, D-312-875-2095.

LOGISTICAL SUPPORT: Complete support facilities available.

CHAMPUS-953-7854
Commissary-953-2343
Family Services-953-3850
Golf Course-263-7588
Locator-953-5027
NCO Club-262-8364
Recreation-953-5675
Theater-953-7411
Chaplain-953-2862
EM Club-953-6399
Fire Dept-953-7360
ITT Office-953-7370
Medical-953-6985
O'Club-264-6423
RV/Camping-953-5161
Visitor Center-953-2014
Child Care-953-6667
Exchange-834-5946
Gas Station-265-7773
Legal-953-2786
MWR-953-5217
Police-953-7222
SATO-263-5500

HEALTH & WELFARE: None. See Maxwell AFB listing, C-334-953-2333. Chapel serving all faiths, C-334-279-4131.

RECREATION: Arts/Crafts EX-3118, Auto Hobby EX-3119, Wood Hobby at Maxwell, Gym EX-3175, Picnic Area EX-4888, Bowling EX-3186, Library EX-3179, Rec Center EX-4802, Youth Activities EX-4802. See Maxwell AFB listing for off-base recreation facilities.

SPACE-A: None. See Maxwell AFB listing, C-334-953-6454, D-312-493-6454, Fax 334-953-4564.

ATTRACTIONS: Alabama state capital, Alabama Shakespeare Festival, Coliseum, Montgomery Museum of Fine Arts, monument to powered flight at Maxwell AFB, First White House of the Confederacy, Civil Rights Memorial, and the new Alabama State Farmers Market..."largest in the southeastern U.S."

U.S. FORCES TRAVEL & TRANSFER GUIDE U.S.A. - 5

ALABAMA

MAXWELL AIR FORCE BASE (AL03R2)
50 LeMay Plaza South
Maxwell Air Force Base, AL 36112-6334

TELEPHONE NUMBER INFORMATION: Main installation numbers: C-334-953-1110, D-312-493-1110.

LOCATION: Take I-85 south to I-65 north. Take Herron St. exit to Bell St. and follow signs to Bell Street Gate Visitor Center. USMRA: Page 36 (E-6). NMC: Montgomery, one-and-a-half miles southeast.

GENERAL INFORMATION: Headquarters Air University (AETC), professional military education center for USAF.

TEMPORARY MILITARY LODGING: Lodging office, Bldg. 157, 351 West Dr., 24 hours daily, C-334-953-2401/7390, D-312-493-2401/7390. Extensive facilities. DV/VIP C-334-953-2095.

LOGISTICAL SUPPORT: Complete support facilities available.

Cafeteria-263-6044	CHAMPUS-953-7854	Chaplain-953-2111
Child Care-953-6667	Commissary-953-6209	Conv Store-265-7773
EM Club-262-8364	Exchange-834-5946	Family Services-953-5002
Gas Station-265-7773	Golf Course-263-9587	ITT Office-953-6351
Legal-953-2786	Locator-953-5027	Medical-953-2333
NCO Club-262-8364	O'Club-264-6423	Package Store-265-7472
Police-953-7222	Public Affairs-953-2014	Retiree Services-953-6725
RV/Camping-953-5496	SATO-264-0076	SDO/NCO-953-2862
Theater-953-7411	Visitor Center-953-4283	

HEALTH & WELFARE: USAF Regional Hospital, Bldg. 50, Emergency C-334-953-2333, 90 beds. Chapel serving all faiths C-334-953-2111.

RECREATION: Aero Club EX-7342, Library EX-5947, Rec Services EX-7320/6369, Skills Development Center (Art/Crafts) EX-6426, Gym EX-5954, Pools EX-5118, Bowling EX-5049, Golf EX-2209, Community Activity Center EX-5496, Youth Center EX-6292, Riding Club EX-7365. Fam-Camp on base, C-334-953-5161, year round, 31 camper spaces w/full hookups; Lake Martin Rec Area, off base near Dadeville, AL C-334-953-5496, D-312-493-5496, year round, 50 camper spaces w/W&E hookups, 12 Mobile Homes, 30 tent spaces; Lake Pippin Maxwell/Gunter Recreation Area near Niceville, FL, year round, C-334-953-5496, D-312-493-5496, 23 camper spaces w/W&E hookups, 10 tent spaces, and 29 Mobile Homes.

SPACE-A: Pax Term/Lounge, Bldg. 844, 0700-1700 Mon-Fri, C-334-953-6454, D-312-493-6454, Fax 334-953-6114. DV/VIP lounge C-334-953-6961. Flights scheduled 24 hours in advance, most via executive aircraft.

ATTRACTIONS: State capital, Shakespeare Theater, historic houses and buildings in Montgomery, including First White House of the Confederacy, Montgomery Museum of Fine Arts, Civil Rights Memorial Monument.

6 - U.S. FORCES TRAVEL & TRANSFER GUIDE U.S.A

ALABAMA

MOBILE COAST GUARD AVIATION TRAINING CENTER (AL08R2)
USCG Aviation Training Center, Mobile, AL 36608-9682

TELEPHONE NUMBER INFORMATION: Main installation numbers: C-334-639-6110, FTS-537-6110, Flight Operations, D-312-436-3635.

LOCATION: Take Airport Blvd. exit west from I-65, eight miles from base, turn right on Schillinger Road, turn left on Tanner Williams Road, one mile. Clearly marked. USMRA: Page 36 (B-9). NMC: Mobile, one mile northwest.

GENERAL INFORMATION: The Aviation Training Center for the US Coast Guard and home for the Gulf Strike Team.

TEMPORARY MILITARY LODGING: Extremely limited. Usually filled by TDY students. C-334-639-6361. See Keesler AFB, MS, C-601-377-33009/4200.

LOGISTICAL SUPPORT: Limited support facilities available.

CDO/OOD-639-6110	**Chaplain-639-6038**	**Commissary-639-6390**
Credit Union-639-6326	**EM Club-639-6359**	**Exchange-639-6390**
Gas Station-639-6496	**Grocery Anx-639-6379**	**Locator-639-6110**
Medical-639-6401	**MWR-639-6130**	**O'Club-639-6358**
Package Store-639-6390	**Public Affairs-639-6428**	

HEALTH & WELFARE: Outpatient clinic appointments C-334-639-6401. Inpatient, see Pensacola Naval Hospital, FL, C-904-452-6788 or see Keesler AFB, MS listing, C-601-377-6337.

RECREATION: Auto Hobby, Rental Equipment, Outdoor Racquet Courts, Weight Room Complex, Jogging Trail, Walter's Park Picnic Area (fee), Swimming Pool (fee). For Info, C-334-639-6136, FTS-537-6136. Operates Dauphin Island Rec Complex, year round, 40 miles south of Mobile on AL-163, 13 furnished cottages, five camper spaces w/full hookups, and 100 camper/tent spaces. For reservations call C-334-861-7113.

SPACE-A: Extremely limited. Main hangar, 0800-1600 Mon-Fri, C-334-639-6161, D-312-436-3635, FTS-537-6444, Fax 334-639-6435, flights to East and Midwest.

ATTRACTIONS: Mobile is one of the largest commercial seaports in the country. Historic houses and beautiful flowers in the Mobile Bay area. Bellingrath Gardens (year round), USS *Alabama*, and Battleship Park.

MOBILE COAST GUARD GROUP (AL16R2)
South Broad Street
Mobile, AL 36615-1390

TELEPHONE NUMBER INFORMATION: Main installation numbers: C-334-441-6217.

LOCATION: From I-10, exit on Broad St., go south approximately three-quarters of a mile to base. USMRA: Page 36 (B-9,10). NMC: Mobile, one mile.

GENERAL INFORMATION: US Coast Guard Group activities.

U.S. FORCES TRAVEL & TRANSFER GUIDE U.S.A. - 7

ALABAMA
Mobile Coast Guard Group, continued

TEMPORARY MILITARY LODGING: None. See Keesler AFB, MS listing, C-601-377-33009/4200.

LOGISTICAL SUPPORT: Limited support facilities available.

All Hands Club-441-5098   Conv Store-441-5097   Exchange-441-5090
Gas Station-441-5097   Locator-441-6217   Package Store-441-5091

HEALTH AND WELFARE: None. See Keesler AFB, MS listing, C-601-377-6337. Also see Pensacola Naval Hospital, FL listing, C-904-452-6788.

RECREATION: Dauphin Island Recreation Area, 40 miles south of Mobile, with 13 cottages, six trailer pads, and unlimited tent spaces. C-334-861-7113.

SPACE-A: None. See Keesler AFB, MS listing, C-601-377-4538, D-312-597-4538.

ATTRACTIONS: Mobile Bay, Battleship Park, *USS Alabama* and other military displays, Bellingrath Gardens.

REDSTONE ARSENAL (AL06R2)
Redstone Arsenal, AL 35898-5020

TELEPHONE NUMBER INFORMATION: Main installation numbers: C-205-876-2151, D-312-746-0011.

LOCATION: Off US-231 go south on Martin Road to main gate. For uniformed personnel, Gate 8 is on Drake Ave, take US-72 onto Jordan Lane, then west on Drake. Drake becomes Goss Rd. on the Arsenal. USMRA: Page 36 (E-1). NMC: Huntsville, adjacent.

GENERAL INFORMATION: Headquarters US Army Missile Command, US Army Ordnance Missile & Munitions Center & School and NASA.

TEMPORARY MILITARY LODGING: Lodging office, Bldg. 244, Goss Rd., 24 hours daily, C-205-876-5713, D-312-746-5713; other SDO, Bldg. 5300, C-205-876-3331. All ranks. DV/VIP call Billeting Office.

LOGISTICAL SUPPORT: Complete support facilities available.

ACS-876-5397   Cafeteria-881-9973/6210   CHAMPUS-955-8888
Chaplain-876-5751   Child Care-876-3704   Commissary-842-2592
Conv Store-881-7862   Exchange-883-6100   Family Services-876-2859
Gas Station-881-7588   Golf Course-876-6888   Legal-876-9015
Locator-876-3331   Medical-876-8287   NCO Club-837-0750
O'Club-830-2582   Package Store-883-7761   Police-876-2222
Public Affairs-876-4161   Recreation 876-4531   Retiree Services-876-2022
SDO/NCO-876-3331   Snack Bar-881-1591   Theater-876-6524
Travel Office-880-3601   Visitor Center-876-4542

HEALTH & WELFARE: Fox Army Community Hospital, Bldg. 4100, C-205-876-8513, emergency and walk-in clinic, 40 beds. Chaplain C-205-876-2337/3433.

RECREATION: Rec Services EX-2501, Arts & Crafts EX-7951, Auto Crafts EX-7727, Golf EX-6888, Rec Center EX-4868, Gym EX-4531, Swimming NCO-EX-6758 Officers-

ALABAMA
Redstone Arsenal, continued

EX-6713, Troop EX-6605, Bowling EX-6634, Martial Arts EX-2501, Sports Office EX-2255, Youth Activities EX-5437. Arsenal campground on post, year round, Outdoor Recreation, Bldg. 5132, C-205-876-6854, 23 camper spaces w/W&E hookups.

SPACE-A: Arsenal Army Airfield, Pax terminal, Bldg. 4809, 0630-1730 daily, C-205-876-4299, D-312-746-2186, Fax 205-842-0562. Flights to limited destinations via executive type aircraft, MEDEVAC C-9, C-130.

ATTRACTIONS: Alabama Space and Rocket Center, Tennessee River.

ALASKA

 Call 1-800-800-4000. Get a military rate by using your Military Living ID # ML3009. Retirees/Active Duty/Reserve/Guard.

ADAK NAVAL AIR FACILITY (AK04R5)
PSC 486, Box 1202
FPO AP 96506-1202

*This base is scheduled to close under the 1995 BRAC.
No closure date has been established.*

TELEPHONE NUMBER INFORMATION: Main installation numbers: C-907-592-4201, D-317-692-4201.

LOCATION: On Adak Island of the Aleutian Island chain, accessible only by air or ship. USMRA: Page 128 (H-8). NMC: Anchorage, 1200 air miles NE. **Note: Closed Station, only assigned personnel and cleared, sponsored guests are allowed on base. Please write to the commander for clearance to visit.**

GENERAL INFORMATION: Naval Security Group Activity, Naval Facility, Patrol Wings and support units.

TEMPORARY MILITARY LODGING: Housing office, 0800-1700 Mon-Fri, C-907-592-8277, D-317-692-8287. All ranks.

LOGISTICAL SUPPORT: Complete support facilities available.

CDO/OOD-592-4201
Exchange-592-8164
Legal-592-8028
NCO Club-592-8392
SDO/NCO-592-4201

Chaplain-592-4169/8203
Fire Dept-592-8141
Medical-592-8383
Police-592-8051
Theater-592-834

EM Club-592-8104
Gas Station-592-8242
MWR-592-4124
Public Affairs-592-4250

HEALTH & WELFARE: Naval Branch Hospital, Emergency C-907-592-8383, 15 beds. Chapel serving all faiths C-907-592-4169/8203.

RECREATION: Arts/Crafts, Auto Hobby, Wood Hobby, Photo Hobby, Boat Basin, Skeet Range, Gym, Roller Rink, Swimming, Racquetball/Handball, Tennis, Hunting/Fishing. Call 592-2648 or 592-2648 for all recreation.

SPACE-A: Pax Term/Lounge, Bldg. 30003, 0800-1700 Mon-Fri, C-907-592-8089, D-317-692-4196, Fax 907-592-8088. Flights to Alaska locations.

ATTRACTIONS: The great outdoors.

CLEAR AIR STATION (AK18R5)
P.O. Box 40013
Clear Air Station, AK 99704-5000

TELEPHONE NUMBER INFORMATION: Main Installation numbers: C-907-585-6409, D-317-585-6416.

ALASKA
Clear Air Station, continued

LOCATION: Located on Fairbanks/Anchorage Highway. USMRA: Page 128 (F-4). NMC: Fairbanks, 80 miles northeast.

GENERAL INFORMATION: 13th Space Warning Squadron.

TEMPORARY MILITARY LODGING: Lodging office, Bldg. 200, C-907-585-6224. All ranks.

LOGISTICAL SUPPORT: Limited support facilities available.

Exchange-585-6457	Fire Dept-585-6321	Locator-585-1110
Medical-585-6414	MWR-585-6276	NCO/O'Club-585-6536
Police-585-6433	Public Affairs-585-6416	

HEALTH & WELFARE: Medical Aid Station C-907-585-6414.

SPACE-A: None. See Eielson Air Force Base listing, C-907-377-1854, D-317-377-1854, Fax 907-377-2287.

ATTRACTIONS: Near Mount McKinley National Park. Hunting, Fishing, and other outdoor activities.

EIELSON AIR FORCE BASE (AK15R5)
3122 Broadway Avenue
Unit 15A
Eielson Air Force Base, AK 99702-1895

TELEPHONE NUMBER INFORMATION: Main installation numbers: C-907-377-1110, D-317-377-1110.

LOCATION: On the Richardson Highway (AK-2). AFB is clearly marked. USMRA: Page 128 (F,G-4). NMC: Fairbanks, 26 miles northwest.

GENERAL INFORMATION: 354th Fighter Wing, 168th Air Refueling Group (ANG), Det 1, 210th Rescue Squadron (ANG), and support activities.

TEMPORARY MILITARY LODGING: Lodging Office, Bldg. 2270, 24 hours daily, C-907-377-1844, D-317-377-1844. All ranks. DV/VIP C-907-377-7686.

LOGISTICAL SUPPORT: Complete support facilities available.

Cafeteria-377-1341	CHAMPUS-377-4130	Chaplain-377-2130
Child Care-377-3237	Comm Club-377-2051	Commissary-377-5134
Conv Store-377-2210	CDO/OOD-377-1500	Exchange-377-4154
Family Services-377-2242	Fire Dept-377-4266	Gas Station-377-3237
Legal-377-4114	Locator-377-1841	Medical-377-2259
MWR-377-2857	Package Store-377-2210	Police-377-5130
Public Affairs-377-2116	Recreation-377-1232	Retiree Services-377-1805
RV/Camping-377-7872	SATO-377-3145	Snack Bar-377-1126
Theater-377-1172	Visitor Center-377-3807	

HEALTH & WELFARE: USAF Clinic, Emergency C-907-377-2296. Inpatient, see Fort Wainwright, listing, C-907-353-5172/5173. Chapels serving all faiths C-907-377-2130.

U.S. FORCES TRAVEL & TRANSFER GUIDE U.S.A. - 11

ALASKA
Eielson Air Force Base, continued

RECREATION: Arts/Crafts EX-1167, Auto Hobby EX-3190, Bowling EX-1129, Flying Club EX-1223, Gym EX-1231, Rec Equip EX-1231, Boat Shop EX-1232, Library EX-3174, Swimming EX-1231, Youth Center 377-3194. Fam-Camp on base, 15 May-7 Sep, C-907-377-1232, D-317-377-1232, 24 camper spaces w/full hookups; Ravenwood Ski Lodge, on base, Nov-Mar, C-907-377-1328, day use only, snow skiing, rec room and support facilities; Birch Lake Recreation Area, 38 miles south of the AFB, May-Sep, C-907-488-6161, D-317-377-4214, 40 camper spaces with E hookups, two deluxe cabins, 16 family cabins, four smaller cabins, and many tent spaces.

SPACE-A: Pax Term/Lounge, Bldg. 1138, 0730-1630 daily, or as required, C-907-377-1854, D-317-377-1854 Fax 907-377-2287, flights to CONUS and Alaska locations.

ATTRACTIONS: Fairbanks and North Pole, Denali National Park, outdoor sports, and recreation.

ELMENDORF AIR FORCE BASE (AK09R5)
Elmendorf Air Force Base, AK 99506-5000

TELEPHONE NUMBER INFORMATION: Main installation numbers: C-907-552-1110, D-317-552-1110.

LOCATION: Off Glenn Highway adjacent to north Anchorage. Take Boniface Parkway Exit. Take either Elmendorf Access Road or Post Road. The base is adjacent to Fort Richardson. USMRA: Page 128 (F-5), page 131 (B,C,D,E-1). NMC: Anchorage, two miles southwest.

GENERAL INFORMATION: Pacific Air Forces Base. Headquarters Alaskan Command, 3rd Wing, Headquarters Alaska NORAD Region, Headquarters 11th Air Force.

TEMPORARY MILITARY LODGING: Lodging office, Bldg. 31250, Acacia Street, 24 hours daily, C-907-552-2454. All ranks. DV/VIP C-907-552-2454.

LOGISTICAL SUPPORT: Complete support facilities available.

CHAMPUS-552-3430
Commissary-552-4877
Family Services-552-2694
Legal-552-3046
NCO Club-753-5190
Police-552-3421
SATO-753-0509
Theater-753-2344

Chaplain-552-4422
EM Club-753-5190
Gas Station-753-2134
Locator-552-4860
O'Club-753-3131
Public Affairs-552-8151
SDO/NCO-552-3013

Child Care-753-5113
Exchange-753-4208
ITT Office-552-5191
Medical-552-2748
Package Store-753-5151
Retiree Services-552-2337
Snack Bar-753-6146

HEALTH & WELFARE: 3rd Wing, 11th Air Force Regional Hospital, Emergency C-907-552-5556, Appointments C-907-552-2778, 110 beds. Chapels serving all faiths C-907-552-4422.

RECREATION: Aero Club 753-4167, Arts/Crafts EX-2470, Bowling EX-4108, Golf EX-3821, Rec Equip EX-2023, Racquetball EX-5353, Tennis EX-8529/5353, Riding Club EX-4987, Jogging Club EX-5353/3504, Field House EX-5353/3504, Library EX-3787, Swimming EX-3504, Community Activity Center EX-8529, Services Squadron EX-2468, Youth Center EX-2266, Riding Stables EX-4987, Ski Area EX-4738. Fam-Camp on

12 - U.S. FORCES TRAVEL & TRANSFER GUIDE U.S.A

ALASKA
Elmendorf Air Force Base, continued

base,May-Sep, C-907-552-3472, D-317-552-3472, 39 camper spaces w/W&E hookups, 10 tent spaces.

SPACE-A: Pax Term/Lounge, Bldg. 32238, 7th Street, 0600-2200 daily, C-907-552-4616, D-317-552-4616, Fax 907-552-3996. Flights to CONUS, Alaska, and foreign locations.

ATTRACTIONS: Anchorage, outdoor sports and recreation, Portage Glacier, Earthquake Park.

FORT GREELY (AK10R5)
"Organization"
502 2nd Street
APO AP 96508

TELEPHONE NUMBER INFORMATION: Main installation numbers: C-907-873-4113, D-317-873-1110.

LOCATION: Off AK-4, six miles south of junction of AK-2 and AK-4. Five miles south of Delta Junction. USMRA: Page 128 (F,G-4). NMC: Fairbanks, 105 miles northwest.

GENERAL INFORMATION: Army Northern Warfare Training Center, Army Cold Region Test Center, and support units.

TEMPORARY MILITARY LODGING: Limited availability with TDY and new arrivals having priority. Lodging office, Bldg. 663, First St, 0730-1600 Mon-Fri, C-907-873-3285, D-317-873-3285. Other hours, SDO, Bldg. 501, C-907-873-4120. All ranks.

LOGISTICAL SUPPORT: Complete support facilities available.

Chaplain-873-4610
Conv Store-869-3110
Family Services-873-3284
Locator-873-3255
O'Club-873-3105
SATO-873-3107
Theater-873-3283
Child Care-873-4593
EM Club-895-3105
Gas Station-869-3210
Medical-873-4498
Police-873-1111
SDO/NCO-873-4720
Commissary-873-4404
Exchange-873-3135
Legal-873-3250
NCO Club-873-3105
Recreation Center-873-1115
Snack Bar-869-3110

HEALTH & WELFARE: US Army Health Clinic, Emergency C-907-873-4498. Inpatient, see Fort Wainwright listing, C-907-353-5172/5173. Chapel serving all faiths C-907-873-4409.

RECREATION: Arts/Crafts EX-3181, Auto Hobby EX-3293, Boat Shop EX-4673, Outdoor Sports Center 873-3183, Rec Center 872-3285, Library 873-3217.

SPACE-A: Use Elmendorf AFB, C-907-552-3337, D-317-552-4616, Fax 907-552-3996.

ATTRACTIONS: Outdoor sports and recreation.

U.S. FORCES TRAVEL & TRANSFER GUIDE U.S.A. - 13

ALASKA

FORT RICHARDSON (AK03R5)
600 Richardson Drive, #5900
Fort Richardson, AK 99505-5900

TELEPHONE NUMBER INFORMATION: Main installation numbers: C-907-384-1110, D-317-384-1110.

LOCATION: Main gate is on Glenn Highway, eight miles south of Eagle River. USMRA: Page 128 (F-5), page 131 (E-1). NMC: Anchorage, eight miles southwest.

GENERAL INFORMATION: Headquarters for US Army, Alaska: Arctic Support Brigade; 1st Battalion (Airborne), 501st Infantry, and other support units.

TEMPORARY MILITARY LODGING: Lodging office, Bldg. 600, Richardson Dr, 0600-2230 Mon-Fri, 1000-1730 Sat-Sun, C-907-384-0436, D-317-384-0436. All ranks.

LOGISTICAL SUPPORT: Complete support facilities available.

ACS-384-1518
Chaplain-384-1468
Conv Store-428-3190
Fire Dept-384-0774
ITR Office-384-1649
Medical-384-0600
Police-384-0823
Retiree Services-1-800-478-7384
SATO-384-1663
Theater-428-1200

Cafeteria-428-1314
Child Care-384-1240
Exchange-428-1233
Gas Station-428-1248
Legal-384-0371
MWR-384-1300
Public Affairs-384-2113
SDO/NCO-384-6665

CHAMPUS-552-3430
Commissary-384-1565
Family Services-384-1518
Golf Course-428-2975/6
Locator-384-0306
Package Store-384-3190
Recreation-384-1649/1480
RV/Camping-384-1480
Snack Bar-428-1314

HEALTH & WELFARE: US Army Troop Medical Clinic, Emergency 911, Appointments C-907-384-0600/0605. Inpatient, see Elmendorf AFB listing, C-907-552-2778. Chapel serving all faiths C-907-384-1468.

RECREATION: Arts/Crafts EX-3717, Auto Hobby EX-3718, Bowling EX-1840, Fitness Center EX-1308, Rec Equip EX-1480, Outdoor Rec Center EX-0001, Golf Course/Ski Slope/Lodge EX-2975/6, Otter Lake Lodge EX-6246, Library EX-1648, Swimming, EX-1301, Skeet Range EX-1480, Youth Center EX-1508/1516. Black Spruce Travel Camp on post, 1 May-1 Sep, C-907-384-1480, 22 camper spaces w/W&E hookups, and 20 camper/tent spaces at Upper Otter Lake Campground; Seward Army Rec Camp at Resurrection Bay near Seward, 133 miles south of post, May-Sep, C-907-384-1649, D-317-384-1649, 50 camper spaces w/W&E hookups, 20 tent sites, 56 motel units plus four cabins.

SPACE-A: None. See Elmendorf AFB listing, C-907-552-4616, D-317-552-4616, Fax 907-552-3996.

ATTRACTIONS: Great outdoors and Anchorage.

14 - U.S. FORCES TRAVEL & TRANSFER GUIDE U.S.A

ALASKA

FORT WAINWRIGHT (AK07R5)
1060 Gaffney Road, #5900
Fort Wainwright, AK 99703-5900

TELEPHONE NUMBER INFORMATION: Main installation numbers: C-907-353-1110, D-317-353-1110.

LOCATION: From Fairbanks, take Airport Way E which leads to the Main Gate of the post. USMRA: Page 128 (F-4). NMC: Immediately adjacent to Fairbanks.

GENERAL INFORMATION: Infantry Brigade, Aviation Brigade, and other support units.

TEMPORARY MILITARY LODGING: Lodging office, Bldg. 1045 (Murphy Hall), Gaffney Rd., 0730-1630 Mon-Fri, C-907-353-6294/7291, D-317-353-6294/7291. All ranks. DV/VIP C-907-353-6671.

LOGISTICAL SUPPORT: Complete support facilities available.

ACS-353-6369
Child Care-356-1550
Exchange-356-1345
Gas Station-353-1263
Legal-353-6534
NCO Club-353-6109
Police-353-7535
Retiree Services-353-2102
SDO/NCO-353-7500
CHAMPUS-353-5340
Commissary-353-7805
Family Services-353-7331
Golf Course-353-6223
Locator-353-6815
O'Club-353-6109
Public Affairs-353-6701
RV/Camping-353-1998
Snack Bar-353-1976
Chaplain-353-6271
Conv Store-356-7259
Fire Dept-353-6485
ITR-353-2652
Medical-353-5281
Package Store-356-1044
Recreation-353-1998
SATO-353-1166
Theater-353-6792

HEALTH & WELFARE: Bassett Army Community Hospital, C-907-353-5143, Appointments C-907-353-5172/5173, 50 beds. Chapels serving all faiths C-907-353-7380/6610.

RECREATION: Arts/Crafts EX-7520, Auto Hobby EX-7436, Bowling EX-6498, Flying Club EX-6671, Golf EX-6223, Gym EX-7080/6748, Ski Lodge EX-6780, Boat Shop/Outdoor Equipment EX-6349, Library EX-7131, Swimming EX-1993, Rec Center EX-7882. Glass Park, on post, year round, C-907-353-2706, D-317-353-2706, camper spaces in open area, no hookups.

SPACE-A: None. See Eielson AFB listing, C-907-377-1854, D-317-377-1854, Fax 907-377-2287.

ATTRACTIONS: Fairbanks North Pole, Golden Days (mid-July), World Eskimo Indian Olympics, Tanana Valley State Fair, Jesse Owens Games, area tours, gold panning, riverboat tours, hiking, rafting, boating, hunting, fishing, camping, Alaskaland, Denali National Park, Mount McKinley (highest point in North America), Northern Lights, Luge Run (Bobsled), skiing, hunting, ice fishing, Chena Hot Springs, Dog Sled Races, Eskimo Winter Olympics, Special Olympics, Nenana Ice Classic, Ice Festival. Continuous daylight in summer; 2-3 hours light in winter.

U.S. FORCES TRAVEL & TRANSFER GUIDE U.S.A. - 15

ALASKA

JUNEAU COAST GUARD AIR STATION (AK19R5)
345 Eagan Drive
Juneau, AK 99801-1701

TELEPHONE NUMBER INFORMATION: Main installation number: C-907-463-2365.

LOCATION: Accessible by air or boat. From the ferry go right (southeast) 13 miles to Eagen Dr., follow signs. USMRA: Page 128 (I-6). NMC: Juneau, in city limits.

GENERAL INFORMATION: Search and Rescue Station.

TEMPORARY MILITARY LODGING: None.

LOGISTICAL SUPPORT: Limited support facilities available.

Consol Club-463-2382   Exchange-463-2385   Medical-463-2146

HEALTH AND WELFARE: Coast Guard Medical Clinic, Federal Bldg., Room 627, C-907-463-2146.

SPACE-A: None. See Sitka Coast Guard Air Station listing, C-907-966-5420, Fax 907-966-5428.

ATTRACTIONS: Beautiful Alaskan countryside. Hunting, fishing, and camping.

KETCHIKAN COAST GUARD BASE (AK21R5)
1300 Stedman Street
Ketchikan, AK 99901-6698

TELEPHONE NUMBER INFORMATION: Main installation numbers: C-907-228-0220.

LOCATION: Accessible only via AK-7, also known as North and South Tongass. Located three miles south of the ferry terminals on AK-7. USMRA: Page 128 (J-7). NMC: Ketchikan, in the city.

GENERAL INFORMATION: Industrial Support Facility, responsible for area search-and-rescue and other Coast Guard operations.

TEMPORARY MILITARY LODGING: None.

LOGISTICAL SUPPORT: Complete support facilities available.

Cafeteria-228-0258	CDO/OOD-228-0221	Exchange-228-0251
CHAMPUS-228-0320	Commissary-228-0251	CPO Club-228-0230
EM Club-228-0254	Family Services-228-0213	Medical-228-0320
MWR-228-0371	NCO Club-228-0254	O'Club-228-0254
Package Store-228-0251	Public Affairs-228-0299	Recreation-228-0371

HEALTH & WELFARE: Coast Guard Clinic, C-907-228-0320.

RECREATION: Auto Hobby EX-0334, off base camping facilities 225-2148, Camping/Rec Equip, Morale Boats, Fitness Center: Call EX-0341.

16 - U.S. FORCES TRAVEL & TRANSFER GUIDE U.S.A

ALASKA
Ketchikan Coast Guard Base, continued

SPACE-A: See Sitka Coast Guard Air Station listing, C-907-966-5420, Fax 907-966-5428.

KODIAK COAST GUARD SUPPORT CENTER (AK08R5)
P.O. Box 195014
Kodiak, AK 99619-5014

TELEPHONE NUMBER INFORMATION: Main installation numbers: C-907-487-5267, D-317-487-5267.

LOCATION: From Kodiak City, take main road southwest for seven miles. Base is on left side. USMRA: Page 128 (E-7). NMC: Kodiak, seven miles northeast.

GENERAL INFORMATION: Support Center, CG Air Station, LORAN Station, and home port for four ships, Electronics Support Unit, Communications Station, Marine Safety Detachment.

TEMPORARY MILITARY LODGING: Guest house, Bldg. N-30, 0800-1700 daily, C-907-487-5446, D-317-487-5446. All ranks. PCS or official duty, all others Space-A. DV/VIP C-907-487-5265.

LOGISTICAL SUPPORT: Complete support facilities available.

CDO/OOD-487-5267
Child Care-487-5481/5482
CPO Club-487-5798
Exchange-487-5373
Gas Station-487-5107
Locator-487-5267
O'Club-487-5798
Public Affairs-487-5700
SATO-487-2500
CHAMPUS-487-5757x131
Commissary-487-5015
EDF-487-5710
Family Services-487-5542
Golf Course-486-7561
Medical-487-5757
Package Store-487-5519
Recreation-487-5108
Snack Bar-487-5988
Chaplain-487-5730/5731
Conv Store-487-5359
EM Club-487-5110
Fire Dept-487-5808
Legal-487-5474
MWR-487-5108
Police-487-5266
Retiree Services-487-5761
Theater-487-5819

HEALTH & WELFARE: USCG Support Center Medical Clinic, Emergency C-907-487-5222. Chapels serving all faiths C-907-487-5730/5731.

RECREATION: Arts/Crafts EX-5471, Auto Hobby EX-5844, Boat House EX-5047, Bowling EX-5401, Gym EX-5272, Teen Center EX-5271. Racquetball, Weight Room and Outdoor Sports EX-5272.

SPACE-A: Pax Term, Hangar #1, 0800-1600 Mon-Fri, C-907-487-5149, D-317-487-5149, Fax 907-487-5273, flights to Alaska locations.

ATTRACTIONS: Hunting and fishing paradise. Home of the largest Kodiak bears.

KULIS AIR NATIONAL GUARD BASE (AK24R5)
5005 Raspberry Road
Anchorage, AK 99502-1998

TELEPHONE NUMBER INFORMATION: Main installation numbers: C-907-249-1176, D-317-626-1176.

U.S. FORCES TRAVEL & TRANSFER GUIDE U.S.A. - 17

ALASKA
Kulis Air National Guard Base, continued

LOCATION: Take International Airport Rd. to Jewel Lake Rd., turn right onto Raspberry Rd.. Main gate is approximately one mile on right. USMRA: Page 128 (F-5), page 131 (A-4). NMC: Anchorage, in city limits.

GENERAL INFORMATION: 176th Communications Flight.

TEMPORARY MILITARY LODGING: None. See Elmendorf AFB listing, C-907-552-2454, D-317-552-2454.

LOGISTICAL SUPPORT: Some support facilities available.

Cafeteria-249-1454	Chaplain-249-1141	Fire Department 249-1139
Legal-249-1100	Locator-249-1176	Medical-249-1415
NCO Club-249-1234	Police-249-1429	Public Affairs 249-1140
SATO-249-1206	SDO/NCO-249-1131	

HEALTH & WELFARE: Medical info, C-907-249-1415. Also see Elmendorf AFB listing, C-907-552-2778.

RECREATION: See Elmendorf AFB listing.

SPACE-A: Base Ops, C-907-249-1225, D-317-626-1225, Fax 907-249-1648.

ATTRACTIONS: Great opportunity for skiing, hunting, fishing, camping, sightseeing, and bird watching.

SITKA COAST GUARD AIR STATION (AK25R5)
Sitka, AK 99835-6500

TELEPHONE NUMBER INFORMATION: Main installation numbers: C-907-966-5431, after hours C-907-966-5420.

LOCATION: Located at end of Airport Rd. on Jponski Island, five miles north of airport terminal. USMRA: Page 128 (I-7). NMC: Juneau, 90 miles by air.

GENERAL INFORMATION: Air Station Sitka primarily involved in search and rescue throughout southeast Alaska. Additionally performs law enforcement, fisheries patrols and aids to navigation support.

TEMPORARY MILITARY LODGING: None.

LOGISTICAL SUPPORT: Limited support facilities available.

Cafeteria-966-5546	CHAMPUS-966-5438	EM Club-966-5516
Exchange-966-5436	Locator-966-5431	Medical-966-5438
O'Club-966-5596	Package Store-966-5436	SDO/NCO-966-5420

HEALTH AND WELFARE: Emergency 911. Air Station Sitka Clinic, C-907-966-5438.

RECREATION: Gym EX-5511, Camping Equip, Rec Equip, Support Services EX-5581.

SPACE-A: Very limited. C-907-966-5420, Fax 907-966-5428.

ALASKA
Sitka Coast Guard Air Station, continued

ATTRACTIONS: Sport fishing and hunting abundant. Sitka National Historical Park, totem poles and Sitka shoreline. Russian Bishop's House; St Michael's Russian Orthodox Church, with many precious icons on display; Castle Hill, site of 1867 transfer of Alaska territory from Russia to the US.

U.S. FORCES TRAVEL & TRANSFER GUIDE U.S.A. - 19

ARIZONA

DOLLAR RENT A CAR Call 1-800-800-4000. Get a military rate by using your Military Living ID # ML3009. Retirees/Active Duty/Reserve/Guard.

DAVIS-MONTHAN AIR FORCE BASE (AZ01R4)
Davis-Monthan Air Force Base, AZ 85707-3010

TELEPHONE NUMBER INFORMATION: Main installation numbers: C-520-750-3900, D-312-361-1110.

LOCATION: From the east on I-10, exit Kolb Rd; north to Golf Links Rd, left to Craycroft Rd, right to main gate. From the west on I-10, exit Alvernon Way; turn left, following road around to the base. (Alvernon Way turns into Golf Links Rd at Ajo intersection.) USMRA: Page 108 (F-9). NMC: Tucson, in city limits.

GENERAL INFORMATION: Air Combat Command Base, AAC Air Ops, and Aerospace Maintenance and Regeneration Center (AMARC).

TEMPORARY MILITARY LODGING: Lodging office, Bldg. 2350, 10th St, 24 hours daily, C-520-750-1500, D-312-361-3230. All ranks. DV/VIP 520-750-3600.

LOGISTICAL SUPPORT: Complete support facilities available.

Cafeteria-790-6150	CHAMPUS-750-5179	Chaplain-750-5411
Child Care-750-3336	Commissary-790-4341	Conv Store-748-8076
Exchange-748-7887	Family Services-750-3368	Gas Station-748-8212
Legal-750-5242	Locator-750-3347	Medical-750-2828
NCO Club-750-3100	O'Club-750-3301	Package Store-747-1365
Police-750-3517	Retiree Services-298-6574	SATO-750-4841
SDO/NCO-750-3121	Theater-748-1157	

HEALTH & WELFARE: USAF Hospital, Emergency C-520-750-3878, 65 beds. Chapel serving all faiths C-520-750-5411.

RECREATION: Library EX-4381, Rec Center/Tickets EX-3717, Swimming EX-3579, Gym EX-3714, Aero Club EX-3603, Golf EX-3734, Bowling EX-3461, Ceramics EX-4385/4028, Saddle Club 885-9049, Wood Hobby EX-3578, Picnic Area EX-3846, Auto Hobby EX-3614. Davis-Monthan Fam-Camp on base, C-520-747-9144, year round, 73 camper spaces w/full hookups, 35 overflow camper spaces w/o hookups.

SPACE-A: Pax Term/Ops in Bldg. 4820, 0700-1600 Mon-Fri, C-520-750-3641, D-312-361-3641, Fax 520-750-7229.

ATTRACTIONS: Old Tucson, movie sets, Reid Park, zoo, Arizona-Sonora Desert, and Pima Air Museum. Also, twice weekly tours at AMARC.

FORT HUACHUCA (AZ02R4)
Fort Huachuca, AZ 85613-5000

TELEPHONE NUMBER INFORMATION: Main installation numbers: C-520-538-7111, D-312-879-0111.

ARIZONA
Fort Huachuca, continued

LOCATION: From I-10 take AZ-90 S to Sierra Vista and main gate of post. USMRA: Page 108 (F,G-9,10). NMC: Tucson, 75 miles northwest.

GENERAL INFORMATION: US Army Intelligence Center and Fort Huachuca, US Army Information Systems Command, and US Army Electronic Proving Ground, Joint Interoperability Test Center.

TEMPORARY MILITARY LODGING: Lodging office, Bldg. 43083, Service Rd, 24 hours daily, C-520-533-2222/5361, D-312-821-5950. Extensive facilities. All ranks. DV/VIP C-520-533-1231, D-312-821-1231.

LOGISTICAL SUPPORT: Complete support facilities available.

CHAMPUS-533-1204	Chaplain-533-5559	Child Care-533-5209
Commissary-533-3360	Conv Store-458-8389	EM Club-533-3876
Exchange-458-7210	Family Services-533-2330	Fire-533-2111
Gas Station-458-9735	ITT Office-533-2404	Legal-533-3181
Locator-533-3636	Medical-538-7200	NCO Club-533-3802
O'Club-533-2193	Police-533-2181/3000	Retiree Services-533-5733
SATO-458-7144	SDO/NCO-533-6100	Snack Bar-533-5759
Theater-533-2950		

HEALTH & WELFARE: Raymond W. Bliss Army Community Hospital, Bldg. 45001, 80 beds. Emergency C-520-533-5152. Chapel serving all faiths, Center C-520-533-5559.

RECREATION: Bowling 533-2849, Golf 538-7160, Gym 533-2948, Library 533-2666, Museum 533-5736, Picnic Reservations 538-8013, Riding 533-5220, Swimming 533-3858/3853, Arts/Crafts 533-2015, Auto Hobby 538-2155, Youth Activities 533-3205, Rec Center 533-2012, Apache Flats Campground on post, C-520-533-7085, D-312-879-7085, year round, 24 camper spaces w/W&E hookups, and a limited number of tent spaces.

SPACE-A: Limited flights from Libby Army Airfield on post via executive aircraft, C-520-538-2860.

ATTRACTIONS: Fort museum. Original cantonment, a National Historical Landmark. Tombstone, is a 25 minute drive on the Charleston Road.

GILA BEND AIR FORCE AUXILIARY FIELD (AZ16R4)
Gila Bend Air Force Auxiliary Field, AZ 85337-5000

TELEPHONE NUMBER INFORMATION: Main installation numbers: C-520-683-6200, D-312-853-5200 (Answered by Gila Bend Security Police).

LOCATION: From I-10 west of Phoenix take exit 112 (Yuma/Gila Bend); south on AZ-85 through Gila Bend; right at Gila Bend AFAF/Ajo sign approximately three-and-a-half miles to the AFAF. USMRA: Page 108 (C-7,8). NMC: Phoenix, 69 miles northeast.

GENERAL INFORMATION: Primarily responsible for Barry M. Goldwater Air Force Gunnery Range, which covers 2.7 million acres.

TEMPORARY MILITARY LODGING: Lodging office, Bldg. 4300, C-520-683-6238, D-312-853-5238.

ARIZONA
Gila Bend Air Force Auxiliary Field, continued

LOGISTICAL SUPPORT: Some support facilities available.

Police-683-6220

HEALTH & WELFARE: None. See Luke AFB listing, C-602-856-2778.

RECREATION: Fam-Camp on base, year round, C-520-683-6238, D-312-853-5238, 35 camper spaces w/full hookups w/cable TV, picnic tables, various tent sites w/o hookups. Outdoor basketball and tennis courts. Picnic Area with horseshoe pits, volleyball court and softball field.

SPACE-A: None. See Luke AFB listing, C-602-856-7131, D-312-853-7131.

ATTRACTIONS: Pleasant weather year round. Mountain areas and Mexico within easy driving distance. Luke AFB, 65 miles away, has full support facilities.

LUKE AIR FORCE BASE (AZ03R4)
7131 North Litchfield Road
Luke Air Force Base, AZ 85309-1534

TELEPHONE NUMBER INFORMATION: Main installation numbers: C-520-856-7411, D-312-896-1110.

LOCATION: From Phoenix, west on I-10 to Litchfield Rd Exit 128, north on Litchfield Rd approximately five miles. Also, from Phoenix, on I-17 to Glendale Ave, west on Glendale Ave to intersection of Glendale Ave and Litchfield Rd, approximately 10 miles. USMRA: Page 108 (D-6,7). NMC: Phoenix, 20 miles east.

GENERAL INFORMATION: Air Education Training Command Base. Largest fighter wing in free world.

TEMPORARY MILITARY LODGING: Lodging office, Bldg. 660, Bong Lane, 24 hours daily, C-520-856-3941. All ranks. DV/VIP EX-C-520-856-5840.

LOGISTICAL SUPPORT: Complete support facilities available.

CHAMPUS-856-7760
Commissary-935-3821
Exchange-935-2671
ITT Office-856-6000
Medical-856-7506
Retiree Services-856-6827
Snack Bar-856-7102
Chaplain-856-6211
Conv Store-935-2414
Family Services-856-6415
Legal-856-6901
O'Club-856-6446
SATO-856-6891
Theater-856-6461
Child Care-856-6339
EM Club-856-7136
Gas Station-935-4953
Locator-856-6405
Police-856-6322
SDO/NCO-856-5800

HEALTH & WELFARE: USAF Hospital, Emergency C-520-856-7506, 40 beds. Appointments C-520-856-2778. Chapels serving all faiths C-520-856-6211/6212.

RECREATION: Arts/Crafts EX-6502, Auto Hobby EX-6107, Wood Hobby EX-6566, Bowling EX-6529, Fitness Center EX-6241, Rec Center EX-7152, Library EX-7191, Youth Center EX-6225. Operates Fort Tuthill Rec Area, 150 miles north on I-17, four miles south of Flagstaff, C-520-774-8893, D-312-896-3401, 21 camper spaces with W&E hookups, 13 camper/tent spaces with no hookups, eight huts, four yurts, 11 A-frames, one furnished

ARIZONA
Luke Air Force Base, continued

cabin, and one Multi Family Chalet; Gila Bend Fam-Camp at Auxiliary Field, C-520-683-6238/6211, D-312-853-5275/5211, 31 spaces with full hookups.

SPACE-A: Pax Term/Lounge, Bldg. 439, 0630-2230 Mon-Fri, 0730-1800 Sat, Sun, Holidays, C-520-856-7131, D-312-853-7131, flights to Midwest and West Coast.

ATTRACTIONS: Colorful Scottsdale nearby. Arizona state capital, fairgrounds and coliseum in Phoenix. ASU in Tempe. Lots of sunshine, hot summers, cool winters.

YUMA ARMY PROVING GROUND (AZ05R4)
Yuma Army Proving Ground, AZ 85365-5000

TELEPHONE NUMBER INFORMATION: Main installation numbers: C-520-328-2020, D-312-899-2020.

LOCATION: Northeast of I-8 turn right on US-95. Southwest of I-10 turn left on US-95. US-95 bisects Army Proving Ground. USMRA: Page 108 (A-6,7,8; B-7,8). NMC: Yuma, 27 miles southwest.

GENERAL INFORMATION: Army Materiel Test Facility with instrumented ranges.

TEMPORARY MILITARY LODGING: Lodging office, Bldg. 1003, 5th St & Barranca Rd, 0700-1800 daily, C-520-328-2127/2129, D-312-899-2127/2129. All ranks. DV/VIP C-520-328-2020.

LOGISTICAL SUPPORT: Complete support facilities available.

ACS-328-2513
Chaplain-328-3465
Comm Club-328-2097
Family Services-328-2711
ITT Office-328-2278
Medical-328-2502
SDO/NCO-328-2020

CDO/OOD-328-2020
Child Care-328-2588
Conv. Store-328-2252
Fire Dept-328-2949
Legal-328-2608
MWR-328-2223
Theater-328-4586

CHAMPUS-328-2502
Commissary-328-2240
Exchange-328-2252
Gas Station-343-1365
Locator-328-2151/2430
Police-328-2720

HEALTH & WELFARE: US Army Health Clinic, Emergency C-520-328-2911, Appointments C-520-328-2502. Inpatient, see San Diego Naval Medical Center, CA listing, C-800-453-0491.

RECREATION: Leisure Travel Office EX-2586/3586/4586, Bowling EX-2790, Fitness Center EX-2400, Swimming EX-2209, Tennis Courts EX-2400, Outdoor Rec EX-4586. Boating on the Colorado River. Yuma Proving Ground Travel Camp on post, C-520-328-3095, D-312-899-3095, 12 camper spaces w/full hookups

SPACE-A: See Yuma MCAS listing for details, C-520-341-2729, D-312-951-2729.

ATTRACTIONS: Isolated post, next to Kofa National Wildlife Refuge and the Colorado River.

U.S. FORCES TRAVEL & TRANSFER GUIDE U.S.A. - 23

ARIZONA

YUMA MARINE CORPS AIR STATION (AZ04R4)
Box 99100
Yuma Marine Corps Air Station, AZ 85369-9100

TELEPHONE NUMBER INFORMATION: Main installation numbers: C-520-341-2011, D-312-951-2011.

LOCATION: From I-8 take Ave 3E south for one mile to base on right, adjacent to Yuma IAP. USMRA: Page 108 (A-8). NMC: Yuma, three miles northwest.

GENERAL INFORMATION: The premier Marine Corps Combat Air Training Base. Near perfect flying conditions and range facilities are available.

TEMPORARY MILITARY LODGING: Lodging office, Sta S-4, Billeting fund, Bldg. 1058, Martini Ave, 24 hours daily, C-520-341-3578/3094, D-312-951-3578/3094. All ranks. Hostess House C-520-341-2262.

LOGISTICAL SUPPORT: Complete support facilities available.

CHAMPUS-341-2916	Chaplain-341-2371	Child Care-341-2350
Commissary-341-2248	Conv Store-341-3567	EM Club-341-2457
Exchange-341-2256	Family Services-341-3421	Gas Station-341-2110
Legal-341-2481	Locator-341-2011	Medical-341-2772
O'Club-341-2711	Package Store-341-3567	Police-341-2205/2361
Public Affairs-341-2275	SATO-341-2755	SDO/NCO-341-2253
SNCO Club-341-2711	Theater-341-2358	

HEALTH & WELFARE: Naval Medical Clinic, Emergency C-520-341-2111, Appointments C-520-341-2772. Inpatient, see San Diego Naval Medical Center, CA listing, C-800-453-0491. Chapels serving all faiths C-520-341-2371.

RECREATION: Special Services EX-2278, Athletic/Picnic Facilities EX-2278, Camping Equip EX-2848, Gym EX-2727, Library EX-2785, Auto Hobby EX-2395, Bowling 726-8320; Swimming EM-EX-2926, Officers-EX-3474. Operates Martinez Lake Rec Area, C-520-341-2278, D-312-951-2007, year round, on the Colorado River, 38 miles north of MCAS off US-95, 17 camper spaces w/W&E hookups, three camper/tent spaces, five cabins and four mobile homes.

SPACE-A: Pax Term/Lounge and Ops, Bldg. 151, 0700-1530 daily, C-520-341-2729, D-312-951-2729.

ATTRACTIONS: Desert type climate, Colorado River.

Other Installations in Arizona

Holbrook Radar Bomb Scoring Site, Holbrook, AZ 86025-1826.
USMRA: Page 108 (G-4,5). C-520-524-3016, Exchange-520-524-3119.
Sky Harbor ANGB, 161st Air Refueling Group, 2001 S. 32nd St. Phoenix, AZ 85034.
USMRA: Page 108 (D-7). C-520-231-8000, D-312-853-9000. SPA-520-231-8162.

24 - U.S. FORCES TRAVEL & TRANSFER GUIDE U.S.A

ARKANSAS

DOLLAR RENT A CAR Call 1-800-800-4000. Get a military rate by using your Military Living ID # ML3009. Retirees/Active Duty/Reserve/Guard.

CAMP JOSEPH T. ROBINSON (AR07R2)
North Little Rock, AR 72199-9600

TELEPHONE NUMBER INFORMATION: Main installation numbers: C-501-212-5100, D-312-962-5100.

LOCATION: Take Burns Park exit off I-40, follow signs to camp (two miles). USMRA: Page 76 (D-5). NMC: North Little Rock, one mile south.

GENERAL INFORMATION: Headquarters Arkansas National Guard, 122nd Army Reserve Command.

TEMPORARY MILITARY LODGING: Lodging office, Bldg. 6300, 6th St and Missouri Ave, 0700-1530 Mon-Thu, 0700-2200 Fri, 0700-1630 Sat, 0600-1530 Sun. C-501-212-5274.

LOGISTICAL SUPPORT: Some support facilities available.

All Ranks Club-758-5076
Fire Department-212-5280
Locator-212-5100
Police-212-5280
Snack Bar-753-9017
Chaplain-212-5926
Golf Course-753-5608
Medical-212-5262
Public Affairs-212-5020
Exchange-753-9017
Legal-212-5030
MWR-753-9017
Restaurant-758-8468

HEALTH AND WELFARE: None. See Little Rock Air Force Base listing, C-501-988-7333. Chapel serving all faiths, C-501-212-5926.

RECREATION: Golf Course 753-5608, Physical Fitness Center, Rec Equip, Gym call 212-5639, swimming pool, lounge, Support Services call 753-9017.

SPACE-A: None. See Little Rock AFB, listing, C-501-988-3684, D-312-731-3684, Fax 501-988-6726.

ATTRACTIONS: State Capitol, Burns Park, Wild River Country, Quapaw District, Little Rock Zoo, Arkansas Arts Center, Governor's Mansion, Old Mill, Pinnacle Mountain, War Memorial Park, Arkansas Travelers baseball.

FORT CHAFFEE (AR04R2)
Fort Chaffee, AR 72905-5000

Scheduled to close October 1997.

TELEPHONE NUMBER INFORMATION: Main installation numbers: C-501-481-2141, D-312-962-2111.

LOCATION: From I-40, take the I-540 exit west in Fort Smith. From I-540, exit onto AR-22 East (Rogers Ave) and continue through the town of Barling to Fort Chaffee, one mile east of Barling. USMRA: Page 76 (A,B-4,5). NMC: Fort Smith, six miles northwest.

U.S. FORCES TRAVEL & TRANSFER GUIDE U.S.A. - 25

ARKANSAS
Fort Chaffee, continued

GENERAL INFORMATION: Active Army and Reserve Component training support, USAR NCO Academy, Regional Training Brigade.

TEMPORARY MILITARY LODGING: Lodging office, Bldg. 1377, Fort Smith Blvd, 0730-0200 Mon-Tue, 0730-2400 Wed-Fri, 0930-1800 Sat-Sun, C-501-484-2252/2917, D-312-962-2252. DV/VIP C-501-484-3216.

LOGISTICAL SUPPORT: Complete support facilities available.

CDO/OOD-484-2666	Conv Store-452-2553	Community Club-484-2340
Exchange-484-2178	Fire Dept-484-2127	Golf Course-484-2326
Locator-484-2460	Medical-484-2488	MWR-484-2550
Police-484-2666	Public Affairs-484-2905	Retiree Services-484-3130
SDO/NCO-484-2666		

HEALTH & WELFARE: St Edward Mercy Medical Center, Emergency C-501-484-6241, Info C-501-484-6100. Chapel serving all faiths.

RECREATION: Golf EX-2326, Gym EX-2550, Library EX-2550, Rec Equip EX-2550, Rec Center EX-2550. Chaffee Trailer Park on post, C-501-484-2770, D-312-962-2770, 39 camper spaces w/full hookups.

SPACE-A: None. See Little Rock AFB, listing, C-501-988-3684, D-312-731-3684, Fax 501-988-6726.

ATTRACTIONS: Ouachita and Ozark National Forests, city of Fort Smith, Arkansas River. Fayetteville, home of the University of Arkansas Razorbacks, offers great opportunity for sporting events.

LITTLE ROCK AIR FORCE BASE (AR02R2)
1250 Thomas Ave
Little Rock Air Force Base, AR 72099-5028

TELEPHONE NUMBER INFORMATION: Main installation numbers: C-501-988-3131, D-312-731-1110.

LOCATION: From US-67/167 to Jacksonville, follow signs to main gate. USMRA: Page 76 (D,E-5). NMC: Little Rock, 18 miles southwest.

GENERAL INFORMATION: Air Combat Command Base, C-130 Training, USAF Combat Aerial Delivery School, Headquarters Arkansas Air National Guard, and other missions.

TEMPORARY MILITARY LODGING: P.O. Box 1192, Bldg. 1024, Cannon Circle, 24 hours daily, C-501-988-6753, D-312-731-6753. DV/VIP 501-988-6828.

LOGISTICAL SUPPORT: Complete support facilities available.

CDO/OOD 988-3200	CHAMPUS-988-7458	Chaplain-988-6014
Child Care-988-6139	Commissary-988-6990	Conv Store-988-4841
EM Club-988-4121	Exchange-988-1150	Family Services-988-6801
Fire Dept-988-3737	Gas Station-988-2301	Golf Course-988-6199
ITT Office-988-3216	Legal-988-6852	Locator-988-6025

ARKANSAS
Little Rock Air Force Base, continued

Medical-988-8811	MWR-988-3365	O'Club-988-1111
Package Store-988-1374	Police-988-3221	Public Affairs-988-3601
Retiree Services-988-6095	RV/Camping-988-3365	SATO-988-4117
Snack Bar-988-8111	Theater-988-6461	

HEALTH & WELFARE: 314th Medical Group, Emergency C-501-988-7333, 15 beds. Chapel serving all faiths C-501-988-6014.

RECREATION: Bowling EX-3793, Rec Center EX-3216. Library, Golf, Swimming, Youth Center, Hobby Shops, Gym and Rec Equip; call main number for extensions. Little Rock Fam-Camp on base, year round, C-501-988-3365, D-312-731-3365, 23 camper spaces w/W&E hookups, six tent spaces.

SPACE-A: Pax Term/Lounge, Bldg. 272, 0730-1630 Mon-Fri, C-501-988-3684, D-312-731-3684, Fax 501-988-6726, flights to CONUS, OCONUS and foreign locations.

ATTRACTIONS: Little Rock, Governor's Mansion, State Capitol, Burns Park, War Memorial Stadium, Arkansas River, and Lake Conway.

PINE BLUFF ARSENAL (AR03R2)
Pine Bluff Arsenal, AR 71602-9500

TELEPHONE NUMBER INFORMATION: Main installation numbers: C-501-540-3000, D-312-966-3000.

LOCATION: Off US-65 northwest of Pine Bluff. Take AR-256, cross AR-365 into main gate of arsenal. USMRA: Page 76 (E-6). NMC: Pine Bluff, eight miles southeast.

GENERAL INFORMATION: An Engineer, Production, Storage, and Test Facility for chemical munitions and related equipment.

TEMPORARY MILITARY LODGING: Lodging office, Bldg. 15-390, Sibert Rd, 0730-1600 daily, C-501-540-3008, D-312-966-3008. DV/VIP facilities available.

LOGISTICAL SUPPORT: Limited support facilities available.

CHAMPUS-540-3410	Exchange-535-1707	Legal-540-3131
Locator-540-3000	Medical-540-3409	Public Affairs-540-3421
Police-540-3505/3506	SATO-540-3613	SDO/NCO-540-3176

HEALTH & WELFARE: US Army Medical Clinic C-501-540-3409. Inpatient, see Little Rock AFB listing, C-501-988-7333. No chapels on the arsenal; all faiths served in Pine Bluff.

RECREATION: Rec Bldg., Golf (9-hole course), Driving Range, Courts and Fields. Rec area on post at Tulley, and Yellow Lakes, limited facilities.

SPACE-A: None. See Little Rock AFB listing, C-501-988-3684, D-312-731-3684.

ATTRACTIONS: Pine Bluff and the Arkansas River. Arkansas...The Natural State.

U.S. FORCES TRAVEL & TRANSFER GUIDE U.S.A. - 27
CALIFORNIA

DOLLAR RENT A CAR — Call 1-800-800-4000. Get a military rate by using your Military Living ID # ML3009. Retirees/Active Duty/Reserve/Guard.

ALAMEDA COAST GUARD SUPPORT CENTER (CA28R4)
Coast Guard Island
Alameda, CA 94501-5100

TELEPHONE NUMBER INFORMATION: Main installation numbers: C-510-437-3191/3151.

LOCATION: From the north: take US-880 south to 16th St/Embarcadero exit; left on Embarcadero follow signs to causeway and island. Signs posted. From the south: take US-880 north to 29th St., exit; Left U-turn at first left, cross overpass, then first right through the light, follow signs around to causeway and island. USMRA: Page 119 (D-5). NMC: Oakland, one mile northwest.

GENERAL INFORMATION: Major Coast Guard Support Base in San Francisco area.

TEMPORARY MILITARY LODGING: Housing office, Bldg. 21, McCullough Dr, 0730-1530 daily, C-510-437-3180; other hours OOD, Bldg. 3, C-510-437-3304. Limited facilities. DV/VIP C-510-437-3303. Duty personnel only.

LOGISTICAL SUPPORT: Most support facilities available.

Chaplain-437-3067
Gas Station-437-3166
Medical-437-3581
Child Care-437-2740
Legal-437-3330
Police-437-3151
Exchange-437-3165
Locator-437-3151
Special Services-437-3577

HEALTH & WELFARE: Outpatient clinics only C-510-437-3581. Inpatient, see Travis AFB listing, C-707-423-3000. Chapels serving all faiths C-510-437-3067.

RECREATION: Gym, Swimming, Auto Hobby Shops, Tennis and Racquetball Courts. Ticket Office-Balboa Travel, Outdoor Recreation Office.

SPACE-A: See Alameda NAS listing, C-510-263-3348, D-312-993-3346.

ATTRACTIONS: San Francisco and the exciting San Francisco Bay Area nearby.

ALAMEDA NAVAL AIR STATION (CA33R4)
Alameda Naval Air Station, CA 94501-5000

Scheduled to close March 1997.

TELEPHONE NUMBER INFORMATION: Main installation numbers: C-510-263-0111, D-312-993-0111.

LOCATION: From Nimitz Highway, CA-880 south, take the Broadway exit. CA-880 north, take Broadway exit (880 north does not say Alameda). Directions to NAS clearly marked. USMRA: Page 119 (D-5). NMC: Oakland, two miles northeast.

CALIFORNIA
Alameda Naval Air Station, continued

GENERAL INFORMATION: Naval Aviation Depot, Fleet Support. Near the San Francisco-Oakland Bay Bridge, on the Oakland side. One home-ported ship, 43 tenant commands.

TEMPORARY MILITARY LODGING: BOQ, Bldg. 17, B St, 24 hours, C-510-263-3649. Navy Lodge, All Ranks, Bldg. 531, C St, C-510-523-4917 or 1-800-NAVY-INN, DV/VIP, EM & Officers, C-510-263-3673/3649.

LOGISTICAL SUPPORT: Complete support facilities available.

CHAMPUS-263-4399	Chaplain-263-3740	Child Care-263-3190
Commissary-263-2727	Conv Store-748-8105	EM Club-263-3217
Exchange-748-8100	Family Services-263-3146	Gas Station-748-8191
Legal-263-3069	Locator-263-0111	Medical-263-4400
O'Club-263-3227	Police-263-3767	SATO-522-4930
SDO/NCO-263-3011	Theater-263-3164	

HEALTH & WELFARE: Naval Branch Medical Clinic, Emergency 9-911. Chapel serving all faiths C-510-263-3740.

RECREATION: Marina EX-3183, Bowling EX-3209, Rec Equip EX-3184, Gym EX-3197, Auto Hobby EX-3173, Swimming EX-3196, MWR Office EX-3151, Youth Center EX-3487. Alameda Marina RV Park on post, year round, C-510-263-3166, D-312-993-3166, 24 camper spaces w/W&E hookups.

SPACE-A: Pax Term/Lounge, Bldg. 77, C-510-263-3346, D-312-993-3346, frequent flights to West Coast Air Stations, infrequent flights to other locations.

ATTRACTIONS: San Francisco & Cable Cars nearby. Great seafood restaurants, and China Town.

ARMED FORCES RESERVE CENTER LOS ALAMITOS/ CA ARMY NATIONAL GUARD (CA39R4)
Building 15, Post Headquarters
Los Alamitos, CA 90720-5001

TELEPHONE NUMBER INFORMATION: Main installation numbers: C-310-795-2000, D-312-972-2011.

LOCATION: Off I-605. Clearly marked. USMRA: Page 117 (E-6,7). NMC: Los Angeles, five miles north.

GENERAL INFORMATION: Armed Forces Reserve Center (AFRC), supporting all active military and reservists from all branches of the Armed Forces, including, retired military, DoD Personnel, certain State active duty and Civil Service personnel, and quasi-military personnel.

TEMPORARY MILITARY LODGING: Transient Quarters, Bldg. 19, Hq AFRC, duty hours, C-310-795-2124, Fax 310-795-2125, D-312-972-2124.

LOGISTICAL SUPPORT: Limited support facilities available.

Beauty-430-3698	Clothing Sales-795-2059	Dry Cleaners-594-5503

U.S. FORCES TRAVEL & TRANSFER GUIDE U.S.A. - 29

CALIFORNIA
AFRC Los Alamitos, continued

Exchange-430-1076
Golf Course-430-9913
Police-795-2100
Snack Bar-775-1296

Fire Department-795-2144
Locator-795-2000
SATO-795-2051

Gas Station-795-1247
Package Store-795-1247
SDO/NCO-795-2090

HEALTH & WELFARE: None. See Los Angeles AFB listing, C-310-363-0964.

RECREATION: None at the AFRC, beaches nearby. See other bases in the Los Angeles and Orange County area.

SPACE-A: C-310-795-2571, D-312-972-2571, Fax 310-795-2566.

ATTRACTIONS: Los Angeles, Hollywood and Orange County.

BARSTOW MARINE CORPS LOGISTICS BASE (CA13R4)
Command Headquarters, Box 110100
Barstow MCLB, CA 92311-5001

TELEPHONE NUMBER INFORMATION: Main installation numbers: C-619-577-6211, D-312-282-6444, L-619-577-6675.

LOCATION: On I-40, one-and-a-half miles east of Barstow. Take I-15 northeast from San Bernardino, or west from Las Vegas, NV. Signs mark direction to MC Logistics Base. USMRA: Page 111 (G-12,13). NMC: San Bernardino, 75 miles southwest.

GENERAL INFORMATION: The Marine Corps Logistics Base serving the western part of the US.

TEMPORARY MILITARY LODGING: Lodging office, Bldg. 171, 0700-1530 daily, C-619-577-6418, D-312-282-6418, Fax C-619-577-6542. Other hours OD, Bldg. 30, Room 8, EX-6611. All ranks. DV/VIP C-619-577-6555, D-312-282-6555. Oasis EX-6550 Active Duty, Retired Military and guests of the same.

LOGISTICAL SUPPORT: Complete support facilities available.

Cafeteria-577-6428
Chaplain-577-6846
Conv Store-256-8974
Family Services-577-6533
ITT Office-577-6541
Locator (Mil)-577-6675
Police-577-6669
SDO/NCO-577-6009

CDO/OOD-577-6611
Child Care-577-6287
EM/NCO Club-577-6532
Fire Dept-577-6731
Legal-577-6874
Medical-577-6591
Public Affairs-577-6430
Snack Bar-577-6264

CHAMPUS-577-6593
Commissary-577-6403
Exchange-256-8974
Gas Station-256-9411
Locator (Civ)-577-6485
O'Club-577-6418
SATO-577-6135

HEALTH & WELFARE: Naval Branch Medical Clinic, Emergency C-619-577-6577, Appointments C-619-577-6591. Inpatient, see Fort Irwin listing, C-619-380-3124. Chapel serving all faiths C-619-577-6402.

RECREATION: Auto Hobby EX-6441, Bowling EX-6264, Ceramics EX-6228, Rec Equip EX-6898, Golf EX-6431, Gym EX-6899, Library EX-6395, Special Services EX-6541, Wood/Rock Hobby EX-6441.

SPACE-A: None. See Edwards AFB listing, C-805-277-4412/4185, D-312-4412-4185.

30 - U.S. FORCES TRAVEL & TRANSFER GUIDE U.S.A

CALIFORNIA
Barstow Marine Corps Logistics Base, continued

ATTRACTIONS: Calico Ghost Town, Solar One, Lake Dolores.

BEALE AIR FORCE BASE (CA47R4)
5900 C Street
Beale Air Force Base, CA 95903-1221

TELEPHONE NUMBER INFORMATION: Main installation numbers: C-916-634-3000, D-312-368-3000.

LOCATION: From CA-70 North, exit south of Marysville, to North Beale Rd; continue for 10 miles until road dead ends at main gate of AFB. USMRA: Page 110 (C,D-5,6). NMC: Yuba City, 12 miles west.

GENERAL INFORMATION: Air Combat Command Base, Space Warning Squadron, aerial reconnaissance, training.

TEMPORARY MILITARY LODGING: Lodging office, 24112 B Street, 24 hours daily, C-916-634-2953, D-312-368-2953. All ranks. DV/VIP C-916-634-2954.

LOGISTICAL SUPPORT: Complete support facilities available.

Cafeteria-788-1070
Commissary-634-2421
Exchange-634-2987
Golf Course-634-2124
Legal-634-2928
Police-634-2131
SATO-634-2940
Tricare-788-0205

Chaplain-634-2306
Consol Club-634-4948
Family Services-634-2860
Information-634-2113
Locator-634-3000
Package Store-634-2982
Snack Bar-788-1550

Child Care-634-4717
Conv Store-788-1271
Gas Station-788-0214
ITT Office-634-2268
Medical-634-4829
Retiree Services-634-2156
Theater-634-2520

HEALTH & WELFARE: USAF Hospital, Emergency C-916-634-4444, 30 beds. Appointments C-916-634-2941. Chapel serving all faiths C-916-634-2306.

RECREATION: Rec Services EX-2273, Aero Club EX-9011, Arts/Crafts EX-2294, Auto Hobby EX-2296, Rec Center EX-2264, Bowling EX-2303, Fitness Center EX-2259, Golf EX-2124, Rod/Gun Club 788-2473, Library EX-2314, Youth Center EX-4719, Rec Equip EX-3340. Swimming at club pools. Beale Fam-Camp on base, year round, C-916-634-3382, D-312-368-3382, 43 camper spaces w/full hookups.

SPACE-A: Pax Term/Lounge, Bldg. 1062, 0700-1600 Mon-Fri, C-916-634-8388, D-312-368-8388, flights to CONUS and overseas via KC-135.

ATTRACTIONS: Sacramento, Sutter's Fort, Zoo, Grass Valley and Nevada City nearby.

CAMP PARKS/PARKS RESERVE FORCES TRAINING AREA (CA97R4)
Bldg. 790
Dublin, CA 94568

TELEPHONE NUMBER INFORMATION: Main installation numbers: C-510-803-5648.

U.S. FORCES TRAVEL & TRANSFER GUIDE U.S.A. - 31

CALIFORNIA
Camp Parks, continued

LOCATION: East Bay Area; westbound 580 to Dublin, CA. USMRA: Page 119 (G-6). NMC: Oakland.

TEMPORARY MILITARY LODGING: None. See Oakland Army Base, C-510-466-3205, D-312-859-3113.

LOGISTICAL SUPPORT: Limited support facilities available.

Community Club-803-5615   Exchange-829-7770   Fire Dept-803-5613
Medical-803-5606   Police-803-5604   Public Affairs-803-5636
Recreation-803-5618

HEALTH & WELFARE: None. See Oakland Army Base listing, C-510-466-2918.

ATTRACTIONS: San Francisco and Bay Area. Many exciting things to see and do in and around Oakland. Jack London Square shopping area at the foot of Broadway in Oakland is a waterfront promenade lined with stores, restaurants and entertainment.

CAMP PENDLETON MARINE CORPS BASE (CA30R4)
Box 555019
Camp Pendleton, CA 92055-5019

TELEPHONE NUMBER INFORMATION: Main installation numbers: C-619-725-4111, D-312-365-4111, FTS-725-4111.

LOCATION: On I-5 which is adjacent to Camp Pendleton main gate. Take "Camp Pendleton Only" off ramp I-5 at Oceanside. USMRA: Page 111 (F-14,15). NMC: Oceanside, adjacent to Base southeast.

GENERAL INFORMATION: The only Marine Corps Amphibious Training Base on the West Coast.

TEMPORARY MILITARY LODGING: Lodging office, Bldg. 1341 (Mainside), 24 hours, daily, C-619-725-3718, D-312-365-5304. All ranks. DV/VIP C-619-725-5194.

LOGISTICAL SUPPORT: Complete support facilities available.

CDO/OOD-725-5617   CHAMPUS-725-1262   Chaplain-725-3777
Child Care-725-6112   Commissary-725-4012   Conv Store-725-6233
EM Club-725-6122   Exchange-725-6233   Family Services-725-5361
Fire Department-725-3333 Gas Station-725-5828   Golf Course-725-4756
ITT-725-5864   ITR-725-7447   Legal-725-6172
Locator-725-5171   Medical-725-1288   MWR-725-5355
O'Club-725-6571   Police-725-3888   Public Affairs-725-5011
Recreation-725-6195   Retiree Services-725-9052 SATO-725-4396
SDO/NCO-725-5617

HEALTH & WELFARE: Naval Hospital, Emergency C-619-725-3258, 600 beds. Appointments C-619-725-1288. Chapel serving all faiths C-619-725-1223.

RECREATION: Auto Hobby EX-5963, Beach Info EX-2463/7935, Bowling EX-5945, Field Archery EX-6288, Flying Club EX-4910, Golf EX-4756, Hobby Shop EX-4880,

32 - U.S. FORCES TRAVEL & TRANSFER GUIDE U.S.A

CALIFORNIA
Camp Pendleton Marine Corps Base, continued

Library EX-5104/5669, Physical Fitness Center EX-6394/2951, Riding Stables EX-5094, Rec Equip EX-5296. Skeet/Trap EX-4832. Special Services EX-6288, Swimming Pool EX-4344/5084, Operates three camping facilities on base, year round: Lake O'Neill Recreation Park on base, year round, C-619-725-4241, D-312-365-4241, five camper spaces with full hookups, 40 camper spaces w/W&E hookups, 20 camper spaces w/W only, 26 camper/tent spaces w/o hookups; Club Del Cottages, C-619-725-2134, 48 cottages, 84 camper spaces w/W&E hookups; San Onofre Recreation Beach on base, year round, C-619-725-7935, d-312-365-7935, 36 mobile homes/cottages, 80 camper spaces w/W&E hookups, 26 camper spaces w/o hookups, 42 camper/tent spaces w/W only.

SPACE-A: None. See El Toro Marine Corps Air Station listing, C-714-726-3920, D-312-997-3920.

ATTRACTIONS: Sandy beaches, Old California Missions, Disneyland, Knott's Berry Farm, Magic Mountain, Sea World, Wild Animal Park, Lion Country Safari, San Diego Zoo, Balboa Park, Maritime Museum, Carlsbad Raceway, Palomar Observatory; race tracks at Hollywood Park, Del Mar, Santa Anita or Los Alamitos.

CAMP ROBERTS (CA98R4)
San Roberts, CA 93451-5000

TELEPHONE NUMBER INFORMATION: Main installation numbers: C-805-238-3100.

LOCATION: On Highway 101, halfway between Los Angeles and San Francisco. USMRA: Page 111 (C-10). NMC: Paso Robles, 12 miles north.

TEMPORARY MILITARY LODGING: Lodging office, C-805-238-8312.

LOGISTICAL SUPPORT: Limited support facilities available.

Chaplain-238-8185   Conf Center-238-8337   Exchange-238-8195
Fire Dept-238-8220   MWR-238-8337   Public Affairs-238-8348
Recreation-238-8167   Snack Bar-238-8120

HEALTH AND WELFARE: None. See Fort Hunter Liggett listing, C-408-386-2516 or Camp San Luis Obispo listing, C-805-546-7600.

RECREATION: Camping facilities on post, C-805-238-8312.

SPACE-A: None. See Lemoore NAS listing, C-209-998-1683, D-312-949-1683, Fax 209-998-3046.

ATTRACTIONS: A short drive to the Hearst Castle, hunting, fishing.

CAMP SAN LUIS OBISPO (CA83R4)
Highway 1, Bldg 738
San Luis Obispo, CA 93403-4360

TELEPHONE NUMBER INFORMATION: Main installation numbers: C-805-594-6500, D-312-630-6500.

CALIFORNIA
Camp San Luis Obispo, continued

LOCATION: On Highway 1 between San Luis Obispo and Morro Bay, USMRA: Page 111 (C-11). NMC: San Luis Obispo, five miles east.

GENERAL INFORMATION: USPFO for California, California Military Academy, National Interagency Counter Drug Institute, California Special Training Institute. Federal Youth Program.

TEMPORARY MILITARY LODGING: Lodging office, Bldg. 738, San Joaquin St. 0800-1600 Mon-Fri, C-805-549-3800, D-312-630-9800.

LOGISTICAL SUPPORT: Limited support facilities available.

Exchange-549-3912
NCO Club-543-4034
Carson Travel-781-8340
Locator-549-6500
O'Club-549-6168
MWR-594-6501
Public Affairs-594-6501

HEALTH AND WELFARE: Emergency, outpatient and inpatient care, Sierra Vista Hospital, C-805-546-7600.

RECREATION: Camp San Luis Obispo RV Park on post, C-805-594-3800, FTS-630-9800, four camper spaces w/full hookups, eight with W&E, tent spaces.

SPACE-A: None. Edwards AFB, listings, C-805-277-4412/4185, D-312-527-2222, Fax 805-277-5544.

ATTRACTIONS: Twelve miles from ocean, scenic central coast. Thirty-five miles from Hearst Castle. Midway between Los Angeles and San Francisco.

CHINA LAKE NAVAL AIR WARFARE SYSTEMS CENTER, WEAPONS DIVISION (CA34R4)
China Lake, CA 93555-6001

TELEPHONE NUMBER INFORMATION: Main installation numbers: C-619-939-2303, D-312-437-2303.

LOCATION: From US-395 or CA-14, take CA-178 to Ridgecrest and the main gate. USMRA: Page 111 (G-10,11,12; H-11). NMC: Los Angeles, 150 miles south.

GENERAL INFORMATION: A major Navy Research, Development, and Test Center for Naval Weapons Systems principally for air warfare. In the upper Mojave Desert.

TEMPORARY MILITARY LODGING: Lodging office, BEQ, C-619-939-3146, D-312-437-3146, BOQ, 0700-2400 daily, C-619-939-2383, D-312-437-3146. All ranks. DV/VIP C-619-939-3039/2338, Fax 619-939-3152.

LOGISTICAL SUPPORT: Complete support facilities available.

CHAMPUS-939-2911
Commissary-939-3138
Fire Dept-939-2402
Legal-939-2203
NCO Club-939-8661
Chaplain-939-3506
Exchange-446-2586
Gas Station-446-5044
Medical-939-8000
O'Club-939-3116
Child Care-939-3171
Family Services-927-1555
Golf Course-939-2990
MWR-932-2010
Police-939-3323

CALIFORNIA
China Lake Naval Air Warfare Systems Center, continued

Public Affairs-939-3511   SATO-446-9047   SDO/NCO-939-2303
Snack Bar-446-2415

HEALTH & WELFARE: Naval Branch Medical Clinic C-619-939-8000. Inpatient, see Edwards AFB listing, C-805-277-3730. Chapel serving all faiths C-619-939-3506.

RECREATION: Auto Hobby EX-2346, Bowling EX-3471, Golf EX-2990, Gym/Swimming EX-2334, Ceramics EX-3252, Wood Hobby EX-3252, Library EX-2595, MWR EX-2010, Youth Center EX-2909.

SPACE-A: Armitage Air Field at Center for test flights. Very limited. C-619-939-2303, D-312-437-5308, Fax 616-446-7204.

ATTRACTIONS: Weapons Exhibit Facility for air-launched Navy & Marine Corps weaponry. Desert type attractions and recreation, isolated area.

CONCORD NAVAL WEAPONS STATION (CA58R4)
10 Delta Street
Concord Naval Weapons Station, CA 94520-5100

TELEPHONE NUMBER INFORMATION: Main installation numbers: C-510-246-2000, D-312-350-0100.

LOCATION: From I-680 take exit in Concord to CA-242/CA-4, exit Chicago Highway, Weapons Station is clearly marked. USMRA: Page 119 (F-2,3). NMC: San Francisco, 35 miles southwest.

GENERAL INFORMATION: Department of Defense Ammunition Trans-shipment and Naval Weapons Support for Pacific Fleet.

TEMPORARY MILITARY LODGING: None. See Treasure Island Naval Station listing, (BEQ) C-415-395-5442, D-312-475-5410 and (BOQ) C-415-395-5273, D-312-475-5274.

LOGISTICAL SUPPORT: Limited support facilities available.

CHAMPUS-246-5869   CDO/ACTO-246-5553   Chaplain-246-5594
Exchange-246-2919   Fire Dept-3911   Housing Mgr-246-5896
Locator-246-2000   Medical-246-2933   MWR-5339
Police-246-5553   Retiree Services-246-5040   SATO(ITT)-246-5795
Sports Club/All Hands-246-2153

HEALTH & WELFARE: Naval Branch Medical Clinic, Emergency C-510-246-3911. Chapel serving all faiths C-510-246-5594.

RECREATION: MWR EX-5341, Tickets (ITT) EX-5795, Gym EX-2021, Auto Hobby EX-2156, Library EX-5338, Rec Equip EX-5338, Swimming EX-2144.

SPACE-A: None. See Travis AFB, C-707-424-1854, D-312-837-1854, Fax 707-424-2048.

ATTRACTIONS: The Weapons Station is a wild life preserve: deer, elk, eagles, quail, foxes, to name a few. Beautiful San Francisco, 35 miles southwest.

U.S. FORCES TRAVEL & TRANSFER GUIDE U.S.A. - 35

CALIFORNIA

CORONADO NAVAL AMPHIBIOUS BASE (CA38R4)
3420 Guadalcanal Road, Bldg. 16
San Diego, CA 92155-5001

TELEPHONE NUMBER INFORMATION: Main installation numbers: C-619-437-2011, D-312-577-2011.

LOCATION: From San Diego, take I-5 south to Coronado-San Diego Bay Bridge ($1 toll for non-carpool, free to motorcycles and carpools). Left on Orange Ave for three miles; pass Hotel del Coronado and watch for signs to base (left turn at third light after hotel). USMRA: Page 118 (C,D-7,8). NMC: San Diego, five miles north.

GENERAL INFORMATION: West Coast Naval Amphibious Training Base, Naval Surface, Expeditionary Warfare Training Group Pacific, Special Warfare Group, and 27 Tenant Commands.

TEMPORARY MILITARY LODGING: Lodging office, Bldg. 500, Tulagi St, 24 hours, C-619-437-3494, D-312-577-3494, BOQ C-619-437-3860, D-312-577-3860, EM C-619-437-3494, Officers C-619-437-3859, Fax 619-577-3475.

LOGISTICAL SUPPORT: Most support facilities available.

All Hands Club-437-3171
Child Care-437-2119
Rec Center-437-5135
ITT Office-437-3018
MWR-437-3339
SATO-435-4414
Theater-437-3014

Camping/Marina-435-8788
CPO Club-437-3857
Exchange-522-7403
Legal-437-2080
Police-437-3432
SDO/NCO-437-3432
TRICARE-437-2526

Chaplain-437-2070
Dental 437-2954
Gas Station-522-7415
Medical-437-3047
Public Affairs-437-3024
Snack Bar-437-2188

HEALTH & WELFARE: Naval Branch Medical Clinic, C-619-437-3047. Chapel (Prot/Cath) C-619-437-2070, (Jewish) C-619-556-1921.

RECREATION: Athletics EX-2185/86, Bowling EX-3016, Camping Gear EX-3028, Catering-437-2181, Discount Ticket Office, Theater, Tennis Courts, Marina, Gym, Swimming, RV Park, Beaches, and Picnic Area. Recreation information EX-3037. Fiddlers Cove, one-and-a-half miles south of base, year round, C-619-435-8788, 50 camper spaces w/W&E hookups.

SPACE-A: None. See North Island NAS listing, C-619-545-9567, D-312-735-9567.

ATTRACTIONS: Downtown Gaslamp District, Horton Plaza Shopping Center, San Diego Bay Area, Seaport Village, San Diego Zoo, Balboa Park, Sea World, and Wild Animal Park.

DEFENSE DISTRIBUTION REGION WEST-SHARPE SITE (CA52R4)
700 East Roth Road, Bldg S-10
Stockton, CA 95296-0002

TELEPHONE NUMBER INFORMATION: Main installation numbers: C-209-982-2000.

CALIFORNIA
Defense Distribution Region West, continued

LOCATION: Off I-5 at Roth Road; or from CA-99 north, left on CA-120, north on Airport Way, left on Roth Road to Depot. USMRA: Page 110 (C-7,8). NMC: Stockton, seven miles north.

GENERAL INFORMATION: Joint Service Command under the Defense Logistics Agency flag to continue the unified mission of supply and support to the military services.

TEMPORARY MILITARY LODGING: None. See Stockton NCS listing, C-209-944-0343.

LOGISTICAL SUPPORT: Limited support facilities available.

CHAMPUS-982-3836	Consol Club-982-2265	Exchange-982-3886
Locator-982-2000	Medical-982-3831	Police-982-2560
Post Rest-982-2262	Retiree Services-982-2213	SATO-982-2233

HEALTH & WELFARE: None. See Travis Air Force Base listing, C-707-423-3000.

RECREATION: Spec Services EX-2237: Arts/Crafts, Library, Swimming, Racquetball and Tennis Courts, Youth Center. Sharpe Travel Camp on post, year round, C-209-982-2232, D-312-462-2232. 12 camper spaces w/full hookups.

SPACE-A: See Alameda NAS listing, C-510-263-3346, D-312-686-3346.

ATTRACTIONS: San Joaquin and Sacramento Valleys. San Francisco and Bay Area, 90 miles west. Reno/Tahoe to north; Yosemite National Park to south.

EDWARDS AIR FORCE BASE (CA48R4)
1 South Rosamond Blvd.
Edwards Air Force Base, CA 93524-1031

TELEPHONE NUMBER INFORMATION: Main installation numbers: C-805-277-1110, D-312-527-1110.

LOCATION: Eighteen miles east of Rosamond, and 30 miles northeast of Lancaster, off CA-14. Also, 10 miles southwest of Boron, off CA-58. USMRA: Page 111 (F,G-12). NMC: Los Angeles, 90 miles southwest.

GENERAL INFORMATION: Air Force Materiel Command Base. Air Force Flight Test Center, USAF Test Pilot School, secondary landing site for space shuttle landings.

TEMPORARY MILITARY LODGING: Lodging office, Bldg. 5602, 24 hours, C-805-277-3394, D-312-527-3394. All ranks. DV/VIP C-805-277-3326.

LOGISTICAL SUPPORT: Complete support facilities available.

Cafeteria-277-3489	CHAMPUS-277-2662	Chaplain-277-6976
Child Care-277-8658	Commissary-277-2336	Conv Store-258-8131
Exchange-258-6573	Family Services-277-2246	Gas Station-258-5037
Golf Course-277-3468	ITT Office-275-5672	Legal-277-4310
Locator-277-2777	Medical-277-2110	MWR-277-4240
Muroc Club-277-2830	Package Store-277-6669	Police-277-3340

U.S. FORCES TRAVEL & TRANSFER GUIDE U.S.A. - 37

CALIFORNIA
Edwards Air Force Base, continued

Public Affairs-277-3510   Retiree Services-277-4931   SATO-277-3623
SDO/NCO-277-3040   Snack Bar-277-2880   Theater-277-4178

HEALTH & WELFARE: USAF Hospital, Bldg. 5500, 25 beds. Emergency C-805-277-2331, Appointments C-805-277-3730. Chapel serving all faiths C-805-277-2110.

RECREATION: Bowling EX-2590, Golf EX-3469, Gym EX-2374/3077, Auto Hobby EX-4275, Ceramics EX-4171, Recreation EX-3546, Wood Hobby EX-3139, Rec Equip EX-2895, Youth Center EX-2217, Library EX-2475. Fam-Camp on base, year round, C-805-277-3394, D-312-527-3394, 26 camper spaces w/full hookups, 10 w/o hookups.

SPACE-A: Pax Term/Lounge, Bldg. 1200, 0600-2200 daily, C-805-277-4412/4185, D-312-527-2222, Fax 805-277-5544, limited flights to CONUS and foreign locations.

ATTRACTIONS: Mojave Desert area. Adjacent to mountain and winter sports areas; 90 minutes from beaches; historic mining and ghost towns nearby.

EL CENTRO NAVAL AIR FACILITY (CA09R4)
El Centro, CA 92243-5001

TELEPHONE NUMBER INFORMATION: Main installation numbers: C-619-339-2524, D-312-958-2524.

LOCATION: Take I-8, two miles west of El Centro, to Forrester Rd exit, one-and-a-half miles to Evan Hewes Highway left (west) for four miles, right on Bennet Rd to main gate. USMRA: Page 111 (H-15,16). NMC: El Centro, seven miles east.

GENERAL INFORMATION: Operates bombing and gunnery ranges in support of fleet operations. Ideal flying conditions.

TEMPORARY MILITARY LODGING: Lodging office, Bldg. 270, B & 2nd Streets, 24 hours daily, C-619-339-2408, D-312-958-8408. DV/VIP Officers, C-619-339-8535, Fax 619-353-1492.

LOGISTICAL SUPPORT: Complete support facilities available.

CHAMPUS-339-2674   Chaplain-339-2457   Child Care-399-2560
Commissary-339-2483   Consol Club 339-2491   Conv Store-339-2670
Exchange-339-2478   Gas Station-339-7535   Legal-339-2594
Medical-339-2675/2674   Package Store-339-2670   Police-339-2525
SDO/NCO-339-2699

HEALTH & WELFARE: Naval Branch Medical Clinic, C-619-339-2675. Chapel serving all faiths C-619-339-2457.

RECREATION: Rec Services EX-2481 for all recreational facilities. 35 self-contained rec vehicles available for rent EX-2481. Campground on base, year round, C-619-339-2489, D-312-958-8489, 59 camper spaces w/full hookups.

SPACE-A: Pax Term, Bldg. 519, 0700-2300 Mon-Sat, C-619-339-2426, D-312-958-8426, limited Space-A flights to CONUS and OCONUS locations.

CALIFORNIA
El Centro Naval Air Facility, continued

ATTRACTIONS: Winter (Jan-Mar) home of the Navy Blue Angels. Imperial Valley, near Mexico.

EL TORO MARINE CORPS AIR STATION (CA22R4)
P.O. Box 95002
Santa Ana, CA 92709-5000

Scheduled to close December 1999

TELEPHONE NUMBER INFORMATION: Main installation numbers: C-714-726-2100, D-312-997-2100.

LOCATION: Take I-5 to Sand Canyon Rd exit; East to Trabuco Rd then right to main gate. USMRA: Page 111(F-14); Page 117(G,H-7,8). NMC: Anaheim, 15 miles northwest.

GENERAL INFORMATION: Marine Corps Air Bases, Western Area, Headquarters 3rd Marine Aircraft Wing, and supporting units.

TEMPORARY MILITARY LODGING: Bldg. 58, 0700-2000 daily, C-714-726-2381, D-312-997-22381. After hours, SDO, C-714-726-3901. All ranks.

LOGISTICAL SUPPORT: Complete support facilities available.

Cafeteria-726-3340
Child Care-726-2153
EM Club-726-2476
Gas Station-726-3340
Locator-726-3736
O'Club-726-2465
Retiree Services-726-2989
Snack Bar-726-3340

CHAMPUS-726-2888
Commissary-726-3828
Exchange-726-3340
ITT Office-726-2626
Medical-726-3175
Package Store-726-3340
SATO-559-1511
SNCO Club-726-2566

Chaplain-726-3825
Conv Store-726-3340
Family Services-726-2771
Legal-726-2507
NCO Club-726-2476
Police-726-2901
SDO/NCO-726-3901
Special Services-726-2571

HEALTH & WELFARE: Naval Branch Medical Clinic, Emergency C-714-726-9911, Appointments C-714-726-3175. Chapels serving all faiths C-714-726-3825.

RECREATION: Aero Club EX-2480, Auto Hobby EX-2481, Gym EX-2993, Bowling EX-2576, Camping Equip EX-2509, Golf EX-2577, Library EX-2569, Stables EX-2911, Swimming EX-2469. Operates Big Bear Recreation Facilities in San Bernardino National Forest, year round, C-714-726-2626, El Toro Campgrounds on base, year round, C-714-726-2626, D-312-997-2626, four camper spaces with full hookups, 11 w/W&E hookups.

SPACE-A: Pax Term/Lounge, Bldg. 624, 0700-2200 Mon-Fri, 0900-1800 Sat-Sun, C-714-726-3920, D-312-997-3920, CONUS, OCONUS and overseas flights.

ATTRACTIONS: Orange County and greater Los Angeles area, Disneyland in Anaheim, Anaheim Stadium (home of the California Angels baseball team), Knott's Berry Farm in Buena Park, Marineland located at the tip of the Palo Verdes peninsula, Movieland Wax Museum in Buena Park, Crystal Cathedral in Garden Grove, beaches, boating.

U.S. FORCES TRAVEL & TRANSFER GUIDE U.S.A. - 39

CALIFORNIA

FORT HUNTER LIGGETT (CA37R4)
Building 205
Fort Hunter Liggett, CA 93928-5000

TELEPHONE NUMBER INFORMATION: Main installation numbers: C-408-386-3000, D-312-686-3000.

LOCATION: From US-101 S exit at King City to CA-14, S to main gate. USMRA: Page 111 (C-10). NMC: San Luis Obispo, 60 miles south.

GENERAL INFORMATION: Sub-Installation of Fort McCoy. Primary training area for 40th Infantry Division (MECH) CALGD, and testing area for USA TEXCOM.

TEMPORARY MILITARY LODGING: Lodging office, Bldg. 105, 0800-1630 daily, C-408-386-2511, D-312-686-2511. All ranks. DV/VIP C-408-386-2025. Other hours, SDO, Bldg. 205, EX-2503.

LOGISTICAL SUPPORT: Limited support facilities available.

ACS-386-2762	CHAMPUS-386-2771	Chaplain-386-4363
Child Care-386-2313	Commissary-386-2190	Community Club-386-2588
Exchange-385-4585	Family Services-386-2762	Fire Dept-386-2527
Gas Station-386-6032	ITT-386-2406	Legal-386-2202
Locator-386-2030	Medical-386-2516	MWR-386-2762
Police-386-2613	Public Affairs-386-2505	Recreation-386-2612
RV/Camping-386-2671	SDO/NCO-386-2503	SATO-386-2406
Snack Bar-386-2645	Theater-386-2645	

HEALTH & WELFARE: US Army Health Clinic, Emergency C-408-386-2516. Chapel serving all faiths C-408-386-2808.

RECREATION: Bowling, Craft Shops, Gym, Hunting and Fishing, Library, Rec Center EX-2406. Primitive Campground on post, year round, C-408-386-1205, 18 primitive spaces w/W hookups.

SPACE-A: None. See Lemoore NAS listing, C-209-998-1683, D-312-949-1683, Fax 209-998-2036.

ATTRACTIONS: Old California, hacienda formerly owned by the Hearst family. San Antonio Mission. Prime hunting and fishing area.

FORT IRWIN NATIONAL TRAINING CENTER (CA01R4)
Fort Irwin National Training Center, CA 92310-5000

TELEPHONE NUMBER INFORMATION: Main installation numbers: C-619-380-4111, D-312-470-4111.

LOCATION: Take I-15 east from Los Angeles for 125 miles or I-15 west from Las Vegas, NV for 150 miles. Fort is north of I-15 near Barstow. Watch for signs. USMRA: Page 111 (G,H-11,12). NMC: San Bernardino, 60 miles southwest.

GENERAL INFORMATION: The US Army National Training Center.

CALIFORNIA
Fort Irwin National Training Center, continued

TEMPORARY MILITARY LODGING: Lodging office, Bldg. 109, 1st Ave. 0800-1630 daily, C-619-380-4599, D-312-470-4599. All ranks. DV/VIP C-619-380-3000. Very limited.

LOGISTICAL SUPPORT: Complete support facilities available.

Chaplain-380-3562
Conv Store-380-2365
Exchange-380-2060
IG-380-3038
Locator-380-3369
O'Club-380-3018
SATO-380-9600
Vet Clinic-380-3025

Child Care-380-1029
Dental-380-3166
Family Services-380-3513
ITT Office-380-3583
Medical-380-3124
Package Store-380-3208
SDO/NCO-380-3750

Commissary-380-3561
EM Club-380-3206
Gas Station-380-1088
Legal-380-3272
NCO Club-380-3018
Police-380-4444/3474
Theater-380-3430

HEALTH & WELFARE: Weed Army Community Hospital, Emergency C-619-380-3777, 25 beds. Appointments C-619-380-3124. Chapels serving all faiths C-619-380-3562/3440/4213.

RECREATION: Bowling EX-4249, Swimming EX-4951-3046, Gym EX-3457, Riding Stables EX-4796, Auto Hobby EX-3531, Library EX-3462, Arts/Crafts EX-3431/3432, Rec Equip EX-3434, Mini-Golf Course/Batting EX-4653, Youth Activities EX-3696, Rec Center EX-3585, Teen Center EX-3696, Morale Support Hq EX-3582.

SPACE-A: None. See China Lake NAWSCWD listing, C-619-939-5301/5282, D-312-437-5308/5267, Fax 619-446-7204.

ATTRACTIONS: Goldstone Deep Space Station. Painted Rock, Opposing Force Museum, Rainbow Basin, and Calico Ghost Town.

FORT MacARTHUR (CA46R4)
San Pedro, CA 90731-2960

TELEPHONE NUMBER INFORMATION: C-310-363-8292, 312-833-8292.

LOCATION: From I-110 (Harbor Freeway) go south to San Pedro, left to Gaffney St, left on 19th St. right to Pacific Ave, on the left approximately 1/4 mile. USMRA: Page. 117 (C-7). NMC: Los Angeles, in city limits.

TEMPORARY MILITARY LODGING: Billeting Manager, Bldg 37, Patton Quadrangle, 24 hours daily, C-310-363-8296. DV/VIP C-310-363-3751.

LOGISTICAL SUPPORT: Limited support facilities available.

Exchange-832-9611   Medical-363-8301   Police-363-8385

HEALTH & WELFARE: None. See Los Angeles AFB listing, C-310-363-0964.

SPACE-A: Available at Los Angeles IAP, C-310-363-0714, D-312-833-0714, Fax 310-216-2670.

ATTRACTIONS: Hollywood and beaches within easy driving distance, major league sports attractions; Los Angeles Dodgers, Los Angeles Lakers, Los Angeles Clippers, and the Los Angeles Kings.

U.S. FORCES TRAVEL & TRANSFER GUIDE U.S.A. - 41

CALIFORNIA

IMPERIAL BEACH
OUTLYING LANDING FIELD (CA100R4)
Imperial Beach, CA 91932-5000

TELEPHONE NUMBER INFORMATION: Main installation numbers: C-619-424-2902.

LOCATION: From I-5 south, right on Palm Ave. left on 13th St., fork right to base. USMRA: Page. 118 (D,E-10). NMC: San Diego, five miles south.

TEMPORARY MILITARY LODGING: None. See Coronado Naval Amphibious Base, Billeting Office C-619-437-3494.

LOGISTICAL SUPPORT: Limited support facilities available.

Commissary-437-9481　　　Exchange-424-2900　　　Service Station-424-2938/8

HEALTH & WELFARE: None. See Coronado NAB listing, C-619-437-3047.

SPACE-A: None. See North Island listing, C-619-545-9567, D-312-735-9567.

ATTRACTIONS: San Diego Bay area, San Diego Zoo, Mexico approximately two miles south.

LEMOORE NAVAL AIR STATION (CA06R4)
700 Avenger Avenue
Lemoore Naval Air Station, CA 93246-5001

TELEPHONE NUMBER INFORMATION: Main installation numbers: C-209-998-0100, D-312-949-0100.

LOCATION: On CA-198, 24 miles east of I-5, 30 miles west of CA-99 in the south central part of the state. USMRA: Page 111 (D-10). NMC: Fresno, 40 miles northwest.

GENERAL INFORMATION: Navy's newest and largest master jet air station.

TEMPORARY MILITARY LODGING: Lodging office, Bldg. 852, Hancock Circle, 24 hours daily, C-209-998-4784, D-312-949-4784. All ranks, and Navy Lodge C-209-998-5791, BOQ, C-209-998-4609, D-312-949-4609, DV/VIP - E-7/9, C-209-998-3344, Fax 209-998-4587.

LOGISTICAL SUPPORT: Complete support facilities available.

Cafeteria-998-3084	CDO/OOD-998-3300	CHAMPUS-998-4490
Chaplain-998-4618	Child Care-998-4919	Commissary-998-4667
Conv Store-998-4939	CPO Club-998-4858/4860	EM Club-998-4872
Exchange-998-4661	Family Services-998-4042	Gas Station-998-4729
ITT Office-998-4700	Legal-998-3873	Locator-998-3789
Medical-998-4481	O'Club-998-4853/4	Police-998-4811
Public Affairs-998-3394	SATO-998-3993	Theater-998-4643

HEALTH & WELFARE: Naval Hospital, Emergency C-209-998-4435/4488/4481, 20 beds. Appointments C-209-998-4448/4449. Chapels serving all faiths C-209-998-4618.

42 - U.S. FORCES TRAVEL & TRANSFER GUIDE U.S.A

CALIFORNIA
Lemoore Naval Air Station, continued

RECREATION: Gym EX-4881/4882/4882, Arts/Crafts EX-4902, Auto Hobby EX-4908, Electronics Hobby EX-4904, Flying Club EX-3526, Bowling EX-4646, Rec Equip EX-4898, Library EX-4633/4634, Rec Center EX-4804, Youth Center EX-4936.

SPACE-A: Pax Term/Lounge, Bldg. 180, 24 hours daily, C-209-998-1683, D-312-949-1683, flights to CONUS Naval Air Stations and other locations.

ATTRACTIONS: Sequoia National Park. Ski areas nearby.

LONG BEACH NAVAL SHIPYARD (CA55R4)
Long Beach, CA 90822-5099

Scheduled to close September 1997.

TELEPHONE NUMBER INFORMATION: Main installation numbers: C-310-547-6202, D-312-360-0111.

LOCATION: Take Long Beach Freeway, CA-710, to Terminal Island exit to Naval Shipyard. Clearly marked. USMRA: Page 117 (C,D-7). NMC: Long Beach, two miles east.

GENERAL INFORMATION: Repair and overhaul surface of non-nuclear ships.

TEMPORARY MILITARY LODGING: Lodging office, Bldg. 422, Military Support, C-310-547-7924, D-312-360-7928. BOQ, C-310-547-6060, D-312-360-6060. DV/VIP EM C-310-547-7928, Officers C-310-547-6060, Fax 310-521-0287. Navy Lodge, C-310-833-2541 or 1-800-NAVY-INN. All ranks.

LOGISTICAL SUPPORT: Complete support facilities available.

CHAMPUS-519-8182	Chaplain-547-6981	Child Care-547-7930
Commissary-547-6510	EM Club-547-7007	Exchange-519-5133
Family Services-547-8220	Gas Station-519-5122	Legal-547-8124
Locator-547-6004	Medical-420-4201	MWR-547-6311
O'Club-547-7208	Package Store-833-0352	Police-547-7640
SATO-832-2097	SDO/NCO-547-6721	

HEALTH & WELFARE: None. See Los Angeles AFB listing, C-310-363-0964. Chapel serving all faiths C-310-547-6981.

RECREATION: Auto Hobby EX-8264, Golf 596-5813, Fitness Center EX-7886, Bowling EX-7656, Sailing/Marina EX-6120, Swimming Officers-EX-6380.

SPACE-A: Available at Los Angeles IAP; C-310-363-0714, D-312-833-0714, Fax C-310-216-2670.

ATTRACTIONS: Greater Los Angeles area, Long Beach and Hollywood. Amphitheater and parks on base.

U.S. FORCES TRAVEL & TRANSFER GUIDE U.S.A. - 43

CALIFORNIA

LOS ANGELES AIR FORCE BASE (CA75R4)
2430 East El Segundo Boulevard
Suite 4049
Los Angeles AFB, CA 90045-4687

TELEPHONE NUMBER INFORMATION: Main installation numbers: C-310-363-1110, D-312-833-1110.

LOCATION: From I-405 (San Diego Freeway) take El Segundo Blvd exit, 200 N Douglas St, El Segundo. USMRA: Page 117 (B-5). NMC: Los Angeles, 10 miles northeast.

GENERAL INFORMATION: Headquarters Air Force Materiel Command, Space and Missile Systems Center, manages R&D, acquisition and launch of DoD space vehicles; 655th Support Group.

TEMPORARY MILITARY LODGING: None. See Long Beach Naval Shipyard listing, C-310-547-7924, D-312-360-7928. BOQ, C-310-547-6060, D-312-360-6060.

LOGISTICAL SUPPORT: Complete support facilities available.

Chaplain-363-1956
Consol Club-363-2230
Gas Station-615-0295
Medical-363-0037
Public Affairs-363-0030

Child Care-363-1792
Exchange-640-0129
Legal-363-2483
Package Store-322-7533
Retiree Services-363-5120

Commissary-833-1426
Family Services-363-1121
Locator-363-1876
Police-363-2123
SATO-363-1064

HEALTH & WELFARE: USAF Clinic C-310-363-0964. Chapel serving all faiths C-310-363-1956.

RECREATION: Auto Hobby EX-1705, Gym EX-2269, Rec Supply EX-2081, discount tickets for some local attractions.

SPACE-A: Available at Los Angeles IAP, 0730-2030 daily, C-310-363-0714, D-312-833-0714, Fax C-310-216-2670. Limited number of flights to CONUS and foreign locations via Air Force contract commercial aircraft. Fam-Camp on base, year round, C-310-363-2081, 15 camper spaces w/W&E hookups.

ATTRACTIONS: Greater Los Angeles area, Hollywood, beaches.

MARINES' MEMORIAL CLUB (CA20R4)
609 Sutter Street
San Francisco, CA 94102-5000

TELEPHONE NUMBER INFORMATION: Main installation numbers: C-415-673-6672. Reservations, 1-800-5-MARINE or 415-673-6604 (direct).

LOCATION: From CA-580, cross the Bay Bridge, take 5th St exit to O'Farrell, right to Powell St, left to Sutter St. USMRA: Page 119 (C-5). NMC: San Francisco, in city limits.

GENERAL INFORMATION: The Marines' Memorial Club is a club/hotel exclusively for uniformed services personnel, active duty & retirees and their guests. **The club is not a part of the government but is a private, non-profit organization and is completely self supporting.** This club/hotel is a living memorial to Marines who lost their lives in the

CALIFORNIA
Marines' Memorial Club, continued

Pacific during WWII. It opened on the Marine Corps' Birthday, November 10, 1946, and chose as its motto "A tribute to those Marines who have gone before; and a service to those who carry on."

LOGISTICAL SUPPORT: Club facilities include coin-operated launderette, valet, exchange store, package store, rooms for private parties, and a dining room and lounge in the Skyroom on the 12th floor, overlooking San Francisco. Convenience store/news stand and coffee shop outside hotel adjacent to entrance. Hotel discount parking on Sutter St. Ask at desk. *Military Living books, maps and atlases are sold in the Club exchange, first floor.*

TEMPORARY MILITARY LODGING: Hotel, all ranks, leave or official duty. Guest rooms (137); deluxe suites (11); family suites (3). Reservations required. C-1-800-5-MARINE or 415-673-6672 (direct). Average room $65-70, average suite $150.

HEALTH AND WELFARE: None. See Alameda NAS, C-510-263-4400.

RECREATION: Theater, library/museum, swimming, gym.

SPACE-A: See Alameda NAS listing, C-510-263-3346, D-312-686-3346.

ATTRACTIONS: In the heart of San Francisco, within walking distance of Cable Cars and Union Square is just one-and-a-half blocks away. Many major attractions.

McCLELLAN AIR FORCE BASE (CA35R4)
3237 Peacekeeper Way
McClellan Air Force Base, CA 95652-1048

This base is scheduled to close under the 1995 BRAC.
No closure date has been established.

TELEPHONE NUMBER INFORMATION: Main installation numbers: C-916-643-2111, D-312-633-1110.

LOCATION: Off I-80 north. From I-80 take Madison Ave or Watt Ave exit. Clearly marked. USMRA: Page 110 (C-6). NMC: Sacramento, nine miles southwest.

GENERAL INFORMATION: Air Force Materiel Command Base. Headquarters Sacramento Air Logistics Center. US Coast Guard Station McClellan. Also AMC, ACC AFCC, and AFRES units.

TEMPORARY MILITARY LODGING: Lodging office, Bldg. 89, 54 O'Malley Ave, 24 hours daily, C-916-643-3267, D-312-633-6223. DV/VIP C-916-643-4311. All ranks.

LOGISTICAL SUPPORT: Complete support facilities available.

Cafeteria-929-9295
Chaplain-643-6021
Conv Store-332-3872
Family Services-643-3815
ITT Office-643-2259
Medical-646-8537
O'Club-643-3526

CDO/OOD-643-2751
Child Care-643-6296
EM Club-922-9657
Gas Station-922-8860
Legal-643-3150
MWR-643-6660
Package Store-643-3080

CHAMPUS-646-9320
Commissary-925-8541
Exchange-920-0537
Golf Course-643-3313
Locator-643-4111
NCO Club-643-5977
Police-643-6160

U.S. FORCES TRAVEL & TRANSFER GUIDE U.S.A. - 45

CALIFORNIA
McClellan Air Force Base, continued

Public Affairs-643-6127   **Recreation-643-6660/2738**   **Retiree Services-643-2207**
SATO-643-4410   **Snack Bar-920-6660**   **Theater-643-8706**

HEALTH & WELFARE: USAF Clinic, C-916-646-8357/8522, Appointments C-916-646-8400. Inpatient C-916-643-7107, D-312-674-1110. Chapel serving all faiths C-916-646-6021.

RECREATION: Arts/Crafts EX-3004, Aero Club EX-3264, Gym EX-2596, Bowling EX-5752, Hobby Shop EX-2323, Golf EX-3313, Library EX-4640, Rec News EX-5311, Rec Equip EX-6034, Outdoor Rec EX-2738, Military Rec Center EX-2259, Swimming EX-3304, Youth Center EX-3946, Picnic Area EX-2596.

SPACE-A: Pax Term, Bldg. 251, 0730-1615 daily, C-916-643-4105, D-312-633-4105, Fax C-916-643-5616, flights to CONUS and foreign locations. Also, try the Coast Guard Air Station Ops at the AFB.

ATTRACTIONS: Lake Tahoe and Reno, NV, San Francisco Bay Area. Air Museum on base, C-916-643-3192, 0900-1500 Mon-Sat, closed Sun and federal holidays.

MIRAMAR NAVAL AIR STATION (CA14R4)
45249 Miramar Way
Miramar Naval Air Station, CA 92145-5005

TELEPHONE NUMBER INFORMATION: Main installation numbers: C-619-537-1011, D-312-577-1011.

LOCATION: From I-15 north of San Diego, take Miramar Way exit. USMRA: Page 118 (C,D-2,3,4); (E,F-2,3). NMC: San Diego, 15 miles southwest.

GENERAL INFORMATION: The Navy's only west coast Master Jet Station. Commander Fighter Wing Pacific, Commander Airborne Early Warning Wing Pacific, Navy Fighter Weapons School (TOPDOME); Commander Carrier Airborne Early Warning Weapons School (TOPDOME), Commander 3rd Marine Air Wing, Commander Marine Air Group 11, Commander Air Group 46.

TEMPORARY MILITARY LODGING: Lodging office, Bldg. M-312 (BOQ), 24 hours daily, C-619-537-4233, D-312-577-4235; Bldg. 638 (BEQ), C-619-537-4233, D-312-577-4235. DV/VIP EM C-619-537-6221, Officers C-619-537-1221, Fax 619-537-4243. Navy Lodge, Bldg. 516, C-619-271-7111 or 1-800-NAVY-INN.

LOGISTICAL SUPPORT: Complete support facilities available.

Cafeteria-695-7278   CHAMPUS-537-4653   Chaplain-537-1333
Child Care-537-4144   Commissary-537-4513   Exchange-695-7200
Family Services-537-4099   Gas Station-695-7251   Legal-537-1241
Medical-537-4653   Navy Relief-537-1807   O'Club-537-4809
OOD-537-1227   Package Store-695-7344   Red Cross-537-4107
Retiree Services-537-4806   SATO-537-4126   Theater-537-4143

HEALTH & WELFARE: Navy Branch Medical Clinic, Emergency C-619-537-4655, Appointments C-619-537-4656. Inpatient, see San Diego Naval Medical Center listing, C-800-453-0491. Chapels serving all faiths C-619-537-1333.

46 - U.S. FORCES TRAVEL & TRANSFER GUIDE U.S.A

CALIFORNIA
Mirimar Naval Air Station, continued

RECREATION: Tickets EX-4126/4141, Rec Services EX-4117, Gym EX-4128, Arts/Crafts/Wood Hobby EX-4134, Bowling EX-1215, Golf EX-4155, Swimming EM-EX-4140, Officers-EX-4154, Picnic (Mills Park) EX-3526, Youth Center EX-4136, Auto Hobby EX-1215, Rec Supply EX-4149, Library EX-1261. RV Park on base, year round, C-619-537-4149, D-312-577-4149, 36 camper spaces w/full hookups, 12 camper spaces with W/E.

SPACE-A: Pax Term/Lounge, Bldg. 476, 0700-2400 daily, C-619-537-4284, D-312-577-4284, Fax 619-537-4261, flights to CONUS locations.

ATTRACTIONS: Old Town San Diego, Sea World, San Diego Zoo, Wild Animal Park, beautiful beaches and boardwalk, Mission Blvd.

MOFFETT FEDERAL AIRFIELD NASA/AMES (CA15R4)
Moffett Federal Airfield, CA 94035-5000

This base is scheduled to close under the 1991 BRAC.
No closure date has been established.

TELEPHONE NUMBER INFORMATION: Main installation numbers: C-415-604-5000, D-312-494-5000.

LOCATION: On Bayshore Freeway, US-101, 35 miles south of San Francisco. USMRA: Page 119 (F-9). NMC: San Jose, seven miles south, San Francisco, 35 miles north.

GENERAL INFORMATION: NASA-AMES Research Center. Santa Clara Naval Air Reserve, and Onizuka AFB Annex are tenants.

TEMPORARY MILITARY LODGING: Lodging office, Bldg. 583, 0800-1600 daily, BEQ C-415-404-8299, D-312-494-8299, BOQ C-415-404-6170, D-312-494-61170, DV/VIP Officers C-415-404-8299, Fax 415-404-6156. Navy Lodge C-415-962-1542 or 800-NAVY-INN. All ranks.

LOGISTICAL SUPPORT: Most support facilities available. NOTE: Support facilities are operated by NASA, or one of the tenants.

NASA/AMES

Cafeteria-604-5969
Public Affairs-604-9000

Locator-604-5000
Visitor Center-604-6274

Moffett Club-604-1680

Onizuka AFS Annex (tenant)

Golf Course-752-4556
MWR-752-4686

ITT Office-604-1686
RV/Camping-752-4556

Medical-603-8251

Santa Clara Navy Air Reserve Station (NARS) (tenant)

CDO/OOD-603-9527
Child Care-940-1884
Exchange-603-9907
SATO-604-1686

CHAMPUS-603-8227
Commissary-603-9976
Family Services-603-8016

Chaplain-603-8073
Conv Store-603-9927
Legal-603-9515

CALIFORNIA
Moffet Federal Airfield NASA/AMES, continued

HEALTH & WELFARE: Air Force Branch Medical Clinic, Emergency C-415-603-8251. Chapels serving all faiths C-415-404-4100.

RECREATION: NASA Field House EX-1686. Racquetball EX-1686, Softball EX-1686, Tennis EX-1686, Auto Hobby EX-8046, Bowling EX-4709, Golf EX-4702, Gym EX-4697, Rec Services 691-1216, Swimming EX-4712, Ticket Office EX-4757, Youth Activities 965-2716.

SPACE-A: Pax Term, Bldg. 158, 24 hours daily, C-415-404-5231, D-312-494-5231, flights to CONUS, OCONUS and foreign locations.

ATTRACTIONS: Paramount Great America Park is five miles south. Located in the heart of the "Silicon Valley." San Jose and Santa Cruz are nearby.

MONTEREY NAVAL POSTGRADUATE SCHOOL (CA16R4)
1 University Circle
Monterey, CA 93943-5000

TELEPHONE NUMBER INFORMATION: Main installation numbers: C-408-656-2441, D-312-878-2441.

LOCATION: Take CA-1 to central Monterey exit, right at light onto Camino Aguajito. Then first right (right fork) onto 10th St., turn left at stop sign onto Sloat Ave., and right at 9th St. gate. Or N on CA-1, Aguajito Rd exit to Mark Thomas Dr, to left on Sloat Ave, right at 9th St gate. USMRA: Page 111 (B-9). NMC: Monterey, in city limits.

GENERAL INFORMATION: Naval Postgraduate School, Defense Resource Management Institute, Fleet Numerical Oceanography Center.

TEMPORARY MILITARY LODGING: Lodging office, Bldg. 220, Herrmann Hall, Stone Rd, 24 hours daily, C-408-656-2441, D-312-878-2441. DV/VIP Officers C-408-656-2441, Fax 408-646-2921.

LOGISTICAL SUPPORT: Most support facilities available.

CDO/OOD-656-2441	CHAMPUS-647-2180	Chaplain-656-2241
Child Care-656-2734	Commissary-242-3418	Conv Store-375-0959
EM Club-656-2359	Exchange-375-3737	Family Services-656-3141
Fire Dept-656-2334	Gas Station-373-7271	Golf Course-656-2167
Legal-656-2506	Locator-656-2441	Medical-656-5234
MWR-656-3223	O'Club-656-2170	Public Affairs-656-2023
Package Store-373-7511	Police-656-2555	Quarterdeck-656-2441
Recreation-656-2275	Retiree Services-242-5595	SATO-656-3357
SDO/SNO-656-2442	Snack Bar-373-0557	

HEALTH & WELFARE: Emergency C-408-242-7631, Appointments C-408-647-5234. Chapels serving Prot/Cath C-408-656-2241.

RECREATION: Rec Office EX-2467, Golf EX-2167, Gym EX-3118, Rec Equip EX-3118, Swimming EX-2275.

SPACE-A: None. See Lemoore NAS listing, C-209-998-1680, D-312-949-1680.

48 - U.S. FORCES TRAVEL & TRANSFER GUIDE U.S.A

CALIFORNIA
Monterey Naval Postgraduate School, continued

ATTRACTIONS: Beaches, seafood, Carmel Valley, Carmel-By-The-Sea, Pebble Beach, Big Sur coastline, Salinas Valley. Beautiful area.

NORTH ISLAND NAVAL AIR STATION (CA43R4)
Building 605, McCain Boulevard
North Island Naval Air Station, CA 92135-7033

TELEPHONE NUMBER INFORMATION: Main installation numbers: C-619-545-8123, D-312-735-8123.

LOCATION: From I-5 exit at Coronado Bridge (toll). Also, from CA-75 north to CA-282 to base. In Coronado. USMRA: Page 118 (B,C-6,7). NMC: San Diego, four miles northeast.

GENERAL INFORMATION: Largest Naval Industrial Complex on the West Coast.

TEMPORARY MILITARY LODGING: Lodging office, Bldg. I (BOQ), 24 hours daily, BEQ, C-619-545-9551, D-312-735-7489, BOQ, C-619-545-7489, D-312-735-7489. Navy Lodge, Bldg. 1402, 24 hours daily, C-619-545-6940, D-312-735-6940. DV/VIP EM C-619-545-9551, Officers C-619-545-7545, Fax 619-545-9072. All ranks.

LOGISTICAL SUPPORT: Complete support facilities available.

CDO/OOD-545-8123
Commissary-545-6566
EM Club-545-7205
Fire Dept-545-8267
ITT Office-545-9576
Medical-545-4265
Police-545-6132
SATO-545-7937

Chaplain-545-8213
Conv Store-522-7277
Exchange-522-7266
Gas Station-522-7281
Legal-545-6270
MWR-545-9206
Public Affairs-545-8167
Snack Bar-522-7266/69

Child Care-545-7226
Consol Club-545-6944
Family Services-545-6071
Golf Course-545-9659
Locator-524-5515
Package Store-545-7279
Recreation-545-9206
Theater-545-8479

HEALTH & WELFARE: Naval Branch Medical Clinic, Emergency C-619-545-4305, Appointments C-619-545-4265. Inpatient, see San Diego Naval Medical Center listing, C-800-453-0491. Chapels serving all faiths except Jewish C-619-545-8215.

RECREATION: Bowling EX-7240, Fitness Center EX-2876, Crew's Pool EX-2880, Golf EX-9659, Library EX-8230, Officers' Pool EX-7228, Skeet/Trap Range EX-7225, Women's Spa 522-2871.

SPACE-A: Pax Term/Lounge, Bldg. 700, 24 hours daily, C-619-545-9567, D-312-735-9567, flights to CONUS. Some to foreign locations.

ATTRACTIONS: Beaches, sport fishing, Old San Diego, Sea World, Bay Area, San Diego Zoo, and Mexico nearby.

U.S. FORCES TRAVEL & TRANSFER GUIDE U.S.A. - 49

CALIFORNIA

NOVATO-DEPARTMENT OF DEFENSE HOUSING FACILITY (HAMILTON NS) (CA89R4)
1000 Main Entrance Rd.
Novato, CA 94949-5000

Scheduled to close September 1996.

TELEPHONE NUMBER INFORMATION: Main installation numbers: C-415-382-4110, D-312-475-4110.

LOCATION: From 580 W (Alameda, Oakland area) to 101 north, to Nave Dr/Hamilton AFB exit. Follow Frontage Rd to white archway (Hamilton AFB) on right side. USMRA: Page 110 (B-7). NMC: San Francisco, 62 miles south.

GENERAL INFORMATION: Coast Guard Pacific Area Strike Team, Hamilton Army Garrison.

TEMPORARY MILITARY LODGING: None. Try the Navy Lodge at Alameda NAS, 1-800-NAVY-INN.

LOGISTICAL SUPPORT: Most support facilities available.

Chaplain-382-4150
Gas Station-382-4190
Medical-883-8985
Quarterdeck-382-4110
Theater-382-4148

Child Care-883-0606
ITT-382-4210
MWR-382-4210
SDO/NCO-382-4110

Exchange-382-4190
Locator-382-4125
Police-883-3697
Snack Bar-382-4190

HEALTH AND WELFARE: None. See Oakland Army Base listing, 510-466-2918.

RECREATION: Auto Hobby 883-0154, Bowling 883-5090, Arts/Crafts, Library, Rec Center, Swimming, Support Services, call 883-5962, Gym 883-0660, Youth Activities 382-4157.

SPACE-A: None. See Travis AFB, CA listing, C-707-424-1854, D-312-837-1854, Fax 707-424-2048.

ATTRACTIONS: Camping, water sports, sightseeing in San Francisco. Wine tasting in the Sonoma and Napa Valleys.

OAKLAND ARMY BASE (CA18R4)
56 Alaska Street
Oakland Army Base, CA 94626-5015

This base is scheduled to close under the 1995 BRAC.
No closure date has been established.

TELEPHONE NUMBER INFORMATION: Main installation numbers: C-510-466-9111, D-312-859-9111.

LOCATION: Near junction of I-80 and I-880, south of San Francisco-Oakland Bay Bridge, look for signs. USMRA: Page. 119 (D-5). NMC: Oakland, two miles southeast.

50 - U.S. FORCES TRAVEL & TRANSFER GUIDE U.S.A

CALIFORNIA
Oakland Army Base, continued

GENERAL INFORMATION: Western Headquarters for Military Traffic Management Command and other Western Area Army support units. Vehicle Processing Center (VPC) for overseas shipment and pick-up (1-800-446-0443).

TEMPORARY MILITARY LODGING: Lodging office, Bldg. 650, 24 hours daily, C-510-466-3205, D-312-859-3113. All ranks. **Fort Mason Officers' Club,** overlooking Fisherman's Wharf in San Francisco, has a limited number of suites and rooms available for officers (all grades); contact the Club Manager for reservations up to 30 days in advance, C-415-441-7700, D-312-859-0111.

LOGISTICAL SUPPORT: Complete support facilities available.

ACS-466-3459
CFAD-466-3516
Commissary-466-2004
Fire Dept-466-2762
Legal-466-2921
O'Club-415-441-7700
Recreation-466-3470
Snack Bar-465-3175

Carlson Travel-466-2100
Chaplain-466-2616
Exchange-836-4277
Gas Station-465-3176
Locator-466-9111
Police-466-3333
Retiree Services-466-2765

CDO/OOD-466-3131
Child Care-466-2687
Family Services-466-3472
Gateway Club-466-3598
Medical-466-2918
Public Affairs-466-3021
SDO/NCO-466-3131

HEALTH & WELFARE: US Army Clinic Health, Emergency C-510-466-2161/2245, Appointments C-510-466-2918. Chapel serving all faiths C-510-466-2616.

RECREATION: Bowling EX-3020, Arts & Crafts Center EX-3541, Youth Center EX-3040, Physical Fitness Center EX-2246/7. Lake Tahoe Oakland Condominiums off base, year round, C-510-444-8107, D-312-859-3113, two three-bedroom condominiums on Lake Tahoe.

SPACE-A: See Travis AFB, C-707-424-1854, D-312-837-1854, Fax 707-424-2048..

ATTRACTIONS: San Francisco and Bay area. Many exciting things to see and do in and around Oakland. Jack London Square shopping area at the foot of Broadway in Oakland is a waterfront promenade lined with stores, restaurants and entertainment.

OAKLAND FLEET & INDUSTRIAL SUPPLY CENTER (CA42R4)
250 Executive Way
Oakland, CA 94625-5000

Scheduled to close February 1998.

TELEPHONE NUMBER INFORMATION: Main installation numbers: C-510-302-2000, D-312-672-2000.

LOCATION: Can be reached from I-880 and CA-24 from the east. Clearly marked. USMRA: Page 119 (D-5). NMC: Oakland, four miles east.

GENERAL INFORMATION: Major Naval West Coast Supply Base, Support Activity for Navy Resale System.

TEMPORARY MILITARY LODGING: None. See Alameda NAS listing, C-510-263-3649, Navy Lodge, C-510-523-4917.

U.S. FORCES TRAVEL & TRANSFER GUIDE U.S.A. - 51

CALIFORNIA
Oakland Fleet & Industrial Supply Center, continued

LOGISTICAL SUPPORT: Limited support facilities available.

CDO/OOD-302-5713
Locator-302-2000
Recreation-302-6759

Exchange-302-5405
MWR-302-6759
Snack Bar-302-6768

Fire Dept-302-6421
Police-302-6421
Public Affairs-302-4794/4967

HEALTH & WELFARE: None. See Travis Air Force Base listing, C-707-423-3000. Chapels available at Oakland Army Base.

SPACE-A: None. See Alameda NAS listing, C-510-263-3346, D-312-686-3346.

ATTRACTIONS: San Francisco, Oakland and Bay area.

ONIZUKA AIR STATION (CA96R4)
1080 Lockheed Way
Sunnyvale, CA 94089

TELEPHONE NUMBER INFORMATION: Main installation numbers: C-408-752-3000, D-312-561-3000.

LOCATION: Clearly marked from Highway 101 or Highway 237, follow signs to base. USMRA: Page 119 (F-9). NMC: San Jose, 10 miles northwest.

GENERAL INFORMATION: 750th Space Group, Det 2 & Det 6, SMC.

TEMPORARY MILITARY LODGING: None. See Moffett Federal Airfield listing BEQ C-415-404-8299, D-312-494-8299, BOQ C-415-404-6170, D-312-494-6170.

LOGISTICAL SUPPORT: Limited support facilities available.

CHAMPUS-603-8227*
Conv Store-752-4061
Golf Course-603-8026*
Locator-752-4539
Police-752-3200

Chaplain-752-4650
Exchange-752-4601
ITT-752-4556
Medical-603-8220*
Public Affairs-752-4026

Comm Club-752-3217
Family Services-752-8010
Legal-752-4622
MWR-752-4556
Retiree Services-603-8047*

*Area code 415.

HEALTH AND WELFARE: Emergency C-408-752-3200. Outpatient care, see Moffett Federal Airfield listing, C-415-603-8251. No chapel on base.

RECREATION: Camping Equip and Rec Equip call 752-4556.

SPACE-A: None. See Moffett Federal Airfield/NASA Ames listing. C-415-404-5231, D-312-494-5231.

ATTRACTIONS: San Francisco, a one hour drive. Monterey (south) and Napa Valley (north), under two hour drives. Day trips to Lake Tahoe, Yosemite National Park.

52 - U.S. FORCES TRAVEL & TRANSFER GUIDE U.S.A

CALIFORNIA

PETALUMA COAST GUARD TRAINING CENTER (CA23R4)
599 Tomales Road
Petaluma, CA 94952-5000

TELEPHONE NUMBER INFORMATION: Main installation numbers: C-707-765-7212/7215.

LOCATION: Exit US-101 North to E Washington Ave, nine miles west to Coast Guard Training Center. USMRA: Page 110 (B-6,7). NMC: San Francisco, 58 miles south.

GENERAL INFORMATION: The major West Coast Coast Guard Training Center.

TEMPORARY MILITARY LODGING: Guest Housing, Bldg. T-134, Nevada Ave, 0730-1600, C-707-765-7248, FTS-623-7248. All ranks.

LOGISTICAL SUPPORT: Complete support facilities available.

Cafeteria-765-7168
Chaplain-765-7330
Consol Club-765-7248
Family Services-765-7326
Locator-765-7212
Package Store-765-7252
RV/Camping-765-7348

CDO/OOD-765-7212
Child Care-765-7334
Exchange-765-7258
Fire Dept-765-7355
Medical-765-7200
Police-765-7215
SATO-765-7362

CHAMPUS-765-7563
Conv Store-765-7252
Driving Range-765-7348
Gas Station-765-7254
MWR-765-7340
Public Affairs-765-7004
Theater-765-7346

HEALTH & WELFARE: Outpatient clinics only, Emergency C-707-765-7200. Chapel serving all faiths C-707-765-7330.

RECREATION: Bowling, Gym, Library, Pool, Golf/Driving Range, Fitness Course. Campsites on base, year round, C-707-765-7348, six camper spaces w/o hookups, 25 tent spaces.

SPACE-A: None. See Travis AFB listing, C-707-424-1854, D-312-837-1854, Fax 707-424-2048.

ATTRACTIONS: The base is a federal game preserve.

POINT MUGU NAVAL AIR WARFARE CENTER, WEAPONS DIVISION (CA40R4)
Point Mugu, CA 93042-5000

TELEPHONE NUMBER INFORMATION: Main installation numbers: C-805-989-1110, D-312-351-1110.

LOCATION: Eight miles south of Oxnard and 40 miles north of Santa Monica, on Pacific Coast Highway (PCH), CA-1. USMRA: Page 111 (E-13). NMC: Los Angeles, 50 miles southeast.

GENERAL INFORMATION: Naval Air Weapons Station, Naval Satellite Operations Center, VXE-6, VX-9, Naval Air Reserve. No general visits permitted.

U.S. FORCES TRAVEL & TRANSFER GUIDE U.S.A. - 53

CALIFORNIA
Point Mugu Naval Air Warfare Center, continued

TEMPORARY MILITARY LODGING: Lodging office, Bldg. 27, D Street, 24 hours, C-805-989-8235, D-312-351-8235. All ranks. VIP EM/Officers C-808-989-8672, Fax 805-989-7470.

LOGISTICAL SUPPORT: Complete support facilities available.

Chaplain-989-7967
Conv Store-989-7189
ITT Office-989-8770
Police-989-7907

Child Care-989-8375
Exchange-989-8896
Legal-989-8233/7309
Theater-989-8249

Commissary-989-7993
Gas Station-989-7791
Medical-989-8815

HEALTH & WELFARE: Naval Medical Branch Clinic, Emergency C-805-989-8821/3331, Appointments C-805-989-4501. Chapels serving all faiths C-805-989-4421/4358/5276.

RECREATION: Auto Hobby EX-7728, Bowling EX-7667, Golf EX-7109, Gym EX-8317, Library EX-7771, Swimming EX-7788, Youth Center EX-7580. Point Mugu Recreation Facilities on base, year round, C-805-989-8407, D-312-351-8407, 51 camper spaces w/full hookups, six camper spaces w/o hookups, 24 motel units.

SPACE-A: Pax Term/Lounge, Base Ops Bldg., 0700-2200 daily, C-805-989-7731, D-312-351-7731, flights to CONUS and foreign locations.

ATTRACTIONS: Beautiful beaches and Los Angeles area nearby. Annual Point Mugu Air Show. Disneyland, Marineland, Movieland, Universal Studios, Queen Mary, and Spruce Goose, Lion Country Safari and more. Ronald Reagan Presidential Library in Simi Valley (C-805-522-8444).

PORT HUENEME NAVAL CONSTRUCTION BATTALION CENTER (CA32R4)
Port Hueneme, CA 93043-4301

TELEPHONE NUMBER INFORMATION: Main installation numbers: C-805-982-4711, D-312-551-4711.

LOCATION: From US-101, exit south on Ventura Rd., right to Pleasant Valley Rd. USMRA: Page 111 (D,E-13). NMC: Los Angeles, 50 miles southeast.

GENERAL INFORMATION: Naval Mobile Construction Battalions and support units.

TEMPORARY MILITARY LODGING: Lodging office, Bldg. 1435, 24 hours, (Enlisted), C-805-982-4497, D-312-551-4497; Bldg. 1164 (Officer), C-805-982-5785. Navy Lodge, Bldg. 1172, C-805-985-2624. (O-6 and above). DV/VIP EM/Officers C-805-982-5785, Fax 805-982-4948.

LOGISTICAL SUPPORT: Complete support facilities available.

CDO/OOD-982-2007
Child Care-982-4849
Exchange-982-4268
Gas Station-982-4755
Legal-982-3124
Mini Mart-982-3186

CHAMPUS-982-6322/7215
Comm Club-982-2872
Family Services-982-5037
Golf Course-982-2620
Locator-982-4732
MWR-982-5554

Chaplain-982-4358
Commissary-982-5199
Fire Dept-982-4595
ITT Office-982-4284
Medical-982-6301
O'Club-982-2756

CALIFORNIA
Port Hueneme NCBC, continued

Police-982-4591
SATO-982-4276

Public Affairs-982-4493
Theater-982-5491

Retiree Services-982-5037

HEALTH & WELFARE: Naval Medical Clinic, C-805-982-6301/3332, Appointments C-805-984-8433. Chapels serving all faiths C-805-982-4421/4358.

RECREATION: Auto Hobby EX-4339, Bowling EX-2619, Community Center EX-4282, Rec Equip EX-5173, Golf EX-2620, Gym EX-5173, Library EX-4411, Museum EX-5163, Skating Rink EX-4606, Swimming EX-4752, Youth Center EX-4218. Point Mugu Rec Area, five miles southeast.

SPACE-A: None. See Point Mugu Missile Test Center listing, C-805-989-7731, D-312-351-7731.

ATTRACTIONS: CEC/SEABEE Museum, beaches, Channel Islands, two marinas.

PRESIDIO OF MONTEREY (CA74R4)
Presidio of Monterey, CA 93944-5006

TELEPHONE NUMBER INFORMATION: Main installation numbers: C-408-242-5000, D-312-878-5000.

LOCATION: From CA-1 in Monterey, exit to Del Monte Blvd, west to Lighthouse Ave. Enter from Lighthouse Ave. USMRA: Page 111 (B-9). NMC: Monterey, in city limits.

GENERAL INFORMATION: Defense Language Institute, Foreign Language Center.

TEMPORARY MILITARY LODGING: C-408-242-5091.

LOGISTICAL SUPPORT: Most support facilities available.

ACS-242-7650/60
Child Care-242-1058
Exchange-242-9602
Golf Course-899-2351
Legal-242-5083/84
MWR-242-6995
Public Affairs-242-5104
SATO-648-8045
Theater-373-2234

CHAMPUS-242-0304
Commissary-242-7671
Fire Department-242-7701
Housing Services-656-2321
Locator-242-5119
Package Store-899-2336
Recreation-242-5447
SDO/SDNCO-242-5119

Chaplain-242-7620
Consol Club-649-1823
Gas Station-372-0702
ITT Office-242-5377
Medical-242-5234
Police-242-5634
RV/Camping-242-5506
Snack Bar-647-9606

HEALTH & WELFARE: Clinic, 0700-1600 Mon-Fri, C-408-647-5234. Chapel serving Protestant/Catholic/Korean C-408-647-5281.

RECREATION: Fitness Center EX-5641, Rec Center EX-5447, Sports Arena EX-5295, Youth Center EX-5277. South Lake Tahoe Recreation Housing off post, year round, C-408-242-5506, D-312-878-5506, one A-Frame chalet, one cabin, two condominiums and motel lodgings.

SPACE-A: None. See Lemoore NAS, CA listing, C-209-998-1680, D-312-949-1680.

ATTRACTIONS: Beaches, seafood, Carmel Valley, Carmel-by-the-Sea, Salinas Valley. Beautiful location on a hill above the bay.

U.S. FORCES TRAVEL & TRANSFER GUIDE U.S.A. - 55

CALIFORNIA

PRESIDIO OF MONTEREY ANNEX (CA36R4)
Presidio of Monterey, CA 93944-5006

TELEPHONE NUMBER INFORMATION: Main installation numbers: C-408-242-2211, D-312-929-1110.

LOCATION: From US-101 Fort Ord exit to main gate of post. USMRA: Page 111 ((B,C-9). NMC: Monterey, seven miles south.

TEMPORARY MILITARY LODGING: None. See Presidio of Monterey listing, C-408-242-5091.

LOGISTICAL SUPPORT: Limited support facilities available.

Commissary-242-7671 Exchange-899-2336 Gas Station-394-2443
Locator-242-2271 Police-242-7851

HEALTH & WELFARE: None. See Presidio of Monterey listing, C-408-647-5234.

SPACE-A: None. See Lemoore NAS, CA listing, C-209-998-1680, D-312-949-1680.

ATTRACTIONS: Beaches, seafood, Carmel Valley, Carmel-by-the-Sea, Salinas Valley. Beautiful location on a hill above the bay.

SAN CLEMENTE ISLAND
NAVAL AUXILIARY LANDING FIELD (CA53R4)
P.O. Box 357054
San Diego, CA 92135-7054

TELEPHONE NUMBER INFORMATION: Main installation numbers: C-619-524-9214, D-312-524-9214.

LOCATION: Visitors must be sponsored by military stationed on the island. USMRA: Page 111 (E-15). NMC: Los Angeles, 50 miles east.

GENERAL INFORMATION: This is a closed base.

TEMPORARY MILITARY LODGING: Billeting Office C-619-524-9202.

LOGISTICAL SUPPORT: Limited support facilities available.

CDO/OOD-524-9212 Consol Club-524-9227 Exchange-524-9147
Fire-524-9212 Police-524-9214

HEALTH & WELFARE: None. See Camp Pendleton listing, C-619-725-1288.

SPACE-A AIR: C-619-524-9183.

ATTRACTIONS: Mansions, beaches, and wildlife.

CALIFORNIA

SAN DIEGO COAST GUARD AIR STATION (CA77R4)
2710 North Harbor Drive
San Diego, CA 92101-1079

TELEPHONE NUMBER INFORMATION: Main installation numbers: C-619-683-6333.

LOCATION: Take I-5 south to Sassafras St/Airport exit. Follow Sassafras St to Grape St, Right Grape St, then right on North Harbor Dr. Front gate one mile on the left. USMRA: Page 118 (C-6). NMC: San Diego, city limits.

GENERAL INFORMATION: Responsible for search and rescue missions, law enforcement, marine environment protection and providing aids to navigation. Marine Safety Office, ATON unit, and Coast Guard Station.

TEMPORARY MILITARY LODGING: None. See San Diego Naval Training Center listing, (BEQ) C-619-524-4788; (BOQ) C-619-524-5382.

LOGISTICAL SUPPORT: Limited support facilities available.

CDO/OOD-683-6470
Family Services-683-6336
Public Affairs-683-6320
CHAMPUS-532-8329
Locator-683-6333
SDO/NCO-683-6470
Exchange-683-6325
Medical-683-6380

HEALTH & WELFARE: Balboa Naval Hospital, Emergency C-619-532-8275, Info C-619-532-6400. No chapel on base.

SPACE-A: CG Hangar, C-619-557-6510. Fixed wing Space-A opportunities extremely limited, also see North Island Naval Air Station listing.

ATTRACTIONS: City of San Diego, Del Mar Racetrack, San Diego Zoo, Balboa Park, Sea World, Mission San Luis Rey.

SAN DIEGO MARINE CORPS RECRUIT DEPOT (CA57R4)
1600 Henderson Avenue, Suite 120
San Diego, CA 92140-5093

TELEPHONE NUMBER INFORMATION: Main installation numbers: C-619-524-1268 x1365.

LOCATION: From I-5 exit Old Town Ave and follow signs. Adjacent to the west side of Lindbergh Field. USMRA: Page 118 (C-6). NMC: San Diego, two miles northeast.

GENERAL INFORMATION: Recruit Depot, Drill Instructor School, Recruiters School. Headquarters 12th Marine Corps Recruiting District, USCG Pacific Area Tactical Law Enforcement Team.

TEMPORARY MILITARY LODGING: Lodging office, Bldg. 625, 0700-2330 daily, C-619-524-4401. All ranks.

LOGISTICAL SUPPORT: Most support facilities available.

U.S. FORCES TRAVEL & TRANSFER GUIDE U.S.A. - 57

CALIFORNIA
San Diego Marine Corps Recruit Depot, continued

CDO/OOD-524-1268 x1276	CHAMPUS-557-7500	Chaplain-524-1324 x1322
Child Care-524-4430	Combined Club-524-6878	Exchange-524-4435
Family Services-524-5728	Fire Department 9-911	Gas Station-296-4043
ITT-524-6772	Legal-524-4089	Locator-524-1720
Medical-524-4079	Museum-524-6038	Package Store-297-2500 x657
Police-524-4202	Public Affairs-524-1268	Recreation 524-6769
RV/Camping-524-6180	SATO-295-7286	Visitor Center-524-6038

HEALTH & WELFARE: Naval Branch Medical Clinic C-619-524-4079. Inpatient, see San Diego Naval Medical Center listing, C-800-453-0491. Chapel serving all faiths C-619-524-1323.

RECREATION: Bowling 524-4446, Camping Equipment 524-6180, Fitness Center 524-4428, Boats 524-5269, Tickets 524-6772, Recreation Services 524-5055.

SPACE-A: None. See North Island NAS listing, C-619-545-9567, D-312-735-9567.

ATTRACTIONS: Sea World, San Diego Zoo, Balboa Park, city of San Diego, Wild Animal Park, Command Museum, Mexico nearby.

SAN DIEGO NAVAL MEDICAL CENTER (CA59R4)
34800 Bob Wilson Drive
San Diego, CA 92134-5000

TELEPHONE NUMBER INFORMATION: Main installation numbers: C-619-532-6400, D-312-522-6400.

LOCATION: Exit from I-5 to Pershing Dr and west on Florida Canyon Dr. to entrance. USMRA: Page 118 (D-6). NMC: San Diego, three miles northeast.

GENERAL INFORMATION: Large Naval medical treatment facility serving the San Diego area.

TEMPORARY MILITARY LODGING: None. See San Diego Naval Station listing, (BEQ) C-619-524-4788; (BOQ) C-619-524-5382. and North Island Naval Air Station listing, BEQ, C-619-545-9551, BOQ, C-619-545-7489.

LOGISTICAL SUPPORT: Limited support facilities available.

CHAMPUS-532-8328	CDO/OOD-532-6400	Child Care-532-6665
Exchange-525-1505	Fire Department-9-911	Medical -532-6400
MWR 532-7245	Public Affairs-532-9380	SATO-532-6607

HEALTH & WELFARE: Emergency 911, Appointments C-800-453-0491, 560 bed inpatient and 200 bed light care facility.

RECREATION: Library 532-7950, Fitness Center 532-7260, Swimming Pool 532-8516, Rec Services Office 532-7245, Tickets 532-7245.

SPACE-A: None. See North Island NAS listing, C-619-545-9567, D-312-735-9567.

ATTRACTIONS: Zoo, Sea World, Balboa Park, city of San Diego, Wild Animal Park, Mexico nearby.

CALIFORNIA

SAN DIEGO NAVAL STATION (CA26R4)
San Diego Naval Station, CA 92136-5000

TELEPHONE NUMBER INFORMATION: Main installation numbers: C-619-556-1011, D-312-526-1011.

LOCATION: Off I-5, seven miles south of San Diego. Take 28th St exit. Station is at 28th & Main Streets. USMRA: Page 118 (D-7,8). NMC: San Diego, in the city.

GENERAL INFORMATION: Pacific Fleet Training Center, Public Works Center, and home port for major ships of the Pacific Fleet.

TEMPORARY MILITARY LODGING: Lodging office, 0730-1630 daily, Bldg. 3362 (BEQ) C-619-556-8672; and Bldg. 3104 (BOQ) C-619-556-8156. DV/VIP C-619-556-8672/8163, Fax 619-556-9325. Navy Lodge near Harbor Dr, 24 hours daily, C-619-234-6142, D-312-958-6142. Reservations: 1-800-628-9466. All ranks.

LOGISTICAL SUPPORT: Complete support facilities available.

Cafeteria-544-2228	CDO/OOD-556-1246/47	CHAMPUS-557-7505
Chaplain-556-1921	Child Care-556-7475	Commissary-556-7202
CPO Club-556-7050	EM Club-556-1915	Exchange-544-2111
Family Services-556-7486	Fire Dept-524-6250	Gas Station-544-2289
Golf Course-556-5162	ITT Office-556-7498	Legal-556-1663
Locator-556-1011	Medical-556-8114	MWR-556-7029
O'Club-556-7948	Package Store-544-2252	Police-556-1841
Public Affairs-556-7356	Retiree Services-556-7404	SATO-231-7361
Theater-556-6062		

HEALTH & WELFARE: Naval Branch Medical Clinic, Emergency C-619-556-8114. Inpatient, see San Diego Naval Medical Center listing, C-800-453-0491. Chapels serving all faiths C-619-532-6025.

RECREATION: Admiral Robinson Center EX-7486, Arts/Crafts EX-7030, Rec Services EX-7029/7455, Auto Hobby EX-5008/9, Sports Director EX-7444, Bowling EX-7486. Admiral Baker Field Campground off base, year round, C-619-556-5525, 27 camper spaces with W&E hookups, 12 camper spaces w/o hookups.

SPACE-A: None. See North Island NAS listing, C-619-545-9567, D-312-735-9567.

ATTRACTIONS: Zoo, Sea World, Balboa Park, City of San Diego, Wild Animal Park, Mexico nearby.

SAN DIEGO NAVAL SUBMARINE BASE (CA79R4)
140 Sylvester Road
San Diego, CA 92106-3521

TELEPHONE NUMBER INFORMATION: Main installation numbers: C-619-553-7533, D-312-553-7533.

LOCATION: Take I-5 or I-8 to Rosecrans exit. Follow to main gate. USMRA: Page 118 (B-6). NMC: San Diego, five miles southeast.

CALIFORNIA
San Diego Naval Submarine Base, continued

GENERAL INFORMATION: Submarine Training Facility, Submarine Development Group One, Submarine Group Five.

TEMPORARY MILITARY LODGING: Lodging office, Bldg. 601, 24 hours daily, BEQ, C-619-553-7533, D-312-553-7533, BOQ, C-619-553-9381, D-312-553-9381. DV/VIP C-619-553-9381, D-312-553-9381, Fax 619-553-0613.

LOGISTICAL SUPPORT: Complete support facilities available.

CHAMPUS-532-8300   Chaplain-553-7201   Conv Store-221-2011
CPO Club-553-7597   EM Club-553-7519   Exchange-221-2011
Family Services-553-7505 Gas Station-221-1095   ITT Office-553-7162
Legal-553-8594   O'Club-553-9384   Police-553-7070
Public Affairs-553-8644 SATO-222-3632   SDO/NCO-553-7533

HEALTH & WELFARE: None. See San Diego Naval Medical Center listing, C-800-453-0491. Chapel serving all faiths C-619-553-7201.

RECREATION: Arts/Crafts EX-7162, Archery EX-7549, Auto Hobby EX-7162, Bowling EX-7521, Camping Equip EX-7549, Ceramics EX-7545, Gym EX-7552, Hobby Shop EX-7549, Library EX-9851, Rec Center EX-7552, Special Services EX-7162, Swimming EX-7552.

SPACE-A: None. See North Island Naval Air Station listing, C-619-545-9567, D-312-735-9567.

ATTRACTIONS: City of San Diego, San Diego Zoo, Balboa Park, Sea World, Mission San Luis Rey. Pacific Ocean, mountains, and deserts within a short driving distance.

SAN DIEGO NAVAL TRAINING CENTER (CA54R4)
33502 Decatur Road, Suite 120
San Diego, CA 92133-1449

Scheduled to close April 1997.

TELEPHONE NUMBER INFORMATION: Main installation numbers: C-619-524-1011/1935, D-312-524-1011.

LOCATION: From I-8 West take Rosecrans exit to Lytton St, left on Lytton to NTC gate #1. From I-5 North take Rosecrans exit, left on Lytton to gate. From I-5 S take Pacific Highway exit to Barnett Ave which becomes Lytton St, turn left to Gate #1. USMRA: Page 118 (B,C-6). NMC: San Diego, four miles east.

GENERAL INFORMATION: West Coast training facility, including both advanced and basic training. Component command includes Service School Command.

TEMPORARY MILITARY LODGING: Lodging office, Bldg. 584 (BEQ), 0600-1600 Mon-Fri, C-619-524-4788, D-312-524-4788 and Bldg. 82 (BOQ) C-619-524-5382, D-312-524-5382. DV/VIP C-619-524-4788/0558, Fax C-619-524-0262.

LOGISTICAL SUPPORT: Complete support facilities available.

CALIFORNIA
San Diego Naval Training Center, continued

CDO/OOD-524-5806	Chaplain-524-5393	Child Care-524-5920
Commissary-524-4171	Exchange-522-7254	Fire Dept-524-9911
Gas Station-221-1049	ITT-524-0330	Legal-524-1924
Locator-524-1011	Medical-524-4948	MWR-524-4530
NCO Club-524-1914	O'Club-524-6287	Package Store-221-2000
Police-524-5806	Public Affairs-524-4210	Recreation-524-4530
SATO-222-6438		

HEALTH & WELFARE: Naval Branch Medical Clinic C-619-524-4948. Inpatient, see San Diego Naval Medical Center listing, C-800-453-0491. Chapel serving all faiths C-619-524-5544.

RECREATION: Library EX-5562, Gym EX-5465, Bowling EX-5479, Sailing EX-6498, Tickets EX-0330, Swimming EX-5378, Rec Equip EX-4530, Marina EX-6498.

SPACE-A: None. See North Island NAS listing, C-619-545-9567, D-312-735-9567.

ATTRACTIONS: Zoo, Sea World, Balboa Park, city of San Diego, Wild Animal Park, Mexico nearby.

SAN PEDRO COAST GUARD SUPPORT CENTER (CA25R4)
San Pedro, CA 90731-5000

TELEPHONE NUMBER INFORMATION: Main installation numbers: C-310-514-6401, FTS-514-6401.

LOCATION: On Coast Guard Base, Terminal Island. USMRA: Page 117 (C-7). NMC: Long Beach, two miles east.

GENERAL INFORMATION: Coast Guard Support Center for the Los Angeles area.

TEMPORARY MILITARY LODGING: Local Housing Authority, PCS, Base PO Box 8, Terminal Island Station, San Pedro, 0700-1600 daily, C-310-514-6450. BEQ only at CG Support Center. All ranks. DV/VIP 310-514-6450.

LOGISTICAL SUPPORT: Limited support facilities available.

CHAMPUS-514-6407	Consol Club-514-6401	Exchange-514-6401
SDO/NCO-514-6401		

HEALTH & WELFARE: None, See Los Angeles AFB listing, C-310-363-0964.

RECREATION: On the beach in the Los Angeles area.

SPACE-A: Available at Los Angeles IAP; see Los Angeles AFB listing, C-310-363-0714, D-312-833-0714, Fax 310-216-2670.

ATTRACTIONS: Greater Los Angeles area.

U.S. FORCES TRAVEL & TRANSFER GUIDE U.S.A. - 61

CALIFORNIA

SANTA CLARA NAVAL AIR RESERVE STATION (CA17R4)
500 Shenandoah Plaza
Moffett Federal Air Field, CA 94035-5000

TELEPHONE NUMBER INFORMATION: Main installation numbers: C-415-604-5000, D-312-359-5000.

LOCATION: On Bayshore Freeway, US-101, 35 miles south of San Francisco. USMRA: Page 119 (F-9). NMC: San Jose, seven miles south.

GENERAL INFORMATION: 129th Air Rescue Group, CANG, and Naval Air Reserve Units. Santa Clara Naval Air Reserve is the Navy local area coordinator for the South Bay area. NAVAIRES Santa Clara is a tenant on Moffett Federal Airfield (operated by NASA).

TEMPORARY MILITARY LODGING: Lodging office, Bldg. 593, 0800-1600 daily, BEQ C-415-404-8299, D-312-494-8299, BOQ C-415-404-6170, D-312-462-6170, DV/VIP C-415-404-8299, D-312-462-8299, Fax 415-404-6156. Navy Lodge C-415-962-1542 or 1-800-NAVY-INN. All ranks.

LOGISTICAL SUPPORT: Complete support facilities available.

CDO/OOD-603-9527
Child Care-940-1884
CPO/O'Club-603-4716
Family Services-603-8016
Golf Course-603-8026
Locator-603-5000
NCO Club-603-8959
Public Affairs-603-9539
Snack Bar-603-9930
CHAMPUS-603-8227
Commissary-603-9976
EM CLub-603-8959
Fire Dept-604-5416
ITT-604-1686
Medical-603-8251
Package Store-603-9927
Retiree Services-603-4069
Chaplain-603-8073
Conv Store-603-9927
Exchange-603-9907
Gas Station-603-9939
Legal-603-9515
MWR-603-9717
Police-604-1623
SATO-604-1686

HEALTH & WELFARE: Air Force Branch Medical Clinic, Emergency C-415-603-8251. Chapels serving all faiths C-415-404-4100.

RECREATION: Auto Hobby EX-8046, Bowling EX-4709, Golf EX-4702, Gym EX-4697, Rec Services 691-1216, Swimming EX-4712, Ticket Office EX-4757, Youth Activities 965-2716.

SPACE-A: Pax Term, Bldg. 158, 24 hours daily, C-415-604-5231, D-312-494-5231, flights to CONUS, OCONUS and foreign locations.

ATTRACTIONS: Paramount's Great America Park, five miles south. Located in the heart of the "Silicon Valley." San Jose and Santa Cruz are nearby.

SEAL BEACH NAVAL WEAPONS STATION (CA80R4)
800 Seal Beach Boulevard
Seal Beach, CA 90740-5050

TELEPHONE NUMBER INFORMATION: Main installation numbers: C-310-626-7301, D-312-873-7301.

LOCATION: Take I-405 to Seal Beach Blvd exit. Turn right (South). Continue to main gate on left. USMRA: Page 117 (E-7). NMC: Long Beach, adjacent.

62 - U.S. FORCES TRAVEL & TRANSFER GUIDE U.S.A

CALIFORNIA
Seal Beach Naval Weapons Station, continued

GENERAL INFORMATION: Not available at press time.

TEMPORARY MILITARY LODGING: C-310-636-7575.

LOGISTICAL SUPPORT: Complete support facilities available.

All Hands Club-626-7105   CDO/OOD-626-7229   Chaplain-626-7229
Fire Department-626-7280 Golf Course-430-9913 Medical-626-7444
MWR-626-7227   Police-626-7210   Public Affairs-626-7215
Recreation-626-7227   Snack Bar-431-8983   Visitor Center-626-7214

HEALTH & WELFARE: Dispensary/Emergency C-310-594-7285, after hours C-310-594-7333. No chapel on base.

RECREATION: Bowling EX-7278, Camping Equip EX-7555/7576, Boy Scout Campsite EX-7215, Gym EX-7278, Library EX-7294, Rec Center/Equip EX-7278, Special Services EX-7215, Youth Activities EX-7278.

SPACE-A: None. See El Toro MCAS listing, C-714-726-3920, D-312-997-3920.

ATTRACTIONS: Greater Los Angeles area, Hollywood.

SIERRA ARMY DEPOT (CA44R4)
First Street, Building P-1
Herlong, CA 96113-9999

TELEPHONE NUMBER INFORMATION: Main installation numbers: C-916-827-4544, D-312-855-4910.

LOCATION: Fifty-five miles northwest of Reno, NV, off US-395. Right on CA-A26 from Reno. When traveling south on US-395, left on CA-A25. USMRA: Page 110 (E-4). NMC: Reno, 55 miles southeast.

GENERAL INFORMATION: Major Army Materiel Command Depot, maintenance and storage activities.

TEMPORARY MILITARY LODGING: Lodging office, Bldg. P-144, duty hours; other hours, Bldg. P-100 (Sec Radio Room), C-916-827-4544/4345. All ranks. DV/VIP EX-4544.

LOGISTICAL SUPPORT: Complete support facilities available.

CHAMPUS-827-4575   Chaplain-827-4138   Commercial Travel-827-4175
Commissary-827-4480   Community Club-827-5325   Conv Store-827-2894
Exchange-827-4388   Family Services-827-4425   Gas Station-827-2894
ITT Office-827-4178   Legal-827-4548   Locator-827-4544
Medical-827-4575   Police-827-4345   Retiree Services-827-4555
SDO/NCO-827-4345/4555   Snack Bar-827-4442   Theater-827-2526

HEALTH & WELFARE: US Army Health Clinic, Emergency C-916-827-4911, Appointments C-916-827-4141. Chapels serving Catholic/Protestant C-916-827-4128.

RECREATION: Auto Hobby EX-4198, Bowling EX-4442, Ceramics EX-4206, Swimming EX-4602, Rec Services EX-4602.

U.S. FORCES TRAVEL & TRANSFER GUIDE U.S.A. - 63

CALIFORNIA
Sierra Army Depot, continued

SPACE-A: None. See Travis AFB listing, C-704-424-1854, D-312-837-1854, Fax 707-424-2048.

ATTRACTIONS: Reno for entertainment, casinos, Lake Tahoe is a one-and-a-half hour drive south.

STOCKTON NAVAL COMMUNICATIONS STATION (CA51R4)
305 Fyffe Avenue
Stockton, CA 95203-4920

NOTE: Station facilities are being reduced due to mission reduction. Call ahead to confirm operation.

TELEPHONE NUMBER INFORMATION: Main installation numbers: C-209-944-0395/0225, D-312-466-7395/7225.

LOCATION: From I-5 north exit at Rough & Ready Island, right at Fresno St to Washington St to station. USMRA: Page 110 (C-7). NMC: Stockton, in the city.

GENERAL INFORMATION: Major Naval Communications Station on the West Coast.

TEMPORARY MILITARY LODGING: Lodging office, Bldg. 128, Hooper & McCloy Ave, 24 hours daily, C-209-944-0343. BOQ/BEQ/DV/VIP Fax 209-944-0214.

LOGISTICAL SUPPORT: Most support facilities available.

CHAMPUS-944-0445
Fire Dept-944-0333
Medical-944-0445
Public Affairs-944-0511/13

Commissary-944-0224
Gas Station-944-0479
MWR-944-0582
Recreation-944-0582

Exchange-944-0200/0393
Golf Course-944-0442
Police-944-0336

HEALTH & WELFARE: Naval Branch Medical Clinic, Emergency C-209-944-0445.

RECREATION: Golf EX-0442, Rec Services EX-0582, Racquetball EX-0330.

SPACE-A: None. See Travis AFB, C-707-424-1854, D-312-837-1854, Fax 707-424-2048.

ATTRACTIONS: Equal distance to Sacramento and San Francisco.

TRAVIS AIR FORCE BASE (CA50R4)
540 Airlift Drive
Travis Air Force Base, CA 94535-5000

TELEPHONE NUMBER INFORMATION: Main installation numbers: C-707-424-1110, D-312-837-1110.

LOCATION: Off I-80 North, take Airbase Parkway exit. Clearly marked. USMRA: Page 110 (B,C-7). NMC: San Francisco, 45 miles southwest.

GENERAL INFORMATION: Air Mobility Command Base, 60th Air Mobility Wing, Headquarters 15th Air Force, 349th Air Mobility Wing (AFRES).

64 - U.S. FORCES TRAVEL & TRANSFER GUIDE U.S.A

CALIFORNIA
Travis Air Force Base, continued

TEMPORARY MILITARY LODGING: Lodging office, Bldg. 404, Sevedge Dr, 24 hours, C-707-437-2987. D-312-837-2987. All ranks. DV/VIP 707-424-3185.

LOGISTICAL SUPPORT: Complete support facilities available.

Cafeteria-437-2092	CHAMPUS-437-7100	Chaplain-424-3217
Child Care-424-0341	Commissary-437-4211	Enlisted Club-424-5071
Exchange-437-4633	Family Services-424-2486	Gas Station-437-2232
Legal-424-3251	Locator-424-2798	Medical-423-3000
O'Club-424-2745	Package Store-437-3692	Police-424-3293
Retiree Services-424-3904	SATO-437-7380	Shoppette-437-6606
Theater-437-3855		

HEALTH & WELFARE: David Grant USAF Medical Center, Emergency C-707-423-3826, 245 beds, Appointments C-707-423-3000. Chapels serving all faiths C-707-424-3217.

RECREATION: Bowling EX-5048, Golf EX-5797, Rec Center EX-5659, Exercise Center EX-5680, Hobby Shops EX-1338, Library EX-3279, Museum EX-5605, Youth Center EX-5392, Aero Club 437-3470, Saddle Club 437-9060. Travis Fam-Camp on base, year round, C-707-424-3583, D-312-837-3583, 70 camper spaces w/full hookups, eight camper/tent spaces w/o hookups.

SPACE-A: Pax Term/Lounge, Bldg. P-3, 24 hours daily, C-707-424-1854 or 1-800-787-2534, D-312-837-1854, Fax 707-424-2048, flights to CONUS, OCONUS, and foreign locations.

ATTRACTIONS: Travis Air Museum, San Francisco 55 miles southwest, Sacramento 45 miles northeast, discount outlet stores in Vacaville, Solano Mall in Fairfield, Busch Brewery, Western Railway Museum.

TREASURE ISLAND NAVAL STATION (CA21R4)
San Francisco, CA 94130-5000

Scheduled to close September 1997.

TELEPHONE NUMBER INFORMATION: Main installation numbers: C-415-395-1000 (0730-1600 Mon-Fri) 415-395-5505 (other hours), D-312-475-5505.

LOCATION: On Treasure Island in San Francisco Bay off I-80 (Oakland Bay Bridge). USMRA: Page 119 (C,D-5). NMC: In San Francisco, two miles to downtown.

GENERAL INFORMATION: Fleet Training Center Detachment, Navy and Marine Corps Reserve Center.

TEMPORARY MILITARY LODGING: Lodging office, 0730-1630 daily, Bldg. 452 (BEQ) C-415-395-5442, D-312-475-5410 and Bldg. 369 (BOQ) C-415-395-5273, D-312-475-5274. DV/VIP C-415-395-5412/5273, Fax 415-395-5666.

LOGISTICAL SUPPORT: Complete support facilities available.

Cafeteria-395-5534	CHAMPUS-395-5818	Chaplain-395-5446
Child Care-395-5796	Commissary-395-5080	EM Club-395-5121
Exchange-395-5515	Family Services-395-5789	Gas Station-395-5540

U.S. FORCES TRAVEL & TRANSFER GUIDE U.S.A. - 65

CALIFORNIA
Treasure Island Naval Station, continued

ITT Office-395-5132   Legal-395-3746   Medical-395-3649
SATO-421-3027   SDO/NCO-395-5505   Theater-395-5144

HEALTH & WELFARE: Naval Branch Medical Clinic, Emergency C-415-395-3649. Chapel serving all faiths C-415-395-6823/6824.

RECREATION: Bowling EX-5136, Marina/Sailing EX-3396, Youth Center EX-5309, Auto Hobby EX-5120, Gear Issue, EX-5132.

SPACE-A: See Travis Air Force Base listing, C-707-424-1854, D-312-837-1854, Fax 707-424-2048.

ATTRACTIONS: Treasure Island Museum, San Francisco, Fisherman's Wharf, Chinatown, cable cars.

TUSTIN MARINE CORPS AIR STATION (CA86R4)
MCAS Tustin
Santa Ana, CA 92710-5001

Scheduled to close December 1997.

TELEPHONE NUMBER INFORMATION: Main installation numbers: C-714-726-2100, D-312-997-2100.

LOCATION: From I-5 (Santa Ana Freeway) left at Sand Canyon exit; to light at Trabuco, right to main gate. USMRA: Page 117 (G-7). NMC: Irvine 10 miles northwest.

TEMPORARY MILITARY LODGING: Billeting Office C-714-726-3001/7984, D-312-997-3001/7984, DV/VIP C-714-726-7301, D-312-997-7301.

LOGISTICAL SUPPORT: Limited support facilities available.

EM Club -726-7219   Exchange-726-3340   Locator-726-3736
Medical-726-7256   NCO Club-726-7219   O' Club-726-7330
Police-726-9911/7666

HEALTH & WELFARE: NAVCARE Clinic, C-714-726-7231.

SPACE-A: None. See El Toro MCAS listing, C-714-726-3920, D-312-997-3920.

ATTRACTIONS: Orange County and greater Los Angeles area, Disneyland in Anaheim, Anaheim Stadium (home of the California Angels baseball team), Knott's Berry Farm in Buena Park, Marineland located at the tip of the Palo Verdes peninsula, Movieland Wax Museum in Buena Park, Crystal Cathedral in Garden Grove, beaches, boating.

TWENTYNINE PALMS MARINE CORPS AIR/GROUND COMBAT CENTER (CA27R4)
Twentynine Palms, CA 92278-5000

TELEPHONE NUMBER INFORMATION: Main installation numbers: C-619-830-6000, D-312-957-6000.

CALIFORNIA
Twentynine Palms, continued

LOCATION: From the west on I-10, exit on CA-62 northeast to base. From the east on I-40 exit south at Amboy. USMRA: Page 111 (H,I-13,14). NMC: Palm Springs, 60 miles southwest.

GENERAL INFORMATION: Largest Marine Corps Base, training and maintenance operation.

TEMPORARY MILITARY LODGING: Bldg. 1565, 5th St, 24 hours daily, C-619-830-6573. All ranks. DV/VIP C-619-830-6109.

LOGISTICAL SUPPORT: Complete support facilities available.

Cafeteria-830-6989	CDO/OOD-830-7200	CHAMPUS-830-2572
Chaplain-830-6464	Child Care-830-7541	Commissary-830-7573
Conv Store-830-6138	EM Club-830-6696	Exchange-830-6163
Family Services-830-7206	Fire Department-830-5239	Gas Station-830-6693
Golf Course-830-6132	ITT Office-830-6163 x264	Legal-830-6111
Locator-830-6000	Medical-830-2872	MWR-830-6870
O'Club-830-6610	Package Store-830-6860	Police-830-6800
Public Affairs-830-6213	Recreation-830-7153	Retiree Services-830-7550
SATO-830-6622	Snack Bar-830-6163	Theater-830-6795
Visitor Center-830-6795		

HEALTH & WELFARE: Branch Naval Hospital, clinics and depts, 40 beds, Emergency C-619-830-7354, Appointments C-619-830-3585. Chapel serving all faiths C-619-830-6456.

RECREATION: Rec Lounge, Gym, Hobby Shops, Youth Activities, Fitness Center, Golf, Riding Stables, Skeet Range, Hunting, Swimming, and more. Call Special Services EX-6597. See El Toro MCAS listing for Big Bear Lake Rec Facility in San Bernardino Mountains.

SPACE-A: None. See Los Angeles IAP listing, C-310-363-0714, D-312-833-0714, Fax 310-216-2670.

ATTRACTIONS: Joshua Tree National Monument, Palm Springs.

VANDENBERG AIR FORCE BASE (CA29R4)
747 Nebraska Avenue, Suite 7
Vandenberg Air Force Base, CA 93437-5000

TELEPHONE NUMBER INFORMATION: Main installation numbers: C-805-734-8232, D-312-276-1611. For extension numbers below: call main installation number and wait for recording, then dial extension or "0" for operator assistance.

LOCATION: Base is located 55 miles north of Santa Barbara, on California Highway 1. USMRA: Page 111 (C-12). NMC: Lompoc, six miles south.

GENERAL INFORMATION: Air Force Space Command, 30th Space Wing.

TEMPORARY MILITARY LODGING: Lodging office, Bldg. 13005, Oregon at L St, 24 hours daily, C-805-734-8232 ext 6-2245, D-312-276-1844. All ranks. Two suites for handicapped. DV/VIP C-805-734-3711.

U.S. FORCES TRAVEL & TRANSFER GUIDE U.S.A. - 67

CALIFORNIA
Vandenberg Air Force Base, continued

LOGISTICAL SUPPORT: Complete support facilities available.

CHAMPUS-EX-6-1878	Chaplain-EX-6-6655	Child Care-EX-6-3237
Commissary-EX-5-8801	Conv Store-734-1055	EM Club-734-4375
Exchange-734-5521	Family Services-EX-6-5484	Gas Station-734-3566
Legal-EX-5-6218	Locator-EX-6-1841	Medical-EX-6-1847
O'Club-734-4311	Police-EX-6-3911	Retiree Services-EX-6-5474
Theater-734-1315	Travel-734-4381	

HEALTH & WELFARE: USAF Hospital, 20 beds, Emergency EX-6-6206. Chapel serving all faiths EX-6-6655.

RECREATION: Aero 734-2733, Arts/Crafts EX-6-6438, Auto Hobby EX-6-6014, Bowling 734-1310, Ceramics EX-6-5209, Golf EX-6-6262, Gym EX-6-3832, Library EX-6-6414, Rec Center EX-6-7976, MWR Supply EX-6-5908, Rod/Gun Club EX-6-4560, Swimming EX-6-3581, Wood Hobby EX-6-4567, Youth Center EX-6-6898. Fam-Camp on base, year round, 805-734-8232-EX-6-8579, D-312-276-8579, 20 camper spaces w/full hookups, 30 camper spaces w/W&E, 19 camper spaces w/o hookups, 15 tent spaces.

SPACE-A: AMC flights extremely limited to nonexistent, C-805-734-8232 EX-6-7742, D-312-276-7742.

ATTRACTIONS: Great beaches, historic missions, Hearst Castle, north of AFB.

Other Installations in California

Channel Islands ANGS, Port Hueneme, CA 93041-4001.
USMRA: Page 111 (D,E-13). C-805-982-4711, Space-A-805-7731.
Humboldt Bay Coast Guard Group, Eureka, CA 95501-5000.
USMRA: Page 110 (A-2,3). C-707-443-2213, Exchange-443-7796.
Lake Tahoe Coast Guard Station, P.O. Box 882, Tahoe City, CA 96145-0882.
USMRA: Page 110 (E-6). C-916-583-7438, RVC-583-7438.
Presidio of San Francisco, Keyes Avenue, Presidio of San Francisco, CA 94129-7000.
USMRA: Page 119 (C-5). C-415-561-2211, D-312-586-1110, Commissary-561-23829, Exchange-922-4605.
March Air Force Base, 2145 Graeber St., Suite 130, March AFB, CA 90045-4687.
USMRA: Page 111 (G-14). C-909-655-1110. D-312-947-1110, BX Mart-655-4311, Space-A-655-2397.
San Diego Fleet Combat Training Center Pacific, 53690 Tomahawk Drive, #144, San Diego, CA 92147-5000.
USMRA: Page 118 (A,B-6). C-619-553-8330, D-312-524-1011.
Tracy Defense Depot Activity, Stockton, CA 95376-5000.
USMRA: Page 110 (C-7). C-209-832-9049.

68 - U.S. FORCES TRAVEL & TRANSFER GUIDE U.S.A

COLORADO

DOLLAR RENT A CAR — Call 1-800-800-4000. Get a military rate by using your Military Living ID # ML3009. Retirees/Active Duty/Reserve/Guard.

BUCKLEY AIR NATIONAL GUARD BASE (CO11R3)
18500 E. Sixth Street
Buckley ANGB, CO 80011-9599

TELEPHONE NUMBER INFORMATION: Main installation numbers: C-303-340-9011, D-312-877-9011.

LOCATION: On East 6th Avenue, off of I-225, clearly marked. USMRA: Page 109 (G-3), page 116 (C,D-3,4). NMC: Denver, 21 miles west.

GENERAL INFORMATION: 140th Training Wing, 200th Airlift Squadron, 2nd Space Warning Squadron, Navy/Marine Reserve Training Center, and Army Aviation Support Facility.

TEMPORARY MILITARY LODGING: None. See Fitzsimons Army Medical Center listing, C-303-361-8903, D-312-943-8903.

LOGISTICAL SUPPORT: Very limited support facilities available.

All Ranks Club-340-9840   Family Services-340-6111   Medical-340-9666
Police-340-9930   Public Affairs-340-9431

HEALTH & WELFARE: None. See Fitzsimons Army Medical Center listing, C-303-361-8525.

SPACE-A: Bldg. 809, 0700-1900 daily, C-303-340-9662/9663, D-312-877-9662/9663, Army flights (MEDEVAC) to CONUS locations.

ATTRACTIONS: Denver nearby. Snow sports, Pro sports teams, National Western Stock Show and Rodeo in January. Fitzsimons Army Medical Center five miles northwest.

FALCON AIR FORCE BASE (CO13R3)
300 O'Malley Ave.
Falcon Air Force Base, CO 80912-3024

TELEPHONE NUMBER INFORMATION: Main installation numbers: C-719-567-4113, D-560-4113.

LOCATION: Approximately 12 miles east of Colorado Springs, east on highway 94 to Enoch Road. NMC: Colorado Springs, 12 miles west.

GENERAL INFORMATION: 50th Space Wing, Ballistic Missile Defense Organization, Space Warfare Center.

TEMPORARY MILITARY LODGING: Located at Peterson Air Force Base. Billeting Office (Bldg 1042) 24 hour front desk, C-719-556-7851; Reservations C-719-556-6293/8048, D-312-834-6293/8048.

COLORADO
Falcon Air Force Base, continued

LOGISTICAL SUPPORT: Limited (Complete support facilities are available at Peterson AFB).

Chaplain-567-3705	Dental-567-5065	Fire Department-567-3370
ITT-567-6050	Legal-567-5050	Police-567-5643
Public Affairs-567-5040	Visitor Center-567-5643	

HEALTH AND WELFARE: Falcon Aid Station (emergency), C-719-567-6666. Also see Peterson AFB listing, C-719-556-1000.

RECREATION: Fitness Center 567-2666. Complete rec facilities are available at Peterson AFB.

ATTRACTIONS: U.S. Air Force Academy, Garden of the Gods, ski resorts (within a 2-3 hour drive).

FITZSIMONS ARMY MEDICAL CENTER (CO10R3)
Aurora, CO 80045-5001

This base is scheduled to close under the 1995 BRAC.
No closure date has been established.

TELEPHONE NUMBER INFORMATION: Main installation numbers: C-303-361-8241, D-312-943-1101, FTS-337-8241.

LOCATION: From I-70 take Peoria Ave (281), exit south, one mile to left on Colfax Ave. Center on left. From I-25 take I-225 north to Colfax Ave, west on Colfax Ave to Center on right. USMRA: Page 116 (C-3). NMC: Denver, eight miles east.

GENERAL INFORMATION: One of the US Army's largest Medical Research, Teaching, and Treatment Facilities.

TEMPORARY MILITARY LODGING: Lodging office and Guest House, ("Fitzsimons Lodge"), Bldg. 400, W Bruns Ave, 0730-2130 Mon-Fri, C-303-361-8903, D-312-943-8903. All ranks. DV/VIP C-303-361-8824.

LOGISTICAL SUPPORT: Complete support facilities available.

ACS-361-8659	Carson Travel-361-8066	CHAMPUS-361-8780
Chaplain-361-3988	Child Care-361-8574	Commissary-361-8270
Community Club-340-8668	Conv Store-340-1066	Exchange-340-1100
Family Services-361-8659	Fire Dept-361-8641	Gas Station-340-1543
Golf Course-340-8622	ITR Office-361-8684	Legal-361-8262
Locator-361-8800	Medical-361-8350	Police-361-3792
Public Affairs-361-3952	Retiree Services-361-8517	SATO-361-8066
SDO/NCO-361-8181	Snack Bar-361-8475	

HEALTH & WELFARE: Emergency C-303-361-8031, Appointment/Info C-303-361-8525, 506 beds. Chapels serving all faiths C-303-361-8121.

RECREATION: Bowling EX-8379, Golf EX-8622, Gym EX-8686, Tickets EX-2135. Dillon Recreation Area off post, C-303-361-8956, D-312-943-8956, 30 camper/tent spaces w/E hookups, three camper/tent spaces without hookups.

COLORADO
Fitzsimons Army Medical Center, continued

SPACE-A: Available at Buckley Air National Guard Base, eight miles east of Denver, Bldg. 809, 0700-1900 daily, C-303-340-9663, D-312-877-9663, Army flights to CONUS locations.

ATTRACTIONS: Many snow ski areas nearby. Denver.

FORT CARSON (CO02R3)
Building 1544
Fort Carson, CO 80913-5000

TELEPHONE NUMBER INFORMATION: Main installation numbers: C-719-526-5811, D-312-691-5811.

LOCATION: From Colorado Springs, take I-25 to exit 135 or CO-115 S to main gate, clearly marked. USMRA: Page 109 (F,G-5,6), page 115 (C,D-6,7). NMC: Colorado Springs, six miles north.

GENERAL INFORMATION: Headquarters 4th Infantry Division, 43rd Support Group, 10th Special Forces Group.

TEMPORARY MILITARY LODGING: Lodging office, Bldg. 731, Woodfill Rd, Colorado Inn, 24 hours daily, C-719-526-4832, D-312-691-4832. All ranks. DV/VIP C-719-526-5811.

LOGISTICAL SUPPORT: Complete support facilities available.

ACS-526-4590
Chaplain-526-0480
Conv Store-526-7923
Fire Dept-526-5615
ITT-526-4495
Medical-526-7000
Police-526-2333
SDO/SNO-526-3400

All Ranks Club-576-7540
Child Care-526-4053
Exchange-526-6177
Gas Station-576-4096
Legal-526-5572
MWR-526-5580
Public Affairs-526-3420

CHAMPUS-526-7000
Commissary-526-5644
Family Services-526-4590
Golf Course-526-4122
Locator-526-0227
Package Store-526-6531
Recreation-526-2083

HEALTH & WELFARE: Evans US Army Community Hospital, Emergency C-719-526-7111, Appointments C-719-526-3762, 154 beds. Chapels serving all faiths C-719-526-3393.

RECREATION: Bowling EX-5542, Arts/Crafts EX-3020, Auto Hobby EX-2147, Events Center 526-6604, Fitness Center 526-2597, Golf EX-4122, Library EX-2350/2842, Little Theater EX-3179, Outdoor Rec EX-2083, Rec Equip EX-2541, Swimming Indoor EX-5739/Outdoor EX-4456. Wood Hobby EX-3487, Youth Activities EX-2680/3546. Turkey Creek Ranch, 12 miles south on CO-115, Rec Area and Ranch House, C-719-526-3905.

SPACE-A: Butts Army Airfield, Bldg. 9601, 0730-1530 Mon-Fri, C-719-526-5300, flights via executive aircraft. Also see Peterson AFB listing.

ATTRACTIONS: USAF Academy, guided tours, Colorado Springs, Pikes Peak, museums, Seven Falls.

U.S. FORCES TRAVEL & TRANSFER GUIDE U.S.A. - 71

COLORADO

PETERSON AIR FORCE BASE (CO06R3)
775 Loring Avenue, Suite 241
Peterson Air Force Base, CO 80914-1294

TELEPHONE NUMBER INFORMATION: Main installation numbers: C-719-556-7321, D-312-834-7011.

LOCATION: Off US-24 (Platte Ave) east of Colorado Springs. Clearly marked. USMRA: Page 109 (G-5), page 115 (D,E-5,6). NMC: Colorado Springs, six miles northwest.

GENERAL INFORMATION: US Space Command, Air Force Space Command, Army Space Command, North American Aerospace Defense Command, 302nd Tactical Airlift Wing (Reserve), 21st Space Wing.

TEMPORARY MILITARY LODGING: Lodging office, Bldg. 1042, Stewart Ave, 24 hours, C-719-556-7851, D-312-834-7851. All ranks. DV/VIP C-719-556-5007.

LOGISTICAL SUPPORT: Complete support facilities available.

CHAMPUS-556-7129	Chaplain-556-4442	Child Care-556-7460
Commissary-556-7765	Conv Store-597-5041	Exchange-596-7270
Family Services-556-6141	Gas Station-597-0350	ITT Office-556-7671
Legal-556-4871	Locator-556-4020	Medical-556-4200
Museum-556-4915	NCO Club-556-4194	O'Club-576-4181
Package Store-596-5685	Police-556-4805	Retiree Services-556-7153
SATO-596-4199		

HEALTH & WELFARE: USAF Clinic, Emergency EX-4333, Appointments C-719-556-1000. Inpatient, see USAF Academy listing, C-719-472-4102. Chapels serving all faiths C-719-556-4442.

RECREATION: Auto Hobby EX-4481, Aero Club EX-4310, Bowling EX-4607, Camping Equip EX-4867, Fitness Center (Gym) EX-4462, Golf EX-7233, Golf Course EX-7414, Hobby Shops EX-7671, Library EX-7462, Swimming EX-4608, Rec Center EX-7941, Rec Equip EX-7751, Skeet/Trap EX-7688, Ski Shop EX-4487, Youth Center EX-7413, Rod/Gun EX-7688.

SPACE-A: Pax Term/Lounge, Bldg. 123, 0630-1730 Mon-Fri, 0700-1600 Sat-Sun, C-719-556-4521, D-312-834-4521, Fax 719-556-4979, flights to CONUS locations.

ATTRACTIONS: Fine Arts Center, Seven Falls, Museums, Pikes Peak Cog Railway in Manitou Springs, ski resorts, US Olympic Training Center.

PUEBLO DEPOT ACTIVITY (CO03R3)
Pueblo, CO 81001-5000

This base is scheduled to close under the 1995 BRAC law.
A closure date has not been established.

TELEPHONE NUMBER INFORMATION: Main installation numbers: C-719-549-4111, D-312-748-4135.

72 - U.S. FORCES TRAVEL & TRANSFER GUIDE U.S.A

COLORADO
Pueblo Depot Activity, continued

LOCATION: Take US-50 E from Pueblo, 13 miles, base is clearly marked. USMRA: Page 109 (G-5,6). NMC: Pueblo, 13 miles west.

GENERAL INFORMATION: A depot activity of the Army Materiel Command.

TEMPORARY MILITARY LODGING: None. See Fort Carson listing, C-719-526-4832, D-312-691-4832.

HEALTH & WELFARE: Dispensary C-719-549-4176. Inpatient, see Fort Carson listing, C-719-526-3762. No chapels at the depot, services in Pueblo.

RECREATION: MWR Office 549-4716.

SPACE-A: None. See Peterson AFB listing, C-719-556-4521, D-312-692-4521, Fax 719-556-4979.

ATTRACTIONS: Sangre de Cristo Arts and Conference Center, Pueblo Reservoir (fishing, boating, water skiing), Nature Center (within city), inter-city bike and hike trails adjoining reservoir, dog track and Pueblo Symphony.

UNITED STATES AIR FORCE ACADEMY (CO07R3)
2304 Cadet Drive, Suite 316
United States Air Force Academy, CO 80840-5016

TELEPHONE NUMBER INFORMATION: Main installation numbers: C-719-472-1818, D-312-259-3110.

LOCATION: West of I-25 north from Colorado Springs. Two gates, about five miles apart, provide access from I-25, clearly marked. USMRA: Page 109 (F-4,5), page 115 (A,B-1,2 C-1,2,3). NMC: Colorado Springs, eight miles south.

GENERAL INFORMATION: US Air Force Academy, education of future Air Force officers, and other tenant units.

TEMPORARY MILITARY LODGING: Lodging office, Bldg. 3130, Academy Dr, C-719-472-3060. All ranks. DV/VIP C-719-472-3540.

LOGISTICAL SUPPORT: Complete support facilities available.

CHAMPUS-472-4983	Chaplain-472-3300	Child Care-472-4733
Commissary-472-5126	Conv Store-472-0395	Exchange-472-0861
Family Services-472-3444	Gas Station-472-0395	Golf Course-472-3456
ITT Office-472-4610	Legal-472-3642	Locator-472-4262
Medical-472-5000	NCO Club-472-4377	O'Club-472-3120
Package Store-472-0554	Police-472-2000	Pro Travel-472-2445/6644
Public Affairs-472-4050	Recreation-472-4356	RV/Camping-687-9098
Snack Bar-472-4252	Visitor Center-472-2569	

HEALTH & WELFARE: USAF Academy Hospital, Emergency C-719-472-4102, Appointments C-719-472-4102, 85 beds. Chapels serving all faiths C-719-472-3300/2636.

RECREATION: Arts/Crafts EX-4538, Auto Hobby EX-4752, Bowling EX-4709, Golf EX-3456, Gym EX-4522, Library EX-4665, Pool EX-4430, Stables EX-4607, Sports

COLORADO
United States Air Force Academy, continued

Tickets 472-1895, Visitor Center (self-guided tours) EX-2555, Falcon Leisure Time Center and Ticket Office EX 3241. Farish Recreation Area off base, C-719-472-4356, D-312-259-4356, 16 camper spaces w/E hookups, 15 camper spaces w/o hookups, four-bedroom lodge, Peregrine Pines Fam-Camp on base, year-round, C-719-472-4356, D-312-259-4356, 45 camper spaces w/full hookups, 33 camper spaces w/o hookups, 11 tent spaces.

SPACE-A: None. See Peterson AFB listing, C-719-556-4521, D-312-692-4521, Fax 719-556-4979.

ATTRACTIONS: Pikes Peak, snow skiing, ghost towns, Colorado Springs.

Other Installations in Colorado

Cheyenne Mountain Air Force Base, Cheyenne Mountain AFB, CO 80914-5515.
No support facilities.
La Junta Air Force Station, 30800 1st Ave., Industrial Park, La Junta, CO 81050-9501. *Scheduled to close July 1996.* USMRA: Page 109 (H-6). C-719-556-4419, D-312-834-4126. Commissary-384-2847.

CONNECTICUT

DOLLAR RENT A CAR. Call 1-800-800-4000. Get a military rate by using your Military Living ID # ML3009. Retirees/Active Duty/Reserve/Guard.

BRADLEY AIR NATIONAL GUARD BASE (CT03R1)
100 Nicholson Road
East Granby, CT 06026-9309

TELEPHONE NUMBER INFORMATION: Main installation numbers: C-860-623-8291, D-312-636-8310.

LOCATION: Take I-91 to exit 40. Follow signs to route 20 (East Granby) and base. USMRA: Page 16 (E-5,6). NMC: Hartford, 10 miles south.

GENERAL INFORMATION: 103rd Fighter Wing, "The Flying Yankees," 118th Tactical Fighter Squadron and other support units and facilities.

TEMPORARY MILITARY LODGING: None. See Westover AFB, MA listing, C-413-593-5421/3006, D-312-589-2700.

LOGISTICAL SUPPORT: Limited support facilities available.

Chaplain-292-2445
Locator-623-8291
Exchange-653-6994
Police-292-2312
Legal-292-2478
Public Affairs-292-2506

HEALTH & WELFARE: None. See New London NSB listing, C-203-449-4877.

SPACE-A: Bradley IAP, Pax Term, 24 hours daily, C-860-292-2356, D-312-636-8356.

ATTRACTIONS: Historic Newgate Prison and the homes of Mark Twain and Harriet Beecher Stowe located within one hour's drive. New England Air Museum adjacent to Bradley IAP.

LONG ISLAND SOUND COAST GUARD GROUP (CT04R1)
120 Woodward Avenue
New Haven, CT 06512-3698

TELEPHONE NUMBER INFORMATION: Main installation numbers: C-203-468-4410.

LOCATION: Take I-95 north to exit 50, right at light, Unit is one mile on right. Take I-95 south to the New Haven Airport exit (Frontage Rd). Pass shopping center, left at second light, Unit is one mile on the right. USMRA: Page 16 (E-9). NMC: New Haven, in city limits.

GENERAL INFORMATION: Captain of the Port, Long Island Sound, Aid to Navigation Team, Long Island Sound, USCGC BOLLARD and CGSTA New Haven.

TEMPORARY MILITARY LODGING: None. See New London Naval Submarine Base listing, Navy Lodge C-203-466-1160, D-312-241-1160, or BEQ/BOQ C-203-449-3117/3416.

CONNECTICUT
Long Island Sound Coast Guard Group, continued

LOGISTICAL SUPPORT: Limited support facilities available.

CDO/OOD-468-4410   **CHAMPUS-468-4415**   **Exchange-468-4433**

HEALTH & WELFARE: None. See New London NSB listing, C-203-449-4877.

SPACE-A: None. See Bradley ANG Base listing.

ATTRACTIONS: New Haven: Yale University, museums, boating, shopping.

NEW LONDON NAVAL SUBMARINE BASE (CT01R1)
Route 12 and Crystal Lake Road
Groton, CT 06349-5000

TELEPHONE NUMBER INFORMATION: Main installation numbers: C-203-449-4636, D-312-241-4636.

LOCATION: From I-95 N take exit 86 to CT-12 & Crystal Lake Rd. Base clearly marked. USMRA: Page 16 (G,H-8), pg 25 (C,D-1). NMC: Hartford, 50 miles northwest.

GENERAL INFORMATION: Naval Submarine School, Naval Underwater Medical Institute, Naval Hospital, Commander Submarine Group Two, Submarine Squadrons Two and Twelve.

TEMPORARY MILITARY LODGING: Navy Lodge, Bldg. CT-380, 77 Dewey Ave, 0700-2300 daily, Check in 1500-1800, Check out 1200, C-203-446-1160, D-312-241-1160. All ranks, BEQ C-203-449-2408, BOQ C-203-449-2105. DV/VIP C-203-449-2105.

LOGISTICAL SUPPORT: Complete support facilities available.

CDO/OOD-449-3444   CHAMPUS-449-4968   Chaplain-449-3232
Child Care-449-3519   Commissary-449-3911   Conv Store-446-8593
CPO Club-449-3721   EM Club-449-3050   Enlisted Galley-449-3679
Exchange-449-3811   Family Services-449-3383 Fire Dept-449-3333
Gas Station-449-3626   Golf Course-449-3763   ITT-449-3238
Legal-449-3741   Locator-449-3087   Medical-449-3428
MWR-449-3238   O'Club-449-3808   Pass Office-449-3224
Package Store-449-3535 Police-449-3222   Public Affairs-449-3889
Recreation-449-3238   Retiree Services-449-3284 SATO-449-3404
Theater-449-3358

HEALTH & WELFARE: Naval Hospital, clinics and depts. Emergency C-203-449-3333, Appointments C-203-449-4877, 24 beds. Chapels serving all faiths C-203-449-3232.

RECREATION: Auto Hobby EX-3582, Bowling EX-3477, Golf EX-3763, Gym EX-4205, Hobby EX-3217, Marina EX-3164, Library EX-3723, Swimming EX-3562, Rec Services EX-3687.

SPACE-A: None. See Bradley ANG Base listing, C-203-292-2356, D-312-636-8356.

ATTRACTIONS: USCG Academy, *Nautilus* Memorial/Submarine Library and Museum.

76 - U.S. FORCES TRAVEL & TRANSFER GUIDE U.S.A

CONNECTICUT

UNITED STATES COAST GUARD ACADEMY (CT02R1)
15 Mohegan Avenue
New London, CT 06320-4195

TELEPHONE NUMBER INFORMATION: Main installation numbers: C-203-444-8474, or 203-437-6809.

LOCATION: From I-95 N take exit 83 in New London. From I-95 south, take exit 82A. Follow signs, clearly marked. USMRA: Page 16 (G,H-8), Page 25 (C-2). NMC: New London, in the city.

GENERAL INFORMATION: The Officer Education and Training Academy for the US Coast Guard.

TEMPORARY MILITARY LODGING: Billeting Office, Bldg. 3130, Academy Dr., 24 hours daily, C-203-446-1160.

LOGISTICAL SUPPORT: Limited support facilities available.

CHAMPUS-444-8432	Chaplain-444-8480	Consol Club-444-8456
Conv Store-444-8492	Credit Union-446-8200	Exchange-444-8488
Gas Station-444-8494	Housing Office-444-8211	Legal-444-8253
Main Gate-444-8614	Medical-444-8400	MWR Office 444-8474
O'Club-444-8140/8459	Pers Spt Center-444-8689	Package Store-444-8491
Police-444-8597	SDO/NCO-444-8450/1	

HEALTH & WELFARE: Outpatient Clinic C-203-444-8400, fire and emergencies C-203-444-8555. Inpatient, see New London NSB listing, C-203-449-4877.

RECREATION: Bowling EX-8470, Library EX-8510, Visitor's Pavilion EX-8611, Gym EX-8600, Equipment Rental EX-8476. Musical Activities EX-8471, Hobby Shop EX-8489, Academy Events Recording 442-1092, and Ticket Office EX-8154.

SPACE-A: None. See Bradley ANG Base listing, C-203-292-2356, D-312-636-8356.

ATTRACTIONS: Visitors are invited to take a self-guided tour of the Academy. The Museum is open from 0900-1700 weekdays throughout the year. From May-Oct, the Visitor's Pavilion and Museum are open daily 0900-1700. When in port, the barque *EAGLE* is open to the public on weekends 1300-1600. During the Spring and Fall, formal reviews by the Corps of Cadets are held on the Washington parade ground.

Other Installations in Connecticut

Camp Rowland Exchange, Bldg. 64 Pinegrove, Niantic, CT 06357-2597.
USMRA: Page 16 (F,G-7). C-203-691-6000, D-312-636-6000. Exchange-739-9672.
West Hartford U.S. Army Reserve, 700 S. Quaker Lane, West Hartford, CT 06110-1242, USMRA: Page 16 (E-7). C-203-236-3393. Exchange-236-3393, Med-231-2009.

DELAWARE

DOLLAR RENT A CAR — Call 1-800-800-4000. Get a military rate by using your Military Living ID # ML3009. Retirees/Active Duty/Reserve/Guard.

DOVER AIR FORCE BASE (DE01R1)
Dover Air Force Base, DE 19902-5501

TELEPHONE NUMBER INFORMATION: Main installation numbers: C-302-677-2113, D-312-445-3000/2113.

LOCATION: From US-113, follow signs to base. Clearly marked. USMRA: Page 42 (I-3,4). NMC: Dover, five miles northwest.

GENERAL INFORMATION: Air Mobility Command Base. Largest air cargo port on the East Coast. AFRES units.

TEMPORARY MILITARY LODGING: Lodging office, Bldg. 805, 14th St, 24 hours daily, C-302-677-2841, D-312-445-5988. All ranks. DV/VIP C-302-677-6649.

LOGISTICAL SUPPORT: Complete support facilities available.

CHAMPUS-677-2530
Commissary-674-4189
Exchange-674-4862
Gas Station-674-4228
Locator-677-3000
O'Club-677-6022
Retiree Services-677-4612
Snack Bar-674-3380

Chaplain-677-3931
Conv Store-674-3551
Family Services-677-6941
Golf Course-677-6036
Medical-677-2600
Police-677-6666
SATO-736-1668
Theater-678-8711

Child Care-677-3716
EM Club-677-6351
Fire Dept-677-4401
Legal-677-3300
NCO Club-677-6351
Public Affairs-667-3379
Services Squadron-677-6901

HEALTH & WELFARE: USAF Hospital, clinics and depts. Acute care clinic (level 4) is open 0700-1830 Mon-Fri; weekends and holidays 0900-1530. Emergency response capabilities are provided 24 hours a day. Routine appointments are scheduled through Family Practice C-302-677-2501, 20 beds. Chapels serving all faiths C-302-677-3931.

RECREATION: Auto Hobby EX-3249, Bowling EX-3946, Equipment Rental EX-3959, Golf EX-6036, Gym EX-3962, Library EX-3992, Swimming EX-3963, Tennis EX-3963, Youth Activities EX-6376, Skeet EX-6380.

SPACE-A: Pax Term, Bldg. 500, 24 hours, C-302-677-2854, D-312-445-2854, Fax 302-677-2953. Flights to CONUS and overseas. Also try New Castle County Airport, Bldg. 2812, 0800-1630 Mon-Fri, C-302-323-3525, D-312-445-3525, flights to CONUS and OCONUS locations. ANG units.

ATTRACTIONS: State capital, Dover Air Force Base Museum, great beaches and the Delaware Bay.

DELAWARE

NEW CASTLE COUNTY AIRPORT/DELAWARE AIR NATIONAL GUARD(DE02R1)
2600 Spruance Drive, Corporate Commons
New Castle, DE 19720-1615

TELEPHONE NUMBER INFORMATION: Main installation numbers: C-302-323-3525, D-312-445-7525.

LOCATION: From I-95 take exit 5 to DE-41 south for one mile to intersection of DE-37 (Corporate Commons Blvd). Turn right Corporate Commons Blvd. then left onto Spruance Drive and follow to gate entrance. USMRA: Page 42 (I-2). NMC: Wilmington, seven miles northeast.

GENERAL INFORMATION: Delaware Air National Guard Base.

TEMPORARY MILITARY LODGING: None. See Aberdeen Proving Ground, MD listing, C-410-278-5148, D-312-298-5148.

LOGISTICAL SUPPORT: Very limited support facilities available.

Exchange-322-5988   Fire Dept-323-3455   Medical-323-3385
Police-323-3440

HEALTH & WELFARE: Outpatient clinic C-302-445-7418/9.

SPACE-A: Pax Term, Bldg. 2812, C-302-323-3525, D-312-445-3525, Fax 302-323-3330. Flights to CONUS and overseas. 0800-1630, ANG units.

U.S. FORCES TRAVEL & TRANSFER GUIDE U.S.A. - 79
DISTRICT OF COLUMBIA

DOLLAR RENT A CAR Call 1-800-800-4000. Get a military rate by using your Military Living ID # ML3009. Retirees/Active Duty/Reserve/Guard.

ANACOSTIA NAVAL STATION (DC02R1)
2701 S. Capitol Street, SW
Washington, DC 20373-5800

TELEPHONE NUMBER INFORMATION: Main installation numbers: C-703-545-6700, D-312-227-0101. (Note: The area code for the following numbers is 202.)

LOCATION: From I-395, exit South Capitol St, cross South Capitol Street Bridge, main entrance is on right. USMRA: Page 55, (F,G-5). NMC: Washington, DC in southeast section.

GENERAL INFORMATION: Naval Media Center, White House Communications Agency, US Navy Ceremonial Guard.

TEMPORARY MILITARY LODGING: Limited transient billeting, C-202-433-8796/0806, D-312-288-8796/0806. Navy Lodge in Bellevue Navy Housing area, Bldg. 4412, C-202-563-6950 or 1-800-NAVY-INN.

LOGISTICAL SUPPORT: Complete support facilities available at adjacent Bolling AFB.

All Hands Club-433-4070
Child Care-433-0771
Fire Dept-433-3334
Police-433-2411
Retiree Services-433-6150

CDO/OOD-433-2231/32
Family Services-433-6150
ITT-433-6666
Public Affairs-433-2218
RV/Camping-433-2269

Chaplain-433-2057
Locator-545-6700
MWR-433-3005
Recreation-433-2269
SDO/SNO-433-2231/32

HEALTH & WELFARE: None. See Washington Navy Yard listing, C-202-433-3792/3407/3757.

RECREATION: Fitness Center-685-0898, Outdoor Rec-433-2269.

SPACE-A: None. See Andrews Air Force Base Listing, C-301-981-1854/3526/3604, D-312-858-1854, Fax 301-981-4241.

ATTRACTIONS: On the Potomac, and in sight of the Capitol and many famous monuments. Museums, and professional sports.

BOLLING AIR FORCE BASE (DC01R1)
20 MacDill Boulevard, Suite 230
Bolling Air Force Base, DC 20332-5100

TELEPHONE NUMBER INFORMATION: Main installation numbers: C-202-545-6700, D-312-297-4080.

LOCATION: Take I-95 (east portion of Capital Beltway, I-495), exit to I-295 north, exit to Portland St, and main entrance to AFB. Also, I-395 north, exit South Capitol St, main entrance to AFB on right. Visitors entrance is at south gate one mile south of main gate.

DISTRICT OF COLUMBIA
Bolling Air Force Base, continued

Clearly marked. USMRA: Page 55 (F-6). NMC: Washington DC, in southeast section of the city.

GENERAL INFORMATION: 11th Wing. Support for Air Force activities of the National Capital Region.

TEMPORARY MILITARY LODGING: Bolling Inn, Bldg. 602, Thiesen St, 24 hours, C-202-767-5316, D-312-297-5316/5741. All ranks. DV/VIP C-202-767-5584, Officer retirees Space-A.

LOGISTICAL SUPPORT: Complete support facilities available.

Cafeteria-562-4419	Clinic-767-5532	CHAMPUS-767-5540
Chaplain-767-5900	Child Care-767-2890	Command Post-767-1111
Commissary-767-4695	Conv Store-562-3105	Exchange-562-3000
Family Services-767-4464	Fire Dept-767-1285	Gas Station-561-0184
Legal-767-4772	Locator-767-4522	Medical-767-5532
NCO Club-767-5222	O'Club-563-8400	Police-767-5558
Public Affairs-767-4781	Recreation-767-7636	Retiree Services-767-5244
RV/Camping-767-9136	SATO-610-5100	Visitor Center-404-5505

HEALTH & WELFARE: USAF Clinic, Emergency C-202-767-5233, Appointments C-202-767-5520. Inpatient, see Andrews AFB, MD listing, C-301-981-7511. Chapels serving all faiths C-202-767-5900.

RECREATION: Arts/Crafts EX-4422, Auto Hobby EX-5471, Bowling 563-4054, Fitness Center EX-5895, Library EX-5578, Marina EX-4651, Rec Equip EX-9136, Rec Center EX-3847, Swimming EX-4286, Youth Center EX-3047.

SPACE-A: None. See Andrews AFB, MD listing, C-301-981-1854/3526/3604, D-312-858-1854, Fax 301-981-4241.

ATTRACTIONS: Washington DC, with its many museums, galleries, monuments and other attractions. Kennedy Center for the Performing Arts.

FORT LESLEY J. McNAIR (DC05R1)
Washington, DC 20319-5050

TELEPHONE NUMBER INFORMATION: Main installation numbers: C-202-545-6700, D-312-222-0101.

LOCATION: At confluence of Anacostia River and Washington Channel, southwest. Enter on P St, SW. Take Maine Ave, SW, to right on 4th St, SW, to dead end at P St. Left, then immediate right into main gate. USMRA: Page 55 (F-5). NMC: Washington DC in southwest section of city.

GENERAL INFORMATION: Headquarters US Army Military District of Washington, Co A, 3rd US Infantry (The Old Guard) "Commander in Chief's Guard," home to the National Defense University, consisting of the National War College (NWC) and the Industrial College of the Armed Forces (ICAF); home to the Inter-American Defense College (IADC).

DISTRICT OF COLUMBIA
Fort Lesley J. McNair, continued

TEMPORARY MILITARY LODGING: Lodging office, Fort Myer, Bldg. 50, Johnson Lane, 24 hours daily, C-703-696-3576/3577. Limited VOQ facilities (Bldg. 54) at Fort McNair. DV/VIP C-703-697-7051, D-312-297-7051.

LOGISTICAL SUPPORT: Most support facilities available.

Chaplain-475-0706
Gas Station-484-5825
Medical-475-1830
Public Affairs-475-0843

Child Care-696-3095
Legal-475-1069
O'Club-484-5801
SDO/NCO-475-0918

Fire Dept-911
Locator-475-2005
Police-475-2018

HEALTH & WELFARE: US Army Health Clinic, Emergency C-202-475-1829, Appointments C-202-475-1831. Inpatient, see Walter Reed Army Medical Center listing, C-202-782-3501. Chapel (Prot/Cath) C-202-475-0706.

RECREATION: Bowling EX-1729, Ball Fields EX-1964, Golf EX-2003, Gym EX-1964, Multi-Craft Shop EX-2000, Swimming EX-0504, Tennis EX-1964.

SPACE-A: None. See Andrews AFB, MD listing, C-301-981-1854/3526/3604, D-312-858-1854, Fax 301-981-4241.

ATTRACTIONS: Included in the original plans for the District of Columbia, and is nearly 200 years old. Second only to West Point in length of service. Site of the trial and execution of President Lincoln's conspirators and where Walter Reed did his research work. Washington waterfront with restaurants, seafood markets, monuments, and scenic Potomac River nearby.

MARINE BARRACKS (DC09R1)
8th and "I" Streets, SE
Washington, D.C. 20390-5000

TELEPHONE NUMBER INFORMATION: Main installation numbers: C-202-433-4073, D-312-288-4073.

LOCATION: At 8th & I Sts. SE. From I-395 north, take 6th St. exit, drive north two blocks to 8th St., turn left. From I-295/I-395 north interchange area, take right split to Downtown/I-395 ramp, exit on 8th St. SE ramp, left at stop sign, right at 8th St. From I-295 south take exit 13, U.S. Naval Station/Suitland Parkway exit, follow exit ramp around to reenter I-295 north, follow instructions as above. From I-495 (Capital Beltway), take Pennsylvania Ave west exit, follow Pennsylvania Ave to 8th St., turn left and follow to I St. USMRA: Page 55 (F,G-5). NMC: Washington DC, in SE section of the city.

GENERAL INFORMATION: USMC light infantry battalion. **Note:** the Marine Barracks is a closed post for all practical purposes. **Facilities are not available unless user, if not permanently stationed at barracks, is escorted by a Marine stationed there.**

TEMPORARY MILITARY LODGING: None. See Bolling AFB listing, C-202-767-5316/5741, D-312-297-5316/5741.

LOGISTICAL SUPPORT: Very limited support facilities available.

DISTRICT OF COLUMBIA
Marine Barracks, continued

Chaplain-433-6201	Exchange-433-4961	ITT-433-2338
Legal-433-6039	MWR-433-2338	NCO Club-433-2528
Police-433-2258/2259	Public Affairs-433-4173	

HEALTH & WELFARE: None. See Washington Navy Yard listing, C-202-433-3792/3407/3757.

SPACE-A: None. See Andrews AFB, MD listing, C-301-981-1854/3526/3604, D-312-858-1854, Fax 301-981-4241.

ATTRACTIONS: Evening Parades are held every Friday, Sunset Parades are held every Tuesday (May through August) for information and reservations call C-202-433-4073. Smithsonian Institution, Lincoln and Jefferson Memorials, Washington Monument, National Archives, Library of Congress, the US Mint, National Gallery of Art, Navy Memorial Museum and the Marine Corps Museum at the Washington Navy Yard and many other attractions.

USO WORLD HEADQUARTERS (DC06R1)
901 M Street, SE
Washington, DC 20374-5096

LOCATION: In the Washington Navy Yard, Bldg. 198. The offices of the USO World Headquarters are on the second and third floors.

RECREATION: Free tickets for shows and sporting events. Ticket and information hot line: 703-696-2551. There are nine Outreach Locations of the USO in the greater Washington DC area serving uniformed personnel and their families. See Appendix E in this book for addresses and telephone numbers.

WALTER REED ARMY MEDICAL CENTER (DC03R1)
6825 16th Street NW
Washington, DC 20307-5000

TELEPHONE NUMBER INFORMATION: Main installation numbers: C-202-782-3501, D-312-291-3501.

LOCATION: From I-495 (Capital Beltway) take Georgia Ave/Silver Spring exit south (also marked US-20 or Georgia Ave) to Medical Center, enter second gate. To reach the Forest Glen support facilities from Georgia Ave south, right turn on to Linden Lane, cross over B&O railroad bridge, support facilities on left (.75 miles from Georgia Ave). USMRA: Page 55 (F-2). NMC: Washington DC, in city limits.

GENERAL INFORMATION: The major Army Medical Research, Teaching, and Treatment Facility. Forest Glen Annex has large Commissary and Exchange and other support facilities.

TEMPORARY MILITARY LODGING: Lodging office, Bldg. 6825, Georgia Ave (at Butternut St), 24 hours daily, C-202-782-2076/2096, D-312-291-2076/2096. All ranks. DV/VIP C-202-782-3117. Guest House EX-3044. Fisher House (Forest Glen Annex), (for families of critically ill patients) C-301-427-6542.

LOGISTICAL SUPPORT: Complete support facilities available.

U.S. FORCES TRAVEL & TRANSFER GUIDE U.S.A. - 83

DISTRICT OF COLUMBIA
Walter Reed Army Medical Center, continued

ACS-782-3412	CHAMPUS-782-6314	Chaplain-782-6308/5
Child Care-(301) 427-5451	Commissary-(301) 427-5401	Consolidated Club-782-3383
Exchange-(301) 427-5401	Family Services-782-3412	Fire Department-782-3318
Gas Station-(301)-565-0900	ITT Office-782-6350	ITR-782-6359
Legal-782-5214/5037	Locator-782-1150	MWR-782-7034/7377
Police-782-3325	Public Affairs-782-7177	Retiree Services-782-3412
SATO-1-800-756-6333	SDO/NCO-782-3383	Snack Bar-4235401/2

HEALTH & WELFARE: Major medical center, 1280 beds, Appointments C-202-782-3501 (Long distance 1-800-433-3574). Chapels serving all faiths C-202-782-6308/05.

PHONE NUMBERS FOR FOREST GLEN ANNEX: Arts/Crafts 427-5100, Exchange 565-0900, Bowling 427-5436, Commissary 427-5013, Gas Station 588-1130, Gym 427-5500, Outdoor Rec 427-5200.

RECREATION: Auto Hobby EX-2433, Fitness Center EX-0536, Library EX-1314, Swimming EX-2324, Tennis EX-2324, Comm Center EX-2216.

SPACE-A: None. See Andrews AFB, MD listing, C-301-981-1854/3526/3604, D-312-858-1854, Fax 301-981-4241.

ATTRACTIONS: Washington DC, White House, Capitol, National Zoo, Washington National Cathedral, Arlington Cemetery, Smithsonian.

WASHINGTON NAVAL SECURITY STATION (DC07R1)
3801 Nebraska Avenue, NW
Washington, DC 20393-5440

TELEPHONE NUMBER INFORMATION: Main installation numbers: C-202-282-0211, D-312-292-0211.

LOCATION: From Virginia cross the Key Bridge, turn left onto Nebraska Ave. Go approximately two-and-a-half miles, station is on your right. USMRA: Page 55 (D,E-3,4).

GENERAL INFORMATION: Naval Security Station, and assigned units.

TEMPORARY MILITARY LODGING: BEQ C-202-282-0254, D-312-292-0254.

LOGISTICAL SUPPORT: Very limited support facilities available.

Medical-282-0206

HEALTH & WELFARE: Branch medical clinic, Emergency C-202-282-0206. Chapel serving all faiths C-202-282-0211.

SPACE-A: None. See Andrews AFB, MD listing, C-301-981-1854/3526/3604, D-312-858-1854, Fax 301-981-4241.

ATTRACTIONS: Washington DC, with its many museums, galleries, monuments and other attractions. Kennedy Center for the Performing Arts.

84 - U.S. FORCES TRAVEL & TRANSFER GUIDE U.S.A

DISTRICT OF COLUMBIA

WASHINGTON NAVY YARD (DC04R1)
901 M Street S.E.
Washington, DC 20374-5000

TELEPHONE NUMBER INFORMATION: Main installation numbers: C-703-545-6700, (Note: The area code for the following numbers is 202.)

LOCATION: Exit I-395/I-695 north at 11th St SE, right turn on M St, west to entrance at 9th St on left side of M St. USMRA: Page 55 (F,G-5). NMC: Washington DC, in southeast section.

GENERAL INFORMATION: Headquarters Naval District Washington, Military Sealift Command, Naval Criminal Investigative Service, and the Navy Band.

TEMPORARY MILITARY LODGING: Lodging office, in the Anacostia complex adjacent to Bolling AFB. From I-95 (Beltway east) take I-295 north, exit at South Capitol St. NDW Anacostia is clearly marked. C-202-433-8796/0806, D-312-288-8796/0806, 0730-1600 daily, other hours EX-2193. Navy Lodge in Bellevue Navy Housing area, adjacent on the south end of Bolling AFB, 24 hours daily, C-202-563-6950/5548.

LOGISTICAL SUPPORT: Most support facilities available.

CDO/OOD-433-2607/2707
Exchange-889-7534
ITT-433-6666
MWR-433-3005
Public Affairs-433-2218
RV/Camping-433-2269

Chaplain-433-2057
Family Services-433-6150
Legal-433-4331
O'Club-433-3041
Recreation-433-2269

Child Care-433-0771
Fire Department-433-3334
Medical-433-3792/3407
Police-433-2411
Retiree Services-433-6150

HEALTH & WELFARE: Dispensary/Emergency C-202-433-3792/3407/3757. Inpatient, see National Naval Medical Center, MD listing, C-301-295-1400. Chapel serving all faiths C-202-433-2057.

RECREATION: Library 433-4132, Fitness Center 433-2063, Recreation Equipment 433-2269, Tennis 433-2829, Swimming 433-2601.

SPACE-A: None. See Andrews AFB, MD listing, C-301-981-1854/3526/3604, D-312-858-1854, Fax 301-981-4241.

ATTRACTIONS: Navy Memorial Museum, Navy Art Gallery, Display Ship *Barry*, Marine Corps Museum. The Navy Summer Pageant (Concerts with video and live performances) every Wednesday night from late June through August, free, reservations required, C-202-433-2218.

Other Installations in the District of Columbia

Armed Forces Hostess Association, Room 1A736 The Pentagon, 6604 Army Pentagon, Washington, DC 20310-6604. USMRA: Page 55 (E-5). C-703-697-3180/6857, D-312-227-6857, Fax 703-693-9510.
U.S. Coast Guard Headquarters, 2100 2nd St., SW, Washington, DC 20593. USMRA: Page 55 (F-5,6). C-202-267-2100, Exchange-267-2095, Med-366-0892.
U.S. Soldiers' and Airmen's Home, 3700 N. Capitol St. NW, Washington, DC 20317-5000. USMRA: Page 55 (F,G-3). C-800-422-9398, Locator-202-722-3112, PAO-722-3556.

U.S. FORCES TRAVEL & TRANSFER GUIDE U.S.A. - 85

FLORIDA

DOLLAR RENT A CAR — Call 1-800-800-4000. Get a military rate by using your Military Living ID # ML3009. Retirees/Active Duty/Reserve/Guard.

CAMP BLANDING (FL42R1)
Route 1, Box 465
Starke, FL 32091-9703

TELEPHONE NUMBER INFORMATION: Main installation number: C-904-533-3100, D-312-960-3100.

LOCATION: Thirty-one miles west of I-95; exit onto Rt. 16. USMRA: Page 38 (F,G-4). NMC: Jacksonville, 30 miles north.

GENERAL INFORMATION: Installation Support Unit, 653rd Engineering Det, 221st Ordnance Detachment, Florida Regional Training Institute, Headquarters 3rd Battalion, 20th Special Forces, 202nd Civil Engineering Squadron, 159th Weather Flight, 159 Weather School, and other support units.

TEMPORARY MILITARY LODGING: Lodging office, Bldg. 2392 Jacksonville Rd, 0800-1630 daily, C-904-533-3381, D-312-960-3381 (Closed Sundays).

LOGISTICAL SUPPORT: Limited support facilities available.

Credit Union-533-2184
Medical-533-3105
NCO Club-533-3319
RV/Camping-533-31040

EM Club-533-3197
Museum-533-3196
O'Club-533-3320

Exchange-533-3513
MWR-533-3104
Police-533-3526

HEALTH AND WELFARE: Medical Info C-904-533-3514. Also see Jacksonville NAS listing, C-904-777-7300. Chapel serving all faiths C-904-533-3231.

RECREATION: Equip, Phys Fitness Center, Rec Equipment. RV Park & Campsites on post, year round, C-904-533-3104, D-312-533-3104, 20 mobile homes, 15 camper spaces w/full hookups, 50 primitive camper/tent spaces w/W hookups.

SPACE-A: None. See Cecil Field NAS listing C-904-778-5536/5481, D-312-860-5536/5481, Fax 904-778-5833.

ATTRACTIONS: Under one hour drives to Gainesville, Jacksonville and St. Augustine, three hours to Disney and the Orlando area.

CECIL FIELD NAVAL AIR STATION (FL06R1)
P.O. Box 111
Cecil Field Naval Air Station, FL 32215-0111

Scheduled to close September 1998.

TELEPHONE NUMBER INFORMATION: Main installation numbers: C-904-778-5627, D-312-860-5627.

FLORIDA
Cecil Field Naval Air Station, continued

LOCATION: Take Normandy (FL-228) exit W off I-295 to main gate. From I-10 take Chaffee Rd exit to Normandy. USMRA: Page 38 (G-3). NMC: Jacksonville, 13 miles east. Base is 14 miles southeast of downtown Jacksonville.

GENERAL INFORMATION: Naval Combat Aircraft Support and Training Base.

TEMPORARY MILITARY LODGING: Lodging office, 24 hours daily, "D" Ave & 4th St, Bldg. 331 (Officers), C-904-778-5255, D-312-860-5255; Bldg. 92 (EM), C-904-778-6191, D-312-860-6191. DV/VIP EX-5255.

LOGISTICAL SUPPORT: Complete support facilities available.

CDO/OOD-778-5627	CHAMPUS-778-6711	Chaplain-778-5239
Child Care-778-5638	Commissary-778-5703	Conv Store-778-0023/0778
CPO Club-778-5390	EM Club-778-6154	Exchange-778-3176
Family Services-778-5239	Fire Dept-778-5233	Gas Station-778-0778
Golf Course-778-5245	ITT Office-778-6112	Legal-778-6088
Locator-778-5240	Medical-778-5406	MWR-778-6004
O'Club-778-5110	Package Store-778-4793	Police-778-5381
Public Affairs-778-6055	Quarterdeck-778-6042	RV/Camping-778-6112
SATO-778-0063		

HEALTH & WELFARE: Naval Branch Medical Clinic, Emergency C-904-778-5212. Inpatient, see Jacksonville NAS listing, C-904-777-7300. Chapels serving all faiths C-904-778-5349.

RECREATION: Golf EX-5245, Rod/Gun EX-5181, Skeet EX-5181, Tickets EX-6112, Auto Hobby EX-5651, Gym EX-5498, Youth Activities 777-8247. Lake Newman, on base, year round, club house and picnic area, EX-6249. Lake Fretwell Recreation Area on base, year round, C-904-778-6112, D-312-860-6112, four camper spaces w/W&E hookups.

SPACE-A: Pax Term/Lounge, Bldg. 47, 24 hours daily, C-904-778-5536/5481, D-312-860-5536/5481, Fax 904-778-5833, flights to CONUS locations. Also see Jacksonville NAS listing.

ATTRACTIONS: Beaches, golf, museums, Busch Gardens tours, minor league baseball and proximity to central Florida tourist attractions.

CLEARWATER COAST GUARD AIR STATION (FL32R1)
15100 Rescue Way
Clearwater, FL 34622-2990

TELEPHONE NUMBER INFORMATION: Main installation numbers: C-813-535-1437 (ask for extensions), D-312-968-4273, FTS-700-826-XXXX.

LOCATION: From I-275, take 60 east to 19 south. Follow signs to air station. USMRA: Page 54 (C-3). NMC: Tampa, 20 miles east.

GENERAL INFORMATION: The Coast Guard Air Station is responsible for search-and-rescue and other Coast Guard operations in the area.

TEMPORARY MILITARY LODGING: None. See MacDill AFB listing, C-813-828-2661, D-312-968-4259.

FLORIDA
Clearwater Coast Guard Air Station, continued

LOGISTICAL SUPPORT: Some support facilities available

CDO/OOD-535-1210/1746 Exchange-535-1437/1410 Medical-535-1606
MWR-535-1181 Public Affairs-535-1145 Recreation-535-1181

HEALTH & WELFARE: None. See St. Petersburg CGG/S listing, C-813-824-7579.

SPACE-A: Limited flights. C-813-535-1437, D-312-968-4273 EX 1181, Fax 813-535-4526.

ATTRACTIONS: Busch Gardens—The Dark Continent, Salvador Dali Museum, The Pier in St. Petersburg, Tampa's Latin Quarter, beaches, water sports.

CORRY STATION NAVAL TECHNICAL TRAINING CENTER (FL19R1)
640 Roberts Avenue
Pensacola, FL 32511-5138

TELEPHONE NUMBER INFORMATION: Main installation numbers: C-904-452-2000, D-312-922-0111.

LOCATION: Off US-98, three miles north of Pensacola NAS. USMRA: Page 38 (A,B-13), page 53 (B-4). NMC: Pensacola, five miles northeast.

GENERAL INFORMATION: Home of the Naval Technical Training Center.

TEMPORARY MILITARY LODGING: BEQ: C-904-452-6609, D-312-922-660.

LOGISTICAL SUPPORT: Most support facilities available.

CHAMPUS-452-6709 Chaplain-452-6376 Child Care-452-6138
Conv Store-453-5311 CPO Club-452-6330 EM Club-452-6347
Exchange-453-5311 ITT Office-452-6143 Legal-452-6334
Locator-452-6512 Medical-452-5242 MWR-452-6568
Police-452-6130 Public Affairs-452-6318 Recreation-453-2129
Retiree Services-452-6529 RV/Camping-453-2129 SATO-452-6291
SDO/NCO-452-6512

HEALTH & WELFARE: None. See Pensacola Naval Hospital listing, C-904-452-6788. Chapels serving all faiths C-904-452-6561.

RECREATION: Archery, Bowling, Hobby Shop, Swimming, Tennis, Rec Center 452-6520. Bronson Field Naval Recreation Park, off base, year round, C-904-453-9435, D-312-453-1147, 138 camper spaces w/W&E, 17 campers for rent, unlimited primitive tent spaces.

SPACE-A: None. See Pensacola NAS listing, C-904-452-3311/2431, D-312-922-3311/2431, Fax 904-452-8105.

ATTRACTIONS: Visit the historic section of Pensacola, beaches. Naval Aviation Museum at NAS Pensacola.

FLORIDA

EGLIN AIR FORCE BASE (FL27R1)
101 West D Avenue, Suite 129
Eglin Air Force Base, FL 32542-5498

TELEPHONE NUMBER INFORMATION: Main installation numbers: C-904-882-1110, D-312-872-1110.

LOCATION: Exit I-10 at Crestview. Follow signs to Niceville and Valparaiso (Eglin AFB). USMRA: Page 39 (B,C,D,-13), page 53 (E-2 F,G,H-1,2,3 H-1,2,3,4). NMC: Fort Walton Beach, seven miles south.

GENERAL INFORMATION: Air Force Materiel Command Base. Largest AFB in the Free World, Air Force Development Test Center, Air Warfare Center, AFRES units.

TEMPORARY MILITARY LODGING: Lodging office, Bldg. 11001, Boatner Rd, 24 hours daily, C-904-882-8761, D-312-872-8761. All ranks. DV/VIP C-904-882-3011. Navy CBQ (Officers & EM) C-904-882-5683, D-312-872-5683 DV/VIP.

LOGISTICAL SUPPORT: Complete support facilities available.

CHAMPUS-882-7249
Commissary-882-3172
Gas Station-678-7222
Locator-882-4478
O'Club-651-1010
SATO-882-8016

Chaplain-882-4426
Exchange-651-2512
ITT Office-882-5930
Medical-882-7242
Police-882-2502
Theater-882-3813

Child Care-882-5519
Family Services-882-2893
Legal-882-4611
NCO Club-678-5127
Retiree Services-882-5916

HEALTH & WELFARE: Regional Hospital, Emergency C-904-882-7227, Appointments C-904-882-4131, 160 beds. Chapel serving all faiths C-904-882-2111.

RECREATION: Golf 882-2695, Hobby Shops 882-3570, Library 882-2460, Youth Activities 882-5074. Also, Swimming, Auto Hobby, Bowling, Gym, Skeet, large and small Game Hunting and Fishing on the AFB. Fam-Camp on base, year round, C-904-882-5058 22 camper spaces w/W&E hookups, 20 tent spaces.

SPACE-A: Pax Term/Lounge, Bldg. 60, 0600-1800 Mon-Fri, 0800-1600 Sat-Sun, C-904-882-4757, D-312-872-4757, Fax 904-882-2655, flights to CONUS locations.

ATTRACTIONS: Fort Walton Beach and beach areas, sport fishing, deep sea fishing, dog races, Pensacola, 35 miles west.

HOMESTEAD AIR RESERVE BASE (FL17R1)
360 Coral Sea Boulevard
Homestead ARB, FL 33039-1299

TELEPHONE NUMBER INFORMATION: Main installation numbers: C-305-224-7000, D-312-791-7000.

LOCATION: Exit 6 off Florida Turnpike, left at bottom of the ramp, approximately one-half mile to traffic light (SW 288th St.), then left to main gate. USMRA: Page 39 (I-14), page (A,B-10). NMC: Miami, 30 miles northeast.

GENERAL INFORMATION: Home of the 482nd Fighter Wing.

FLORIDA
Homestead Air Reserve Base, continued

TEMPORARY MILITARY LODGING: Billeting Office C-305-224-7168. Hours of operation are from 0700-2100; holiday hours are 0900-1800.

LOGISTICAL SUPPORT: Some support facilities available.

CDO/OOD-224-7023	CHAMPUS-265-3104	Chaplain-224-7093
Consol Club-224-7517	Conv Store-224-7464	Exchange-224-7464
Family Services-224-7329	Fire Dept-224-7117	Legal-224-7063
Locator-224-7000	Package Store-224-7464	Police-224-7115
Public Affairs-224-7303	Retiree Services-224-7580	SATO-224-7051

HEALTH & WELFARE: None. See Miami CGAS listing, C-305-953-2266.

RECREATION: Gym.

SPACE-A: Pax Terminal/lounge Bldg. 558, C-305-224-7518, D-312-791-7518, flights to CONUS locations.

ATTRACTIONS: Biscayne Bay, deep sea fishing, Everglades National Park, horse and dog racing, boating, and water sports.

HURLBURT FIELD (FL18R1)
131 Bartley Street, Suite 326
Hurlburt Field, FL 32544-5000

TELEPHONE NUMBER INFORMATION: Main installation numbers: C-904-882-1110 (Eglin Base info), D-312-579-1110.

LOCATION: Off US-98, five miles west of Fort Walton Beach. Clearly marked. USMRA: Page 39 (C-13), page 53 (H-4). NMC: Pensacola, 40 miles west.

GENERAL INFORMATION: Air Force Special Operations Command Base, on the Eglin AFB reservation, US Special Operations Command AF Component, 16th Special Operations Wing, Air Force Air Ground Operations School, USAF Special Operations School.

TEMPORARY MILITARY LODGING: Billeting Office, Bldg. 90509, 24 hours daily, C-904-884-6245, D-312-579-6245/7115. All ranks. DV/VIP C-904-884-2308.

LOGISTICAL SUPPORT: Most support facilities available.

CHAMPUS-884-3912	Chaplain-884-7795	Child Care-884-6937
Commissary-884-7762	Conv Store-581-0030	Exchange-581-0030
Family Services-884-6201	Fire Dept-884-1357	Gas Station-581-2224
Golf Course-884-6940	ITT Office-884-7848	Legal-884-7821
Medical-884-7882	NCO Club-884-6469	O'Club-884-7507
Package Store-884-6370	Police-884-7114	Public Affairs-884-7464
Recreation-884-7397	Omega-581-6223	SATO-884-6344
SDO/NCO-884-7774	Theater-884-7648	

HEALTH & WELFARE: Clinic, Emergency C-904-884-7882, Appointments C-904-884-7882. Inpatient, see Eglin AFB listing, C-904-882-4131. Chapel serving all faiths C-904-884-7795.

FLORIDA
Hurlburt Field, continued

RECREATION: Auto Hobby EX-6674, Bowling EX-6470, Hobby Shops EX-6492, Library EX-6947, Marina EX-6939, Swimming EX-6866, Youth Center EX-6355. See Eglin AFB listing for Rec Areas.

SPACE-A: Try Base Ops, C-904-884-7806. Also see Eglin AFB listing C-904-884-4757/5783, D-312-872-4757/5783.

ATTRACTIONS: Sport fishing, water sports. Pensacola (west) and Panama City (east), both short drives.

JACKSONVILLE NAVAL AIR STATION (FL08R1)
P.O. Box 102
Jacksonville Naval Air Station, FL 32212-5000

TELEPHONE NUMBER INFORMATION: Main installation numbers: C-904-772-2345/2346, D-312-942-2345/2346.

LOCATION: Access from US-17 south. USMRA: Page 38 (G-3), page 50 (B,C-6,7). NMC: Jacksonville, nine miles northeast.

GENERAL INFORMATION: Fixed and rotary wing anti-submarine warfare aircraft support and training, Naval Hospital, Naval Aviation Depot, Naval Supply Center.

TEMPORARY MILITARY LODGING: Lodging office, Bldg. 11, 24 hours daily, C-904-772-3138 (EM), 904-772-3537 (Officer). DV/VIP C-904-772-3147/3148. Navy Lodge: C-904-772-6000, D-312-942-6000 or 1-800-NAVY-INN.

LOGISTICAL SUPPORT: Complete support facilities available.

CDO/OOD-772-2338
Child Care-772-5529
EM Club-772-3521
Fire Dept-772-2451
ITT Office-772-3318
Medical-777-7300
O'Club-772-3041
Public Affairs-772-4032
RV/Camping-772-3227
Vet Clinic-772-3786

CHAMPUS-573-3300
Commissary-573-5010
Exchange-777-7200
Gas Station-772-2797
Legal-772-3481
MWR-772-3112
Package Store-777-7286
Recreation-772-3112
SATO-778-1411

Chaplain-772-3051/3440
Conv Store-777-7285
Family Services-772-2766
Golf Course-772-3249
Locator-772-2340
Navy Campus-772-2477
Police-772-2661
Retiree Services-772-5783
Snack Bar-772-2936

HEALTH & WELFARE: Naval Hospital, Emergency C-904-772-2423, Appointments C-904-777-7300, 310 beds. Chapels serving all faiths C-904-772-3051/3440.

RECREATION: Archery 778-7582, Athletic Director EX-3239, Fitness Center EX-3518, Auto Hobby Shop EX-3227, Library EX-3415, Marina EX-3260, Bowling EX-3403, Golf EX-3249, RV Park EX-3227, Storage EX-3227, Swimming EX-2930, Wood Shop EX-3681. RV Park on base, year round, C-904-772-3227, D-312-942-3227, eight camper spaces w/full hookups, eight camper spaces w/W&E, 14 camper/tent spaces w/o hookups.

SPACE-A: Pax Term/Lounge, Bldg. 118, 24 hours daily, C-904-772-3956, D-312-942-3956, Fax 904-942-2514, flights to CONUS and Caribbean area.

FLORIDA
Jacksonville Naval Air Station, continued

ATTRACTIONS: Golfing, beaches, deep sea fishing, St Augustine, Orlando. Museum of Science and History in Jacksonville, art museums, planetarium.

KEY WEST NAVAL AIR STATION (FL15R1)
Key West Naval Air Station, FL 33040-5000

TELEPHONE NUMBER INFORMATION: Main installation numbers: C-305-293-2268, D-312-483-2268.

LOCATION: Take Florida Turnpike, US-1 south to exit signs for Key West NAS on Boca Chica Key, seven miles north of Key West. USMRA: Page 39 (G-16). NMC: Miami, 150 miles north.

GENERAL INFORMATION: Tactical aircraft and rescue aircraft operations; pilot training. Coast Guard, reserve and other services support detachments.

TEMPORARY MILITARY LODGING: Lodging office, Bldg. C2076 24 hours daily, C-305-293-4100. (BOQ) C-305-293-5571, BEQ: C-305-293-2488. Navy Lodge: C-305-292-7556 or 1-800-NAVY-INN.

LOGISTICAL SUPPORT: Complete support facilities available. All EX through switchboard.

All Hands Club-293-2807	CDO/OOD-293-2268	CHAMPUS-293-4543
Chaplain-293-2318	Child Care-293-4376	Exchange-292-7201
Family Service-293-4408	Legal-293-4310	Locator-293-2256
Medical-293-2444	Mini Mart-293-7216	MWR-293-2112
O'Club-293-4205	Police-293-2531	RV/Camping-293-4434

HEALTH & WELFARE: Florida Keys Memorial Hospital, Assistance C-305-293-2444, Ambulance Service C-305-293-2337. Chapels serving all faiths C-305-293-2318.

RECREATION: Auto Hobby EX-2615, Bowling EX-2976, Flying Club EX-5081, Gym EX-2480, Marina EX-3161, Rec Center EX-2112/3039, Water Rec EX-2468. Sigsbee RV Park on base, year round, C-305-293-4434, 70 camper spaces w/full hookups, 200 camper space w/W, unlimited tent spaces.

SPACE-A: Check at Control Tower, 0800-1600 daily, C-305-293-2751/2769, D-312-483-2751/2769, flights to CONUS locations.

ATTRACTIONS: Boating, sport fishing, water sports, Audubon House, Ernest Hemingway Home and Museum, Mel Fisher's Museum, Aquarium. Sigsbee RV Park on base, year round, C-305-293-3161.

MacDILL AIR FORCE BASE (FL02R1)
8208 Hangar Loop Drive, Suite 51
MacDill Air Force Base, FL 33621-5502

TELEPHONE NUMBER INFORMATION: Main installation numbers: C-813-828-1110, D-312-968-1110.

FLORIDA
MacDill Air Force Base. continued

LOCATION: Take I-75 south to I-275 south, exit at Dale Mabry Highway (US-92), south five miles to MacDill AFB main gate. USMRA: Page 38 (E,F-8), page 54 (E,F-3,4). NMC: Tampa, five miles north.

GENERAL INFORMATION: Air Combat Command Base. Headquarters US Special Operations Command, and US Central Command, 6th Air Base Wing.

TEMPORARY MILITARY LODGING: Lodging office, Bldg. 411, corner Garden Dr & Tampa Blvd, 24 hours daily, C-813-828-2661, D-312-968-4259. All ranks. DV/VIP C-813-828-2056.

LOGISTICAL SUPPORT: Complete support facilities available.

ACS-828-4413	Cafeteria-840-0511	CHAMPUS-828-5220
Chaplain-828-3621	Child Care-828-3332	Commissary-828-3196
Conv Store-840-2077	EM-828-3357	Exchange-840-0511
Family Services-828-2221	Fire Dept-828-3438	Gas Station-839-7089
Golf Course-828-4494	ITT-828-2478	Legal-828-4421
Locator-828-2444	Medical-828-3334	NCO Club-828-3357
O'Club-837-1031	Package Store-840-2323	Police-828-3322
Public Affairs-828-2215	Retiree Services-828-4555	RV/Camping-828-3864
SATO-828-4327	Snack Bar-840-2211	Theater-828-3973

HEALTH & WELFARE: USAF Regional Hospital, Emergency C-813-839-3344, Appointments C-813-839-5711, 75 beds. Chapels serving all faiths C-813-828-3621.

RECREATION: MWR EX-2821, Arts/Crafts EX-4413, Auto Hobby EX-4553, Bowling EX-3008, Golf EX-4494, Gym EX-4496, Library EX-3607, Marina EX-4983, Rec Center EX-4518, Youth Activities EX-4244. Coon's Creek Recreation Area on base, year round, C-813-840-6919, D-312-968-4982, 199 camper spaces w/full hookups, 57 camper spaces w/W&E hookups, 33 spaces w/o hookups, and 34 tent spaces w/o hookups.

SPACE-A: Pax Term/Lounges, Hangar 4, 0730-1630 Mon-Fri, C-813-828-2310, D-312-968-2310, Fax 813-828-3202, flights to CONUS locations and MEDEVAC. Also, USCG Air Station, St Petersburg, C-813-534-1437 EX-219, may have flights.

ATTRACTIONS: Busch Gardens, Disney World, professional sports (football,hockey, baseball (spring training)), sport fishing, water sports.

MAYPORT NAVAL STATION (FL13R1)
Mayport Naval Station, FL 32228-0112

TELEPHONE NUMBER INFORMATION: Main installation numbers: C-904-270-5011, D-312-960-5011.

LOCATION: From Jacksonville take Atlantic Blvd (FL-10) east to Mayport Rd (FL-A1A), left to Naval Station. USMRA: Page 38 (H-3), page 50 (G-3,4). NMC: Jacksonville, 10 miles west.

GENERAL INFORMATION: Homeport for 23 ships.

TEMPORARY MILITARY LODGING: Lodging office, Bldg. 1586, Bailey Ave, 24 hours daily, C-904-247-1376, D-312-960-5707, BEQ: C-904-270-5575, D-312-960-5575,

FLORIDA
Mayport Naval Station, continued

BOQ: C-904-270-5423, D-312-960-5423. All ranks. DV/VIP (EM) C-904-270-5707, D-312-960-5707, (Officers) C-904-270-5423, D-312-960-5423.

LOGISTICAL SUPPORT: Complete support facilities available.

CHAMPUS-270-5575
Commissary-249-7362
EM Club-270-7197
Gas Station-270-5712
Locator-270-5401
Police-270-5583
SDO/NCO-270-5401

Chaplain-270-5212
Conv Store-270-5548
Exchange-247-5752
ITT Office-270-5145
Medical-270-5303
Retiree Services-270-5910
Snack Bar-270-5760/5625

Child Care-270-5339
CPO Club-270-5432
Family Services-270-6600
Legal-270-5245
O'Club-270-5313
SATO-270-5427

HEALTH & WELFARE: Naval Branch Medical Clinic, Emergency C-904-270-5444, Appointments C-904-270-5306. Inpatient, see Naval Hospital, Jacksonville NAS listing, C-904-777-7300. Chapels serving all faiths C-904-270-5212.

RECREATION: Arts and Crafts EX-5540, Auto Hobby EX-5392, Bowling EX-5377, Golf EX-5380, Gym EX-5451, Intramural Sports EX-5451, Library EX-5393, Swimming EX-5425, Rec Center EX-5680, Tennis EX-5717.

SPACE-A: See Jacksonville NAS listing, C-904-772-3956, D-312-942-3956, Fax 904-942-2514.

ATTRACTIONS: Zoo, beaches, deep sea fishing. Three-hour drive to Orlando.

MIAMI COAST GUARD AIR STATION (FL30R1)
Opa Locka, FL 33054-2397

TELEPHONE NUMBER INFORMATION: Main installation numbers: C-305-953-2100, FTS-820-1180.

LOCATION: Take exit 14 from I-95 onto NW 135th St (Opa Locka Blvd, also FL-916) west to Lejeune Rd., then north to the airport. Turn left on Wright, Air Station is at the end of the road. USMRA: Page 39 (J-13), page 51 (D-6). NMC: Miami, 10 miles southeast.

GENERAL INFORMATION: A Coast Guard Air Station with regional search-and-rescue and drug-interdiction responsibilities.

TEMPORARY MILITARY LODGING: None. See Key West NAS listing, C-305-293-4100. (BOQ) C-305-293-5571, BEQ: C-305-293-2488.

LOGISTICAL SUPPORT: Limited support facilities available.

All Hands Club-953-2291
Commissary-953-2290
Medical-953-2265/2266
Public Affairs-953-2151

CDO/OOD-953-2280
Exchange-688-6851
MWR-953-2115
SDO/NCO-953-2130/2140

CHAMPUS-953-2265/2266
Family Services-953-2110
Package Store-953-2290

HEALTH & WELFARE: Coast Guard Air Station Clinic C-305-953-2266. No chapel on base.

RECREATION: For recreational activities call 305-953-2115.

FLORIDA
Miami Coast Guard Air Station, continued

SPACE-A: None. No regularly scheduled flights from the Air Station. See Key West Naval Air Station listing, C-305-293-2751/2769, D-312-483-2751/2769.

ATTRACTIONS: Hollywood/Rembroke Pines Area, city of Miami, Gratigny Park, Spanish Monastery, Vizcaya Art Museum, Hialeah Park, Miami Seaquarium, Miami Serpentarium, Dade City Art Museum, beaches.

MIAMI COAST GUARD BASE (FL31R1)
100 MacArthur Causeway
Miami Beach, FL 33139-5119

TELEPHONE NUMBER INFORMATION: Main installation numbers: C-305-535-4300, FTS-820-0300.

LOCATION: Take I-95 to MacArthur Causeway (also I-359) east. USMRA: Page 39 (J-13), page 51 (B-4,5). NMC: Miami Beach, in city limits.

GENERAL INFORMATION: The Coast Guard Base in Miami is responsible for regional search-and-rescue and drug-interdiction missions.

TEMPORARY MILITARY LODGING: None. See Key West NAS listing. C-305-293-4100. (BOQ) C-305-293-5571, BEQ: C-305-293-2488.

LOGISTICAL SUPPORT: Limited support facilities available.

CHAMPUS-535-4350   Exchange-535-4354   Medical-535-4350
SDO/NCO-535-4361

HEALTH & WELFARE: General medical services (medical/dental) available during normal working hours, Corpsman available 24 hours, **Active Duty personnel only.**

SPACE-A: None. See Key West NAS listing, C-305-293-2751/2769, D-312-483-2751/2769.

ATTRACTIONS: City of Miami (tours available), Gratigny Park, Spanish Monastery, Vizcaya Art Museum, beaches, water sports.

ORLANDO NAVAL TRAINING CENTER (FL11R1)
Orlando, FL 32813-8360

Scheduled to close December 1998.

TELEPHONE NUMBER INFORMATION: Main installation numbers: C-407-646-4111, D-312-791-4111.

LOCATION: From I-4 in Orlando take FL-50 (Colonial Dr) east about three miles; then north on Bennet Rd for one-half mile to NTC. USMRA: Page 38 (H-7), page 53 (D-1). NMC: Orlando, in city limits.

GENERAL INFORMATION: Training Center, schools. Annex is adjacent to Orlando IAP on site of the old McCoy AFB, 10 miles south.

FLORIDA
Orlando Naval Training Center, continued

TEMPORARY MILITARY LODGING: Lodging office, Bldg. 375 1200 Leahy St., 0730-1600 duty days, C-407-646-5614, D-312-791-5614.

LOGISTICAL SUPPORT: Complete support facilities available.

Cafeteria-646-5826/4330	CDO-646-4501	CHAMPUS-646-5833
Chaplain-646-5185	Child Care-646-5135	Conv Store-646-4456
EM Club-646-4206	Exchange-646-5511	Family Services-646-5283
Gas Station-646-5979	ITT Office-646-5164	Legal-646-5181
Locator-646-4501	Medical-646-4946	O'Club-646-4529
Package Store-646-4406	Police-646-4444	Retiree Services-646-4617
SATO-895-4664	Snack Bar-646-4291	Theater-646-5502

HEALTH & WELFARE: Medical Clinic, Appointments C-407-643-4982. Chapels serving all faiths C-407-646-4922.

RECREATION: Auto Hobby EX-5920/857-1380, Bowling EX-5048, Ceramics EX-5808, Sailing EX-4492, Flying Club 898-3311, Golf EX-5736, Gym EX-5161, Library EX-5137, Swimming EX-5196, Water Sports EX-5850, Wood Hobby EX-5024. Lake Baldwin Picnic Grounds EX-5161. Travel Trailer Park on base, year round, C-407-857-2120, 48 camper spaces w/full hookups, 13 spaces w/W&E, 10 spaces w/o hookups.

Chaplain-857-3280   Commissary-857-3550   Mini Mart-859-4890
Package Store-859-4890

SPACE-A: None. See Patrick AFB listing, C-407-494-5631, D-312-854-5631, Fax 407-494-7991.

ATTRACTIONS: The playground of Florida, Disney World, Busch Gardens, Cypress Gardens, Sea World, Epcot Center, Universal Studios, Church St Station.

PANAMA CITY COASTAL SYSTEMS STATION, NAVAL SURFACE WARFARE CENTER (FL35R1)
6703 West Highway 98
Panama City, FL 32407-5000

TELEPHONE NUMBER INFORMATION: Main installation numbers: C-904-234-4100, D-312-436-4100.

LOCATION: Located on US-98 at the foot of the Hathaway Bridge in Panama City Beach. USMRA: Page 39 (D-14). NMC: Panama City, adjacent.

GENERAL INFORMATION: The Station is a Navy Research and Development Laboratory responsible for coastal and harbor defense activities.

TEMPORARY MILITARY LODGING: BEQ, Bldg. 304, C-904-234-4756, BOQ, Bldg. 349, C-904-234-4556, 24 hours daily. DV/VIP (Officers) C-904-234-5464, D-312-436-5464.

LOGISTICAL SUPPORT: Limited support facilities available.

Consol Club-234-4374   Exchange-235-2778   Medical-234-4177
Police-234-4332

96 - U.S. FORCES TRAVEL & TRANSFER GUIDE U.S.A

FLORIDA
Panama City Coastal Systems Station, NSWC, continued

HEALTH & WELFARE: Medical Info, C-904-234-4177. See Tyndall AFB listing, C-904-283-4277/2023.

RECREATION: Fitness Center EX-4370. Panama City CSS Outdoor Recreation/Marina, C-904-234-4402, 29 camper spaces w/full hookups, three mobile homes.

SPACE-A: See Pensacola NAS listing, C-904-452-3311/2431, D-312-922-3311/2431, Fax 904-452-8105.

ATTRACTIONS: Beaches, water sports.

PATRICK AIR FORCE BASE/ CAPE CANAVERAL AIR STATION (FL03R1)
1201 Minuteman Street
Suite C-133
Patrick Air Force Base, FL 32925-3237

TELEPHONE NUMBER INFORMATION: Main installation numbers: C-407-494-1110, D-312-854-1110.

LOCATION: Take I-95 south to exit 73 (Wickham Rd), three miles to FL-404 (Pineda Causeway), left on South Patrick Dr to Patrick AFB. USMRA: Page 38 (I-8) NMC: Orlando.

GENERAL INFORMATION: Air Force Space Command Base, 45th Space Wing, support to DoD and NASA.

TEMPORARY MILITARY LODGING: Billeting Office, Bldg. 720, 820 Falcon Ave, 24 hours daily, C-407-494-6570, D-312-854-7597. All ranks. DV/VIP 494-4506.

LOGISTICAL SUPPORT: Complete support facilities available.

CHAMPUS-494-8112
Commissary-494-4060
EM Beach Club-494-7491
Fire Department-494-7642
ITT-494-5158
Medical-494-8229
O'Club-494-4011
Public Affairs-494-5933
RV/Camping-494-2042
SDO/NCO-494-7001

Chaplain-494-4073
Conv Store-494-4555
Exchange-799-1300
Gas Station-494-2655
Legal-494-7815
MWR-494-8382
Package Store-494-6686
Recreation-853-1287
SATO-494-4155
Theater-494-2057

Child Care-494-7028
Dinette-494-4248
Family Services-494-4907
Golf Course-494-7856
Locator-494-4542
NCO Club-494-7491
Police-494-2008
Retiree Services-494-5464
Snack Bar-494-5614
Visitor Center-494-2659

HEALTH & WELFARE: 45th Medical Group Hospital, Emergency C-407-494-8134, Appointments C-407-494-8241, 25 beds. Chapels serving all faiths C-407-494-4073.

RECREATION: MWR EX-6695, Auto Hobby EX-2537, Bowling EX-2958, Aero Club EX-4356, Golf EX-7856, Gym EX-6697, Hobby Shops EX-2482, Library EX-6881, Swimming EX-6796, Rec Center EX-5523, Skeet EX-4787, Youth Center EX-4747. Manatee Cove Campground on base, year round, C-407-494-4787, D-312-854-4787, 56 camper spaces w/W&E, five spaces w/o hookups.

FLORIDA
Patrick Air Force Base, continued

SPACE-A: Pax Term/Lounge, Bldg. 800, 0730-1630 Mon-Fri, C-407-494-5631, D-312-854-5631, Fax 407-494-7991, flights to CONUS and Caribbean locations.

ATTRACTIONS: Air Force Space Museum, John F. Kennedy Space Center, Disney World, Daytona Beach, Epcot Center, Spaceport USA, Sea World.

PENSACOLA NAVAL AIR STATION (FL14R1)
190 Radford Blvd.
Pensacola Naval Air Station, FL 32508-5217

TELEPHONE NUMBER INFORMATION: Main installation numbers: C-904-452-0111, D-312-922-0111.

LOCATION: Four miles south of US-98, and 12 miles south of I-10. Take Navy Blvd from US-98 or US-29 directly to NAS. USMRA: Page 39 (A,B-13,14), page 53 (A,B-4,5). NMC: Pensacola, eight miles north.

GENERAL INFORMATION: Chief of Naval Education & Training, Naval Aviation Schools Command, home of Navy Blue Angels, Navy Public Works Center.

TEMPORARY MILITARY LODGING: Lodging office, 24 hours daily; Bldg. 600 BOQ (Officers), C-904-452-2755/2756, D-312-922-2755/2756. Lodging office, Bldg. 3472 (BEQ), C-904-452-3438, D-312-922-3438. Navy Lodge, C-800-628-9466. DV/VIP C-904-452-2755/6.

LOGISTICAL SUPPORT: Complete support facilities available.

CDO/OOD-452-2353	CHAMPUS-452-6711	Chaplain-452-2341
Child Care-452-2211	Commissary-452-6889	Conv Store-453-2483
CPO Club-452-800	EM Club-452-8000	Exchange-458-3317
Family Services-452-5990	Fire Dept-452-2896	Gas Station-458-3221
Golf Course-452-2454	ITT Office-452-4229	Legal-452-4321
Locator-452-0111	Medical-452-5662	MWR-452-3806
NCO Club-452-8000	O'Club-455-2276	Omega-453-8922
Package Store-455-4155	Police-452-2453	Public Affairs-452-2311
Recreation-452-2317	Retiree Services-452-5991	RV/Camping-452-2635
Snack Bar-452-3899	Visitor Center-452-3757	

HEALTH & WELFARE: Naval Branch Medical Clinic, C-904-452-5214. Inpatient, see Pensacola Naval Hospital listing, C-904-452-6788. Chapels serving all faiths C-904-452-2341.

RECREATION: Athletics EX-4391, Auto Hobby EX-2039, Beach EX-4391, Bowling EX-4630, Marina (Sherman Cove) EX-3369, Golf EX-2455, Gym 452-4391, Hobby Shops EX-2039, Library EX-4362, Sailing EX-3369, Swimming 452-8293, Youth Activities 452-2417. Oak Grove Park on base, year round, C-904-452-2535, D-312-922-2535, 12 cabins, 42 camper spaces w/W&E hookups, 15 tent sites.

SPACE-A: Pax Term/Lounge, Bldg. 1852, 24 hours daily, C-904-452-3311, D-312-922-3311, Fax 904-452-8105flights to CONUS locations.

FLORIDA
Pensacola Naval Air Station, continued

ATTRACTIONS: Sport fishing, water sports, golf, National Museum of Naval Aviation, Fiesta of Five Flags, Fort Pickens, Fort Barrancas, annual Blue Angels Marathon, annual Blue Angels Homecoming Air Show (Nov).

PENSACOLA NAVAL HOSPITAL (FL20R1)
6000 West Highway 98
Pensacola, FL 32512-0003

TELEPHONE NUMBER INFORMATION: Main installation numbers: C-904-452-6601, D-312-922-6601.

LOCATION: On US-98 between Navy Blvd and Fairfield Dr in Pensacola. USMRA: Page 39 (A,B-13), page 53 (B-4). NMC: Pensacola.

GENERAL INFORMATION: The Naval Hospital, built in 1976, supports four naval aviation and technical training bases.

TEMPORARY MILITARY LODGING: None. See Pensacola NAS, BOQ C-904-452-2755, C-904-452-3438 and Whiting Field NAS, C-904-623-7605/6, D-312-868-7605/6.

LOGISTICAL SUPPORT: Limited support facilities available. Most support is at Pensacola NAS.

CDO/OOD-452-6601	CHAMPUS-452-6709	Chaplain-452-6481
Conv Store-455-9649	Legal-452-6844	Public Affairs-452-6796
Snack Bar-452-6267		

HEALTH & WELFARE: Complete range of clinics and depts, Emergency 904-452-6788. Most clinics 0730-1600 daily.

RECREATION: None. See Pensacola NAS and Corry NTTC listings.

SPACE-A: None. See Pensacola NAS listing, C-904-452-3311, D-312-922-3311.

ATTRACTIONS: The Blue Angels, beaches, fishing.

ST. PETERSBURG COAST GUARD GROUP/STATION (FL33R1)
600 8th Avenue SE
St. Petersburg, FL 33701-5030

TELEPHONE NUMBER INFORMATION: Main installation numbers: C-813-824-7638, 1-800-732-6864.

LOCATION: Take I-275 to I-175 east, exit 9, right to Group/Station. Located adjacent to Albert Whitted Airport. USMRA: Page 38 (E-8), page 54 (D-5). NMC: St. Petersburg, in city limits.

TEMPORARY MILITARY LODGING: None. See MacDill AFB listing, C-813-828-2661, D-312-968-4259.

LOGISTICAL SUPPORT: Complete support facilities available.

FLORIDA
St Petersburg Coast Guard Group/Station, continued

All Hands Club-7658	Barber Shop-896-2816	CDO/OOD-824-7519
CHAMPUS-824-7579	Chaplain-823-3454	Consol Club-824-7658
CPO/O' Club-824-7582	Exchange-896-2816	Family Services-824-7684
Galley-824-7651	Locator-824-7506	Medical-824-7579
Minimart-824-7667	MWR-824-7598	Package Store-896-2816
Police-825-7599	Public Affairs-824-7564	Retiree Services-824-7504
SDO/NCO-824-7501		

HEALTH & WELFARE: Dispensary/Emergency (0730-1530) C-813-824-7579, other hours C-813-824-7501. Inpatient, see MacDill AFB listing, C-813-839-5711.

RECREATION: Swimming pool with picnic area.

SPACE-A: None. See MacDill AFB listing, C-813-838-2310, D-312-968-2310, Fax 813-828-3202.

ATTRACTIONS: Close to beaches, boating, fishing, skin diving, scuba diving, snorkeling, water skiing, St Petersburg sights, professional sports (NHL Tampa Bay Lightning, NFL Tampa Bay Buccaneers, MLB -in 1998- Tampa Bay Devil Rays), MLB spring training, minor league baseball, Salvador Dali Museum.

SAUFLEY FIELD (FL34R1)
NETPMSA
6490 Saufley Field Road
Pensacola, FL 32509-5237

TELEPHONE NUMBER INFORMATION: Main installation numbers: C-904-452-1628, D-312-922-1628.

LOCATION: From I-10 exit to FL-297 (Pine Forest Rd) south to a right on Saufley Field Rd and the base. USMRA: Page 39 (A,B-13), page 53 (A,B-3). NMC: Pensacola, in the city.

GENERAL INFORMATION: Host unit at Saufley Field is the Naval Education and Training Program Management Support Activity (NETPMSA). Tenant units include the Defense Activity for Non-Traditional Education Support (DANTES), Federal Prison Camp, Finance and Accounting Service Center, Naval Reserve Center, and other minor units.

TEMPORARY MILITARY LODGING: None. See Pensacola Naval Air Station listing, BEQ C-904-452-3438, D-312-922-3438/2755. BOQ C-904-452-2755, D-312-922-2755. DV/VIP C-904-452-4609/2756.

LOGISTICAL SUPPORT: Very limited support facilities available.

CMO Club-452-1556   Chaplain-452-2341   SDO-452-1628

HEALTH & WELFARE: Dental C-904-452-5600, Medical Emergency C-904-452-3333.

RECREATION: Rec Services 452-1071 (Corry Annex) includes racquetball, handball, tennis; Golf EX-1097, Gym EX-1071.

SPACE-A: None. See Pensacola Naval Air Station listing, C-904-452-3311, D-312-922-3311, Fax 904-452-8105.

FLORIDA
Saufley Field, continued

ATTRACTIONS: Gulf Islands National Seashore (Fort Pickens, Fort Barrancas, Fort Barrancas Advanced Redoubt), Naval Museum of Aviation.

SHADES OF GREEN ON WALT DISNEY WORLD® RESORT (FL49R1)
P.O. Box 22789
Lake Buena Vista, FL 32830-2789

TELEPHONE NUMBER INFORMATION: Main installation numbers: C-407-824-3400, FAX 407-824-3460.

LOCATION: From Orlando take I-4 west, exit 26B, Walt Disney World, follow Magic Kingdom Resort signs, go through Magic Kingdom toll booth, stay in far right lane following signs to resort and hotels, at first light turn left, Seven Seas Dr past Polynesian Resort, come to three way stop, turn right on Floridian Way, driveway is first road to the left, Magnolia Palm Dr. USMRA: Page 38 (G-7), page 53 (A-2). NMC: Orlando, 15 miles northeast.

GENERAL INFORMATION: The Army announced on November 3, 1993 that it had leased the Disney Inn at Walt Disney World in Lake Buena Vista, Florida, to serve as an Armed Forces Recreation Center (AFRC). The Disney Inn was renamed "Shades of Green on Walt Disney World Resort." It is very popular with families because of its large rooms (288) and easy access to transportation to various parts of Disney World.

TEMPORARY MILITARY LODGING: Reservations required. Military personnel, active, retired, Guard & Reserve, family members and DoD employees may make reservations by calling (407) 824-3600 or FAX (407) 824-3665. Write for reservation and information packet: Shades of Green on Walt Disney World Resort, P.O. Box 22789, Lake Buena Vista, FL 32830-2789. The inn has 288 large rooms each appointed with two queen-size beds, sofa-bed, private bath. There are 2 outdoor pools & a kiddy pool, tennis courts, and easy access to Walt Disney World transportation. RATES: E1-5 $55. E6-9, O1-3, WO1-CW3 $79. O4-6, CW4-5 $89. O7-10 $95. GS1-10 $79. GS11-15 $89. NAF Civilians $79-95. Rates are for double occupancy. Single room subtract $2. There will be an added charge of $10 per additional adult above two per room. Season of Operation: Year round.

LOGISTICAL SUPPORT: None. See Orlando Naval Training Center.

Gift Shop-824-3400

HEALTH & WELFARE: None. See Orlando NTC, C-407-643-4982.

SPACE-A: None. See Patrick AFB, C-407-494-5631, D-312-854-5631.

ATTRACTIONS: A child's dream come true, a visit to Walt Disney World, Epcot Center and Disney MGM Studios Theme Park. If that is not enough to keep you busy, there is golf, swimming, and tennis all without leaving the resort.

FLORIDA

TYNDALL AIR FORCE BASE (FL04R1)
445 Suwannee Road, Suite 101
Tyndall Air Force Base, FL 32403-5541

TELEPHONE NUMBER INFORMATION: Main installation numbers: C-904-283-1110, D-312-523-1110.

LOCATION: Take I-10, exit to US-231 south to US-98 east. Clearly marked. USMRA: Page 39 (E-14). NMC: Panama City, 10 miles northwest.

GENERAL INFORMATION: Air Education and Training Command Base, 1st Air Force, 325th Fighter Wing, Southeast Air Defense Sector, USAF Civil Engineering Support Agency.

TEMPORARY MILITARY LODGING: Billeting Office, Bldg. 1332, Suwanne and Oak Dr, 24 hours daily, C-904-283-4210/4211, D-312-523-4210/4211. All ranks. DV/VIP C-904-283-2232.

LOGISTICAL SUPPORT: Complete support facilities available.

CHAMPUS-283-3883
Command Post-283-2115
EM Club-283-4444
Fire Dept-283-2852
ITT Office-283-2230
Medical-283-2778
O'Club-283-4357
Public Affairs-283-2983
RV/Camping-283-2798
Snack Bar-283-4110
Chaplain-283-2925
Commissary-283-4825
Exchange-283-4110
Gas Station-286-5826
Legal-283-4681
MWR-283-2501
Package Store-286-5886
Recreation-283-2501/2983
SATO-283-2581
Theater-283-2594
Child Care-283-4747
Conv Store-286-5852
Family Services-283-2963
Golf Course-283-2565
Locator-283-2138/4210
NCO Club-283-4444
Police-283-2558
Retiree Services-283-2737
SDO/NCO-283-4145
Visitor Center-283-3860

HEALTH & WELFARE: USAF Acute Care Clinic C-904-283-2333, 30 beds, Appointments C-904-283-4277/2023, 50 beds. Chapels serving all faiths C-904-283-2925.

RECREATION: Auto Hobby, Beach, Bowling, Flying Club, Golf, Gym, Hobby Shops, Library, Marina, Swimming, Tennis and Theater EX-2495. Youth Center EX-4326. Fam-Camp on base, year round, C-904-283-2798, D-312-523-2798, 3 cottages, 76 camper spaces w/full hookups, 14 camper spaces w/W&E, eight tent spaces.

SPACE-A: Try Base Ops C-904-283-4244. Also see Pensacola NAS listing.

ATTRACTIONS: Panama City and beautiful white sand beaches.

WHITING FIELD NAVAL AIR STATION (FL05R1)
7550 USS Essex Street
Milton, FL 32570-6155

TELEPHONE NUMBER INFORMATION: Main installation numbers: C-904-623-7011, D-312-868-7011.

LOCATION: From US-90 east exit, FL-87 north for eight miles to NAS. USMRA: Page 39 (B-13). NMC: Pensacola, 30 miles southwest.

FLORIDA
Whiting Field Naval Air Station, continued

GENERAL INFORMATION: Naval Aviation Training, fixed- and rotary-wing aircraft.

TEMPORARY MILITARY LODGING: Lodging office, Bldg. 2942, 24 hours daily, C-904-623-7605/6, D-312-868-7605/6. All ranks. DV/VIP C-904-623-7201/7605.

LOGISTICAL SUPPORT: Complete support facilities available.

CDO/OOD-623-7437	CHAMPUS-623-7657	Chaplain-623-7395
Child Care-623-7472	Commissary-623-7131	Consolidated Club-623-7288
Exchange-623-8066	Family Services-623-7234	Fire Dept-623-7331
Gas Station-623-8088	Golf Course-623-7348	Legal-623-7231
Locator-623-7437	Medical-623-7151	MWR-623-7221
Package Store-623-7198	Police-623-7431	Public Affairs-623-7651
Recreation-623-7502	Retiree Services-623-7177	

HEALTH & WELFARE: Naval Branch Medical Clinic, Military sick call C-904-623-7151. Inpatient, see Pensacola Naval Hospital listing, C-904-452-6788. Chapels serving all faiths C-904-623-7211.

RECREATION: Boat Dock EX-2383, Bowling EX-7545, Golf EX-7348, Gym EX-7718, Hobby Shops EX-7445, Library EX-7274, Racquetball EX-7412. See Pensacola NAS for travel camp.

SPACE-A: None. See Pensacola NAS listing, C-904-452-3311, D-312-922-3311.

ATTRACTIONS: Deep sea fishing, water sports, golf, dog races, stock car racing, Pensacola Symphony Orchestra.

Other Installations in Florida

Canaveral Air Force Station, Patrick AFB, FL 32925-5000.
USMRA: Page 38 (I-7). C-407-494-1110, D-312-467-1110. Exchange-853-3196, Consol Club-853-1234.
Cortez U.S. Coast Guard Station, 4530 124th St., Court West, Cortez, FL 34215-9999
USMRA: Page 39 (E,F-9). C-813-794-1262, 800-232-0154. Exchange-795-2805.
Fort Myers Beach Coast Guard Station, 719 San Carlos Dr., Fort. Myers, FL 33931-2221.
USMRA: Page 39 (F,G-11). C-813-463-5754. Exchange-463-8963.
Jupiter U.S. Coast Guard Station, US-1, Lighthouse Park, Jupiter, FL 33469.
USMRA: Page 39 (J-10). C-407-746-5402. Exchange-746-5402.
Mayport Coast Guard Base, P.O. Box 385, Mayport, FL 32267-0385
USMRA: Page 38 (H-3), page 50 (F-3). C-904-247-7301, D-312-960-5780. Exchange-247-8738.
New Smyrna Beach Coast Guard Station, P.O. Box 370, New Smyrna Beach, FL 32069-0370.
USMRA: Page 38 (I-6). C-904-428-9085. Exchange-427-2786.
Panama City Coast Guard Station, Panama City, FL 32407-5000.
USMRA: Page 39 (D-14). Exchange, Medical-234-4177.

U.S. FORCES TRAVEL & TRANSFER GUIDE U.S.A. - 103

GEORGIA

DOLLAR RENT A CAR Call 1-800-800-4000. Get a military rate by using your Military Living ID # ML3009. Retirees/Active Duty/Reserve/Guard.

ALBANY MARINE CORPS LOGISTICS BASE (GA17R1)
Albany Marine Corps Logistics Base, GA 31704-1128

TELEPHONE NUMBER INFORMATION: Main installation numbers: C-912-439-5000, D-312-460-5000.

LOCATION: Off US-82, take Mock Rd south from 5-Points to Fleming Road. Go east to main gate. USMRA: Page 37 (C-8). NMC: Albany, three miles west.

GENERAL INFORMATION: The East Coast main Marine Corps Supply Base.

TEMPORARY MILITARY LODGING: Housing office, Bldg. 3600, 0800-1630 daily. C-912-439-5614, D-312-567-5314.

LOGISTICAL SUPPORT: Most support facilities available.

CHAMPUS-435-0472   Chaplain-439-5282   Commissary-435-1721
Conv Store-435-1471   Exchange-888-6801   Family Services-439-5276
Gas Station-436-8352   Legal-439-5212   Locator-439-5000/5206
Medical-435-0806/5984   Nursery-439-5247   NCO Club-439-5223
O'Club-439-5239   Package Store-435-7567   Police-439-5181
SATO-435-1946   SDO/NCO-439-5206   Snack Bar-435-1471
Theater-439-5166

HEALTH & WELFARE: Naval Medical Clinic, Emergency C-912-435-0806, Appointments C-912-435-5984. Inpatient, see Moody AFB listing, C-912-257-3816. Chapel serving all faiths C-912-439-5282.

RECREATION: Skeet Range EX-5234, Golf EX-5211, Hobby Shops EX-5226, Bowling EX-5233, Gym EX-5246, Library EX-5242, Swimming EX-5234, Rod/Gun Club EX-5000. Covella Pond Picnic Area EX-5234.

SPACE-A: None. See Moody AFB listing, C-912-257-2465, D-312-460-2465.

ATTRACTIONS: Drum & Bugle Corps. Tallahassee, FL, easy drive south.

ATHENS NAVAL SUPPLY CORPS SCHOOL (GA12R1)
1425 Prince Avenue
Athens, GA 30606-5000

TELEPHONE NUMBER INFORMATION: Main installation numbers: C-706-354-1500, D-312-588-1500.

LOCATION: From Atlanta, take I-85 north to highway 316, east to Athens perimeter loop. Follow loop west to Prince Ave exit, right onto Prince Ave. Base is on the right. USMRA: Page 37 (D-3), page 49 (A-1). NMC: Atlanta, 70 miles west.

GENERAL INFORMATION: Navy Supply Corps School, Personnel Support Detach.

GEORGIA
Athens Naval Supply Corps School, continued

TEMPORARY MILITARY LODGING: Lodging office, Brown Hall, 0800-1600 daily, BEQ/BOQ/DV/VIP C-706-354-7360, D-312-588-7360, Fax 706-354-7360.

LOGISTICAL SUPPORT: Limited support facilities available.

CDO/OOD-354-1500	CHAMPUS-354-7321	Chaplain-354-7208
Child Care-543-6113	Commissary-354-7371	Conv Store-354-8761
CPO Club-354-7381	Exchange-354-3850	Gas Station-354-8761
Medical-354-7321	MWR-354-7363	O' Club-354-7381
Package Store-354-8761	Police-354-7355	Public Affairs-354-7316
Recreation-354-7374	Retiree Services-354-7335	SATO-354-7369

HEALTH & WELFARE: Naval Branch Clinic, (0730-1130 and 1230-1600 only) C-706-354-7321. Inpatient, see Fort Gordon listing, C-706-791-7300. Chapel serving all faiths C-706-354-7208.

RECREATION: Gym EX-7377, Library EX-7217, Swimming EX-7300, Tennis EX-7205.

SPACE-A: None. See Atlanta NAS listing, C-404-919-4903, D-312-925-4903, Fax 404-919-5105.

ATTRACTIONS: Athens, University of Georgia, Naval Supply Corps Museum.

ATLANTA NAVAL AIR STATION (GA16R1)
1000 Halsey Avenue
Marietta, GA 30060-5099

TELEPHONE NUMBER INFORMATION: Main installation numbers: C-770-919-5392, D-312-925-5392.

LOCATION: From I-75, take exit 111 Windy Hill. Proceed west on Windy Hill to Atlanta Road. Take right (N) on Atlanta Road to Richardson Road. Take right (E). Main Gate on left. USMRA: Page 37 (B-3), page 49 (A-1). NMC: Atlanta, 15 miles southeast.

GENERAL INFORMATION: Navy and Marine Corps tactical aircraft and crew training.

TEMPORARY MILITARY LODGING: Lodging office, Bldg. 54, 24 hours daily. Very limited. BEQ/BOQ/DV/VIP C-770-919-6393, D-312-925-5393, Fax 770-421-5546.

LOGISTICAL SUPPORT: Most support facilities available.

CDO/OOD-919-6392	CHAMPUS-919-5314	Chaplain-919-6472
Child Care-919-6590	CPO Club-919-6508	Exchange-919-5488
Family Services-919-6735	Gas Station-427-4400	ITT Office-919-6499
Legal-919-6396	Medical-919-5300	MWR-919-6510
NCO Club-919-6508	O' Club-919-6508	Police-919-5394
Package Store-419-0776	Police-919-6394	Public Affairs-919-6406
Recreation-919-6510	Retiree Services-919-6735	RV/Camping-974-6309
SATO-424-3909	Visitor Center-919-6735	

HEALTH & WELFARE: Naval Branch Clinic, Emergency C-770-919-5304, Appointments C-770-919-5302. Inpatient, see Robins AFB listing, 912-926-2354. Chapels serving all faiths C-770-919-5472/3/4.

GEORGIA
Atlanta Naval Air Station, continued

RECREATION: Auto Hobby Shop EX-5485, Bowling EX-5493, Fitness Center EX-5735, Flying Club EX-5507. Also Operates Lake Allatoona Navy Recreation site, off base, C-404-421-5502, D-312-925-5502, nine cabins, one camper w/W&E, 10 camper spaces w/W&E hookups, three tent spaces.

SPACE-A: C-770-919-5359, D-312-925-5359, Fax 770-919-5105.

ATTRACTIONS: Atlanta, Stone Mountain State Park, Six Flags Over Georgia, and other attractions are within 30 miles of NAS.

CAMP FRANK D. MERRILL (GA23R1)
Wahsega Road
Dahlonega, GA 30533-9499

TELEPHONE NUMBER INFORMATION: Main installation numbers: C-706-864-3327, D-312-797-5770.

LOCATION: From GA 400 take Highway 60 north to Dahlonega, follow 60 and US 19 approximately three miles take left on Wahsega Rd. Camp is approximately nine miles. USMRA: Page 37 (C-2). NMC: Gainseville 25 miles south.

GENERAL INFORMATION: Mountain training phase of Ranger School.

TEMPORARY MILITARY LODGING: Small lodging facility (two units), C-706-864-3327 EX-187. All ranks. (Can be bumped by incoming assigned duty status personnel).

LOGISTICAL SUPPORT: Limited support facilities available.

All Ranks Club-EX-158   CHAMPUS-EX-189   Commissary-EX-109
Exchange-EX-188   Fire Dept-EX-130   Medical-EX-189
Public Affairs-EX-102   SDO-864-3327

HEALTH & WELFARE: Small, limited clinic, C-706-864-3327. Emergencies: St. Joseph Hospital, C-404-864-6136. Outpatient, see Fort. McPherson listing, C-404-752-2184.

RECREATION: Swimming Pool, Gym, racquetball, sauna EX-126. Picnic areas, horseshoe ring, outdoor grills.

SPACE-A: See Dobbins AFB listing, C-770-919-4903, D-312-925-4903, Fax 770-919-5105.

ATTRACTIONS: Old gold mining town of Dahlonega-site of first gold rush, Blue Ridge Mountains, State parks, Appalachian Trail, North Georgia College-formerly a military college-built in 1873, abundant opportunity for hunting and fishing. One hour drive to Atlanta.

DOBBINS AIR RESERVE BASE (GA13R1)
1492 First Street
Dobbins Air Reserve Base, GA 30069-5010

TELEPHONE NUMBER INFORMATION: Main installation numbers: C-770-919-5000, D-312-925-1110.

GEORGIA
Dobbins Air Reserve Base, continued

LOCATION: From I-75 north exit to Delk Rd (exit 111) to Dobbins ARB. Clearly marked. USMRA: Page 37 (B-3), Page 49 (A-1). NMC: Atlanta, 16 miles northeast.

GENERAL INFORMATION: Air Force Reserve Base, Headquarters 22nd Air Force (AFRES), 94th Airlift Wing (AFRES).

TEMPORARY MILITARY LODGING: Lodging Office, Dobbins Inn, Bldg. 800, 1295 Barracks Ct., 24 hours daily, C-770-919-4745, D-312-925-4745. All ranks. DV/VIP 770-919-4520.

LOGISTICAL SUPPORT: Limited support facilities available.

Consol Club-919-5040　　Exchange-428-3054　　Locator-919-5000
Medical-919-5300　　　　Police-919-4908　　　　SATO-919-4848
SDO/NCO-919-5000

HEALTH & WELFARE: Dispensary/Emergency C-770-919-5302. Inpatient, see Robins AFB listing, C-912-926-2354. Chapels serving all faiths C-770-919-4955/4956 (Prot/Cath), C-770-873-1731 (Jewish).

RECREATION: Flying Club, Gym, Swimming, Tennis EX-4870. Lakeside Fam Camp on base, year round, C-770-919-4870, D-312-925-4870, 16 camping spaces w/W&E hookups.

SPACE-A: Pax Term/Lounge, Bldg. 737, 0700-2300 daily, C-770-919-4903, D-312-925-4903, Fax 770-919-5105. Flights to CONUS locations. Reserve units.

ATTRACTIONS: Jimmy Carter Presidential Library, Stone Mountain, Six Flags, Metro Atlanta, Underground Atlanta, Atlanta Braves baseball.

FORT BENNING (GA11R1)
Fort Benning, GA 31905-5065

TELEPHONE NUMBER INFORMATION: Main installation numbers: C-706-544-2218, D-312-784-2218.

LOCATION: Off I-185 and US-27/280. USMRA: Page 37 (B-6). NMC: Columbus, five miles northwest.

GENERAL INFORMATION: Army Infantry Center and School, Army Infantry Training Brigade, School of the Americas, 75th Ranger Regiment, 29th Infantry Regiment, 36th Engineer Group, 11th Infantry Regiment, 3rd Brigade, 24th Infantry Division, Ranger Training Brigade, U.S. Army Marksmanship Unit, U.S. Physical Fitness School.

TEMPORARY MILITARY LODGING: Lodging office, Bldg. 399, 24 hours daily. C-706-689-0067, D-312-835-3145. All ranks. DV/VIP 706-545-5724.

LOGISTICAL SUPPORT: Complete support facilities available.

CHAMPUS-544-3401　　　Chaplain-545-2080　　　　Child Care-689-8698
Commissary-544-3663　　Conv Store-682-0473　　　EM Club-689-0887
Exchange-682-0826　　　Family Services-545-1169　Gas Station-687-6520
Legal-545-3281　　　　　Locator-545-5216　　　　　Medical-544-2041
NCO Club-687-0600　　　O'Club-682-0640　　　　　Package Store-687-9674

GEORGIA
Fort Benning, continued

Police-545-5222   Retiree Services-545-2715   SATO-682-0622
SDO/NCO-545-2218   Snack Bar-687-0349   Theater-682-0562

HEALTH & WELFARE: Martin Army Community Hospital, clinics and depts, Emergency C-706-544-1502, Appointments C-706-544-2041, 500 beds. Chapel serving all faiths C-706-545-2050.

RECREATION: Arts/Crafts, Bowling, Golf 687-1940, Gym, Hobby Shops, Intramural Sports, Library, Pool, Tennis, Rod/Gun Club, Youth Center, Rec Center, all 545-4436/3677. Uchee Creek Rec Area on post, year round, C-706-545-4053, D-312-835-4053, 22 cabins, 38 camper spaces w/full hookups, 27 camper spaces w/W&E hookups. Also, operates Destin Army Infantry Center Recreation Area, FL, on Choctawatchee Bay, year round, C-904-837-6423, Reservations 1-800-642-0466, 43 camper spaces w/full hookups, 23 camper spaces w/o hookups, 22 cottages, 54 motel units.

SPACE-A: Lawson Army Airfield on post, limited flights via executive Army aircraft, C-706-545-3524, D-312-835-3524.

ATTRACTIONS: National Infantry Museum on post, Springer Opera House, Columbus, Callaway Gardens, Pine Mountain, Ford Little White House.

FORT GILLEM (GA21R1)
Building 101, Hood Avenue
Forest Park, GA 30050-5000

TELEPHONE NUMBER INFORMATION: Main installation numbers: C-404-362-7311, D-312-797-7311.

LOCATION: From I-75, east on I-285 to I-675, south to Fort Gillem exit, right to Anvil Block Rd, go one-half mile to US-23; turn right and immediate left at light to main gate, south for three miles to the main gate. Fort is five miles from Hartsfield (Atlanta) IAP. USMRA: Page 37 (C-4), page 49 (C-4). NMC: Atlanta, 10 miles northwest.

GENERAL INFORMATION: Subpost of Fort McPherson. Headquarters 2nd US Army, 2nd US Army Recruiting Brigade (SW), 3rd CID Region, Army CID Lab, Army and Air Force Exchange Distribution Region, and other tenant agencies.

TEMPORARY MILITARY LODGING: Lodging office, Bldg. 817, Hood Ave, 0730-1600 Mon-Fri, C-404-363-5431, D-312-797-5431. All ranks. DV/VIP 404-363-5431.

LOGISTICAL SUPPORT: Most support facilities available.

Chaplain-362-7395   Commissary-363-5126   EM Club-363-3530
Exchange-363-5430   Family Services-362-7764   Fire Dept-363-5532
ITT Office-363-5584   NCO Club-363-3530   O'Club-363-3830
Package Store-363-9047   Police-363-5981   Recreation-363-5853
SATO-363-5737

HEALTH & WELFARE: None. See Fort McPherson listing, C-404-752-2184. Inpatient, see Robins AFB listing, C-912-926-2354. Chapels serving all faiths C-404-363-7395.

RECREATION: Bowling EX-5460, Golf EX-5853, Gym EX-5853, Library EX-2568, Rec Center EX-5853, Skeet EX-5316, Tennis EX-5853, Youth Center EX-5520.

GEORGIA
Fort Gillem, continued

SPACE-A: None. See Dobbins AFB listing, C-404-919-4903, D-312-925-4903, Fax 404-919-5105.

ATTRACTIONS: Atlanta Braves, Six Flags, Stone Mountain.

FORT GORDON
HEADQUARTERS US ARMY SIGNAL CENTER (GA09R1)
Building 29808, Chamberlain Avenue
Fort Gordon, GA 30905-5650

TELEPHONE NUMBER INFORMATION: Main installation numbers: C-706-791-0110, D-312-780-0110.

LOCATION: Between US-78/278 and US-1. Gates are on both US-78 & US-1. USMRA: Page 37 (F-4). NMC: Augusta, 12 miles northeast.

GENERAL INFORMATION: 15th Regimental Signal Brigade, Regimental Noncommissioned Officer Academy, Dwight David Eisenhower Army Medical Center, 63rd Signal Battalion, 67th Signal Battalion, 73rd Ordnance Battalion, 513th Military Intelligence Brigade, Regional Signal Intelligence Operations Center.

TEMPORARY MILITARY LODGING: Lodging office, Griffith Hall, Bldg. 250, Chamberlain Ave, 0730-2400 daily, C-706-791-2277/3103, D-312-780-2277. Stinson Guest House C-706-793-7160.

LOGISTICAL SUPPORT: Complete support facilities available.

ACS-791-3579
Child Care-791-2701
EM Club-793-0220
Gas Station-793-8363
Locator-791-4675
O'Club-791-2205
Public Affairs-791-7003
SDO/NCO-791-4517
CHAMPUS-791-6261
Commissary-791-3718
Exchange-793-7171
ITR Office-791-3704
Medical-791-5811
Package Store-793-5366
Retiree Services-791-4745
Signal Club-771-6921
Chaplain-791-4683
Conv Store-793-1160
Family Services-791-6967
Legal-791-7813
NCO Club-791-6780
Police-791-4380
SATO-793-0626
Theater-791-3982

HEALTH & WELFARE: Dwight David Eisenhower Army Medical Center, Information: C-706-791-5811, Family Practice Appointments: C-706-791-7300. Chapels serving all faiths C-706-791-6667/4220.

RECREATION: Bowling EX-3446, Gyms EX-2864/3692, Golf 791-2433, Library EX-2449, Riding Stables EX-4864, Rec Center 541-1057, Swimming EX-3034, Fish and Wildlife EX-5025, Youth Activities EX-5104. Recreation Area off base, year round, C-706-541-1057, nine cabins, eight mobile homes, one bunk house, 60 camper spaces w/full hookups, 30 camper spaces w/E, 50 tent spaces.

SPACE-A: May be obtained through the Fort Gordon Operational Support Airlift. C-706-791-6251/2019.

ATTRACTIONS: Augusta Masters Golf Tournament, many golf courses, and historical sites in old Augusta.

U.S. FORCES TRAVEL & TRANSFER GUIDE U.S.A. - 109

GEORGIA

FORT McPHERSON (GA08R1)
Bldg 65
Fort McPherson, GA 30330-5000

TELEPHONE NUMBER INFORMATION: Main installation numbers: C-404-752-3113, D-312-572-3113.

LOCATION: Off I-75, take Lakewood Freeway (GA-166), exit west past MARTA Station to main gate. USMRA: Page 49 (B-3). NMC: Atlanta, in city limits.

GENERAL INFORMATION: Headquarters Forces Command, Headquarters Third Army, US Army Reserve Command.

TEMPORARY MILITARY LODGING: Billeting Office, Lodging T-22, 0630-2330 daily. C-404-752-3833/2253, D-312-572-2253/3833. DVQ: C-404-669-6196. All ranks. DV/VIP 404-752-4145.

LOGISTICAL SUPPORT: Complete support facilities available.

ACS-752-4070	CHAMPUS-752-2044	Chaplain-752-2004
Child Care-752-3945	Commissary-752-2231	Exchange-753-6258
Gas Station-753-2114	Legal-752-2626/3394	Medical-752-2184
O'Club-752-3828	Package Store-753-4537	Police-752-3050/HELP
Retiree Services-752-2183	SDO/NCO-752-2980/3602	

HEALTH & WELFARE: US Army Health Clinic, C-404-752-3139, Appointments C-404-752-2184 (Ret C-404-752-2183). Chapels serving all faiths C-404-752-3954/2315.

RECREATION: Arts/Crafts EX-2221, Auto Hobby EX-2070, Bowling EX-2479, Golf EX-2178/2078, Gym EX-3034, Library EX-2665, Rec Center EX-3677, Tickets EX-3677/4392, Youth Center EX-2763. Operates Lake Allatoona Army Recreation Area, off post, year round, C-770-974-3413, 13 camper spaces w/full hookups, six camper and 15 tent spaces, three apartment units, 25 cabins.

SPACE-A: None. See Dobbins AFB listing, C-404-919-4903, D-312-925-4903, Fax 404-919-5105.

ATTRACTIONS: Six Flags, Cyclorama, pro sports, Stone Mountain, 1996 Olympics.

FORT STEWART (GA15R1)
Fort Stewart, GA 31314-5000

TELEPHONE NUMBER INFORMATION: Main installation numbers: C-912-767-1110, D-312-870-1110.

LOCATION: On US-84. Accessible from US-17 or I-95. Also GA-119 or GA-144 crosses the post but may be closed occasionally. USMRA: Page 37 (G-7). NMC: Savannah, 35 miles northeast.

GENERAL INFORMATION: Hq 24th Infantry Division and Army support units.

110 - U.S. FORCES TRAVEL & TRANSFER GUIDE U.S.A

GEORGIA
Fort Stewart, continued

TEMPORARY MILITARY LODGING: Billeting Office, Bldg. 4951, 0730-2400 daily, C-912-767-8384, D-312-870-8384. Other hours, SDO, Bldg.1, C-912-767-8666. All ranks. DV/VIP 912-767-8610.

LOGISTICAL SUPPORT: Complete support facilities available.

ACS/AER-767-5058/5059	Chaplain-767-8801	Child Care-767-2311
Commissary-767-4191	Conv Store-876-8434	Consolidated Club-767-2837
EM Club-767-5604	Exchange-876-2850	Family Services-767-8549
Fire Dept-767-7003	Gas Station-876-8434	Golf Course-767-2370
ITT Office-767-4363	Legal-767-8809	Locator-767-2862
Medical-767-66633	Package Store-368-5080	Police-767-2822
Public Affairs-767-5457	Retiree Services-767-5013	SATO-767-3642
SDO/NCO-767-8666	Snack Bar-876-2782	Theater-767-7083
Tri Care-767-6015	Visitor Center-767-5058	

HEALTH & WELFARE: Winn Army Community Hospital, clinics and depts, Emergency C-912-767-6666, Appointments C-912-767-6609, 165 beds. Chapel serving all faiths C-912-767-4219.

RECREATION: Arts/Crafts EX-2515, Archery/Rifle Range EX-5032, Auto Hobby EX-3527, Bowling EX-4127/4866, Comm Rec Center EX-2191, Golf EX-2370, Gym EX-3031/8894/7090, Library EX-2828, Music Center EX-2180, Indoor Swimming EX-3034, Outdoor Swimming EX-8575, Performing Arts EX-3410, Rec Equip EX-2988, Skeet EX-3519, Teen Club EX-2815, Youth Center EX-4491. Holbrook Pond Recreation Area and Campground on post, year round, C-912-767-2717, D-312-870-2717, 20 camper spaces w/W&E hookups, 20 camper spaces w/W hookups.

SPACE-A: Try Savannah IAP, C-912-964-1941, D-312-860-8210, flights to CONUS and OCONUS destinations via C-130H aircraft. Also see Hunter Army Airfield.

ATTRACTIONS: Tybee, Jekyll, and St. Catherines Islands off coast of Georgia; fishing, beaches, and boating; Savannah and other historic sites; Cumberland Island National Seashore; Okefenokee Swamp National Wildlife Refuge. Hunting and fishing on Fort Stewart.

HUNTER ARMY AIRFIELD (GA10R1)
1252 Strachan Drive
Savannah, GA 31409-5003

TELEPHONE NUMBER INFORMATION: Main installation numbers: C-912-767-1110, D-312-870-1110.

LOCATION: From I-95 to GA-204 east for 13 miles to Savannah. Turn left onto Stephenson Ave, to Wilson Ave Gate to Installation. USMRA: Page 37 (H-7). NMC: Savannah, in southwest part of city.

GENERAL INFORMATION: Aviation and other Army support battalions, Ranger Battalion.

TEMPORARY MILITARY LODGING: Lodging office, Bldg. 6010, Duncan & Leonard St, 0730-2400 Mon-Fri, 0800-1700 Sat, Sun, Holidays, C-912-352-5910/5834, D-312-971-

GEORGIA
Hunter Army Airfield, continued

5910/5834, other hours, Bldg. 1201, 352-5140. All ranks. DV/VIP C-912-355-8610, D-312-870-8610.

LOGISTICAL SUPPORT: Complete support facilities available.

ACS-352-5163	CHAMPUS-352-5552	Chaplain-352-5111
Child Care-352-5261	Commissary-352-5007	Conv Store-354-0075
Dining Facility-352-6209	Exchange-352-5336	Family Services-352-5259
Fire Dept-352-5600	ITT Office-352-6439	Legal-352-5115
Locator-767-2863	Medical-352-5551	NCO Club-352-5262
O'Club-352-5270	Package Store-354-8752	Police-352-6133
Public Affairs-352-5994	SATO-352-5610	SDO/NCO-352-5000
Snack Bar-354-7946	Theater-352-5556	

HEALTH & WELFARE: Tuttle Army Health Clinic, Emergency C-912-233-5700/5551. Inpatient, see Fort Stewart listing, C-912-767-6609. Chapels serving all faiths C-912-352-5111.

RECREATION: Rec Center EX-5430, Bowling EX-5205/6279, Gym EX-5078/6351, Auto Crafts EX-6244, Craft Shops EX-5025, Racquet Courts, Library EX-5816/5688, Swimming EX-5562, Golf (18 hole) EX-5622, Ball Fields, Skeet/Trap Range EX-6148, Rec Equipment EX-5274/5722. Lotts Island Army/Air Force Travel Camp on post, year round, C-912-352-5274, D-312-870-5722, 15 camper/tent spaces w/W hookups.

SPACE-A: Very Limited. Army Ops, Hunter AAF, limited flights via executive aircraft, C-912-352-5030. Also, Savannah CGAS at Hunter AAF Ops, limited flights, C-912-352-6035.

ATTRACTIONS: Historic Savannah, period homes, General Sherman's headquarters, Cotton Exchange, Fort Pulaski and Fort McAllister.

KINGS BAY NAVAL SUBMARINE BASE (GA03R1)
1063 USS Tennessee Ave
Kings Bay, GA 31547-2606

TELEPHONE NUMBER INFORMATION: Main installation numbers: C-912-673-2000, D-312-573-2111.

LOCATION: Off I-95 north of GA/FL border. Take Exit 1 which leads right into base, or Exits 2A or 2B, east to Kings Bay Road and follow the road north to base. USMRA: Page 37 (G-9). NMC: Jacksonville, FL, 40 miles south.

GENERAL INFORMATION: East Coast Submarine Base, Headquarters Submarine Squadron 20. Home of the East Coast Trident submarines and headquarters of Submarine Group 10 Commander.

TEMPORARY MILITARY LODGING: Lodging office, Bldg. 1051-N, James Madison Rd, 0800-1630 Mon-Fri, C-912-673-2163, D-312-573-2163. DV/VIP 912-673-2165, Fax 912-673-2752. Navy Lodge, Bldg. 0158, C-912-882-6868.

LOGISTICAL SUPPORT: Most support facilities available.

Cafeteria-882-6229	CDO/OOD-673-2020	CHAMPUS-673-2928 ext.4228
Chaplain-673-4501	Child Care*-2043	Commissary-673-3310
Conv Store-882-6944	CPO Club*-8999	EM Club*- 8999

112 - U.S. FORCES TRAVEL & TRANSFER GUIDE U.S.A

GEORGIA
Kings Bay Naval Submarine Base, continued

Exchange-882-6098	Family Services-673-4512	Fire Dept-673-2263
Gas Station-882-6945	Golf Course*-8476	ITT*-2289
Legal-673-2025	Locator*-3980	Medical-673-4247/4215
MWR*-ext. 2041	NCO Club*-ext. 8999	O' Club*-8999
Package Store*-3104	Police-673-2265	Public Affairs-673-4714
Recreation*-8103	Retiree Services*-4517	SATO*-2230
Snack Bar-882-6229	Visitor Center*-2272	

*Dial 673-2001 then the number listed.

HEALTH & WELFARE: Medical/Dental Clinics, Emergency C-912-673-3333. Inpatient, see Jacksonville NAS, FL listing. C-904-777-7300. Chapel serving all faiths C-912-673-4501.

RECREATION: Bowling, Gym, Golf, Swimming, Racquetball Courts, Outdoor Sport Fields, Rec Equip, Auto Hobby, Ceramics, Library, Picnic Area, Tennis Courts, Boat and Camping Trailer Rental, Fresh and Salt Water Fishing.

SPACE-A: None. See Jacksonville NAS, FL listing, C-904-772-3956/3825, D-312-942-3956/3825, Fax 904-942-2514.

ATTRACTIONS: Beautiful beaches, sport fishing, hunting, Cumberland Island, and Jekyll and St Simons Islands are one hour drives north.

MOODY AIR FORCE BASE (GA02R1)
5251 Berger Street, Suite 3
Moody Air Force Base, GA 31699-1795

TELEPHONE NUMBER INFORMATION: Main installation numbers: C-912-257-4211, D-312-460-1110.

LOCATION: On GA-125, 10 miles north of Valdosta. Also, can be reached from I-75, via GA-122. USMRA: Page 37 (D,E-9). NMC: Valdosta, 10 miles south.

GENERAL INFORMATION: Air Combat Command Base, New Composite Wing—52nd Airlift Squadron.

TEMPORARY MILITARY LODGING: Billeting Office, Bldg. 3131, Cooney St, 24 hours daily, C-912-257-3893, D-312-460-3893. All ranks. DV/VIP 912-257-3480.

LOGISTICAL SUPPORT: Complete support facilities available.

Cafeteria-257-3031	CHAMPUS-257-3799	Chaplain-257-3211
Child Care-257-3935	Cmd Post-257-3503	Commissary-257-3365
Conv Store-257-3876	Exchange-257-3431	Family Services-257-3333
Gas Station-257-3451	Legal-257-3414	Locator-257-3585/3516
Medical-257-2778	NCO Club-257-3794	O'Club-257-3351
Package Store-257-4166	Police-257-3200/3108	Retiree Services-257-3315
SATO-257-3307	Snack Bar-257-3093	Theater-257-3557

HEALTH & WELFARE: USAF Hospital, Acute Care Clinic C-912-257-3232, Appointments C-912-257-3816, 15 beds. Chapels serving all faiths C-912-257-3211/3646.

GEORGIA
Moody Air Force Base, continued

RECREATION: Bowling EX-3872, Golf EX-3297, Auto Hobby EX-3056, Ceramics EX-3452, Wood Hobby EX-3452, Library EX-3539, Fitness Center EX-3348, Rec Center EX-3280, Swimming EX-3560/3864, Youth Center EX-3067. Grassy Pond Rec Area off base, year round, C-912-559-5840, D-312-460-5840, 13 cabins, 18 camper spaces w/full hookups, many tent spaces.

SPACE-A: Pax Term, Bldg. 8153, 0700-2300 Mon-Fri, 0800-1600 Sat, Sun, Holidays, C-912-257-2465, D-312-460-2465, flights to CONUS locations. Also see Jacksonville NAS, FL listing.

ATTRACTIONS: Crystal Lake, 40 miles north.

ROBINS AIR FORCE BASE (GA14R1)
215 Page Road, Suite 106
Robins Air Force Base, GA 31098-1662

TELEPHONE NUMBER INFORMATION: Main installation numbers: C-912-926-1113, D-312-468-1001.

LOCATION: Off US-129 on GA-247 at Warner Robins. Access from I-75 S. USMRA: Page 37 (D-6). NMC: Macon, 18 miles northwest.

GENERAL INFORMATION: Air Force Materiel Command Base. Warner Robins Air Logistics Center and AFRES headquarters stationed here.

TEMPORARY MILITARY LODGING: Lodging office, Bldg. 557, Club Dr, 24 hours daily, C-912-926-2100, D-312-468-2100. All ranks. DV/VIP 912-926-2761.

LOGISTICAL SUPPORT: Complete support facilities available.

Cafeteria-922-8635	CHAMPUS-923-6118	Chaplain-926-2821
Child Care-923-6349	Commissary-926-2126	Conv Store-923-5085
Exchange-923-5536	Family Services-926-1256	Fire Dept-926-5323
Gas Station-923-7292	Golf Course-923-7334	Legal-926-5995
Locator-926-6027	Medical-926-3845	MWR-926-5491
NCO Club-923-5581	O'Club-922-3011	Package Store-926-3142
Police-926-2187	Public Affairs-926-2137	Retiree Services-926-2019
SATO-926-5363	Snack Bar-922-0136	Theater-926-2919
Visitor Center-926-4208		

HEALTH & WELFARE: USAF Hospital, Emergency C-912-926-3845, Information C-912-926-2354, 30 beds. Chapels serving all faiths C-912-926-2821/2166.

RECREATION: MWR Rentals EX-4001, Community Center EX-2105, Bowling EX-2112, Library EX-5378, Gym EX-2128, Hobby Shops EX-3004/5282, Golf EX-4103, Swimming EX-2105. Picnic Area, Skeet Range, Stables, Nature Center, Youth Center EX-4500, Aero Club EX-4867. Fam-Camp on base at Luna Lake, year round, C-912-926-4500, D-312-468-4500, 16 camper spaces with W&E hookups, 12 tent spaces.

SPACE-A: Pax Term/Lounge, Bldg. 127, 0700-1700 hours daily, C-912-926-3166, D-312-468-3166 Fax 912-926-4255, flights to CONUS locations.

GEORGIA
Robbins Air Force Base. continued

ATTRACTIONS: Macon, 4th largest city in Georgia, Andersonville Trail, Ocmulgee National Park, Robins AFB Museum of Aviation.

U.S. FORCES TRAVEL & TRANSFER GUIDE U.S.A. - 115

HAWAII

DOLLAR RENT A CAR. Call 1-800-800-4000. Get a military rate by using your Military Living ID # ML3009. Retirees/Active Duty/Reserve/Guard.

BARBERS POINT NAVAL AIR STATION (HI01R6)
Building 1
Barbers Point Naval Air Station, HI 96862-5050

Scheduled to close July 1999.

TELEPHONE NUMBER INFORMATION: Main installation numbers: C-808-684-6266, D-315-484-6266.

LOCATION: Take H-1 west (toward Waianae) to Barbers Point NAS/Makakilo exit, south for a half mile to main gate. USMRA: Page 129 (C-7). NMC: Honolulu, 15 miles east.

GENERAL INFORMATION: Tactical naval aircraft squadrons, Coast Guard Air Station and support units.

TEMPORARY MILITARY LODGING: Lodging office, Bldg. 1788, Bealleau Woods, off Enterprise, 24 hours daily, C-808-684-0687, D-315-484-0687. BEQ C-808-684-2290, D-315-484-2290, BOQ C-808-684-3191, D-315-484-3191, All ranks. DV/VIP: EM C-808-684-2290, Officers C-808-684-3191, Fax 808-684-0704.

LOGISTICAL SUPPORT: Complete support facilities available.

All Hands Club-682-4925
Chaplain-684-3111
EM Club-682-5243
Fire Department-471-7117
Legal-684-4202
MWR-684-8283
Police-684-6223
RV/Camping-682-2019
CDO/OOD-684-6266
Child Care-682-5246
Exchange-682-7330
Gas Station-682-5143
Locator-684-1005
OFC/CPO-682-4925
Public Affairs-684-7101
SATO-682-4551
CHAMPUS-474-4406
Commissary-684-0702
Family Services-684-7290
Golf Course-682-3088
Medical-684-4300
Package Store-682-3074
Recreation-682-2010/19
Snack Bar-682-5146

HEALTH & WELFARE: Naval Branch Medical Clinic C-808-684-4300, Emergency C-808-684-8244, Appointments C-808-684-6201. Inpatient, see Tripler Medical Center listing, C-808-834-8000. Chapel serving all faiths C-808-684-3111/3188.

RECREATION: Bowling, International Sports Shop, Golf, Fitness Center, Library, Swimming, Rec Center 684-8281, Tennis, Picnic Area. Recreation Area on base, year round, C-808-682-2019, 24 two-bedroom cottages, 21 camper spaces w/water faucet only.

SPACE-A: None. See Hickam AFB, C-808-449-1515/1854, D-315-448-1515/1854, Fax 808-448-1503.

ATTRACTIONS: Honolulu, beaches, island tours.

HAWAII

BARKING SANDS
PACIFIC MISSILE RANGE FACILITY (HI22R6)
P.O. Box 128
Kekaha, Kauai, HI 96752-0128

TELEPHONE NUMBER INFORMATION: Main installation numbers: C-808-335-4254, D-315-471-6254.

LOCATION: Six miles west of Kekaha on Kaumualii Highway. USMRA: Page 129 (B-2). NMC: Lihue, 30 miles east.

GENERAL INFORMATION: Naval Base with the following tenant activities: 154th Composite Group, 115th Aircraft Warning Squadron Hawaii ANG, National Bureau of Standards, Naval Undersea Warfare Engineering Station, Sandia National Laboratories, Dept of Agriculture. Operations and maintenance.

TEMPORARY MILITARY LODGING: Lodging office, Bldg. 1261, Tartar Dr, 0730-1600 daily, C-808-335-4383, D-315-471-6383, Fax 808-335-4304; Beach cottages C-808-335-4446.

LOGISTICAL SUPPORT: Complete support facilities available.

Cafeteria-335-4249
Consol Club-335-4708/09
Fire Department-335-04372
Locator-335-4254
O'Club-335-4219
Public Affairs-335-4740
Theater-335-4210

CDO/OOD-335-4254/4743
CPO Club-335-4166
Gas Station-335-4347
Medical-335-4203
Package Store-335-4202
Recreation-335-4446
Visitor Center-335-4221

Child Care-335-4453
Exchange-335-4300
Legal-335-4732
MWR-335-4446
Police-335-4649/4523
Snack Bar-335-4708

HEALTH & WELFARE: Outpatient, Garden Island Medical Group, Inc, Waimea C-808-338-1645; Inpatient, Kauai Veterans Memorial Hospital C-808-338-9431. CHAMPUS advisor, Hawaii Medical Service Association, C-808-944-2281. No chapel on base.

RECREATION: Arts/Crafts 335-4303, Auto Hobby 335-4439, Bowling 335-4379, Camping Equipment 335-4379, Ceramics 335-4303, Off-Post Camping 335-6061, Gym 335-4379, Racquetball/Tennis 335-4446, Recreation Equipment 335-4379, Recreation Center 335-4379, MWR 335-4446, Swimming 335-4391, Wood Hobby 335-4438. Beach cottages on base, year round, C-808-335-4255, D-312-471-6255, 10 two-bedroom cottages.

SPACE-A: Air Ops, Bldg. 300, C-808-335-4310, D-315-471-6310.

ATTRACTIONS: Beaches, hiking and camping; beautiful countryside, views, sunsets; Kalalau Lookout..."Wettest spot on Earth,"..."The Garden Island."

BELLOWS AIR FORCE STATION (HI18R6)
220 Tinker Road
Waimanalo, HI 96795-1010

TELEPHONE NUMBER INFORMATION: Main installation numbers: C-808-259-8080.

HAWAII
Bellows Air Force Station, continued

LOCATION: On the eastern shore of Oahu. From Honolulu, take H-1 east to HI-61, north to HI-72, south to AFS. Clearly marked. USMRA: Page 129 (E-7). NMC: Kaneohe, nine miles northwest.

GENERAL INFORMATION: Pacific Air Force Base, recreation center for uniformed services personnel and families, and Marine training area.

TEMPORARY MILITARY LODGING: Bellows Recreation Center, 220 Tinker Rd, From U.S. mainland 1-800-437-2607, C-808-259-8080, Fax 808-259-5972.

LOGISTICAL SUPPORT: Limited support facilities available.

Exchange-259-5913   Police-259-4200   Recreation-259-4121
Snack Bar-259-4110

HEALTH & WELFARE: None. See Kaneohe MCAS listing, C-808-257-3133. Inpatient, see Tripler Medical Center listing, C-808-834-8000. No chapel on base.

RECREATION: Golf Driving Range EX-4121, Recreation equipment checkout and miniature golf EX-4121. Beach cottages on base, year round, C-808-259-8841/5749 or 1-800-259-8841, 97 cottages.

SPACE-A: None. See Hickam AFB listing, C-808-449-1515/1854, D-315-449-1515/1854, Fax 808-448-1503.

ATTRACTIONS: Great beaches on windward side of Island of Oahu. Watch out for the strong undertow. Blow Hole is nearby, and beautiful Kaneohe Bay.

CAMP H. M. SMITH MARINE CORPS BASE (HI15R6)
Camp H. M. Smith, HI 96861-5001

TELEPHONE NUMBER INFORMATION: Main installation numbers: C-808-477-5106, D-315-477-5106.

LOCATION: Off H-1 west in Halawa Heights. Take Halawa Heights Road. Clearly marked. USMRA: Page 129 (D-7), page 131 (C-1). NMC: Honolulu, 10 miles southeast.

GENERAL INFORMATION: Headquarters US Pacific Command, Headquarters Commander Marine Forces Pacific and support units.

TEMPORARY MILITARY LODGING: None, see Fort Shafter listing, C-808-839-2336, D-315-438-1102.

LOGISTICAL SUPPORT: Most support facilities available.

CHAMPUS-474-4406   Chaplain-477-6461   EM Club-477-0807
Exchange-488-1234   Family Services-474-2220   Gas Station-477-6358
Legal-477-6362   Locator-477-0344   Medical-477-5036
O'Club-484-9322   Police-477-6330   Retiree Services-471-3345
SATO-487-1567   SDO/NCO-477-5106   SNCO Club-484-9322

HEALTH & WELFARE: Emergency C-808-477-6411. Inpatient, see Tripler Army Medical Center listing, C-808-834-8000. Chapel serving all faiths C-808-477-6461.

HAWAII
Camp H.M. Smith Marine Corps Base, continued

RECREATION: Bowling EX-6382, Riding EX-9417, Fitness Center EX-5197, Racquet Sports EX-5176, Rec Equip EX-5197, Special Services EX-5141, Swimming EX-5067, Tickets EX-5143. Camp Hawkins Campground 484-9417.

SPACE-A: None. See Hickam AFB listings, C-808-449-1515/1854, D-315-449-1515/1854, Fax 808-448-1503.

ATTRACTIONS: Beautiful view of Honolulu and Pearl Harbor.

FORT DeRUSSY HALE KOA HOTEL AFRC (HI08R6)
2055 Kalia Road
Honolulu, HI 96815-1998

TELEPHONE NUMBER INFORMATION: Main installation numbers: C-808-955-0555 (24 hours); 800-367-6027 from CONUS (0800-1600 hours daily HI time except holidays).

LOCATION: On Fort DeRussy at 2055 Kalia Road, Waikiki Beach, Oahu. Fort DeRussy is between Ala Moana Blvd, Kalakaua Ave & Saratoga Rd, nine miles east of Honolulu IAP. USMRA: Page 129 (D,E-7,8), pg 131 (F-4). NMC: Honolulu, in city limits.

GENERAL INFORMATION: Hale Koa Hotel and Armed Forces Recreation Center, Fort DeRussy Military Museum.

TEMPORARY MILITARY LODGING: The Hale Koa Hotel, two towers with 815 guest rooms, A/C and all modern resort hotel facilities. First class beachfront resort built by and run for active duty and retired uniformed personnel of all services. Rates from $48 to $132 per room per night, double occupancy. *For complete details on eligibility, rate structure and facilities, see Military Living's *"Temporary Military Lodging Around The World"* or *"Military RV, Camping & Rec Areas Around The World"*. Reservations may be made up to one year in advance.

LOGISTICAL SUPPORT: Most support facilities available.

Activity Desk-955-0555	Coffee House-955-0555	Dining Room-955-0555
Exchange-955-0060	Lounge-955-0555	Tour Office-955-0555
Snack Bar-955-0555		

HEALTH & WELFARE: None. see Tripler Army Medical Center listing, C-808-834-8000. Chapel located on Fort DeRussy, one-half block from Hale Koa Hotel.

RECREATION: Athletic Fields, Racquetball, Handball, Tennis, Swimming, Volleyball, Fitness Center.

SPACE-A: None. See Hickam AFB listing, C-808-449-1854, D-315-449-1854, Fax 808-448-1503.

ATTRACTIONS: Zoo, resort hotels, entertainment, beaches, water sports, military museum. Hale Koa Hotel entertainment includes: Magic Show with Mexican/Italian dinner buffet, Luau on the beach and Tama's Polynesian Revue.

U.S. FORCES TRAVEL & TRANSFER GUIDE U.S.A. - 119

HAWAII

FORT SHAFTER (HI09R6)
Fort Shafter, HI 96858-5100

TELEPHONE NUMBER INFORMATION: Main installation numbers: C-808-471-7110.

LOCATION: Take H-1 west, exit at Fort Shafter. Clearly marked. USMRA: Page 129 (D-7), Page 131 (D,E-1,2). NMC: Honolulu, seven miles east.

GENERAL INFORMATION: US Army Pacific Command (USARPAC).

TEMPORARY MILITARY LODGING: Lodging office, Bldg. 453B, Burr Rd, 0730-1600 Mon-Fri, C-808-839-2336, D-315-438-1102. After hours, DSO, Bldg. T-100, EX-9912. All ranks. DV/VIP EX-1577.

LOGISTICAL SUPPORT: Complete support facilities available.

ACS-438-9285
Child Care-438-1151
Exchange-845-9655
ITT Office-438-1985
Package Store-845-9655
Retiree Services-438-2798
Theater-438-9979

CHAMPUS-831-4450
Commissary-438-2903
Fire Dept-471-7117
Legal-438-2945
Police-438-7114
SATO-841-1941

Chaplain-8364599
Consol Club-438-1974
Gas Station-848-0404
Locator-655-2299
Public Affairs-438-2471
SDO/NCO-438-2255

HEALTH & WELFARE: None. see Tripler Medical Center listing, C-808-834-8000. Chapels serving all faiths C-808-438-1939.

RECREATION: Athletic Fields 433-6443, Bowling 438-9996, Golf 438-9587, Hobby Shops 438-1071, Handball/Racquetball 438-1152, Special Services 655-9238, Rec Center 438-1152, Swimming 438-1798, Tennis 655-9238, Youth Activities 438-1159.

SPACE-A: None. See Hickam AFB listing.

ATTRACTIONS: Honolulu, USS Arizona National Memorial, National Memorial Cemetery of the Pacific (Punch Bowl), Pearl Harbor.

HICKAM AIR FORCE BASE (HI11R6)
800 Scott Circle
Hickam Air Force Base, HI 96853-5328

TELEPHONE NUMBER INFORMATION: Main installation numbers: C-808-471-7110, D-315-471-7110.

LOCATION: Adjacent to the Honolulu IAP. Accessible from H-1 or Nimitz Highway. Clearly marked. USMRA: Page 129 (D-7) Page 131 (B,C-2,3,4). NMC: Honolulu, six miles east.

GENERAL INFORMATION: Pacific Air Force Base. Headquarters PACAF, 65th Airlift Squadron, 15th Air Base Wing Support Units.

TEMPORARY MILITARY LODGING: Lodging office, Bldg. 1153, 24 hours daily, C-808-449-2603, D-315-449-2603. All ranks. DV/VIP C-808-449-1781.

120 - U.S. FORCES TRAVEL & TRANSFER GUIDE U.S.A

HAWAII
Hickam Air Force Base, continued

LOGISTICAL SUPPORT: Complete support facilities available.

Cafeteria-422-8000	Chaplain-449-1754	Child Dev Center-449-6898
Commissary-449-7693	Conv Store-422-8404	Exchange-422-1304
Family Services-449-2494	Fire Dept-449-7117	Gas Station-422-8744
Golf Course-449-2525	Legal-449-1737	Locator-449-0165
Medical-448-6000	MWR-449-6721	NCO Club-449-1292
O'Club-449-1998	Police-449-2200	Public Affairs-449-2490
Recreation-449-1334	Retiree Services-449-9896	SATO-422-0548
Snack Bar-422-8008	Theater-449-2239	TRICARE-448-6120
Visitor Center-449-1083		

HEALTH & WELFARE: USAF Clinic, Emergency C-808-449-7116, Appointments C-808-449-9901, Acute Care Services C-808-448-6189. Inpatient, see Tripler Medical Center listing, C-808-834-8000. Chapel serving all faiths C-808-449-1754.

RECREATION: Arts/Crafts EX-2148, Auto Hobby EX-2554, Athletic Fields EX-6686, BMX Track EX-6721, Bowling EX-2702, Fitness Center EX-1044, Golf EX-6490/2093, Gym EX-6711, Tickets and Tours EX-2230, Marina EX-5215, Rec Center EX-3354, Rec Equip EX-6870, MWR EX-6721, Skating Rink/Skateboard Center EX-6721, Swimming EX-6573/1070, Tennis EX-2598/5389, Library EX-2831, Outdoor Rec EX-5215, Youth Center EX-1492.

SPACE-A: Pax Term/Lounge, Bldg. 2028, 24 hours daily, C-808-22-2729, D-315-449-1854, Fax 808-448-1503. Flights to CONUS and overseas locations.

ATTRACTIONS: Honolulu, Waikiki Beaches and Pearl Harbor.

HONOLULU COAST GUARD BASE
AND COAST GUARD HOUSING RED HILL (HI21R6)
Honolulu, HI 96819-4398

TELEPHONE NUMBER INFORMATION: Main installation numbers: C-808-541-2490/1, D-315-430-0111. NOTE: Prefix of 833 or 839 indicates activity is located at Red Hill.

LOCATION: Take H-1 and exit at HI-64 south to Sand Island Access Road to base. USMRA: Page 129 (D-7) Page 131 (C,D-1,2). NMC: Honolulu, in city limits.

GENERAL INFORMATION: The largest operating unit in the 14th Coast Guard District is located at Sand Island. Personnel perform all Coast Guard functions with the exception of ice-breaking.

TEMPORARY MILITARY LODGING: None. See Hickam Air Force Base listing, C-808-449-2603, D-315-449-2603.

LOGISTICAL SUPPORT: Limited support facilities available.

Consol Club-541-2475	Exchange-541-2499	Gas Station-833-2448/72
Package Store-541-2499	SATO-541-2468	

HEALTH & WELFARE: Dispensary C-808-541-2405.

HAWAII
Honolulu Coast Guard Base, continued

RECREATION: Gym/Weight Room EX-2415, Tennis EX-2415, Racquet Courts 833-9632, Swimming 833-9632, Tennis 833-9632, Athletic Field EX-2413, Auto Hobby EX-2416, Tickets EX-2413, Special Services 833-9632, Teen Club 833-7850.

SPACE-A: None. See Hickam AFB listing, C-808-449-1854, D-315-449-1854, Fax 808-448-1503.

ATTRACTIONS: Honolulu, island tours, helicopter tours, USS Arizona Memorial and USS Bowfin Submarine Exhibit, Waikiki Beach, Diamond Head, National Memorial Cemetery of the Pacific.

KANEOHE MARINE CORPS BASE (HI12R6)
Box 63002
Kaneohe Bay, HI 96863-5001

TELEPHONE NUMBER INFORMATION: Main installation numbers: C-808-471-7110, D-315-471-7110.

LOCATION: At end of H-3 on the Windward side of Oahu. Off Mokapu Blvd and Kaneohe Bay Drive. Clearly marked. USMRA: Page 129 (E-6). NMC: Honolulu, 14 miles southwest.

GENERAL INFORMATION: 3rd Combat Service Support Group, Air Support Element of the 1st Marine Aircraft Wing, a number of separate battalions and other units.

TEMPORARY MILITARY LODGING: Lodging office, Bldg. 3038, 0630-1800 Mon-Fri, 0900-1800 Sat, Sun, Holidays, C-808-257-2409, D-315-457-2409. All ranks. DV/VIP 477-6891.

LOGISTICAL SUPPORT: Complete support facilities available.

CHAMPUS-257-2145	Chaplain-257-3552/3506	Child Care-254-5335
Commissary-257-2383	EM Club-254-4648	Exchange-254-5871
Family Services-254-1592	Gas Station-254-6764	Golf Course-254-1745
ITT Office-254-3304	Legal-257-2160/2168	Medical-257-3133
MWR-254-7515	O'Club-254-5166	Package Store-254-4913
PMO-257-7114/2124	Public Affairs-257-2728	SDO/NCO-257-1829
Seven-Day Store-254-3946	SNCO Club-254-5592	Theater-254-2113

HEALTH & WELFARE: Naval Branch Medical Clinic, Emergency C-808-257-3133. Inpatient, see Tripler Army Medical Center listing, C-808-834-8000. Chapels serving all faiths C-808-257-3506.

RECREATION: Athletic Fields EX-2458, Beaches EX-2716, Bowling (K-Bay Lanes) EX-4980, Golf EX-1745, Gym EX-2658, Handball/Racquetball EX-2516, Library EX-6301, Marina EX-5606, Scuba Locker EX-5709, Station Pool EX-6278, Tennis EX-2516. Beach Cottages and Campsites on base, year round, C-808-254-2806, D-315-430-3513, 24 studio units, 11 cottages,; 4 camper spaces w/W hookups.

SPACE-A: None. See Hickam AFB listing, C-808-449-1854, D-315-449-1854, Fax 808-448-1503.

ATTRACTIONS: Kaneohe Bay, beaches, outdoor sports, historical sites, and wildlife refuges.

HAWAII

KILAUEA MILITARY CAMP AFRC (HI17R6)
Bldg. 40 Attn: Reservations
Hawaii Volcanoes National Park, HI 96718-5000

TELEPHONE NUMBER INFORMATION: Main installation numbers: C-808-967-7315.

LOCATION: On island of Hawaii, 216 air miles southeast of Honolulu, 32 miles from Hilo IAP. Scheduled bus transportation to camp: reservations required Hilo to KMC. USMRA: Page 129 (I,J-6,7). NMC: Hilo, 32 miles northwest.

GENERAL INFORMATION: Armed Forces Recreation Center, Kilauea Military Camp (KMC). A resort for uniformed services personnel, retirees, DoD civilians and their families.

TEMPORARY MILITARY LODGING: Lodging office, 0800-1630 Mon-Thu, 0800-1830 Fri, C-808-967-8333/43; direct from Oahu C-438-6707. All ranks. 52 cabins, six apartments and two dormitories. Reservations required.

LOGISTICAL SUPPORT: Limited support facilities available.

Cafeteria-967-8355   Country Store-967-8364   Gas Station-967-8362
SDO/NCO-967-7315

HEALTH & WELFARE: US Army Troop Medical Clinic, C-808-967-8368. Inpatient, see Tripler Medical Center listing, C-808-834-8000. Catholic and Protestant services each Sunday.

RECREATION: Bowling, Bicycle Rental, Golf, Rec Room, Snack Bar, Koa Bar, Lectures, Mini Health Center, Multi-Purpose Court (Basketball, Volleyball), Tennis (two courts on camp), Rental Equip for Hiking, Tennis, Golf, and other sports. Tours—check with registration desk. Call C-808-438-6707/808-967-8333.

SPACE-A: None. See Hickam AFB listing, C-808-449-1854, D-315-449-1854, Fax 808-448-1503.

ATTRACTIONS: Tours of the Big Island—Hawaii, Hilo, Black Sands Beach, Kona, Hawaii Volcanoes National Park, active lava flows. Hula shows. Helicopter rides.

LUALUALEI NAVAL MAGAZINE (HI23R6)
3 Constellation Street
Waianae, HI 96792-4301

TELEPHONE NUMBER INFORMATION: Main installation numbers: C-808-474-4340, D-315-474-4340.

LOCATION: Follow H-1 Freeway west towards Waianae to Ewa exit. Follow Fort Weaver Rd south to Iroquois Point Rd. Turn left and travel to West Loch Branch gate. USMRA: Page 129 (B,C-7), page 131 (A,B-3,4). NMC: Honolulu, 20 miles southeast.

GENERAL INFORMATION: NUWES, SUBASE Pearl Harbor MK48 Torpedo Shop, USAO, DIO, Munitions Branch.

HAWAII
Lualualei Naval Magazine, continued

TEMPORARY MILITARY LODGING: Lodging office, Bldg. 600, Iroquois Point Dr (BEQ Gate), 0600-2300 Sun-Thu, 0700-2400 Fri-Sat, C-808-474-7908, D-315-474-7908, Fax 808-474-7919.

LOGISTICAL SUPPORT: Complete support facilities available.

CDO/OOD-474-4340	CMO Club-474-7928	Exchange-668-3386 LB
Fire Dept-474-7829	Galley-474-7844	Police-668-3261 LB
Snack Bar-668-3586 LB		474-1381 WB

Note: LB = Lualualei Branch, WB = West Loch Branch.

HEALTH & WELFARE: Barbers Point Naval Branch Medical Clinic C-808-684-8245. Inpatient, see Tripler Medical Center listing, C-808-834-8000.

RECREATION: Auto Hobby 499-2421, Camping Equip EX-7933, Rec Equip EX-7933, Rec Center EX-7933, Special Services EX-7933, Swimming EX-7933. See Barbers Point NAS and Bellows AFS listings for camping/rec areas.

SPACE-A: None. See Hickam AFB listing, C-808-449-1854, D-315-449-1854, Fax 808-448-1503.

ATTRACTIONS: Beaches, outdoor rec activities, tourist attractions.

PEARL HARBOR NAVAL BASE (HI19R6)
Box 110
Pearl Harbor Naval Base, HI 96860-5020

TELEPHONE NUMBER INFORMATION: Main installation numbers: C-808-471-7110, D-315-430-0111.

LOCATION: Off H-1 adjacent to Honolulu IAP. Clearly marked. USMRA: Page 129 (C,D-7), Page 131 (A-1,2,3; B-2,3; C-2). NMC: Honolulu, five miles east.

GENERAL INFORMATION: Headquarters Pacific Fleet, Headquarters Submarine Force Pacific, Naval Shipyard, support units and home port for approximately 40 ships.

TEMPORARY MILITARY LODGING: Lodging office, USS Arizona Hall, Bldg. 1623, 24 hours daily, C-808-471-8053, D-315-474-5210. BEQ C-808-471-0148, D-315-474-5210, BOQ C-808-474-1201, D-315-474-5210, All ranks. DV/VIP 808-474-5210, Fax 808-423-1704.

LOGISTICAL SUPPORT: Complete support facilities available.

All Hands Club-471-8455	All Hands Club-474-7235	ACS-471-9125
CDO/OOD-471-1222	CHAMPUS-474-4406	Chaplain-471-3971
Child Care-422-7133	Commissary-471-0263	Conv Store-423-3217
EM Club-471-0841	Exchange-423-3344	Family Services-474-4222
Fire Dept-471-7117	Gas Station-423-3229	Golf Course-471-0348
ITT Office-474-7521	Legal-471-0291	Medical-471-9541
MWR-471-0818	Package Store-423-3254	Police-471-7114
Public Affairs-471-0281	Recreation-474-1198	SATO-423-8770
Theater-471-0726		

124 - U.S. FORCES TRAVEL & TRANSFER GUIDE U.S.A

HAWAII
Pearl Harbor Naval Base, continued

HEALTH & WELFARE: Naval Medical Clinic, Emergency C-808-471-7116. Inpatient, see Tripler Medical Center listing, C-808-834-8000. Chapel serving all faiths C-808-471-3971.

RECREATION: Athletic Fields 474-0786, Bloch Arena 474-0786, Bowling 471-2162, Dependents Activities Center 471-0392, Golf 471-03478, Special Services Office 471-3169/474-6156, Swimming 471-9307, Tennis/Racquetball 471-0610, Video Games 471-2581.

SPACE-A: None. See Hickam AFB listing, C-808-449-1854, D-315-449-1854, Fax 808-448-1503.

ATTRACTIONS: USS Arizona Memorial and Visitor Center, and USS Bowfin Submarine Exhibit.

PEARL HARBOR NAVAL STATION (HI20R6)
Pearl Harbor, HI 96860-5000

TELEPHONE NUMBER INFORMATION: Main installation numbers: C-808-471-7110.

LOCATION: From Honolulu IAP, take Highway one west. Follow signs for Pearl Harbor/Hickam AFB. Take exit for Pearl Harbor and ask guard at Nimitz gate for further directions. USMRA: Page 129 (C-7). NMC: Honolulu five miles east.

GENERAL INFORMATION: Naval Logistics Support and Receiving Station.

TEMPORARY MILITARY LODGING: Bldg. 1315, 0700-1600 daily, C-808-471-1226. BEQ C-808-471-9188, D-315-471-9188, BOQ C-808-471-0445, D-315-471-0445. DV/VIP C-808-422-9494, Fax 808-491-2944.

LOGISTICAL SUPPORT: Complete support facilities available.

CHAMPUS-474-4406
Commissary-471-0263
EM Club-471-0841
Gas Station-423-3229
ITT Office-474-6156
Medical-471-9541
Package Store-423-3254
Quarterdeck-474-6249
SATO-423-8770
Visitor Center-471-3627

Chaplain-471-3971
Conv Store-423-3250
Exchange-423-3344
Golf Course-471-0348
Legal-471-0291
MWR-471-0818
Police-474-7182
Restaurant-471-0593
Snack Bar-471-1746

Child Care-422-7133
CPO Club-471-8166
Family Services-474-2220
Galley-474-8488
Locator-471-7110
O'Club-471-1702
Public Affairs-471-0818
Retiree Services-449-9896
Theater-471-0726

HEALTH & WELFARE: Makalepa Base Clinic, C-808-471-9541, Emergency C-808-471-7116, Appointments C-808-471-7117. Chapel serving all faiths C-808-471-3971.

RECREATION: Auto Hobby EX-9072, Bowling 474-2162, Camping & Rec Gear rental 472-7582, Dive Shop 422-PADI, Golf Course EX-0348, Library EX-8238, Gym/Aerobics EX-1198, Rec Center 474-0787, Marina EX-9680, Swimming Pool EX-9723/474-7122, YMCA EX-3398, Youth Activities EX-1409/474-3071.

HAWAII
Pearl Harbor Naval Station, continued

SPACE-A: None. See Hickam AFB listing, C-808-449-1854, D-315-449-1854, Fax 808-448-1503.

ATTRACTIONS: Diamond Head, beaches, island tours, Polynesian Cultural Center.

SCHOFIELD BARRACKS (HI13R6)
Schofield Barracks, HI 96857-6000

TELEPHONE NUMBER INFORMATION: Main installation numbers: C-808-471-7110, D-315-430-0111.

LOCATION: Off H-2 or HI-99 in the center of the island of Oahu. Clearly marked. USMRA: Page 129 (C-6). NMC: Honolulu, 20 miles southeast.

GENERAL INFORMATION: 25th Infantry Division (Light) and U.S. Army Hawaii.

TEMPORARY MILITARY LODGING: Lodging office, Bldg. 692, McCornack Rd, 0730-1600 Mon-Fri, C-808-624-9877 All ranks. The new Inn at Schofield Barracks C-808-624-9650 is complete with 192 guest rooms.

LOGISTICAL SUPPORT: Complete support facilities available.

Chaplain-655-0739
Conv Store-624-9825
Family Services-655-4663
Locator-438-2484
O'Club-624-5600
Snack Bar-624-2692
Child Care-655-3471
EM Club-624-2230
Gas Station-624-9857
Medical-655-4747
Package Store-624-2692
Theater-655-0603
Commissary-655-2369
Exchange-622-1773
Legal-655-0804
NCO Club-655-2251
Police-655-7114

HEALTH & WELFARE: US Army Health Clinic, Emergency C-808-655-4747, Appointments C-808-665-0915. Inpatient, see Tripler Medical Center listing, C-808-834-8000. Chapels serving all faiths C-808-655-9307.

RECREATION: Arts/Crafts EX-9042, Archery EX-4804, Athletic Fields EX-0900, Bowling EX-0757, Golf EX-9833, Gym EX-0900, Hobby Shops EX-0898/9042/9368, MWR Office EX-4804, Rec Equip EX-0143, Rec Center EX-9091, Library EX-0145, Swimming EX-9698, Youth Center EX-4641, Scuba EX-0143, Tennis EX-0852, Tickets EX-9972. See Bellows AFS and Fort Shafter listings for camping/rec areas.

SPACE-A: None. See Hickam AFB listing, C-808-449-1854, D-315-449-1854, Fax 808-448-1503.

ATTRACTIONS: Sugar cane and pineapple fields. Tropic Lightning Museum.

TRIPLER MEDICAL CENTER (HI03R6)
Tripler Medical Center, HI 96859-5000

TELEPHONE NUMBER INFORMATION: Main installation numbers: C-808-433-6661, D-315-433-6661.

HAWAII
Tripler Medical Center, continued

LOCATION: Take H-1 west from Honolulu to Tripler exit. Turn right on Jarrett White Rd to Tripler MC. USMRA: Page 129 (D-7) Page 131 (D-1,2). NMC: Honolulu, three miles southeast.

GENERAL INFORMATION: Tripler Medical Center is the largest military medical center in the Pacific area of operations. Tripler treats service members from all branches of the military.

TEMPORARY MILITARY LODGING: Lodging office, Bldg. 228B, Jarrett White Rd, 0600-2200 Mon-Fri, 0800-1600 Sat-Sun, C-808-433-2336, D-315-433-2336. All ranks. DV/VIP 433-2336.

LOGISTICAL SUPPORT: Complete support facilities available.

CHAMPUS-433-6330	Chaplain-433-5727	Commissary-438-1367
Exchange-833-1267	Gas Station-833-1250	ITT Office-438-1985
Legal-433-5311	Medical-433-6661	O'Club-833-1268
Patient Rep-433-6336	Retiree Services-438-2798	SATO-834-1486
SDO/NCO-433-6661	Snack Bar-833-1259	

The Aliamanu Military Reservation, a nearby housing area, has a large Exchange Shoppette 833-6997, and a Gas Station 833-6997.

HEALTH & WELFARE: Army Hospital, Ambulance C-808-433-5700, Emergency C-808-433-6629, Appointments C-808-834-8000. Chapel serving all faiths C-808-433-5727.

RECREATION: Swimming EX-5257, Gym EX-6443, Tennis EX- 6443, Racquetball/ Handball EX-6443, Golf Driving, Special Services EX-5772, Library EX-6968.

SPACE-A: None. See Hickam AFB listing, C-808-449-1854, D-315-449-1854, Fax 808-448-1503.

ATTRACTIONS: USS Arizona National Memorial, Pearl Harbor. Great view of Honolulu.

WAHIAWA NAVAL COMPUTER AND TELECOMMUNICATIONS AREA MASTER STATION, EASTERN PACIFIC [NCTAMS EASTPAC] (HI16R6)
500 Center Street
Wahiawa, HI 96786-3050

TELEPHONE NUMBER INFORMATION: Main installation numbers: C-808-653-5385, D-315-453-5385.

LOCATION: H-2 to Wahiawa, station is three miles north. USMRA: Page 129 (C-6). NMC: Honolulu, 20 miles southeast.

GENERAL INFORMATION: Naval Communications for Pacific area.

TEMPORARY MILITARY LODGING: BEQ C-808-653-5367, D-315-453-5367, Fax 808-653-4600.

LOGISTICAL SUPPORT: Limited support facilities available.

HAWAII
Wahiawa (NCTAMS), continued

CDO/OOD-653-5385
Child Care-653-5305
Family Services-653-0203
ITT Office-621-0733
Medical-653-5340
Police-653-0234
SATO-621-0733

CHAMPUS-474-4406
EM Club-653-5470
Fire Dept-653-5479
Legal-653-5397
Mini-Mart-653-5364
Public Affairs-653-5569

Chaplain-653-5577
Exchange-653-5364
Gas Station-653-5451
Locator-653-5385
MWR-653-5485
Recreation-653-5485

HEALTH & WELFARE: Naval Branch Medical Clinic, Emergency and Appointments C-808-653-5340/50. Chapels serving all faiths C-808-653-5577.

RECREATION: Arts/Crafts EX-5574, Bowling EX-5576, Gym EX-5542, Racquet Sports EX-5542, Rec Equip EX-5542, Special Services EX-0191, Swimming EX-5306.

SPACE-A: None. See Hickam AFB listing, C-808-449-1854, D-315-449-1854, Fax 808-448-1503.

ATTRACTIONS: Short drive to Honolulu, beach areas.

WAIANAE ARMY RECREATION CENTER (HI05R6)
85-010 Army Street
Waianae, HI 96792-5000

TELEPHONE NUMBER INFORMATION: Main installation numbers: C-808-696-4158 (Oahu), 1-800-847-6771 (Outer Island), 1-800-333-4158 (Mainland). D-315-430-0111.

LOCATION: HI-1 west to HI-93, west to Waianae. USMRA: Page 129 (B-6). NMC: Honolulu, 35 miles southeast.

GENERAL INFORMATION: Recreation center on the beach operated by the Army for all uniformed personnel and their families both active and retired.

TEMPORARY MILITARY LODGING: Lodging office, Bldg. 4070, 0900-1600 Mon-Fri, C-808-696-4158 (Oahu), 1-800-847-6771 (Outer Island), 1-800-333-4158 (Mainland). Thirty-nine cabins. All ranks. DV/VIP, one house.

LOGISTICAL SUPPORT: Limited support facilities available.

Beach Club-696-4778
Police-696-2811
WHRC Manager-696-6026

CHAMPUS-433-6330
Package Store-696-2886

ITT-655-9971
SATO-624-9513

HEALTH & WELFARE: None. see, Tripler Army Medical Center listing, C-808-834-8000.

RECREATION: Beach Club. All beach front sports/recreation, some recreation equipment available.

SPACE-A: None. See Hickam AFB listing, C-808-449-1854, D-315-449-1854, Fax 808-448-1503.

ATTRACTIONS: Beautiful beaches. Swimming, surfing, windsurfing.

128 - U.S. FORCES TRAVEL & TRANSFER GUIDE U.S.A
HAWAII

WHEELER ARMY AIRFIELD (HI14R6)
Wheeler Army Airfield, HI 96854-5000

TELEPHONE NUMBER INFORMATION: Main installation numbers: C-808-471-7110, D-315-471-7110.

LOCATION: Off H-2 or HI-99 in the center of the island of Oahu. Adjacent to Schofield Barracks. USMRA: Page 129 (C-6). NMC: Honolulu, 20 miles southeast.

GENERAL INFORMATION: Aviation Support for 25th INF DIV (Light), Air National Guard Aircraft Control and Warning Squadron and support units.

TEMPORARY MILITARY LODGING: None. See Schofield Barracks listing, C-808-624-9877, The new Inn at Schofield Barracks C-808-624-9650

LOGISTICAL SUPPORT: Most support facilities available.

Consol Club-656-1718   Exchange-624-9817   Gas Station-624-3451
Locator-438-2484   Medical-655-0915   Police-655-2146
Snack Bar-624-2375

HEALTH & WELFARE: Dispensary/Emergency C-808-655-0915, Appointments C-808-655-5201. Inpatient, see Tripler Medical Center listing, C-808-834-8000.

RECREATION: Athletic Fields, Bowling, Golf, Auto Hobby, Fitness Center, Gym, Special Services, Tennis, Racquetball/Handball, Armed Services "Y", Youth Activities, Library.

SPACE-A: None. See Hickam AFB listing, C-808-449-1854, D-315-449-1854, Fax 808-448-1503.

ATTRACTIONS: Numerous activities on Oahu and other islands. Pineapple and sugar cane fields.

Other Installations in Hawaii

Aliamanu Military Reservation, 1875 Aliamanu Dr., Aliamanu, HI 96854-5000.
USMRA: Page 131 (C-2). C-808-833-1185, MWR-836-0338, Service Station-833-6997.
Barbers Point Coast Guard Air Station, Barbers Point, HI 96862-5000, club facilities.
USMRA: Page 129 (C-7). C-808-682-2614, Exchange-682-2731.
Fort Ruger, Cannon Club, Honolulu, HI 96814-5000.
USMRA: Page 129 (E-8), page 131 (G-4). C-808-737-5996.
Hilo Big Island Exchange, 1300 Kekuanaua St., Bldg. 505, Hilo, HI 96720-5000.
USMRA: Page 129 (J-6). C-808-935-3449.
Maui Exchange, 1686 Kaahumanu Ave., Wailukku, HI 96793-5000.
USMRA: Page 129 (G-4). C-808-244-3006, Exchange-244-3006.

IDAHO

DOLLAR RENT A CAR — Call 1-800-800-4000. Get a military rate by using your Military Living ID # ML3009. Retirees/Active Duty/Reserve/Guard.

GOWEN FIELD (ID04R4)
4040 Guard Street
Boise, ID 83705-5004

TELEPHONE NUMBER INFORMATION: Main installation numbers: C-208-422-5011, D-312-941-5011.

LOCATION: From I-84 west, take Orchard St exit (exit 52). Turn left and remain on road as it goes behind the airport. Watch for "Gowen Field" sign near tanks. Turn left into Main Gate. USMRA: Page 98 (B-8). NMC: Boise, five miles north.

GENERAL INFORMATION: Headquarters, Idaho Army and Air National Guard, US Naval and Marine reserves, Army Armor Training Center, Combat Vehicle Transition Training Team, Regional Training Site, Maintenance, 124th Fighter Group, 116th Cavalry Brigade.

TEMPORARY MILITARY LODGING: Lodging office, Bldg. 669, 0800-1700 daily, C-208-422-6023, D-312-941-6023.

LOGISTICAL SUPPORT: Most support facilities available.

CHAMPUS-422-5027
Exchange-422-5676
Legal-422-5474
MWR-422-6703
Police-422-5366
Retiree Services-422-5817
Theater-422-6245

Chaplain-422-6467/5394
Family Services-422-5067
Locator-422-5011
NCO Club-422-5674
Public Affairs-422-5268
SATO-422-5000

Conv Store-422-5676
Fire Dept-422-5867
Medical-422-5369
O'Club-422-5667/5668
Recreation-422-5381
Snack Bar-422-5674

HEALTH AND WELFARE: None. See Mountain Home AFB listing, C-208-828-2276. Chapel serving all faiths C-208-422-5394.

RECREATION: Physical Fitness Center 422-6046, Swimming 422-5673, Softball field.

SPACE-A: None. See Mountain Home AFB listing, C-208-828-2304, D-312-728-2304, Fax 208-828-4128.

ATTRACTIONS: Boise River: trout and bass fishing, swimming, waterskiing, windsurfing, skin diving, tubing, City of Trees, with five large parks along the river. Zoo, Rose Garden, State Historical Museum, Art Museum. Bogus Basin ski area (both nordic and alpine skiing), snowmobiling.

MOUNTAIN HOME AIR FORCE BASE (ID01R4)
Mountain Home Air Force Base, ID 83648-5000

TELEPHONE NUMBER INFORMATION: Main installation numbers: C-208-828-2111, D-312-728-1110.

IDAHO
Mountain Home Air Force Base, continued

LOCATION: From Boise, take I-84 southeast, 39 miles to Mountain Home exit, follow road through town to Airbase Rd, 10 miles to main gate. USMRA: Page 98 (C-9). NMC: Boise, 51 miles northwest.

GENERAL INFORMATION: Air Combat Command Base. B-1B, F-15C, F-15E, F-16, & KC-135R Air intervention aircraft composite wing. Air-to-ground and air-to-air combat.

TEMPORARY MILITARY LODGING: Lodging office, Bldg. 2604, Falcon St, 24 hours daily, C-208-832-4661, D-312-728-6451. All ranks. DV/VIP C-208-832-4536, D-312-728-4536.

LOGISTICAL SUPPORT: Complete support facilities available.

CHAMPUS-828-7800	Chaplain-828-6417	Child Care-828-2443
Commissary-828-2286	Conv Store-828-6921	Exchange-832-4353
Family Services-828-2964	Fire Dept-828-1105/6	Gas Station-832-4459
Legal-828-2238	Locator-828-6647	Medical-828-2778
NCO/EM Club-828-2105	O'Club-828-2597	Package Store-828-6921
Police-828-2256	SATO-832-2276	SDO/NCO-828-2071
Snack Bar-828-6546	Theater-828-2431	

HEALTH & WELFARE: USAF Hospital, Emergency C-208-828-7100, Appointments C-208-828-2276, 20 beds. Chapels serving all faiths C-208-828-6417.

RECREATION: Youth Center EX-2501, Library EX-2326, Bowling EX-6329, Gym EX-2381, Swimming EX-6620, Golf EX-6151, Auto Hobby EX-2295, Arts/Crafts EX-6680, Rec Center EX-2246, Skeet/Trap EX-6093, Stables EX-4093, Rec Equip EX-2237, Outdoor Program EX-6333. Fam-Camp on base, year round, C-208-828-6333, D-312-728-6333, 22 camper spaces w/full hookups, 10 tent spaces, Strike Dam Marina off base, C-208-828-6333, Marina only. Island Park Recreation Area off base, five travel trailers. Operates Grant's Village, Yellowstone National Park, WY, off base, 15 May-15 Sep, C-208-828-6333, D-312-728-6333, six travel trailers w/full hookups.

SPACE-A: Pax Term/Lounge, Bldg. 262, 0730-1630 Mon-Fri, C-208-828-2304, D-312-857-2304, Fax 208-828-4128, flights to CONUS locations. Also, Boise Air Terminal, limited Space-A, Reserve Units, C-208-389-5303, D-312-941-5303.

ATTRACTIONS: Snow skiing, hunting, and fishing. Boise, capital city of Idaho.

ILLINOIS

DOLLAR RENT A CAR — Call 1-800-800-4000. Get a military rate by using your Military Living ID # ML3009. Retirees/Active Duty/Reserve/Guard.

CHARLES MELVIN PRICE SUPPORT CENTER (IL04R2)
Granite City, IL 62040-1801

TELEPHONE NUMBER INFORMATION: Main installation numbers: C-618-452-4212, D-312-892-4212.

LOCATION: From I-70 take McKinley Bridge exit, cross Mississippi River, follow signs to Center. From I-270, cross river bridges and take first Granite City exit (Route 3 north) to Center. USMRA: Page 64 (C,D-7). NMC: St Louis, seven miles west.

GENERAL INFORMATION: Army Area Support Center, Army Materiel Command aviation and other materiel procurement and logistical activities. Military Traffic Management Command POV processing center.

TEMPORARY MILITARY LODGING: Lodging office, Bldg. 102, Niedringhaus St, 0730-1615 daily, C-618-452-4287, D-312-892-4287. Other hours, Security Office, Bldg. 221, C-618-452-4224. All ranks.

LOGISTICAL SUPPORT: Complete support facilities available.

ACS-452-4260	CHAMPUS-314-425-4851	Chaplain-452-4277
Child Care-452-4480	Commissary-452-4232	Comm Club-452-5595
Exchange-452-5230	Family Services-452-4260	Gas Station-452-4388
ITT Office-314-263-1060	Medical-331-4851	Mil Pers-452-4422
Package Store-452-6112	Police-452-4224	POV Center-452-4650/4651
Retiree Services-452-4472	SATO-314-263-3415	SDO/NCO-452-4247

HEALTH & WELFARE: None. See Scott AFB listing, 618-256-1847. Chapel serving all faiths C-314-452-4277.

RECREATION: Auto Hobby EX-4279, Bowling EX-4319, Golf EX-4444, Library EX-4332, Rec Center EX-4398, Swimming EX-4221, Gym EX-4209.

SPACE-A: None. See Scott AFB listing, C-618-256-1854, D-312-576-1854, Fax 618-256-1948.

ATTRACTIONS: Gateway Arch, Mississippi River Tours, St Louis, Lacledes Landing, Hockey, Grants Farm, Busch Stadium, Six Flags, Kiel Auditorium, VP Fair (July), Fox Theater, Soulard Market area, museums, USS Inaugural Minesweeper.

GREAT LAKES NAVAL TRAINING CENTER (IL07R2)
2701 Sheridan Road
Great Lakes Naval Training Center, IL 60088-5000

TELEPHONE NUMBER INFORMATION: Main installation numbers: C-708-688-3500, D-312-792-3500.

ILLINOIS
Great Lakes Naval Training Center, continued

LOCATION: From I-94 north or US-41 north of Chicago, exit to IL-137 east to Sheridan Road, turn right into the gate. Clearly marked. USMRA: Page 64 (G-1). NMC: Chicago, 30 miles south.

GENERAL INFORMATION: Naval Training Center, Service School Command, Recruit Training Command, Naval Hospital, Hospital Corps School, Headquarters US Military Entrance Processing Command.

TEMPORARY MILITARY LODGING: Lodging office, Bldg. 834, 0700-1600 daily, C-708-688-2170, D-312-792-2710. Navy Lodge, Bldg. 2500, C-708-689-1485, Fax 708-689-1489. Bldg. 219-H (BEQ at Naval Hospital), 24 hours daily, C-708-688-5800, D-312-792-5800. All ranks. DV/VIP C-708-688-3777, Fax 708-688-5815.

LOGISTICAL SUPPORT: Complete support facilities available.

Cafeteria-578-6120	CDO/OOD-688-3939/3300	CHAMPUS-688-5457/60/65
Chaplain-688-5610	Child Care-688-5662	Commissary-688-2644
Conv Store-578-6247/6221	EM Club-688-4641	Exchange-578-6100
Family Services-688-3603	Fire Dept-688-3333	Gas Station-578-6198
Golf Course-688-4593	ITT-688-3537	Legal-688-3340/1
Locator-688-3415	Medical-688-5618	MWR-688-2110
Package Store-578-6247	Police-688-3333	Port-O-Call-688-6946
Public Affairs-688-2430	Recreation-688-2110	Retiree Services-688-5434
RV/Camping-688-2110	SATO-688-3481/5316	SDO/SNO-688-3500
Snack Bar-578-6120	Theater-688-6763	USO-688-5591/2274
Visitor Center-688-5670		

HEALTH & WELFARE: US Naval Hospital, Emergency C-708-688-5618, Appointments C-708-688-5600. Chapels serving all faiths C-708-688-5410/4537, Chaplain-688-2384.

RECREATION: Bowling EX-5612, Golf EX-4593, Rec Center EX-5573, Auto Hobby, Craft Shops, Swimming, Tennis. Picnic area and boating at Nunn Beach on Lake Michigan, EX-2110/2457.

SPACE-A: None. See Glenview NAS listing, C-708-657-2326, D-312-932-2326, Fax 708-657-2929.

ATTRACTIONS: Excellent seasonal recreation available on Lake Michigan and in the Chain O'Lakes area.

O'HARE AIR RESERVE STATION (IL11R2)
928 Airlift Group, 6626 N. Patton Road
O'Hare IAP ARS, IL 60666-5023

Scheduled to close July 1997.

TELEPHONE NUMBER INFORMATION: Main installation numbers: C-312-825-6000, D-312-930-1110.

LOCATION: Located in the northeast corner of O'Hare IAP. Main gate 500 feet west of intersection of US-45 (Mannheim Rd) & IL-72 (Higgins Rd). Taxi is the only transportation to/from civilian terminals. USMRA: Page 69 (C,D-3,4). NMC: Chicago, 18 miles southeast.

ILLINOIS
O'Hare Air Reserve Station, continued

GENERAL INFORMATION: Reserve/Guard Base.

TEMPORARY MILITARY LODGING: None. See Great Lakes NTC listing, (BOQ), C-708-688-3777, D-312-932-2275; (BEQ), C-708-688-2170, D-312-932-2453.

LOGISTICAL SUPPORT: Limited support facilities available.

Consol Club-825-6448   Exchange-825-6449   Police-825-6223
Retiree Services-825-6060   SATO-825-5215

HEALTH & WELFARE: None. See Great Lakes NTC listing, C-708-688-5600.

SPACE-A: Base Ops, Bldg. 60, 0700-1530 Mon-Fri, C-312-825-6623, D-312-930-6623, non-ANG only. Bldg. 19, 0730-1600 Mon-Fri, C-312-825-6983, D-312-930-6983, ANG only. Flights to CONUS, OCONUS (limited) and overseas (limited).

ATTRACTIONS: City of Chicago, Wrigley Field, Chicago Cubs and White Sox baseball, Chicago Bears football, Chicago Bulls basketball, Frank Lloyd Wright Home and Studio, Racetrack, Brookfield Zoo, Ned Brown Forest Preserve.

ROCK ISLAND ARSENAL (IL08R2)
Rock Island Arsenal, IL 61299-5000

TELEPHONE NUMBER INFORMATION: Main installation numbers: C-309-782-6001, D-312-793-6001.

LOCATION: From I-74 north in Moline exit to 3rd Ave west and follow signs to Arsenal Island located in middle of Mississippi River. USMRA: Page 64 (C-2). NMC: Quad Cities of Rock Island and Moline in IL and Davenport and Bettendorf in IA.

GENERAL INFORMATION: Headquarters Rock Island Arsenal and Industrial Operations Command.

TEMPORARY MILITARY LODGING: Housing Office, Bldg 102, C-309-782-2376, D-312-793-2376, Fax 309-782-2550.

LOGISTICAL SUPPORT: Most support facilities available.

Arsenal Club-788-4860   Cafeteria-793-4337   Child Care-782-2828
Commissary-782-4798   Exchange-788-4940   Family Services-782-3828
Legal-782-8432   Locator-782-3004   Medical-782-0801
Police-782-2846

HEALTH & WELFARE: US Army Health Clinic, Emergency C-309-782-0801, Appointments C-309-782-0805. Chapel serving all faiths C-309-782-4736.

RECREATION: Auto Hobby 782-4950, Gym 782-6787, Outdoor Rec 782-8630, Fitness Center 782-6787, Skeet 782-2014.

SPACE-A: None. See O'Hare IAP/ARS listing, C-312-825-6623, D-312-930-6623.

ATTRACTIONS: Rock Island Arsenal Museum, National Cemetery, Confederate Cemetery, Colonel Davenport House.

134 - U.S. FORCES TRAVEL & TRANSFER GUIDE U.S.A

ILLINOIS

SCOTT AIR FORCE BASE (IL02R2)
Scott Air Force Base, IL 62225-5000

TELEPHONE NUMBER INFORMATION: Main installation numbers: C-618-256-1110, D-312-576-1110.

LOCATION: Off I-64, take exit 19 east or 19A west to IL-158 south, two miles and watch for signs to AFB entry. USMRA: Page 64 (D-8). NMC: St Louis, 25 miles west.

GENERAL INFORMATION: Headquarters for US Transportation Command; Air Mobility Command; Air Force Command, Control, Communications, and Computer Agency; Air Weather Service; Defense Commercial Communications Office; and USAF Medical Center Scott.

TEMPORARY MILITARY LODGING: Scott Inn, Bldg. 1510, Scott Dr, 24 hours daily, C-618-744-1200, D-312-576-1844. All ranks. DV/VIP EX-5555.

LOGISTICAL SUPPORT: Complete support facilities available.

CHAMPUS-256-7521	Chaplain-256-3303	Child Care-256-2669
Commissary-256-2783	Exchange-744-0888	Family Services-256-3616
Fire Department-256-5130	Gas Station-746-2184	Golf Course-744-1400
Legal-256-2358	Locator-256-1841	Medical-256-1847
MWR-256-2067	NCO Club-744-1777	O'Club-744-1333
Package Store-256-5942	Police-256-2223	Public Affairs-256-4241
Recreation-256-2067	Retiree Services-256-5092	RV/Camping-256-2067
SATO-256-5397	Snack Bar-744-1177	Theater-256-5177

HEALTH & WELFARE: USAF Medical Center, Emergency C-618-256-7595, Appointments C-618-256-1847 (800-826-4939 - IL only), 55 beds. Chapels serving all faiths C-618-256-3303/5144.

RECREATION: Arts/Crafts EX-4230, Auto Hobby EX-4566, Bowling 256-4054, Golf EX-1400, Fitness Center EX-4020, Gym EX-4524, Rec Equip EX-2067, Library EX-5100/3028, Swimming EX-2579, Youth Center EX-2115. Fam-Camp on base, year round, C-618-256-2056, D-312-576-2056, 24 camper spaces w/W&E hookups.

SPACE-A: Pax Term/Lounge, Bldg. P-8, 0445-2400 daily, C-618-256-3017, D-312-576-3017, (Daily flight recording, C-618-256-1854, D-312-576-1874), Fax 618-256-1948, flights to CONUS, overseas flights board at Lambert-St Louis Airport AMC Counter C-314-263-6270.

ATTRACTIONS: St Louis nearby, Mississippi River.

Other Installation in Illinois

Capital Airport Air National Guard Base, Springfield, IL 62707-5000, USMRA: Page 64 (D-5). C-217-753-8850, Exchange-753-8394, Med-753-8221/2.

INDIANA

Call 1-800-800-4000. Get a military rate by using your Military Living ID # ML3009. Retirees/Active Duty/Reserve/Guard.

CAMP ATTERBURY (IN05R2)
Edinburg, IN 46124-1096

TELEPHONE NUMBER INFORMATION: Main installation numbers: C-812-526-9711, D-312-786-2499.

LOCATION: From I-65, take exit 76 (31 north), left at Hospital Road. Enter post on Kings Drive at guard shack. USMRA Page 65 (E-6,7). NMC: Indianapolis 45 miles north.

GENERAL INFORMATION: Indiana National Guard Training Site

TEMPORARY MILITARY LODGING: None. See Crane NASWC listing, C-812-854-1176, D-312-482-1176.

LOGISTICAL SUPPORT: Limited support facilities available.

Consol Club-526-1159   Exchange-526-1140   MWR-526-1101
NCO-526-1143   O'Club-526-1141   Public Affairs-526-1306

HEALTH & WELFARE: None. See Crane Division NSWC listing, C-812-854-1220.

RECREATION: Campgrounds on post, year round, C-812-526-1101 26 camper spaces w/W&E hookups.

SPACE-A: None. See Scott AFB, IL listing, C-618-256-1854, D-312-576-1854, Fax 618-256-1958.

ATTRACTIONS: Indianapolis 45 miles north, Camp Atterbury Veterans Memorial Park, Camp Atterbury Prisoner of War Chapel.

CRANE DIVISION
NAVAL SURFACE WARFARE CENTER (IN03R2)
300 Highway 361
Crane, IN 47522-5001

TELEPHONE NUMBER INFORMATION: Main installation numbers: C-812-854-1225, D-312-482-1110.

LOCATION: From US-231 exit to IN-45 or IN-645 to enter the Center from the west. USMRA: Page 65 (D-8). NMC: Bloomington, 34 miles northeast.

GENERAL INFORMATION: A major Naval Weapons and Ammunition Support Center.

TEMPORARY MILITARY LODGING: Limited lodging, Bldg. 2682, BEQ/BOQ/DV/VIP, C-812-854-1176, D-312-482-1176, Fax 812-854-3313, 0730-1500 Mon-Fri. All ranks.

LOGISTICAL SUPPORT: Complete support facilities available.

INDIANA
Crane Division Naval Surface Warfare Center, continued

Cafeteria-854-1381
Commissary-854-3297
Exchange-854-1392
ITT Office-854-6059
Package Store-854-1392
Retiree Services-854-1222
SDO/NCO-854-1225

CDO/OOD-854-1225
Consol Mess-854-3435
Fire Dept-854-1235
Locator-854-2511
Police-854-3300
RV/Camping-854-1368
Visitor Center-854-4521

CHAMPUS-854-1220
Conv Store-854-1864
Gas Station-854-1864
Medical-854-1597
Public Affairs-854-1640
SATO-854-1244

HEALTH & WELFARE: Dispensary/Emergency C-812-854-1220.

RECREATION: Bowling EX-1586, Rec Center EX-1586, Tickets EX-1586, Library EX-1526, Golf EX-1242. MWR Campgrounds on base, 1 April-31 Oct, C-812-854-1368, D-312-482-1368, 52 camper spaces w/full hookups, 20 tent spaces.

SPACE-A: None. See Scott AFB, IL listing, C-618-256-1854, D-312-576-1854, Fax 618-256-1958.

ATTRACTIONS: Indiana University, Bloomington, Lake Greenwood Nature Trail.

Other Installations in Indiana

Fort Benjamin Harrison Indianapolis, IN 46216-5450. USMRA: Page 65 (E-5). Exchange-549-5698, Commissary-549-5293, Public Affairs-542-2912.
Grissom Air Reserve Base, Grissom ARB, IN 46971-5000.
USMRA: Page 65 (E-3), C-317-688-5211, Exchange 689-5270, Space-A 688-2861.
Stout Field, Indianapolis, IN 46216-5000. C-317-247-3300, D-312-724-2300.

U.S. FORCES TRAVEL & TRANSFER GUIDE U.S.A. - 137

IOWA

DOLLAR RENT A CAR Call 1-800-800-4000. Get a military rate by using your Military Living ID # ML3009. Retirees/Active Duty/Reserve/Guard.

CAMP DODGE (IA02R2)
Johnston, IA 51031-1902

TELEPHONE NUMBER INFORMATION: Main installation numbers: C-515-252-4011. D-312-946-2011

LOCATION: From I-35/I-80, take Merle Hay/Camp Dodge exit (exit 131); north on Iowa 401 approximately four miles to camp. USMRA: Page 77 (E-5). NMC: Des Moines, five miles.

GENERAL INFORMATION: State Headquarters Iowa National Guard, Iowa Law Enforcement Academy (State Dept of Public Safety).

TEMPORARY MILITARY LODGING: Lodging office, Bldg. A-8 (facilities), 7th St and Des Moines Ave 24 hours daily, C-515-252-4238, D-312-946-2238. 1630-0800, call Security C-515-240-3742.

LOGISTICAL SUPPORT: Some support facilities available.

CHAMPUS-252-4454 Chaplain-252-4378* Exchange-252-4382
ITT-270-2445 Legal-252-4279 Medical-252-4235*
Museum-252-4531* Public Affairs-252-4582 SDO/NCO-252-4011
Security-240-3472 SATO-270-2445

*These facilities are not manned by full-time personnel, call Public Affairs at 252-4582 for info.

HEALTH AND WELFARE: Camp Dodge Troop Medical Center, Emergency C-515-240-3742/3740 (Security); Outpatient and inpatient care VA Med Center, Des Moines, C-515-255-2173. Chapel serving all faiths C-515-252-4378.

RECREATION: Swimming 276-1106. Ball diamonds.

SPACE-A: None. See Offutt AFB, NE listing, C-402-294-6235/7111, D-312-271-6235/7111, Fax 402-294-6715.

ATTRACTIONS: Camp Dodge is adjacent to the Saylorville Recreational Area, which provides boating, fishing, camping, hiking, and bicycling. Des Moines, with full cultural and entertainment activities. Adventureland Theme Park, White Water University Park, aquarium, zoo, State Fairgrounds.

Other Installations in Iowa

Des Moines Exchange, Bldg. 106, 217 E. Army, Des Moines, IA 50315-5000.
USMRA: Page 77 (E-5). C-515-287-9210, Exchange-287-7671.
Sioux City Gateway Airport, Sergeant Blugg, IA 51054-1002.
USMRA: Page 77 (A-4). C-712-255-3511, Exchange-277-2042, Med-255-3511.

138 - U.S. FORCES TRAVEL & TRANSFER GUIDE U.S.A

KANSAS

DOLLAR RENT A CAR — Call 1-800-800-4000. Get a military rate by using your Military Living ID # ML3009. Retirees/Active Duty/Reserve/Guard.

FORBES FIELD (KS01R3)
Forbes Field Air National Guard Base, 5920 E Street
Topeka, KS 66619-5370

TELEPHONE NUMBER INFORMATION: Main installation numbers: C-913-861-4210, D-312-720-4210.

LOCATION: From I-70, take Highway 75 south exit. Main gate located at second stop light on Highway 75. USMRA: Page 78 (I-4). NMC: Topeka, three miles north.

GENERAL INFORMATION: 190th Air Refueling Group, 117th Air Refueling Squadron, 127th Weather Flight.

TEMPORARY MILITARY LODGING: None. See Fort Riley listing, C-913-289-2830/6903, D-312-856-2880.

LOGISTICAL SUPPORT: Some support facilities available.

CHAMPUS-861-4130   Chaplain-861-4001   Exchange-861-4962
Fire Dept-861-4501 Legal-861-4002   Locator-861-4210
Medical-861-4522   MWR-861-0144   Police-861-4080
Public Affairs-861-4195 RV/Camping-235-3388

HEALTH & WELFARE: Very limited. C-913-861-4518. See Fort Riley listing, C-913-239-7777.

RECREATION: Golf Course 862-0114, Lake Shawnee C-913-235-3388, Museum 862-3303, Rod/Gun Club 861-4002.

SPACE-A: Limited, infrequent flights. Call C-913-231-4210, D-312-720-4210, Fax 913-861-4555.

ATTRACTIONS: Combat Air Museum on post. Topeka, Heartland Park Race Track, Kansas Expocenter, Topeka zoo, Kansas Museum of History.

FORT LEAVENWORTH (KS04R3)
600 Thomas Avenue
Fort Leavenworth, KS 66027-1389

TELEPHONE NUMBER INFORMATION: Main installation numbers: C-913-684-4021, D-312-552-4021.

LOCATION: From I-70, exit US-73 north to Leavenworth. From I-29, exit Highway 92 west to Leavenworth. Fort is adjacent to city of Leavenworth. USMRA: Page 72 (J-3). NMC: Kansas City, 30 miles southeast.

GENERAL INFORMATION: Combined Arms Center, US Disciplinary Barracks, Command and General Staff College, Headquarters 35th Infantry Division (Mech).

KANSAS
Fort Leavenworth, continued

TEMPORARY MILITARY LODGING: Lodging office, Bldg. 695, 214 Grant Ave, 24 hours daily, C-913-684-4091, D-312-552-4091, Fax 913-684-4397. All ranks. DV/VIP C-913-684-4064.

LOGISTICAL SUPPORT: Complete support facilities available.

ACS-684-4357	Cafeteria-651-6573	CHAMPUS-684-6210
Chaplain-684-2210	Child Care-684-2322	Commissary-684-4903
Consol Club-651-7011	Conv Store-651-7183	EM Club-684-2895
Exchange-651-7271	Family Services-684-4357	Gas Station-651-6541
Golf Course-651-7176	ITR Office-684-2580	Legal-684-4944
Locator-684-3651	Medical-684-6224/6110	MWR-684-3719
Package Store-651-7183	Police-684-2111	Public Affairs-684-5604
Recreation-684-3719	Retiree Services-684-2041	SDO/SNO-684-4154
Snack Bar-651-6586	Theater-684-4683	Travel-684-3236

HEALTH & WELFARE: Munson Army Community Hospital, clinics and depts, Emergency C-913-684-6110, Appointments C-913-684-6224, Acute Care Clinic C-913-684-6110, 55 beds. Chapel serving all faiths C-913-684-2017.

RECREATION: Arts/Crafts-684-3377, Bowling-651-2195, Fitness Center-684-3895, Flying Club-651-6808, Gym-684-3895/2037, Library-758-3101, Stables-651-4487, Swimming-684-2187/3088/3998, Tennis-684-3845, Youth Services-684-5121.

SPACE-A: Sherman Army Airfield, Pax Term/Lounge, Bldg. 132, 0730-1630 Mon-Fri, C-913-684-2396, D-312-552-2396, flights to CONUS locations.

ATTRACTIONS: Frontier Army Museum, Agriculture Hall of Fame in Bonner Springs, Harry S. Truman Library & Museum in Independence MO, Kansas City Royals, Kansas City Chiefs.

FORT RILEY (KS02R3)
Fort Riley, KS 66442-5000

TELEPHONE NUMBER INFORMATION: Main installation numbers: C-913-239-3911, D-312-856-1110.

LOCATION: Clearly marked off I-70. USMRA: Page 78 (G,H-3,4). NMC: Topeka, 50 miles east.

GENERAL INFORMATION: Headquarters for 1st Infantry Division (Mech) and Fort Riley, Fort Riley Readiness Group.

TEMPORARY MILITARY LODGING: Lodging office, Bldg. 45, Barry Ave, 24 hours daily, C-913-239-2830, D-312-856-2830. All ranks. DV/VIP C-913-239-3926/3037.

LOGISTICAL SUPPORT: Complete support facilities available.

ACS-239-9437	CHAMPUS-239-7720	Chaplain-239-2828/3359
Child Care-239-4480	Commissary-239-6621	Community Club-784-5999
Conv Store-784-6037	Exchange-784-4439	Family Services-239-2560
Fire Dept-239-4257	Gas Station-784-5081	Golf Course-239-5412
ITR Office-239-5614	Leaders Club-784-5999	Legal-239-3117

140 - U.S. FORCES TRAVEL & TRANSFER GUIDE U.S.A

KANSAS
Fort Riley, continued

Locator-239-9867/9868	Medical-239-7777	MWR-239-2612
Package Store-784-5182	Police-239-3053	Public Affairs-239-3032
Retiree Services-239-3667	SDO/EOC-239-2222	Snack Bar-784-2231
Theater-239-9454	Travel-239-2586	Visitor Center-239-2672

HEALTH & WELFARE: Irwin Army Community Hospital, Emergency C-913-239-7777, 250 beds. Chapel serving all faiths C-913-239-3730.

RECREATION: Multi-Crafts EX-9205, Auto Hobby EX-4028, Skating Rink EX-2243, Library EX-2392, Gyms EX-3868/5562/5771/4683, Tennis EX-3288, Youth Center EX-2840, Wood Hobby EX-6415, Flying Club EX-2205, Swimming EX-9441, Riding Club EX-6651, Outdoor Rec EX-6189, Rec Equip EX-6189. Moon Lake Rec Area on post, EX-6189, no camping facilities.

SPACE-A: Marshall Army Airfield, Bldg. 743, 24 hours daily, C-913-239-2530, D-312-856-2530, flights via executive aircraft. Also, try Forbes Field ANG Base, Topeka, Bldg. 611, C-913-862-1234, D-312-720-4210, Flying Training Missions to CONUS and OCONUS locations.

ATTRACTIONS: Custer House, US Cavalry Museum, and First Territorial Capitol.

McCONNELL AIR FORCE BASE (KS03R3)
McConnell Air Force Base, KS 67221-5000

TELEPHONE NUMBER INFORMATION: Main installation numbers: C-316-652-6100, D-312-743-1110.

LOCATION: Take I-35 to Wichita, exit at Kellogg St (US-54) west to Rock Rd south and McConnell AFB. USMRA: Page 78 (G-6). NMC: Wichita, six miles northwest.

GENERAL INFORMATION: Air Mobility Command Base, 22nd Air Refueling Wing.

TEMPORARY MILITARY LODGING: Lodging office, Bldg. 193, Manhattan St, 24 hours daily, C-316-683-7711, D-312-743-6500. All ranks. DV/VIP C-316-693-6500.

LOGISTICAL SUPPORT: Complete support facilities available.

CHAMPUS-5018	Chaplain-652-3562	Child Care-652-4223
Commissary-652-5625	Conv Store-685-0291	Exchange-685-0231
Family Services-652-3729	Fire-117	Gas Station-652-5196
ITT Office-652-4005	Legal-652-3590	Locator-652-3555
Medical-652-5050	NCO Club-6183	O' Club-6182
Public Affairs-652-3141	Package Store-685-5198	Police-652-3975
SATO-4002	The Club-652-4147	Visitor Center-4712/13

HEALTH & WELFARE: USAF Super Clinic, Appointments C-316-652-5050. Chapel serving most faiths C-316-652-3562.

RECREATION: Arts/Crafts EX-3809, Bowling Alley EX-6187, Golf EX-4038, Indoor Pool EX-4004, Rec Equip EX-4425, Library EX-4207, Youth Center EX-4071.

KANSAS
McConnell Air Force Base, continued

SPACE-A: Pax Term/Lounge, Bldg. 1112, 24 hours daily, C-316-652-3840, D-312-743-3840, Fax 316-652-4957, flights to CONUS, OCONUS and overseas via KC-135R aircraft.

ATTRACTIONS: Rebuilt downtown core area has resulted in an outstanding civic and cultural complex, Zoo, Museums of Art and History, Botanical Garden.

KENTUCKY

DOLLAR RENT A CAR — Call 1-800-800-4000. Get a military rate by using your Military Living ID # ML3009. Retirees/Active Duty/Reserve/Guard.

FORT CAMPBELL (KY02R2)
Fort Campbell, KY 42223-5000

TELEPHONE NUMBER INFORMATION: Main installation numbers: C-502-798-2151, D-312-635-1110.

LOCATION: In the southwest part of Kentucky, four miles south of intersection of US-41A and I-24, 10 miles northwest of Clarksville, TN. USMRA: Page 40 (E,F-7). NMC: Hopkinsville, 15 miles north.

GENERAL INFORMATION: 101st Airborne Division (Air Assault), Air Assault School, 5th SFG (A), 101st Corps Support Group Regiment, 160th Special Operation Aviation Regiment.

TEMPORARY MILITARY LODGING: Lodging office, Bldg. 1581, 26th & Indiana, C-502-798-5281/618. Reservations C-615-431-5107, D-312-635-2865, 0730-1600 Mon-Fri. All ranks. DV/VIP- C-615-431-8924.

LOGISTICAL SUPPORT: Complete support facilities available.

ACS-798-5127
Chaplain-798-6124
Conv Store-439-1914
Family Services-798-5127
Golf Course-798-4906
Locator-798-1110
NCO Club-439-1772
Police-798-7110
Retiree Services-798-5680
SDO/NCO-798-9793
Visitor Center-798-7463

Cafeteria-631-3779
Child Care-798-2164
EM Club-439-3897
Fire Dept-798-7171
ITT Office-798-7436
Medical-798-8400
O'Club-431-5603
Public Affairs-798-3025
RV/Camping-798-2629
Snack Bar-431-6239

CHAMPUS-798-8280
Commissary-798-2606
Exchange-439-1841
Gas Station-439-1689
Legal-798-5011
MWR-798-2917
Package Store-431-3622
Recreation-798-7466
SATO-431-5660
Theater-798-2917

HEALTH & WELFARE: Blanchfield Army Community Hospital, Emergency C-502-798-8000/8400, Appointments C-502-798-8287/439-8287. Chapels serving all faiths C-502-798-8464/8777.

RECREATION: Arts/Crafts EX-6693, Auto Hobby EX-6317, Bowling EX-5887/4993, Golf EX-4906, Gym EX-5894, Rec Equip EX-3919/6806, Stables EX-2629/2487, Outdoor Rec EX-3126/5590, Library EX-5729, Swimming EX-6290, Rec Center EX-6383/4616/7446/5818, Tennis EX-6973/5225, Show Center EX-6087. Eagles' Rest/Fletchers Fork Travel Camp on post, year round, C-502-798-3126/5590 D-312-635-3126/5590, 75 camper spaces w/W&E hookups, four cabins.

SPACE-A: Campbell Army Airfield, Pax Term, Zone H/I, 24 hours daily, C-502-798-2146, Fax 502-798-9288, flights via executive aircraft.

ATTRACTIONS: A growing recreational area in Nashville..."Home of the Grand Ole Opry," Land Between the Lakes (170,000-acre national recreational and environmental education area).

KENTUCKY

FORT KNOX (KY01R2)
P.O. Box 995
Fort Knox, KY 40121-5000

TELEPHONE NUMBER INFORMATION: Main installation numbers: C-502-624-1181, D-312-464-1181.

LOCATION: From I-65 in Louisville, exit Gene Snyder Expressway west to US-31 west, go south to Fort Knox. From I-64, exit I-264 (Waterson Expressway west) to US-31 west, south to Fort Knox. From I-71, exit I-65 south to Gene Snyder Expressway to US-31 west then south to Fort Knox. USMRA: Page 40,41 (H,I-3,4). NMC: Louisville, 25 miles north.

GENERAL INFORMATION: Army Armor Center, Training Brigades, HQ USAREC, and HQ, 2 ROTC Region.

TEMPORARY MILITARY LODGING: Lodging office, Bldg. 4770 (Newgarden Tower), Dixie Highway 31 west. 24 hours daily, C-502-942-1000. All ranks. DV/VIP EX-3138/3943.

LOGISTICAL SUPPORT: Complete support facilities available.

Cafeteria-942-0805/0230	CHAMPUS-624-9050	Chaplain-624-5255/4524
Child Care-624-8320	Commissary-624-8525	EM Club-942-8067
Exchange-942-0278	Family Services-624-6291	Gas Station-942-0841/8338
ITT Office-942-1437	Legal-624-2771	Locator-624-1141
Medical-624-9999/9000	NCO Club-942-0409	O'Club-942-8383
Package Store-942-0166	Police-624-2111/112	Retiree Services-624-4315
SATO-942-2509	SDO/NCO-624-4481/4421	Theater-942-7999/6832

HEALTH & WELFARE: Ireland Army Community Hospital, Emergency C-502-624-9000, Appointments C-502-624-9148. Chapel serving all faiths C-502-624-4524.

RECREATION: Arts/Crafts EX-4725, Auto Hobby EX-5410/5338, Bowling EX-4740/6840, Golf EX-4218/942-0984, Gym EX-3316/3641, Rec Equip EX-2314, Outdoor Rec EX-7754, Field House EX-2214, Library EX-1232/4723, Swimming EX-4033, Rec Center EX-8254, Tennis EX-2214/4033. Camp Carlson Army Travel Camp on post, year round, C-502-624-4836, D-312-464-4836, seven camper spaces w/full hookups, 18 camper spaces w/W&E hookups, four family cabins, four youth cabins 25 tent spaces.

SPACE-A: Godman Army Airfield, Pax Term, Bldg. 5220, 24 hours daily, C-502-624-5545, D-312-464-5545, Fax 502-624-2421, flights via executive aircraft to CONUS locations.

ATTRACTIONS: Mammoth Cave, Louisville, Hodgenville..."Birthplace of Abraham Lincoln," and Bardstown...site of "My Old Kentucky Home," all within 50 miles. Patton Museum at Chaffee Ave entrance to Fort Knox opens at 0900 to 1630 Mon-Fri year round, with special hours: 1 May through 30 Sept 1000-1800, 1000-1430 on Sat, Sun and holidays.

Other Installations in Kentucky

Standiford Field Air National Guard Base, 1019 Old Grade Lane Louisville, KY 40213-2678, USMRA: Page 41 (I-3). C-502-364-9400, BX-364-9420, Public Affairs-364-9431, Space-A-364-9459.

144 - U.S. FORCES TRAVEL & TRANSFER GUIDE U.S.A

LOUISIANA

DOLLAR RENT A CAR — Call 1-800-800-4000. Get a military rate by using your Military Living ID # ML3009. Retirees/Active Duty/Reserve/Guard.

BARKSDALE AIR FORCE BASE (LA01R2)
50 Vandenberg Ave, Suite 108
Barksdale Air Force Base, LA 71110-2079

TELEPHONE NUMBER INFORMATION: Main installation numbers: C-318-456-1110, D-312-781-1110.

LOCATION: Exit I-20 at Airline Dr, go south to Old Minden Rd (1/4 mile), left on Old Minden Rd (one block), then right on North Gate Drive (one mile) to North Gate of AFB. USMRA: Page 79 (B-2). NMC: Shreveport, one mile west. Co-located with Bossier City and Shreveport.

GENERAL INFORMATION: Air Combat Command Base, Headquarters 8th Air Force, 2nd Wing, B-52, KC-135, and KC-10 Aircraft, AFRES units.

TEMPORARY MILITARY LODGING: Lodging office, Bldg. 5155, Hangarline Rd, 24 hours daily, C-318-747-4708, D-312-781-3091. All ranks. DV/VIP C-318-456-2151.

LOGISTICAL SUPPORT: Complete support facilities available.

CHAMPUS-456-6572
Commissary-456-8378
EM Club-456-4467
Fire Dept-456-1117
Legal-456-2561
O'Club-456-4926
Public Affairs-456-3065
RV/Camping-456-2679
Theater-456-3666
Chaplain-456-2111
Command Post-456-22151
Exchange-746-2554
Gas Station-742-1929
Locator-456-3555
Package Store-742-2284
Recreation-456-2636
SATO-741-3095
Visitor Center-456-3587
Child Dev Center-456-4139
Conv Store-746-2284
Family Sppt Center-456-8331
Golf Course-456-2263
Medical-456-6161
Police-456-2551
Retiree Services-456-4480
SDO/NCO-456-2151

HEALTH & WELFARE: USAF Hospital, Emergency C-318-456-6161, Appointments C-318-456-6555. Chapels serving all faiths C-318-456-2111.

RECREATION: Bowling EX-4133, Golf EX-3832, Aero Club, Auto Hobby, Rec Equip, Wood Hobby, Swimming, Tennis, Youth Center, Riding, Rod/Gun Club, Community Centre EX-8911. Fam-Camp on base, year round, C-318-456-2679, D-312-781-2679, 18 camper spaces w/W&E hookups, four w/o hookups.

SPACE-A: Pax Term/Lounge, Bldg. 6404, 0630-1630 Mon-Fri, C-318-456-3738, D-312-781-3738, flights to CONUS, OCONUS and overseas via KC-135/10 aircraft.

ATTRACTIONS: Moderate climate. Great water sports. Horse racing (Louisiana Downs) Apr-Nov, NCAA sanctioned Independence Bowl late in December, Riverboard Casinos open 24 hours daily.

U.S. FORCES TRAVEL & TRANSFER GUIDE U.S.A. - 145

LOUISIANA

CAMP BEAUREGARD (LA12R2)
Pineville, LA 71360-5000.

TELEPHONE NUMBER INFORMATION: Main installation numbers: C-318-640-2080, D-312-485-8222.

LOCATION: Off US-171, nine miles south of Leesville. USMRA: Page 79 (D-4). NMC: Alexandria, 45 miles northeast.

TEMPORARY MILITARY LODGING: Lodging office, C-318-640-2080 ext 269/302.

LOGISTICAL SUPPORT: Limited support facilities available.

Chaplain-2080
EXchange-641-9661
Locator-2080

Consol Club-EX-219
Family Services-EX-248
Medical-EX-296

EM Club-640-8164
Fire-2080
NCO Club-EX-277

HEALTH & WELFARE: Camp Beauregard outpatient clinic, C-318-640-2080 EX 258/296.

SPACE-A: None. See Fort Polk listing, C-318-531-4831/7328, D-312-863-4831/7328.

ATTRACTIONS: Baton Rouge, state capital, approximately 100 miles southeast. New Orleans, approximately 160 miles southeast.

FORT POLK/JOINT READINESS TRAINING CENTER (LA07R2)
Fort Polk, LA 71459-5000.

TELEPHONE NUMBER INFORMATION: Main installation numbers: C-318-531-2911, D-312-863-1110, FTS: 528-1110.

LOCATION: Off US-171, nine miles south of Leesville. USMRA: Page 79 (C-4). NMC: Alexandria, 45 miles northeast.

GENERAL INFORMATION: Headquarters Joint Readiness Training Center, 2nd Armored Cavalry Regiment, 108th ADA and Warrior Brigade.

TEMPORARY MILITARY LODGING: Lodging office, Magnolia House, Bldg. 522, Utah Ave, 24 hours daily, C-318-531-2941/537-9591. All ranks.

LOGISTICAL SUPPORT: Complete support facilities available.

ACS-531-1941
Child Care-531-2149
Exchange-537-1001
Gas Station-537-8269
ITT-531-1975
Medical(ER)-531-3368
Police-531-2677
Retiree Services-531-4515
Shoppette-537-5234
Visitor Center-531-2941

CHAMPUS-531-3974
Commissary-531-2088
Family Services-531-1941
Golf Course-531-4661
Legal-531-2580
MWR-531-1948
Public Affairs-531-2714
RV/Camping-565-4235
Travel-537-0658

Chaplain-531-7338/6179
Conv Store-537-1050/8865
Fire Dept-531-2026
ITR-531-1795-4
Locator-531-1272
Package Store-535-0456
Recreation-531-5350
SDO/NCO-531-1727
Theater-531-2087

LOUISIANA
Fort Polk JRTC, continued

HEALTH & WELFARE: Bayne-Jones Army Community Hospital, Emergency C-318-531-3368/3361, Appointments C-318-531-3000. Chapel serving all faiths C-318-531-4228/2332.

RECREATION: Auto Hobby EX-6149, Bowling EX-6273, Golf EX-4661, Gyms EX-2145, Library EX-2665, Outdoor Rec EX-5350, Rec Center EX-1975, Youth Center EX-6907. Ball Fields, Skeet/Trap Range, Arts/Crafts, Fitness Course, Theater presentations, tours. Toledo Bend Recreation Site off post, year round, C-318-531-1974, 15 camper spaces w/W&E hookups, 12 mobile homes. South Fort Mobile Home Park on post, year round, C-318-531-2941, 10 camper spaces w/full hookups.

SPACE-A: Polk Army Airfield, Base Ops, 0700-2200 Mon-Fri, during JRTC rotations 24 hours a day. C-318-531-4831/7328, D-312-863-4831/7328.

ATTRACTIONS: Fort Polk Military Museum. Baton Rouge, state capital, 155 miles southeast. New Orleans, 232 miles southeast.

JACKSON BARRACKS (LA13R2)
New Orleans, LA 70146-5000.

TELEPHONE NUMBER INFORMATION: Main installation numbers: C-504-271-6262, D-312-485-8210.

LOCATION: From I-10 east to Claiborne exit to Jackson Barracks. USMRA: Page 90 (F-3,4). NMC: New Orleans, in city limits.

TEMPORARY MILITARY LODGING: Lodging office C-504-278-6207, D-312-485-6207.

LOGISTICAL SUPPORT: Limited support facilities available.

EM Club-278-6490   Exchange-271-6245

HEALTH & WELFARE: None. See New Orleans NSA listing, C-504-678-2670.

SPACE-A: None. See New Orleans NAS listing, C-504-393-3213, D-312-363-3213, Fax 502-393-3734.

ATTRACTIONS: City of New Orleans, Superdome, New Orleans French Quarter, Mississippi River, Riverboat cruises, New Orleans Zoo, Aquarium. Audubon Park.

NEW ORLEANS COAST GUARD SUPPORT CENTER (LA10R2)
4640 Urquhart St
New Orleans, LA 70117-4698

TELEPHONE NUMBER INFORMATION: Main installation numbers: C-504-942-3020, FTS-942-3033.

LOCATION: From I-10 go south on Elysian Fields Ave, left on Claiborne Ave, right on Poland St, left on Urquhart St to main gate. USMRA: Page 79 (H-6,7) Page 90 (E-3). NMC: New Orleans, city limits.

U.S. FORCES TRAVEL & TRANSFER GUIDE U.S.A. - 147

LOUISIANA
New Orleans Coast Guard Support Center, continued

GENERAL INFORMATION: Provides industrial and repair support to primarily the Eighth CG District Host Command to many tenants, including CG Group New Orleans, CG Station and CG Aids to Navigation Team NOLA, and others.

TEMPORARY MILITARY LODGING: None. See New Orleans Naval Air Station listing, C-504-678-3842, D-312-363-3841, DV/VIP-504-678-3842.

LOGISTICAL SUPPORT: Limited support facilities available.

CDO/OOD-942-3020   Exchange-942-7220   Medical-942-3021

HEALTH & WELFARE: Charity Hospital, Emergency 911.

SPACE-A: None. See Keesler AFB, MS listing, C-601-377-4538, D-312-597-4538.

ATTRACTIONS: City of New Orleans, Superdome, Jefferson Downs Racetrack, Audubon Park, New Orleans Zoo, Bayou Segnette State Park.

NEW ORLEANS NAVAL AIR STATION/ JOINT RESERVE BASE (LA11R2)
New Orleans, LA 70143-5012

TELEPHONE NUMBER INFORMATION: Main installation numbers: C-504-678-3011, D-312-678-3011.

LOCATION: Off LA-23 in Belle Chasse. Clearly marked. USMRA: Page 79 (H-7) Page 90 (F-6). NMC: New Orleans, 10 miles north.

GENERAL INFORMATION: Navy Fighter, Logistics, and Patrol Aircraft Squadrons, Coast Guard Air Station, Air Force Reserve and ANG units, and US Customs Service.

TEMPORARY MILITARY LODGING: Lodging office, Bldg. 22 (Olson Ave) and Bldg. 40 (4th St), 24 hours daily, C-504-678-3842, D-312-363-3841. Fax 504-393-1959, DV/VIP C-504-678-3842.

LOGISTICAL SUPPORT: Most support facilities available.

CHAMPUS-361-2676
Conv Store-678-3506
Duty Office-678-3253
Fire Dept-678-3105
HighTops Bar-678-3509
Locator-678-3253
NCO Club-678-3509
Police-678-3827
Retiree Services-361-2134
Snack Bar-678-3514

Chaplain-678-3525
CDO/OOD-678-3253
EM Club-678-3509
Gas Station-678-3506
ITT-678-3695
Medical-678-3660
O'Club-678-3844
Public Affairs-678-3260
RV/Camping-678-3448

Child Care-678-3654
CPO Club-678-3844
Exchange-678-3510
Golf Course-678-3453
Legal-678-3266
MWR-678-3231
Package Store-678-3510
Recreation-678-3230
SATO-361-2330

HEALTH & WELFARE: Naval Medical Clinic, Emergency Room care not available. NAS Branch clinic appointments. EX 3661 (Active Duty Only), NSA Medical Clinic appointments. 678-2670 (Retired and Dependents). Inpatient care, see Keesler AFB, MS listing, C-601-377-6337.

LOUISIANA
New Orleans Naval Air Station/Joint Reserve Base, continued

RECREATION: Auto Hobby EX-3448, Bowling EX-3514, Golf EX-3453, Gym EX-3230, Rec Equip EX-3230. Campground on base, year round, C-504-678-3448, D-312-363-3448, 17 camper spaces w/full hookups, two camping trailers, one mobile home, 10 tent spaces.

SPACE-A: Pax Term/Lounge, Bldg. 1, 0700-2300 hours daily, C-504-678-3213, D-312-363-3213, Fax 504-678-3734, flights to CONUS, OCONUS and overseas.

ATTRACTIONS: New Orleans French Quarter, Mississippi River, New Orleans Zoo, Aquarium, Swamp Tours, River Boat Casinos.

NEW ORLEANS NAVAL SUPPORT ACTIVITY (LA06R2)
2300 General Meyer Avenue
New Orleans, LA 70142-5007

TELEPHONE NUMBER INFORMATION: Main installation numbers: C-504-678-5011, D-312-363-5011.

LOCATION: On the Westbank of the Mississippi River. From I-10 east, take Mississippi River Bridge to the Westbank. Take Gen DeGaulle east exit after passing over bridge and turn left at Shirley Dr which leads to NSA. USMRA: Page 90 (E,F-3,4). NMC: New Orleans, five miles east.

GENERAL INFORMATION: Headquarters for both the Naval and Marine Corps Reserve.

TEMPORARY MILITARY LODGING: Navy Lodge, Bldg. 702, 0700-2000 daily, C-504-366-3266. BEQ, C-504-678-2220, D-312-678-2220, BOQ, C-504-678-2264, D-312-678-2264, DV/VIP C-504-678-2264, D-312-678-2264, Fax 504-678-2663. All ranks.

LOGISTICAL SUPPORT: Complete support facilities available.

CDO/OOD-678-2655	CHAMPUS-678-2675	Chaplain-678-2244
Child Care-678-2450	Commissary-678-2182	CPO Club-678-2218
EM Club-678-2219	Exchange-678-2702	Family Services-678-2647
Gas Station-678-2747	ITT Office-678-2208	Locator-678-5011
Legal-678-2520	MWR-678-2269	O'Club-678-2218
Package Store-678-2749	Police-678-2570	Public Affairs-678-2540
Retiree Services-678-2134	SATO-678-2330	

HEALTH & WELFARE: Primary Care C-504-678-2390, Emergency 911, Appointments C-504-678-2670. Inpatient, see Keesler AFB listing, C-601-377-6337. Chapel serving all faiths C-504-678-2244.

RECREATION: Rec Equip EX-2527, Swimming EX-2654, Courts EX-2527, Hobby Shops EX-2207, Bowling EX-2204. RV Park on base, year round, C-504-678-2269, 16 camper spaces w/W&E hookups.

SPACE-A: None. See New Orleans NAS listing, C-504-678-3213, D-312-678-3103.

ATTRACTIONS: New Orleans French Quarter, Bourbon Street, Sports, New Orleans Zoo, River Boat Cruises, Aquarium, Superdome.

U.S. FORCES TRAVEL & TRANSFER GUIDE U.S.A. - 149

MAINE

DOLLAR RENT A CAR — Call 1-800-800-4000. Get a military rate by using your Military Living ID # ML3009. Retirees/Active Duty/Reserve/Guard.

BANGOR AIR NATIONAL GUARD BASE/ BANGOR IAP (ME10R1)
Bangor, ME 04401-3099

TELEPHONE NUMBER INFORMATION: Main installation numbers: C-207-990-7700 (ask for extensions), D-312-698-7700.

LOCATION: Located in Bangor city limits. Northbound from I-95 take exit 47, Ohio St, drive west two blocks and turn left, one block to right turn on Union St (ME-222), pass Bangor IAP, turn left on Griffin Road, entrance is 300 yards on right. USMRA: Page 18 (E-6,7). NMC: Bangor, in city limits.

GENERAL INFORMATION: Air National Guard Air Refueling Wing with KC-135E aircraft, Over-the-Horizon Backscatter Radar Operations Center.

TEMPORARY MILITARY LODGING: The Army National Guard operates the "Pine Tree Inn," 24 hours daily, C-207-942-2081, D-312-698-7700. Located at 22 Cleveland Ave on Bangor IAP adjacent to Bangor ANG Base. All ranks.

LOGISTICAL SUPPORT: Most support facilities available.

CHAMPUS-EX-458 **Child Care-941-0466** **Commissary-990-7751**
Exchange-990-7233 **Retiree Services-EX-458** **SATO-EX-355**

HEALTH & WELFARE: None. See Winter Harbor Naval Security Group Activity listing, C-207-963-5534.

RECREATION: None. See Winter Harbor Naval Security Group listing.

SPACE-A: Pax Term, Bldg. 491, 0730-1600 Mon-Fri, C-207-990-7212/7247, D-312-698-7212/7247, Fax 207-990-7216. Flights to CONUS and overseas.

ATTRACTIONS: Lobster and other seafood, Penobscot Marine Museum in Searsport, Acadia National Park, Bar Harbor, Mt Desert Island, beaches, and boating.

BRUNSWICK NAVAL AIR STATION (ME07R1)
Brunswick Naval Air Station, ME 04011-5000

TELEPHONE NUMBER INFORMATION: Main installation numbers: C-207-921-1110, D-312-476-1110.

LOCATION: From I-95 north, exit Coastal Route 1 north. Take route 1 four miles to Cooks Corner. Turn right to main gate of BNAS. USMRA: Page 18 (C-9). NMC: Portland, 30 miles southwest.

GENERAL INFORMATION: Maritime Patrol, Search and Rescue, and Survival Schools are located here. The last active duty military installation in the northeast.

MAINE
Brunswick Naval Air Station, continued

TEMPORARY MILITARY LODGING: Lodging office, Bldg. 512, Sewall Rd, 24 hours daily, C-207-921-2245, D-312-476-2245, Fax 207-792-0232. Navy Lodge, Topsham Annex, 0730-2200 daily, C-207-921-2206. All ranks. DV/VIP C-207-921-2214.

LOGISTICAL SUPPORT: Complete support facilities available.

Cafeteria-921-2455	CHAMPUS-921-2901	Chaplain-921-2223
Child Care-921-2610	Commissary-921-7121	Conv Store-921-2179
CPO Club-921-2291	EM Club-921-2121	Exchange-921-2387
Family Services-921-2273	Legal-921-2331	Locator-921-1110
Medical-921-2610	Package Store-921-2128	Police-921-2585
Retiree Services-921-2609	SDO/NCO-921-2214	

HEALTH & WELFARE: Naval Branch Clinic, Emergency C-207-921-2610, Appointments C-207-921-2243. Chapels serving all faiths C-207-921-2231/2223.

RECREATION: Rec Equip EX-2738, Bowling EX-2145, Auto Hobby EX-2488, Crafts EX-2168, Golf EX-2155, Ski Shop EX-2155.

SPACE-A: Pax Term/Lounge, Bldg. 200, 24 hours daily, C-207-921-2682/2689, D-312-476-2682/2689, limited flights to CONUS and overseas.

ATTRACTIONS: Great snow skiing on the coast of Maine, just two hours north. Lobsters and other seafood. Maine Maritime Museum in Bath, Summer Music Theater in Brunswick.

CUTLER NAVAL COMPUTER & TELECOMMUNICATIONS STATION (ME08R1)
HCR 69, Box 198
East Machias, ME 04630-1000

TELEPHONE NUMBER INFORMATION: Main installation numbers: C-207-259-8203, D-312-476-7203.

LOCATION: From I-95 take Alt US-1 to Ellsworth ME, US-1 east to East Machias, right on ME-191 to base at Cutler. USMRA: Page 18 (G,H-7). NMC: Bangor, 100 miles west.

GENERAL INFORMATION: The world's most powerful transmitter. Provides fleet communications.

TEMPORARY MILITARY LODGING: BEQ/BOQ C-207-259-8201/8284, Fax 207-259-7231.

LOGISTICAL SUPPORT: Most support facilities available.

Cafeteria-259-8225	CDO/OOD259-8229/8226	CHAMPUS-259-8219/09
Chaplain-259-8388	Commissary-259-8270	Consol Club-259-8277
Exchange-259-8244	Fire Dept-259-8260	ITT Office-259-8201
Locator-258-8203	Medical-259-8209/219	Police-259-8267
Rec Services-259-8284	Snack Bar-259-8277	

HEALTH & WELFARE: Naval Branch Medical Clinic, Appointments C-207-259-8209/219, Emergency after hours EX-229.

U.S. FORCES TRAVEL & TRANSFER GUIDE U.S.A. - 151

MAINE
Cutler Naval Computer & Telecommunications Station, continued

RECREATION: Bowling EX-275, Hobby Shop EX-285. Sprague's Neck on base, year round, C-207-259-8284, D-312-476-7284, one log cabin (Running water and indoor sanitary facilities 15 May-15 Sep), 10 camper spaces w/o hookups.

SPACE-A: None. See Bangor ANG Base listing, C-207-990-7212/7247, D-312-698-7212/7247, Fax 207-990-7216.

ATTRACTIONS: Skiing, hiking.

SOUTH PORTLAND COAST GUARD BASE (ME11R1)
259 High Street
South Portland, ME 04106-0007

TELEPHONE NUMBER INFORMATION: Main installation numbers: C-207-767-0320.

LOCATION: Exit I-95 to I-295 north, exit I-295 to Broadway, east to South Portland. Watch for signs to the base. USMRA: Page 18 (B,C-9). NMC: South Portland, in city limits.

GENERAL INFORMATION: Industrial Base/SAR Station.

TEMPORARY MILITARY LODGING: None. See Brunswick Naval Air Station listing, C-207-921-2245, D-312-476-2245, Fax 207-792-0232.

LOGISTICAL SUPPORT: Some support facilities available.

CDO/OOD-767-0303	**Consol Club-767-0374**	**Exchange-767-4757**
Locator-767-0320	**Medical-767-0339**	**MWR-767-0311**
Personnel-767-0331		

HEALTH & WELFARE: Dispensary (0800-1500 Mon-Fri) C-207-767-0339. Inpatient, see Brunswick NAS listing, C-207-921-2243.

SPACE-A: None. See Brunswick NAS listing, C-207-921-2682/2689, D-312-476-2682/2689.

ATTRACTIONS: City of Portland.

WINTER HARBOR
NAVAL SECURITY GROUP ACTIVITY (ME09R1)
10 Eabbri Green, Suite 10
Winter Harbor, ME 04693-7001

TELEPHONE NUMBER INFORMATION: Main installation numbers: C-207-963-5534/5535, (ask for extensions) D-312-476-9287.

LOCATION: From Ellsworth, take US-1 north to ME-186 east to Acadia National Park. Naval Security Station on Schoodic Point in the park. USMRA: Page 18 (F-8). NMC: Bangor, 45 miles northwest.

GENERAL INFORMATION: Provides communications security and performs other security activities for Navy units.

MAINE
Winter Harbor Naval Security Group Activity, continued

TEMPORARY MILITARY LODGING: Lodging office, Bldg. 84, 0730-2230 daily, C-207-963-5534 EX-223, D-312-476-9223. All ranks.

LOGISTICAL SUPPORT: Complete support facilities available.

CDO/OOD-963-5534	CHAMPUS-EX-297	Chaplain-EX-279
Child Care-EX-265	Club(all ranks) EX-283/4	Commissary-EX-259
Conv Store-EX-254	Exchange-EX-254	Fire Dept-EX-229
Gas Station-963-7391	Legal-EX-210	Locator-963-5534
Medical-EX-297	MWR-963-5537	Police-EX-225
Public Affairs-EX-224	Recreation-EX-287	RV/Camping-EX-287

HEALTH & WELFARE: Naval Branch Medical Clinic, Emergency C-207-963-7206 EX-297 or C-207-963-5534. Chapel serving all faiths C-207-963-5534 EX-279.

RECREATION: MWR, C-207-963-5537/5534, EX-287, D-312-476-9287. Bowling Center, Auto Hobby Shop, Weight and Exercise Rooms, Gear Issue 963-5537, Saunas, Racquetball and Tennis Courts, Hiking Trails, Car Wash, Child Development Center. Winter Harbor Recreation Area on base, 15 Apr-15 Oct, C-207-963-5537, D-312-476-9287/9288, five camper spaces w/W&E hookups, one camper space w/o hookups, three tent spaces, six recreation cabins and five mobile homes.

SPACE-A: None. See Bangor ANG Base listing, C-207-990-7212/7247, D-312-698-7212/7247, Fax 207-990-7216.

ATTRACTIONS: Boating and fishing, hiking, swimming, golfing, fall foliage, downhill and cross-country skiing, fresh seafood, August blueberry harvest.

Other Installations in Maine

Camp Keyes, Augusta, ME 04333-0033.
USMRA: Page 18 (C-8). C-207-626-4271, D-312-476-1110, Exchange-626-4213.
Rockland Coast Guard Station, 34 Tillson Ave., Rockland, ME 04841-3498.
USMRA: Page 18 (D-8). C-207-596-6667, Exchange-594-7731.
Southwest Harbor Coast Guard Group, P.O. Box 5000, Southwest Harbor, ME 04679-5000. USMRA: Page 18 (E,F-8). C-207-244-5517, Exchange-244-5670.

U.S. FORCES TRAVEL & TRANSFER GUIDE U.S.A. - 153

MARYLAND

DOLLAR RENT A CAR Call 1-800-800-4000. Get a military rate by using your Military Living ID # ML3009. Retirees/Active Duty/Reserve/Guard.

ABERDEEN PROVING GROUND (MD11R1)
Aberdeen Proving Ground, MD 21005-5055

TELEPHONE NUMBER INFORMATION: Main installation numbers: C-410-278-1110, D-312-298-5201.

LOCATION: Aberdeen Area: From I-95, take exit 85 to MD-22 east for two miles to main gate. Edgewood Area: From I-95, take exit 77 to MD-24 for two miles to main gate. Also, from US-40 right (if coming from Baltimore) on MD 755 (Edgewood Rd) then right on US-24 to main gate. USMRA: Page 42 (G-2,3). NMC: Baltimore, 23 miles southwest.

GENERAL INFORMATION: US Army Test & Evaluation Command, Army Research Laboratory, U.S. Army Ordnance Center & School, School of Military Packaging Technology, Army Environmental Center, 203rd Military Intelligence Battalion, U.S. Army Center for Health Promotion and Preventive Medicine, Army Materiel Systems Analysis Activity, Chemical and Biological Defense Command, 389th Army Band.

TEMPORARY MILITARY LODGING: Aberdeen Area: Lodging office, Bldg. 2207, Bel Air St, 24 hours daily, C-410-278-5148, D-312-298-5148. All ranks. DV/VIP C-410-278-1038. Edgewood Area: Lodging office, C-410-617-3848

LOGISTICAL SUPPORT: Complete support facilities available.

ABERDEEN AREA

ACS-278-4372/7474/7478
Exchange-272-6828
Medical-278-4671
Package Store-272-6269

Chaplain-278-4333
Family Services-278-4530
NCO Club-272-8873
Shoppette-272-1681

Commissary-278-7561
Locator-278-5138
O'Club-272-3062

EDGEWOOD AREA

ACS-671-3362
Family Services-671-3362

Chaplain-671-4109
Medical-671-3001

Commissary-671-2114
O'Club-671-5400

HEALTH & WELFARE: Aberdeen Area: US Army Health Clinic, Emergency C-410-278-332, Appointments C-410-278-4671. Inpatient, see Fort George G. Meade listing, C-301-677-8151. Chapel serving all faiths C-410-278-4333. Edgewood Area: US Army Health Clinic, Emergency C-410-278-3332. Chapel serving all faiths C-410-671-4109.

RECREATION: Aberdeen Area: Arts & Crafts EX-4207, Auto Hobby EX-5178, Boat Dock EX-3344, Bowling EX-4041, Golf EX-4794, Gym EX-4216, Library EX-3417, Rec Center EX-2621, Rec Equip EX-4124, Boating Club 272-4124. Edgewood Area: Flying Club 676-2882, Golf EX-2213, Gym EX-3375, Library EX-3650, Rec Center EX-2713, Rec Equip EX-2713, Boat Club 671-7320, Riding club EX-6500. Skipper's Point Recreational Area on post, year round, C-410-278-4124, D-312-298-4124, six camper spaces w/o hookups, 15 tent spaces.

SPACE-A: None. See Andrews AFB listing, C-301-981-1854/3526, D-312-858-1854, Fax 301-981-4241.

MARYLAND
Aberdeen Proving Ground, continued

ATTRACTIONS: Ordnance Museum. Baltimore a short drive away, one of the world's largest ports. Fort McHenry, where Francis Scott Key composed the "Star Spangled Banner."

ANDREWS AIR FORCE BASE (MD02R1)
1535 Command Drive
Andrews AFB, MD 20331-5000

TELEPHONE NUMBER INFORMATION: Main installation numbers: C-301-981-1110, D-312-858-1110/6161.

LOCATION: From I-95 (east portion of Capital Beltway, I-495), take exit 9; first traffic light after leaving exit ramp turn left. At next traffic light turn right into main gate of AFB. Also, from I-395 north, exit South Capitol St, cross Anacostia River on South Capitol St, bear left to Suitland Parkway east, exit Parkway at Morningside on Suitland Rd east to main gate of AFB. Clearly marked. USMRA: Page 42 (E-5) Page 55 (I,J-6,7). NMC: Washington, DC, six miles northwest.

GENERAL INFORMATION: Air Mobility Command Base. 89th Airlift Wing and support units, 459th Airlift Wing (AFRES), D.C. Air National Guard, Naval Air Facility, and Air National Guard Support Center.

TEMPORARY MILITARY LODGING: Lodging, the Gateway Inn, office, Bldg. 1375, Arkansas Rd, 24 hours daily, C-301-423-1412, D-312-858-4614. All ranks. DV/VIP C-301-423-4525.

LOGISTICAL SUPPORT: Complete support facilities available.

Cafeteria-568-2381/2357
Child Care-981-3035
Family Center-981-7087
Golf Course-981-4404
Locator-981-6161
NCO Club-981-3799
Retiree Services-981-2726
SDO/NCO-981-5058
Theater-981-2273

CHAMPUS-981-5615
Commissary-981-7105
Fire Dept-981-4985
ITT Office-981-6560
Medical-981-2411
O'Club-420-5091
RV/Camping-981-4413
Shoppette-568-2364
Visitor Center-981-0689

Chaplain-981-2111
Exchange-568-2222
Gas Station-981-0868
Legal-981-3622
MWR-981-5663
Police-981-9334
SATO-202-433-8326
Snack Bar-568-0180/2357

HEALTH & WELFARE: Malcolm Grow USAF Medical Center, Emergency C-301-981-2333, Appointments C-301-981-7511, 235 beds. Chapel serving all faiths C-301-981-2111.

RECREATION: Aero Club EX-6900, Auto Hobby EX-3917/6643, Bowling EX-6452, Golf EX-4404, Gym EX-7101, Library EX-6454, Multi-Craft EX-2697, Racquetball EX-7101, Rec Center EX-6560, Skeet/Trap EX-5985, Swimming EX-4944, Tennis EX-5710, Youth Center EX-5636. Fam-Camp on base, year round, C-301-981-4109, 11 camper spaces w/full hookups.

SPACE-A: Pax Term/Lounge, Bldg. 1245, 0600-2200 hours daily, C-301-981-1854, D-312-858-1854, Fax 301-981-4241, flights to CONUS locations.

ATTRACTIONS: Aerial gateway to Washington, DC, home of "Air Force One"...the President's aircraft. Monuments, White House, parks, and museums.

U.S. FORCES TRAVEL & TRANSFER GUIDE U.S.A. - 155

MARYLAND

CURTIS BAY COAST GUARD YARD (MD01R1)
2401 Hawkins Point Road
Baltimore, MD 21226-1797

TELEPHONE NUMBER INFORMATION: Main installation numbers: C-410-636-4117 (ask for extensions).

LOCATION: Take I-695 to exit 1, bear to your right, right on Hawkins Point Rd, left into Coast Guard Yard. USMRA: Page 42 (F-3) Page 49 (C-4). NMC: Baltimore, two miles north.

GENERAL INFORMATION: The Coast Guard's only shipbuilding and repair facility. Curtis Bay Station, CG Group Baltimore, two homeported ships.

TEMPORARY MILITARY LODGING: No central Lodging office, CGES office, Bldg. 28A (BOQ), C-410-636-7373; Transient Family Lodging, Guest Housing Manager, C-410-636-4187, 0900-1500 Mon-Fri, other hours, OOD/JOOD, Bldg. 33, C-410-636-7493. All ranks. Space available.

LOGISTICAL SUPPORT: Most support facilities available.

CHAMPUS-636-3144	Chaplain-636-7715	Drydock Club-636-7382
Exchange-636-4198	Family Services-636-3159	Legal-636-7250
Medical-636-3144	O'Club-636-7356	OOD/JOOD-636-7493
Police-636-3695		

HEALTH & WELFARE: USCG Yard Clinic, Emergency C-410-636-3144. Inpatient, see Fort George G. Meade listing, C-301-677-8151. Chapels serving all faiths 410-636-7715.

RECREATION: Auto Hobby EX 3785, Bowling EX 3968, Marina EX-2656, Rec Center, Special Services Office, Swimming EX 7494.

SPACE-A: Try Martin State Airport, ANG Base Ops (135th TAG), during flight processing, C-410-780-8308, D-312-235-8308, flights to CONUS, OCONUS and overseas locations. This organization is not staffed to process requests for Space-A travel on a regular basis.

ATTRACTIONS: Oriole Park at Camden Yards, Inner Harbor (Aquarium, Science Center, Baltimore Zoo) maritime and streetcar museums, Baltimore Arena, Fort McHenry, World Trade Center.

FORT DETRICK (MD07R1)
Bldg. 810
Fort Detrick, MD 21702-5000

TELEPHONE NUMBER INFORMATION: Main installation numbers: C-301-619-8000, D-312-343-8000.

LOCATION: From Washington DC, take I-270 north to US-15 north. From Baltimore, take I-70 west to US-15 north. From US-15 north, in Frederick, exit Seventh St. Clearly marked to post. USMRA: Page 42 (D-2). NMC: Baltimore, 50 miles east and Washington DC, 50 miles southeast.

MARYLAND
Fort Detrick, continued

GENERAL INFORMATION: US Army Medical Research and Materiel Command, US Army Medical Research Institute of Infectious Diseases, 1110th Signal Battalion Telecommunications Center, Quad-Service Medical Logistics.

TEMPORARY MILITARY LODGING: Lodging office, Bldg. 810, Schreider Street, 0745-1630 Mon-Fri, C-301-619-2154, D-312-343-2154. All ranks. DV/VIP C-301-619-7114.

LOGISTICAL SUPPORT: Most support facilities available.

ACS-619-2197	CHAMPUS-619-7175	Chaplain-619-7371
Child Care-619-3300	Commissary-619-2521	Community Center-619-2823
Exchange-619-2262	Family Services-619-2197	Fire Dept-619-7318
Gas Station-662-7777	Legal-619-2221	Locator-619-8000/1110
Medical-619-7175	NCO-619-7114	Police-619-7114
Public Affairs-619-2018	Recreation-619-2711	RV/Camping-619-2759
SDO/NCO-619-7114	Travel-631-2073	

HEALTH & WELFARE: US Army Health Clinic, Appointments C-301-619-7175. Inpatient, see Fort George G. Meade listing, C-301-677-8151. Chapel serving Protestants and Catholics C-301-619-7371.

RECREATION: Arts/Crafts EX-2292, Auto Hobby EX-2759, Bowling EX-2816, Driving Range EX-2964, Field House/Gym EX-2498, Fishing Pond EX-2498, Fitness Center EX-2374, Library EX-7519, Skeet Range/3D Archery Range EX-2823, Swimming EX-2374, Tennis EX-2498, Youth Center EX-2901.

SPACE-A: None. See Andrews AFB listing, C-301-981-1854, D-312-858-1854, Fax 301-981-4241.

ATTRACTIONS: Baltimore, Washington, and Gettysburg are easy drives. Near snow ski resorts. Quaint shops and excellent restaurants in Historic Frederick.

FORT GEORGE G. MEADE (MD08R1)
HQ, Bldg. 2738, Ernie Pyle Avenue
Fort George G. Meade, MD 20755-5000

TELEPHONE NUMBER INFORMATION: Main installation numbers: C-410-677-6261, D-312-923-6261.

LOCATION: Off Baltimore-Washington Parkway, I-295, exit MD-198 east, Fort Meade Rd. Clearly marked. USMRA: Page 42 (E,F-4). NMC: Baltimore (15 miles) and Washington DC (25 miles).

GENERAL INFORMATION: Headquarters First Army (East), National Security Agency, 694th Intelligence Group, Naval Securities Group Activities, Defense Information School, and Army Field Band.

TEMPORARY MILITARY LODGING: Lodging office, Bldg. 4707, Ruffner Rd, Brett Hall, 24 hours daily, C-410-677-6529/5884, D-312-923-6529/5884. All ranks.

LOGISTICAL SUPPORT: Complete support facilities available.

MARYLAND
Fort George G. Meade, continued

ACS-677-5540	CHAMPUS-677-8982	Car Care-672-2879
Chaplain-677-6704/6703	Child Care-677-6312	Commissary-677-7463
Conv Store-674-6896	EM Club-677-4546/7576	Exchange-674-7170
Family Services-677-6948	ITT-677-7354	Legal-677-9536
Locator-677:Civ-7657	Medical-677-2570/3911	MWR-677-2988
Army-4547	NCO Club-677-4546/7576	O'Club-677-5298
AF-0298	Package Store-674-6988	Police-677-6622/6623
MC-0266	Public Affairs-677-1361/62	Recreation-677-5822
Navy-0336	Retiree Services-677-7433	RV/Camping-677-3810
SATO-677-4871	SDO/SNO-677-4805	Snack Bar-672-7332
Theater-677-5324		

HEALTH & WELFARE: Kimbrough Army Community Hospital, Emergency C-410-677-2520/3911, Appointments C-301-677-8151. Chapels serving all faiths C-410-677-6703/04.

RECREATION: Auto Hobby EX-5542, Bowling EX-5541, Rec Equip EX-3825, Sports Arena 677-3716, Golf EX-4333, Gym EX-3042, Library EX-4509, Multi-Craft EX-7809, Outdoor Rec EX-3810, Picnic Area EX-3810, Swimming EX-3716, Tennis EX-3042, Youth Center EX-1847.

AAFES
Army & Air Force Exchange Service
Fort Meade Exchange
(410) 674-7170
Easy stop off I-95 or the Baltimore-Washington Parkway

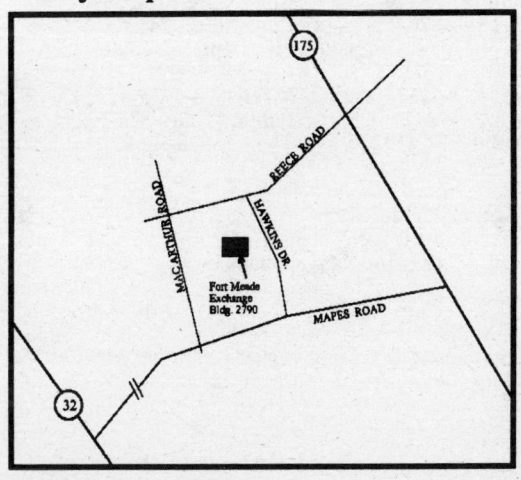

Features

- Main Exchange   [E]
- Gas Station   [gas pump icon]
- Shoppette   [S]
- Class 6   [VI]

MARYLAND
Fort George G. Meade, continued

SPACE-A: None. See Andrews AFB listing, C-301-981-1854/3526, D-312-858-1854, Fax 301-981-4241.

ATTRACTIONS: Museum on post, horse races at Laurel.

FORT RITCHIE (MD13R1)
Bldg. 343, Fort Ritchie, MD 21719-5010

This base is scheduled to close under the 1995 BRAC.
No closure date has been established.

TELEPHONE NUMBER INFORMATION: Main installation numbers: C-301-878-1300, D-312-277-1300.

LOCATION: From US-15 north, exit at Thurmont to MD-550 north for seven miles to Cascade, and main gate. Also, from Hagerstown, take MD-64 east to MD-491 north to MD-550 north to Cascade and main gate. USMRA: Page 42 (C,D-1). NMC: Hagerstown, 16 miles southwest.

GENERAL INFORMATION: Headquarters Defense Information Systems Agency-Western Hemisphere, US Army Information Systems Engineering Command—Continental United States; Headquarters, 1108th US Army Signal Brigade, and US Army Garrison, Fort Ritchie.

TEMPORARY MILITARY LODGING: Fort Ritchie Guest House Bldg. 520, West Banfill Ave & Cushman Ave, 0800-1845 Mon-Fri, 0800-1645 Sat, Sun, and holidays, C-301-241-4445 or 878-5171, DC Dial 878-5171, D-312-988-5171. The Community Club has comfortable accommodations with views of lower Lake Royer, call the Guest House for reservations.

LOGISTICAL SUPPORT: Complete support facilities available.

CHAMPUS-878-5118
Commissary-878-5881
Exchange-241-4600
Gas Station-241-4334
Locator-878-5685
Package Store-878-4290
Retiree Services-878-5747
Travel Office-878-4396

Chaplain-878-5146
Comm Club-878-4361
Family Services-878-5040
ITR Office-878-5577
Medical-878-4132/5439
Police-878-4500
Snack Bar-878-4192

Child Care-878-5380
Conv Store- 241-4334
Fire Dept-241-4500
Legal-878-5771
MWR-878-5233
Public Affairs-878-5874
Theater-878-5867

HEALTH & WELFARE: US Army Health Clinic, Emergency C-301-241-4500, Appointments C-301-878-4132/4455. Inpatient, see Walter Reed Army Medical Center, Washington, DC listing, C-800-433-3574. Chapel serving all faiths C-301-878-5070.

RECREATION: Arts/Crafts EX-4212, Auto Hobby EX-5891, Bowling EX-4192, Community Center EX-5881, Golf EX-4192, Gym EX-4485, Library EX-5060, Outdoor Rec EX-4186, Ski Club EX-4186, Swimming EX-4186, Tennis EX-4186, Wood Hobby EX-4212, Youth Activities EX-5500. Outdoor Recreation Center on post, year round, C-301-878-4186, D-312-977-4186, lake, picnic area, boat rental, tennis, swimming, fishing, ice skating, nearby ski resorts.

MARYLAND
Fort Ritchie, continued

SPACE-A: None. See Andrews AFB listing, C-301-981-1854, D-312-858-1854, Fax 301-981-4241.

ATTRACTIONS: Several snow ski areas nearby, historic Gettysburg, PA. Historic Civil War sites surround the area.

INDIAN HEAD
NAVAL SURFACE WARFARE CENTER (MD04R1)
101 Strauss Avenue
Indian Head, MD 20640-5000

TELEPHONE NUMBER INFORMATION: Main installation numbers: C-301-743-4000, D-312-354-4000.

LOCATION: Take I-495 (Capital Beltway) east, exit to MD-210 south for 25 miles to station. USMRA: Page 42 (D-5,6). NMC: Washington DC, 25 miles north.

GENERAL INFORMATION: Naval Explosive Ordnance Disposal Technology Center.

TEMPORARY MILITARY LODGING: Lodging office, Bldg. 969, Jackson St, 0730-2330, daily, BEQ/BOQ, C-301-743-4845, D-312-364-4845. Fax 301-743-4838.

LOGISTICAL SUPPORT: Limited support facilities available.

CDO/OOD-743-4845	CHAMPUS-743-4601	Chaplain-743-4340
Child Care-743-4458	Club (all ranks)-743-4648	Exchange-743-4851
Family Services-743-5180	Fire Dept-743-4370	Golf Course-743-4662
ITT Office-743-4875	Legal-743-6668	Locator-743-4000
Medical-743-4601	Police-743-4381	SATO-743-7116
SDO/NCO-743-4438		

HEALTH & WELFARE: Naval Branch Medical Clinic, Emergency C-301-743-4601. Inpatient, see Andrews AFB listing, C-301-981-7511. Chapel serving all faiths C-301-743-3183.

RECREATION: Rec Office EX-4850/4761, Gym EX-4850, Golf course EX-4662, Bowling EX-4761, Auto Hobby EX-6314, Racquetball EX-1396, Library EX-4747, Weight Room EX-1396/4661.

SPACE-A: None. See Andrews AFB listing. C-301-981-1854, D-312-858-1854, Fax 301-981-4241.

ATTRACTIONS: New amphitheater along side the Potomac has summer concerts and special events. The Potomac River and Washington, DC, 28 miles north.

NATIONAL NAVAL MEDICAL CENTER (MD06R1)
8901 Wisconsin Ave
Bethesda, MD 20889-5600

TELEPHONE NUMBER INFORMATION: Main installation numbers: C-301-295-4611, D-312-295-4611.

160 - U.S. FORCES TRAVEL & TRANSFER GUIDE U.S.A

MARYLAND
National Naval Medical Center, continued

LOCATION: From I-495 (Capital Beltway) take Wisconsin Ave exit south one mile to Naval Medical Center on left. USMRA: Page 55 (D,E-1). NMC: Washington, DC, one mile southeast.

GENERAL INFORMATION: The Navy's largest and most advanced medical center, Uniformed Services University of the Health Sciences.

TEMPORARY MILITARY LODGING: Housing office, Bldg. 8, 0800-1630 daily, BEQ/BOQ/DV/VIP C-301-295-5855/1111. D-312-295-0321/0307. Navy Lodge, Bldg. 52, 0800-2200 daily, C-301-654-1795, for reservations call 1-800-NAVY-INN, Fax 301-295-5955. All ranks.

LOGISTICAL SUPPORT: Complete support facilities available except Commissary.

Cafeteria-295-2618
Chaplain-295-1501
EM Club-295-0256
ITT-295-0030
Medical-295-4810
Package Store-654-6382
SATO-295-5101

CDO/OOD-295-4611
Child Care-295-0014
Exchange-295-0871/6362
Legal-295-2215
MWR-295-0030
Police-295-1246

CHAMPUS-295-5143/5144
Conv Store-295-6362
Gas Station-295-6359
Locator-295-5202
O'Club-652-6318
Public Affairs-295-5727

HEALTH & WELFARE: National Naval Medical Center, Emergency C-301-295-4810, Appointments C-301-295-1400, Info C-301-295-5387, 500 beds. Chapel serving all faiths C-301-295-1511.

RECREATION: Bowling EX-2060, Gym EX-0031, Library EX-1184, Rec Services EX-0031, Swimming EX-0031, Tennis EX-0031, Picnic area on S Palmer Rd.

SPACE-A: None. See Andrews AFB listing, C-301-981-1854, D-312-858-1854, Fax 301-981-4241.

ATTRACTIONS: National Zoo in nearby Rock Creek Park. Wisconsin Ave S ends in the Georgetown section of Washington, DC. Washington National Cathedral is off Wisconsin Ave at Massachusetts Ave.

PATUXENT RIVER NAVAL AIR STATION (MD09R1)
Patuxent River, MD 20670-5409

TELEPHONE NUMBER INFORMATION: Main installation numbers: C-301-342-3000/1000, D-312-342-3000.

LOCATION: From I-95 (east portion of Capital Beltway, I-495) take exit 7A to Branch Ave (MD-5) south. Follow MD-5 until it becomes MD-235 near Oraville, on to Lexington Park, and the NAWC. Main gate is on MD-235 and MD-246 (Cedar Point Rd). USMRA: Page 42 (F,G-6,7). NMC: Washington DC, 65 miles northwest.

GENERAL INFORMATION: Naval Air Warfare Center Aircraft Division and Naval Air Station.

TEMPORARY MILITARY LODGING: No central billeting office. See ITT, Bldg. 458, Room 5, 0900-1630 daily, BEQ/BOQ/DV/VIP C-301-342-3631/3601, D-312-342-

U.S. FORCES TRAVEL & TRANSFER GUIDE U.S.A. - 161

MARYLAND
Patuxent River Naval Air Station, continued

631/3601, Navy Lodge C-301-737-2400, 1-800-NAVY-INN. Housing office, Bldg. 423, 0730-1600 daily, Fax 301-342-1015. All ranks.

LOGISTICAL SUPPORT: Complete support facilities available.

CDO/OOD-342-1095
Child Care-342-7639
CPO Club-342-3657/3685
Family Services-342-4911
Golf Course-342-3597
Locator-342-4911
O'Club-342-3656
Public Affairs-342-7512
RV/Camping-326-4216
Theater-342-3572

CHAMPUS-342-1457
Commissary-342-3789
EM Club-342-3657/3685
Fire Dept-342-3333
ITT Office-342-3508
Medical-342-1436
Package Store-342-9315
Recreation-342-3510/3521
SATO-342-1051 ext.115
Visitor Center-342-3231

Chaplain-342-3812/5050
Conv Store-342-8715
Exchange-342-7483
Gas Station-342-5828
Legal-342-1045/1046
MWR-342-3510
Police-342-3277
Retiree Services-342-4911
Snack Bar-342-5608

HEALTH & WELFARE: Naval Hospital, Emergency C-301-342-1422, Appointments C-301-342-1500. Chapels serving all faiths C-301-342-3812.

RECREATION: Auto Hobby EX-3507, Bowling EX-3994, Ceramics EX-3160, Rec Equip EX-3519, Golf EX-3597, Gym EX-3519/3508, Library EX-1927, Marina EX-3573, Stables EX-3296, Swimming EX-4225/5960, Wood Hobby EX-3569, Youth Center EX-3329. Goose Creek/West Basin Recreation Area on base, Feb-Nov, C-301-342-5408, D-312-342-3232, 14 camper spaces w/W&E hookups, 46 camper/tent spaces w/o hookups.

SPACE-A: Pax Term/Lounge, Bldg. 103, 24 hours daily, C-301-342-3836/7, D-312-342-3836/7, flights to CONUS locations.

ATTRACTIONS: Calvert Cliffs Nuclear Power Plant Museum, Calvert Marine Museum, Naval Air Test & Evaluation Museum, Potomac River-St Clement's Island Museum, St Mary's City, Sotterley Plantation, Cecil's Mill, Point Lookout State Park, Seafood Festivals.

SOLOMONS NAVY RECREATION CENTER (MD05R1)
PO Box 147
Solomons, MD 20688-0147

TELEPHONE NUMBER INFORMATION: Main installation numbers: C-410-326-4216, DC Metro: 1-800-NAVY-230.

LOCATION: On Patuxent River in Solomons. From I-95 (east portion of Capital Beltway, I-495) exit 11A, Pennsylvania Ave and MD 4 for 65 miles southeast. Clearly marked. USMRA: Page 42 (F,6). NMC: Washington DC, 65 miles northwest.

GENERAL INFORMATION: A Navy operated/managed rec center of 262 acres on delta where Patuxent River merges with Chesapeake Bay. Open year round.

TEMPORARY MILITARY LODGING: Reservation office, Bldg. 411, outside main gate, 0900-1800 daily (later hours in summer), reservations numbers above. Call for peak season reservation priority information. 53 units include: furnished cottages, 1-5 bedrooms, equipped kitchens. Most have one bath, some have two. TVs, telephones not provided. Linens not provided but may be rented.

MARYLAND
Solomons Navy Recreation Center, continued

LOGISTICAL SUPPORT: Limited. The following support facilities available: ice vending, campers' store (summer season), and laundry. Exchange, commissary, located at Patuxent River NAWC.

SDO/NCO-326-3566   **Security-326-2436**

HEALTH & WELFARE: None. See Patuxent River NAS listing, C-301-342-1500.

RECREATION: Swimming Pools, Beach, Fitness Center, Basketball, Volleyball, Tennis, Marina, Picnic Areas, Table Tennis, Movies, Gear Issue, Amusement Machines Arcade, Fishing Pier. 146 camper spaces w/full hookups, 151 camper spaces w/W&E, seven electric only camper spaces and 56 camper/tent spaces w/o hookups, 15 tent spaces. C-410-326-4216.

SPACE-A: None. See Patuxent River NAS listing, C-301-342-3836, D-312-342-3836.

ATTRACTIONS: Solomons Island area, historic St Mary's City, and Cliffs of Calvert. Excellent area for crabbing, fishing, sailing and boating.

UNITED STATES NAVAL ACADEMY
ANNAPOLIS NAVAL STATION (MD10R1)
348 Kinkaid Road
Annapolis, MD 21402-5073

TELEPHONE NUMBER INFORMATION: Main installation numbers: C-410-293-1000, D-312-281-1000.

LOCATION: Off US-50/301, clearly marked. Naval Station is off US-50/301 east, clearly marked. USMRA: Page 42 (F-4), page 48 (D,E,F,G-1,2,3). NMC: Annapolis, within city limits.

GENERAL INFORMATION: Navy education facility for officers and their support.

TEMPORARY MILITARY LODGING: BEQ, Bldg. 168, 0800-1600 Sun, Mon & holidays, 0800-2300 Tue-Sat, C-410-293-2587, D-312-281-3906. BOQ, Bldg. 2, 0800-1600 Sun, Mon & holidays, 0800-2300 Tue-Sat, C-410-293-3906, D-312-281-3906. DV/VIP C-410-293-1500.

LOGISTICAL SUPPORT: Complete support facilities available.

CDO/OOD-293-9068	CHAMPUS-293-2276	Chaplain-293-9100
Child Care-293-9390	Clipper Club-267-3660	Commissary-293-2494
Conv Store-757-2120	Exchange-757-0005	Family Services-293-2641
Fire Dept-293-3333	Gas Station-757-2120	Golf Course-757-2022
ITT Office-267-4059	Legal-293-9025	Locator-293-2385
Medical-293-2061	MWR-293-3660	O'Club-293-2611
Package Store-293-3232	Police-293-9300	Public Affairs-293-2291
Retiree Services-293-2641	RV/Camping-293-9200	SATO-268-7203
SDO/NCO-293-3972	Theater-293-1100	Visitor Center-263-6933

HEALTH & WELFARE: Naval Branch Medical Clinic, Emergency C-410-293-2561, Appointments C-410-293-3617. Inpatient, see National Naval Medical Center, listing, C-301-295-1400. Chapels serving all faiths C-410-293-2891.

U.S. FORCES TRAVEL & TRANSFER GUIDE U.S.A. - 163

MARYLAND
United States Naval Academy, continued

RECREATION: Auto Hobby EX-3731, Bowling EX-3034, Rec Equip EX-3580, Golf 757-2022, Hobby Shops EX-3731, Gym EX-3850/2518, Library EX-2311, Marina EX-3731, Rec Center EX-2518/3691, Swimming EX-3691/2518, Youth Activities EX-3580/3691. Fam-Camp on base, Mar-Nov, C-410-293-9200, D-312-281-9200, 14 camper spaces w/W&E hookups.

SPACE-A: None. See Andrews AFB listing, C-301-981-1854, D-312-858-1854, Fax 301-981-4241.

ATTRACTIONS: Walking tour of the Naval Academy, museum, tour of historic Annapolis, city dock area, and the Maryland Capitol building.

Other Installations in Maryland

Cheltenham Naval Communications Station, Washington, DC 20397-5310.
USMRA: Page 42 (E-5). C-301-238-2380, Consol Club-238-2436, MWR-238-2444, Package Store-238-2407.
Martin State Airport/Warfield Air National Guard, Bldg. 1110, 2701 Eastern Blvd, Baltimore, MD 21220-2899.
USMRA: Page 42 (F,G-3). C-410-780-8210, Exchange 780-6270, Space-A-780-8551.

164 - U.S. FORCES TRAVEL & TRANSFER GUIDE U.S.A

MASSACHUSETTS

DOLLAR RENT A CAR Call 1-800-800-4000. Get a military rate by using your Military Living ID # ML3009. Retirees/Active Duty/Reserve/Guard.

BOSTON COAST GUARD SUPPORT CENTER (MA12R1)
427 Commercial Street
Boston, MA 02109-1027

TELEPHONE NUMBER INFORMATION: Main installation numbers: C-617-223-3257.

LOCATION: From the south on MA-93 or I-90 (Massachusetts Turnpike), exit at Atlantic Ave (which becomes Commercial St), follow for one mile, Center is on the right. From the north on I-93 exit at Charlestown/Sullivan exit, cross Charlestown Bridge, take first left onto Commercial St, Center is two blocks on the left. USMRA: Page 24 (E-4,5). NMC: Boston, in city limits.

GENERAL INFORMATION: Logistic support for major cutters homeported here. Tenant Commands include Marine Safety Office, Group Boston, Ships Repair Detachment, Electronic Maintenance Detachment, Reserve Center Boston.

TEMPORARY MILITARY LODGING: MAA office, Bldg. 4, 427 Commercial St, 0730-1500 Mon-Fri, C-617-223-3171, FTS-223-3171.

LOGISTICAL SUPPORT: Limited support facilities available.

CDO/OOD-223-3313   **CHAMPUS-223-3250**   **Chaplain-223-3164**
Consol Club-223-3265 **Exchange-223-3135**   **Galley-223-3267**
Medical-223-3250

HEALTH & WELFARE: USCG Support Center Clinic C-617-223-3250. Inpatient, Brighton Marine Hospital C-617-782-3400. Chapel serving all faiths C-317-223-3164.

RECREATION: Camping Equipment, Fitness Center, Gym EX-3125.

SPACE-A: None. See Hanscom AFB listing, C-617-377-11433, D-312-478-11433, Fax 617-377-2383.

ATTRACTIONS: City of Boston: Fenway Park, JFK Library and Museum, Blue Hills Reservation, Prospect Hill Ski Area, many universities, Aquarium, Franklin Park Zoo, "Boston Pops," Museum of Science, Computer Museum.

HANSCOM AIR FORCE BASE (MA06R1)
ESC/PA
9 Eglin Street
Hanscom Air Force Base, MA 01731-5000

TELEPHONE NUMBER INFORMATION: Main installation numbers: C-617-377-4441, D-312-478-5980.

MASSACHUSETTS
Hanscom Air Force Base, continued

LOCATION: From I-95, take exit 30B (MA-2A) west for two miles then turn right at the Hanscom Field Sign. USMRA: Page 17 (J-3) Page 24 (A-2). NMC: Boston, 17 miles southeast.

GENERAL INFORMATION: Air Force Materiel Command Base. Hq, Electronics Systems Center, Geophysics Directorate.

TEMPORARY MILITARY LODGING: Lodging office, Bldg. 1427, 24 hours daily, C-617-377-2112, D-312-478-2112. All ranks. DV/VIP EX-5151.

LOGISTICAL SUPPORT: Complete support facilities available.

Cafeteria-377-2189	CHAMPUS-377-4701	Chaplain-377-3538/5144
Child Care-377-2858	Commissary-377-2544	Conv Store-274-8588
Exchange-377-5258	Family Services-377-3436	Gas Station-377-5155
ITT Office-377-3262	Legal-377-2362	Locator-377-5111/4441
Medical-377-2333	NCO Club-377-2123	O'Club-377-5740
Package Store-377-3675	Police-377-4357/2314	Public Affairs-377-5191
Retiree Services-377-2476	SATO-377-2631	Snack Bar-377-2395
SDO/NCO-377-5144	Theater-377-5200	

HEALTH & WELFARE: USAF Clinic, Emergency C-617-377-2333, Appointment C-617-377-4706. Chapel serving all faiths C-617-377-3538.

RECREATION: Activity Schedule EX-2687, Aero Club EX-5160, Auto Hobby EX-2612, Bowling EX-2237, Gym EX-3435/3639, Hobby Shops EX-2612, Rec Services EX-3901, Rec Equipment EX-3348, Services Club EX-2610, Swimming EX-2455, Library EX-2177, Rec Center EX-2610. Fam-Camp off base, year round, C-617-377-4670, 35 camper spaces w/full hookups, 21 camper spaces w/W&E, 10 tent spaces. Fourth Cliff Rec Area off base, C-617-837-9269, or 1-800-468-9547, 11 camper spaces w/full hookups, three cabins.

SPACE-A: Pax Term, Bldg. 1714, Mon-Fri: 0630-2300, Sat-Sun: 0900-1700, C-617-377-1143, D-312-478-1143, (Daily flight recording C-617-377-3333, D-312-478-3333) Fax 617-377-2383, flights to Andrews AFB, MD and other East Coast locations. Uses runways of Lawrence G. Hanscom Field adjoining the base.

ATTRACTIONS: The Bedford flag..."Oldest flag in America." Concord, North Bridge, Lexington, historic sites and taverns.

NATICK SOLDIER SYSTEMS COMMAND (MA11R1)
15 Kansas Street
Natick, MA 01760-5000

TELEPHONE NUMBER INFORMATION: Main installation numbers: C-508-233-4001, D-312-256-4001.

LOCATION: Exit from I-90 (Massachusetts Pike), exit 13, Natick to MA-30 east to MA-27 south. Or exit MA-9 west for six miles to MA-27 south. Watch for signs to the Center's main entrance off Kansas St. USMRA: Page 17 (J-4). NMC: Boston, 25 miles east.

GENERAL INFORMATION: Natick is a US Army AMC Research, Development and Engineering Center.

166 - U.S. FORCES TRAVEL & TRANSFER GUIDE U.S.A

MASSACHUSETTS
Natick Soldier Systems Command, continued

TEMPORARY MILITARY LODGING: None. See Hanscom AFB, C-617-377-2112, D-312-478-2112.

LOGISTICAL SUPPORT: Most support facilities available.

ACS-233-4798	Exchange-233-4797	Family Services-233-4798
Legal 233-4322	Locator-233-4001	MWR-233-4960
NCO Club-233-5583	O'Club-233-4791	Police-233-4201
SATO-233-4299		

HEALTH & WELFARE: Dispensary C-508-651-4155.

RECREATION: Auto Hobby, Weight Room, Rec Services, Swimming, Sailing EX-4960.

SPACE-A: None. See Hanscom AFB listing, C-617-377-1143, D-312-478-1143, Fax 617-377-2383.

ATTRACTIONS: Cities of Boston and Cambridge, Boston National Historical Park, *USS Constitution* and Museum, many other historical sites and museums.

OTIS AIR NATIONAL GUARD BASE (MA07R1)
Otis Air National Guard Base, MA 02542-5024

TELEPHONE NUMBER INFORMATION: Main Installation Numbers: C-508-968-6300, D-557-6300, FTS-642-6300.

LOCATION: Off MA-28 at the base of Cape Cod. USMRA: Page 17 (M-7). NMC: Boston, 70 miles northwest.

GENERAL INFORMATION: Air Force Air National Guard, Army National Guard, Coast Guard Air Station.

TEMPORARY MILITARY LODGING: Temporary quarters, Bldg. 5204, C-508-968-6461.

LOGISTICAL SUPPORT: Limited support facilities available.

Barber Shop-968-6685	CHAMPUS-968-6570	Child Care-968-6450
Consol Club-968-6330	Conv Store-968-6683	Exchange-968-6648
Exchange-968-6662	Gas Station-968-6639	ITT Office-968-6448
Package Store-968-6662	Post Office-968-4278	SDO/NCO-968-6330
Theater-968-6452		

HEALTH & WELFARE: USCG Cape Cod Clinic C-508-968-6570. Inpatient, see Newport Naval Education and Training Center, RI listing, C-401-841-3111. Chapel serving all faiths C-508-968-4901.

RECREATION: Golf Course (9 hole) EX-6454, Auto Hobby EX-6449, Library EX-6456, Rec Equipment EX-6448, Ceramics EX-4045, Tennis, Stables, Teen Center EX-6451. Cape Cod Vacation Apartments on base, year round, 12 town house apartments, 18 suites, two single rooms, C-617-223-8047. Also Cuttyhunk Island Rec Facility off base on Cuttyhunk Island, year round, two apartments. All apartments furnished. Reservations by application are required. More requests are received for the Cuttyhunk apartments than can be approved,

MASSACHUSETTS
Otis Air National Guard Base, continued

C-508-968-5461, FTS-642-6461. See Military Living's *Military RV, Camping & Rec Areas Around the World* for additional information.

SPACE-A: Base Ops/CG Hangar, 0800-1600 Mon-Fri (weekend hours vary), C-508-968-4831, D-312-557-4831, Fax 509-968-6321, CONUS flights.

ATTRACTIONS: Beautiful Cape Cod, near Plymouth and other historic towns. Beaches and water sports.

SOUTH WEYMOUTH NAVAL AIR STATION (MA05R1)
1134 Main Street
South Weymouth, MA 02190-5000

Scheduled to close September, 1996.

TELEPHONE NUMBER INFORMATION: Main installation numbers: C-617-682-2993 (Rings at Hanscom AFB switchboard for South Weymouth NAS), D-312-955-2933.

LOCATION: From MA-3 (Pilgrims Highway) take exit 16 to MA-18 south to 5th traffic light, turn left. USMRA: Page 17 (L-4) Page 24 (G,H-10). NMC: Boston, 15 miles northwest.

GENERAL INFORMATION: Training of Navy and Marine Corps Combat Air Reserve Units.

TEMPORARY MILITARY LODGING: Lodging office, Shea Memorial Dr, 0730-1600 Mon-Fri, BEQ/BOQ/DV/VIP C-617-682-2738/2928, D-312-955-2928. All ranks. DV/VIP 617-682-2738, Fax 617-682-2594. Space very limited on weekends.

LOGISTICAL SUPPORT: Most support facilities available.

CDO/OOD-682-2933	CHAMPUS-682-2675	Chaplain-682-2943
Child Care-682-2934	CPO Club-682-2566	EM Club-682-2566
Exchange-331-1636	Family Services-682-2581	Fire Dept-682-2812
Gas Station-331-1636	ITT-682-2546	Legal-682-2540
Locator-682-2906	Medical-682-2674	O'Club-682-2938
Package Store-331-1636	Police-682-2610	Public Affairs-682-2607
Retiree Services-682-2590	SATO-682-2978	Snack Bar-682-2980

HEALTH & WELFARE: Naval Branch Medical Clinic, Emergency C-617-682-2674. Chaplain C-617-682-2604.

RECREATION: Auto Hobby EX-2886, Swimming EX-2848, Bowling EX-2921.

SPACE-A: Pax Term/Lounge, Hangar 1, 0700-2300 daily, C-617-682-2713, D-312-955-2713, flights to CONUS locations.

ATTRACTIONS: Historic Quincy is nearby. Massachusetts Bay and Boston are easy drives north and northwest. Cape Cod to the south.

168 - U.S. FORCES TRAVEL & TRANSFER GUIDE U.S.A

MASSACHUSETTS

WESTOVER AIR RESERVE BASE (MA03R1)
Westover Air Reserve Base, MA 01022-5000

TELEPHONE NUMBER INFORMATION: Main installation numbers: C-413-557-1110, D-312-589-1110.

LOCATION: Take exit 5 off I-90 (Massachusetts Turnpike) in Chicopee. Westover is on MA-33, north of I-90; signs mark way to base. USMRA: Page 16 (F-4). NMC: Springfield, eight miles south.

GENERAL INFORMATION: Air Force Reserve Base. 439th Airlift Wing, Army Reserve, Navy Reserve, Marine Corps Reserve, and Air Force Reserve units.

TEMPORARY MILITARY LODGING: Lodging office, Bldg. 2200, Outer Dr. (VOQ) C-413-557-2700, D-312-589-2700, 24 hours daily. SDO, 557-3557. All ranks. DV/VIP C-413-557-5421.

LOGISTICAL SUPPORT: Complete support facilities available.

CHAMPUS-557-3918	Commissary-593-3288	Consol Club-593-5531
Exchange-593-5941	Fire Dept-557-3818	Gas Station-593-3288
Legal-557-3513	Locator-557-3874	Medical-557-3565
MWR-557-3958	Police-557-3557	Public Affairs-557-2020
Retiree Services-557-3918	RV/Camping-557-2974	Shoppette-593-3288
Snack Bar-557-3896	SDO/NCO-557-3571	

HEALTH & WELFARE: Dispensary C-413-557-3565. Chaplain C-413-557-3031 (available on Reserve weekends).

RECREATION: Bowling EX-3010, Gym EX-3958.

SPACE-A: Very limited. Pax Term, Bldg. 7091, Base Ops, 0700-2300 daily, C-413-557-2951, D-312-589-2951, flights to CONUS and OCONUS locations on transient aircraft.

ATTRACTIONS: Springfield, Mt. Tom Snow Ski Resort, Holyoke. Basketball Hall Of Fame in Springfield.

Other Installations in Massachusetts

Camp Edwards, Camp Edwards, MA 02542-5003.
USMRA: Page 17 (M-6,7). C-508-968-5886, Consol Club-968-5879.
Nantucket Coast Guard LORAN Station, Natick, MA 01760-5000.
USMRA: Page 17 (O-9). C-508-257-6645, Exchange-257-6564.

U.S. FORCES TRAVEL & TRANSFER GUIDE U.S.A. - 169

MICHIGAN

DOLLAR RENT A CAR Call 1-800-800-4000. Get a military rate by using your Military Living ID # ML3009. Retirees/Active Duty/Reserve/Guard.

ALPENA COMBAT READINESS TRAINING CENTER (MI16R2)
5884 A Street
Alpena, MI 49707-8125

TELEPHONE NUMBER INFORMATION: Main installation numbers: C-517-354-6291, D-312-741-3291.

LOCATION: Five miles west of Alpena on M-32. USMRA: Page 66 (F-4). NMC: Alpena, five miles west.

GENERAL INFORMATION: Air National Guard Training Base.

TEMPORARY MILITARY LODGING: None. See Camp Grayling listing, C-517-348-3661, D-312-722-3661, Fax 517-348-3844.

LOGISTICAL SUPPORT: Some support facilities available.

Exchange-354-6272   Police-354-6210   SATO-354-6290

HEALTH & WELFARE: None. See Traverse City CGAS listing, C-616-922-8282.

SPACE-A: Bldg. 10, C-517-354-6305, D-312-741-3305.

ATTRACTIONS: Lake Huron shore, fishing, hunting, and camping.

CAMP GRAYLING TRAINING SITE (MI10R2)
Grayling, MI 49739-0001

TELEPHONE NUMBER INFORMATION: Main installation numbers: C-517-348-3611. D-312-623-3708

LOCATION: Located three miles west of city of Grayling, just off of I-75. USMRA: Page 66 (D-5). NMC: Grayling, three miles east.

GENERAL INFORMATION: Guard and reserve training center with approximately 147,000 acres of prime infantry, tank, helicopter, artillery, mortar and A/G training area.

TEMPORARY MILITARY LODGING: Lodging office, Bldg. 560, 0700-1700 daily, C-517-348-3661, D-312-722-3661, Fax 517-348-3844.

LOGISTICAL SUPPORT: Some support facilities available. (517-348-7621-EX)

Cafeteria-EX-3242   Chaplain-348-3699   EM Club-EX-3229
Exchange-348-4781   Locator-348-3611   Medical-348-3621
NCO Club-EX-3305   O'Club-348-9033   Police-EX-3764

170 - U.S. FORCES TRAVEL & TRANSFER GUIDE U.S.A

MICHIGAN
Camp Grayling Training Site, continued

HEALTH AND WELFARE: None. See Traverse City CGAS listing, C-616-922-8282. Chapel serving all faiths C-517-348-3699.

RECREATION: Camp Grayling Trailer Park on post, 15 May-15 Sep, C-517-348-7621 EX-3389, 70 camper spaces w/full hookups, 10 tent spaces.

SPACE-A: None. See Alpena Combat Readiness Training Center listing, C-517-354-6305, D-312-741-3305.

ATTRACTIONS: Lake Margrethe, boat launch and beach area, nearby. Huron National Forest, Lake Michigan, Lake Huron, skiing, water recreation. Upper Peninsula 90 miles north, Canada 130 miles north.

DETROIT COAST GUARD GROUP (MI13R2)
110 Mt. Elliott Avenue
Detroit, MI 48207-4380

TELEPHONE NUMBER INFORMATION: Main installation numbers: C-313-568-9525.

LOCATION: From 94 East or West, take the Mt. Elliott exit and travel south. The base is located at 110 Mt. Elliott. USMRA: Page 70 (E-4) NMC: Detroit, in city limits.

GENERAL INFORMATION: Host unit for Group Detroit Offices, Aids to Navigation Detroit, Marine Safety Office Detroit, USCGC Bristol Bay, Reserve Group Detroit, and Reserve Unit Detroit.

TEMPORARY MILITARY LODGING: None. See Selfridge ANGB listing, C-810-307-4062, D-312-273-4062.

LOGISTICAL SUPPORT: Very limited support facilities available.

CHAMPUS-568-9526   **Exchange-259-6217**   **Medical-568-9526/7**

HEALTH & WELFARE: None. See Selfridge ANGB listing, C-810-307-4650.

RECREATION: None. See Selfridge ANGB listing.

SPACE-A: None. See Selfridge ANGB listing, C-810-307-5884, D-312-273-5884.

ATTRACTIONS: Detroit, Lake Huron, and Canada.

GRAND HAVEN COAST GUARD GROUP (MI06R2)
650 Harbor Avenue
Grand Haven, MI 49417-1752

TELEPHONE NUMBER INFORMATION: Main installation numbers: C-616-847-4500.

LOCATION: From I-96 east, to US-31 south in Grand Haven, west on Jackson St and follow it along the waterfront to the Group Office. From US-31 north, go west on Franklin

U.S. FORCES TRAVEL & TRANSFER GUIDE U.S.A. - 171

MICHIGAN
Grand Haven Coast Guard Group, continued

St to Harbor Dr, turn left and follow the road to the Group Office. USMRA: Page 66 (B-8). NMC: Muskegon, 12 miles north.

GENERAL INFORMATION: The center of Coast Guard operations for the western shore of Lake Michigan from Michigan City, IN to Frankfort, MI.

TEMPORARY MILITARY LODGING: None.

LOGISTICAL SUPPORT: Limited support facilities available.

CDO/OOD-847-4500   CHAMPUS-847-4520   Exchange-846-0490
Family Services-847-4503 Package Store-847-0490   Public Affairs-847-4504

HEALTH & WELFARE: Medical Office (0730-1600) C-616-847-4520. No military clinics or hospitals. Nearest civilian medical facility is North Ottawa Community Medical Center, C-616-842-3600 (outside Grand Haven area 800-678-6624). No chapel on base.

RECREATION: Downhill skiing, cross country skiing, ice skating, boating, fishing, golf, beaches, indoor swimming, tennis courts, YMCA programs, trap/skeet shooting, bicycling, canoeing. Operates Point Betsie Recreation Cottage in Frankfort, C-616-847-4530.

SPACE-A: None. See Selfridge ANGB listing, C-810-307-5884, D-312-273-5884.

ATTRACTIONS: Grand Haven State Park, world's largest musical fountain, Annual Coast Guard Anniversary Festival (city has been recognized by Congress as Coast Guard City, USA).

SAULT STE MARIE COAST GUARD GROUP (MI15R2)
337 Water Street
Sault Ste Marie, MI 49783-9501

TELEPHONE NUMBER INFORMATION: Main installation numbers: C-906-635-3217, FTS-372-0217.

LOCATION: Take I-75 north to exit 392, merge onto I-75 Business Spur/Ashmun St. Follow Ashmun St until it ends at St Mary's River. Turn right on Water St, base is three blocks on left. USMRA: Page 66 (E-1,2). NMC: Detroit, 350 miles south.

GENERAL INFORMATION: Vessel Traffic Safety Search Rescue Group, Group Sault Radio telecommunications, Captain of the Port-marine safety, environmental pollution, general administration, ID card issuing activity, ATON/STA small boat stations.

TEMPORARY MILITARY LODGING: None.

LOGISTICAL SUPPORT: Limited support facilities available.

Cafeteria-635-3267   CHAMPUS-635-3225   Exchange-635-3276
Quarterdeck-635-3229   SDO/NCO-635-3233

HEALTH & WELFARE: War Memorial Hospital, C-906-635-4460. No chapel on base.

RECREATION: None available on base.

172 - U.S. FORCES TRAVEL & TRANSFER GUIDE U.S.A

MICHIGAN
Sault Ste Marie Coast Guard Group, continued

SPACE-A: None. See Alpena Combat Readiness Training Center listing, C-517-354-6305, D-312-741-3305.

ATTRACTIONS: Hunting and fishing.

SELFRIDGE AIR NATIONAL GUARD BASE (MI01R2)
29423 George Avenue
Selfridge ANG Base, MI 48045-5029

TELEPHONE NUMBER INFORMATION: Main installation numbers: C-810-307-4011, D-312-273-4011.

LOCATION: Take I-94 north from Detroit to Selfridge exit, then east on MI-59 to main gate of base. USMRA: Page 66 (G-9) Page 70 (G-1). NMC: Detroit, 10 miles southwest.

GENERAL INFORMATION: Air National Guard units, Reserve units of Air Force, Navy, Marine Corps and Army. Coast Guard Air Station Detroit.

TEMPORARY MILITARY LODGING: Lodging office, Bldg. 410, George Ave, 24 hours daily, C-810-307-4062, D-312-273-4062. DV/VIP C-810-307-4062. All ranks.

LOGISTICAL SUPPORT: Complete support facilities available. Some support also available at Detroit Arsenal.

CHAMPUS-307-5261	Chaplain-307-4761	Child Care-307-4711
Commissary-307-5570	Conv Store-307-4256	Exchange-307-5789
Family Services-307-5903	Gas Station-307-4256	Locator-307-4021
Medical-307-4650	O'Club-307-4785	Package Store-307-5072
Police-307-4673	SATO-307-7651	Snack Bar-307-4397
SDO/NCO-307-4011		

HEALTH & WELFARE: US Army Health Clinic, Emergency 911 or C-810-307-5000, Appointment C-810-307-4650. Inpatient, see Wright-Patterson AFB, OH listing, C-513-257-2968 Chapel serving all faiths C-810-307-4761.

RECREATION: Auto Hobby EX-4535, Wood Hobby EX-4535, Multi-Crafts EX- 5155, Rec Center EX-4524/4564, Youth Activities EX-4524/4564, Bowling EX-5941, Swimming/Tennis EX-5765, Picnic Area 463-3070, Golf Course and Outdoor Sports Center EX-4344. Selfridge Outdoor Rec Area, on base, Apr-Sep, C-810-463-3070, D-312-273-3070, marina only, no camping.

SPACE-A: Information, C-810-307-5884, D-312-273-5884.

ATTRACTIONS: Air Museum, Detroit, Canadian cities of Windsor and Sarnia.

TRAVERSE CITY COAST GUARD AIR STATION (MI07R2)
Traverse City, MI 49684-3586

TELEPHONE NUMBER INFORMATION: Main installation numbers: C-616-922-8214, FTS-922-8214.

U.S. FORCES TRAVEL & TRANSFER GUIDE U.S.A. - 173

MICHIGAN
Traverse City Coast Guard Air Station, continued

LOCATION: Located across from Cherry Capital Airport. From US-31 north go south on Airport Access Rd. Air Station will be on the left. USMRA: Page 66 (C-5). NMC: Traverse City, in city limits.

GENERAL INFORMATION: A large rescue air station covering the northern Great Lakes area.

TEMPORARY MILITARY LODGING: None. See Camp Grayling listing, C-517-348-3661, D-312-722-3661.

LOGISTICAL SUPPORT: Limited support facilities available.

Exchange-922-8330   ID Cards-922-8228   Medical-922-8282
Operations-922-8211   SDO/NCO-922-8214

HEALTH & WELFARE: Medical office, Emergency C-616-922-8282. No chapel at station.

SPACE-A: None. See Alpena CRTC, C-517-354-6305, D-312-742-3305.

ATTRACTIONS: Fresh water lakes, local golf courses, ski areas nearby. Sleeping Bear Dunes National Lakeshore, Peshawbetown Indian Village, Old Mission Lighthouse, Manistee National Forest.

Other Installations in Michigan

Battlecreek Air National Guard Base, 3445 Phantom Ave., Battlecreek, MI 49015-5509. USMRA: Page 66 (D-9). C-616-969-3210, Exchange-969-3372.
Detroit Arsenal, Warren, MI 48090-5000.
USMRA: Page 70 (E-2). C-810-574-5000, Medical-574-5771.

174 - U.S. FORCES TRAVEL & TRANSFER GUIDE U.S.A

MINNESOTA

DOLLAR RENT A CAR — Call 1-800-800-4000. Get a military rate by using your Military Living ID # ML3009. Retirees/Active Duty/Reserve/Guard.

CAMP RIPLEY (MN02R2)
PO Box 150
Little Falls, MN 56345

TELEPHONE NUMBER INFORMATION: Main installation number: C-612-632-7000.

LOCATION: Clearly marked off Highway 371. USMRA: Page 80 (C,D-6), NMC: Little Falls, seven miles south.

TEMPORARY MILITARY LODGING: None. See Minneapolis-St Paul IAP/ARS listing, C-612-725-5320, D-312-825-5320.

LOGISTICAL SUPPORT: Some support facilities available.

Exchange-632-7382
NCO Club-632-7255
SATO-632-7465

Family Services-632-7296
O'Club-632-7239
Snack Bar-632-7412

Medical-632-7378
Police-632-7665

HEALTH & WELFARE: None.

SPACE-A: None. See Minneapolis-St Paul IAP listing, C-612-725-5552, D-312-825-5552.

ATTRACTIONS: Hunting, fishing and camping.

MINNEAPOLIS-ST PAUL INTERNATIONAL AIRPORT AIR RESERVE STATION (MN01R2)
760 Military Highway
Minneapolis, MN 55450-2000

TELEPHONE NUMBER INFORMATION: Main installation numbers: C-612-725-5011, D-312-825-5011.

LOCATION: From I-35 E or MN-55 S to crosstown MN-62, exit at 34th Ave and entrance. USMRA: Page 89 (C-3,4). NMC: Minneapolis-St Paul, in city limits.

GENERAL INFORMATION: Air Reserve Station, co-located Air Force Reserve Wing, and ANG Airlift Wing, Navy, Marine Corps and other reserve units.

TEMPORARY MILITARY LODGING: Lodging office, Bldg. 711, 0700-2200 hours Mon-Fri, 0630-1700 Sat, C-612-725-5320, D-312-825-5320. All ranks.

LOGISTICAL SUPPORT: Limited support facilities available.

Exchange-726-9023
NCO Club-725-5390
Police-725-5402

Family Support-725-8057
O'Club-725-5403
Public Affairs-725-5337

Gas Station-726-9025
Omega Travel-726-1995
Recreation-725-5316

MINNESOTA
Minneapolis-St Paul IAP/ARS, continued

HEALTH & WELFARE: No health, chapel, or commissary facilities available at this base. VA Medical Center, 54th St & 48th Ave, C-612-725-2000.

SPACE-A: Base Ops, Bldg. 821, 0730-1600 daily, C-612-725-5552/8018, D-312-825-5552/8018, and ANG Base Ops Bldg. 684, C-612-725-5681/5149, D-312-825-5681/5149. Flights to CONUS and OCONUS locations, mostly training flights on weekends.

ATTRACTIONS: Minneapolis-St Paul (Twin Cities) on the Mississippi and Minnesota Rivers. Many lakes within the cities with walking and bicycling trails.

Other Installations in Minnesota

Duluth Air National Guard Base, 4680 Viper St., Duluth, MN 55811-6031. USMRA: Page 80 (F-5). C-218-727-6886, Exchange-727-8365.

176 - U.S. FORCES TRAVEL & TRANSFER GUIDE U.S.A

MISSISSIPPI

DOLLAR RENT A CAR — Call 1-800-800-4000. Get a military rate by using your Military Living ID # ML3009. Retirees/Active Duty/Reserve/Guard.

CAMP SHELBY TRAINING SITE (MS07R2)
1001 Lee Avenue
Camp Shelby, MS 39407-5500

TELEPHONE NUMBER INFORMATION: Main installation numbers: C-601-558-2000, D-312-921-2540.

LOCATION: From Hattiesburg, take Highway 49 south, follow signs. USMRA: Page 43 (F-8). NMC: Hattiesburg, 10 miles north.

GENERAL INFORMATION: Training Site Headquarters, Regional School Support Detachment, Mississippi Military Academy.

TEMPORARY MILITARY LODGING: Bldg. 6606, 0730-1600 daily, C-601-558-2540, D-312-921-2540. All ranks.

LOGISTICAL SUPPORT: Most support facilities available.

Chaplain-558-2378
Exchange-558-2349
Medical-558-2805
O'Club-558-2749
Theater-558-2593

Conv Store-558-2506
Gas Station-558-2506
Museum-558-2757
Package Store-558-2349

EM Club-558-2578
Locator-558-2000
NCO Club-558-2427
Security-558-2472

HEALTH & WELFARE: Medical info C-601-558-2805. Chapel serving all faiths C-601-558-2378.

RECREATION: Equipment Rental EX-2697, Rec Center EX-2397, Special Services EX-2397, Swimming EX-2220, Softball, Tennis, and Basketball. Lake Walker Family Campground on post, year round, C-601-558-2397, D-312-921-2397, 25 camper spaces w/full hookups.

SPACE-A: None. See Meridian NAS listing, C-601-679-2505, D-312-637-2505, Fax 601-637-2038.

ATTRACTIONS: Kamper Park and Zoo, Hattiesburg Historical Society, Paul S. Johnson State Park.

COLUMBUS AIR FORCE BASE (MS01R2)
Columbus Air Force Base, MS 39710-5000

TELEPHONE NUMBER INFORMATION: Main installation numbers: C-601-434-7322, D-312-742-1110.

LOCATION: Clearly marked off US-45. USMRA: Page 43 (G-3). NMC: Columbus, 10 miles south.

U.S. FORCES TRAVEL & TRANSFER GUIDE U.S.A. - 177

MISSISSIPPI
Columbus Air Force Base, continued

GENERAL INFORMATION: Air Education and Training Command Base. Undergraduate pilot training.

TEMPORARY MILITARY LODGING: Lodging office, Bldg. 956, B St, 24 hours daily, C-601-434-2548, D-312-742-2548. All ranks. DV/VIP 601-434-7002.

LOGISTICAL SUPPORT: Complete support facilities available.

CHAMPUS-434-2130
Commissary-434-7101
Exchange-434-2988
Gas Station-434-6161
Locator-434-2841
NCO Club-434-7927
Police-434-7129
SATO-434-6866
Theater-434-2930

Chaplain-434-2500
Conv Store-434-6864
Family Services-434-2790
Golf Course-434-7932
Medical-434-2101
O'Club-434-2489
Public Affairs-434-7067
SDO/NCO-434-7020

Child Care-434-2479
EM Club-434-7927
Fire Dept-434-2263
Legal-434-7030
MWR-434-7437
Package Store-434-7816
Retiree Services-434-2790
Snack Bar-434-6498

HEALTH & WELFARE: USAF Hospital, Emergency C-601-434-2101, Appointment C-601-434-2847, 7 beds. Chapel serving all faiths C-601-434-2500.

RECREATION: Rec Services EX-7437, Auto Hobby EX-7842, Bowling EX-2825, Golf EX-7932, Ceramics EX-7836, Gym EX-2722, Rec Center EX-7859, Sportsman's Lodge EX-2441, Wood Hobby EX-7837, Youth Center EX-2504, MWR EX-2316, Rec Equipment EX-2505, Library EX-2934.

SPACE-A: Limited. See Meridian NAS listing, C-601-679-2505, D-312-637-2505, Fax 601-637-2038..

ATTRACTIONS: Period historic homes, Columbus, and northeast Mississippi.

GULFPORT NAVAL CONSTRUCTION BATTALION CENTER (MS03R2)
5200 CBC 2nd Street
Gulfport, MS 39501-5001

TELEPHONE NUMBER INFORMATION: Main installation numbers: C-601-871-2555, D-312-868-2555.

LOCATION: Take US-49 south to Gulfport. Follow signs to Center. From US-90 exit to Broad Ave. From I-10 exit to US-49. USMRA: Page 43 (F-10). NMC: New Orleans, 70 miles west.

GENERAL INFORMATION: Naval Construction Training Center, 20th Naval Construction Regiment, and Construction Battalions.

TEMPORARY MILITARY LODGING: Lodging office, 0700-1600 daily. Bldg. 314 BOQ, C-601-871-2505, 1-800-628-9466, D-312-868-2505. Bldg. 317 BEQ, C-601-871-2506, D-312-868-2505. Navy Lodge, C-601-864-3101. DV/VIP C-601-865-2202, D-312-363-2205, Fax 601-871-2130.

LOGISTICAL SUPPORT: Complete support facilities available.

178 - U.S. FORCES TRAVEL & TRANSFER GUIDE U.S.A

MISSISSIPPI
Gulfport Naval Construction Battalion Center, continued

Cafeteria-864-5530	CHAMPUS-871-2821	Chaplain-871-2454
Child Care-871-3114	Commissary-871-2040	Conv Store-863-4506
CPO Club-871-2616	EM Club-871-2396	Exchange-871-2619
Family Services-871-2581	Fire Dept-871-2333	Gas Station-864-5527
Golf Course-871-2494	ITT Office-871-2231	Legal-871-2626
Locator-871-2555	Medical-871-2806	MWR-871-2538
NCO Club-871-2396	O'Club-871-2616	Package Store-864-5527
Police-871-2433	Public Affairs-871-2393	Recreation-871-2696
Retiree Services-871-2647	SATO-864-9219	SDO/NCO-871-2555
Theater-871-2489	Visitor Center-871-3164	

HEALTH & WELFARE: Naval Branch Medical Clinic, Emergency C-601-871-2809. Inpatient, see Keesler AFB listing, C-601-377-2530. Chapel serving all faiths C-601-871-2454.

RECREATION: Auto Hobby EX-2804, Bowling EX-2739, Crafts EX-2560, Wood Hobby EX-2518, Golf EX-2494, Gym EX-2353/2668, Library EX-2409, Racquetball EX-2668, Rec Lake/Park EX-2231, Rec Equipment EX-2519, Swimming EX-2768, Youth Center EX-2251.

SPACE-A: None. See Keesler AFB listing, C-601-377-4538, D-312-597-4538.

ATTRACTIONS: Gulf Coast, beaches, and water sports. Cities of Mobile and New Orleans, short drives.

JACKSON IAP/THOMPSON FIELD (MS09R2)
141 Military Drive
Jackson, MS 39208-8881

TELEPHONE NUMBER INFORMATION: Main installation numbers: C-601-936-3633, D-312-731-9210.

LOCATION: Off I-20 and US-49, clearly marked. USMRA: Page 43 (D-6). NMC: Jackson, five miles west.

GENERAL INFORMATION: Mississippi Air National Guard, 172nd Airlift Group.

TEMPORARY MILITARY LODGING: None. See Meridian NAS listing, C-601-679-2186/5955/2386, D-312-637-2186/5955/2386, Fax 601-679-2745.

LOGISTICAL SUPPORT: Very limited support facilities available.

Consol Club-936-8468   Exchange-932-3930   Fire Dept-731-9411
Medical-936-8351

HEALTH & WELFARE: Outpatient Clinic, C-601-936-8351, D-312-731-8351.

SPACE-A: Very limited unscheduled flights, C-601-936-8372, D-312-731-9372, Fax 601-936-8605.

ATTRACTIONS: Historic Homes, Vicksburg National Battlefield Park 30 miles west.

U.S. FORCES TRAVEL & TRANSFER GUIDE U.S.A. - 179

MISSISSIPPI

KEESLER AIR FORCE BASE (MS02R2)
720 Chappie James, Suite 101
Keesler Air Force Base, MS 39534-2603

TELEPHONE NUMBER INFORMATION: Main installation numbers: C-601-377-1110, D-312-597-1110.

LOCATION: From I-10 exit 46, follow signs to base. From US-90, north on White Ave to main gate. USMRA: Page 43 (F-10). NMC: Biloxi, in city limits.

GENERAL INFORMATION: Air Education and Training Command Base, Training Wing, USAF Medical Center, and AFRES units.

TEMPORARY MILITARY LODGING: Lodging office, Larcher Blvd, 24 hours daily Bldg. 2101, Muse Manor, 0715-1600 Mon-Fri, C-601-377-2631/3663, All ranks.

LOGISTICAL SUPPORT: Complete support facilities available.

CHAMPUS-377-6001
Commissary-377-2830
Gas Station-432-2404
Medical-377-6550
Package Store-436-3683
Retiree Services-377-3871
Sub Shop-436-3124

Chaplain-377-2110
Exchange-435-1341
Legal-377-3510
NCO Club-377-3439
Police-377-3720
SATO-377-2230
Theater-377-2383

Child Care-377-3324
Family Services-377-4293
Locator-377-2798
O'Club-377-2219
Public Affairs-377-2783
SDO/NCO-377-1110

HEALTH & WELFARE: USAF Medical Center, Emergency C-601-377-6016, Appointment C-601-377-2530, Off base C-601-374-6800, 335 beds. Chapel serving all faiths C-601-377-6237.

RECREATION: Bowling EX-2817, Golf EX-3832, Gym, Swimming and Outdoor Sports EX-2800, Youth Center EX-3349, Library Ex-2181, Vandenberg Rec Center EX-3646. Marina on base, year round Kessler Fam Camp on base, year round, C-601-377-3160, D-312-597-3160, 20 camper spaces w/full hookups.

SPACE-A: Pax Term/Lounge, Bldg. 0233, 0600-2300 daily, C-601-377-4538, D-312-597-4538, flights to CONUS locations.

ATTRACTIONS: Gulf Coast beaches, seafood, Pensacola, FL, New Orleans, LA, and Mobile, AL, all within easy driving distance.

KEY FIELD AIR NATIONAL GUARD BASE (MS05R2)
6255 M Street
Meridian, MS 39307-7112

TELEPHONE NUMBER INFORMATION: Main installation numbers: C-601-484-9000, D-312-778-9210.

LOCATION: From 20 West, take 11 South, Air National Guard signs clearly marked. USMRA: Page 43 (F-6). NMC: Meridian, within the city limits.

GENERAL INFORMATION: Mississippi Air National Guard.

180 - U.S. FORCES TRAVEL & TRANSFER GUIDE U.S.A

MISSISSIPPI
Key Field Air National Guard Base, continued

TEMPORARY MILITARY LODGING: None. See Meridian NAS listing, C-601-679-2186/5955/2386, D-312-637-2186/5955/2386, Fax 601-679-2745.

LOGISTICAL SUPPORT: Very limited support facilities available.

Exchange-485-3072   Medical-484-9206

HEALTH & WELFARE: Outpatient Clinic, C-601-484-9206, D-312-694-9206.

SPACE-A: Very limited, C-601-484-9726, D-312-778-9210.

ATTRACTIONS: Historic Homes, Vicksburg National Battlefield Park 120 miles west.

MERIDIAN NAVAL AIR STATION (MS04R2)
1155 Rosenbaum Avenue, Suite 13
Meridian Naval Air Station, MS 39309-5003

TELEPHONE NUMBER INFORMATION: Main installation numbers: C-601-679-2211, D-312-637-2211.

LOCATION: Take MS-39 north from Meridian, for 12 miles to four-lane access road. Clearly marked. Right for three miles to NAS main gate. USMRA: Page 43 (G-6). NMC: Meridian, 15 miles southwest.

GENERAL INFORMATION: Naval Air Training Wing, Naval Technical Training Center, Marine Aviation Training Support Group, and Regional Counter-drug Training Academy.

TEMPORARY MILITARY LODGING: Lodging office, 24 hours daily. Bldg. 218 (CBQ), Fuller Rd, BEQ C-601-679-2186, D-312-637-2186, BOQ C-601-678-5955, D-312-637-5955, DV/VIP C-601-637-2386, D-312-446-2386, Fax 601-679-2745.

LOGISTICAL SUPPORT: Complete support facilities available.

CDO-679-2528	CHAMPUS-679-2315	Chaplain-679-2139
Child Care-679-2652	Commissary-679-2554	Conv Store-679-2568
Consol Club-679-2650	Exchange-679-8461	Family Services-679-2358
Fire Dept-679-2352	Gas Station-679-2664	ITT Office-679-2326
Legal-679-2590	Locator-679-2301	Medical-679-2683
MWR-679-2551	Package Store-679-2653	Police-679-2528
Public Affairs-679-2602	Snack Bar-679-2531	

HEALTH & WELFARE: Naval Branch Medical Clinic, Emergency C-601-679-2683, Appointment C-601-679-2402. Chapels serving all faiths C-601-679-2319/2405.

RECREATION: Auto Hobby EX-2609, Wood Hobby EX-2609, Bowling EX-2651, Golf EX-2129/2526, Gym EX-2379, Stables EX-2507, Library EX-2623, Swimming EX-2379/2551, Racquetball EX-2720, Rec Equipment EX-2562, Sportsmen's Association EX-2666, Youth Center EX-2687.

SPACE-A: Pax Terminal, Bldg. 1, 1400-0300 M-Th, 1400-2200 F, C-601-679-2505, D-312-637-2505, Fax 601-637-2038. Flights to CONUS destinations via Admin Aircraft.

MISSISSIPPI
Meridian Naval Air Station, continued

ATTRACTIONS: Lake Okatibbee, 10 miles west, Jimmie Rodgers Museum and Monument in Meridian.

PASCAGOULA NAVAL STATION (MS06R2)
Bldg. 10
Pascagoula, MS 39567-5000

TELEPHONE NUMBER INFORMATION: Main installation numbers: C-601-761-2140, D-312-358-2140.

LOCATION: From I-10 east, exit 69, four miles south to Highway 90, four miles west to Ingalls Access Road, one mile to Naval Station Causeway, three miles to the gate. USMRA: Page 43 (G-10). NMC: Pascagoula two miles east.

GENERAL INFORMATION: Shore Intermediate Maintenance Activity, Fleet Industrial Supply Center Detachment, Branch Medical Clinic, Branch Dental Clinic, Personnel Support Detachment.

TEMPORARY MILITARY LODGING: None. However, a 154-person combined Bachelor Quarters is sometimes used as temporary lodging. C-601-761-2182, D-312-358-2182. Also see Keesler AFB listing, C-601-377-2631/3663.

LOGISTICAL SUPPORT: Very limited support facilities available.

CDP/OOD-761-2020
Exchange-761-5133
Legal-761-2372
MWR-761-2134

CHAMPUS-761-2365
Family Services-761-4281
Locator-761-2017

Chaplain-761-2010
Fire Dept-761-2028
Medical-761-2363

HEALTH & WELFARE: Outpatient Clinic, C-601-761-2363, D-312-358-2363.

RECREATION: Fitness Center, Ball fields.

SPACE-A: None. See Keesler AFB listing, C-601-377-4538, D-312-597-4538.

ATTRACTIONS: Gulf Islands National Seashore, Sheppard State Park, and beautiful beaches.

WATERWAYS EXPERIMENT STATION (MS10R2)
Vicksburg, MS 39180

TELEPHONE NUMBER INFORMATION: Main installation number: C-601-636-3111.

LOCATION: From I-20, exit 1-C, one mile south. USMRA: Page 43 (C-6). NMC: Vicksburg, MS, five miles west.

TEMPORARY MILITARY LODGING: None.

LOGISTICAL SUPPORT: Limited support facilities available.

Cafeteria-634-2560
SDO/NCO-634-2513

CHAMPUS-634-5790

Exchange-634-2377/2136

MISSISSIPPI
Waterways Experiment Station, continued

HEALTH AND WELFARE: Medical info C-601-634-5790. No chapel on base.

RECREATION: Fitness Center on base.

SPACE-A: Try Vicksburg Municipal Airport, Pax Term, 0730-1600, C-601-638-6550, or Jackson IAP, 0730-1600, C-601-936-8300, D-312-731-9372.

ATTRACTIONS: Visitors facility, guided tours 1000 & 1400 daily (two tours per day). City of Vicksburg: historic tours, National Military Park, toy soldiers museum, houses of the Old South, and riverboat casino gambling.

Other Installations in Mississippi

Armed Forces Retirement Home (U.S. Naval Home Facility), Gulfport, MS 39507-1597.
USMRA: Page 43 (F-10), C-601-897-4000, Exchange-897-4000.
Gulfport-Biloxi Reg Apt/ANGB, 4715 Hewes Ave., Bldg 1, Gulfport, MS 39507-4324.
USMRA: Page 43 (F-10), C-601-868-6200, D-312-363-6200, Exchange-868-6200, Med-868-6200.
Vicksburg Municipal Airport, Vicksburg, MS 39180-9616.
USMRA: Page 43 (C-6), C-601-638-6550, Space-A-638-6550.

U.S. FORCES TRAVEL & TRANSFER GUIDE U.S.A. - 183

MISSOURI

DOLLAR RENT A CAR Call 1-800-800-4000. Get a military rate by using your Military Living ID # ML3009. Retirees/Active Duty/Reserve/Guard.

FORT LEONARD WOOD (MO03R2)
Hoge Hall, Building 3200
Fort Leonard Wood, MO 65473-5000

TELEPHONE NUMBER INFORMATION: Main installation numbers: C-314-596-0131, D-312-581-0110.

LOCATION: Two miles south of I-44, adjacent to St Robert & Waynesville, at Fort Leonard Wood exit. USMRA: Page 81 (E-6). NMC: Springfield, 85 miles southwest.

GENERAL INFORMATION: Basic Training installation and Army Training Center for Engineer Corps personnel.

TEMPORARY MILITARY LODGING: Lodging office, Bldg. 315, Room 126, Missouri Ave, 24 hours daily, C-314-596-6169, or 1-800-677-8356. All ranks. DV/VIP C-314-563-6183.

LOGISTICAL SUPPORT: Complete support facilities available.

Cafeteria-329-3601
Child Care-596-1028
Conv Store-329-2777
Exchange-329-2200
Gas Station-329-3373
Legal-596-0629
MWR-329-3300
Public Affairs-563-4015
RV/Camping-596-4223
Theater-596-1267/2531

CHAMPUS-596-9427
Commissary-596-0689
Davis Club-329-7426
Family Services-596-7177
Golf Course-596-4770
Locator-596-0677
Open Mess-329-6500
Package Store-329-6333
SATO(Carlson)-329-4141
Visitor Center-596-8015

Chaplain-596-7121
Community Services-596-0186
Engineers Club-596-6533
Fire Dept-596-0886
ITT Office-329-3231
Medical-596-0414
Police-596-6141
Retiree Services-596-0947
SDO/NCO-563-6126

HEALTH & WELFARE: General Leonard Wood Army Community Hospital, clinics and depts, Emergency C-314-596-2157, Appointment C-314-596-9179. Chapel serving all faiths C-314-596-1490.

RECREATION: Arts/Crafts EX-0242, Auto Hobby EX-0243, Bowling EX-1498, Gym EX-2810, Library EX-4113, Outdoor Rec EX-4223, Riding Academy EX-5631, Stables EX-5631, Youth Activities EX-3031, Rec Center, ITT, Field House, Outdoor Trails, Swimming, Stadium, Tennis. Lake of the Ozarks Recreation Area off post, 16 March 29 Oct, C-314-346-5640, 16 camper spaces w/W&E hookups, 21 camper/tent spaces w/o hookups, 28 mobile homes.

SPACE-A: Forney Army Airfield, Base Ops, 24 hours daily, C-314-596-0165/4819, D-312-581-0165, Fax 314-596-0166, flights to CONUS.

ATTRACTIONS: Near Lake of the Ozarks recreational areas.

MISSOURI

MARINE CORPS ACTIVITIES AT RICHARDS-GEBAUR AIRPORT (MO02R2)
Richards-Gebaur Airport, MO 64147-5000

This base was in the process of converting to Marine Corps control at press time.

TELEPHONE NUMBER INFORMATION: Headquarters C-816-843-3800.

LOCATION: From US-71 south, take Belton-Air Base exit, west on County Line Road (or 155th St) to base. Between Granview & Belton. USMRA: Page 81 (B-5) Page 89 (B-5). NMC: Kansas City, 17 miles north.

GENERAL INFORMATION: Marine Corps Activities.

TEMPORARY MILITARY LODGING: Lodging office, Bldg. 250, Kensington St, 0730-2330 daily, C-816-843-3855/3850-2125, D-312-894-3855/3850.

LOGISTICAL SUPPORT: Very limited support facilities available.

Consol Club-331-1601   **Exchange-331-2019**

HEALTH & WELFARE: None. See Whiteman AFB listing, C-816-687-1847.

RECREATION: MWR equipment rental 843-3870.

SPACE-A: None. See Rosecrans Memorial Airport, St Joseph, ANG, Bldg. 17, 0730-1600 Mon-Fri, C-816-271-1260, D-312-720-9260, flights via C-130 aircraft to CONUS locations.

ATTRACTIONS: Kansas City, the city of fountains. Harry S. Truman Library and home in Independence a short drive away, KC Royals and KC Chiefs pro sports teams.

ST LOUIS COAST GUARD BASE (MO05R2)
5550 Bircher Boulevard, Suite 101
#2 Union Seventy Center
St Louis, MO 63120-5000

TELEPHONE NUMBER INFORMATION: Main installation numbers: C-314-679-0141, FTS: 279-6800.

LOCATION: Take I-70 west, exit Bircher Blvd, turn left then seven miles to Union Seventy Center. USMRA: Page 81 (G-5) Page 91 (B-3,4). NMC: St Louis, five miles.

GENERAL INFORMATION: Three WLR Class Buoy Tenders, two Reserve Units.

TEMPORARY MILITARY LODGING: None. See Scott AFB, IL listing, C-618-744-1200, D-312-576-1844.

LOGISTICAL SUPPORT: Limited support facilities available.

EM Club-832-5021   **Exchange-845-2467**   **Locator-832-5941**

HEALTH & WELFARE: USAF Medical Center, Scott AFB, IL, C-618-256-7500.

U.S. FORCES TRAVEL & TRANSFER GUIDE U.S.A. - 185

MISSOURI
St Louis Coast Guard Base, continued

RECREATION: Limited recreational activities.

SPACE-A: None. See Scott AFB, IL listing.

ATTRACTIONS: St Louis, Gateway Arch, USS *Inaugural* Minesweeper, planetarium, U.S. Grant's farm.

WHITEMAN AIR FORCE BASE (MO04R2)
555 Mitchell Avenue, Suite 214
Whiteman Air Force Base, MO 65305-5000

TELEPHONE NUMBER INFORMATION: Main installation numbers: C-816-687-1110, D-312-975-1110.

LOCATION: From I-70 east exit to US-13 south to US-50 east for 10 miles, then right on Route J which leads to AFB. USMRA: Page 81 (C-5). NMC: Kansas City, 60 miles northwest.

GENERAL INFORMATION: Air Combat Command Base. 509th Bomb Wing and Air Force Reserve 442nd Fighter Wing.

TEMPORARY MILITARY LODGING: Lodging office, Bldg. 3011, Mitchell Ave, 24 hours daily, C-816-687-1844, D-312-975-1844, DV/VIP C-816-687-6543. All ranks.

LOGISTICAL SUPPORT: Complete support facilities available.

Am Express Travel 563-4441
Chaplain-687-3652
Conv Store-563-5445
Food Court-563-3167
Locator-687-1841
Package Store-563-5445
Theater-687-5110
Child Care-687-5592
Exchange-563-3003
Gas Station-687-5445
Medical-687-2118
Police-687-3700
The Club-687-4422
CHAMPUS-687-4350
Commissary-687-5655
Family Services-687-3660
Legal-687-6809
MWR-687-5617
Retiree Services-687-6457

HEALTH & WELFARE: For medical care appointment during duty hours, call C-816-687-1847 or 1-800-537-7405 within the 816 area code.

RECREATION: Community Activity Center EX-5617, Youth Center EX-5586, Golf EX-5572, Bowling EX-5114, Swimming EX-5502, Fitness Center EX-5496, Library EX-5614, Auto Hobby EX-5689.

SPACE-A: Base Ops, C-816-687-3101, D-312-975-3010, flights to CONUS locations.

ATTRACTIONS: Outdoor sports, Lake of the Ozarks region. Kansas City.

MISSOURI

Other Installations in Missouri

Lambert-St Louis IAP, St Louis, MO 63145-0305.
USMRA: Page 81 (G-5). C-314-263-6400, Space-A-263-6270.
Rosecrans Memorial Airport/ANG, 705 Memorial Dr., St Joseph, MO 64503-9307.
USMRA: Page 81 (B-3). C-816-236-3300, Space-A-271-3260.
Scott-Page Exchange, Bldg. 101, 9700 Page Blvd, St. Louis, MO 63132-5000.
USMRA: Page 91 (A-2). C-314-427-8188, Exchange-427-8188.
St Louis Post Exchange, St. Louis, MO 63120-5000.
USMRA: Page 81 (G-5). C-314-389-1445, Exchange-389-1445.

U.S. FORCES TRAVEL & TRANSFER GUIDE U.S.A. - 187

MONTANA

DOLLAR RENT A CAR Call 1-800-800-4000. Get a military rate by using your Military Living ID # ML3009. Retirees/Active Duty/Reserve/Guard.

MALMSTROM AIR FORCE BASE (MT03R3)
21, 77th Street North
Malmstrom Air Force Base, MT 59402-5000

TELEPHONE NUMBER INFORMATION: Main installation numbers: C-406-731-1110, D-312-632-1110.

LOCATION: From I-15 take 10th Ave south, exit to AFB. From the east take Malmstrom exit off US-87/89 to AFB. Clearly marked. USMRA: Page 99 (D,E-4). NMC: Great Falls, one mile west.

GENERAL INFORMATION: Air Mobility Command and Air Force Space Command Base, 43rd Air Refueling Group, and 341st Missile Wing (AFSPC).

TEMPORARY MILITARY LODGING: Lodging office, Bldg. 1680, 24 hours daily C-406-731-3895, DV/VIP 727-8600.

LOGISTICAL SUPPORT: Complete support facilities available.

Cafeteria-731-4607	CHAMPUS-731-4396	Chaplain-731-3721
Child Care-731-2417	Commissary-731-3675	Community Center-731-4633
Conv Store-761-8004	Exchange-761-8004	Family Services-731-4900
Fire Dept-911	Gas Station-761-7333	ITT-731-4634
Legal-731-2878	Locator-731-4121/	Medical-731-4412
MWR-731-3263	after hours-727-3895	NCO Club-761-4155
O'Club-761-6430	Package Store-761-8004	Police-911
Public Affairs-731-4044	Recreation-731-3691	Retiree Services-731-4142
RV/Camping-731-3394	Snack Bar-761-8004/3194	Theater-731-3236
Travel-731-2934	Visitor Center-731-3892	

HEALTH & WELFARE: USAF Clinic, Bldg. 2040, Emergency C-406-731-1110-EX-118, Appointment C-406-731-3425, Ambulance C-406-731-1110-EX-118. Chapel serving all faiths C-406-731-3721.

RECREATION: Arts/Crafts EX-3691, Auto Hobby EX-3777, Bowling EX-2494, Library EX-2748, Rec Center EX-2248, Wood Hobby EX-3232, Youth Center EX-2422, Sports Arena EX-3621, Outdoor Rec EX-3263. Fam-Camp on base, May-Oct, C-406-731-3263, D-312-632-3263, 24 camper spaces w/full hookups, five camper/tent spaces w/o hookups. Wagner's Guest Camp & Ranch off base, May-Sep, C-406-731-3263, D-312-632-3263, seven trailers.

SPACE-A: Pax Term, Base Ops, Bldg. 360, 24 hours daily, C-406-731-2861, D-312-632-2861, KC-135R MEDEVAC and other flights, most to CONUS locations.

ATTRACTIONS: Big Sky Country, snow skiing, wildlife, fish and game.

MONTANA AIR NATIONAL GUARD BASE (MT06R3)
120th Fighter Wing
2800 Airport Avenue B
Great Falls, MT 59404-5570

TELEPHONE NUMBER INFORMATION: Main installation numbers: C-406-791-6220, D-312-279-2220, FAX: C-406-791-6488.

LOCATION: Great Falls International Airport. Airport exit is off I-15, and is one mile south of the 10th Ave S exit. USMRA: Page 99 (D-4). NMC: Great Falls, one mile.

GENERAL INFORMATION: Montana Air National Guard, 120th Fighter Wing.

TEMPORARY MILITARY LODGING: None. See Malmstrom AFB listing, C-406-731-3895, DV/VIP 727-8600.

LOGISTICAL SUPPORT: Limited support facilities available.

Cafeteria-791-6224
Legal-791-6180
Public Affairs-791-6228
Snack Bar-791-6224

Chaplain-791-6300
Locator-791-6220
SATO-791-6477

Exchange-791-6299
Police-791-6336
SDO/NCO-791-6202

HEALTH AND WELFARE: Chapel serving all faiths C-406-791-6300.

SPACE-A: None. See Malmstrom AFB, MT listing, C-406-731-2861, D-312-632-2861.

ATTRACTIONS: C.M. Russel Museum, Paris Gibson Art Gallery, Malmstrom Aircraft Museum, Heritage Park, Giant Springs State Park.

Other Installations in Montana

Fort Harrison Site, Helena, MT 59601-5000.
USMRA: Page 99 (D-5). C-406-444-7910, Exchange-444-7910.

U.S. FORCES TRAVEL & TRANSFER GUIDE U.S.A. - 189

NEBRASKA

DOLLAR RENT A CAR Call 1-800-800-4000. Get a military rate by using your Military Living ID # ML3009. Retirees/Active Duty/Reserve/Guard.

NEBRASKA AIR NATIONAL GUARD BASE (NE05R3)
2420 West Butler Avenue
Lincoln, NE 68524-1897

TELEPHONE NUMBER INFORMATION: Main installation numbers: C-402-458-1110, D-312-946-1110.

LOCATION: Adjacent to Lincoln Municipal Airport, right on I-80. USMRA: Page 82 (I-5). NMC: Lincoln, two miles southeast.

GENERAL INFORMATION: 155th Air Refueling Wing. Air National Guard.

TEMPORARY MILITARY LODGING: None. See Offutt AFB listing, C-402-294-3671/9000, D-312-3671/9000.

LOGISTICAL SUPPORT: Limited support facilities available.

Chaplain-458-1121
Legal-458-1122
O'Club-458-1126
Exchange-474-3454
Medical-458-1485
Police-458-1150
Fire Dept-458-1338
NCO/EM Club-458-1125
SDO/NCO-458-1266

HEALTH AND WELFARE: None. See Offutt AFB listing, C-402-294-6477/5510.

RECREATION: Running track, softball diamond.

SPACE-A: PAX terminal C-402-458-1233/1260.

ATTRACTIONS: Home of state government, University of Nebraska, Elephant Hall at University of Nebraska, Nebraska State Historical Society Museum, and Lincoln Children's Zoo. Many fine restaurants, hotels/motels and area lakes with camping. "The Clean City."

OFFUTT AIR FORCE BASE (NE02R3)
Offutt Air Force Base, NE 68113-5000

TELEPHONE NUMBER INFORMATION: Main installation numbers: C-402-294-1110, D-312-271-1110.

LOCATION: From I-80 exit to US-75 south to AFB exit, 6.5 miles south of I-80/US-75 interchange. USMRA: Page 82 (I,J-5). NMC: Omaha, eight miles north.

GENERAL INFORMATION: Air Combat Command Base. 55th Wing, Headquarters US STRATCOM, Air Force Global Weather Central, and other support units.

TEMPORARY MILITARY LODGING: Lodging office, Bldg. 44, Grants Pass St, 24 hours daily, C-402-294-3671/9000, D-312-271-3671/9000. All ranks. DV/VIP EX-4461.

LOGISTICAL SUPPORT: Complete support facilities available.

NEBRASKA
Offutt Air Force Base, continued

EM Club-291-6785	Exchange-291-9100	Cafeteria-291-9596
Chaplain-294-6244	Child Care-294-2203	CHAMPUS-294-7424
Commissary-294-5920	Conv Store-292-0218	Family Services-294-3111
Gas Station-291-8745	Legal-294-3732	Locator-294-5125
Medical-294-7371	NCO Club-292-1600	O'Club-292-1560
Package Store-292-7097	Police-294-6110\	Retiree Services-294-7693
Theater-294-5951		

HEALTH & WELFARE: USAF Hospital, Emergency C-402-294-7334, Appointment AD C-402-294-6477, Dep C-402-292-5510. Chapels serving all faiths C-402-294-6244/6051.

RECREATION: Aero Club EX-3503, Auto Hobby EX-5564, Arts/Crafts EX-3872, Bowling EX-2514, Golf EX-3362/292-1680, Gym EX-5904, Library EX-2533, Photo Hobby EX-3872, Rec Center EX-6247, Swimming EX-2274/3593/6466, Wood Hobby EX-3318, Youth Center EX-5152. Fam-Camp on base, year round, C-402-294-2108, D-312-271-2108, 10 camper spaces w/full hookups.

SPACE-A: Pax Term/Lounge, Bldg. T-47, 0500-2100 Mon-Fri, 0700-1900 Sat-Sun, C-402-294-6235, D-312-271-6235, Fax 402-294-4070, flights to CONUS and OCONUS locations.

ATTRACTIONS: City of Omaha, Old Market area, Boys Town.

Other Installations in Nebraska

Camp Ashland, Ashland, NE 68003-9801.
USMRA: Page 82 (I-5). C-402-944-2607, Exchange-944-2750, 944-2110.

U.S. FORCES TRAVEL & TRANSFER GUIDE U.S.A. - 191

NEVADA

DOLLAR RENT A CAR Call 1-800-800-4000. Get a military rate by using your Military Living ID # ML3009. Retirees/Active Duty/Reserve/Guard.

FALLON NAVAL AIR STATION (NV02R4)
4755 Pasture Road
Fallon Naval Air Station, NV 89496-5000

TELEPHONE NUMBER INFORMATION: Main installation numbers: C-702-426-5161, D-312-830-5161.

LOCATION: From US-50 exit to US-95 south at Fallon, for three miles to left on Union St to NAS. USMRA: Page 113 (C-4). NMC: Reno, 72 miles west.

GENERAL INFORMATION: Fleet training squadrons, Home of Strike Warfare Center, Center for Tactical Warfare, Strike Fighter Wing Detachment, VFA-127.

TEMPORARY MILITARY LODGING: Lodging office, 24 hours daily, BOQ C-702-423-2147/6671, D-312-830-2526, BEQ C-702-426-2515, D-312-830-2515. Other hours, BOQ, C-702-426-2521. All ranks. DV/VIP C-702-423-6671, Fax 702-426-2408.

LOGISTICAL SUPPORT: Complete support facilities available.

CDO/OOD-426-2714
Chaplain-426-2813
Conv Store-426-2489
EM Club-426-2445
Fire Dept-426-3411
ITT Office-426-2865
Medical-426-3110
Police-426-2853

Cafeteria-426-2501
Child Care-426-5808
CPO Club-426-2482
Exchange-426-2400
Gas Station-426-2583
Legal-426-2711
MWR-426-2550
Public Affairs-426-2880

CHAMPUS-426-3102
Commissary-426-3420
Credit Union-426-2500
Family Services-426-3333
ID cards-426-2808
Locator-426-5161
O'Club-426-2841
Recreation-426-2869

HEALTH & WELFARE: Naval Branch Medical Clinic, Emergency 911, Appointment C-702-426-3110. Chapel serving all faiths C-702-426-2813.

RECREATION: Bowling, Rec Equipment, Gym, Library, Swimming, Auto Hobby, Picnic Area, Car Rental, Special Services Office EX-2865. Fallon RV Park and Recreation Area on base, year round, C-702-426-2598, D-312-830-2598, 16 camper spaces w/W&E hookups.

SPACE-A: Pax Term, hangar 5, 0630-2245 Mon-Fri, 0800-1800 Sat, 1000-1800 Sun, C-702-426-3415, D-312-830-3415, flights to CONUS and OCONUS locations.

ATTRACTIONS: Reno, Carson City, Virginia City, and Lake Tahoe nearby.

INDIAN SPRINGS AIR FORCE AUXILIARY FIELD (NV03R4)
3770 Duffer Drive
Indian Springs, NV 89018-5000

TELEPHONE NUMBER INFORMATION: Main installation numbers: C-702-652-0201, D-312-682-0201.

NEVADA
Indian Springs Air Force Auxiliary Field, continued

LOCATION: Off US-95, 47 miles northwest Nellis AFB. USMRA: Page 113 (F-8). NMC: Las Vegas, 45 miles southeast.

GENERAL INFORMATION: Forward operating location and emergency landing airfield for Nellis AFB.

TEMPORARY MILITARY LODGING: None. See Nellis AFB listing, C-702-643-2710, D-312-682-2711, DV/VIP C-702-643-2987.

LOGISTICAL SUPPORT: Limited support facilities available.

Exchange-652-0326   Medical-879-6214/6246

HEALTH & WELFARE: Medical Aid Station, Emergency C-702-652-0286 between 0730-1630 Mon-Fri, after duty hours C-702-562-0213 (Fire Dept). Inpatient and non-emergency care, see Nellis AFB listing, C-702-653-2778. Chapel serving all faiths at Nellis AFB, C-702-562-2950.

RECREATION: None. See Nellis AFB listing.

SPACE-A: None. See Nellis AFB listing, C-702-652-1854, D-312-682-1854, Fax 702-652-1561.

ATTRACTIONS: Desert area, Tolyabe National Forest and Lee Canyon ski area, south of US-95, nearby.

NELLIS AIR FORCE BASE (NV01R4)
Nellis Air Force Base, NV 89191-5000

TELEPHONE NUMBER INFORMATION: Main installation numbers: C-702-652-1110, D-312-682-1110.

LOCATION: Off I-15. Also, accessible from US-91/93. Clearly marked. USMRA: Page 113 (G-9). NMC: Las Vegas, eight miles southwest.

GENERAL INFORMATION: Air Combat Command Base. Air Warfare Center, Combat Fighter units. USAF Air Demonstration Squadron, "The Thunderbirds."

TEMPORARY MILITARY LODGING: Lodging office, Bldg. 780, Fitzgerald St, 24 hours daily, C-702-643-2710, D-312-682-2711. All ranks. DV/VIP C-702-643-2987.

LOGISTICAL SUPPORT: Complete support facilities available.

CHAMPUS-653-2500	Chaplain-652-2950	Child Care-652-4241
Commissary-643-7919	Conv Store-644-6375	EM Club-652-9733
Exchange-644-2044	Family Services-652-6070	Fire Dept-652-9630
Gas Station-643-1686	Golf Course-652-2602	Legal-652-4213
Locator-652-8134	Medical-652-2778	O'Club-652-9188
Package Store-644-1433	Police-652-2311	Public Affairs-652-2750
Retiree Services-652-8712	SATO-644-5400	SDO/NCO-652-2638
Theater-652-5020	Visitor Center-652-3216	

U.S. FORCES TRAVEL & TRANSFER GUIDE U.S.A. - 193

NEVADA
Nellis Air Force Base, continued

HEALTH & WELFARE: Nellis Federal Hospital, Emergency C-702-653-2343, Appointment C-702-653-2778, 119 beds. Chapel serving all faiths C-702-652-2950.

RECREATION: Arts/Crafts EX-2849, Auto Hobby EX-2284, Bowling EX-2170, Golf EX-2602, Gym EX-6433, Library EX-9210, Rec Center EX-5014, Rec Equipment EX-2514, Youth Center EX-6015. Lucky Seven Fam-Camp off base, year round, C-702-643-3060.

SPACE-A: Pax Term/Lounge, Bldg. 1044, 0730-1630 daily, C-702-652-1854, D-312-682-1854, Fax 702-652-1561, flights to CONUS locations.

ATTRACTIONS: Las Vegas, Lake Mead National Recreation Area, Mt. Charleston, Hoover Dam, Red Rock Canyon, Spring Mountain Ranch, Valley of Fire, beautiful deserts.

NEVADA AIR NATIONAL GUARD BASE (NV06R4)
Reno, NV 89502-5000

TELEPHONE NUMBER INFORMATION: Main installation numbers: C-702-788-4500, D-312-830-4500.

LOCATION: Reno-Cannon International Airport exit off I-395. Co-located at the IAP. USMRA Page 113 (B-4). NMC: Reno, within city limits.

GENERAL INFORMATION: Air National Guard activities.

TEMPORARY MILITARY LODGING: None. See Fallon NAS listing, C-703-423-2147/6671, D-312-830-2526/2515, Fax 702-426-2408.

LOGISTICAL SUPPORT: Limited support facilities available.

Cafeteria-788-4573   CHAMPUS-788-4510   Consol Club-788-4570
Police-788-4549   SATO-788-4667   SDO/NCO-788-4550
Snack Bar-788-4573

HEALTH AND WELFARE: Outpatient and inpatient care, VA Hospital, C-702-786-7200. Chapel serving all faiths one weekend per month.

RECREATION: None available on base.

SPACE-A: See Fallon NAS listing, C-702-426-3415, D-312-830-3415.

ATTRACTIONS: Lake Tahoe, skiing, Casinos, gambling.

194 - U.S. FORCES TRAVEL & TRANSFER GUIDE U.S.A

NEW HAMPSHIRE

DOLLAR RENT A CAR Call 1-800-800-4000. Get a military rate by using your Military Living ID # ML3009. Retirees/Active Duty/Reserve/Guard.

NEW BOSTON AIR STATION (NH04R1)
317 Chestnut Hill Road
Amherst, NH 03031-1514

TELEPHONE NUMBER INFORMATION: Main installation number: C-603-471-2000, D-312-489-2000.

LOCATION: From I-93 north, take I-293 west to Route 101 west to Route 114 north to New Boston Road. USMRA: Page 23 (F-10). NMC: Manchester, eight miles northeast.

TEMPORARY MILITARY LODGING: None. See Hanscom Air Force Base, MA (30 miles southeast) listing, C-617-377-2112.

LOGISTICAL SUPPORT: Very limited.

Fire Department-471-2470 MWR-471-2452 Police-471-2450
Public Affairs-471-2211 Recreation-471-2452 RV/Camping-471-2234

HEALTH & WELFARE: None. See Hanscom AFB, MA listing, C-617-377-4706.

RECREATION: New Boston Recreation Area on base, June-Sep, C-603-471-2452/2234, D-312-489-2452/2234, three mobile homes, 12 camper spaces w/W&E hookups, 42 camper/tent spaces w/o hookups.

SPACE-A: None. See Hanscom AFB listing, C-617-377-1143, D-312-478-1143, or Pease ANGB listing, C-603-430-3323, D-312-852-3323.

ATTRACTIONS: Snow Skiing, hiking.

PEASE AIR NATIONAL GUARD BASE (NH01R1)
Newington, NH 03803-0157

TELEPHONE NUMBER INFORMATION: Main installation numbers: C-603-430-2453, D-312-852-2453.

LOCATION: From I-95 north to Spaulding Turnpike, then follow signs. Base is at intersection of Spaulding Turnpike & Gosling Road. USMRA: Page 23 (H-9). NMC: Portsmouth, three miles northeast.

GENERAL INFORMATION: 157th Air Refueling Group, New Hampshire Air National Guard.

TEMPORARY MILITARY LODGING: None. See Portsmouth Naval Shipyard listing, C-207-438-1513, D-312-684-1513.

LOGISTICAL SUPPORT: Very limited support facilities available.

Exchange-436-0302

NEW HAMPSHIRE
Pease Air National Guard Base, continued

HEALTH & WELFARE: None. See Portsmouth Naval Shipyard listing, C-207-438-1799.

SPACE-A: Pax Term/Lounge, Bldg. 247, C-603-430-3323, D-312-852-3323, flights to CONUS, OCONUS and overseas.

ATTRACTIONS: City of Portsmouth, harbor, beaches, skiing in White Mountains is a one hour drive.

PORTSMOUTH NAVAL SHIPYARD (NH02R1)
Portsmouth Naval Shipyard, NH 03801-5000

TELEPHONE NUMBER INFORMATION: Main installation numbers: C-207-438-1000, D-312-684-1000.

LOCATION: From I-95 north, cross Piscataqua River Bridge into Maine. Take exit 2 to US-236 to US-1 south to US-203, left onto Walker St. to gate 1. From I-95 south, take exit 2, follow above directions. Located on an island on Piscataqua River between Portsmouth and Kittery, ME. USMRA: Page 23 (H-9). NMC: Portsmouth, in city limits.

GENERAL INFORMATION: A Naval Shipyard and Repair Facility.

TEMPORARY MILITARY LODGING: Lodging office, C-207-438-1513/2015, Fax 207-438-3580.

LOGISTICAL SUPPORT: Limited support facilities available.

CHAMPUS-438-3862	Chaplain-438-1970	Child Care-438-3804
Commissary-438-5532	CPO Club-438-2455	Exchange-438-2341
ITT Office-438-2351	Legal-438-2703	Locator-438-2436
Medical-438-2555	MWR-438-2351	O'Club-438-2269
Pizza Parlor-438-3536	Police-438-2002	Public Affairs-438-1525
SDO/NCO-438-2200	Visitor Center-438-3550	

HEALTH & WELFARE: Naval Medical Clinic, Emergency C-207-438-4940, Appointment C-207-438-1799. Chapel serving all faiths C-207-438-1970, Police Emergency C-207-438-2444.

RECREATION: Rec Services/Marina 438-1583, Rec Equipment EX-1514, Library EX-2769, Tennis EX-2404, Bowling EX-2404, Handball/Racquetball EX-2404, Gym EX-2360, Sailing/Boat Rental EX-1514, Auto Hobby EX-2981, Wood Hobby EX-1820, Fitness Center EX-2402.

SPACE-A: None. See Pease ANGB listing, C-603-430-3323, D-312-852-3323.

ATTRACTIONS: Beaches, snow skiing nearby.

196 - U.S. FORCES TRAVEL & TRANSFER GUIDE U.S.A

NEW JERSEY

DOLLAR RENT A CAR Call 1-800-800-4000. Get a military rate by using your Military Living ID # ML3009. Retirees/Active Duty/Reserve/Guard.

BAYONNE MILITARY OCEAN TERMINAL (NJ10R1)
Foot of 32nd Street
Bayonne, NJ 07002-5302

Scheduled to close September 1998.

TELEPHONE NUMBER INFORMATION: Main installation numbers: C-201-823-5111, D-312-247-5111.

LOCATION: From New Jersey Turnpike, exit 14A to NJ-169 east to main gate. Follow green and white signs. USMRA: Page 26 (C-5,6). NMC: New York City, 10 miles northeast.

GENERAL INFORMATION: An activity of the Military Traffic Management Command, Eastern Area, whose headquarters is co-located at terminal.

TEMPORARY MILITARY LODGING: Liberty Lodge, C-201-823-8700.

LOGISTICAL SUPPORT: Limited support facilities available.

ACS-823-7737
Comm Club-823-7603
Locator-823-5111/0111
SDO/NCO-823-7207

Chaplain-823-7265
Exchange-339-4520
Medical-823-7371

Child Care-823-5980
Legal-823-7122
Police-823-6666/6000

HEALTH & WELFARE: US Army Health Clinic, C-201-823-7371. Family Support Branch, C-201-823-5643. Inpatient, Uniformed Services Medical Treatment Facility, Baley-Seton Hospital, Staten Island, NY, C-212-447-3010. Chapel serving all faiths C-201-823-7265.

RECREATION: Gym, Rec Equipment EX-7767, Community Recreation Branch EX-5672, ITR office EX-5319.

SPACE-A: None. See McGuire AFB listing, C-609-724-3078, D-312-440-3078, Fax 609-724-4621.

ATTRACTIONS: New York City, Atlantic City, Liberty State Park with ferries to Statue of Liberty, Jersey Shore.

CAPE MAY COAST GUARD TRAINING CENTER (NJ13R1)
1 Munro Avenue
Cape May, NJ 08204-5002

TELEPHONE NUMBER INFORMATION: Main installation numbers: C-609-898-6900.

LOCATION: Take Garden State Parkway or US-9 to Cape May. In Cape May, take Pittsburgh Ave to Pennsylvania Ave to main gate of Center. USMRA: Page 19 (D-10). NMC: Atlantic City, 45 miles northeast.

U.S. FORCES TRAVEL & TRANSFER GUIDE U.S.A. - 197

NEW JERSEY
Cape May Coast Guard Training Center, continued

GENERAL INFORMATION: Coast Guard Training Center for Recruits, Center, Cape May Air Station, several Coast Guard ships.

TEMPORARY MILITARY LODGING: Housing office, 0800-1630 hours daily, C-609-898-6922, FTS-884-6922. All ranks.

LOGISTICAL SUPPORT: Limited support facilities available.

CDO/OOD-898-6915	CHAMPUS-898-6966	Chaplain-898-6974
Child Care-898-6922	Comm Club-898-6937	Commissary-898-6940
CPO Club-898-6344	Exchange-898-6940	Family Services-898-6925
Fire Dept-898-6415	ITT Office-898-6989	Legal-898-6902
Locator-898-6900	Medical-898-6959	MWR-898-6922
Package Store-898-6940	Police-898-6225	Public Affairs-898-6969
Recreation-898-6922	RV/Camping-898-6922	SATO-884-3197
SDO/NCO-898-6915	Theater-898-6922	Visitor Center-898-6922

HEALTH & WELFARE: USCG Hospital, clinics and depts, Emergency C-609-898-6959, Appointment C-609-898-6959, 25 beds. Medical services are Space-A for dependents and retirees. Chapel serving all faiths C-609-898-6974.

RECREATION: Gym EX-6973, Swimming EX-6973. Wildwood Campground on base, 1 May -15 Oct, C-609-898-6922, eight camper spaces w/W&E hookups, eight tent spaces w/o hookups.

SPACE-A: None. See McGuire AFB listing, C-609-724-3078, D-312-440-3078, Fax 609-724-4621.

ATTRACTIONS: Beaches, Atlantic City Resort. Auto/Passenger ferry from Cape May to Lewes, DE, operates year round.

EARLE NAVAL WEAPONS STATION (NJ11R1)
Colts Neck, NJ 07722-5007

TELEPHONE NUMBER INFORMATION: Main installation numbers: C-908-866-2000, D-312-449-2000.

LOCATION: From New Jersey Turnpike (I-95), exit 8 to NJ-33, east through Freehold to NJ-537, east to NJ-34, south to main gate. Or exit Garden State Parkway to NJ-33, west to NJ-34, north to Station. USMRA: Page 19 (F,G-5). NMC: Newark, 50 miles north.

GENERAL INFORMATION: Naval Ammunition, Storage and Trans-shipment site with loading facilities near Sandy Hook at Leonardo.

TEMPORARY MILITARY LODGING: Very limited in bachelor-type quarters. Officers C-908-866-2167, EM C-908-866-2434, Fax 908-462-7723.

LOGISTICAL SUPPORT: Limited support facilities available.

All Hands Club-866-2438	CDO/OOD-866-2500	CHAMPUS-866-2303
Chaplain-866-2405	Child Care-866-2530	Consol Club-866-2436
Exchange-866-2349	Family Services-866-2115	Fire Dept-866-2260
ITT Office-866-2167	Legal-866-2066	Medical-866-2685

NEW JERSEY
Earle Naval Weapons Station, continued

MWR-866-2350	Package Store-866-2417	Police-866-2069
Public Affairs-866-2171	Recreation-866-2402	Retiree Services-866-2115
SATO-866-2886	SDO/NCO-866-2500	

HEALTH & WELFARE: Naval Branch Medical Clinic C-908-866-2300. Inpatient, see Patterson Army Health Clinic, Acute Care Clinic, Fort Monmouth listing, C-908-532-3851. Chapel serving all faiths C-908-866-2405.

RECREATION: Auto Hobby EX-2105, Bowling EX-2394, Gym EX-2119/2351, Library EX-2103, Hobby Shops EX-2469, Youth Activities EX-2351, Special Services EX-2350/2389.

SPACE-A: None. See McGuire AFB listing, C-609-724-3078, D-312-440-3078, Fax 609-724-4621.

ATTRACTIONS: The New Jersey Shore nearby. New York City, Atlantic City, Six Flags Great Adventure Theme Park.

FORT DIX ARMY GARRISON (NJ03R1)
Fort Dix, NJ 08640-5000

TELEPHONE NUMBER INFORMATION: Main installation numbers: C-609-562-1011, D-312-944-1110, FTS-484-1011.

LOCATION: From NJ Turnpike (I-95), exit 7, right onto NJ-206, short distance left on NJ-68, continue to General Circle & main gate. USMRA: Page 19 (E,F-6). NMC: Trenton, 17 miles northwest.

GENERAL INFORMATION: Army Reserve Training Center.

TEMPORARY MILITARY LODGING: Lodging office, Bldg. 5255, Maryland Ave & First St, 24 hours daily, C-609-562-4849, D-312-944-4849. All ranks. DV/VIP C-609-562-5059/6293.

LOGISTICAL SUPPORT: Complete support facilities available.

Cafeteria-723-2671	CHAMPUS-562-6482	Chaplain-562-2020
Child Care-723-1009	Club Dix-723-272	Commissary-724-2301
Conv Store-723-0464	EM Club-562-4896	Exchange-723-6100
Family Services-562-2767	Gas Station-723-0464	ITT Office-562-4848
Legal-562-4148	Locator-562-1011	Medical-562-3142
NCO Club-562-3272	O'Club-723-7700	Package Store-723-5488
Police-562-6001	Retiree Services-562-5430	SATO-562-4707
Snack Bar-723-6100	SDO/NCO-562-2643/2645	Theater-562-3986

HEALTH & WELFARE: Walson Air Force Community Hospital, clinics and depts, Emergency C-609-562-2695. Chapel serving all faiths C-609-562-2020.

RECREATION: Arts/Crafts EX-5691, Auto Hobby EX-6762, Bowling EX-6895, Golf EX-5443, Library EX-3587, Rod/Gun Club EX-4676, Swimming EX-2863, Teen Club EX-5061, Youth Activities EX-5061. Brindle Lake Travel Camp on post, year round, C-609-562-6667, D-312-944-6667, 10 spaces w/o hookups.

U.S. FORCES TRAVEL & TRANSFER GUIDE U.S.A. - 199

NEW JERSEY
Fort Dix Army Garrison, continued

SPACE-A: None. See McGuire AFB listing, C-609-724-3078, D-312-440-3078, Fax 609-724-4621.

ATTRACTIONS: Atlantic City and Philadelphia, short drives.

FORT MONMOUTH (NJ05R1)
Fort Monmouth, NJ 07703-5016

TELEPHONE NUMBER INFORMATION: Main installation numbers: C-908-532-9000, D-312-992-9000.

LOCATION: Take New Jersey Turnpike to Garden State Parkway, exit 105 for Eatontown, NJ-35 north to main gate. USMRA: Page 19 (G-5). NMC: New Brunswick, 23 miles northwest.

GENERAL INFORMATION: Army Communications-Electronics Command, other supporting electronics organizations, US Military Academy Preparatory School.

TEMPORARY MILITARY LODGING: Lodging office, Bldg. 270, Allen & Barton Ave, 0745-2400 daily, C-908-532-1635/1092, D-312-992-1635. All ranks. DV/VIP-C-908-532-1635.

LOGISTICAL SUPPORT: Complete support facilities available.

ACS-532-2076
CHAMPUS-532-3203
Commissary-532-1260
Exchange-542-7235
Gas Station-542-7417
Legal-532-4371
MWR-532-7810
Package Store-532-5353
Recreation-532-2374
Theater-542-4317

All Hands Club-532-3892
Chaplain-532-2066
Conv Store-542-5353
Family Services-532-2076
Golf Course-532-4307
Locator-532-1492
O'Club-532-4561
Police-532-1112/911
Retiree Services-532-4673
Visitor Center-532-6078

CDO/OOD-532-1100
Child Care-532-8069
EM Club-532-3892
Fire Department-532-1265
ITR Office-532-3892
Medical-532-3851
Ombudsman-532-6078
Public Affairs-532-1258
SDO/NCO-532-1100

HEALTH & WELFARE: Patterson Army Health Clinic, Acute Care Clinic, C-908-532-3851, 35 beds. Chapel serving all faiths C-908-532-2066.

RECREATION: Bowling EX-3805, Physical Fitness Center EX-2848, Golf EX-4307, Library EX-3172, Swimming EX-3275, Outdoor Rec EX-2374, Auto Hobby EX-3301, Multi-Crafts EX-3159, Photo Hobby EX-3159, Community Center EX-2695.

SPACE-A: None. See McGuire AFB listing, C-609-724-3078, D-312-440-3078, Fax 609-724-4621.

ATTRACTIONS: New Jersey beaches nearby, Monmouth Park Racetrack, New York City, Atlantic City.

NEW JERSEY

LAKEHURST NAVAL AIR WARFARE CENTER (NJ08R1)
Lakehurst, NJ 08733-5000

TELEPHONE NUMBER INFORMATION: Main installation numbers: C-908-323-2011, D-312-624-1110.

LOCATION: Take the Garden State Parkway south to NJ-70, west to junction of NJ-547, turn right and proceed one mile to base. USMRA: Page 19 (F-6). NMC: Trenton, 30 miles northwest.

GENERAL INFORMATION: Naval Air Warfare Center Aircraft Division, Naval Air Engineering Station.

TEMPORARY MILITARY LODGING: Lodging office, Bldg. 480-481, 24 hours daily, BEQ/BOQ/DV/VIP C-908-323-2266, D-312-624-2266, Fax 908-323-2269. All ranks.

LOGISTICAL SUPPORT: Complete support facilities available.

Chaplain-323-2272/2539   Child Care-323-2406/2034   COM-323-2340
Commissary-323-2516   Conv Store-323-2909   Exchange-323-7680/7683
Family Services-323-1223/4 Galley-323-2554   Legal-323-2571/2170
Medical-323-2231   Package Store-657-5100   Police-323-2457/2332
Public Affairs-323-2620

HEALTH & WELFARE: Naval Branch Medical Clinic, Emergency C-908-323-2231. Inpatient, see Fort Dix listing, C-609-562-2695. Chapel serving all faiths C-908-323-2272.

RECREATION: Golf EX-7483, Bowling EX-2027. Gym, Rec Equipment, Library, Picnic Area, Swimming, Theater, Auto Hobby call EX-2468.

SPACE-A: Pax Terminal C-908-323-2438, D-312-624-2438, Fax 908-323-7802.

ATTRACTIONS: Atlantic City, New Jersey beaches, Six Flags Great Adventure Theme Park, Manhattan, Philadelphia.

McGUIRE AIR FORCE BASE (NJ09R1)
2901 Falcon Lane
McGuire Air Force Base, NJ 08641-5000

TELEPHONE NUMBER INFORMATION: Main installation numbers: C-609-724-1100, D-312-440-1110.

LOCATION: From New Jersey Turnpike (I-95), exit 7 to NJ-206 southeast to AFB. Adjacent to Fort Dix. Clearly marked. USMRA: Page 19 (E-6). NMC: Trenton, 18 miles northwest.

GENERAL INFORMATION: Air Mobility Command base. Airlift Wing, Air Refueling Group, East Coast Mobility Center, ANG and AFRES units.

TEMPORARY MILITARY LODGING: Lodging office, Bldg. 2717, 24 hours daily, C-609-724-2954, D-312-440-2954. All ranks. DV/VIP C-609-724-2405.

U.S. FORCES TRAVEL & TRANSFER GUIDE U.S.A. - 201

NEW JERSEY
McGuire Air Force Base, continued

LOGISTICAL SUPPORT: Complete support facilities available.

Cafeteria-723-5056	CHAMPUS-562-4040	Chaplain-724-3811
Child Care-724-3806	Commissary-724-4155	Conv Store-723-3933
Exchange-723-6100	Family Services-724-3294	Gas Station-724-4608
Golf Course-724-2169	ITT Office-723-3111	Legal-724-4601
Locator-724-2345	Medical-724-5509	MWR-724-3737
NCO Club-724-2396	O'Club-724-3297	Package Store-724-3888
Police-724-2001	Public Affairs-724-2104	Retiree Services-724-2459
SATO-724-3131	SDO/NCO-724-3935	Theater-724-3240
Visitor Center-724-3154		

HEALTH & WELFARE: None. See Walson Air Force Community Hospital, Fort Dix, C-609-562-2695. Chapel serving all faiths C-609-724-3811.

RECREATION: Bowling EX-3345, Aero Club 723-3943, Library EX-4319, Golf EX-3330, Gym EX-2158, Rec Center EX-3736, Special Services Office EX-3208, Youth Center EX-3940. Fam-Camp on base, year round, C-609-724-2145, D-312-440-2145, six camper spaces w/W&E hookups.

SPACE-A: Pax Term/Lounge, Bldg. 1706, C-609-724-3078, D-312-440-3078, Fax 609-724-4621, flights to CONUS and overseas.

ATTRACTIONS: New Jersey Shore, Atlantic City and Philadelphia nearby.

PICATINNY ARSENAL - (US ARMAMENT RESEARCH, DEVELOPMENT AND ENGINEERING CENTER) (NJ01R1)
Bldg. 1
Picatinny Arsenal, NJ 07806-5000

TELEPHONE NUMBER INFORMATION: Main installation numbers: C-201-724-4021, 800-831-2759, D-312-880-4021.

LOCATION: Take I-80 west, exit 34B to Rt. 15 north, follow signs to Center, one mile north. From I-80 east, exit 34 to Rt. 15 follow signs to Center. USMRA: Page 19 (E-2). NMC: Newark, 30 miles east.

GENERAL INFORMATION: Research and Development element of the Army Armament Munitions and Chemical Command located at Picatinny Arsenal.

TEMPORARY MILITARY LODGING: Lodging office, Bldg. 3359, Lower Belt Rd, 0800-1630 Mon-Fri, C-201-724-2633/3506, D-312-880-2633/3506. All ranks. DV/VIP EX-7026.

LOGISTICAL SUPPORT: Complete support facilities available.

Cafeteria-989-2420	CHAMPUS-724-2113	Chaplain-724-4139
Child Care-724-4337	Commissary-724-2918	Exchange-989-2518
Family Services-724-4315	Fire Dept-724-4544	Gas Station-724-3902
Golf Course-989-2466	ITT-724-4186	Legal-724-6598
Locator-724-2852	Medical-724-2113	NCO Club-724-2639
O'Club-989-2460	Police-724-6666	Public Affairs-724-6364
Recreation-724-4186	SATO-328-0525	Visitor Center-724-2407

NEW JERSEY
Picatinny Arsenal, continued

HEALTH & WELFARE: US Army Health Clinic, Emergency C-201-724-4611, Appointment C-201-724-2113. Inpatient, Uniformed Services Medical Treatment Facility, Bayley-Seton Hospital C-718-390-5811, Staten Island NY, C-212-447-3010. Chaplain serving all faiths C-201-724-4139.

RECREATION: Crafts EX-4014, Rental Center EX-4016, Bowling EX-4629, Rod/Gun Club, Ski Club EX-4014 (Ski slope on north end of arsenal). Lake Denmark Rec Area on post, late June-Sep, C-201-724-4014, D-312-880-4014, 12 mobile homes, three camper spaces w/W&E hookups, 15 camper spaces w/o hookups, and 16 tent spaces.

SPACE-A: None. Use Philadelphia IAP, C-215-897-5600/5644, D-312-443-5600/5644, Fax 215-897-5627.

ATTRACTIONS: Lake Country, skiing, New York City nearby.

Other Installations in New Jersey

Atlantic City International Airport, Pleasantville, NJ 08232-9500.
USMRA: Page 19 (E-8). C-609-645-6000, Exchange-484-5115.
Camp Pedricktown Support Installation Exchange, Scheduled to close under the 1995 BRAC. No closure date has been established, Bldg. 380, Rt 130 Pedricktown, NJ 08067-5000. USMRA: Page 19 (C-7). C-609-299-4303, Exchange-299-4303.
Sea Girt National Guard Exchange, Bldg. 57, Sea Girt, NJ 08750-5000.
USMRA: Page 19 (G-6). C-908-542-7235/7406, NGX-542-7235/7406.

U.S. FORCES TRAVEL & TRANSFER GUIDE U.S.A. - 203

NEW MEXICO

DOLLAR RENT A CAR — Call 1-800-800-4000. Get a military rate by using your Military Living ID # ML3009. Retirees Active Duty Reserve Guard.

CANNON AIR FORCE BASE (NM02R3)
100 S. DL Ingram Boulevard, Suite 102
Cannon Air Force Base, NM 88103-5216

TELEPHONE NUMBER INFORMATION: Main installation numbers: C-505-784-3311, D-312-681-1110.

LOCATION: From Clovis, west on US-60/84 to AFB. From NM-467 enter the Portales gate. USMRA: Page 114 (H-5). NMC: Clovis, seven miles east.

GENERAL INFORMATION: Air Combat Command Base. Fighter Wing, F-111, EF-111A, and F-16 Operations.

TEMPORARY MILITARY LODGING: Lodging office, Bldg. 1801B, Olympic St, 24 hours daily, C-505-784-2918, D-312-681-2918. All ranks. DV/VIP C-505-784-2727. Advance reservations C-505-784-4833.

LOGISTICAL SUPPORT: Complete support facilities available.

CHAMPUS-784-4085
Commissary-784-2160
Family Services-784-2452
Locator-784-4932
O'Club-784-2477
SATO-784-2304
Theater-784-2582
Chaplain-784-2507
Conv Store-784-3421
Gas Station-784-5177
Medical-784-4033
Package Store-784-2993
SDO/NCO-784-2253
Child Care-784-2704
Exchange-784-3387
Legal-784-2211
NCO Club-784-2853
Police-784-4111
Snack Bar-784-2280

HEALTH & WELFARE: 27th FW Hospital, clinics and depts, Emergency C-505-784-4033, Appointment C-505-784-2778, 35 beds. Chapel serving all faiths C-505-784-2507.

RECREATION: Bowling EX-2280, Golf EX-2800, Gym EX-2466, Auto Hobby EX-2170, Library EX-2786, Youth Center EX-2747.

SPACE-A: Extremely limited Space-A. Pax Term/Lounge, Bldg. 135, 0700-2300 Mon-Fri, 0700-2100 other days, C-505-784-2935, D-312-681-2935, flights to CONUS. Extremely limited.

ATTRACTIONS: Carlsbad Caverns, Sierra Blanca ski resort, and Clovis.

HOLLOMAN AIR FORCE BASE (NM05R3)
490 First Street, Suite 2800
Holloman Air Force Base, NM 88330-8287

TELEPHONE NUMBER INFORMATION: Main installation numbers: C-505-475-5411, D-312-867-5411.

NEW MEXICO
Holloman Air Force Base, continued

LOCATION: Exit US-70/82, eight miles southwest of Alamogordo. Route to AFB clearly marked. USMRA: Page 114 (D,E-7). NMC: Las Cruces, 50 miles southwest.

GENERAL INFORMATION: Air Combat Command Base. Headquarters Fighter Wing, and many support activities.

TEMPORARY MILITARY LODGING: Billeting Office, Bldg. 583, W New Mexico Ave, 24 hours daily, C-505-475-6123, D-312-867-3311. All ranks. DV/VIP C-505-475-5573/5574.

LOGISTICAL SUPPORT: Complete support facilities available.

Cafeteria-479-2698	CHAMPUS-475-7700	Chaplain-475-7211
Child Care-475-7505	Commissary-475-5127	Conv Store-479-2381
Exchange-479-6164	Family Services-475-3944	Gas Station-479-6004
Legal-475-7216	Locator-475-7510	Medical-475-3268
NCO Club-475-3226	O'Club-475-3611	Package Store-479-2201
Police-475-7397	Public Affairs-475-5406	SATO-475-3245
SDO/NCO-475-3226	Shoppette-479-2381	Snack Bar-479-2779
Theater-475-3286	Visitor Center-475-5920	

HEALTH & WELFARE: USAF Acute care clinic with eight beds, Emergency C-505-475-3268, Appointment C-505-479-2778, Dental C-505-475-3742. Chapel serving all faiths C-505-475-7211/7024.

RECREATION: Bowling EX-7378, Golf EX-3574, Gym EX-3229, Auto Hobby EX-7438, Consol Hobby EX-3760, Library EX-3939, Rec Equipment EX-7328, Rec Supply EX-5369, Youth Center EX- 3753, Aero Club EX-5813, Stables EX-3848, Swimming EX-3639. Fam-Camp, on base, year round, C-505-475-5369, D-312-867-5369, 12 camper spaces w/full hookups.

SPACE-A: Pax Term/Lounge, Bldg. 571, 24 hours daily, C-505-475-5411, D-312-867-5411, limited flights to CONUS locations.

ATTRACTIONS: Sierra Blanca ski area. El Paso TX and Ciudad Juarez, Mexico easy drive south. International Space Hall of Fame and White Sands National Monument in Alamogordo; Horse Racing, Ruidoso; Carlsbad Caverns, Whites City.

KIRTLAND AIR FORCE BASE (NM03R3)
2000 Wyoming Boulevard SE.
Kirtland Air Force Base, NM 87117-5606

TELEPHONE NUMBER INFORMATION: Main installation numbers: C-505-846-0011, D-312-246-0011.

LOCATION: From I-40 east, exit on Wyoming Blvd, south for two miles to Wyoming gate to AFB. USMRA: Page 114 (D-4). NMC: Albuquerque, one mile northeast.

GENERAL INFORMATION: Air Force Materiel Command Base. Air Force Operational Test and Evaluation Center, Phillips Lab, Defense Nuclear Agency Field Command, ANG and AFRES units and other units.

NEW MEXICO
Kirtland Air Force Base, continued

TEMPORARY MILITARY LODGING: Lodging office, Bldg. 22016, Club Dr, 24 hours daily, C-505-846-9652, D-312-246-1497. All ranks. DV/VIP C-505-846-4119.

LOGISTICAL SUPPORT: Complete support facilities available.

CHAMPUS-846-3335
Commissary-846-9558
Fire Dept-846-8069
ITT-846-2924
Medical-846-3730
O'Club-265-5165
Public Affairs-846-5991
RV/Camping-846-1275/1499
Theater-846-SHOW(7647)

Chaplain-846-5691
Exchange-846-9642
Gas Station-265-9093
Legal-846-4217
MWR-846-2059
Package Store-265-7301
Recreation-846-4123/4124

Child Care-846-1103
Family Services-846-0741
Golf Course-846-1169
Locator-846-0011
NCO Club-846-1467
Police-846-7913
Retiree Services-846-1536
SATO-846-7171/2914

HEALTH & WELFARE: USAF Hospital on VA Campus, clinics and depts, Emergency C-505-846-3730, 40 beds.

RECREATION: Bowling EX-6851, Library EX-1532, Golf EX-1169, Gym EX-1102/1068, Auto Hobby EX-1104, Arts/Crafts EX-1067, Sandia Skeet Club 846-0196, Youth Center EX-2042, Wood Hobby EX-1861. Fam-Camp on base, year round, C-505-846-1275, D-312-246-1275, 20 camper spaces, w/full hookups, three camper spaces w/water hookups, 29 camper spaces w/o hookups.

SPACE-A: Pax Term/Lounge, Bldg. 333, 0715-1600 Mon-Fri, C-505-846-0889, D-312-246-0889, Recorded flight information, 505-846-0785, flights to CONUS locations.

ATTRACTIONS: National Atomic Museum, Albuquerque, world's longest free span tram, Old Town founded in 1706, variety of Indian Pueblos, Albuquerque International Hot Air Balloon Fiesta each October, State Fair each September..."4th largest in US," ski resorts, Santa Fe, Indian cliff dwellings, Santa Fe Opera.

WHITE SANDS MISSILE RANGE (NM04R3)
Bldg. 122 Augusta Street
White Sands Missile Range, NM 88002-5047

TELEPHONE NUMBER INFORMATION: Main installation numbers: C-505-678-2121, D-312-258-2211.

LOCATION: From US-70, follow signs to White Sands Missile Range, (WSMR). Clearly marked. USMRA: Page 114 (D-6,7,8). NMC: El Paso TX, 45 miles south.

GENERAL INFORMATION: Army Test and Evaluation Command, NASA, and other tenants and support activities.

TEMPORARY MILITARY LODGING: Billeting Office, 0745-1530 daily, C-505-678-4559, D-312-258-4559. All ranks. DV/VIP C-505-678-1028.

LOGISTICAL SUPPORT: Complete support facilities available.

ACS-678-6767
Chaplain-678-2615/2031
Community Club-678-2057

Cafeteria-678-2081
Child Care-678-7882
Conv Store-678-2072

CHAMPUS-678-3099
Commissary-678-2358
Exchange-678-2072

NEW MEXICO
White Sands Missile Range, continued

Family Services-678-1663	Fire Dept-117	Gas Station-678-4877
ITT Office-678-1111	ITR-6784134	Legal-678-1263
Locator-678-1630	Medical-678-1231	MWR-678-1256
Package Store-678-2072	Police-678-1234	Public Affairs-678-1134
Retiree Services-678-3221	SATO-678-4778	SDO/NCO-678-2031
Theater-678-2483	Visitor Center-678-8824	

HEALTH & WELFARE: McAfee Army Health Center, Emergency C-505-678-2882, Info C-505-678-1231. Chapel serving all faiths C-505-678-2615.

RECREATION: Arts/Crafts EX-5321, Auto Hobby EX-5800, Bowling EX-3465, Golf EX-1759, Gym EX-3374, Library EX-5820, Swimming EX-3870, Rec Equipment EX-1713, Rec Center EX-4134. Volunteer Park Travel Camp Site on post, year round, C-505-678-1713, D-312-258-1713, eight camper spaces w/full hookups.

SPACE-A: None. See the Fort Bliss, TX listing, C-915-568-8048, D-312-978-0831.

ATTRACTIONS: White Sands National Monument and Space Center in Alamogordo.

U.S. FORCES TRAVEL & TRANSFER GUIDE U.S.A. - 207

NEW YORK

DOLLAR RENT A CAR — Call 1-800-800-4000. Get a military rate by using your Military Living ID # ML3009. Retirees Active Duty Reserve Guard.

BROOKLYN COAST GUARD AIR STATION (NY18R1)
Floyd Bennett Field
Brooklyn, NY 11234-7097

TELEPHONE NUMBER INFORMATION: Main installation numbers: C-718-615-2422, FTS-644-0422.

LOCATION: Take Belt Parkway to exit 11, south to Flatbush Ave. Watch for main entrance on the left. USMRA: Page 26 (F-7). NMC: Brooklyn, in city limits.

GENERAL INFORMATION: US Coast Guard Helicopter Base located in a National Park.

TEMPORARY MILITARY LODGING: Extremely limited transient quarters. Call main number for information.

LOGISTICAL SUPPORT: Most support facilities available.

All Hands Club-615-2480
Exchange-377-0380
MWR-615-2457
Police-692-1220
SDO/NCO-615-241009
Visitor Center-338-5799
Cafeteria-615-2456
Locator-615-2420
O'Club-615-2476
Public Affairs-615-2406
Snack Bar-615-2469
Conv Store-615-2469
Medical-615-2457
Package Store-615-2469
Recreation-615-2535
Travel-703-9548

HEALTH & WELFARE: Sick Bay, Edwards Hall C-718-615-2457. Inpatient, Uniformed Services Medical Treatment Facility, Bayley-Seton Hospital, Staten Island, C-718-390-6000.

RECREATION: Pool, Baseball, Boat Ramp, Model Plane Field, Auto Hobby, Wood Hobby, Volleyball, Picnic Area, Archery, Camping, Putting Green: Call Rec Services EX-2453.

SPACE-A: Limited, via helicopter, C-718-615-2410. See McGuire AFB, NJ C-609-724-3078, D-312-440-3078, Fax 609-724-4621

ATTRACTIONS: City of New York with its many restaurants, shows and museums, including the *Intrepid* Sea-Air-Space Museum.

FORT DRUM (NY06R1)
Fort Drum, NY 13602-5000

TELEPHONE NUMBER INFORMATION: Main installation numbers: C-315-772-6011, D-312-341-6011.

LOCATION: From Syracuse, take I-81 north to exit 48 (past Watertown), and follow signs to Fort Drum. USMRA: Page 21 (J-3). NMC: Watertown, eight miles southwest.

NEW YORK
Fort Drum, continued

GENERAL INFORMATION: Headquarters 10th Mountain Division (Light Infantry) and Fort Drum, and supporting units.

TEMPORARY MILITARY LODGING: Lodging office, Bldg. T-2227, 24 hours daily, C-315-772-5435, D-312-341-5435. All ranks. DV/VIP C-315-772-5010. Also, The Inn at Fort Drum at 4205 Po Valley Rd, C-315-773-7777.

LOGISTICAL SUPPORT: Complete support facilities available.

Cafeteria-772-5960	CHAMPUS-772-5111	Chaplain-772-5591
Commissary-772-5294	Conv Store-773-7594	EM Club-772-7673
Exchange-773-0061	Family Services-772-6709	Gas Station-773-8025
ITT Office-772-8222	Legal-772-5261	Locator-772-5869
Medical-772-8162	NCO Club-772-7673	O'Club-772-6222
Package Store-773-6989	Police-772-5157	Retiree Services-772-6434
SATO-772-5750/4864	SDO/NCO-772-5647	Theater-772-5571

HEALTH & WELFARE: Guthrie Ambulatory Health Clinic, Emergency C-315-772-5236, Appointment C-315-772-4350. Chapel serving all faiths C-315-772-5591.

RECREATION: Crafts EX-4325, Auto Hobby EX-5785, Bowling EX-6601, Gym EX-9674. Small ski slope and cross-country ski trails. Remington Pond Rec Area on post, Apr-Nov, wilderness area, C-315-772-5169, D-312-341-5169, six camper spaces w/o hookups.

SPACE-A: Wheeler-Sack Army Airfield, Bldg. P-2059, 0700-1700 hours, C-315-772-5681, D-312-341-5681, flights via executive aircraft to CONUS locations.

ATTRACTIONS: Sackets Harbor Battlefield (site of War of 1812 battle), Thousand Islands, Lake Ontario and Canada nearby.

FORT HAMILTON (NY02R1)
Headquarters New York Area Command & Fort Hamilton
Brooklyn, NY 11252-5700

TELEPHONE NUMBER INFORMATION: Main installation numbers: C-718-630-4401, D-312-232-4401.

LOCATION: From Belt Parkway, exit 2 (Fort Hamilton Parkway) to 100th St, right to Fort Hamilton Parkway, right to main gate. USMRA: Page 26 (D-7). NMC: New York, in city limits.

GENERAL INFORMATION: New York Area Command providing facilities and support for Army and DoD activities in the New York City metro area.

TEMPORARY MILITARY LODGING: Lodging office, Bldg. 109, 0800-1630 hours daily, C-718-630-4564, D-312-232-4564. All ranks. DV/VIP C-716-630-4324. Also, Navy Lodge at Gateway National Park (formerly New York Naval Station), C-718-442-0413.

LOGISTICAL SUPPORT: Complete support facilities available.

ACS-630-4754	CHAMPUS-630-4754	Chaplain-630-4969
Child Care-630-4040	Commissary-921-4007	Community Club-630-4903

NEW YORK
Fort Hamilton, continued

Exchange-748-3440	Family Services-630-4332	Gas Station-680-2773
ITT-630-4911	Legal-630-4024	Locator-630-4958
Medical-630-4036	MWR-630-4778	Package Store-680-7093
Police-630-4445	Public Affairs-630-4820	Retiree Services-630-4930
SATO-230-2706	Snack Bar-748-3440	Theater-748-3440

HEALTH & WELFARE: Ainsworth Army Health Clinic, Emergency C-718-630-4555, Appointment C-718-630-4268. Inpatient, Uniformed Services Medical Treatment Facility, Bayley-Seton Hospital, Staten Island, C-718-390-6000. Chaplain serving all faiths C-718-630-4969.

RECREATION: Arts/Crafts EX-4942, Auto Hobby EX-4150, Youth Activities EX-4123, Library EX-4875, Rec Center Ex-4476, Bowling EX-4440, Museum-EX-4349, Sports, EX-4793.

SPACE-A: None. See Stewart ANGB, C-914-563-2965/3298, D-312-247-2965/3298.

ATTRACTIONS: Historic fort, New York City nearby, Harbor Defense Museum. Limited support facilities at Fort Totten (housing area) in Queens.

FORT TOTTEN (NY20R1)
Fort Totten, NY 11359-1016

This base is scheduled to close under the 1995 BRAC.
No closure date has been established.

TELEPHONE NUMBER INFORMATION: Main installation numbers: C-718-352-5700, D-312-456-0700.

LOCATION: From Manhattan: Whitestone Bridge to Cross Island Parkway. Take Bell Blvd exit and follow signs to fort. From Long Island: Take Cross Island Parkway to Bell Blvd exit and proceed to fort. USMRA: Page 26 (G-3). NMC: New York City, 10 miles southwest.

GENERAL INFORMATION: Headquarters of the 77th Regional Support Command.

TEMPORARY MILITARY LODGING: None. See Fort Hamilton listing, C-718-630-4564, D-312-232-4564.

LOGISTICAL SUPPORT: Limited support facilities available.

Exchange-352-8314   Police-352-5793   SDO/NCO-352-5804

HEALTH & WELFARE: None. See Fort Hamilton listing, C-718-630-4268.

RECREATION: None available on base.

SPACE-A: None. See McGuire AFB, NJ listing, C-609-724-3078, D-312-440-3078, Fax 609-724-4621.

ATTRACTIONS: New York City. Fort has been in existence since 1857.

210 - U.S. FORCES TRAVEL & TRANSFER GUIDE U.S.A

NEW YORK

MITCHEL COMPLEX (NY21R1)
Garden City, NY 11530-5000

TELEPHONE NUMBER INFORMATION: Main installation numbers: C-516-222-1285, after hours 222-1270.

LOCATION: From the north: Northern State Parkway to Meadowbrook Parkway, Stewart Ave exit to light, right to next light, left to Mitchell field. From the south: Verrazano Bridge to Belt Parkway, stay left to Southern State Parkway, Stewart Ave exit as above. USMRA: Page 26 (I,J-4). NMC: NYC, 27 miles west.

GENERAL INFORMATION: Mitchel Field and Mitchel Manor Housing Areas with supporting facilities. The two areas are approximately two-and-a-half miles apart.

TEMPORARY MILITARY LODGING: None. Use Gateway National Park, C-718-442-0413 (Navy Lodge).

LOGISTICAL SUPPORT: Limited support facilities available.

CHAMPUS-222-1282	Child Care-222-1614	Commissary-222-0880
Exchange-222-1293	Family Services-486-1922	Police-222-1285
Retiree Services-222-1282	SDO/NCO-222-1285	Theater-222-1610

HEALTH & WELFARE: None. See Fort Hamilton listing, C-718-630-4268.

RECREATION: Camping Equipment EX-1611, Community Center EX-0282, Gym EX-1611, Swimming EX-1611, Youth Activities EX-0282.

SPACE-A: None. See McGuire AFB, NJ listing, C-609-724-3078, D-312-440-3078, Fax 609-724-4621.

ATTRACTIONS: New York City Cradle of Aviation Museum on base (hangar 384), NYC. Departure site for Charles Lindbergh's first nonstop, solo transatlantic flight.

NEW YORK COAST GUARD SUPPORT CENTER (NY01R1)
Bldg. 110
Governors Island, NY, NY 10004-5000

TELEPHONE NUMBER INFORMATION: No base operator. Direct calls only.

LOCATION: Take free Governors Island Ferry from Battery Park area of Manhattan. USMRA: Page 26 (D-5). NMC: New York, one mile northwest.

GENERAL INFORMATION: Coast Guard Support Center.

TEMPORARY MILITARY LODGING: Super 8 Governors Island Guest House, C-212-269-8878. All ranks. DV/VIP, C-212-668-7197.

LOGISTICAL SUPPORT: Complete support facilities available.

CDO/OOD-668-7015	CHAMPUS-668-7405	Chaplain-668-7313
Child Care-668-6499	Commissary-668-7338	CPO Club-668-7266
EM Club-668-7397	Exchange-668-7311	Family Services-668-6444

U.S. FORCES TRAVEL & TRANSFER GUIDE U.S.A. - 211

NEW YORK
New York Coast Guard Support Center, continued

Fire Dept-668-7300
ITT-668-3402
Medical-668-7167/7347
Package Store-668-7311
Recreation-668-7255

Gas Station-425-2970
Legal-668-7651
MWR-668-7255
Police-668-7474
Theater-668-7401

Golf Course-668-7329
Locator-668-7786
O'Club-668-7266
Public Affairs-668-7114

HEALTH & WELFARE: USCG Clinic, Emergency EX-7243. Inpatient, Uniformed Services Medical Treatment Facility, Bayley-Seton Hospital, Staten Island, C-718-390-6000. Chapels serving all faiths EX-7313.

RECREATION: Bowling EX-7315, Crafts EX-7248, Golf EX-7319, Gym EX-7255, Library EX-7394, Picnic Grounds EX-7255, Swimming EX-7255, Tennis EX-3401, Tickets EX-7255.

SPACE-A: None. See McGuire AFB NJ listing, 609-724-3078, D-312-440-3078, Fax 609-724-4621.

ATTRACTIONS: New York City, Action Park.

NIAGARA FALLS AIR RESERVE STATION (NY12R1)
2720 Kirkbridge Drive
Niagara Falls International Airport/ARS, NY 14304-5000

TELEPHONE NUMBER INFORMATION: Main installation numbers: C-716-236-2000, D-312-238-2014.

LOCATION: Take I-190 to Niagara Falls, exit Porter Packard Road. Turn right onto Porter Packard and stay on it until it becomes Lockport. Turn right at main gate. USMRA: Page 20 (D-6). NMC: Niagara Falls, six miles west.

GENERAL INFORMATION: 914th Airlift Wing, 107th Air Refueling Group.

TEMPORARY MILITARY LODGING: Lodging office, Bldg. 312, Flint Ave, 0700-2300 daily, C-716-236-2014, D-312-489-2014 or 1-800-456-4990. All ranks. DV/VIP C-716-236-2136/2139.

LOGISTICAL SUPPORT: Most support facilities available.

Chaplain-236-2381
Legal-236-2134
Package Store-236-2100
Recreation-236-2328

Consol Club-236-2027
Locator-236-2002
Police-236-2280
SATO-236-2039

Exchange-236-2100
Medical-236-2086
Public Affairs-236-2136
Snack Bar-236-2329

HEALTH & WELFARE: Dispensary/Emergency C-716-236-2086. Chapel serving all faiths C-716-236-2096.

RECREATION: Limited on base.

SPACE-A: Pax Term/Lounge, Bldg. 800, 0800-1600 Mon-Fri, C-716-236-2174/2371, D-312-489-2174/2371, Fax C-716-236-2380, flights to CONUS and overseas via AFRES aircraft.

ATTRACTIONS: Niagara Falls, Canada.

NEW YORK

SENECA ARMY DEPOT ACTIVITY (NY03R1)
5786 State Route 96
Romulus, NY 14541-5001

This base is scheduled to close under the 1995 BRAC.
No closure date has been established.

TELEPHONE NUMBER INFORMATION: Main installation numbers: C-607-869-1110, D-312-489-5110.

LOCATION: Fifty-five miles southeast of Rochester, 12 miles south of Geneva, on NY-96A. USMRA: Page 20 (H-7). NMC: Geneva, 12 miles north, Rochester, 55 miles northwest.

GENERAL INFORMATION: Coast Guard Loran Station.

TEMPORARY MILITARY LODGING: Lodging office, Bldg. B-116, 0830-1630 hours daily, C-607-869-1211/1314, D-312-489-5314. All ranks.

LOGISTICAL SUPPORT: Complete support facilities available.

CHAMPUS-869-1243   Fire Dept-869-1436   NCO Club-869-1438
O'Club-869-1666   Police-869-1448   Public Affairs-869-1353
RV/Camping-869-1211

HEALTH & WELFARE: None. See Niagara Falls ARS listing, C-716-236-2086.

RECREATION: Lakeshore Travel Camp on post, year round, C-607-869-1211, D-312-489-5211, six camper spaces w/W&E, two camper spaces w/E hookups, 21 mobile homes.

SPACE-A: None. See Niagara Falls Air Reserve Station listing, C-716-236-2174/2371, D-312-489-2174/2371, Fax C-716-236-2380.

ATTRACTIONS: Finger Lakes region of NY.

SOLDIERS', SAILORS', AND AIRMEN'S CLUB (NY17R1)
283 Lexington Ave.
New York, NY 10016-3540

TELEPHONE NUMBER INFORMATION: C-1-800-678-TGIF (8443), 212-683-4353/4354, Fax 212-683-4374.

LOCATION: From the Lincoln Tunnel, east on 34th or 36th St to Third Ave. Left on 37th St (one block), left on Lexington Ave, club is on the left at mid-block. USMRA: Page 26 (E-4). NMC: New York, in city limits.

GENERAL INFORMATION: Open to all Servicemen/women, Active Duty, Reserve, National Guard, service academy/ROTC students, all retirees, former service personnel with honorable discharge, allied member forces, and their dependents. Note: Unaccompanied spouses and widows with ID may use facilities on a Space-A basis. Guests are required to provide an ID Card or proof of Honorable Discharge.

NEW YORK
Soldiers', Sailors' and Airmen's Club, continued

TEMPORARY MILITARY LODGING: Club open 24 hours. Reservations for weekends suggested. Rates range from $25-35 depending rank. Note: There is no elevator, guests must be able to climb stairs. Continental breakfast on weekends and holidays. Rates range from $25-$35 per night.

LOGISTICAL SUPPORT & RECREATION: Facilities include lounges, library, TV rooms, pool room, and canteen.

HEALTH AND WELFARE: None. See Fort Hamilton, NY listing, C-718-630-4268.

SPACE-A: See McGuire AFB, NJ listing, C-609-724-3078, D-312-440-3078, Fax C-609-724-4621.

ATTRACTIONS: The SS&A has been in this location since 1926. Here's your chance to visit the Big Apple to shop and see the sights. There is controlled access, a helpful staff. Definitely one of New York's best kept secrets! Also, Historic Murray Hill section, Midtown Manhattan. five blocks from Grand Central Station and Empire State Building. Residential area, many fine restaurants, close to 5th Avenue shopping and theatre district.

AUTHOR'S NOTE: The **Soldiers', Sailors' and Airmen's Club** is a tax exempt, not-for-profit organization founded in 1919 to serve the needs of service personnel while visiting New York City. It is the only club of its kind in the city.

SUFFOLK COUNTY AIR NATIONAL GUARD BASE/ FRANCIS GABRESKI AIR NATIONAL GUARD STATION (NY25R1)
150 Riverhead Road
Westhampton Beach, NY 11978

TELEPHONE NUMBER INFORMATION: Main installation numbers: C-516-288-7300, D-312-456-7300.

LOCATION: Two miles south of Sunrise Highway. USMRA: Page 20 (F-2). NMC: Westhampton Beach, in city limits.

TEMPORARY MILITARY LODGING: None. Military rates available at surrounding commercial motels.

LOGISTICAL SUPPORT: Most support facilities available.

CDO/OOD-288-7416	Chaplain-288-7566	EM Club-288-7481
Exchange-288-7557	Fire Dept-288-7534	Legal-288-7587
Medical-288-7447	O'Club-288-7481	Package Store-288-7557
Police-288-7478	Public Affairs-288-7400	

HEALTH & WELFARE: None.

SPACE-A: Pax Term, Bldg 369, Monday through Friday 0730-1600, C-516-288-7416, D-312-456-7416.

ATTRACTIONS: Beaches nearby, gateway to "The Hamptons," New York City, with its many attractions, is just 70 miles east.

214 - U.S. FORCES TRAVEL & TRANSFER GUIDE U.S.A
NEW YORK

STEWART ARMY SUBPOST (NY09R1)
New Windsor, NY 12553-9000

TELEPHONE NUMBER INFORMATION: Main installation numbers: C-914-563-3323, D-312-247-1110.

LOCATION: From I-87 take Newburgh exit to Union Ave, south to NY-207. Follow signs to Stewart Airport and Subpost. USMRA: Page 21 (M-10). NMC: New York City, 60 miles south.

GENERAL INFORMATION: Support activity for US Military Academy, West Point.

TEMPORARY MILITARY LODGING: Lodging office, Bldg. 2605, 6th and D Sts, Five Star Inn, 24 hours daily, C-914-563-3311, D-312-247-3311/3524. All ranks.

LOGISTICAL SUPPORT: Complete support facilities available. See USMA, West Point listing for further support facilities.

Chaplain-564-5291
Conv Store-564-7601
Family Services-563-3485
Police-564-6031
Child Care-563-3522
EM Club-564-7590
Medical-563-2113
Commissary-938-3663
Exchange-564-7601
O'Club-564-6661

HEALTH & WELFARE: US Army Health Clinic C-914-563-2113. Inpatient, see United States Military Academy, West Point listing, C-914-938-4004. Chapels serving all faiths C-914-563-3310/3429.

RECREATION: Library EX-3501, Youth Center EX-3544, Swimming EX-3485, Bowling EX-3447, Gym EX-3565, Picnic/Archery EX-3485, Multi-Crafts EX-3584, Auto Hobby EX-3420, Community Recreation EX-3485.

SPACE-A: At press time, Space-A on C-5s at Stewart IAP, 105th Military Airlift Group, still is not available because of lack of ground equipment and personnel. Check on new Space-A opportunities with Marine Reserve Unit Operations, C-914-563-2965/2966, D-312-247-2965/2966. Mostly CONUS flights; no dependents.

ATTRACTIONS: Historic USMA, West Point, and Hudson River Valley.

UNITED STATES MILITARY ACADEMY, WEST POINT (NY16R1)
West Point, NY 10996-5000

TELEPHONE NUMBER INFORMATION: Main installation numbers: C-914-938-4011, D-312-688-1110.

LOCATION: Off I-87 or US-9 west. Clearly marked. USMRA: Page 21 (M,N-10) Page 28 (D-3). NMC: New York City, 50 miles south.

GENERAL INFORMATION: Military Educational Institution, Corps of Cadets and support units.

NEW YORK
United States Military Academy, West Point, continued

TEMPORARY MILITARY LODGING: Hotel Thayer, Bldg. 674, 24 hours daily, C-914-446-4731, D-312-688-2632 or 1-800-247-5047. All ranks. DV/VIP C-914-938-4315/4316 Five Star Inn, C-914-563-3311.

LOGISTICAL SUPPORT: Complete support facilities available.

CHAMPUS-938-4838
Commissary-938-3663
Family Services-938-2023
Legal-938-4541
Police-938-3312
SATO-446-6400
Visitor Center-938-2638

Child Care-938-4523
Conv Store-938-3035
Gas Station-446-5556
Locator-938-4412
Public Affairs-938-2006
SDO/NCO-938-3500
West Point Club-446-5506

Comm Club-938-5120
Exchange-446-5406
ITR Office-938-2070
Medical-938-5169
Retiree Services-938-4217
Theater-938-4159

HEALTH & WELFARE: William L. Keller Army Community Hospital, Emergency C-914-938-4004, Info C-914-938-5169, 65 beds. Chapels serving all faiths C-914-938-3412.

RECREATION: Golf EX-2435, Ski Slope EX-3726, Youth Center EX-3208, Swimming EX-2946/5158, Lodge EX-4335, Gym EX-2338, Tate Skating Rink EX-2991, Community Recreation Division Rental EX-2503, Bowling EX-2140, Library EX-2974, Rec Office EX-3809/4455, Rec Center EX-3601/2070, Crafts EX-4812/2074. Round Pond Recreation Area off base, 15 Apr-15 Nov, C-914-938-2503, D-312-688-2503, 26 camper spaces w/W&E, 20 tent spaces.

SPACE-A: None. See Stewart Army Subpost listing, C-914-563-2965/2966, D-312-2247-2965/2966.

ATTRACTIONS: Tours of historic USMA, West Point. Hudson River Valley.

WATERVLIET ARSENAL (NY19R1)
Watervliet, NY 12189-4050

TELEPHONE NUMBER INFORMATION: Main installation numbers: C-518-266-1110, D-312-974-1110.

LOCATION: Take I-787 to exit 6 to 19th St. Watch for signs to the arsenal. USMRA: Page 21 (N-7). NMC: Albany, six miles south.

GENERAL INFORMATION: Watervliet is an Army R&D and artillery/cannon production facility. Oldest continually active arsenal in the US.

TEMPORARY MILITARY LODGING: None. See Westover ARB, MA listing C-413-557-2700, D-312-589-2700.

LOGISTICAL SUPPORT: Most support facilities available.

ACS-266-5103
Exchange-266-5371
Medical-266-4195

Cafeteria-266-5473
Family Services-266-5920
Police-266-4334

Comm Club-266-5917
Legal-266-5298
Public Affairs-266-5090

HEALTH & WELFARE: US Army Health Clinic C-518-266-4195.

NEW YORK
Watervliet Arsenal continued

RECREATION: Pitch and Putt Golf Course, Tennis, Swimming, Racquetball Court, Health Facility, Shop: call Rec Services EX-5017.

SPACE-A: None. See Stewart Army Subpost C-914-563-2965, D-312-247-2965.

ATTRACTIONS: Albany (New York's Capital), Rivers Park (Industrial Heritage Tour), Saratoga Race Track, Saratoga Performing Arts Center, State Museum, Peebles Island State Park, Watervliet Arsenal Museum.

Other Installations in New York

Buffalo Coast Guard Group, 1 Furhmann Blvd, Buffalo, NY 14203-3189.
USMRA: Page 20 (D-6). C-716-846-4156, Exchange-856-4143.
Camp Smith, Bldg. 546, Peekskill, NY 10566-5000.
USMRA: Page 28 (D,E-5,6). C-914-734-7377, Exchange-734-9665.
Gateway National Park, Staten Island, NY 10304-5000.
USMRA: Page 26 (C-7). Navy Lodge C-718-442-0413.
Griffiss Airfield, 592 Hangar Road, Suite 202, Griffiss AFB, NY 13441-4520.
USMRA Page 21 (J,K-5,6). C-315-330-1110, Space-A-330-7400/7450, extremely limited.
Hancock Field ANGB, Syracuse, NY 13211-7099.
USMRA: Page 21 (I-6). C-315-454-4330, Exchange-454-6100.
Roslyn Air National Guard Station, Harbor Hill Road, Roslyn, NY 11576-2399.*This base is scheduled to close under the 1995 BRAC. No closure date has been established.*
USMRA: Page 26 (I-4). C-516-625-6946, Exchange-625-6946.
Schenectady County Airport/National Guard Base/Scotia Naval Administrative Unit, 1 Amsterdam Rd, Scotia, NY 12302-9460. USMRA: Page 21 (M,N-6). C-518-381-3600, Commissary-381-5935, Exchange-381-6640, Space-A-381-7420.
Shinnecock Coast Guard Station, Foster Avenue, Hampton Bays, NY 11946-3298.
USMRA: Page 20 (G-2). C-516-728-0343, Exchange-728-4350.
United States Merchant Marine Academy, Steamboat Road, Kings Point, NY 11024-1699. C-516-773-5000, Public information line-773-5527, Group tours-773-5387.

U.S. FORCES TRAVEL & TRANSFER GUIDE U.S.A. - 217

NORTH CAROLINA

DOLLAR RENT A CAR — Call 1-800-800-4000. Get a military rate by using your Military Living ID # ML3009. Retirees/Active Duty/Reserve/Guard.

CAMP LEJEUNE MARINE CORPS BASE (NC10R1)
Box 20004
Camp Lejeune Marine Corps Base, NC 28542-0004

TELEPHONE NUMBER INFORMATION: Main installation numbers: C-910-451-1113, D-312-484-1113.

LOCATION: Main gate is six miles east of junction of US-17 and NC-24, off NC-24. USMRA: Page 45 (L,M-5). NMC: Jacksonville, three miles northwest.

GENERAL INFORMATION: USMC Forces Atlantic, II MEF. 2nd Marine Division, 2nd Force Service Support Group.

TEMPORARY MILITARY LODGING: Lodging office, Bldg. 2617, 24 hours daily, C-910-451-1385/2146, D-312-484-1385/2146. Hostess House, C-910-451-3041. DV/VIP C-910-451-2523.

LOGISTICAL SUPPORT: Complete support facilities available.

Cafeteria-451-2592	CHAMPUS-451-4150/4152	Chaplain-451-3210/5633
Commissary-451-2172	Conv Store-451-5491	CPO Club-451-2839
EM Club-451-2872	Exchange-451-2481	Family Services-451-5340
Gas Station-451-2443	Golf Course-451-1668	ITT Office-451-5398
Legal-451-1903	Locator-451-3074	Medical-451-4300
O'Club-451-2465	Police-451-2555	Public Affairs-451-5655
Recreation-451-2108	Retiree Services-451-5927	SATO-451-2192/5889
SDO/NCO-451-2528	Theater-451-1759	Visitor Center-451-2197

HEALTH & WELFARE: Naval Hospital, Emergency C-910-451-4840, Appointment C-910-451-4630, 205 beds. Chapel serving all faiths C-910-451-4070.

RECREATION: Arts/Crafts EX-2077, Auto Hobby EX-1550, Golf EX-5445/1668, Gym EX-3516/1612/3768/5288/1870, Boating EX-1956/7386/8307, Riding Stables EX-2238, Library EX-5724, Swimming EX-2024/0768/1441, Trap/Skeet Range EX-3889, Beach EX-7273, Fishing/Hunting EX-5226. Onslow Beach Campsites & Recreation Area on base, year round, C-910-451-7473/7502, D-312-484-7473/7502, 51 camper spaces w/full hookups, 19 tent spaces 17 mobile homes, eight apartments and four beach houses for use of AD on PCS orders only.

SPACE-A: None. See Cherry Point MCAS listing, C-919-466-3232, D-312-582-3232.

ATTRACTIONS: Raleigh, NC, state capital, 116 miles northeast. Wilmington, 45 miles south. Both offer many museums, historical areas and gardens. Beaches on base.

218 - U.S. FORCES TRAVEL & TRANSFER GUIDE U.S.A
NORTH CAROLINA

CAPE HATTERAS COAST GUARD GROUP (NC09R1)
P.O. Box 604
Buxton, NC 27915-0604

TELEPHONE NUMBER INFORMATION: Main installation number: C-919-995-3676.

LOCATION: From US-158 or US-64, take NC-12 to Buxton (approximately 50 miles south of Nags Head). East on Old Lighthouse Road, five miles to base. USMRA: Page 45 (P-3). NMC: Elizabeth City, 110 miles northwest.

GENERAL INFORMATION: Coast Guard Group.

TEMPORARY MILITARY LODGING: Recreational Quarters, C-919-995-6435.

LOGISTICAL SUPPORT: Very limited support facilities available.

Exchange-995-6431   Medical-995-6426   RVC-995-6435

HEALTH & WELFARE: Coast Guard Clinic, C-919-995-6426. Inpatient see Portsmouth Naval Medical Center listing, C-804-399-1100.

RECREATION: Cape Hatteras Coast Guard Recreational Quarters, year round, C-919-995-3676. Six units that sleep five, and two suites.

SPACE-A: None. See Cherry Point MCAS listing, C-919-466-3232, D-312-582-3232.

ATTRACTIONS: Within walking distance of the historic Cape Hatteras Lighthouse. Excellent beaches, fishing, and wind surfing.

CHARLOTTE DOUGLAS IAP/ NORTH CAROLINA AIR NATIONAL GUARD BASE (NC20R1)
5225 Morris Field Dr.
Charlotte, NC 28208-5797

TELEPHONE NUMBER INFORMATION: Main installation numbers: C-704-391-4100, D-312-583-9210.

LOCATION: From I-77 take exit 6 A/B to Billy Graham Parkway (US-521) north to Morris Field Drive (three-and-a-half miles), turn left. Base is on your right. USMRA: Page 44 (G-4). NMC: Charlotte, three miles east.

GENERAL INFORMATION: Headquarters of the North Carolina Air National Guard.

TEMPORARY MILITARY LODGING: None. See Fort Bragg listing, C-910-436-2211.

LOGISTICAL SUPPORT: Limited support facilities available.

Chaplain-391-4179   EM Club-391-4426   Fire Department-391-4206
Legal-391-4260   O' Club-39104427   Police-391-4152
Public Affairs-391-4141   SATO-391-4163

U.S. FORCES TRAVEL & TRANSFER GUIDE U.S.A. - 219

NORTH CAROLINA
Charlotte Douglas IAP, continued

HEALTH & WELFARE: None. See Fort Jackson, SC listing, C-803-751-5308/2183.

SPACE-A: Base Operations C-704-391-4177, D-312-583-9177, Fax 704-391-4322. Unscheduled flights to CONUS and overseas.

ATTRACTIONS: None. This is co-located at an international airport.

CHERRY POINT MARINE CORPS AIR STATION (NC02R1)
PSC Box 8013
Cherry Point, NC 28533-0013

TELEPHONE NUMBER INFORMATION: Main installation numbers: C-919-466-2811, D-312-582-2811

LOCATION: On NC-101 between New Bern and Morehead City. US-70 connects with NC-101 at Havelock. USMRA: Page 45 (N-4). NMC: Jacksonville, 50 miles southwest.

GENERAL INFORMATION: Second Marine Aircraft Wing and Naval Aviation Depot.

TEMPORARY MILITARY LODGING: Lodging office, 24 hours daily, Bldg. 3673 (Officers), Bldg. 214 (EM), 24 hours daily, C-919-466-3060/5245, D-312-582-3060/5245. All ranks. DV/VIP C-919-447-5169.

LOGISTICAL SUPPORT: Complete support facilities available.

CDO/OOD-466-5236/4313	CHAMPUS-466-0122	Chaplain-466-4001
Child Care-466-3783	Commissary-447-2061	Conv Store-447-7041
Exchange-447-7041	Family Services-466-4401	Fire Dept-466-2241
Gas Station-447-2402	Golf Course-466-3044	ITT Office-466-2197
Legal-466-2310	Locator-466-2109/2026	Medical-466-0266
MWR-466-2431	O'Club-447-2395	Package Store-447-7041
Police-466-3615	Public Affairs-466-4241	Recreation-466-4232/2197
Retiree Services-466-5836	RV/Camping-466-2197	Omega Travel-466-5814
SDO/NCO-466-5236	Snack Bar-447-7041	SNCO Club-466-3087
Theater-466-3884	Visitor Center-466-5921	

HEALTH & WELFARE: Naval Hospital, Emergency C-919-466-0255, 23 beds. Chapel serving all faiths C-919-466-4000.

RECREATION: Arts/Crafts EX-3965, Bowling EX-3910, Boat Docks EX-5812, Library EX-3552, Swimming EX-2209, Rec Center EX-4331, Picnic Area EX-2197. MWR Fam-Camp on base, year round, C-919-466-2197, D-312-582-2197, 15 camper spaces w/full hookups.

SPACE-A: Pax Term/Lounge, Bldg. 199, 0600-2300 daily, C-919-466-3232/2379, D-312-582-3232/2379, flights to CONUS and overseas.

ATTRACTIONS: Outer Banks of NC, hunting, fishing, swimming, beaches and outdoor recreation of all types. New Bern, first colonial capital of NC, 17 miles north. Morehead City, 19 miles southeast, is a large commercial fishing port.

NORTH CAROLINA

ELIZABETH CITY COAST GUARD SUPPORT CENTER (NC03R1)
Elizabeth City, NC 27909-5000

TELEPHONE NUMBER INFORMATION: Main installation numbers: C-919-335-6224.

LOCATION: Take I-65 east to VA-104, south to US-17, south to Elizabeth City, left on Halstead Blvd, three miles to main gate of Center. USMRA: Page 45 (O-1). NMC: Elizabeth City, in city limits.

GENERAL INFORMATION: Air Station, Aviation Technical Training and Repair Center for the Coast Guard, National Strike Force Coordination Center.

TEMPORARY MILITARY LODGING: Lodging office, Bldg. 5, 0800-1630 daily, C-919-335-6286. Six two-bedroom trailers, reservations required, C-919-335-6548. All ranks.

LOGISTICAL SUPPORT: Most support facilities available.

CHAMPUS-335-6460
Consol Club-335-6301
Gas Station-335-6187
Package Store-335-6187
SDO/NCO-335-6130

Chaplain-335-6202
EM Club-335-6388
Locator-335-6130
Police-335-6398
Travel (AAA)-335-6321

Conv Store-335-6187
Exchange-335-6269
Medical-335-6460
Retiree Services-335-6224

HEALTH & WELFARE: USCG Clinic, Emergency C-919-335-6460, Appointment C-919-335-6460. Inpatient see Portsmouth Naval Medical Center listing, C-804-399-1100. Chapel serving all faiths C-919-335-6202.

RECREATION: Gym, Swimming, Auto Hobby, Boat Ramp, Ceramics, Racquetball, Tennis, Beaches. Weeksville Campsites on base, year round, C-919-335-6548, six mobile homes and four camper spaces w/full hookups.

SPACE-A: Coast Guard Air Station, Air Ops Center, 0800-1600 Mon-Fri, C-919-335-6332, D-312-935-1520, FTS: 931-0332, flights to CONUS and overseas.

ATTRACTIONS: Outer Banks of North Carolina, fresh seafood, beaches.

FORT BRAGG (NC05R1)
Fort Bragg, NC 28307-5000

TELEPHONE NUMBER INFORMATION: Main installation numbers: C-910-396-0011, D-312-236-0011.

LOCATION: Take I-95, exit to NC-24 west for 15 miles. NC-24 runs through Post as Bragg Blvd. From US-401 (Fayetteville Bypass) exit to All American Expressway, five miles to Fort. USMRA: Page 345 (I,J-4). NMC: Fayetteville, 10 miles southeast.

GENERAL INFORMATION: XVIII Airborne Corps, Airborne Division, Army Special Operations Command, Field Artillery Brigade, Corps Support Command, Joint Special Operations Command, other support units.

U.S. FORCES TRAVEL & TRANSFER GUIDE U.S.A. - 221

NORTH CAROLINA
Fort Bragg, continued

TEMPORARY MILITARY LODGING: Lodging office, Bldg. D-3601 (Moon Hall), Room 101, 24 hours daily, C-910-436-2211, D-312-236-5575. All ranks. DV/VIP C-910-436-2804.

LOGISTICAL SUPPORT: Complete support facilities available.

ACS-396-8682	Cafeteria-436-4901	CHAMPUS-432-4424/2741
Chaplain-396-1121	Child Care-396-6979	Commissary-396-2428
Conv Store-436-0800/4600	EM Club-436-3200	Exchange-436-4888
Family Services-396-6316	Fire Dept-396-1504	Gas Station-497-3985
Golf Course-436-3811	ITT Office-396-1278	Legal-396-1445
Locator-396-3601	Medical-432-1351	MWR-396-2077
NCO-436-4200	O'Club-436-0111	Package Store-436-0404
Police-396-0391	Public Affairs-396-5600	Recreation-396-2077
Retiree Services-396-5304	RV/Camping-396-3502	SATO-436-5808
SDO/NCO-396-6100	Theater-436-5323	Visitor Center-396-2815

HEALTH & WELFARE: Womack Army Medical Center, Emergency 432-0301/0302, Appointment 432-1351, 325 beds. Chapel serving all faiths 396-1121.

RECREATION: Hobby Shops: Auto EX-4397/432-5696/497-1257. Bowling 436-1432/497-3428, Golf 436-3390/497-1752, Field House/Swimming EX-4468/2231, 432-6489/3573/6493/1712/1031. Rec Equipment EX-1065/1340, Stables 497-1257, Library EX-3526, Music Center EX-4373, Sport Parachute Club 436-5858, Green Beret Parachute Club 436-4056, Rod/Gun Club 436-3323, Youth Center EX-1278. Smith Lake Army Travel Campground on Post, year round, C-910-396-5979, D-312-236-5979, 13 camper spaces w/full hookups, 11 w/W&E hookups.

SPACE-A: None. See Pope AFB, NC listing, C-910-394-4429/2803, D-312-486-4429/2803, Fax 910-394-2474.

ATTRACTIONS: Pinehurst Resort is nearby. JFK Special Warfare Museum and 82nd Airborne Division Museum on Post.

FORT MACON COAST GUARD GROUP (NC18R1)
Atlantic Beach, NC 28512-0237

TELEPHONE NUMBER INFORMATION: Main installation numbers: C-919-247-4598.

LOCATION: Take US-70 to Atlantic Beach/Morehead City Bridge. Left at traffic light in Atlantic Beach onto NC-58 (Fort Macon Rd). Proceed to entrance at end of road on right. USMRA: Page 45 (N-5). NMC: New Bern, 30 miles northwest.

GENERAL INFORMATION: Homeport of USCGC's *Primrose, Block Island, Staten Island, Gentian,* and *ANT Primrose.*

TEMPORARY MILITARY LODGING: None. See Camp Lejeune listing, C-910-451-1385/2146, D-312-484-1385/2146.

LOGISTICAL SUPPORT: Limited support facilities available.

222 - U.S. FORCES TRAVEL & TRANSFER GUIDE U.S.A

NORTH CAROLINA
Fort Macon Coast Guard Group, continued

Cafeteria-247-7981　　CHAMPUS-247-4551　　Exchange-247-4591
Medical-247-4551　　　SDO/NCO-247-4598

HEALTH & WELFARE: Clinic C-919-247-4551. Inpatient, see Cherry Point MCAS listing C-919-466-0255. No Chapel on base.

RECREATION: Camping/Rec Equipment EX-4598. Water activities year round.

SPACE-A: None. See Cherry Point Marine Corps Air Station listing, C-919-466-3232, D-312-582-3232.

ATTRACTIONS: Resort town of Atlantic Beach, beaches, fishing, Fort Macon State Park, Cape Lookout National Seashore.

NEW RIVER MARINE CORPS AIR STATION (NC06R1)
PSC Box 21002
Jacksonville, NC 28545-1002

TELEPHONE NUMBER INFORMATION: Main installation numbers: C-910-451-1113/1115, D-312-484-1113/1115.

LOCATION: Off US-17, two miles south of Jacksonville. Clearly marked. USMRA: Page 45 (L,M-5). NMC: Jacksonville, two miles northeast.

GENERAL INFORMATION: Marine Aircraft Groups, Marine Air Traffic Control Squadron, and Marine Wing Support Squadron, Headquarters Squadron.

TEMPORARY MILITARY LODGING: Lodging office, Bldg. 705, duty hours, C-910-451-6621, D-312-484-6568. All ranks. DV/VIP C-910-451-6621.

LOGISTICAL SUPPORT: Complete support facilities available.

CDO/OOD-451-0539　　　CHAMPUS-451-4152　　　Chaplain-451-6801
Child Care-451-6712　　　Commissary-451-6395　　Conv Store-451-0539
EM Club-451-0589　　　　Exchange-451-0539　　　Family Services-451-6110
Fire Dept-451-6620　　　　Gas Station-451-6092　　Legal-451-6160
Locator-451-6568　　　　　Medical-451-6511　　　　MWR-451-6573
O'Club-451-6409　　　　　Package Store-451-0539　Police-451-6111
Public Affairs-451-6196　　Recreation-451-6410　　　RV/Camping-451-6578
Theater-451-6292

HEALTH & WELFARE: Naval Branch Medical Clinic, Emergency C-919-451-6511. Inpatient, Camp Lejeune MCB, C-910-451-4630. Chapels serving all faiths at Camp Lejeune MCB C-910-451-4070.

RECREATION: Arts/Crafts EX-6711, Auto Hobby EX-6709, Gym EX-6714, Library EX-6942, Bowling EX-6582, Rec Equipment EX-6387, Ceramics EX-6711, Wood Hobby EX-6690, Marina EX-6578, Swimming EX-6436. Marina on base, year round, C-910-451-6578, D-312-484-6578, six camper spaces w/W hookups.

SPACE-A: Limited. Helicopter aircraft here. See Cherry Point MCAS listing.

NORTH CAROLINA
New River Marine Corps Air Station, continued

ATTRACTIONS: Great North Carolina beaches. Cape Lookout National Seashore to the northeast.

POPE AIR FORCE BASE (NC01R1)
259 Maynard Street.
Pope Air Force Base, NC 28308-2391

TELEPHONE NUMBER INFORMATION: Main installation numbers: C-910-394-0001, D-312-486-1110.

LOCATION: Take I-95, exit 55 to NC-87/24 west. Follow signs to Pope AFB and Fort Bragg. USMRA: Page 45 (J-4). NMC: Fayetteville, 12 miles southeast.

GENERAL INFORMATION: Air Combat Command Base, 624th Air Mobility support Group, 23rd Wing (composite wing), 18th Air Support Operations Group, Combat Control School, and AFRES units.

TEMPORARY MILITARY LODGING: Lodging office, 302 Ethridge St, 24 hours daily, C-910-394-4131, D-312-486-4131. All ranks. DV/VIP C-910-394-4739.

LOGISTICAL SUPPORT: Complete support facilities available.

CHAMPUS-394-2182
Commissary-497-6777
Family Services-394-2119
Golf Course-394-2325
Medical-394-2278
Police-394-2808
Retiree Services-394-2174
Visitor Center-394-4616

Chaplain-394-2677
Consol Club-394-2154
Fire Dept-394-2464
Legal-394-2341
MWR-394-2145
Public Affairs-394-4183
SATO-436-4700

Child Care-394-4323
Exchange-436-4888
Gas Station-497-6615
Locator-394-4822
Package Store-497-8181
Recreation-394-2779
Theater-394-2679

HEALTH & WELFARE: USAF Clinic, Emergency C-910-394-2232. Inpatient, see Fort Bragg listing, C-910-432-3719. Chapel serving all faiths C-910-394-2676.

RECREATION: Auto Hobby EX-2293, Bowling EX-2891, Golf EX-2325, Rec Equipment EX-4730, Library EX-2791, CAC EX-2779. Fam-Camp, operated by Fort Fisher AFS, on NC-421 at Kure Beach year round, C-910-458-6546/6549, D-312-656-2212, nine camper spaces w/full hookups.

SPACE-A: Pax Term/Lounge, 1427 Surveyor St, 24 hours daily, C-910-394-4429/2803, D-312-486-4429/2803, Fax 910-394-2474, flights to CONUS and OCONUS locations.

ATTRACTIONS: Raleigh, Durham, and Chapel Hill are easy drives. Myrtle Beach, SC is two-and-a-half hours south. Mountains three hours west. Great hunting and fishing areas.

SEYMOUR JOHNSON AIR FORCE BASE (NC11R1)
1570 Wright Avenue
Seymour Johnson Air Force Base, NC 27531-2468

TELEPHONE NUMBER INFORMATION: Main installation numbers: C-919-736-5400, D-312-488-1110.

224 - U.S. FORCES TRAVEL & TRANSFER GUIDE U.S.A

NORTH CAROLINA
Seymour Johnson Air Force Base, continued

LOCATION: From US-70 Bypass, take Seymour Johnson AFB exit onto Berkeley Blvd to main gate. Clearly marked. USMRA: Page 45 (L-3). NMC: Raleigh, 50 miles west.

GENERAL INFORMATION: Air Combat Command Base.

TEMPORARY MILITARY LODGING: Lodging office, Bldg. 3804, 24 hours daily, Wright Ave, C-919-736-6705, D-312-488-6705. All ranks. DV/VIP call Billeting.

LOGISTICAL SUPPORT: Complete support facilities available.

CHAMPUS-736-5650	Chaplain-736-5211	Child Care-736-6289
Commissary-736-6183	Exchange-735-9786	Family Services-736-5404
Gas Station-734-7358	Golf Course-736-6249	Legal-736-6256
Locator-736-5584	Medical-736-2778	NCO Club-734-2757
O'Club-735-8546	Package Store-734-2948	Police-736-6413/5473
Public Affairs-736-6352	Retiree Services-736-6377	Shoppette-735-9364
Theater-736-6164	Visitor Center-736-6237	

HEALTH & WELFARE: USAF Hospital, clinics and depts, Acute Care Clinic C-919-736-5577, Appointment C-919-736-2778, 20 beds. Chapel serving all faiths C-919-736-5211.

RECREATION: Arts/Crafts EX-5423, Auto Craft EX-5284, Bowling EX-6669, Golf EX-6249, Gym EX-6643, Outdoor Recreation EX-5405, Library EX-5739, Community Center EX-6745. Fam-Camp on Base, year round, C-919-736-5405, D-312-488-5405, eight camper spaces w/full hookups. Rogers Bay Family Campway off base, year round, C-919-736-5263, D-312-488-5263, six travel trailers. Also operates Fort Fisher Air Force Recreation Area, year round, C-910-458-6546/6549. Sixteen camper spaces w/full hookups, 26 cottages, six mobile homes, lodge with 27 rooms and 13 suites, and 20 tent spaces.
SPACE-A: Pax Term, Bldg. 4507, 0800-1600 Mon-Fri, C-919-736-6729, D-312-488-6729, flights to CONUS and overseas.

ATTRACTIONS: NC Research Triangle of Raleigh, Durham and Chapel Hill.

U.S. FORCES TRAVEL & TRANSFER GUIDE U.S.A. - 225

NORTH DAKOTA

DOLLAR RENT A CAR — Call 1-800-800-4000. Get a military rate by using your Military Living ID # ML3009. Retirees/Active Duty/Reserve/Guard.

CAMP GILBERT C. GRAFTON
ARMY NATIONAL GUARD TRAINING SITE (ND03R3)
Rural Route 5, Box 278A
Devils Lake, ND 58301-9235

TELEPHONE NUMBER INFORMATION: Main installation numbers: C-701-662-0200, D-312-344-5226.

LOCATION: From Highway 2 at Devils Lake go to Highway 20-S, entrance is four miles on right. USMRA: Page 83 (G-3). NMC: Devils Lake, four miles north.

GENERAL INFORMATION: Army National Guard Training Site.

TEMPORARY MILITARY LODGING: Billeting, C-701-662-0239, 0700-1600 hours daily.

LOGISTICAL SUPPORT: Limited support facilities available.

Consol Club-662-2171
Locator-662-0200
O'Club-662-0221
Snack Bar-662-0285

EM Club-662-0221
Medical-662-5323
Police-662-5323

Exchange-662-0314
NCO Club-662-0221
RV/Camping-662-0239

HEALTH AND WELFARE: Medical clinic C-701-662-5323.

RECREATION: Boat rental, golf, swimming, and hunting and fishing.

SPACE-A: None. See Grand Forks AFB listing, C-701-747-4376/4409, D-312-362-4376/4409, Fax 701-747-6540.

ATTRACTIONS: Base has shoreline with Devils Lake, an excellent site for hunting and fishing.

CAVALIER AIR STATION (ND08R3)
HCR 3, Box 260, Building 830
Cavalier AS, ND 58220-9314

TELEPHONE NUMBER INFORMATION: Main installation numbers: C-701-993-3292, D-312-330-3292.

LOCATION: North on I-29. Take Highway 5, Cavalier exit. Go west 18 miles to town of Cavalier, through town continuing west on Highway 5 another 18 miles to site, on left side of road. USMRA: Page 83 (I-2). NMC: Grand Forks, ND 75 miles south.

GENERAL INFORMATION: 10th Space Warning Squadron.

TEMPORARY MILITARY LODGING: None. See Grand Forks listing, C-701-747-3070, D-312-362-3070.

NORTH DAKOTA
Cavalier Air Station, continued

LOGISTICAL SUPPORT: Limited support facilities available.

Exchange-993-3224   Fire Dept-993-3671   MWR-993-3201
Police-993-3365   Recreation-993-3201   SDO/NCO-993-3292
Snack Bar-993-3228

HEALTH AND WELFARE: Cavalier Clinic, C-701-265-8338, Inpatient, Pembina County Memorial, C-701-265-8461.

RECREATION: Bowling EX-3229, Camping Equipment EX-3201, MWR EX-3201, Gym EX-3376.

SPACE-A: None. See Grand Forks AFB listing, C-701-747-4376/4409, D-312-362-4376/4409, Fax 701-747-6540.

ATTRACTIONS: Icelandic State Park, Pembina gorge, and Frost Fire mountain. The Red River Valley is one of the most fertile areas of the Midwest. Very good fishing, hunting, skiing, and camping. Close to major cultural center in Winnipeg.

GRAND FORKS AIR FORCE BASE (ND04R3)
660 1st Avenue, Suite 2
Grand Forks Air Force Base, ND 58205-5154

TELEPHONE NUMBER INFORMATION: Main installation numbers: C-701-747-3000, D-312-362-3000.

LOCATION: From I-29, take US-2 west exit for 14 miles to Grand Forks, County Rd B-3 (Emerado/Air Base) one mile to AFB. USMRA: Page 83 (I-3). NMC: Grand Forks, 15 miles east.

GENERAL INFORMATION: Air Mobility Command Base. 319th Air Refueling Wing and 321st Missile Group.

TEMPORARY MILITARY LODGING: Lodging office, Bldg. 117, I St and 6th Ave, 24 hours daily, C-701-747-3070, D-312-362-3070. All ranks. DV/VIP C-701-747-4513.

LOGISTICAL SUPPORT: Complete support facilities available.

CHAMPUS-747-5323   Chaplain-747-3074   Child Care-747-3042
Commissary-747-3090   Comm Services-747-3112   EM Club-747-3392
Exchange-594-5542   Family Services-747-3240 Fire Dept-747-6304
Gas Station-594-5951   Golf Course-747-4279   Legal-747-3606
Locator-747-3344   Medical-747-5468   O'Club-747-3131
Package Store-594-5206 Police-747-5351   Public Affairs-747-5016
Retiree Services-747-6197 RV/Camping-747-3688   SATO-594-5141
Snack Bar-594-2695   Theater-747-3101   Visitor Center-747-4283

HEALTH & WELFARE: USAF Hospital, clinics and depts, Emergency C-701-747-5601, Appointment C-701-747-5302, 20 beds. Chapel serving all faiths C-701-747-3076.

RECREATION: Arts/Crafts EX-3481, Auto Hobby EX-3394, Bowling EX-3074, Library EX-3046, Rec Center EX-3112. Fam-Camp, on base, 1 May-1 Oct, C-701-747-3688, 21 camper spaces w/full hookups.

NORTH DAKOTA
Grand Forks Air Force Base, continued

SPACE-A: Pax Term/Lounge, Bldg. 528, 24 hours daily, C-701-747-4409/4410, D-312-362-4409/4410, Fax 701-747-6540. Flights to CONUS, OCONUS and overseas.

ATTRACTIONS: Outdoor sports and recreation. Canada is 140 miles north of the base on I-29.

MINOT AIR FORCE BASE (ND02R3)
Minot Air Force Base, ND 58705-5000

TELEPHONE NUMBER INFORMATION: Main installation numbers: C-701-723-1110, D-312-453-1110.

LOCATION: On US-83, north of Minot. USMRA: Page 83 (D-2). NMC: Minot, 15 miles south.

GENERAL INFORMATION: Air Combat Command Base, 91st Missile Wing (Associate Wing), 5th (Main) Bomb Wing.

TEMPORARY MILITARY LODGING: Lodging office, Bldg. 173, 24 hours daily, C-701-723-2184, D-312-453-3108. All ranks. DV/VIP C-701-723-3474.

LOGISTICAL SUPPORT: Complete support facilities available.

Cafeteria-727-4625
Child Care-723-3750
EM Club-727-3806
Fire Dept-723-2461
ITT Office-727-6171
Medical-723-5000
Police-723-3096
Retiree Services-723-4365
Snack Bar-727-9132

CHAMPUS-723-5176
Commissary-723-4559
Exchange-727-4717
Gas Station-727-4876
Legal-723-3026
NCO Club-727-6157
Public Affairs-723-6212
SATO-723-2108
Theater-723-3802

Chaplain-723-2456/2457
Conv Store-727-4973
Family Services-723-4728
Golf Course-723-3164
Locator-723-1841
O'Club-727-3731
Recreation-723-4670
SDO/NCO-723-3102
Visitor Center-723-3093

HEALTH & WELFARE: 5th Medical Group, Emergency C-701-723-5627, Appointment C-701-723-5475. Chapel serving all faiths C-701-723-3633.

RECREATION: Arts/Crafts EX-3640, Auto Hobby EX-2127, Bowling EX-2610, Golf EX-6864, Gym EX-3174/2124, Rec Equipment EX-2175, Library EX-3344, Rec Center EX-4670, Tennis EX-2786, Tickets EX-4670, Outdoor Rec EX-3648, Swimming EX-3388 (Summer only).

SPACE-A: Pax Term/Lounge, Bldg. 746, Base Ops, 24 hours daily, C-701-723-2348/1854, D-312-453-2348/1854, flights to CONUS and overseas.

ATTRACTIONS: Trestle Valley Ski Area, outdoor recreation. Canada easy drive north via US-83.

NORTH DAKOTA

Other Installations in North Dakota

Fraine Barracks NGHQ, Office of the Adjutant General, 030 Fraine Barracks, P.O. Box 5511, Bismarck, ND 58506-5511
USMRA: Page 83 (E-5,6). C-701-224-5100, D-312-344-5100, Exchange-224-5119, Legal-224-5194, Public Affairs-224-5106
Hector Field ANGB, 1400 28th Ave., N., Fargo, ND 58105-5536
USMRA: Page 83 (J-5). C-701-237-6030, D-312-362-8110. Exchange-241-7184, Club-241-7181.
Raymond J. Bohn Armory (ND Army National Guard HQ), Office of the Adjutant General, 4200 E. Divide, P.O. Box 5511, Bismarck, ND 58506-5511.
USMRA: Page 83 (E-5,6). C-701-224-5104, Exchange-224-5168, Public Affairs-224-5106, Retiree Services-224-5138, SATO-224-8615.
Rickenbacker Air National Guard Base, 7556 South Perimeter Road, Rickenbacher ANGB, OH 43217-5887. USMRA: Page 67 (D-7). C-614-492-4223, Space-A-492-4595.

U.S. FORCES TRAVEL & TRANSFER GUIDE U.S.A. - 229

OHIO

DOLLAR RENT A CAR Call 1-800-800-4000. Get a military rate by using your Military Living ID # ML3009. Retirees/Active Duty/Reserve/Guard.

CLEVELAND COAST GUARD MARINE SAFETY OFFICE (OH07R2)
1055 East 9th Street
Cleveland, OH 44114-1092

TELEPHONE NUMBER INFORMATION: Main installation numbers: C-216-522-4404, FTS-216-522-4404.

LOCATION: Take I-71 north or I-90 east to OH-2 west. Exit at East 9th St and travel north towards Lake Erie on East 9th St. From I-77 north, also exit onto East 9th St. USMRA: Page 67 (F-3). NMC: Cleveland, in city limits.

GENERAL INFORMATION: *USCG Cutter Neah Bay*, Electronics Repair Shop, USCG Station Cleveland Harbor.

TEMPORARY MILITARY LODGING: None.

LOGISTICAL SUPPORT: Limited support facilities available.

CHAMPUS-522-7587   **O'Club-687-1755**   **Package Store-687-1756**
"Otto Graham" Exchange*

* The Exchange/Package store is about a 10 minute drive from CGMSO at 13920 West Parkway Drive, C-216-671-3500. It has exchange items and some uniform items for the five armed services.

HEALTH & WELFARE: Outpatient, Lutheran Medical Center C-216-363-2353. Inpatient, Lutheran Hospital C-216-281-2500. Chapel serving all faiths.

RECREATION: None available on base.

SPACE-A: None. See Wright-Patterson AFB, listing, C-513-257-7741, D-312-787-7741, Fax 513-476-1580.

ATTRACTIONS: Rock and Roll Hall of Fame and Museum. Major League baseball, football, soccer, and basketball teams, Great Lakes, NASA Lewis Research Center, West Side Market, world-class symphony orchestra, ballet and opera.

DEFENSE CONSTRUCTION SUPPLY CENTER (OH05R2)
3990 East Broad Street
Columbus, OH 43216-5000

TELEPHONE NUMBER INFORMATION: Main installation numbers: C-614-692-3131, D-312-850-3131.

LOCATION: From I-270 (Beltway) take exit 39 to Broad Street west, main gate at 3990 Broad Street. Mailing address: PO Box 3990. USMRA: (D-6). NMC: Columbus, in city limits.

230 - U.S. FORCES TRAVEL & TRANSFER GUIDE U.S.A

OHIO
Defense Construction Supply Center, continued

GENERAL INFORMATION: Logistical Support for construction supplies, weapons systems, and equipment for DoD.

TEMPORARY MILITARY LODGING: Limited facility near O'Club C-614-692-4758.

LOGISTICAL SUPPORT: Most support facilities available..

Cafeteria-692-1423	CDO/OOD-692-2166	CHAMPUS-692-2227
Exchange-231-0976	Fire Dept-692-2026	Golf Course-239-6669
ITR-692-1111	Legal-692-3284	Locator-692-3131
Medical-692-2227	MWR-692-2011	O'Club-239-0482
Police-692-3722	Public Affairs-692-2328	Recreation-692-3084
Retiree Services-692-4165	RV/Camping-692-1111	SATO-692-1447

HEALTH & WELFARE: US Air Force Health Clinic C-614-692-2227. Inpatient, see Wright-Patterson AFB listing, C-513-257-2969.

RECREATION: Gym, racquetball, golf course w/driving range, and pool.

SPACE-A: None. See Wright-Patterson AFB listing, C-512-257-7741, D-312-787-7741, Fax 513-476-1580.

ATTRACTIONS: State Fairgrounds, Ohio Historical Center, Franklin Park Conservatory, Ohio State University, Center of Science and Industry, Palace Theatre, German Village, Brewery District, and Columbus Museum of Art.

NEWARK AIR FORCE BASE (OH04R2)
813 Irving Wick Drive W
Newark, OH 43057-0031

Scheduled to close September 1996.

TELEPHONE NUMBER INFORMATION: Main installation numbers: C-614-522-2171, D-312-346-1110.

LOCATION: From I-70 exit to OH-79 north to Heath, main entrance from Irving-Wick Drive. USMRA: Page 67 (E-6). NMC: Newark, three miles north.

GENERAL INFORMATION: Air Force Materiel Command Base. The Air Force Aerospace Guidance and Metrology Center.

TEMPORARY MILITARY LODGING: None. See Wright-Patterson AFB listing, C-512-257-3451, D-312-787-3451.

LOGISTICAL SUPPORT: Limited support facilities available.

Cafeteria-522-7666	CHAMPUS-522-7633	Consol Club-522-7239
Exchange-522-7213	Locator-522-2171	Medical-522-7333
Police-522-7200	Public Affairs-522-7243	Recreation-522-7766
SDO/NCO-522-7503		

HEALTH & WELFARE: Dispensary/Emergency C-614-522-7333/117. Inpatient, see Wright-Patterson AFB listing, C-513-257-2969. No chapel on base.

U.S. FORCES TRAVEL & TRANSFER GUIDE U.S.A. - 231

OHIO
Newark Air Force Base, continued

RECREATION: Jogging, Track, Handball/Racquetball EX-7220.

SPACE-A: None. Try Mansfield Lahm Airport, Bldg. 101 (ANG Base), 0745-1630 Mon-Fri, C-419-522-0124, D-312-696-6124, flights to CONUS, OCONUS and overseas.

ATTRACTIONS: Heisey Museum, Moundbuilders and Flint Ridge Parks, Buckeye Lake, Denison and Newark Campus of Ohio State University. Columbus easy drive.

TOLEDO AIR NATIONAL GUARD (OH03R2)
2660 S. Eber Road
Swanton, OH 43558

TELEPHONE NUMBER INFORMATION: Main installation number: C-419-868-4078.

LOCATION: Take Ohio Turnpike to exit 3A, turn left, go to Eber Road, turn right, go about one mile. Base is clearly marked. USMRA: Page 67 (B,C-3). NMC: Toledo.

TEMPORARY MILITARY LODGING: None. See Selfridge ANGB, MI listing, C-810-307-4062, D-312-273-4062.

LOGISTICAL SUPPORT: Limited support facilities available.

Chaplain-868-4017   Exchange-867-9939   Medical-868-4045
Police-868-4099

ATTRACTIONS: Toledo Mudhens (minor league baseball).

WRIGHT-PATTERSON AIR FORCE BASE (OH01R2)
Wright-Patterson Air Force Base, OH 45433-5542

TELEPHONE NUMBER INFORMATION: Main installation numbers: C-513-257-1110, D-312-787-1110.

LOCATION: South of I-70, off I-675 at Fairborn. Also, access from OH-4. AFB clearly marked. USMRA: Page 67 (B-7). NMC: Dayton, 10 miles southwest.

GENERAL INFORMATION: Air Force Materiel Command Base. Test Wing, Foreign Aerospace Technology Center, Air Force Institute of Technology, USAF Medical Center, and Aeronautical Systems Center.

TEMPORARY MILITARY LODGING: Lodging office, Bldg. 825, Schlatter Dr & Childlaw Rd, 24 hours daily, C-513-257-3451, D-312-787-3451. All ranks. DV/VIP C-513-257-3110.

LOGISTICAL SUPPORT: Complete support facilities available.

Chaplain-257-7941	Child Care-257-2173	Commissary-257-7420
Conv Store-254-3549	Day Care Center-257-3107	EM Club-257-2001
Exchange-879-5730	Family Services-257-6934	Gas Station-257-3760
Legal-257-6142	Locator-257-3231	Medical-257-2969
NCO Club-257-7292	O'Club-257-2216	Package Store-257-3705
Police-257-6226	Snack Bar-879-4317	Theater-257-4697

OHIO
Wright-Patterson Air Force Base, continued

HEALTH & WELFARE: USAF Medical Center, Emergency C-513-257-2969, 301 beds. Chapel serving all faiths C-513-257-7941.

RECREATION: Arts/Crafts EX-7025, Auto Hobby EX-4937, Bowling EX-7796, Gym EX-4225/3607, Rec Equipment EX-4222, Aero Club EX-7950, Fishing/Hunting EX-2001, Library EX-4815, Swimming EX-4225, Rec Center EX-2001, Tennis EX-7248, Youth Center EX-55053, Picnic Area EX-2001, Stables 253-3810. Fam-Camp on base, year round, C-513-257-9889, D-312-787-9889, 16-20 camper spaces w/W&E hookups (no water in winter).

SPACE-A: Pax Term/Lounge, Bldg. 206, Area C, Skeel Ave, 0530-2000 Mon-Fri, other days 0800-1600, C-513-257-7741, D-312-787-7741, flights to CONUS and OCONUS locations. Also, flights to CONUS and OCONUS locations from Youngstown Municipal Airport, AFRES Base Ops, C-216-392-1236, D-312-346-1236, Fax: 216-392-1097.

ATTRACTIONS: Air Force Museum on base. Wright Brothers Memorial, Dayton. Other aviation attractions in Dayton area.

YOUNGSTOWN AIR RESERVE BASE (OH11R2)
910 AW
3976 King Graves Road
Vienna, OH 4473-0910

TELEPHONE NUMBER INFORMATION: Main installation numbers: C-216-392-1000, D-312-346-1000.

LOCATION: Off Route 11, near I-81. Base is clearly marked. USMRA: Page 67 (H-3). NMC: Youngstown.

TEMPORARY MILITARY LODGING: C-216-392-1268.

LOGISTICAL SUPPORT: Most support facilities available.

Chaplain-392-1393
Fire Dept-392-1117
NCO Club-392-1295
Public Affairs-392-1236

Exchange-392-1395
Legal-392-1037
O'Club-392-1295

Family Services-392-1201
MWR-392-1295
Police-392-1277

HEALTH & WELFARE: None. See Cleveland CG Marine Safety Office listing, C-216-363-2353.

SPACE-A: Pax Term, C-216-392-1236, D-312-346-1236, Fax: C-216-392-1097, D-312-346-1097.

ATTRACTIONS: Geauga Lake amusement park is nearby.

Other Installations in Ohio

Camp Perry Training Site, Bldg. 600, Port Clinton, OH 43452-5000.
USMRA: Page 67 (D-3). C-419-635-4114, Exchange-635-5116, TML-635-4114.
Cleveland North Coast Guard Exchange, 13920 West Parkway, Cleveland, OH 44135-5000. USMRA: Page 67 (F-3). C-216-671-3500, Consol Club-687-1755, Exchange-671-3500.
Mansfield-Lahm Airport, Mansfield, OH 44901-5000.
USMRA: Page 67 (E-4,5). C-419-521-0124, Exchange-526-5358, Medical-521-0124, Space-A-521-0124.
Toledo Coast Guard Station, Bay View Park, Toledo, OH 43611-5000.
USMRA: Page 67 (C-3). C-419-729-2034, Exchange-729-5911.

OKLAHOMA

DOLLAR RENT A CAR — Call 1-800-800-4000. Get a military rate by using your Military Living ID # ML3009. Retirees/Active Duty/Reserve/Guard.

ALTUS AIR FORCE BASE (OK02R3)
100 Inez Blvd
Altus Air Force Base, OK 73523-5000

TELEPHONE NUMBER INFORMATION: Main installation numbers: C-405-482-8100, D-312-866-1110.

LOCATION: From US-62 traveling west from Lawton, turn right at first traffic light in Altus and follow the road to the main gate northeast of Falcon Road. USMRA: Page 84 (E-5). NMC: Lawton, 56 miles east.

GENERAL INFORMATION: Air Education and Training Command Base. C-141, C-5, and KC-135 aircrew training missions. Worldwide Air Refueling Mission.

TEMPORARY MILITARY LODGING: Billeting Office, Bldg. 82, 24 hours daily, C-405-481-7356, D-312-866-7356, also 1-800-528-1218. All ranks. DV/VIP C-405-481-7044.

LOGISTICAL SUPPORT: Complete support facilities available.

CHAMPUS-481-5313
Commissary-481-7329
Exchange-482-8733
Gas Station-482-7002
Locator-481-7250
O'Club-481-6224
Public Affairs-481-7700
RV/Camping-481-6704

Chaplain-481-7485
Conv Store-481-7095
Family Services-481-7460
Golf Course-481-7207
Medical-482-5222
Package Store-481-6276
Recreation-481-6600
SATO-481-6466

Child Care-481-7502
EM Club-481-7034
Fire Dept-481-6333
Legal-481-7294
MWR-481-5812
Police-481-7444
Retiree Services-481-5671
Theater-481-7341

HEALTH & WELFARE: USAF Hospital, clinics and depts, Emergency C-405-482-5222, Appointment C-405-481-5970, 15 beds. Chapel serving all faiths C-405-482-7485.

RECREATION: Arts/Crafts EX-7048, Auto Hobby EX-6326, Bowling EX-6300, Golf EX-7207, Gym EX-7153, Library EX-6302, Base Pool EX-6377, O'Club Pool EX-6281, EM Club Pool EX-5106. Fam-Camp, on base, year round, C-405-481-6704, D-312-866-6704, four camper spaces w/full hookups, three camper spaces w/E hookups.

SPACE-A: Pax Term/Lounge, Bldg. 178, 0730-1630 Mon-Fri, C-405-481-6350/6428, D-312-866-6350/6428, Fax 405-481-5065, flights to CONUS and overseas.

ATTRACTIONS: Western prairie country. Lake Altus, 15 miles north. Outdoor sports.

CAMP GRUBER (OK03R3)
P.O. Box 29
Braggs, OK 74423-0029

TELEPHONE NUMBER INFORMATION: Main installation numbers: C-918-487-6001.

OKLAHOMA
Camp Gruber, continued

LOCATION: Exit I-40 at Webber Falls (exit 287), take Highway 64 to Gore, OK, take state highway 10 to Braggs. First entrance to camp after passing through Braggs. USMRA: Page 84 (I-4). NMC: Muskogee, 12 miles north.

GENERAL INFORMATION: Urban Warfare School, Small Arms Ranges.

TEMPORARY MILITARY LODGING: Lodging office, Bldg. 155, 4th St and Anzio Dr, 0730-1600 Mon-Fri, C-918-487-6066, FTS-487-6067.

LOGISTICAL SUPPORT: Limited support facilities available.

Exchange-487-5643 Locator-487-6066 Package Store-487-5643
Police-487-6021 RV/Camping-487-6066

HEALTH AND WELFARE: None, refer to civilian services. Emergency and inpatient care, Muskogee Regional Medical Center, C-918-682-5501. Outpatient care, Muskogee Immediate Care, C-918-682-0721.

RECREATION: None available on base.

SPACE-A: None. See Tinker AFB listing, C-405-739-4360/4339, D-312-339-4360/4339, Fax 405-739-4317.

ATTRACTIONS: Located in western edge of Ozark Mountains. Rolling hills, lakes, fishing and water recreation, Native American culture, Cherokee Heritage Center, Trail of Tears dramatization, all short drives.

FORT SILL (OK01R3)
Fort Sill, OK 73503-5000

TELEPHONE NUMBER INFORMATION: Main installation numbers: C-405-442-8111, D-312-639-7090.

LOCATION: From I-44 at Lawton, take US-62/277, four miles northwest to post. Clearly marked. USMRA: Page 84 (E, F-5). NMC: Wichita Falls, TX, 50 miles south.

GENERAL INFORMATION: Headquarters, US Army Field Artillery Center, US Army Field Artillery School, and support units.

TEMPORARY MILITARY LODGING: Billeting Office, Bldg. 5676, Fergusson Road, 24 hours daily, C-405-442-5000/07, D-312-639-5000. All Ranks. DV/VIP C-405-442-4825.

LOGISTICAL SUPPORT: Complete support facilities available.

Carlson Travel-357-6616 Cafeteria-353-6209 CHAMPUS-458-2484
Chaplain-442-3302/5795 Child Care-442-2320 Class Six-355-4053
Commissary-442-2305 Conv Store-355-7601 EM Club-355-3021
Exchange-248-7504 Family Services-442-5018 Gas Station-353-3419
ITR Office-442-6211 Legal-442-5058/5059 Locator-442-3693/6172
Medical-442-0500 NCO Club-248-0417 O'Club-442-5300
Police-442-2101 Retiree Services-442-4009 SDO/NCO-442-4912
Snack Bar-248-7025 Theater-442-4572

OKLAHOMA
Fort Sill, continued

HEALTH AND WELFARE: Reynolds Army Community Hospital, clinics and depts, Emergency C-405-442-0770. Chapel serving all faiths C-405-442-2615.

RECREATION: Arts/Crafts 442-5687, Auto Hobby EX-2549, Bowling EX-2882, Golf EX-2723, Gym EX-6652/6712, Rec Equipment 355-8270, Library EX-3806, Rec Center EX-6745, Youth Center EX-6745.

SPACE-A: Henry Post Army Airfield, Bldg. 4907, 0700-1800 Mon-Fri, C-405-442-5808/3385, D-312-639-5808/3385, Fax 405-442-5643, flights via executive aircraft to CONUS locations. Also, try Will Rogers ANG Base, Bldg. 1011. 0630-1700 Mon-Thu, C-405-686-5550, D-312-940-5550, flights to CONUS and OCONUS locations.

ATTRACTIONS: Lawton, Geronimo's burial place is two miles from the fort, US Army Field Artillery and Fort Sill Museum.

McALESTER ARMY AMMUNITION PLANT (OK09R3)
1 C Tree Road
McAlester, OK 74501-5000

TELEPHONE NUMBER INFORMATION: Main installation numbers: C-918-421-3490, D-312-956-7490.

LOCATION: Off Indian Nation Turnpike, west of US-69. The southeast Oklahoma area is mostly rolling pasture with timber-covered hills and creek bottoms. USMRA: Page 84 (I-5). NMC: Tulsa, 90 miles north.

GENERAL INFORMATION: Produces, stores, renovates, and issues ammunition, explosives, and ordnance items to all branches of the Armed Forces

TEMPORARY MILITARY LODGING: Lodging office C-918-421-2480, D-312-956-6480, Fax 918-421-2489.

LOGISTICAL SUPPORT: Complete support facilities available.

ACS-421-3490
Comm Club-421-3587
Fire Dept-421-2221
Medical-421-2495
Police-421-3370
RV/Camping-421-3484
CHAMPUS-421-2496
Exchange-421-2388
ITT Office-421-2418
MWR-421-3262
Public Affairs-421-2591
SDO/NCO-421-2642
Child Care-421-2204
Family Services-421-3490
Legal-421-2439
Package Store-421-2388
Recreation-421-3262
Snack Bar-421-2384

HEALTH & WELFARE: US Army Health Clinic, C-918-421-2496. Inpatient, see Tinker AFB listing, C-405-734-6841.

RECREATION: Auto Hobby, Boat Rental, Bowling, Gym, Rec Equipment, Library, Pool, Rec Center, Tennis, Youth Activities. Murphy's Meadow on base, year round, C-918-421-3484/2673, D-312-956-3484/2673, 34 camper spaces w/W&E hookups.

SPACE-A: None. See Tinker AFB listing, C-405-739-4360/4339, D-312-339-4360/4339, Fax 405-739-4317.

ATTRACTIONS: Lake Eufaula.

OKLAHOMA

TINKER AIR FORCE BASE (OK04R3)
3001 Staff Drive, Suite 1AG78A
Tinker Air Force Base, OK 73145-3010

TELEPHONE NUMBER INFORMATION: Main installation numbers: C-405-732-7321, D-312-884-1110. **NOTE:** Prefix for extensions listed below is 734.

LOCATION: Southeast Oklahoma City, off I-40. Use gate 1 off Air Depot Blvd. Clearly marked. USMRA: Page 84 (G-4). NMC: Oklahoma City, 12 miles northwest.

GENERAL INFORMATION: Air Force Materiel Command Base. Major Logistics Center for the Air Force. Navy Stratcom E-6 Wing. AWACS E-3 Sentry Wing. AFRES Tanker Wing.

TEMPORARY MILITARY LODGING: Billeting Office, Bldg. 5604, 24 hours daily, C-405-734-2822/5095, D-312-884-2822/5095. All ranks. DV/VIP C-405-734-5511.

LOGISTICAL SUPPORT: Complete support facilities available.

Cafeteria-734-3161	CHAMPUS-734-2615	Chaplain-734-2111
Child Care-734-3116	Commissary-734-5212	Conv Store-733-3445
Exchange-734-3035	Family Services-739-2505	Gas Station-734-3040
Legal-739-5811	Locator-734-2456	Medical-734-8250
NCO Club-734-3435	O'Club-734-3418	Package Store-734-3466
Police-734-3737/2000	Retiree Services-739-2795	Snack Bar-734-3486
Theater-734-3400	Travel-739-5057	

HEALTH & WELFARE: USAF Hospital, clinics and depts, Emergency C-405-734-8250, Appointment Dep C-405-737-6841, AD C-405-734-8366, 30+ beds. Chapel serving all faiths C-405-734-2111.

RECREATION: Arts/Crafts EX-5615, Auto Hobby EX-5616, Bowling EX-3484, Golf EX-2909, Gym EX-5607, Handball EX-5607, Boat Rental EX-2289, Fishing EX-2289, Library EX-7837, Outdoor Rec Center EX-2289, Swimming EX-5607, Riding Club 737-4775, Youth Center EX-7866. Fam-Camp on base, year round, C-405-734-2289, D-312-884-2289, 29 camper spaces w/W&E hookups, five tent spaces.

SPACE-A: Pax Term/Lounge, Bldg. 268, Mon-Fri 0715-1800, C-405-739-4360/4339, D-312-339-4360/4339, Fax 405-739-4317, flights to CONUS and overseas locations.

ATTRACTIONS: Oklahoma City (the capital), Kirkpatrick Planetarium, Oklahoma Air Space Museum, Omniplex Science Museum, National Cowboy Hall of Fame and Western Heritage Center, Oklahoma City Zoo, Remington Park Racetrack, arts and entertainment.

VANCE AIR FORCE BASE (OK05R3)
246 Brown Parkway
Vance Air Force Base, OK 73705-5000

TELEPHONE NUMBER INFORMATION: Main installation numbers: C-405-237-2121, D-312-940-7110.

LOCATION: Off of US-81 south. Clearly marked. USMRA: Page 84 (F-3). NMC: Oklahoma City, 90 miles southeast.

OKLAHOMA
Vance Air Force Base, continued

GENERAL INFORMATION: Air Education and Training Command Base. Flying Training Wing, Undergraduate Pilot Training.

TEMPORARY MILITARY LODGING: Lodging office, Bldg. 714, Williams Road, 24 hours daily, C-405-249-7358, D-312-940-7358. All ranks.

LOGISTICAL SUPPORT: Complete support facilities available.

CHAMPUS-249-7746	**Chaplain-249-7211**	**Child Care-249-7310**
Commissary-249-7428	**Exchange-237-6765**	**Family Services-249-7322**
Gas Station-237-7445	**Legal-249-7404**	**Locator-249-7791/7358**
Medical-249-7416	**NCO Club-237-7311**	**O'Club-237-2326**
Package Store-237-6765	**Police-249-7415**	**Retiree Services-249-6177**

HEALTH & WELFARE: USAF Clinic, Emergency C-405-237-6117, Appointment C-405-237-7416. Inpatient, see Tinker AFB listing, C-405-734-6841. Chapel serving all faiths C-405-237-7211.

RECREATION: Arts/Crafts EX-7402, Auto Hobby EX-7508, Bowling EX-7331, Gym EX-7830/7670, Library EX-7368, Youth Center EX-7474.

SPACE-A: C-405-237-7424, D-312-940-7110.

ATTRACTIONS: National Cowboy Hall of Fame, Kirkpatrick Planetarium, National Softball Hall of Fame, Humphrey Heritage Village/Museum of the Cherokee Strip, Railroad Museum of Oakland, Midgley Museum, Leonardo's Discovery Warehouse, George's Museum of Antique Cars, the Zoo, and Frontier City.

Other Installations in Oklahoma

Will Rogers Air National Guard Base, Will Rogers ANGB, OK 73169-1040.
USMRA: Page 84 (G-4). C-405-686-5210, Space-A-686-5550.

U.S. FORCES TRAVEL & TRANSFER GUIDE U.S.A. - 239

OREGON

DOLLAR RENT A CAR — Call 1-800-800-4000. Get a military rate by using your Military Living ID # ML3009. Retirees/Active Duty/Reserve/Guard.

ASTORIA COAST GUARD GROUP/AIR STATION (OR05R4)
2185 SE., 12th Place
Warrenton, OR 97146-5000

TELEPHONE NUMBER INFORMATION: Main installation number: C-503-861-6192.

LOCATION: Take highway 30 from Portland west to Astoria. Go through Astoria and across the Young River Bridge. Follow signs, plainly marked. USMRA: Page 100 (B-1). NMC: Portland, 100 miles east.

GENERAL INFORMATION: Coast Guard Group is based in Astoria, The Coast Guard Air Station is based in Warrenton.

TEMPORARY MILITARY LODGING: None.

LOGISTICAL SUPPORT: Some support facilities available.

Chaplain-861-6225
Exchange-325-0108
MWR-861-6237
Commissary-325-0108
Gas Station-325-0108
Public Affairs-861-6123
Conv Store-861-3350
Medical-861-6240

HEALTH & WELFARE: Coast Guard Health Services Clinic, C-503-861-6240.

RECREATION: Morale Welfare and Recreation Office 861-6237

SPACE-A: None. See Portland IAP/ANGB listing, C-503-335-4390/4421, D-312-638-4390, Fax 503-335-5098.

ATTRACTIONS: The Columbia River. Minutes from: Washington State, Saddle Mountain State Park, and Clatsop and Tillamook National Forests.

KINGSLEY FIELD (OR03R4)
302 Vandenberg Drive, Suite 38
Klamath Falls, OR 97603-0400

TELEPHONE NUMBER INFORMATION: Main installation numbers: C-541-885-6308, D-312-830-6110.

LOCATION: Take I-5 through Medford to highway 140E to south side bypass. Go East approximately four-and-a-half miles to the airport. USMRA: Page 100 (D-8). NMC: Medford, 80 miles west.

GENERAL INFORMATION: Near the Oregon/California border, Southern Oregon's only military installation.

TEMPORARY MILITARY LODGING: Billeting Office, Kingsley Lodge, Building 208, McConnell Circle, 0800-1600 Mon-Fri (closed 1200-1300), C-541-885-6365.

OREGON
Kingsley Field, continued

LOGISTICAL SUPPORT: Extremely limited support facilities available.

Consol Club-885-6484 **Exchange-885-6371**

HEALTH & WELFARE: Clinic C-885-6308.

RECREATION: Hiking in nearby national forests.

SPACE-A: Limited. C-541-885-6686, D-312-830-6686.

ATTRACTIONS: Crater Lake, Lava Beds, Oregon Caves, Freemont National Forest, Rogue River National Forest, Winema National Forest.

NORTH BEND COAST GUARD GROUP (OR02R4)
2000 Connecticut Avenue
North Bend, OR 97459-2399

TELEPHONE NUMBER INFORMATION: Main installation numbers: C-503-756-9210/9220, D-312-891-9210/9220.

LOCATION: Take OR-101 to Virginia St., west one mile to Maple, turn right, two blocks (follow signs). USMRA: Page 100 (A-5,6). NMC: Eugene, 80 miles northeast.

TEMPORARY MILITARY LODGING: None.

LOGISTICAL SUPPORT: Limited support facilities available.

CHAMPUS-756-9235 **Commissary-888-5285** **Exchange-888-5285**
Family Services-756-9258 **Medical-756-9234** **MWR-756-9282**
Package Store-888-5285 **Public Affairs-756-9214** **SDO/NCO-756-9210**

HEALTH & WELFARE: None.

SPACE A: None. See Portland IAP/ANGB listing, C-503-335-4390/4421, D-312-638-4390, Fax 503-335-5098.

ATTRACTIONS: Oregon Dunes National Recreation Area.

PORTLAND AIR NATIONAL GUARD BASE (OR01R4)
6801 NE Cornfoot Road
Portland, OR 97218-2797

TELEPHONE NUMBER INFORMATION: Main installation number: C-503-335-4000.

LOCATION: Go south on I-205 to NE Airport Way exit, west on NE Airport Way to Alderwood, south on Alderwood to Cornfoot Road. Co-located with Portland International Airport. USMRA: Page 100 (C-2), page 103 (C-1). NMC: Portland, in city limits.

GENERAL INFORMATION: Oregon Air National Guard, 142nd Fighter Group, 244th and 272nd Combat Communications Squadrons, 939th and 304th Air Rescue Wings, Civil Air Patrol.

U.S. FORCES TRAVEL & TRANSFER GUIDE U.S.A. - 241

OREGON
Portland Air National Guard Base, continued

TEMPORARY MILITARY LODGING: None.

LOGISTICAL SUPPORT: Limited support facilities available.

Chaplain-335-4449
Fire Dept-335-4889
Police-335-4752
Travel-335-4265

Consol Club-335-5151
Medical-335-4757
Public Affairs-335-4104

Exchange-249-0997
MWR-335-4176
Retiree Services-335-4945

HEALTH & WELFARE: Medical info C-503-335-4757. Chapel 503-335-4449.

RECREATION: Camping Equipment 335-4748, Rec Center 335-4748.

SPACE-A: Portland IAP, ANG Ops, 24 hours daily, C-503-335-4390, D-312-638-4390, Fax 503-335-5098, transit aircraft.

ATTRACTIONS: Greater Portland area.

Other Installations in Oregon

Coos Bay Coast Guard Exchange, 1684 Ocean Blvd., Coos Bay, OR 97420-5000.
USMRA: Page 100 (A-6). C-541-888-5285, Exchange-888-5285.
Portland Coast Guard Marine Safety Office/Group, 6767 N. Basin Ave., Portland, OR 97217-3992. USMRA: Page 100 (C-2), page 103 (B-2). C-503-240-9310, Exchange-286-3510.

242 - U.S. FORCES TRAVEL & TRANSFER GUIDE U.S.A

PENNSYLVANIA

DOLLAR RENT A CAR — Call 1-800-800-4000. Get a military rate by using your Military Living ID # ML3009. Retirees/Active Duty/Reserve/Guard.

CARLISLE BARRACKS (PA08R1)
US Army War College
Carlisle Barracks, PA 17013-5050

TELEPHONE NUMBER INFORMATION: Main installation numbers: C-717-245-3131, D-312-242-3131.

LOCATION: From I-81 exit 17 to US-11, two miles southwest to Carlisle, signs clearly marked to Barracks and Army War College. USMRA: Page 22 (F-6). NMC: Harrisburg, 18 miles northeast.

GENERAL INFORMATION: Army War College and Army Military History Institute.

TEMPORARY MILITARY LODGING: Lodging office, Bldg. 7, 0700-1800 Mon-Fri, 0900-1700 Sat-Sun, C-717-245-4245, D-312-242-4245. All ranks. DV/VIP C-717-245-4818.

LOGISTICAL SUPPORT: Complete support facilities available.

ACS- 245-4357
Child Care-245-3701
Exchange-245-2463
Golf Course-243-3262
Locator-245-3131
Police-245-4115
Retiree Services-245-4501
Theater-245-4108

CHAMPUS-245-4112
Commissary-245-3409
Family Services-245-4357
ITT Office-245-3309
Medical-245-3007
Public Affairs-245-4101
SATO-245-3158

Chaplain-245-3318
Comm Spt Center-245-3215
Fire Dept-245-4419
Legal-245-4940
Package Store-245-4325
Recreation-245-4116
SDO/NCO-245-4342

HEALTH & WELFARE: Dunham Army Health Clinic, Emergency C-717-245-3007. Inpatient, see Walter Reed Army Medical Center, Washington, DC listing, C-800-433-3574. Chapel serving all faiths C-717-245-3318.

RECREATION: Art Center EX-3319, Morale Support Office EX-4343, Golf 243-3262, Bowling EX-4109, Gym EX-3418/3475, Wood Hobby EX-3466, Swimming EX-3560.

SPACE-A: None. Use Harrisburg IAP, ANG area, 0730-1630 Mon-Fri, C-717-948-2268, D-312-430-9268, Fax 717-948-2599.

ATTRACTIONS: Hessian Powder Magazine Museum and Omar N. Bradley Museum; Amish Country and Gettysburg Battlefield nearby.

CHARLES E. KELLY SUPPORT FACILITY (PA12R1)
6 Lobaugh Street
Oakdale, PA 15071-5000

TELEPHONE NUMBER INFORMATION: Main installation numbers: C-412-777-1336/1173, D-312-242-1336/1173.

PENNSYLVANIA
Charles E. Kelly Support Facility, continued

LOCATION: From I-279 take I-79 south to Carnegie exit (exit 13). Bear right and travel approximately two-and-a-half miles through town of Rennerdale. Follow signs. USMRA: Page 22 (A-6). NMC: Pittsburgh, 13 miles east.

GENERAL INFORMATION: A local area Army Support Center.

TEMPORARY MILITARY LODGING: None. See Pittsburgh IAP/ARS C-412-269-8229/8230.

LOGISTICAL SUPPORT: Most support facilities available.

CHAMPUS-777-1176   Commissary-777-1239/1174   Exchange-777-1316
Four Seasons-EX-1321   Package Store-777-1318   Recreation-777-1350
Retiree Services-777-1177   SATO-693-8710   Snack Bar-777-1329

HEALTH & WELFARE: None.

RECREATION: Community Center EX-1313, Gymnasium EX-1350.

SPACE-A: Use Pittsburgh IAP/ARS, C-412-269-8000, D-312-277-8000.

ATTRACTIONS: City of Pittsburgh, The Shops at Station Square, Carnegie Science Center, the Boardwalk, the Gateway Clipper Fleet boats and a magnificent view of the city atop Mount Washington. Pittsburgh Pirates baseball, Penguins hockey, and Steelers football.

DEFENSE DISTRIBUTION REGION EAST (PA06R1)
14 Dedication Drive
New Cumberland, PA 17070-5001

TELEPHONE NUMBER INFORMATION: Main installation numbers: C-717-770-6011, D-312-977-6011.

LOCATION: From I-83, exit 18 to PA-114, east for one mile to Old York Road, left three-quarters-of-a-mile to Ross Ave, right for one mile to main gate of depot. USMRA: Page 22 (G-6). NMC: Harrisburg, seven miles northeast.

GENERAL INFORMATION: Defense Logistics Agency.

TEMPORARY MILITARY LODGING: Lodging office, Bldg. 268, J Ave, 0700-1700 hours daily, C-717-770-7035, D-312-977-7035. All ranks. DV/VIP C-717-770-7192.

LOGISTICAL SUPPORT: Complete support facilities available.

Cafeteria-770-7165/6693   CHAMPUS-770-7281   Chaplain-770-6111
Child Care-770-7360   Commissary-770-6540   Consol Club-770-7802
Conv Store-774-4482   Exchange-774-4482   Family Services-770-6203
Fire Dept-770-6632   Gas Station-774-4066   Golf Course-770-5199
ITR Office-770-7670   Legal-770-6310   Locator-770-6770
Medical-782-7281   MWR-770-6118   Package Store-774-4482
Police-770-6222   Public Affairs-770-6223   Recreation-770-7718
SATO-770-6468   Snack Bar-770-5125

244 - U.S. FORCES TRAVEL & TRANSFER GUIDE U.S.A

PENNSYLVANIA
Defense Distribution Region East, continued

HEALTH & WELFARE: US Army Health Clinic, Emergency EX-7281. Inpatient, see Walter Reed Army Medical Center, Washington, DC listing, C-800-433-3574.

RECREATION: Auto Hobby EX-6664, Bowling EX-7325, Fitness Center EX-6428, Golf EX-5199, Gym EX-6428, Rec Equipment EX-7625, Library EX-7121, Outdoor Recreation EX-7718, Swimming EX-6476, Rec Center EX-7625, Youth Center EX-4413.

SPACE-A: None. Use Philadelphia IAP, C-215-897-5600, D-312-443-5600.

ATTRACTIONS: State Capitol in Harrisburg, Harley Davidson Plant (York, PA), Hershey Park, Gettysburg Battlefield, Pennsylvania Dutch Country.

DEFENSE PERSONNEL SUPPORT CENTER (PA02R1)
2800 South 20th Street,
Philadelphia, PA 19145-5099

Scheduled to relocate June 1999.

TELEPHONE NUMBER INFORMATION: Main installation numbers: C-215-737-2411, D-312-444-2411.

LOCATION: From I-95 take Broad Street exit, go two miles to intersection of 20th Street and Oregon Ave, follow signs. USMRA: Page 27 (D-6). NMC: Philadelphia, within city limits.

GENERAL INFORMATION: Provides defense personnel and their eligible dependents with $4 billion worth of food, clothing and textiles, medicines, and medical equipment.

TEMPORARY MILITARY LODGING: None. See Willow Grove NAS/JRB listing, C-215-442-5800, D-312-991-5800, DV/VIP C-215-443-1776.

LOGISTICAL SUPPORT: Limited support facilities available.

Cafeteria-737-3932	Carlson Travel-737-2650	CDO/OOD-737-2341
CHAMPUS-737-2324	Exchange-737-3925	Locator-737-2411
Medical-737-2251	MWR-737-3932	O'Club-737-3939
Police-737-2222	Public Affairs-737-2311	Recreation-737-3936
Retiree Services-737-2429	Snack Bar-737-3933	

HEALTH & WELFARE: US Army Health Clinic, C-215-737-2251.

RECREATION: Fitness Center EX-3936, Rec Services EX-3936.

SPACE-A: None. Use Philadelphia IAP, C-215-897-5600, D-312-443-5600.

ATTRACTIONS: Independence Hall, Betsy Ross House, Liberty Bell Pavilion. Edgar Allen Poe National Historic Site. Museums, professional sports, tours.

U.S. FORCES TRAVEL & TRANSFER GUIDE U.S.A. - 245

PENNSYLVANIA

FORT INDIANTOWN GAP (PA04R1)
1 Garrison Road
Fort Indiantown Gap, PA 17003-5040

Scheduled to close October 1998

TELEPHONE NUMBER INFORMATION: Main installation numbers: C-717-861-2000, D-312-491-2000.

LOCATION: From I-81 take exit 29 B, north on PA-934 to post. USMRA: Page 22 (G-6). NMC: Harrisburg, eight miles southwest.

GENERAL INFORMATION: US Army Garrison, Pennsylvania Department of Military Affairs, Reserve Component training and area support.

TEMPORARY MILITARY LODGING: Lodging office, Bldg. T-0-1, 0800-2330 daily, C-717-861-2512, D-312-491-2512. All ranks. DV/VIP C-717-861-2552.

LOGISTICAL SUPPORT: Most support facilities available.

ACS- 861-2610
Child Care-861-8351
Family Services-861-2610
ITR Office-861-2622
Medical-861-2091
Police-861-2160
RV/Camping-861-2622
Snack Bar-865-2044

CHAMPUS-861-2091
Comm Club-861-2173
Fire Dept-861-2349
Legal-861-2294
MWR-861-2060
Public Affairs-861-2193
SATO-861-2755

Chaplain-861-2241
Exchange-861-2058
Gas Station-865-6938
Locator-861-2000
Package Store-865-0024
Retiree Services-861-2610
SDO/NCO-861-2160

HEALTH & WELFARE: US Army Health Clinic C-717-865-2091. Inpatient, see Walter Reed Army Medical Center, Washington, DC listing, C-800-433-3574.

RECREATION: Auto Hobby 861-2477, Bowling 861-2061, Education Center 861-2513, Flying Activity 861-2813, Gym 861-2860, Library 861-2030, Outdoor Rec 861-2622.

SPACE-A: None. Use Philadelphia IAP, C-215-897-5600, D-312-443-5600.

ATTRACTIONS: Hershey Amusement Park, Pennsylvania Dutch Country, Lebanon and origin of Lebanon Bologna.

LETTERKENNY ARMY DEPOT (PA03R1)
Chambersburg, PA 17201-4150

This base is scheduled to close under the 1995 BRAC.
No closure date has been established.

TELEPHONE NUMBER INFORMATION: Main installation numbers: C-717-267-8111, D-312-570-5110.

LOCATION: From I-81 exit 8 W to PA-997 West left and enter depot at gate 6. USMRA: Page 22 (E-7). NMC: Harrisburg, 55 miles northeast.

PENNSYLVANIA
Letterkenny Army Depot, continued

GENERAL INFORMATION: Army Depot that maintains Army materiel, ammunition and general supplies. DoD tactical missile maintenance center.

TEMPORARY MILITARY LODGING: Lodging office, Bldg. 500-16, Coffey Ave, 0730-1615 Mon-Fri, C-717-267-8890, D-312-570-8890. All ranks. DV/VIP C-717-267-8659.

LOGISTICAL SUPPORT: Most support facilities available.

Cafeteria-264-1321
Comm Center-267-8478
Legal-267-9889
Police-267-8800
Chaplain-267-8628
Exchange-264-1713
Locator-267-8366
Retiree Services-267-9725
Child Care-267-8846
Family Services-267-9051
Medical-267-8416
Travel-267-1315

HEALTH & WELFARE: US Army Health Clinic C-717-267-8416. Inpatient, see Walter Reed Army Medical Center, Washington, DC listing, C-800-433-3574. Chapel serving all faiths C-717-267-8628.

RECREATION: Auto Hobby EX-5571, Gym EX-9383, Swimming EX-5561. Army Travel Camp on post, 1 Apr-31 Oct, C-717-267-9494/9620, D-312-570-9494/9620, eight camper spaces, w/W&E hookups.

SPACE-A: None. Use Philadelphia IAP, C-215-897-5600, D-312-443-5600.

ATTRACTIONS: Gettysburg Battlefield, Hershey Park, Potomac C&O Canal, Carlisle Barracks and War College.

MECHANICSBURG NAVAL INVENTORY CONTROL POINT (PA07R1)
PO Box 2020
Mechanicsburg, PA 17055-0788

TELEPHONE NUMBER INFORMATION: Main installation numbers: C-717-790-2000, D-312-430-2000.

LOCATION: From I-83 exit 20 to US-11, four miles. Or from PA Turnpike (I-76), exit 16 (Carlisle), eight miles to Center. USMRA: Page 22 (F,G-6). NMC: Harrisburg, 10 miles northeast.

GENERAL INFORMATION: Logistics Support Activity for Naval ships parts.

TEMPORARY MILITARY LODGING: None. See Carlisle Barracks listing C-717-245-4245.

LOGISTICAL SUPPORT: Most support facilities available.

Cafeteria-790-3537
Golf Course-790-1610
Exchange-790-2608
Police-790-3351
Child Care-790-5683
Medical-790-3461
O'Club-790-3505
SATO-795-6286
Fire Dept-790-3467
MWR-790-1610
Package Store-790-2608
SDO/NCO-790-4444

U.S. FORCES TRAVEL & TRANSFER GUIDE U.S.A. - 247

PENNSYLVANIA
Mechanicsburg Naval Inventory Control Point, continued

HEALTH & WELFARE: Naval Branch Medical Clinic, Emergency C-717-790-3461. Inpatient, see National Naval Medical Center, MD listing, C-202-295-1400. No chapel facilities.

RECREATION: Limited facilities on base, see Carlisle Barracks listing.

SPACE-A: None. Use Harrisburg IAP, 0730-1600 Mon-Fri, C-717-948-2268, D-312-430-9268, Fax 717-948-2599.

ATTRACTIONS: Gettysburg Battlefield.

PHILADELPHIA COAST GUARD GROUP (PA19R1)
1 Washington Ave.
Philadelphia, PA 19147

TELEPHONE NUMBER INFORMATION: Main installation number: C-215-271-4800, Fax 215-271-4919.

LOCATION: Exit 16 off I-95. Follow signs. USMRA: Page 27 (D,E-6). NMC: Philadelphia, within city limits.

TEMPORARY MILITARY LODGING: None. See Willow Grove NAS/JRB listing, C-215-442-5800, D-312-991-5800, DV/VIP C-215-443-1776.

LOGISTICAL SUPPORT: Limited support facilities available.

CDO/OOD-271-4940   **Exchange-271-4921**   **Fire Dept-271-4927**
Police-271-4971

HEALTH & WELFARE: None. See Defense Personnel Support Center listing, C-215-737-2251.

SPACE-A: None. Use Philadelphia IAP, C-215-897-5600/5644, D-312-443-5600/5644.

ATTRACTIONS: Independence Hall, Betsy Ross House, Liberty Bell Pavilion. Edgar Allen Poe National Historic Site. Museums, professional sports, tours.

PITTSBURGH IAP/AIR FORCE
RESERVE INSTALLATION (PA15R1)
2475 Defense Ave.
Coraopolis, PA 15108-4403

TELEPHONE NUMBER INFORMATION: Main installation numbers: C-412-474-8000, D-312-277-8000.

LOCATION: Take Business Route 60 to exit 3 from Pittsburgh. Follow signs. USMRA: Page 22 (A-5,6). NMC: Pittsburgh, 15 miles southeast.

TEMPORARY MILITARY LODGING: C-412-474-8230

LOGISTICAL SUPPORT: Limited support facilities available.

248 - U.S. FORCES TRAVEL & TRANSFER GUIDE U.S.A

PENNSYLVANIA
Pittsburgh IAP/AFRI, continued

Chaplain-424-8204	Exchange-424-8207	Fire Dept-911
Legal-424-8265	Police-424-8255	Public Affairs-424-8750
Recreation-424-8245	Retiree Services-424-8558	Travel-424-8197
Snack Bar-424-8737		

HEALTH & WELFARE: None.

SPACE-A: Pax Term info, AFRES, C-412-474-8000, D-312-277-8000.

ATTRACTIONS: City of Pittsburgh, The Shops at Station Square, Carnegie Science Center, Carnegie Museum, The Boardwalk, the Gateway Clipper Fleet boats and a magnificent view of the city atop Mount Washington. Pittsburgh Pirates baseball, Penguins hockey, and Steelers football.

TOBYHANNA ARMY DEPOT (PA05R1)
11 Hap Arnold Boulevard
Tobyhanna, PA 18466-5000

TELEPHONE NUMBER INFORMATION: Main installation numbers: C-717-895-7000, D-312-795-7000, FTS-590-7000.

LOCATION: Take I-80 to I-380 west, exit 7 to depot. USMRA: Page 22 (I-4). NMC: Scranton, 24 miles northwest.

GENERAL INFORMATION: Army Communications-Electronics Depot.

TEMPORARY MILITARY LODGING: Lodging office, Bldg. 1001, Admin Loop, 0800-1630 daily, C-717-895-7970, D-312-795-7970. All ranks. DV/VIP 717-895- 6223.

LOGISTICAL SUPPORT: Complete support facilities available.

ACS-895-6128	Cafeteria-895-7998	CHAMPUS-895-7225
Chaplain-895-6397	Commissary-895-7246	Comm Club-895-8478
Exchange-895-7716	Family Services-895-7069	Fire Dept-895-7300
Gas Station-895-7401	ITT-895-6559	Legal-895-7210
Locator-895-7409	Medical-895-7225	MWR-895-7584
Package Store-895-7592	Police-895-7550	Public Affairs-895-6552
Recreation-895-7584	Retiree Services-895-7019	SATO-895-6318
SDO/NCO-895-7550	Theater-895-7584	

HEALTH & WELFARE: US Army Health Clinic, Emergency C-717-895-7282. Inpatient, see Fort Dix, NJ listing, C-609-562-2695. Chapel serving all faiths C-717-895-7319.

RECREATION: Arts/Crafts EX-7584, Auto Hobby EX-6609, Rec Equipment EX-7092, Library EX-7316, Youth Activities EX-7634.

SPACE-A: Army flights C-717-895-7000. Also see McGuire AFB, NJ listing, C-609-724-3078, D-312-440-3078, Fax 609-724-4623.

ATTRACTIONS: Scranton and Wilkes-Barre nearby, several ski areas, Pocono Mountains.

U.S. FORCES TRAVEL & TRANSFER GUIDE U.S.A. - 249

PENNSYLVANIA

WARMINSTER NAVAL AIR WARFARE CENTER (PA17R1)
Warminster, PA 18974-5000

Scheduled to close July 1996

TELEPHONE NUMBER INFORMATION: Main installation numbers: C-215-441-2000, D-312-441-2000.

LOCATION: Take PA Turnpike (I-276) exit 27 north to PA 611 past Willow Grove, east on highway 132 approximately five miles. USMRA: Page 22 (J-6). NMC: Philadelphia, 27 miles south.

GENERAL INFORMATION: Naval Aviation Research and Development Center, Funding, Contract and Printing Offices.

TEMPORARY MILITARY LODGING: None. See Willow Grove NAS listing, C-215-442-5800, D-312-991-5800, Fax 215-442-5817.

LOGISTICAL SUPPORT: Limited support facilities available.

Cafeteria-441-1600	EM Club-441-2510	Medical-441-3789
Police-441-2298	SATO-441-2729	

HEALTH & WELFARE: Small limited clinic, C-215-441-3789. Emergency C-215-433-1600, Willow Grove NAS.

RECREATION: Auto Hobby, Camping Equipment, Gym, Swimming Pool, All EX-2510, Flying Club EX-2591.

SPACE-A: None. See Willow Grove NAS listing, C-215-443-6217, D-312-991-6216/7, Fax 215-443-6188.

ATTRACTIONS: Philadelphia historical sites, Sesame Place Amusement Park.

WILLOW GROVE NAVAL AIR STATION/ JOINT RESERVE BASE (PA01R1)
Willow Grove, PA 19090-5000

TELEPHONE NUMBER INFORMATION: Main installation numbers: C-215-443-1000, D-312-991-1000.

LOCATION: PA Turnpike, exit 27, to NAS. USMRA: Page 22 (I,J-6). NMC: Philadelphia, 21 miles south.

GENERAL INFORMATION: Naval Air Reserve Unit training.

TEMPORARY MILITARY LODGING: Lodging office, Bldg. 609, 24 hours daily, C-215-442-5800, D-312-991-5800, Fax 215-442-5817. All ranks. DV/VIP 215-443-1776.

LOGISTICAL SUPPORT: Most support facilities available.

PENNSYLVANIA
Willow Grove Naval Air Station/JRB, continued

Cafeteria-443-6282
Child Care-443-6080
EM Club-443-6089
Legal-443-6056
O'Club-443-6081
SDO/NCO-443-6454

CHAMPUS-443-6376
Conv Store-443-6026
Exchange-443-6031
Locator-443-6854
Package Store-443-6078

Chaplain-443-6002
CPO Club-443-6089
ITT Office-443-6082
Medical-443-6362
Police-443-6067

HEALTH & WELFARE: Naval Branch Medical Clinic, Emergency C-215-443-1600, Appointment C-215-443-6373/75. Chapel serving all faiths C-215-443-6002.

RECREATION: Bowling EX-6092, Fitness Center EX-6066, Gym EX-6082, Rec Equipment EX-6066, Swimming EX-6079. Operates Lake Laurie Campground, NJ, C-215-443-6082, D-312-991-6082, two campers w/full hookups.

SPACE-A: Pax Term/Lounge, Hangar 80, 0730-1600 Wed-Sun, C-215-433-6216, D-312-991-6216, Fax 215-443-6188, flights to CONUS and overseas.

ATTRACTIONS: New Jersey beaches are a one and a half hour drive; Pocono Mountain resorts, a one hour drive.

Other Installations in Pennsylvania

Chambersburg Municipal Airport, Chambersburg, PA 17201-4170.
USMRA: Page 22 (E-7). C-717-267-8788, Space A-267-8788.
Harrisburg IAP, Middletown, PA 17057-5086.
USMRA: Page 22 (G-6). C-717-948-2200, Exchange-948-2415, Medical-948-2234, Space A-948-2268.

U.S. FORCES TRAVEL & TRANSFER GUIDE U.S.A. - 251

RHODE ISLAND

DOLLAR RENT A CAR Call 1-800-800-4000. Get a military rate by using your Military Living ID # ML3009. Retirees/Active Duty/Reserve/Guard.

NEWPORT NAVAL EDUCATION AND TRAINING CENTER (RI01R1)
61 Capodanno Drive
Newport, RI 02841-1513

TELEPHONE NUMBER INFORMATION: Main installation numbers: C-401-841-2311, D-312-948-2311.

LOCATION: From US-1 exit to RI-138 east over Jamestown/Newport bridge (toll) to Newport. Follow signs to Navy Base, gate No 1. USMRA: Page 17 (J-8), Page 25 (B,C-1,2,3). NMC: Newport, adjacent.

GENERAL INFORMATION: Naval War College, Surface Warfare Officers School, Naval Justice School, Naval Hospital, Naval Undersea Warfare Center, other training and support activities.

TEMPORARY MILITARY LODGING: Lodging office, 24 hours daily; Bldg. 684 (Officers) C-401-841-3156; Bldg. 447 (EM), C-401-841-4410. Navy Lodge, Bldg. 685, 0700-2300 daily, C-401-849-4500. All ranks. DV/VIP C-401-841-3715, Fax 401-849-3906.

LOGISTICAL SUPPORT: Complete support facilities available.

Cafeteria-841-1360
Child Care-841-4562
CPO Club-841-3877
Family Services-841-2283
Locator-841-4001
Package Store-846-3080
Retiree Services-841-4089
Snack Bar-846-7671/814

CHAMPUS-841-2671
Commissary-841-2111
EM Club-841-3994
ITT Office-841-3116
Medical-841-3771
Police-841-3241/3242
SATO-847-8800

Chaplain-841-2234
Conv Store-846-2831
Exchange-846-2555
Legal-841-3766
O'Club-846-2515
Public Affairs-841-3538
SDO/NCO-841-3456

HEALTH & WELFARE: Naval Hospital, clinics and depts, Emergency C-401-841-3111. Chapel serving all faiths C-401-841-2234.

RECREATION: Auto Hobby EX-3026, Gym EX-3154, Rec Equipment EX-2638, Yacht Club EX-3283, Swimming EX-3957, Rec Center EX-4293.

SPACE-A: Use Quonset State Airport, ANG Area, 0800-1600 Mon-Fri, C-401-866-1405, D-312-476-3420.

ATTRACTIONS: Beaches, Newport Music Festivals, Tennis Hall of Fame, mansion tours.

Other Installations in Rhode Island

Quonset Point State Airport, 1 Minuteman Way, North Kingston, RI 02852-7502. USMRA: Page 17 (J-7). C-401-886-1420, NCO Club-886-1143, Space-A-886-1420.

252 - U.S. FORCES TRAVEL & TRANSFER GUIDE U.S.A

SOUTH CAROLINA

DOLLAR RENT A CAR — Call 1-800-800-4000. Get a military rate by using your Military Living ID # ML3009. Retirees/Active Duty/Reserve/Guard.

BEAUFORT MARINE CORPS AIR STATION (SC01R1)
P.O. Box 55001 Giger Boulevard
Beaufort Marine Corps Air Station, SC 29904-5000

TELEPHONE NUMBER INFORMATION: Main installation numbers: C-803-522-7100, D-312-832-7100.

LOCATION: From I-95 exit take any Beaufort exit and follow signs. Sixteen miles to MCAS. Clearly marked. USMRA: Page 44 (G-9). NMC: Savannah, GA, 40 miles south.

GENERAL INFORMATION: Marine Aircraft Group-31, Marine Air Control Squadron-2, Marine Corps Support Squadron-273.

TEMPORARY MILITARY LODGING: BOQ, Bldg. 431, 24 hours daily, C-803-522-7676/7658, D-312-832-7676/7658. All ranks. DV/VIP C-803-522-7158. De Treville House 522-1663.

LOGISTICAL SUPPORT: Most support facilities available.

Cafeteria-522-1753
Child Care-522-7290
Family Services-522-7353
Legal-522-7330
O'Club-522-7541
Public Affairs-522-7201
Staff Club-522-7726

CHAMPUS-525-5343
Conv Store-522-1231
Gas Station-522-1752
Locator-522-7188
Package Store-522-1601
SDO/NCO-522-7121

Chaplain-522-7775
Exchange-522-1891
ITT-522-7340
Medical-522-7311/7424
Police-522-7373
Snack Bar-522-1861

HEALTH & WELFARE: Naval Branch Clinic, Emergency C-803-522-7311, Appointments C-803-522-7782. Inpatient, see Beaufort Naval Hospital, located between MCAS and Parris Island Recruit Depot, C-803-525-5600. Chapel serving all faiths C-803-522-7775.

RECREATION: Bowling EX-7106, Gym EX-7192, Special Services EX-7400, Picnic Area EX-7340, Boat Rental EX-7570, Library EX-7682, Swimming EX-7573, Rec Center EX- 7340.

SPACE-A: Pax Term/Lounge, Bldg. 860, 0700-2300 Mon-Fri, 1000-1800 Sat, 1200-2000 Sun, C-803-522-7143, D-312-832-7143, Fax 803-522-7221, flights to CONUS and OCONUS locations.

ATTRACTIONS: Beaches, seafood, period homes, Savannah, Charleston.

CHARLESTON AIR FORCE BASE (SC06R1)
102 East Hill Boulevard, Room 223
Charleston Air Force Base, SC 29404-5154

TELEPHONE NUMBER INFORMATION: Main installation numbers: C-803-566-6000, D-312-673-6000.

SOUTH CAROLINA
Charleston Air Force Base, continued

LOCATION: From I-26 East, exit to West Aviation Ave to traffic light, continue through light to second light right, follow road around end of runway to gate 2 (River Gate). USMRA: Page 44 (H-8,9). NMC: Charleston, 10 miles southeast.

GENERAL INFORMATION: Air Mobility Command Base. Active Duty Airlift Wing, Air Force Reserve Airlift Wing and Air National Guard Fighter Detachment.

TEMPORARY MILITARY LODGING: Lodging office, Bldg. 322, Simpson St & Davis Dr, 24 hours daily, C-803-556-3806, (552-9900-room number after duty hour) D-312-673-3806. All ranks.

LOGISTICAL SUPPORT: Complete support facilities available.

CHAMPUS-566-3971
Commissary-566-5709
Fire Dept -566-3778
Legal-566-5502
MWR-566-3800
Package Store-767-4594
Recreation-566-3337
Shoppette-767-4594

Chaplain-566-2536
Exchange-552-5000
Gas Station-767-4594
Locator-566-3282
NCO Club-566-2930
Police-566-3600/2695
Retiree Services-566-2228
Theater-566-333

Child Care-566-4366
Family Services-566-4408
Golf Course-566-4174
Medical-566-4003
O'Club-566-3920
Public Affairs-566-5608
RV/Camping-566-5270/5271
Travel-566-3091

HEALTH & WELFARE: USAF Clinic, Emergency C-803-566-2802. Inpatient, see Beaufort Naval Hospital, located between MCAS and Parris Island Recruit Depot, C-803-525-5600. Chapel serving all faiths, C-803-566-2536.

RECREATION: Arts/Crafts EX-4936, Auto Skills Shop EX-4942, Bowling EX-3315, Fitness Center EX-3347, Library EX-3320, Swimming EX-5271, Rec Center EX-3337, Tennis EX-3347, Youth Center EX-2684. Shady Oaks Family Campground on base, year round, C-803-566-5270, D-312-673-5270, 23 camper spaces w/W&E hookups.

SPACE-A: Pax Term/Lounge, Bldg. 164, 0500-2300 daily, C-803-566-3082, D-312-673-3082, Fax 803-566-3060, flights to CONUS and overseas.

ATTRACTIONS: Beautiful sandy beaches, period homes, gardens.

CHARLESTON COAST GUARD BASE (SC16R1)
196 Tradd Street
Charleston, SC 29401-1899

TELEPHONE NUMBER INFORMATION: Main installation numbers: C-803-724-7600/723-9378, D-312-794-2086/563-2086.

LOCATION: In downtown Charleston. USMRA: Page 44 (H-9). NMC: Charleston, in city limits.

GENERAL INFORMATION: Performs search-and-rescue operations.

TEMPORARY MILITARY LODGING: None. See Charleston Air Force Base listing, C-803-556-3806, D-312-673-3806.

LOGISTICAL SUPPORT: Complete support facilities available.

254 - U.S. FORCES TRAVEL & TRANSFER GUIDE U.S.A

SOUTH CAROLINA
Charleston Coast Guard Base, continued

CDO/OOD-724-7619/76	CHAMPUS-724-7653	Chaplain-720-7723
EM Club-724-7674	Exchange-722-8817	Locator-724-7608
Medical-724-7653	NCO Club-724-7674	Package Store-722-8817

HEALTH & WELFARE: None. See Beaufort Naval Hospital, located between MCAS and Parris Island Recruit Depot, C-803-525-5600.

SPACE-A: None. See Charleston AFB listing, C-803-803-566-3082, D-312-673-3082, Fax 803-566-3060.

ATTRACTIONS: Charleston..."One of America's most historic cities" features miles of beautiful, sandy beaches, gardens, fresh water lakes, great fishing.

CHARLESTON NAVAL WEAPONS STATION (SC11R1)
2316 Red Bank Road, Suite 100
Goose Creek, SC 29445-8601

TELEPHONE NUMBER INFORMATION: Main installation numbers: C-803-764-7901, D-312-794-7901.

LOCATION: Exit 203 off I-26, US-78, to US-52, to SC-37 (Red Bank Road) to main gate. USMRA: Page 44 (H-8,9). NMC: Charleston, 25 miles south.

GENERAL INFORMATION: Provides materiel and technical support for ammunition and assigned weapons and weapon systems. It operates an explosive ordnance out-loading facility. Manages Navy family housing for Charleston area.

TEMPORARY MILITARY LODGING: BEQ C-803-764-7646. Also, see Charleston Air Force Base listing, C-803-556-3806, D-312-673-3806.

LOGISTICAL SUPPORT: Most support facilities available.

Chaplain-764-7222	Child Care-764-7408	Commissary-764-7015
Exchange-764-7042	Family Services-764-7294	Gas Station-764-7573
Package Store-764-7314		

HEALTH & WELFARE: Naval Branch Medical Clinic, C-803-764-7634. Inpatient, see Beaufort Naval Hospital, located between MCAS and Parris Island Recruit Depot, C-803-525-5600. Chapel serving all faiths C-803-764-7222.

RECREATION: Morale Welfare Recreation 764-7601. Gym/Fitness Center 764-7530, Bowling, Golf, Hunting/fishing, Picnic Area, Racquetball, Swimming, and Theater.

SPACE-A: None. See Charleston AFB listing, C-803-566-3082, D-312-673-3082, Fax 803-566-3060.

ATTRACTIONS: Historic Charleston (25 miles south), and scenic Myrtle Beach (100 miles northeast).

U.S. FORCES TRAVEL & TRANSFER GUIDE U.S.A. - 255

SOUTH CAROLINA
FORT JACKSON (SC09R1)
Fort Jackson, SC 29207-5060

TELEPHONE NUMBER INFORMATION: Main installation numbers: C-803-751-7511, D-312-734-1110.

LOCATION: Exit from I-20 north of fort, or from US-76/378 at the main gate. From I-20 and I-77 interchange take newly constructed Beltway to Percival Road, right onto Percival Road to Gate 2. USMRA: Page 44 (G-6). NMC: Columbia, 12 miles southwest.

GENERAL INFORMATION: Two Training Brigades for training recruits, one Combat Service Support Training (AIT) Brigade, Army Reception Station, and Reserve Command.

TEMPORARY MILITARY LODGING: Kennedy Hall, Bldg. 2785, Semmes & Lee Rd, 0700-2300 daily, C-803-751-6223/6149, D-312-734-6223/6149. Palmetto Hall, Bldg 600 C-803-751-5205/4429, D-312-734-5205/4429. All ranks. DV/VIP C-803-751-6618, D-312-734-5218.

LOGISTICAL SUPPORT: Complete support facilities available.

ACS-751-5256	CHAMPUS-751-2425	Chaplain-751-3121
Child Care-751-6222/6221	Commissary-751-6347	Conv Store-782-0590
Exchange-787-1950	Family Services-751-5256	Fire Dept-751-3117
Gas Station-782-3725/86939	Golf Course-787-4437	ITT Office-751-6219/6602
Legal-751-7657	Locator-751-7571	Medical-751-2160
MWR-782-8876	NCO Club-782-1932	O'Club-787-5819
Package Store-782-1614	Police-751-3113	Public Affairs-751-7650
Retiree Services-751-6715	SDO/NCO-751-7611	Snack Bar-751-4759
Theater-751-7488	Travel-782-5121	

HEALTH & WELFARE: Moncrief Army Community Hospital, clinics and depts, Emergency C-803-751-4444, Appointments C-803-751-5308/2183, 410 beds. Chapels serving all faiths C-803-751-3121.

RECREATION: Arts/Crafts EX-6359, Auto Hobby EX-5653/5755, Bowling EX-4656/4959, Golf EX-6367, Gym EX-5878, Library EX-4816/5589, Rec Equip EX-5481, Rifle Range EX-6954, Riding Club EX-6357, Youth Activities EX-4114/4829, Swimming EX-4796/7472/7084, Rec Center EX-5743/4057, Outdoor Rec Dir EX-4948, Picnic Area EX-6606/4215. Weston Lake Recreation Area & Travel Camp on post, year round, C-803-751-5253, D-312-734-5253, 13 camper spaces w/full hookups, five camper spaces w/W&E, 10 tent spaces w/W&E, seven cabins.

SPACE-A: None. See Charleston AFB listing, C-803-566-3082, D-312-673-3082, Fax 803-566-3060.

ATTRACTIONS: Outdoor sports and recreation. Columbia, the state capital. Ernie Pyle Media Center located on Fort Jackson, a memorial to the slain World War II correspondent. Museum traces South Carolina and Fort Jackson history.

SOUTH CAROLINA

McENTIRE AIR NATIONAL GUARD BASE (SC18R1)
1325 South Carolina Road
Eastover, SC 29044-50017

TELEPHONE NUMBER INFORMATION: Main installation number: C-803-776-5121, D-312-583-8301.

LOCATION: On SC highway 378 between Sumter and Columbia, SC. USMRA: Page 44 (G-6,7). NMC: Columbia, SC, 15 miles west.

GENERAL INFORMATION: 169th Tactical Fighter Group, 240th Combat Communications Squadron.

TEMPORARY MILITARY LODGING: None. See Shaw Air Force Base listing, C-803-668-3210, or 1-800-769-7429.

LOGISTICAL SUPPORT: Limited support facilities **available during drill weekends only.**

Chaplain-695-6265E
Fire Dept-695-6287
NCO Club-695-6326
Public Affairs-695-6208

EM Club-695-6326
Legal-695-6210
O'Club-695-6326

Exchange-695-6517
Medical-695-6296
Police-695-6284

HEALTH AND WELFARE: None. See Fort Jackson listing, C-803-751-5308/2183.

SPACE-A: C-803-695-6210, D-312-583-8210.

ATTRACTIONS: Charleston, Myrtle Beach 100 miles., Columbia: State Capital, State Fairgrounds, gardens, zoo.

PARRIS ISLAND MARINE CORPS RECRUIT DEPOT (SC08R1)
Parris Island, SC 29905-5000

TELEPHONE NUMBER INFORMATION: Main installation numbers: C-803-525-2111, D-312-832-2111.

LOCATION: From I-95 south, exit at Beaufort to SC-170 or US-21, both east to SC-280 to SC-281 which leads to main gate of depot. USMRA: Page 44(G-10). NMC: Savannah, GA 43 miles southwest.

GENERAL INFORMATION: Recruit Depot for USMC male recruits east of Mississippi and all female recruits.

TEMPORARY MILITARY LODGING: Billeting, 24 hours daily, C-803-525-2976/3460, D-312-832-2976/3460: Bldg. 200 (Hostess House), Bldg. 254 (TLQ), Bldg. 331 (BEQ), Bldg. 289 (BOQ). All ranks. DV/VIP C-803-525-2594.

LOGISTICAL SUPPORT: Complete support facilities available.

CHAMPUS-525-5343
Commissary-525-2679

Chaplain-522-3533
Conv Store-525-2248

Child Care-525-3514
EM Club-525-2461

SOUTH CAROLINA
Parris Island Marine Corps Recruit Depot, continued

Exchange-525-3301
Gas Station-525-2248
Legal-525-2559
MWR-525-3301
Police-525-3444
SDO/NCO-525-3712
Special Services-525-3301

Family Services-525-3791
Golf Course-525-2240
Locator-525-3358
O'Club-525-2905
Public Affairs-525-3240
Snack Bar-525-2810
Theater-525-2377

Fire Dept-525-3637
ITT Office-525-3301
Medical-525-3351
Package Store-525-3611
SATO-525-2627
SNCO Club-525-2452
Visitor Center-525-3650

HEALTH & WELFARE: Naval Branch Medical Clinic, Emergency C-803-525-3351, Appointments C-803-525-2617. Inpatient, see Beaufort Naval Hospital, located between MCAS and Parris Island Recruit Depot, C-803-525-5600. Chapel serving all faiths C-803-525-2424.

RECREATION: Arts/Crafts EX-2204, Auto Hobby EX-3205, Bowling EX-2290, Golf EX-2240, Boat Basin EX-3670, Fitness Center EX-3395, Rod/Gun Club EX-3635, Library EX-3261, Swimming EX-3347/3447/3530.

SPACE-A: None. See Beaufort MCAS listing, C-803-522-7143, D-312-832-7143, Fax 803-522-7221.

ATTRACTIONS: Great beaches on the Atlantic Ocean. Museum on base. Visitors Center building 283.

SHAW AIR FORCE BASE (SC10R1)
Shaw Air Force Base, SC 29152-5000

TELEPHONE NUMBER INFORMATION: Main installation numbers: C-803-668-8110, D-312-965-1110.

LOCATION: Off US-76/378, eight miles west of Sumter. Clearly marked. USMRA: Page 44 (H-6). NMC: Columbia, 35 miles west.

GENERAL INFORMATION: Air Combat Command. 9th Air Force Headquarters, 20th Fighter Wing.

TEMPORARY MILITARY LODGING: Lodging office, Bldg. 471, Myers St, 24 hours daily, C-803-668-3210, D-312-965-3210. Switchboard, C-803-666-3658, D-312-965-3210. All ranks. DV/VIP C-803-668-3210.

LOGISTICAL SUPPORT: Complete support facilities available.

CDO/OOD-668-3330
Child Care-668-2305
EM/NCO Club-666-3651
Gas Station-666-3140
Medical-668-2571
Police-668-3200
Snack Bar-666-2115

CHAMPUS-668-2589
Commissary-668-3207
Exchange-666-3481
Legal-668-2505
O'Club-666-3661
Retiree Services-668-3036
Theater-668-3914

Chaplain-668-3224
Conv Store-666-3215
Family Services-668-3533
Locator-668-2811
Package Store-666-3167
SATO-668-3644/3293

HEALTH & WELFARE: USAF Hospital, clinics and depts, Emergency C-803-668-2571, Appointments C-803-668-2778, 25 beds. Chapel serving most faiths C-803-668-3224.

SOUTH CAROLINA
Shaw Air Force Base, continued

RECREATION: Arts/Crafts EX-2362, Auto Hobby EX-2929, Bowling EX-3553, Aero Club EX-2057, Fitness Center EX-2941, Golf EX-3950, Rec Equip EX-2204, Rod/Gun Club EX-2492, Library EX-3084, Rec Center EX-2205, Swimming EX-3520, Youth Center EX-5420. Wateree Recreation Area off base, year round, C-803-668-3245, D-312-965-3245, 20 camper spaces w/W&E hookups, 12 cabins and 10 tent spaces.

SPACE-A: Bldg. 1578, Base Ops, 0800-1500 daily, C-803-668-3818, D-312-965-3818, Fax 803-668-4156, D-312-965-2796, infrequent flights to CONUS locations.

ATTRACTIONS: Sumter Iris Gardens. Columbia is an easy drive. Myrtle Beach is a one-and-a-half hour drive. Outdoor sports and recreation.

Other Installations in South Carolina

Beaufort Naval Hospital, Beaufort, SC 29902-6148.
USMRA: Page 44 (G-9). C-803-525-5600, Medical-525-5600, Exchange-525-5600, TML-522-7658/7676.
Charleston International Airport, Suite 124, 5500 International Blvd., Charleston, SC 29418-6924. USMRA: Page 44 (H-9). C-803-566-5794/5, Space A-566-5794/5795.

U.S. FORCES TRAVEL & TRANSFER GUIDE U.S.A. - 259

SOUTH DAKOTA

DOLLAR RENT A CAR — Call 1-800-800-4000. Get a military rate by using your Military Living ID # ML3009. Retirees/Active Duty/Reserve/Guard.

BELLE FOURCHE AIR FORCE STATION (SD03R3)
Box 139
Belle Fourche AFS, SD 57717-8801

TELEPHONE NUMBER INFORMATION: Main installation numbers: C-605-385-2241, D-312-675-2241.

LOCATION: From I-90 to highway 85 north to station. USMRA: Page 85 (A-4). NMC: Rapid City, 60 miles southeast.

TEMPORARY MILITARY LODGING: None. See Ellsworth AFB listing, C-605-385-2844, D-312-675-2844.

LOGISTICAL SUPPORT: Limited support facilities available.

Commissary-892-3431   EM Club-892-2427   Exchange-892-3431

HEALTH & WELFARE: None. See Ellsworth AFB listing, C-605-385-3333.

RECREATION: Hiking in nearby Black Hills National Forest or Bear Butte State Park, fishing in Belle Fourche River or Reservoir.

SPACE-A: None. See Ellsworth AFB listing, C-605-385-1052, D-312-675-1052, Fax 605-385-1063.

ATTRACTIONS: Black Hills National Forest, Badlands, Mount Rushmore, Crazy Horse Monument, Bear Butte State Park, Belle Fourche River and Reservoir.

ELLSWORTH AIR FORCE BASE (SD01R3)
1958 Scott Dr., Ste 1
Ellsworth Air Force Base, SD 57706-4710

TELEPHONE NUMBER INFORMATION: Main installation numbers: C-605-385-1000, D-312-675-1000.

LOCATION: Two miles north of I-90, exit 63. Ten miles east of Rapid City. Clearly marked. USMRA: Page 85 (B-5). NMC: Rapid City, 10 miles west.

GENERAL INFORMATION: Air Combat Command Base, 28th Bomb Wing, B-1B base.

TEMPORARY MILITARY LODGING: Billeting Office, Bldg. 1103, Risner Dr, 24 hours daily, C-605-385-2844, D-312-675-2844. All ranks. DV/VIP C-605-385-1205, D-312-675-1205.

LOGISTICAL SUPPORT: Complete support facilities available.

Cafeteria-923-1623   CHAMPUS-385-3259   Chaplain-385-1597/7630
Child Care-385-2488   Commissary-385-4364   Consolidated Club-385-1764
Conv Store-923-5231   Exchange-923-4774   Family Services-385-1348

SOUTH DAKOTA
Ellsworth Air Force Base, continued

Gas Station-923-1489	Golf Course-923-4999	Legal-385-2329
Locator-385-1379	Medical-385-7630	MWR-385-1315
Package Store-385-1664	Police-385-4001	Public Affairs-385-5056
Recreation-385-1613	Retiree Services-385-5050	RV/Camping-385-2999
SATO-923-1466	Theater-385-1684/1685	Visitor Center-385-2894

HEALTH & WELFARE: USAF Hospital, clinics and depts, Emergency C-605-385-7630, Appointments C-605-385-3333, 15 beds. Chapel serving all faiths C-605-385-1597.

RECREATION: Arts/Crafts 385-2899, Auto Hobby EX-7630, Fitness Center EX-2266, Riding Club 923-1454, Library EX-1686, Rec Center EX-1613, Bowling EX-2536. Fam-Camp on base, 15 May-15 Oct, C-605-385-2999, D-312-675-2999, 24 camper spaces w/full hookups, 12 camper spaces w/E hookups, six tent spaces.

SPACE-A: Pax Term/Lounge, Bldg. 7506, 24 hours daily, C-605-385-1052/2861, D-312-675-1052, Fax 605-385-1063, flights to CONUS, OCONUS and overseas locations.

ATTRACTIONS: Air and Space Museum, and three small fishing lakes on base, Black Hills, Badlands, Deadwood (Casinos), and Mt. Rushmore nearby. An outdoor sports and recreation paradise.

U.S. FORCES TRAVEL & TRANSFER GUIDE U.S.A. - 261

TENNESSEE

DOLLAR RENT A CAR — Call 1-800-800-4000. Get a military rate by using your Military Living ID # ML3009. Retirees/Active Duty/Reserve/Guard.

ARNOLD AIR FORCE BASE (TN02R2)
100 Kindel Drive, Suite B213
Arnold Air Force Base, TN 37389-2213

TELEPHONE NUMBER INFORMATION: Main installation numbers: C-615-454-3000, D-312-340-5011.

LOCATION: From US-231 north of Huntsville, take TN-55 east to AEDC access highway in Tullahoma. From I-24 take AEDC exit 117, four miles south of Manchester. Clearly marked. USMRA: Page 41 (I-9). NMC: Chattanooga, 65 miles southeast; Nashville, 65 miles northwest.

GENERAL INFORMATION: Air Force Materiel Command. Arnold Engineering Development Center, nation's largest complex of wind tunnels, altitude rocket test cells, space environment chambers, and other related R&D test and evaluation facilities.

TEMPORARY MILITARY LODGING: Lodging office, Bldg. 3027, 0600-2200 Mon-Fri, 1000-2000 Sat, 1200-2200 Sun, C-615-454-3099, D-312-340-3099. All ranks.

LOGISTICAL SUPPORT: Complete support facilities available.

All Ranks Club-454-3090
Commissary-455-7249
ITT-454-3128
Medical-454-5351
Retiree Services-454-4574

CHAMPUS-454-5351
Exchange-455-7153
Legal-454-7153/7814
Police-454-5222
SDO/NCO-454-7752

Chaplain-454-3470
Fire Dept-454-56548
Locator-454-3000
Public Affairs-454-5586
Travel-454-4798

HEALTH & WELFARE: Dispensary/Emergency C-615-454-5351. Inpatient, see Redstone Arsenal, AL, C-205-876-8513. No Chapels on base.

RECREATION: Arts/Crafts, Tennis, Sailing/Boat Rental: all EX-6084. 9-hole golf course open year round, C-615-455-5870. Fitness Center, C-615-454-6440, D-312-340-6440. Fam-Camp on base, 1 Apr-1 Oct, C-615-454-6084, D-312-340-6084, 26 camper spaces w/W&E hookups, 57 tent spaces.

SPACE-A: Base Ops, C-615-454-7752, D-312-340-7752, very limited flights to CONUS locations. Also, try Nashville International Airport, ANG area, 0800-1700 Mon-Fri, C-615-399-6581, D-312-340-6581, flights to CONUS and OCONUS locations.

ATTRACTIONS: Chattanooga and Lookout Mountains are an easy drive southeast. Home of Grand Ole Opry, Opryland, Nashville.

262 - U.S. FORCES TRAVEL & TRANSFER GUIDE U.S.A
TENNESSEE

McGHEE TYSON AIR NATIONAL GUARD BASE (TN07R2)
Knoxville, TN 37950-5000

TELEPHONE NUMBER INFORMATION: Main installation numbers: C-615-985-3210, D-312-588-3210.

LOCATION: From US-129, take McGhee Tyson Airport exit. Clearly marked. USMRA: Page 41 (L-8). NMC: Knoxville, 10 miles north.

TEMPORARY MILITARY LODGING: Lodging office, C-615-985-3300. All ranks.

LOGISTICAL SUPPORT: Limited support facilities available.

Exchange-985-3400

HEALTH & WELFARE: McGhee Tyson Outpatient services, C-985-4277.

SPACE-A: Base Ops, C-615-985-4403, D-312-266-4403, flights to CONUS and OCONUS locations.

ATTRACTIONS: Great Smokey Mountains National Park, Cherokee National Forest, and Douglas Lake.

MEMPHIS NAVAL SUPPORT ACTIVITY (TN01R2)
7800 Third Avenue
Millington, TN 38054-5045

TELEPHONE NUMBER INFORMATION: Main installation numbers: C-901-873-5111, D-312-966-5111.

LOCATION: From US-51 north, follow signs. USMRA: Page 40 (B-9,10). NMC: Memphis, 11 miles southwest.

GENERAL INFORMATION: Naval and Marine Corps Aviation Training Groups.

TEMPORARY MILITARY LODGING: Lodging office, Bldg. S-1, 24 hours daily, C-901-873-5459/5348, D-312-966-5459/5348, Fax 901-873-7271. All ranks. DV/VIP, C-901-873-5459/5384.

LOGISTICAL SUPPORT: Complete support facilities available.

Cafeteria-872-1170	CHAMPUS-873-5824	Chaplain-873-5341
Child Care-873-5745	Commissary-873-5122	Conv Store-872-1334
CPO Club-873-5664/5442	EM Club-873-5131	Exchange-872-7716/0138
Family Services-873-5075	Gas Station-872-2241	Legal-873-5201
Locator-873-5111	Medical-873-5444	O'Club-873-5115
Package Store-873-1660	Police-873-5533	Public Affairs-873-5761
Retiree Services-873-5195	SATO-872-0104	Theater-873-5749

HEALTH & WELFARE: Naval Hospital, clinics and depts, Emergency C-901-873-5444, Appointments C-901-873-5801, 230 beds. Chapel serving all faiths C-901-873-5828.

TENNESSEE
Memphis Naval Support Activity, continued

RECREATION: Bowling EX-5779, Golf EX-5168, Gym EX-5383, Rod/Gun Club EX-5665, Library EX-5683, Swimming EX-5187, Rec Center EX-5498, Tennis EX-5163, Stables EX-5301. Rec Area on base, C-901-872-1573, D-312-966-5163, 12 camper spaces.

SPACE-A: None. Try Memphis IAP, ANG Area, C-901-541-7131/7132, D-312-966-8131/8132, Fax 901-541-7230, flights to CONUS and OCONUS locations.

ATTRACTIONS: Graceland, Peabody Hotel, Mud Island, Libertyland, The Orpheum, Overton Square, Memphis Zoo, and historic Beale Street..."Home of the Blues."

TENNESSEE NATIONAL GUARD ARMORY, HOUSTON BARRACKS (TN09R2)
3041 Sidco Drive (P.O. Box 41502)
Nashville, TN 37204-1502

TELEPHONE NUMBER INFORMATION: Main installation numbers: C-615-532-3061/3062, D-312-778-3061/3062.

LOCATION: I-65 south, to Armory Drive exit, USMRA: Page 40 (G,H-8). NMC: Nashville, four miles northwest.

GENERAL INFORMATION: Headquarters Tennessee Army National Guard and Tennessee Air National Guard, 194th Engineer Brigade.

TEMPORARY MILITARY LODGING: None. See Fort Campbell, KY listing, C-502-798-5281/618. Reservations C-615-431-5107, D-312-635-2865.

LOGISTICAL SUPPORT: Very limited support facilities.

Exchange-532-3297   Legal-532-3054   SATO-532-3294

HEALTH & WELFARE: See Fort Campbell, KY listing, C-502-798-8287/439-8287.

SPACE-A: Try Nashville IAP, Bldg. 723, 0700-1530, C-615-361-4600, D-312-446-6438. Flights to CONUS and OCONUS locations via ANG C-130A aircraft.

ATTRACTIONS: Opryland, Grand Ole Opry, Shopping, Sightseeing, The District.

Other Installations in Tennessee

Chattanooga Armory Exchange, 1801 Holtz Claw Ave. Chattanooga, TN 37404-5000.
USMRA: Page 41 (J-10). C-423-265-8941, Exchange-265-9941.
Defense Distribution Region Central, 2163 Airways Blvd. Memphis, TN 38114-5210.
USMRA: Page 40 (A-10), page 51 (B-3). C-901-775-6011, Consol Club-775-6343, Exchange-985-3400.
Kingsport Site Exchange, 4401 W. Stone Dr., Kingsport, TN 37660-1050.
USMRA: Page 41 (O-7). C-423-247-8721, Exchange-247-8721.
Nashville IAP/Tennessee ANGB, 240 Knapp Blvd, Nashville, TN 37217-25378.
USMRA: Page 40 (G, H-8). C-615-399-6000, Exchange-399-5638, Space A-399-6581.
Smyrna Exchange, Bldg. 607, A St., Smyrna, TN 37167-5000.
USMRA: Page 40 (H-8). C-615-459-6034, Exchange-459-6034.

TEXAS

DOLLAR RENT A CAR — Call 1-800-800-4000. Get a military rate by using your Military Living ID # ML3009. Retirees/Active Duty/Reserve/Guard.

BROOKS AIR FORCE BASE (TX26R3)
Brooks Air Force Base, TX 78235-5000

TELEPHONE NUMBER INFORMATION: Main installation numbers: C-210-536-1110, D-312-240-1110.

LOCATION: At the intersection of I-37 and Military Drive (Loop 13). USMRA: Page 91 (C-4). NMC: San Antonio, five miles northwest.

GENERAL INFORMATION: Air Force Materiel Command base. Human Systems Center, research laboratories, USAF School of Aerospace Medicine and support units.

TEMPORARY MILITARY LODGING: Lodging office, Bldg. 214, 24 hours daily, C-210-536-1844, D-312-240-1844. All ranks. DV/VIP C-210-536-3238.

LOGISTICAL SUPPORT: Complete support facilities available.

Brooks Club-536-3782
Child Care-536-2736
Exchange-533-9161
Human Resrcs-536-3821
Locator-536-1841
Public Affairs-536-3234
SDO/NCO-536-3278

CHAMPUS-536-2928
Commissary-536-2727
Family Services-536-2531
ITT Office-536-2077
Medical-536-1847
Retiree Services-536-2116
Snack Bar-536-2671/2140

Chaplain-536-3824
Conv Store-533-9161
Gas Station-532-2191
Legal-536-3301
Police-536-2851
SATO-536-1800/3230
Vet Clinic-536-2723

HEALTH & WELFARE: USAF Clinic, Emergency 911, 536-0911 (from housing), 8911 (from TML), Appointments C-210-536-1847. Inpatient, see Lackland AFB listing, C-210-670-7100. Chapel serving all faiths C-210-536-3824.

RECREATION: Auto Hobby EX-2624, Bowling EX-3763, Ceramics EX-2120, Golf EX-2636, Sports and Fitness Center EX-2342, SVS Office EX-3691, Library EX-2634, Picnic Area EX-2881, Swimming EX-3744, Community Center EX-2847, Wood Hobby EX-2120, Youth Center EX-2515. Fam-Camp on base, year round, C-210-536-1844, D-312-240-1844, seven camper spaces w/full hookups, eight camper spaces w/W&E hookups.

SPACE-A: None. See Kelly AFB listing, C-210-925-8714/5, D-312-945-8714/5.

ATTRACTIONS: Close to San Antonio, Sea World of Texas, museums, missions, The Alamo, San Antonio Zoo, Sea World, Fiesta Texas.

CAMP MABRY (TX39R3)
2210 West 35th Street
Austin, TX 78703

TELEPHONE NUMBER INFORMATION: Main installation numbers: C-512-465-5001.

U.S. FORCES TRAVEL & TRANSFER GUIDE U.S.A. - 265

TEXAS
Camp Mabry, continued

LOCATION: From Dallas, take I-35 to Austin, right onto 38 1/2 Street exit (turns onto 35th Street West). Cross over Loop 1, installation is on the right. USMRA: Page 87 (K-5). NMC: Austin, in city limits.

GENERAL INFORMATION: Texas National Guard Headquarters.

TEMPORARY MILITARY LODGING: Lodging office, C-512-465-5500.

LOGISTICAL SUPPORT: Most support facilities available.

CHAMPUS-465-5145   Family Services-465-5000   Legal-465-5057
Police-465-5001   Public Affairs-465-5059   Retiree Services-465-5090
SATO-452-5222   Snack Bar-706-6720

HEALTH & WELFARE: None. See Fort Hood listing, C-817-288-8888.

SPACE-A: Robert Gray Army Airfield, Bldg. 13, 0800-1700 Mon-Fri, C-817-288-9281, D-312-738-9281, Fax 817-288-1930, occasional flights available within US, C-817-288-9718 after 1800 hours.

CORPUS CHRISTI NAVAL AIR STATION (TX10R3)
11001 D Street
Suite 143
Corpus Christi Naval Air Station, TX 78419-5021

TELEPHONE NUMBER INFORMATION: Main installation numbers: C-512-939-2811, D-312-861-1110.

LOCATION: On TX-358, southeast side of Corpus Christi. The south gate is on NAS Drive. USMRA: Page 87 (K-8). NMC: Corpus Christi, 10 miles west.

GENERAL INFORMATION: Naval Air Training Command, Coast Guard Air Station, and Corpus Christi Army Depot.

TEMPORARY MILITARY LODGING: Lodging office, 24 hours daily, Bldg. 1281, Ocean Drive C-512-939-2388/89 D-312-861-2388/89, Fax C-512-939-3275. Navy Lodge, Bldg. 1281, 0800-1800 Mon-Fri, 0900-1800 Sat-Sun, C-512-937-6361. All ranks. DV/VIP C-512-939-2388/89, Fax 512-939-3275.

LOGISTICAL SUPPORT: Complete support facilities available.

CDO/OOD-939-2383   CHAMPUS-939-3238   Chaplain-939-3751
Child Care-939-8702   Commissary-939-3177   CPO Club-939-2541
Conv Store-939-3122   EM Club-939-2541   Exchange-939-2166
Family Services-939-3722 Fire Dept-939-3333   Gas Station-939-7910
Golf Course-939-3250   ITT Office-939-3637   Legal-939-3531/3532
Locator-939-2383   Medical-939-3446   MWR-939-2267/3497
NCO-939-2541   O' Club-939-2541   Package Store-939-2166
Police-939-2480   Public Affairs-939-3420   Recreation-939-3497
Retiree Services-939-3113 RV/Camping-937-5071   SATO-937-8806
Snack Bar-939-3444   Theater-939-3497   Visitor Center-939-3722

TEXAS
Corpus Christi Naval Air Station, continued

HEALTH & WELFARE: Naval Hospital, Emergency C-512-939-3735, Appointments C-512-939-3154, 195 beds. Chapel serving all faiths C-512-939-3751.

RECREATION: Arts/Crafts EX-3169, Auto Hobby EX-3470, Golf EX-3250, Gym EX-3164, Camping Equip 937-5071, Party House EX-2444, Skeet Range EX-2444, Picnic Area EX-2444, Library EX-3574. Shields Park Recreation Area on base, year round, C-512-937-5071, 24 camper spaces w/W&E, five tent spaces.

SPACE-A: Pax Term, Hangar 58, 0800-1700 Mon-Fri, C-512-939-2505, D-312-861-2505, flights to CONUS locations. Also, check with CGAS, C-512-939-2052.

ATTRACTIONS: Bay and gulf water sports. Also, symphony, museums, and historical homes.

DALLAS NAVAL AIR STATION (TX12R3)
Dallas Naval Air Station, TX 75211-5000

NOTE: Dallas NAS will move to Fort Worth NAS/Joint Reserve Base in 1996. Dallas NAS will close after the move is complete. Call ahead to ensure that the facility you need is still operating.

TELEPHONE NUMBER INFORMATION: Main installation numbers: C-214-266-6111, D-312-874-6111.

LOCATION: Exit from I-30 at loop 12, west of Dallas, go south on loop 12 to Jefferson Ave exit, NAS on left (south) side of Ave. Near Grand Prairie. USMRA: Page 88 (E-3). NMC: Dallas, 15 miles northeast.

GENERAL INFORMATION: Tactical Naval and Marine Corps Aircraft Units, and ANG and Army Reserve Air Units here.

TEMPORARY MILITARY LODGING: Lodging office, Bldg. 209, 24 hours daily, C-214-266-6155, D-312-874-61355, Fax 214-266-6608. All ranks. DV/VIP C-214-266-6103/6104.

LOGISTICAL SUPPORT: Most support facilities available.

Cafeteria-266-6524
Conv Store-266-6409
Family Services-266-6137
Legal-266-6105
Medical-266-6284
Retiree Services-266-6137
Snack Bar-266-6405
Chaplain-266-6132
Desert Storm Club-6424
Gas Station-266-6440
Locator-266-6111
Package Store-266-6409
SATO-266-6639
Child Care-266-6275
Exchange-266-6411
ITT Office-266-6108
McDonalds-264-2402
Police-266-6139
SDO/NCO-266-6120/6215

HEALTH & WELFARE: Naval Branch Medical Clinic, Emergency C-214-266-6284, Appointments, C-214-266-6284. Chapel serving all faiths, C-214-266-6132.

RECREATION: Auto Hobby, Bowling, Rec Equip, Athletic Dir EX-6109. Mountain Creek Lake and Marina on base, year round, C-214-266-6427, D-312-874-6427.

SPACE-A: Pax Term/Lounge, Bldg. 20, 0700-2200 daily, C-214-266-6651, D-312-874-6651, Fax 214-266-6253, flights to CONUS locations.

TEXAS
Dallas Naval Air Station, continued

ATTRACTIONS: Dallas. Theater Center, Cotton Bowl, Zoo, Aquarium, Museum of Natural History, Telephone Pioneer Museum of Texas, Professional Sports.

DYESS AIR FORCE BASE (TX14R3)
650 Second Street
Dyess Air Force Base, TX 79607-1960

TELEPHONE NUMBER INFORMATION: Main installation numbers: C-915-696-0212, D-312-461-1110.

LOCATION: Main gate is three miles east of I-20 and US-277. USMRA: Page 87 (I-3). NMC: Abilene, six miles northeast.

GENERAL INFORMATION: Air Combat Command Base. 7th Wing and support units.

TEMPORARY MILITARY LODGING: Lodging office, 441 Fifth St., Dyess Inn, 24 hours daily, C-915-692-8610, D-312-461-8610. All ranks. DV/VIP C-915-696-5610.

LOGISTICAL SUPPORT: Complete support facilities available.

Cafeteria-698-1720
Child Care-696-4337
Conv Store-692-4771
Gas Station-692-6721
Medical-696-4677
Police-696-2131
CHAMPUS-696-5114
Commissary-696-2434
Exchange-692-8976
Legal-696-3305
O'Club-696-2405
SATO-696-4743
Chaplain-696-4224
Consol Club-696-4311
Family Services-696-5996
Locator-696-3098
Package Store-696-3497
Theater-696-4320

HEALTH & WELFARE: USAF Hospital, Emergency C-915-696-2334, Appointments C-915-696-4677, 40 beds. Chapel serving all faiths C-915-696-4224.

RECREATION: Arts/Crafts EX-4175, Auto Hobby EX-4179, Bowling EX-4166, Golf EX-5067, Gym EX-4306, Rec Equip EX-2402, Library EX-2618, Rec Center EX-4305, Swimming EX-3346, Stables EX-3471, Youth Center 696-4797.

SPACE-A: Pax Term/Lounge, 674 Alert Ave., 24 hours daily, C-915-696-3108/2237, D-312-461-3108/2237, flights to CONUS, OCONUS and foreign locations.

ATTRACTIONS: Abilene, outdoor sports, Abilene Zoo, and Dyess Linear Air Park.

FORT BLISS (TX06R3)
Fort Bliss, TX 79916-0058

TELEPHONE NUMBER INFORMATION: Main installation numbers: C-915-568-2121, D-312-978-2121.

LOCATION: Accessible from I-10 or US-54. USMRA: Page 86 (B,C-5,6). NMC: El Paso, within city limits.

GENERAL INFORMATION: Air Defense Artillery Center and School, Sergeants Major Academy, 11th Air Defense Artillery Brigade, 3rd Armored Cavalry Regiment, 6th Air Defense Artillery Brigade, Range Command, 1st Combined Arms Support Battalion, William Beaumont Army Medical Center, and other units.

TEXAS
Fort Bliss, continued

TEMPORARY MILITARY LODGING: Lodging office, Bldg. 251, Club Rd, 24 hours daily, C-915-568-4888, D-312-978-4888. All ranks. DV/VIP C-915-568-5319/5225. New YMCA Residence Center on William Beaumont Medical Center, C-915-562-8461. Fort Bliss Inn, room. C-915-565-7777.

LOGISTICAL SUPPORT: Complete support facilities available.

Carlson Travel-562-2340	CHAMPUS-569-2536	Chaplain-568-5992
Child Care-562-3843	Commissary-568-4022	Conv Store-562-3774
Exchange-562-7200	Family Service-568-4614	Gas Station-562-2353
ITR Office-568-7506	Legal-568-6513	Locator-568-1113
Medical-569-2450	NCO Club-562-5969	O'Club-568-2738
Package Store-566-8371	Police-568-2115/6	Retiree Services-568-2632
SDO/NCO-568-4233/1501		

HEALTH & WELFARE: William Beaumont Army Medical Center, Emergency C-915-569-2209, 340 beds. Chapels serving all faiths C-915-568-3194/5992 and C-915-568-5106/1519.

RECREATION: Auto Hobby EX-7280/1172, Bowling EX-6272/1685, Golf 562-1273/2066, Gym EX-6281/8693, Rec Equip EX-7705, Music/Theater EX-2595/7427, Picnic Area EX-6097, Saddle Club EX-8648, Rod/Gun Club EX-2983, Library EX-2489, Swimming EX-7431, Tickets EX-6498/5210, Youth Center EX-5437, Rec Center EX-3881/8276. RV Park on post, year round, C-915-568-4693, D-312-978-4693, 73 camper spaces w/full hookups, eight tent spaces.

SPACE-A: Biggs Army Airfield, Bldg. 11210, 0600-2200 Mon-Fri, 0800-1600 Sat-Sun, C-915-568-8097, D-312-978-8097, limited CONUS flights.

ATTRACTIONS: Four museums (Fort Bliss, Air Defense Artillery, 3rd Armored Cavalry Regiment, and Non-commissioned Officer) on post, Carlsbad Caverns National Park, White Sands National Monument, Ciudad Juarez. El Paso Symphony, El Paso Diablos (minor league baseball, Double-A), and Tigua Indian Reservation.

FORT HOOD (TX02R3)
Fort Hood, TX 76544-5000

TELEPHONE NUMBER INFORMATION: Main installation numbers: C-817-287/288-1110, D-312-737/738-1110. NOTE: Prefix for extensions listed below is 287.

LOCATION: From I-35 north, exit to US-190 west, nine miles to Killeen. Main gate is clearly marked. USMRA: Page 87 (K-4,5). NMC: Killeen, at main entrance.

GENERAL INFORMATION: Armored Corps Headquarters, and headquarters for 1st Cavalry Division and 4th Infantry Division (Mechanized), 6th Cavalry Brigade, 13th Corps Support Command, 3rd Signal Brigade, 89th Military Police Brigade, 504th Military Intelligence Group, 3rd Air Support Group (AF), 31st Air Defense Artillery Brigade, Medical Activity, Dental Activity, and TEXCOM (Test Activity) and the Combat Aviation Training Brigade.

TEMPORARY MILITARY LODGING: Lodging office, Bldg. 36006, Wratten Dr, 24 hours daily, C-817-287-3815/27008, D-312-738-3815/27008, Fax 817-288-7604. DV/VIP C-817-287-5001.

TEXAS
Fort Hood, continued

LOGISTICAL SUPPORT: Complete support facilities available.

ACS-287-3071	CDO/OOD-287-2520/2506	CHAMPUS-288-8155
Chaplain-287-1625	Child Care-287-5448	Commissary-287-4575
Conv Store-532-3089	EM Club-287-6737	Exchange-532-5962
Family Services-287-4031	Gas Station-532-7353	Golf Course-287-3466/4
ITT Office-287-7310	Legal-287-5297	Locator-287-2137/7486
Medical-288-8000	MWR-287-8109	NCO Club-532-3317
O'Club-532-5329	Package Store-532-5239	Police-287-2176
Public Affairs-287-0103	Recreation-288-4636	Retiree Services-287-5210
RV/Camping-287-4447	SATO-532-8958	SDO/NCO-287-2520/25
Snack Bar-532-7293	Theater-287-3350	Visitor Center-287-4936

HEALTH & WELFARE: Darnall Army Community Hospital, Ambulance C-817-288-8111, Emergency C-817-288-8113, Appointments C-817-288-8888, 225 beds. Chapels serving all faiths C-817-287-1624/5283.

RECREATION: Arts/Crafts 288-2970, Auto Hobby EX-2725, Bowling EX-3424, Golf EX-4130/3466, Rec Equip EX-4126, Skating Center EX-5623, Hunting/Fishing EX-5841, Archery EX-4907, Library EX-5202/2739 & 288-9520, Marina EX-8300, Pool EX-5037/288-9882, Swimming/Beach EX-6644, Rec Center EX-288-7911 & 288-9828/0353, Youth Activities EX-2330, Boat Rental EX-5526, Music Center EX-6116. Dirt Riders Club 532-4552, Hunt/Saddle Club, Riding Club, Rod/Gun Club, Sport Parachute Club EX-5847. West Fort Hood Travel Camp on post, year round, C-817-288-9926, D-312-738-9926, 64 camper spaces w/full hookups, 20 tent spaces. Belton Lake Recreation Area on post, year round, C-817-287-2523, D-312-737-2523, 10 cottages, 11 camper spaces w/full hookups, 48 camper spaces w/W&E hookups, 41 tent spaces.

SPACE-A: Robert Gray Army Airfield, Bldg. 13, 0800-1700 Mon-Fri, C-817-288-9281, D-312-738-9281, Fax 817-288-1930, occasional flights available within US.

ATTRACTIONS: State capital, Austin. Hunting and fishing.

FORT SAM HOUSTON (TX18R3)
Fort Sam Houston, TX 78234-5000

TELEPHONE NUMBER INFORMATION: Main installation number: C-210-221-1211.

LOCATION: Accessible from I-410 or I-35. USMRA: Page 91 (C,D-2,3). NMC: San Antonio, in city limits.

GENERAL INFORMATION: Headquarters 5th Army, Headquarters 90th Army Reserve Command, Headquarters US Army Medical Command, US Army Medical Dept and School, Brooke Army Medical Center, US Army Dental Command, US Army Veterinary Command, 41st Combat Support Hospital.

TEMPORARY MILITARY LODGING: Lodging office, Bldg. 592, Dickman Rd, 24 hours daily, C-210-221-6125/6262, D-312-471-6125/6262, Fax C-210-221-6275. All ranks.

LOGISTICAL SUPPORT: Complete support facilities available.

ACS-221-2705	CHAMPUS-916-9989	Chaplain-221-9680
Child Care-221-5002	Commissary-221-4690	Conv Store-225-0216

TEXAS
Fort Sam Houston, continued

EM Club-224-2721
Fire Dept-221-2727
ITT Office-221-0703
Locator-221-3315
O'Club-224-4211
Retiree Services-221-5958
Snack Bar-228-9071

Exchange-225-5566
Gas Station-228-9001
ITR-221-2333
Medical-916-6141
Package Store-223-3427
Carlson Travel-225-5261

Family Services-221-2705
Golf Course-222-9386
Legal-221-2353
NCO Club-224-2721
Police-221-0463
SDO/NCO-221-2810

HEALTH & WELFARE: Brooke Army Medical Center, Emergency C-512-221-6466, Appointments C-210-916-6771. Chapel serving all faiths C-512-221-1688.

RECREATION: Arts/Crafts EX-7125, Auto Hobby 224-7046, Bowling EX-3683/4740, Golf EX-5863/4388, Gym EX-2593, Outdoor Rec EX-3703/224-7162, Stables 224-7207, Hunting/Fishing EX-7367, Library EX-3702, Swimming EX-3290/5993, Rec Center EX-4829/2892/4743/2333, Theater (Plays) EX-5953, Youth Center EX-7882, Music and Theater EX-2186. Canyon Lake Army Recreation Area, off post, year round, C-210-221-0703/2333, D-312-471-0703/2333, 32 camper spaces w/W&E hookups, 32 mobile homes.

SPACE-A: None. See Kelly AFB listing, 210-925-8714/5, D-312-945-8714/5.

ATTRACTIONS: San Antonio, Botanical Gardens. Gulf Coast and Mexico nearby, Natural Bridge Caverns. Sea World, Fiesta Texas Amusement Park, Historic Fort Sam Houston, The Alamo, San Antonio Riverwalk.

FORT WORTH NAVAL AIR STATION/JOINT RESERVE BASE (TX21R3)
Building 1215
Fort Worth Naval Air Station/Joint Reserve Base, TX 76127-5000

TELEPHONE NUMBER INFORMATION: Main installation numbers: C-817-782-7445, D-312-739-7445.

LOCATION: On TX-183. From Fort Worth, west on I-30, exit at Carswell AFB/Horne St. Follow signs to main gate. USMRA: Page 88 (A-3). NMC: Fort Worth, seven miles east.

GENERAL INFORMATION: Air Combat Command Base. Bomb Wing and AFRES units.

TEMPORARY MILITARY LODGING: Lodging office, Bldg. 3140, 6th St & Meandering Road, 24 hours daily, C-817-782-5449, D-312-739-5274, Fax C-817-782-7606. All ranks. DV/VIP C-817-782-7614.

LOGISTICAL SUPPORT: Complete support facilities available.

CHAMPUS-782-4827
Commissary-782-5446
Exchange-738-1943
Legal-782-7595
O'Club-782-5631
Retiree Services-782-5661
Snack Bar-731-2075

Chaplain-782-7301
Conv Store-731-4187
Family Services-782-7877
Locator-782-7082/5000
Package Store-738-0462
SATO-782-5579
Theater-782-5450

Child Care-782-5753
EM Club-782-5293
Gas Station-738-1002
Medical-782-4000
Police-782-5200
SDO/NCO-782-5555

TEXAS
Fort Worth Naval Air Station/Joint Reserve Base, continued

HEALTH & WELFARE: Emergency C-817-782-4050, Appointments C-817-782-4500. Chapel serving all faiths C-817-782-7301.

RECREATION: Arts/Crafts EX-7114, Auto Hobby EX-7114, Bowling EX-5505, Fitness Center EX-7770, Golf 738-8402, Rec Equip EX-7972, Marina EX-7972, MWR Office EX-5411, Rec Center EX-7077, Swimming EX-7770/7869, Tennis EX-7770, Library EX-5230, Youth Center EX-5498.

SPACE-A: Pax Term/Lounge, Bldg. 1423, 0730-1630 Mon-Fri, C-817-782-5649/7513, D-312-739-5649/7513, flights to CONUS, OCONUS and foreign locations.

ATTRACTIONS: Zoo, Fort Worth Botanic Gardens, Museum of Science and History. Dallas, Six Flags over Texas.

GOODFELLOW AIR FORCE BASE (TX24R3)
184 Lancaster Ave., Suite J
Goodfellow Air Force Base, TX 76908-5000

TELEPHONE NUMBER INFORMATION: Main installation numbers: C-915-654-3231, D-312-477-3217.

LOCATION: Off US-87 or US-277. Clearly marked. USMRA: Page 86 (H-6,7). NMC: San Angelo, two miles northwest.

GENERAL INFORMATION: Air Education and Training Command.

TEMPORARY MILITARY LODGING: Lodging office, Bldg. 3305, Kearney Blvd, 24 hours daily, C-915-654-3332/3206, D-312-477-3332/3206. All ranks.

LOGISTICAL SUPPORT: Complete support facilities available.

CHAMPUS-654-3276
Commissary-653-3357
Family Service-654-3420
Locator-654-3231
NCO Club-655-3256
Police-654-3504
SATO-655-5139

Chaplain-654-3424
Conv Store-655-5794
Gas Station-655-5793
Medical-654-3049
O'Club-654-5327
Public Affairs-654-3876
SDO/NCO-654-3044

Child Care-654-3239
Exchange-655-3361
Legal-654-3203
MWR-654-3853
Package Store-654-3249
Retiree Services-654-3813
Theater-654-3206

HEALTH & WELFARE: Appointments C-915-654-3150. Inpatient, see Dyess AFB listing, 915-696-4677. Chapel serving all faiths C-915-654-3424.

RECREATION: Arts/Crafts EX-3233, Auto Hobby EX-3233, Bowling EX-3227, Gym EX-3242, Rod/Gun Club EX-3246, Library EX-3232, Swimming EX-3226, Rec Center EX-3247, Theater EX-3206. Fort Worth NAS/JRB Recreation Camp, off base, year round Thu-Mon, C-915-944-1012, D-312-477-3217, 19 camper spaces w/W&E hookups.

SPACE-A: Limited. See Dyess AFB listing, C-915-696-3108, D-312-461-3108.

ATTRACTIONS: Lakes, Fort Concho and city of San Angelo.

TEXAS

INGLESIDE NAVAL STATION (TX30R3)
1455 Ticonderoga, Suite W123
Ingleside, TX 73862-5001

TELEPHONE NUMBER INFORMATION: Main installation numbers: C-512-776-4201, D-312-776-4201.

LOCATION: I-37 south to Route 361 to Route 1069. USMRA: Page 87 (K,L-8). NMC: Corpus Christi, 37 miles south

TEMPORARY MILITARY LODGING: Lodging office, C-512-776-4420, D-312-776-4420, Fax 512-776-4519.

LOGISTICAL SUPPORT: Limited support facilities available.

Exchange-776-4534

HEALTH & WELFARE: Branch Medical Clinic, C-512-776-4200.

SPACE-A: Limited. See Corpus Christi listing, C-512-939-2505, D-312-861-2505.

ATTRACTIONS: Bay and gulf water sports. Also, symphony, museums, and historical homes.

KELLY AIR FORCE BASE (TX03R3)
807 Buckner Drive
Suite 1
Kelly Air Force Base, TX 78241-5842

TELEPHONE NUMBER INFORMATION: Main installation numbers: C-210-925-1110, D-312-945-1110.

LOCATION: All of the following, I-10, I-35, I-37, I-410 intersect with US-90. From US-90 take either the Gen Hudnell or Gen McMullen exit and go south to AFB. USMRA: Page 91 (B-3,4). NMC: San Antonio, seven miles northeast.

GENERAL INFORMATION: Air Force Materiel Command Base. San Antonio Air Logistics Center, Air Intelligence Agency, Electronic Warfare Center, Air Force News Center, AFRES and ANG units.

TEMPORARY MILITARY LODGING: Lodging office, Bldg. 1676, 24 hours daily, C-210-925-1844/924-7201, D-312-945-8931. All ranks. DV/VIP 210-925-7678.

LOGISTICAL SUPPORT: Complete support facilities available.

Cafeteria-925-4990
Child Care-925-5747
Family Services-925-4181
Golf Course-925-4006
Locator-925-1841
NCO Club-924-8354
Public Affairs-925-7951
SATO-925-7371
CHAMPUS-925-8206
Commissary-925-6991
Fire Dept-925-5526
ITT Office-925-4584
Medical-925-6333
O'Club-924-8254
Retiree Services-925-9314
SDO/NCO-925-6906
Chaplain-925-7874
Exchange-924-9247
Gas Station-924-2960
Legal-925-3095
MWR-925-7144
Police-925-6811
RV/Camping-925-5725
Visitor Center-925-5551

TEXAS
Kelly Air Force Base, continued

HEALTH & WELFARE: USAF Clinic, Emergency C-210-925-4544, Appointments C-210-925-8811. Inpatient, see Lackland AFB listing, C-210-670-7100. Chapel serving all faiths C-210-925-7874.

RECREATION: Arts/Crafts EX-8346, Auto Hobby EX-3872, Bowling EX-5933/ 5480, Golf EX-4006, Gym EX-4846, Rec Services Office EX-4584, Aero Club EX-3825, Library EX-4116, Swimming EX-4846, Youth Center EX-8100. Fam-Camp on base, year round, C-210-925- 5725, 30 camper spaces w/full hookups.

SPACE-A: Pax Term/Lounge, Bldg. 1614, 0700-1800 Mon-Fri, 0800-1600 Sat-Sun, C-210-925-8714/8715, D-312-945-8714/5, flights to CONUS, OCONUS and foreign locations.

ATTRACTIONS: The Alamo, River Walk, Tower of the Americas, San Antonio Zoo, Institute of Texas Cultures and McNay Art Museum.

KINGSVILLE NAVAL AIR STATION (TX22R3)
802 Dealey Avenue, Suite 103
Kingsville, TX 78363-5027

TELEPHONE NUMBER INFORMATION: Main installation numbers: C-512-595-6136, D-312-861-6136.

LOCATION: Off US-77 south, exit to TX-425 southeast to main gate. USMRA: Page 87 (K-9). NMC: Corpus Christi, 30 miles northeast.

GENERAL INFORMATION: Training Air Wing # 2, two squadrons, and support units.

TEMPORARY MILITARY LODGING: Lodging office, Bldg. 3729, duty hours, C-512-595-6321/6309, D-312-861-6321/6309, Fax 512-595-6428. All ranks. DV/VIP C-512-595-6136/6321.

LOGISTICAL SUPPORT: Complete support facilities available.

CHAMPUS-595-6238	Chaplain-595-6331	Child Care-595-6176
Commissary-595-6241	Conv Store-595-6106	CPO Club-595-6121
EM Club-595-6121	Exchange-595-6361	Family Services-595-6333
Gas Station-595-6106	ITT Office-595-6449	Legal-595-6426
Medical-595-6305	O'Club-595-6121	Package Store-595-6473
Police-595-6217	Retiree Services-595-6533	SDO/NCO-595-6136

HEALTH & WELFARE: Naval Branch Medical Clinic, Emergency C-512-595-6911, Appointments C-512-595-6342. Inpatient, see Corpus Christi NAS listing, C-512-939-3154. Chapel serving all faiths C-512-595-6331.

RECREATION: Arts/Crafts, Auto Hobby, Bowling, Nautilus Center, Tennis, Gym, Swimming, Picnic Area, hunting at Escondido Ranch: call EX-6171/6172.

SPACE-A: Very limited, C-512-595-6108, D-312-861-6108. Also see Corpus Christi NAS listing.

ATTRACTIONS: Gulf Coast, Corpus Christi, King Ranch, and fishing in Baffin Bay.

274 - U.S. FORCES TRAVEL & TRANSFER GUIDE U.S.A
TEXAS

LACKLAND AIR FORCE BASE (TX25R3)
2000 Bong Ave.
Suite 2
Lackland Air Force Base, TX 78236-5110

TELEPHONE NUMBER INFORMATION: Main installation numbers: C-210-671-1110, D-312-473-1110.

LOCATION: Off US-90 south. Loop 13 (Military Drive) bisects Lackland AFB. USMRA: Page 87 (J-6,7), page 91 (A,B-3). NMC: San Antonio, six miles northeast.

GENERAL INFORMATION: Air Training Command Installation, Host: 37th Training Wing, Basic and technical training, Defense Language Institute English Language Center, Inter-American Air Forces Academy, Tenant: 59th Medical Wing (Wilford Hall Medical Center).

TEMPORARY MILITARY LODGING: Lodging office, Bldg. 10203, 24 hours daily, C-210-671-4277. All ranks. DV/VIP C-210-671-3622.

LOGISTICAL SUPPORT: Complete support facilities available.

CDO/OOD-671-4225
Child Care-671-3168
Exchange-674-8965
Family Spt-671-3069
ITT Office-671-3133
Medical-670-7100
O'Club-671-2524
Public Affairs-671-2907
SATO-673-9057
Visitor Center-671-3024

CHAMPUS-670-6858
Commissary-671-2830
Family Services-671-3722
Gas Station-673-0848
Legal-671-3367
MWR-671-3395
Package Store-674-0848
Recreation-671-4269
Snack Bar-671-4047

Chaplain-671-4104
Conv Store-674-0848
Fire Dept-671-2921
Golf Course-671-3466
Locator-671-1841
NCO Club-671-2110
Police-671-2018
Retiree Services-671-2728
Theater-673-8077

HEALTH & WELFARE: Wilford Hall Medical Center C-210-670-7100, Emergency C-210-670-7331, 690 beds. Chapel serving all faiths C-210-670-7373.

RECREATION: Arts/Crafts EX-2515, Auto Hobby EX-3549, Bowling EX-2271, Golf EX-3466, Gym EX-2554, Rec Equip EX-3106, Rod/Gun Club 674-7831, Library EX-2678, Swimming EX-3445, Rec Center EX-2619. Fam-Camp on base, year round, C-210-671-3106, D-312-473-3106, 24 camper spaces w/full hookups.

SPACE-A: None. See Kelly AFB listing, C-210-925-8714/8715, D-312-945-8714/8715.

ATTRACTIONS: City of San Antonio, Zoo, River Walk, The Alamo, El Mercado La Villita, Institute of Texan Cultures, Spanish missions, McNay Art Institute, Sea world of Texas, Fiesta Texas.

LAUGHLIN AIR FORCE BASE (TX05R3)
Laughlin Air Force Base, TX 78843-5227

TELEPHONE NUMBER INFORMATION: Main installation numbers: C-210-298-3511, D-312-732-1110.

U.S. FORCES TRAVEL & TRANSFER GUIDE U.S.A. - 275

TEXAS
Laughlin Air Force Base, continued

LOCATION: Take US-90 west from San Antonio, 150 miles or US-277 south from San Angelo, 150 miles to Del Rio area. The AFB is clearly marked off US-90. USMRA: Page 86 (H-9). NMC: Del Rio, six miles northwest.

GENERAL INFORMATION: Air Training Command Base. Undergrad Pilot Training, Flying Training Wing.

TEMPORARY MILITARY LODGING: Lodging office, Bldg. 470, 7th St, 24 hours daily, C-210-298-5731, D-312-732-5731. All ranks. DV/VIP C-210-298-5041.

LOGISTICAL SUPPORT: Complete support facilities available.

CDO/OOD-298-5167	CHAMPUS-298-6301	Chaplain-298-5111
Child Care-298-5419	Commissary-298-5821	Conv Store-298-3867
Exchange-298-3627	Family Services-298-5222	Fire Dept-298-5035
Gas Station-298-3867	Golf Course-298-5451	Legal-298-5172
Locator-298-3511	Medical-298-6362	MWR-298-5810
NCO Club-298-5407	O'Club-298-5374	Package Store-298-2111
Police-298-5100	Public Affairs-298-5988	SATO-298-2078
SDO/NCO-298-5167	Snack Bar-298-3001	Theater-298-5144

HEALTH & WELFARE: USAF Hospital, Emergency C-210-298-6333, Appointments C-210-298-5562. Chapel serving all faiths C-210-298-5111.

RECREATION: Arts/Crafts, Bowling EX-5526, Golf EX-5451, Gym EX-5251/5326, Marina 775-5971, Rec Center EX-5474. Skeet Range EX-5830, Stables EX-5830, Fam-Camp on base, year round, C-210-298-5474, D-312-732-5474, 15 camper spaces w/full hookups. Also operates Lake Amistad Rec Area, off base near, year round, C-210-775-5971, D-312-732-5971, six camper spaces w/hookups.

SPACE-A: C-210-298-5308, D-312-732-5308.

ATTRACTIONS: On the Mexican border at Ciudad Acuna, Mexico. Lake Amistad, Alamo Village.

RANDOLPH AIR FORCE BASE (TX19R3)
1 Washington Circle, Suite 4
Randolph Air Force Base, TX 78150-4562

TELEPHONE NUMBER INFORMATION: Main installation numbers: C-210-652-1110, D-312-487-1110.

LOCATION: From I-35, Pat Booker Rd exit. USMRA: Page 91 (E-2). NMC: San Antonio, five miles southwest.

GENERAL INFORMATION: Air Education and Training Command Base. 12th Flying Training Wing, Headquarters Air Training Command, Air Force Military Personnel Center, Hq Air Force Recruiting Service, and support units.

TEMPORARY MILITARY LODGING: Lodging office, Bldg. 118, 24 hours daily, C-210-652-1844, D-312-487-1844. All ranks. DV/VIP 652-4126.

LOGISTICAL SUPPORT: Complete support facilities available.

TEXAS
Randolph Air Force Base, continued

CHAMPUS-652-5524	Chaplain-652-6121/4659	Child Care-652-4946
Commissary-652-6545	Exchange-652-2681	Family Services-652-3060
Gas Station-658-1515	Legal-652-6781	Locator-652-1841
Medical-652-2734	NCO Club-658-3557	O'Club-658-7445
Package Store-658-4544	Police-652-5700	Retiree Services-652-6880
SATO-658-3585	SDO/NCO-652-1859	Shoppette-658-1717
Snack Bar-658-1440	Theater-652-3278	

HEALTH & WELFARE: USAF Clinic C-210-652-4373, Appointments C-210-652-2273. Inpatient, see Lackland AFB listing, C-210-670-7100. Chapels serving all faiths C-210-652-4659/6121.

RECREATION: Art/Crafts EX-2788, Auto Hobby EX-2952, Bowling EX-6271, Gym 652-2955/5955, Golf EX-4570, MWR Office EX-3012/3125, MWR Supply EX-3702, Hunt/Saddle EX-2346, Library 652-2617, Rec Equip 652-5268, Rec Center 652-2301, Youth Activities EX-3298, Skeet Range EX-2064. Off Base Recreation Area, year round (closed Mon-Tue), C-210-652-4125, 10 camper spaces w/W&E hookups, 45 tent spaces w/o hookups, 11 primitive shelters w/E hookups.

SPACE-A: Pax Term/Lounge, Hangar 7, east side, 0600-1800 Mon-Fri, Sat and Sun as required, C-210-652-1854/3725, D-312-487-1854/3725, Fax 210-652-5618, flights to CONUS locations.

ATTRACTIONS: San Antonio, New Braunfels and Canyon Lake. Rec areas are nearby.

RED RIVER ARMY DEPOT (TX09R3)
Building 15, Main Street
Texarkana, TX 75507-5000

TELEPHONE NUMBER INFORMATION: Main installation numbers: C-903-334-2141, D-312-829-2141, FTS-730-9031.

LOCATION: Off I-30, take Red River Army Depot exit. Route clearly marked. USMRA: Page 87 (N-2). NMC: Texarkana, 20 miles east.

GENERAL INFORMATION: Army Depot Activity for maintenance for armored vehicles, ammunition, and missiles.

TEMPORARY MILITARY LODGING: Lodging office, Bldg. 228, 0745-1645 daily, C-903-334-3976/3227, D-312-829-3976/3227. All ranks. DV/VIP C-903-334-2316.

LOGISTICAL SUPPORT: Most support facilities available.

CHAMPUS-334-2155	Comm Club-334-2350	Exchange-334-2396
Fam Services-334-2466	Legal-334-3258	Medical-334-2155
Police-334-2911	Retiree Services-334-2726	SDO/NCO-334-2911

HEALTH & WELFARE: US Army Health Clinic, Emergency C-903-334-2650, Appointments C-903-334-2155. Inpatient, see Barksdale AFB listing, C-318-456-6555.

RECREATION: Arts/Crafts EX-2441, Wood/Auto Shop EX-2088, Golf EX-2359, Gym EX-2733, Rod/Gun Club EX-2379/4868, Rec Services EX-3506. Elliott Lake Recreation

TEXAS
Red River Army Depot, continued

Area on post, year round, C-903-334-2254, D-312-829-2254, 16 camper spaces w/full hookups, 16 camper spaces w/W&E, 16 cabins, 20 tent spaces, five wooded screen shelters.

SPACE-A: None. See Little Rock AFB, AR listing, C-501-988-3684, D-312-731-3684.

ATTRACTIONS: Near Texarkana, TX/AR, outdoor sports and recreation.

REESE AIR FORCE BASE (TX20R3)
111 First Street, Suite 6
Reese Air Force Base, TX 79489-5301

Scheduled to close September 1997.

TELEPHONE NUMBER INFORMATION: Main installation numbers: C-806-885-4511, D-312-838-4511.

LOCATION: From I-289 (Loop) take 4th Street, six miles west. The road terminates at AFB, main gate is one block north. USMRA: Page 86 (F-4). NMC: Lubbock, six miles east.

GENERAL INFORMATION: Air Education Training Command. Flying Training Wing, Undergraduate Pilot Training, and support activities.

TEMPORARY MILITARY LODGING: Lodging office, Bldg. 1142, K St, 24 hours daily, C-806-885-3155, D-312-838-3155. All ranks. DV/VIP C-806-885-6187.

LOGISTICAL SUPPORT: Complete support facilities available.

Cafeteria-885-3226
Child Care-885-3317
EM Club-885-3156
Fire Dept-885-3311
ITT Office-885-3787
Medical-885-3245
Package Store-885-2427
Recreation-885-3787
SDO/NCO-885-3754
Visitor Center-885-6652
CHAMPUS-885-3581
Commissary-885-3315
Exchange-885-4581
Gas Station-885-4965
Legal-885-3505
NCO Club-885-3156
Police-885-3333
Retiree Services-885-3168
Snack Bar-885-2331
Chaplain-885-3237
Conv Store-885-2427
Family Services-885-3306
Golf Course-885-3819
Locator-885-3678
O'Club-885-3466
Public Affairs-885-3410
SATO-885-6144
Theater-885-3144

HEALTH & WELFARE: USAF Clinic C-806-885-3515, Appointments C-806-885-3245, No beds. Chapel serving all faiths C-806-885-3237.

RECREATION: Arts/Crafts EX-3241, Auto Hobby EX-3142, Bowling EX-3116, Golf EX-3819, Gym EX-3207, Rec Equip EX-3815, Picnic Area EX-3787, Rod/Gun Club EX-3412, Library EX-3344, Swimming EX-3371/3667, Rec Center EX-3787, Youth Center EX-3820.

SPACE-A: Pax Term/Lounge, Base Ops, Bldg. 79, 0700-1900 Mon-Thu, 2100 Fri, 0900-1600 Sat, 1000-1700 Sun. C-806-885-3105, D-312-838-3105, Fax 806-885-1028, used primarily for student training sortie preparation. Open only to accommodate student training operations. Closed when not supporting student training. Occasional Space-A flights available to CONUS locations. Commercial air and bus transportation from Lubbock is limited. No rail connections.

TEXAS
Reese Air Force Base, continued

ATTRACTIONS: Texas Tech University and Lubbock Christian College, Ranching Heritage Center, planetarium, museum. Agriculture and ranching. Outdoor recreation and hunting in season.

SHEPPARD AIR FORCE BASE (TX37R3)
419 G Avenue, Suite 3
Sheppard Air Force Base, TX 76311-2943

TELEPHONE NUMBER INFORMATION: Main installation numbers: C-817-676-2511, D-312-736-2511.

LOCATION: Take US-281 north from Wichita Falls, exit to TX-325 which leads to main gate. Clearly marked. USMRA: Page 87 (J-1). NMC: Wichita Falls, five miles southwest.

GENERAL INFORMATION: Air Education and Training Command. Sheppard Training Center, 80th Flying Training Wing & support units. 82nd Training, Logistics, Support, and Medical Groups. 782nd Training Group, 882nd Training Group, and 982nd Training Group.

TEMPORARY MILITARY LODGING: Lodging office, Bldg. 766, Ave H, 24 hours daily, C-817-855-7370, D-312-736-2631. All ranks. DV/VIP C-817-855-2123.

LOGISTICAL SUPPORT: Complete support facilities available.

Chaplain-676-2111	Child Care-676-2038	Commissary-676-2901
Conv Store-855-4341	EM Club-676-6427	Exchange-855-4318
Family Services-676-2300	Fire Dept-676-2310	Gas Station-855-4341
Golf Course-676-6369	ITT-676-2876	Legal-676-4262
Locator-676-1841	Medical-676-1847	MWR-676-2089
NCO Club-676-6427	O'Club-676-6460	Package Store-855-6502
Police-676-2981	Public Affairs-676-2732	Recreation-676-6210
Retiree Services-676-5088	SATO-676-4267	Snack Bar-855-5451
SDO/NCO-676-2621	Theater-676-4426	TRICARE-851-2709
Visitor Center-676-7441		

HEALTH & WELFARE: 82nd Medical Group (Sheppard Hospital), Emergency C-817-676-2333, Appointments C-817-676-1847, 90 beds. Chapel serving all faiths C-817-676-4370.

RECREATION: Arts/Crafts EX-6667, Auto Hobby EX-4110, Bowling EX-2677, Golf EX-6369, Gym EX-6133, Picnic Area EX-2876, Library EX-6152, Swimming EX-6494, Rec Center EX-6210, Skeet/Trap Range/Gun Club EX-6852. Sheppard Recreation Annex, off base, year round, C-903-523-4613, eight camper spaces w/full hookups, 16 camper spaces w/W&E hookups, 43 cabins, one mobile home.

SPACE-A: Pax Term/Lounge, Bldg. 1360, duty hours, C-817-676-2180/6474, D-312-736-2180/6474, flights to CONUS locations.

ATTRACTIONS: Wichita Falls and outdoor sports.

TEXAS

Other Installations in Texas

Biggs Field, 11210 CSM E. Slewitzke St., Biggs AAF, TX 79908-0053.
USMRA: Page 86 (B-6). C-915-568-2121, Gas Station-562-8442, Exchange-562-7200, Space A-568-8097.
Camp Bullis, Fort Sam Houston Training Site, TX 78234-5066.
USMRA: Page 87 (J-6); Page 91 (B,C-1). Exchange-698-1183.
Ellington Field ANGB/Houston CGAS, 14657 Sneider St., Houston, TX 77034-5586.
USMRA: Page 89 (D-4,5). C-713-929-2222, Exchange-484-5892.
Galveston Coast Guard Base, P.O. Box 1912, Galveston, TX 77553-1912.
USMRA: Page 87 (N-6). C-409-763-0724, CDO/OOD-766-5641, Chaplain-766-5667, Exchange-763-2203, Family Services-766-4751, Medical-766-5661, Public Affairs-766-5622.
Headquarters Army & Air Force Exchange Service, 3911 South Walton Walker Blvd, Dallas, TX 75236-1598. USMRA: Page 88 (F-4). C-214-312-2011, Exchange-312-2011.
Houston CG Marine Safety Office, 9640 Clinton Drive, Galena Park, TX 77547-0446.
USMRA: Page 89 (C-3). C-713-672-5100, Exchange-672-6639.
Waco Shoppette, 1801 Exchange Parkway, Waco, TX 76712-5000.
USMRA: Page 87 (K-4). C-817-666-8309, Exchange-666-8309.

UTAH

DOLLAR RENT A CAR — Call 1-800-800-4000. Get a military rate by using your Military Living ID # ML3009. Retirees/Active Duty/Reserve/Guard.

CAMP W.G. WILLIAMS (UT11R4)
17800 South Camp Williams Road
Riverton, UT 84065-4999

TELEPHONE NUMBER INFORMATION: Main installation numbers: C-801-576-3850, D-312-766-3669.

LOCATION: From I-15 take exit 296 (Draper/Riverton), turn west onto highway 111. Turn left at second traffic light, drive approximately seven miles, and Camp Williams is on the left. USMRA: Page 112 (D-4). NMC: Salt Lake City, 25 miles north.

GENERAL INFORMATION: Utah Regional Training Academy. Camp Williams is a National Guard training base.

TEMPORARY MILITARY LODGING: Lodging office, Bldg. 802, 1000-1700 Mon-Fri, 1000-1400 Sat-Sun. C-801-576-3674, D-312-766-3674.

LOGISTICAL SUPPORT: Limited support facilities available.

Cafeteria-576-3722
Medical-576-3871
O'Club-254-7623
Recreation-576-3674
Visitor Center-576-3669

Exchange-576-3815
MWR-576-3937
Police-576-3669
SATO-576-0285

Locator-576-3669
NCO Club-576-3722
Public Affairs-576-3978
Snack Bar-576-3722

HEALTH AND WELFARE: None. See Hill AFB listing, C-801-777-4061.

RECREATION: Physical Fitness Center 576-3864, Rec Equipment 576-3674.

SPACE-A: See Hill AFB listing, C-801-777-1854/2887, D-312-458-1854/2887, Fax 801-775-3249.

ATTRACTIONS: Salt Lake City: Temple Square, planetarium, Hogle Zoo, Trolley Square for shopping, Delta Center for pro sports. Close to skiing and hiking.

DUGWAY PROVING GROUND (UT04R4)
Dugway Proving Ground, UT 84022-5000

TELEPHONE NUMBER INFORMATION: Main installation numbers: C-801-831-2151, D-312-789-2151. **NOTE:** When calling from Salt Lake City the prefix is 522 instead of 831.

LOCATION: Isolated but can be reached from I-80. Take Skull Valley Road (exit 77) for 40 miles south. USMRA: Page 112 (B,C-4,5). NMC: Salt Lake City, 80 miles northeast.

GENERAL INFORMATION: Major Army Test and Evaluation Command. Range and evaluation units.

UTAH
Dugway Proving Ground, continued

TEMPORARY MILITARY LODGING: Lodging office, Bldg. 5228, Valdez Circle, 0730-1845 Mon-Thu, 0700-1545 Fri. C-801-831-2333, D-312-789-2333. All ranks. DV/VIP C-801-831-2020.

LOGISTICAL SUPPORT: Complete support facilities available.

CHAMPUS-831-3311
Commissary-831-2164
Exchange-831-4491
ITT Office-831-2318
Medical-831-2222
SATO-831-2131

Chaplain-831-2431
Comm Club-831-2901
Family Services-831-2278
Legal-831-3716
Package Store-831-4491
SDO/NCO-831-3535

Child Care-831-3345
Conv Store-831-4773
Gas Station-831-4773
Locator-831-3545/1110
Police-831-5161

HEALTH & WELFARE: US Army Health Clinic, Emergency C-801-831-2211/22, Appointments C-801-831-2222. Inpatient, see Hill AFB listing, C-801-777-4061. Chapels serving all faiths C-801-831-2431.

RECREATION: Car Care Center EX-2654, Bowling EX-2687, Post Fitness Center EX-2705, Youth Center EX-2177, Library EX-2178, Outdoor Rec Center EX-2318.

SPACE-A: Try Salt Lake City IAP, ANG area, 0800-1700 Mon-Fri, C-801-595-2274 D-312-790-9174, Fax 801-595-2271. Flights to CONUS and OCONUS locations.

ATTRACTIONS: Great Salt Lake, Salt Lake City, historic Mormon sites, museums, and skiing.

HILL AIR FORCE BASE (UT02R4)
Hill Air Force Base, UT 84056-5824

TELEPHONE NUMBER INFORMATION: Main installation numbers: C-801-777-7221, D-312-777-7221.

LOCATION: Adjacent to I-15 between Ogden and Salt Lake City. Take exit 336, east on UT-193 to south gate. USMRA: Page 112 (D-3). NMC: Ogden, eight miles north.

GENERAL INFORMATION: Air Force Materiel Command Base, Headquarters Ogden Air Logistics Center. Also, 388 FW (ACC) and 419 FW (AFRES), both flying F-16.

TEMPORARY MILITARY LODGING: Lodging office, Bldg. 146, D St, 24 hours daily, C-801-777-1844, D-312-777-1844. All ranks. DV/VIP C-801-777-5565.

LOGISTICAL SUPPORT: Complete support facilities available.

CHAMPUS-777-6206
Commissary-777-2300
Family Services-777-2301
Locator-777-1841
O'Club-773-4924
Public Affairs-777-5201
SATO-777-4677

Chaplain-777-2106
Conv Store-773-4673
Gas Station-773-3600
Medical-777-5285
Package Store-777-2169
Restaurant-777-4165
Theater-777-2328

Child Care-777-6321
Exchange-773-1207
Legal-777-6756
NCO Club-773-3166
Police-777-3056
Retiree Services-777-5735

HEALTH & WELFARE: USAF Hospital, Emergency C-801-777-5285, Appointments C-801-777-4061 (AD), C-801-777-1847 (Dep). Chapels serving all faiths C-801-777-2106.

UTAH
Hill Air Force Base, continued

RECREATION: Arts/Crafts EX-2649, Auto Hobby EX-3476, Bowling EX-6565, ITT EX-2892, Golf EX-3272, Gym EX-2761, Hess Fitness Center EX-2761, Rod/Gun Club EX-6767, Library EX-3833, Swimming EX-4617, Rec Center EX-3525, Youth Center EX-2419. Fam-Camp on base, 1 Apr-31 Oct, C-801-777-1844/2601, D-312-458-1844/2601, 14 camper spaces w/full hookups, 14 camper spaces w/o hookups. Carter Creek Recreation Area, off base, Jul-Oct, C-801-777-3525/3661, D-312-458-3525/3661, six cabins, four trailers, four camper spaces w/W&E hookups, three tent spaces. Hillhaus Lodge off base, C-801-621-2202, D-312-458-3525, four suites, three rooms, and one loft.

SPACE-A: Pax Term/Lounge, Bldg. 405 Area 1, 0600-2200 daily, C-801-777-1854/2887, D-312-458-1854/2887, Fax 801-775-3249. Flights to CONUS locations.

ATTRACTIONS: Salt Lake City, snow skiing. Park City, Temple Square.

OGDEN DEFENSE DEPOT (UT09R4)
500 W. 12th Street
Ogden, UT 84407-5000

Scheduled to close in 1997.

TELEPHONE NUMBER INFORMATION: Main installation numbers C-801-399-7011, D-312-352-7011.

LOCATION: From I-15 north, exit 12th St east, one mile to gate on left. USMRA: Page 112 (D-2). NMC: Ogden, in city limits.

TEMPORARY MILITARY LODGING: Lodging office C-801-399-6030, D-312-352-6030.

LOGISTICAL SUPPORT: Limited support facilities available.

Consol Clubs-399-7278
Locator-399-7011
Police-399-7453
Snack Bar-399-7688/6975
Fire Department-399-7311
MWR-399-7297
Public Affairs-399-7482
Legal-399-7759
Officers Club-399-7278
Recreation-399-7771

HEALTH AND WELFARE: Ogden Army Health Clinic C-801-399-7513.

SPACE-A: None. See Hill AFB listing, C-801-777-1854/2887, D-312-777-1854/2887, Fax 801-775-3249.

ATTRACTIONS: Salt Lake City, snow skiing, Park City, Temple Square.

TOOELE ARMY DEPOT (UT05R4)
Tooele, UT 84074-5008

TELEPHONE NUMBER INFORMATION: Main installation numbers: C-801-833-3211, D-312-790-1110.

LOCATION: From west I-80, exit 99, to UT-36 south for about 15 miles to main entrance. USMRA: Page 112 (C-4). NMC: Salt Lake City, 40 miles northeast.

U.S. FORCES TRAVEL & TRANSFER GUIDE U.S.A. - 283

UTAH
Tooele Army Depot, continued

GENERAL INFORMATION: Army Depot for maintenance, general supplies and ammunition.

TEMPORARY MILITARY LODGING: Lodging office, Bldg. 1, Hq Loop, 0630-1700 daily, C-801-833-2124, D-312-790-2124. All ranks.

LOGISTICAL SUPPORT: Most support facilities available.

ACS-833-2852   CHAMPUS-1-800-842-4333 Comm Club-833-2582
Exchange-833-2394   Family Services-833-2852 Fire Department-833-2015
ITT Office-833-3129   Legal-833-2536   Locator-833-2094
Medical-833-2572   MWR-833-2039   Package Store-833-2394
Police-833-2559   Public Affairs-833-3216 Recreation-833-2039
Retiree Services-833-2249 SATO-833-3251   SDO/SNO-833-2304
Theater-833-2582

HEALTH & WELFARE: US Army Medical Clinic, Emergency C-801-833-2666, Appointments C-801-833-2572. Inpatient, see Hill AFB listing, C-801-777-4061.

RECREATION: Arts/Crafts EX-2940, Auto Hobby EX-2873, Bowling EX-2849/882-9922, Sports EX-2005, ITT EX-3219, Gym EX-3189, Sports Rental EX-2107, Swimming EX-3189, Stables EX-3345. Oquirrh Hills Travel Camp on post, May-Oct, C-801-833-3129, D-312-790-3129, 14 camper spaces w/W&E hookups, eight tent spaces.

SPACE-A: None. See Hill AFB listing, C-801-777-1854/2887, D-312-458-1854/2887, Fax 801-777-3249.

ATTRACTIONS: Salt Lake City nearby, Utah desert, and mountains are available for rock climbing, exploration, camping, motorcycling, hiking, and/or sightseeing.

Other Installations in Utah

Salt Lake City International Airport, Salt Lake City, UT 84116-5000.
USMRA: Page 112 (D-3); Page 116 (B-2). C-801-595-2200, Exchange-355-1923, Medical-595-2337, Space A-595-2274.

VERMONT

Call 1-800-800-4000. Get a military rate by using your Military Living ID # ML3009. Retirees/Active Duty/Reserve/Guard.

Installations in Vermont

Camp Johnson, Bldg. 17 Colchester, VT 05446-5000.
USMRA: Page 23 (A-4). C-802-655-3030, Exchange-655-3030.
Ethan Allen Firing Range, Jericho, VT 05465-9706.
USMRA: Page 23 (B-4). C-802-899-2811, Exchange-899-2811.

U.S. FORCES TRAVEL & TRANSFER GUIDE U.S.A. - 285

VIRGINIA

DOLLAR RENT A CAR Call 1-800-800-4000. Get a military rate by using your Military Living ID # ML3009. Retirees/Active Duty/Reserve/Guard.

ALEXANDRIA COAST GUARD TELECOMMUNICATION AND INFORMATION SYSTEMS COMMAND (VA44R1)
Alexandria, VA 22310-3999

TELEPHONE NUMBER INFORMATION: Main installation numbers: C-703-313-5400.

LOCATION: Take I-95 to Telegraph Rd exit. Travel south on Telegraph Road four miles to Base on left. USMRA: Page 47 (M-5). NMC: Washington, DC, 15 miles northeast.

GENERAL INFORMATION: TISCOM, Ceremonial Honor Guard, Navigation Systems Center.

TEMPORARY MILITARY LODGING: None. See Fort Belvoir listing, C-703-805-2333 or 1-800-295-9750.

LOGISTICAL SUPPORT: Limited support facilities available.

Consol Club-313-5990   Exchange-313-5992   Medical-313-5446
Retiree Services-313-5434

HEALTH & WELFARE: Dispensary C-703-313-5446 (duty hours). Inpatient, see Fort Belvoir listing, C-703-805-0510. No chapel on base.

RECREATION: Auto Hobby EX-5994, Picnic Grounds EX-5987, Rec Equipment EX-3614, Special Services EX-3602.

SPACE-A: None. See Andrews AFB, MD listing, C-301-981-1854/3526, D-312-858-1854, Fax 301-981-4241.

ATTRACTIONS: Mount Vernon, Old Town Alexandria, Washington, DC.

ARMED FORCES STAFF COLLEGE (VA48R1)
Norfolk, VA 23511

TELEPHONE NUMBER INFORMATION: Main installation numbers: (Quarterdeck 24-hours) C-804-444-5150, D-312-564-5150.

LOCATION: From I-64 east to I-564 to Terminal Blvd. Armed Forces Staff College will be on the corner of Terminal and Hampton Blvd. USMRA: Page 52 (F-6). NMC: Norfolk, in city limits.

GENERAL INFORMATION: Armed Forces Staff College.

TEMPORARY MILITARY LODGING: Bldg. SC 407. C-804-444-5311, D-312-564-5311. Officers only.

LOGISTICAL SUPPORT: Most support facilities available.

VIRGINIA
Armed Forces Staff College, continued

Chaplain-444-5183 Child Care-444-5588 Exchange-440-2000
Family Services-444-5183 O'Club-423-4713 Police-444-5255
Exchange (Marianas Hall)-440-2070

HEALTH & WELFARE: Sewells Point - Sick Call 677-6254, Acute Care 677-6290.

RECREATION: Library EX-5155, Fitness Center EX-1198, Rec Equip Rental EX-5443, Youth Activities EX-5443.

SPACE-A: None. See Norfolk Naval Base listing, C-804-444-4118/4148, D-312-564-4118/4148, Fax 804-445-6563.

ATTRACTIONS: Virginia Beach nearby, entertainment and restaurants.

CHEATHAM ANNEX FLEET AND INDUSTRIAL SUPPLY CENTER (VA02R1)
108 Sanda Avenue
Williamsburg, VA 23185

TELEPHONE NUMBER INFORMATION: Main installation numbers: C-804-887-4000, D-312-953-4000.

LOCATION: From I-64 take exit 242B to US-199 East to main gate of Cheatham Annex. USMRA: Page 47 (N-8). NMC: Williamsburg, six miles west.

GENERAL INFORMATION: Annex of Norfolk Fleet and Industrial Supply Center, Depot activity for Naval supplies and other special programs.

TEMPORARY MILITARY LODGING: Lodging office, MWR, Bldg. 284, 0700-1530 Mon-Fri, C-804-887-7224/7101, D-312-953-7224/7101. All ranks. DV/VIP C-804-887-7108.

LOGISTICAL SUPPORT: Some support facilities available.

Conv Store-887-3582 Exchange-887-3582 Gas Station-887-3582
Golf Course-887-7159 ITT Office-887-7101 Police-887-7222
Medical-887-7222 MWR-887-7101 SDO/NCO-887-7222

HEALTH & WELFARE: Medical Emergency C-804-887-7222. Also, see Langley AFB listing, C-804-764-6801.

RECREATION: Auto Hobby EX-7418, Swimming EX-7102, Golf EX-7159, MWR Office EX-7101/2. Recreation Cabins and RV Park on base, year round, C-804-887-7224, D-312-953-7224, 19 camper spaces w/full hookups, 12 cabins.

SPACE-A: None. See Norfolk Naval Base listing, C-804-444-4118/4148, D-312-564-4118 /4148, Fax 804-445-6563.

ATTRACTIONS: Historic Williamsburg, Jamestown, and Yorktown are nearby. Water Country USA, Busch Gardens, Mariners' Museum, and Virginia Living Museum within 30 minutes. Paramount's Kings Dominion is 75 minutes away.

U.S. FORCES TRAVEL & TRANSFER GUIDE U.S.A. - 287

VIRGINIA

CHESAPEAKE NAVAL SECURITY GROUP ACTIVITY NORTHWEST (VA42R1)
1320 Northwest Boulevard, Suite 100
Chesapeake, VA 23322-4094

TELEPHONE NUMBER INFORMATION: Main installation numbers: C-804-421-8000, D-312-564-1336.

LOCATION: Five miles West of VA-168 at NC/VA border, turn right onto Ballahack Road, and follow to base gate (a left on Relay Road). Located between Moyock NC and Great Bridge VA. USMRA: Page 47 (N,O-10). NMC: Norfolk, VA, 35 miles north.

GENERAL INFORMATION: Naval Security and Communications Activity.

TEMPORARY MILITARY LODGING: BEQ/BOQ C-804-421-8331, D-312-564-1336, DV/VIP C-804-421-8331, D-312-564-1336, Fax 804-421-8235, Code 32.

LOGISTICAL SUPPORT: Complete support facilities available.

CDO/OOD-421-8000	Chaplain-421-8204	Child Care-421-8266
Conv Store-421-8254	CPO Club-421-8290	EM Club-421-8250
Exchange-421-8254	Family Services-421-8770	Fire Dept-421-8243
Galley-421-8276	Gas Station-421-8252	Legal-421-8375
Medical-421-8220	MWR-421-8260	O'Club-421-8285
Package Store-421-8252	Police-421-8334	Public Affairs-421-8328
Recreation-421-8260	RV/Camping-421-8262	Snack Bar-421-8250

HEALTH & WELFARE: Dispensary C-804-421-8220, Dental C-804-421-8225.

RECREATION: Gym EX-8303, Fitness Center EX-8263, Swimming EX-8303, Rec Services EX-8260. Stewart Campground, on base, 1 May-1 Dec, C-804-421-8262, D-312-564-1336-EX-262, 18 camper spaces w/E hookups.

SPACE-A: None, see Norfolk Naval Base listing, C-804-444-4118/4148, D-312-564-4118/4148, Fax 804-445-6563.

ATTRACTIONS: Casemate Museum at Fort Monroe, Portsmouth Naval Shipyard Museum, Mariners' Museum, Nauticus Marine Museum, and Busch Gardens and Williamsburg are nearby.

DAHLGREN NAVAL SURFACE WARFARE CENTER (VA06R1)
17320 Dahlgren Road
Dahlgren, VA 22448-5100

TELEPHONE NUMBER INFORMATION: Main installation numbers: C-540-653-8291, D-312-249-8291.

LOCATION: From I-95 in Fredericksburg, east on VA-3 to VA-206 (17 miles), left at Arnolds Corner, east to Dahlgren (11 miles). Also, US-301 south to VA-206, east to main gate of Center. USMRA: Page 47 (M-6). NMC: Washington, DC, 38 miles north.

288 - U.S. FORCES TRAVEL & TRANSFER GUIDE U.S.A

VIRGINIA
Dahlgren Naval Surface Warfare Center, continued

GENERAL INFORMATION: Naval Surface Weapons RDT&E Center.

TEMPORARY MILITARY LODGING: Lodging office, Bldg. 217, 0700-1530 daily, C-540-653-7671, D-312-249-7671. All ranks. DV/VIP C-540-653-8153.

LOGISTICAL SUPPORT: Complete support facilities available.

Cafeteria-663-3841	CHAMPUS-663-8241	Chaplain-663-8297
Child Care-663-4994	Commissary-663-7318	EM Club-663-8785
Exchange-663-2121	Family Services-663-1839	Fire Dept-911
Gas Station-663-2050	Golf Course-663-3002	Gen Mess-663-8277
ITT-663-8785	Legal-663-7121	Locator-663-8291
Medical-663-8241	MWR-663-7777	O'Club-663-1916
Police-663-8501	Public Affairs-663-8689	Recreation-663-7777
Retiree Services-663-1839	RV/Camping-663-8580	SATO-663-0074
SDO/NCO-663-8531	Snack Bar-663-2720	Theater-663-7777

HEALTH & WELFARE: Naval Branch Medical Clinic, Emergency C-540-663-8241. Inpatient, see Fort Belvoir listing, C-703-805-0510. Chapel serving all faiths C-540-663-8297.

RECREATION: Rec Equip EX-8585, Library EX-7474, Tennis EX-8580, Bowling EX-7327, Golf EX-3002, Gym EX-8580, Swimming EX-8088.

SPACE-A: None. See Andrews AFB MD listing, C-301-981-1854/3526, D-312-858-1854, Fax 301-981-4241.

ATTRACTIONS: Center is on the Potomac River. Washington, DC, easy drive.

DAM NECK FLEET COMBAT TRAINING CENTER ATLANTIC (VA25R1)
1912 Regulus Ave
Virginia Beach, VA 23461-2098

TELEPHONE NUMBER INFORMATION: Main installation numbers: C-804-433-2000, D-312-433-2000.

LOCATION: On ocean front, off Oceana Blvd. USMRA: Page 47 (O-9,10) page 52 (J-7,8). NMC: Virginia Beach, two miles northeast.

GENERAL INFORMATION: Fleet Combat Training Center with tenant commands, Naval Guided Missiles School, and Naval Surface Warfare Center East Coast Operations.

TEMPORARY MILITARY LODGING: Lodging office, Bldg. 566-C, duty hours. BEQ C-804-491-2449/0602. BOQ C-804-433-6691/6546, D-312-433-6691/6766. All ranks. DV/VIP C-804-433-7718.

LOGISTICAL SUPPORT: Most support facilities available.

Chaplain-433-6602	CDO-433-6234	Conv Store-433-7754
Exchange-433-6496	Gas Station-433-7794	Locator-433-6000
Medical-433-6327	O'Club-433-6141	Police-433-6186

VIRGINIA
Dam Neck Fleet Combat Training Center, continued

HEALTH & WELFARE: Naval Branch Medical Clinic, Emergency C-804-433-6327. Also, see Portsmouth Naval Medical Center listing, C-804-399-1100. Chapels serving all faiths C-804-433-6602.

RECREATION: Bowling EX-6341, Swimming EX-6551, Golf EX-2866, Gym EX- 6101, Library EX-6565, Beach. Stewart Campground off base, 35 miles south of Norfolk, in Chesapeake, operated by and located on Naval Security Group Activity near Atlantic beaches, Apr-Oct (Nov-Mar, self-contained only), C-804-421-8262, D-312-564-1336 EX-262, 18 camper spaces w/E hookups.

SPACE-A: None. See Oceana NAS listing, C-804-433-2903/2260, D-312-433-2903/2260.

ATTRACTIONS: Virginia Beach, water sports. Close to Norfolk, Williamsburg.

DEFENSE GENERAL SUPPLY CENTER (VA30R1)
Richmond, VA 23297-5000

TELEPHONE NUMBER INFORMATION: Main installation numbers: C-804-279-3861, D-312-695-1110.

LOCATION: From I-95 (Richmond-Petersburg Turnpike) exit 64 or 67 to US-1/301. Clearly marked on US-1/301. USMRA: Page 47 (L-8). NMC: Richmond, eight miles north.

GENERAL INFORMATION: General Supply Center of the Defense Logistics Agency.

TEMPORARY MILITARY LODGING: None. See Fort Lee listing, C-804-733-4100, D-312-687-6698.

LOGISTICAL SUPPORT: Complete support facilities available.

Cafeteria-271-9497	CHAMPUS-279-3821	Commissary-279-3733
Exchange-279-2654	Gas Station-279-1478	Locator-279-3811
Medical-279-3821	O'Club-279-4607	Package Store-279-1498
Police-279-4888	SDO/NCO-279-3805	Snack Bar-279-3572

HEALTH & WELFARE: Clinic C-804-279-3821.

RECREATION: None outdoors; Canadian elk roam the 20-acre pasture of the Center. Pool, tennis courts, gymnasium, fitness center.

SPACE-A: None. See Langley AFB listing, C-804-764-4698/4311, D-312-574-4698/4311, Fax 804-764-5941.

ATTRACTIONS: Historic Richmond short drive north, Edgar Allen Poe Museum, First White House of the Confederacy. Museum of the Confederacy, Virginia Museum of Fine Arts, Science Museum of Virginia, St. John's Church, King's Dominion and Busch Gardens amusement parks, and various Civil War battlefields.

VIRGINIA

FORT A. P. HILL (VA17R1)
Bowling Green, VA 22427-5000

TELEPHONE NUMBER INFORMATION: Main installation numbers: C-804-633-8760, D-312-934-8760.

LOCATION: From I-95, take Bowling Green/Fort A P Hill exit, US-17 (bypass) east to VA-2 south to Bowling Green, take VA-301 northeast to main gate. Also, exit I-95 to VA-207 north to VA-301 north and to main gate. USMRA: Page 47 (L,M-6,7). NMC: Fredericksburg, 14 miles northwest.

GENERAL INFORMATION: Army Active, Reserve and ANG Training Center, Marine, Navy, Air Force Reserve Officer Training Corps, and other Civilian Organizations.

TEMPORARY MILITARY LODGING: Lodging office, Bldg. TT-0114, 0800-1630 Mon-Fri from Oct-Mar, daily from Apr-Sep. C-804-633-8335, D-312-578-8335. All ranks. DV/VIP C-804-633-8205.

LOGISTICAL SUPPORT: Limited support facilities available.

CDO/OOD-633-8205	Chaplain-633-8269	Comm Club-633-8398
EM Club-633-8378	Exchange-633-8690	Fire Dept-633-8317
Locator-633-8433	Medical-633-8339	MWR-633-8219
Police-633-8425	Recreation-633-8219	Public Affairs-633-8324/8120
RV/Camping-633-8219	SDO/NCO-633-8201	Snack Bar-633-8690
Theater-633-8375/8219		

HEALTH & WELFARE: US Army Health Clinic, Emergency C-804-633-8216.

RECREATION: Rec Center, Pool, Hunting, Skeet Range, Fishing, Golf driving range Recreation Facilities on post, year round, C-804-633-8219, D-312-934-8219, 48 camper spaces w/full hookups, four log cabins, and "The Lodge" (nine bedrooms).

SPACE-A: None. See Andrews AFB, MD listing, C-301-981-1854/3526, D-312-858-1854, Fax 301-981-4241.

ATTRACTIONS: Nearby historic Fredericksburg and Civil War battlefields.

FORT BELVOIR (VA12R1)
9820 Flagler, Suite 201
Fort Belvoir, VA 22060-5932

TELEPHONE NUMBER INFORMATION: Main installation numbers: C-703-545-6700, D-312-227-0101.

LOCATION: From I-95 S or US-1 S take Fort Belvoir exits. Signs clearly mark support facilities. USMRA: Page 47 (L,M-5); Page 55 (B,C-8). NMC: Washington, 10 miles northeast.

GENERAL INFORMATION: Defense Systems Management College, Defense Mapping School, Army Management Staff College and support units.

VIRGINIA
Fort Belvoir, continued

TEMPORARY MILITARY LODGING: Lodging office, Bldg. 470, 24 hours daily, C-703-805-2333 or 1-800-295-9750, D-312-665-9750, Fax C-703-805-3566. All ranks. DV/VIP C-703-805-2640.

LOGISTICAL SUPPORT: Complete support facilities available.

ACS-805-2277/4590
Child Care-806-4344/6540
EM Club-780-0962
Fire Dept-805-1107
ITR-805-2654
Medical-805-0510
O'Club-780-0930
Public Affairs-805-5001
SATO-799-5680/3400
Theater-806-5237

CHAMPUS-805-0644/0542
Commissary-781-0536
Exchange-781-7070
Gas Station-806-4581
Legal-805-4018
MWR-805-4137
Package Store-780-0954
Recreation-805-3714
SDO/NCO-805-3101

Chaplain-806-4316
Conv Store-805-5155
Family Services-805-2908
Golf Course-806-4043/5892
Locator-805-2043/3758
NCO Club-780-0962
Police-806-3104
Retiree Services-805-3673
Snack Bar-805-3069

HEALTH & WELFARE: Dewitt Army Hospital, Emergency C-703-805-0510, 120 beds. Chapels serving all faiths C-703-806-3177.

RECREATION: Arts/Crafts 806-4143, Auto Hobby 806-4088, Bowling 805-3068, Rec Equip 805-2378, Golf 806-6016, Gym 805-3594, Library 805-3323, Marina 781-8282, Picnic Area 805-3781, Rec Center 805-3714, Swimming 805-2620, Tennis 805-2538, Wildlife Refuge 806-4007, Youth Center 805-4605.

SPACE-A: Davison Army Airfield, Bldg. 1327, 0730-1600 daily, C-703-806-7546, D-312-656-7546, Fax 703-806-7297, flights to CONUS locations.

ATTRACTIONS: Washington, DC, Smithsonian Institution.

FORT EUSTIS (VA10R1)
Building 213
Fort Eustis, VA 23604-5015

TELEPHONE NUMBER INFORMATION: Main installation numbers: C-804-878-1110; D-312-927-1110.

LOCATION: From I-64, exit 250A to VA-105, west to Fort Eustis. USMRA: Page 47 (N-9); Page 52 (B,C-2,3). NMC: Newport News, 13 miles southwest.

GENERAL INFORMATION: Army Transportation Center.

TEMPORARY MILITARY LODGING: Lodging office, Bldg. 2110, Pershing Ave, 24 hours daily, C-804-878-5807, D-312-927-5807. All ranks. DV/VIP C-804-878-6030.

LOGISTICAL SUPPORT: Complete support facilities available.

ACS-878-3638
Child Care-878-3794
Consol Club-887-5700
Fire Dept-878-4281
ITT Office-878-3694
Medical-878-7511

CHAMPUS-878-7861
Commissary-878-5966
Exchange-887-0293
Gas Station-887-0392
Legal-878-2205
MWR-878-3285

Chaplain-878-1304
Conv Store-887-0882
Family Services-878-3638
Golf Course-878-2965
Locator-878-5215
Package Store-887-0882

VIRGINIA
Fort Eustis, continued

Police-878-4554
SDO/NCO-878-5050
Travel-878-5577

Public Affairs-878-4920
Snack Bar-887-0494

Retiree Services-878-2953
Theater-878-3436

HEALTH & WELFARE: McDonald Army Hospital, Emergency C-804-878-7675, TRICARE-677-6000. Chapels serving all faiths C-804-878-1317.

RECREATION: Auto Hobby EX-5440, Bowling EX-5482, Flying Club EX-3722, Go-Cart Track EX-5883, Golf EX-2965, Gym EX-4380, Library EX-5017, Marina EX-2610, Swimming EX-5544, Tennis EX-2097, Saddle Club EX-2835, Skeet Range EX-5822, Youth Activities EX-4448.

SPACE-A: None. See Langley AFB listing, C-804-764-4698/4311, D-312-574-4698/4311, Fax 804-764-5941.

ATTRACTIONS: On the James River, historic Williamsburg nearby, Busch Gardens, Water Country USA, US Transportation Museum (free), Mariners' Museum, Nauticus, and the Virginia Air & Space Center.

FORT LEE (VA15R1)
911 C Ave.
Fort Lee, VA 23801-1515

TELEPHONE NUMBER INFORMATION: Main installation numbers: C-804-765-3000, D-312-539-3000.

LOCATION: From I-95 take Fort Lee/Hopewell exit, and follow VA-36 to main gate. USMRA: Page 47 (L-8). NMC: Petersburg, three miles west.

GENERAL INFORMATION: Combined Arms Support Command, Quartermaster Center and School, Defense Commissary Agency, Army Logistics Management College, Army Information Systems Software Development Center-Lee, and reserve units.

TEMPORARY MILITARY LODGING: Lodging office, Bldg. P-8025, Mahone Ave, 24 hours daily, C-804-733-4100, D-312-687-6698. All ranks. DV/VIP C-804-733-4293.

LOGISTICAL SUPPORT: Complete support facilities available.

ACS-734-6388
Chaplain-734-1187
Conv Store-861-6241
Family Services-734-6388
Golf Course-734-1228
Locator-734-6855
NCO Club-765-1539
Police-765-3988
Retiree Services-734-6973
Snack Bar-734-6861

Cafeteria-861-6480
Child Care-734-6376
EM Club-765-2314
Fire Dept-734-7025
ITR-734-6622
Medical-734-9000
O'Club-861-7545
Public Affairs-765-3100
SATO-734-7019
Theater-734-6630

CHAMPUS-734-9448
Commissary-765-2260
Exchange-861-5970
Gas Station-861-6794
Legal-765-1500
MWR-734-6622
Package Store-861-3297
Recreation-765-2212
SDO/NCO-734-7993

HEALTH & WELFARE: Kenner Army Community Hospital, Emergency C-804-734-9346, Appointments C-804-765-3400/734-9166, 120 beds. Chapels serving all faiths C-804-734-2937.

VIRGINIA
Fort Lee, continued

RECREATION: Arts/Crafts EX-6858, Auto Hobby EX-6859, Bowling EX-6860, Golf EX-2899, Fitness Center EX-765-3070, Gym EX-6636, Rec Equip EX-2212, Riding Club EX-6396, Rod/Gun Club EX-2212, Music Center EX-6623, Library EX-6846, Swimming EX-6747, Live Theater EX-6630, Youth Center EX-3763.

SPACE-A: None. See Langley AFB listing, C-804-764-4698/4311, D-312-574-4698/4311, Fax 804-764-5941.

ATTRACTIONS: Quartermaster Museum, Petersburg National Battlefield Park, Colonial Williamsburg, Richmond's Virginia and Poe Museums and Monument Avenue; Petersburg's Blandford Church and Cemetery and Trapezium House, Colonial Heights' Lee Headquarters (Violet Bank), and Hopewell's Appomattox Manor.

FORT MONROE (VA13R1)
Headquarters, Building 77, ATZG-PAO
Fort Monroe, VA 23651-5000

TELEPHONE NUMBER INFORMATION: Main installation numbers: C-804-727-2111, D-680-2111.

LOCATION: From I-64 exit at Hampton and follow tour signs through Phoebus to fort. USMRA: Page 47 (N-9), page 52 (F-4). NMC: Hampton, one mile north.

GENERAL INFORMATION: Headquarters Army Training & Doctrine Command, US Army Reserve Officers' Training Corps (ROTC) Cadet Command, Joint Warfighting Center, Mobility Concepts Agency, Naval Surface Weapons Center, Continental Army Band, and support units.

TEMPORARY MILITARY LODGING: Lodging office, Bldg. T-179, Murray St, 0800-1645 Mon-Fri, C-804-727-2128, D-680-2128. All ranks. DV/VIP C-804-727-3596.

LOGISTICAL SUPPORT: Complete support facilities available.

CHAMPUS-727-2701
Commissary-727-3326
Gas Station-722-4843
Medical-727-3305
Police-727-2238
Theater-727-2793

Chaplain-727-2611
Exchange-722-0794
Legal-727-3616
O'Club-727-2406/2432
Retiree Services-727-2093
Travel-800-918-3456

Child Care-727-2698
Family Services-727-3878
Locator-727-2111
Package Store-727-2487
SDO/NCO-727-2256

HEALTH & WELFARE: US Army Health Clinic, Emergency C-804-727-2840, Appointments C-804-727-2219. Inpatient, see Langley AFB listing, C-804-764-6801. Chapels serving all faiths C-804-727- 2611/4157.

RECREATION: Arts/Crafts EX-2728, Auto Hobby 727-2311, Bowling EX-2939, Fishing/Boating EX-4308, Fitness Center/Gym EX-3090, Library EX-2909, Swimming EX-4181, Youth Center EX-3957, "The Colonies" Travel Park on post, year round, C-804-727-2384, D-312-680-2384, 13 camper spaces w/full hookups.

SPACE-A: None. See Langley AFB listing, C-804-764-4698/4311, D-312-574-4698/4311, Fax 804-764-5941.

294 - U.S. FORCES TRAVEL & TRANSFER GUIDE U.S.A

Fort Monroe, continued

ATTRACTIONS: Williamsburg, Jamestown, Norfolk, Casemate Museum.

FORT MYER (VA24R1)
Building 59
Fort Myer, VA 22211-5000

TELEPHONE NUMBER INFORMATION: Main installation numbers: C-703-545-6700, D-312-222-0101. Note: Prefix for the extensions listed below is 696.

LOCATION: Adjacent to Arlington National Cemetery. Take Fort Myer exit from Washington Blvd, at 2nd St, or enter from US-50 (Arlington Blvd) first gate. Also, exit from Boundary Drive to 12th St North entrance near the Iwo Jima Memorial. USMRA: Page 55 (E-5). NMC: Washington, DC, one mile northeast.

GENERAL INFORMATION: Headquarters Command Fort Myer, Headquarters 3rd Infantry (Old Guard), Headquarters US Army Band, and support units.

TEMPORARY MILITARY LODGING: Lodging office, Bldg. T-49, Jackson St, 24 hours daily, C-703-696-3576, D-312-226-3576. All ranks. DV/VIP C-703-696-7051.

AAFES
Army & Air Force Exchange Service

Fort Myer Exchange

(703) 522-4575

Close to the Pentagon

Features

- Main Exchange
- Gas Station
- Shoppette
- Class 6

U.S. FORCES TRAVEL & TRANSFER GUIDE U.S.A. - 295

VIRGINIA
Fort Myer, continued

LOGISTICAL SUPPORT: Complete support facilities available.

ACS-696-3510	CHAMPUS-696-3656	Chaplain-696-3532
Child Care-696-3095	Commissary-696-3674	Consol Club-527-1300
Exchange-696-7201	Fire Dept-911	Gas Station-522-2584
Legal-696-0761	Locator-475-2005	Medical-696-3466
MWR-696-8864	NCO CLub-527-1300	O'Club-524-3037
Police-696-3089	Public Affairs-696-3944	Recreation-696-8849
Retiree Services-696-5948	Snack Bar-528-4766	SDO/NCO-696-3250

HEALTH & WELFARE: Andrew Rader US Army Health Clinic, Emergency C-703-545-3628, Appointments C-703-545-3464/3078. No ambulance service or facilities for life-threatening emergencies. Inpatient, see Fort Belvoir listing, C-703-805-0510. Chapels serving all faiths, C-703-545-3535.

RECREATION: Arts/Crafts EX-3385, Auto Hobby EX-3387, Bowling EX-3567, Community Center EX-3470, Fitness Center EX-0649, Gym EX-9655, Library EX-3608, Museum EX-6670, Rec Center EX-3470, Swimming EX-3226, Youth Activities EX-3199.

SPACE-A: None. See Andrews AFB, MD listing, C-301-981-1854/3526, D-312-858-1854, Fax 301-981-4241.

ATTRACTIONS: Arlington National Cemetery, Tomb of the Unknown Soldier, barracks and activities of the Old Guard, Old Guard Museum, Iwo Jima Memorial, Netherlands Carillon, Washington, DC.

FORT PICKETT (VA16R1)
Building 472, Military Road
Blackstone, VA 23824-5000

Scheduled to close September 1996.

TELEPHONE NUMBER INFORMATION: Main installation numbers: C-804-292-8621, D-312-438-8621.

LOCATION: On US-460, one mile from Blackstone. Clearly marked. USMRA: Page 47 (K-9). NMC: Petersburg 40 miles northeast, Richmond, 60 miles northeast.

GENERAL INFORMATION: Provides and maintains maneuver and training areas that reflect current doctrine of the active and reserve components of the Army and other military services.

TEMPORARY MILITARY LODGING: Lodging office, Bldg. T-469, Military Rd, 0730-1600 Mon-Fri, C-804-292-2443, D-312-438-2443. All ranks. DV/VIP C-804-292-2454.

LOGISTICAL SUPPORT: Most support facilities available.

CHAMPUS-292-2528	Chaplain-292-2601	Comm Club-292-2336
Comm Services-292-2233	Exchange-292-5489	Fire Dept-292-2217
Gas Station-292-5537	Legal-292-2168	Locator-292-2266
Medical-292-2528	MWR-292-2613	Package Store-292-5489
Police-292-8444	Recycling-292-2208	Retiree Services-292-2306

VIRGINIA
Fort Pickett, continued

RV/Camping-292-8309   SATO-292-2303/8340   SDO/NCO-292-8444
Theater-292-8466

HEALTH & WELFARE: US Army Health Clinic, Emergency C-804-292-2211.

RECREATION: Bowling EX-8518, Hunting/Fishing EX-2618, Swimming EX-8538, Sports EX-8626, Crafts EX-2616, Racquetball Court. Travel Camp on post, year round, C-804-292-2443, D-312-438-2443, 15 camper spaces w/full hookups, six tent spaces.

SPACE-A: None. See Langley AFB listing, C-804-764-4698/4311, D-312-574-4698/4311, Fax 804-764-5941.

ATTRACTIONS: Dollhouse Museum, Petersburg Civil War Battlefields, Appomattox Court House National Historic Park.

FORT STORY (VA08R1)
Fort Story, VA 23459-5000

TELEPHONE NUMBER INFORMATION: Main installation numbers: C-804-422-7305, D-312-438-7305.

LOCATION: From the south exit of Chesapeake Bay Bridge Tunnel (US-13), east on US-60 (Atlantic Ave) to Fort Story. Clearly marked. From I-64 take US-60 east. From VA-44 (Norfolk-VA Beach Expressway) exit US-58, turn left, N. Atlantic Ave (US-60) to 89th St to Fort Story. USMRA: Page 47 (O-9); Page 52 (I,J-5,6). NMC: VA Beach, three miles south.

GENERAL INFORMATION: Sub-Installation of Fort Eustis. Army Transportation Units, Test Activity, Army Logistics, and Over-the-Shore Training & Test Site.

TEMPORARY MILITARY LODGING: Lodging office, Atlantic Avenue, 0730-2330 daily, C-804-422-7321, D-312-927-9321. All ranks. DV/VIP Fort Eustis C-804-878-5206, D-312-927-5206/5207.

LOGISTICAL SUPPORT: Complete support facilities available.

ACS-422-7311   CHAMPUS-464-7869   Chaplain-422-7552/7665
Child Care-422-7413   Conv Store-428-0188   Exchange-422-7858
Family Services-422-7311 Fire Department-422-7456   Fort Story Club-422-7583
Gas Station-428-7071   ITT Office-422-7472/7555   Legal-422-7391
Locator-422-7682   Medical-422-7822   Package Store-422-7869
Police-422-7141   Public Affairs-422-7755   SDO/NCO-422-7454/7482
Theater-422-7472

HEALTH & WELFARE: None. See Portsmouth Naval Medical Center listing, C-804-399-1100. Chapels serving all faiths C-804-422-7552/7665.

RECREATION: Auto Craft EX-7713, Bowling EX-7458, Sports EX-7052, Rec Center EX-7472, Rec Equip EX-7472, Tennis EX-7975, Library EX-7525, Tickets EX-7472. Cape Henry Travel Camp on post, year round, C-804-422-7601, D-312-438-7601, 24 camper spaces w/W&E hookups, 13 log cabins, three Kamping Kabins.

VIRGINIA
Fort Story, continued

SPACE-A: None. See Norfolk Naval Base listing, C-804-444-4118/4148, D-312-564-4118/4148, Fax 804-445-6563.

ATTRACTIONS: Virginia Beach City and resort beaches nearby. See the Cross at Cape Henry (located on Fort Story), site of the first stop of English settlers in the USA, and the Old Cape Henry Lighthouse, a registered Historical Landmark.

HENDERSON HALL USMC (VA21R1)
1555 Southgate Road
Arlington, VA 22214

TELEPHONE NUMBER INFORMATION: Main installation numbers: C-703-694-1235, D-312-224-1235.

LOCATION: From Columbia Pike, VA-244, exit to South Orme St, Sheraton National Hotel at corner, west to dead end, right to second gate left. Also, from Memorial Drive (VA-27) exit to Columbia Pike, first traffic light right onto Southgate Rd, enter first gate on right. Across Southgate Road from Navy Annex. USMRA: Page 55 (E-5). NMC: Washington, DC, one mile northeast.

GENERAL INFORMATION: Headquarters Battalion USMC, HQMC and support units. Provides support to personnel at HQMC (Navy Annex across the street).

TEMPORARY MILITARY LODGING: None. See Fort Myer listing, C-703-696-3576, D-312-226-3576.

LOGISTICAL SUPPORT: Most support facilities available.

Chaplain-614-9280	Child Care-692-0042	EM Club-614-2125
Exchange-979-8420	Family Services-614-7200	ITT Office-979-842 ext 116
Legal-614-3800	Medical-614-1229	Police-614-2200
Public Affairs-614-2200	SDO/NCO-746-0950	

HEALTH & WELFARE: Clinic C-703-694-2726. Inpatient, see National Naval Medical Center, MD listing, C-301-295-1400.

RECREATION: Gym EX-2969, Racquetball 727-2706, Swimming EX-2706, Rec Equip 727-2706.

SPACE-A: None. See Andrews AFB, MD listing, C-301-981-1854/3526, D-312-858-1854, Fax 301-981-4241.

ATTRACTIONS: Adjacent to Arlington National Cemetery and Pentagon. Iwo Jima Memorial, Netherlands Carillon, Kennedy Center for the Performing Arts, Lincoln Memorial, Washington DC with its many sights, museums and galleries.

JUDGE ADVOCATE GENERAL'S SCHOOL (VA01R1)
600 Massie Road
Charlottesville, VA 22903-1781

TELEPHONE NUMBER INFORMATION: Main installation numbers: C-804-972-6300, D-312-274-7115, ext 300.

VIRGINIA
Judge Advocate General's School, continued

LOCATION: Take Route 29 to Arlington Street to Massie Road, located on University of Virginia. USMRA: Page 47 (J-7). NMC: Charlottesville, in city limits.

GENERAL INFORMATION: Army Judge Advocate General's School.

TEMPORARY MILITARY LODGING: Lodging office, room 156B, 0800-1630 Mon-Fri, C-804-972-6334, D-312-274-7110.

LOGISTICAL SUPPORT: Limited support facilities available.

Exchange-972-6324   Locator-972-6325   SDO/NCO-972-6300

HEALTH & WELFARE: None. See Fort Lee listing, C-804-727-2219. Religious services on campus.

RECREATION: All the facilities of the University of Virginia, with special permission.

SPACE-A: None. See Andrews AFB, MD listing, C-301-981-1854/3526, D-312-858-1854, Fax 301-981-4241.

ATTRACTIONS: Historic University of Virginia, and city of Charlottesville.

LANGLEY AIR FORCE BASE (VA07R1)
159 Sweeney Blvd.
Suite 100
Langley Air Force Base, VA 23665-2292

TELEPHONE NUMBER INFORMATION: Main installation numbers: C-804-764-9990, D-312-574-1110.

LOCATION: From I-64 E in Hampton take Armistead Ave exit, keep right to stop light; right onto LaSalle Ave and enter AFB. USMRA: Page 47 (N-9); Page 52 (E-3). NMC: Hampton, one mile west.

GENERAL INFORMATION: Air Combat Command Base. Headquarters Air Combat Command, Headquarters Air Division Air Combat Command, 1st Fighter Wing, and support units.

TEMPORARY MILITARY LODGING: Lodging office, Bldg. 75, Nealy Ave, 24 hours daily, C-804-764-4051, D-312-574-4051. All ranks. DV/VIP C-804-764-3467.

LOGISTICAL SUPPORT: Complete support facilities available.

CHAMPUS-764-6987   Chaplain-764-7847   Child Care-764-3449
Commissary-766-1304   Conv Store-766-1249   EM Club-764-1220
Exchange-766-1253   Family Services-764-4875   Fire Dept-764-3068
Gas Station-766-1286   ITT-764-2983   Legal-764-3276
Locator-764-5615   MWR-764-3999   O'Club-766-1361
Package Store-764-1330   Police-764-5091   Public Affairs-764-2018
Retiree Services-764-7386 SATO-764-5989   SDO/NCO-764-7771
Snack Bar-766-1237   Theater-764-2580   Visitor Center-764-4169

VIRGINIA
Langley Air Force Base, continued

HEALTH & WELFARE: First Medical Group Hospital, Emergency C-804-764-6801, 50 beds. Chapels serving all faiths C-804-764-7847.

RECREATION: Arts/Crafts EX-4647, Wood Hobby EX-3978, Auto Hobby EX-4607, Bowling EX-2433, Golf EX-4547, Gym EX-5791, Rec Equip EX-4616, Flying Club EX-7486, Marina EX-7220, Scuba Club EX-2312, Rifle Club EX-2312, Skeet Club EX-3769, Eagle Park EX-5792, Library EX-2906, Swimming EX-5791, Rec Center EX- 7175, Youth Center EX-2300. Bethel Park Rec Area, off base, 1 Apr-31 Oct, C-804-764-7170, D-312-574-7170, no camper spaces (expected to be completed by fall 1996).

SPACE-A: Pax Term/Lounge, Bldg. 754B, 0600-1800 Mon-Fri. C-804-764-4698/4311, D-312-574-4698/4311, Fax 804-764-5941, flights to CONUS locations.

ATTRACTIONS: Virginia Tidewater Area, Norfolk nearby. Great fishing, beaches, and water sports.

LITTLE CREEK NAVAL AMPHIBIOUS BASE (VA19R1)
1450 D Street
Norfolk, VA 23521-2438

TELEPHONE NUMBER INFORMATION: Main installation numbers: C-804-464-7000, D-312-680-7000.

LOCATION: From I-64 south to Northampton Blvd exit to base, exit VA-225. From Chesapeake Bay Bridge/Tunnel US-60 west to base. USMRA: Page 47 (N,O-9); Page 52 (G,H-5,6). NMC: Norfolk, 11 miles southwest.

GENERAL INFORMATION: Expeditionary Warfare Training Group Atlantic, Special Warfare Group Atlantic, and homeport for approximately 30 ships.

TEMPORARY MILITARY LODGING: Lodging office, 24 hours daily; Bldg. 3408 (BOQ) C-804-464-7522/3; Bldg. 3601 (BEQ) C-804-464-7577/8601. Navy Lodge, Bldg. 3531, C-804-464-1194. All ranks. DV/VIP C-804-464-5901, Fax 804-464-8635.

LOGISTICAL SUPPORT: Complete support facilities available.

CHAMPUS-464-8189	Chaplain-464-7427	Child Care-464-7868
Commissary-460-2939	Conv Store-464-3090	CPO Club-464-7789
EM Club-464-7949	Exchange-363-3202	Family Services-464-7563
Galley-464-7546	Gas Station-363-3119	ITT Office-464-7665
Legal-464-7331	Locator-464-7226	Medical-464-7850/7793
O'Club-460-1111	Police-464-7438	SATO-464-2392
SDO/NCO-464-7385	Snack Bar-464-2663	

HEALTH & WELFARE: Naval Branch Medical Clinic, Emergency C-804-464-7850, Appointments C-804-464-7850. Inpatient, see Portsmouth Naval Medical Center listing, C-804-399-1100. Chapels serving all faiths C-804-464-7427/7429.

RECREATION: MWR Dir EX-7905, Auto Hobby EX-7339, Ceramics Hobby EX- 7998, Wood Hobby EX-7605, Bowling EX-7952, Golf EX-8526, Gym EX-4821, Rec Equip EX-7735, Ballet/Slimnastic Classes EX-7665, Picnic Area EX-7369, Tennis EX-8118, Fishing Boat (Gator III) EX-7140, Boats/Campers EX-7516, Library EX-7998, Swimming

VIRGINIA
Little Creek Naval Amphibious Base, continued

EX-8139. MWR RV Park on base, year round, C-804-464-7516, D-312-680-7516, 45 camper spaces w/W&E hookups, 6 tent spaces.

SPACE-A: None See Norfolk Naval Base listing, C-804-444-4118/4148, D-312-564-4118/4148, Fax 804-445-6563.

ATTRACTIONS: Water sports, beaches, fishing, Norfolk.

NORFOLK NAVAL BASE (VA18R1)
Norfolk, VA 23511-5000

TELEPHONE NUMBER INFORMATION: Main installation numbers: C-804-444-0000, D-312-564-0000, FTS: 954-0111.

LOCATION: Take I-64 west, Naval Base exit I-564, follow signs. USMRA: Page 52 (F-5,6). NMC: Norfolk, in city limits.

GENERAL INFORMATION: CINC Atlantic Fleet, SACLANT (NATO), FMF Atlantic, Surface and Submarine Forces Atlantic, Air Forces Atlantic, Armed Forces Staff College, and the world's largest Naval Base comprised of Norfolk NAS, Norfolk Naval Station, Naval Computer and Telecommunications Area Master Station Atlantic, Naval Aviation Depot, Fleet Industrial Supply Center, and Camp Elmore Marine Corps Base.

TEMPORARY MILITARY LODGING: Lodging office, Bldg. I-A (BEQ), 0730-1600 Mon-Fri, C-804-444-4425. Bldg. A-128 (BOQ), 24 hours daily, C-804-444-4151/3250; NAVSTA BOQ EX-3250; NAS BOQ EX-7466. Navy Lodge, 24 hours daily, C-804-489-2656. All ranks. DV/VIP C-804-444-3250, Fax 804-445-6599.

LOGISTICAL SUPPORT: Complete support facilities available.

Cafeteria-440-2243
Child Care-444-3379
CPO Club-444-2125
Family Services-444-2102
Golf Course-444-5572
Locator-444-0000
O'Club-440-0773
Public Affairs-322-2853
RV/Camping-444-7218
Snack Bar-440-2119

CDO/OOD-322-2866
Commissary-423-8286
EM Club-440-5483
Fire Dept-444-3333
ITT-445-6663
Medical-444-1531
Package Store-440-2119
Quarter Deck-322-2866
SATO-440-0397
Theater-440-5304

Chaplain-444-7361
Conv Store-444-2383
Exchange-440-2214
Gas Station-440-2268
Legal-444-4497
MWR-444-3670
Police-444-2324
Retiree Services-444-2102
SDO/NCO-322-2866
TRICARE-677-6000

HEALTH & WELFARE: Clinic/Emergency C-804-444-1532, Appointments C-804-667-6000. Inpatient, see Portsmouth Naval Medical Center listing, C-804-399-1100. Chapels serving all faiths C-804-444-7361.

RECREATION: Arts/Crafts EX-3846, Auto Hobby EX-8383, Bowling EX-7908, Golf EX-5572/5267, Gym EX-2276/7218, Rec Equip EX-2536, Rec Park EX-4184, Sailing EX-2918, Fishing EX-4392, Rec Office EX-7218/2276, Library EX-2888, Rec Center EX-0897, Tickets 445-6663.

SPACE-A: Norfolk NAS, Bldg. LP-84, 24 hours daily, C-804-444-4118/4148, D-312-564-4118/4148, Fax 804-445-6563, flights to CONUS, OCONUS and foreign locations.

U.S. FORCES TRAVEL & TRANSFER GUIDE U.S.A. - 301

VIRGINIA
Norfolk Naval Base, continued

ATTRACTIONS: Largest naval base in the world. Local attractions include: Hampton Roads Naval Museum, Gardens by the Sea, MacArthur Memorial, Williamsburg, City of Norfolk, and Waterside Downtown Norfolk.

NORFOLK NAVAL SHIPYARD (VA26R1)
Portsmouth, VA 23709-5000

TELEPHONE NUMBER INFORMATION: Main installation numbers: C-804-496-3000, D-312-961-0111.

LOCATION: From I-264 in Portsmouth exit on Effingham St south to enter the Shipyard. USMRA: Page 52 (F-7). NMC: Portsmouth, in city limits.

GENERAL INFORMATION: World's largest shipyard devoted exclusively to warship repair work.

TEMPORARY MILITARY LODGING: Lodging office, 24 hours daily, Bldg 1504, C-804-396-4449, D-312-961-4449, Fax C-804-396-4968. All ranks.. Chesepeake Inn, Bldg 1530, C-804-398-8500. DV/VIP C-804-396-8605.

LOGISTICAL SUPPORT: Complete support facilities available.

CHAMPUS-398-5100	Chaplain-396-5021	Child Care-396-5863
Commissary-396-6309	Consol Club-396-5054	Exchange-397-2220
Gas Station-397-4319	ITT Office-396-7639	Legal-396-8625
Locator-396-3000	Medical-398-3226	Package Store-399-6673
Police-396-7266	Public Affairs-396-9550	Retiree Services-396-4484
SATO-398-0636	SDO/NCO-396-3221	Snack Bar-397-2220

HEALTH & WELFARE: Naval Branch Medical Clinic, Appointments C-804-396-3226, Ambulance C-804-396-3678. Inpatient, see Portsmouth Naval Medical Center listing, C-804-399-1100. Chapels serving all faiths C-804-396-5021, Duty chaplain C-804-444-7156.

RECREATION: MWR Office 396-3835, Bowling 396-3808/7051, Athletic Facilities 396-3845/3835, Gym 396-3845, Pool Tables 396-3835, Library 444-1571, Swimming 396-3835.

SPACE-A: None. See Norfolk Naval Base listing, C-804-444-4118/4148, D-312-564-4118/4148, Fax 804-445-6563.

ATTRACTIONS: Virginia Beach nearby. Tidewater outdoor sports. Naval Shipyard Museum, Mariners' Museum, college sports, Triple-A baseball.

OCEANA NAVAL AIR STATION (VA09R1)
Virginia Beach, VA 23460-5120

TELEPHONE NUMBER INFORMATION: Main installation numbers: C-804-433-2000, D-312-433-2000.

LOCATION: From I-64 exit to Norfolk-Virginia Beach Expressway (VA-44 E), east on Virginia Beach Blvd. Bordered by Oceana Blvd (VA-615) and London Bridge Rd. Also,

302 - U.S. FORCES TRAVEL & TRANSFER GUIDE U.S.A

VIRGINIA
Oceana Naval Air Station, continued

bordered by Potters and Harpers Roads. USMRA: Page 47 (O-9); Page 52 (I,J-7). NMC: Virginia Beach, in city limits.

GENERAL INFORMATION: Home to all F-14 Tomcats and A-6 Intruders on the East Coast. Headquarters for Commander Fighter Wing, U.S. Atlantic Fleet, and Commander Attack Wing, U.S. Atlantic Fleet.

TEMPORARY MILITARY LODGING: Lodging office, Bldg. 460, 24 hours daily, BEQ C-804-433-2555, D-312-433-2574, BOQ/DV/VIP C-804-425-0500, D-312-423-3293, Fax 804-433-2784.

LOGISTICAL SUPPORT: Complete support facilities available.

CHAMPUS-433-3328
Commissary-428-2931
Exchange-491-4260
Legal-433-3116
NCO Club-433-2637
Police-433-3123

Chaplain-433-2871
Conv Store-491-4267
Family Services-433-2912
Locator-433-2366
O'Club-428-0036
SATO-422-0487

Child Care-433-3164
EM Club-433-2453
Gas Station-491-4283
Medical-677-7000
Package Store-433-2840
SDO/NCO-433-2366

HEALTH & WELFARE: Naval Branch Medical Clinic, Emergency C-804-433-2221, Appointments C-804-433-2336/2151. Inpatient, see Portsmouth Naval Medical Center listing, C-804-399-1100. Chapels serving all faiths C-804-433-2871.

RECREATION: Auto Hobby EX-3403, Bowling EX-2167, Golf EX-2866, Gym EX-2695, Rifle/Pistol, Skeet/Trap EX-2875, Fishing Boat/Campers EX-3215, Picnic Area EX-3381, Stables EX-3266, Athletic/Rec Office EX-2695, Spec Services EX-3381, Library EX-2401, Swimming Office-EX-3285, EM-EX-2825.

SPACE-A: Pax Term/Lounge, Bldg. 100, 24 hours daily, C-804-433-2903/2260, D-312-433-2902/2260, flights to CONUS and OCONUS locations.

ATTRACTIONS: Virginia Beach, resort beaches, and entertainment nearby.

PENTAGON (VA41R1)
Washington, DC 20310-5000

TELEPHONE NUMBER INFORMATION: Main installation numbers: C-703-545-6700, D-312-227-0101.

LOCATION: From I-395 S, exit to South Parking or from Columbia Pike (VA-244) exit to South Parking. North Parking accessible from Boundary Channel Drive, exit from I-395 S. Visitor parking entrance is from Boundary Channel Dr and is paid parking. Due to tightened security the River and Mall entrances are accessible only by walking from other parking areas. Bus, METRO, and taxi service from Concourse. Concourse and all entrances have directions posted to support activities/facilities. USMRA: Page 55 (E-5). NMC: Washington, DC, adjacent.

GENERAL INFORMATION: Headquarters Department of Defense, Joint Chiefs of Staff and the military departments. The world's largest office building, 17.5 miles of corridors, employing about 27,000 people.

U.S. FORCES TRAVEL & TRANSFER GUIDE U.S.A. - 303

VIRGINIA
Pentagon, continued

TEMPORARY MILITARY LODGING: See Fort Myer, VA listing, C-703-696-3576, D-312-226-3576, DV/VIP C-703-696-7091.

LOGISTICAL SUPPORT: Very limited. Most are commercial activities.

CHAMPUS-695-3597   Chaplain-695-3336   Exchange-695-7637
ITT-AF-697-9866   ITT-AR-697-3816   Legal-AF-695-2450
Legal-AR-697-3170   Legal-NA-695-1332   Medical-697-6594/4598

HEALTH & WELFARE: Military clinics: AR-697-6594, AF-697-4598, civ-697-4778. Inpatient, see Walter Reed Army Medical Center, Washington DC listing, C-800-433-3574. Chapel, Room 3A1054, 695-3336. Armed Forces Hostesses Association, Room 1A736, 697-6857/3180, volunteers, info on the area.

RECREATION: Athletic Center, North Parking entrance, membership club, 521-5020, has work-out rooms, jogging, racquet sports, swimming, sauna and health rooms. Library 695-5346. Rec Services: USA: Room 3A146, 697-3816; USAF: Room 5E367, 697-9866; OSD/JCS Welfare & Rec: Room 3C1055, 695-5338. Ski Club 697-9866, Carlson Travel 979-5500.

SPACE-A: None. See Andrews AFB, MD listing, C-301-981-1854/3526, D-312-858-1854, Fax 301-981-4241.

ATTRACTIONS: The Pentagon guided one-hour tour is an exciting tourist attraction (office on Concourse). Free tours leave approximately every 30 minutes, 695-1776. Great military art on the corridor walls and in Hall of Heroes (Medal of Honor winners).

PORTSMOUTH COAST GUARD SUPPORT CENTER (VA43R1)
4000 Coast Guard Boulevard
Portsmouth, VA 23703-2199

TELEPHONE NUMBER INFORMATION: Main installation numbers: C-804-483-8532, D-312-483-8532.

LOCATION: From I-664 exit to High St through Churchland, left on Cedar Lane, right on West Norfolk Blvd, left on Coast Guard Blvd. to gate. USMRA: Page 47 (N-9), page 52 (F-6). NMC: Norfolk eight miles southeast.

TEMPORARY MILITARY LODGING: None. See Norfolk Naval Base listing, (BEQ) C-804-444-4425. (BOQ), C-804-444-4151/3250.

LOGISTICAL SUPPORT: Limited support facilities available.

All Hands Club-483-8536   CDO/OOD-483-8428   CHAMPUS-483-8462
Chaplain-483-8699   Exchange-483-8618   MWR-483-8670
Public Affairs-483-8594   Recreation-483-8671

HEALTH & WELFARE: Portsmouth CG Outpatient Clinic C-804-483-8596.

SPACE-A: None. See Norfolk Naval Base listing, C-804-444-4118/4148, D-312-564-4118/4148, Fax 804-445-6563.

304 - U.S. FORCES TRAVEL & TRANSFER GUIDE U.S.A

VIRGINIA
Portsmouth Coast Guard Support Center, continued

ATTRACTIONS: Tours: Portsmouth Harbor, MacArthur Memorial, Naval Museums.

PORTSMOUTH NAVAL MEDICAL CENTER (VA27R1)
Portsmouth, VA 23708-5000

TELEPHONE NUMBER INFORMATION: Main installation numbers: C-804-398-5008, D-312-564-0111.

LOCATION: Off I-264 in Portsmouth, take Effingham St exit to medical center. USMRA: Page 52 (F-7). NMC: Norfolk, two miles north.

GENERAL INFORMATION: The oldest medical center in the Navy; providing continuous medical care since 1830. One of four major teaching hospitals in the Navy. Supports the entire Tidewater area. Undergoing major construction/renovation project through year 2003 to add parking garage, support facilities, BEQ's, and large replacement hospital.

TEMPORARY MILITARY LODGING: None. See Norfolk Naval Base listing, (BEQ) C-804-444-4425. (BOQ), C-804-444-4151/3250.

LOGISTICAL SUPPORT: Limited support facilities available.

CDO/OOD-398-5008
EM Club-398-5881
Fire Dept-398-5444
Locator-398-5624
O'Club-398-5935
Police-398-7534
SATO-396-0640

CHAMPUS-398-7377/87
Exchange-397-5857
ITT-398-5439
Medical-398-5064
Patient Info-398-5002
Public Affairs-398-7986
Theater-398-5858

Chaplain-398-5550
Family Services-398-7801/2
Legal-398-5452
MWR-398-5094
Package Store-397-5857
Retiree Services-398-7689

HEALTH & WELFARE: Naval Hospital, Emergency C-804-398-5064, Appointments C-804-399-1100, 446 beds. Chapels serving all faiths C-804-398-5550.

RECREATION: Special Services Office EX-5094/5, Bowling EX-5100, Library EX-5858.

SPACE-A: None. See Norfolk Naval Base listing, C-804-444-4118/4148, D-312-564-4118/4148, Fax 804-445-6563.

ATTRACTIONS: Tours: Portsmouth Harbor, MacArthur Memorial, Naval Museums.

QUANTICO MARINE CORPS BASE (VA11R1)
Quantico, VA 22134-5001

TELEPHONE NUMBER INFORMATION: Main installation numbers: C-703-784-2121, D-312-278-2121.

LOCATION: From I-95 take exit 150A (Quantico/Triangle). US-1 is adjacent to the base. Directions to the base are clearly marked. USMRA: Page 47 (L-5,6). NMC: Washington, DC, 30 miles north.

GENERAL INFORMATION: Home to the Marine Corps Combat Development Command and various tenant commands.

U.S. FORCES TRAVEL & TRANSFER GUIDE U.S.A. - 305

VIRGINIA
Quantico Marine Corps Base, continued

TEMPORARY MILITARY LODGING: Hostess House, Bldg 3072, C-703-784-2983, D-312-278-2983, All ranks. DV/VIP C-703-784-4477.

LOGISTICAL SUPPORT: Complete support facilities available.

CDO/OOD-784-2707	CHAMPUS-784-2491	Chaplain-784-2131
Child Care-784-2299	Commissary-784-2476	Conv Store-640-6615
EM Club-784-4262	Exchange-640-8800	Family Services-784-2650
Fire Dept-784-2637	Gas Station-640-7700	Golf Course-784-2424
ITT Office-784-2789	Legal-784-3122	Locator-784-2681
Medical-784-2525	MWR-784-3007	NCO Club-784-4262
O'Club-784-2676	Package Store-640-8816	Police-784-2251
Pro Travel Corp-784-7101	Public Affairs-784-2741	Recreation-784-2014
Retiree Services-784-2511	RV/Camping-784-5270	Theater-784-2638
Visitor Center-784-2506		

HEALTH & WELFARE: Naval Medical Clinic, Emergency 911, Information C-703-784-2525. Inpatient, see Fort Belvoir listing, C-703-805-0510. Chapels serving all faiths C-703-784-2131.

RECREATION: Auto Hobby EX-2729, Bowling EX-2210, Special Interest Clubs EX-3196, Golf EX-2424, Gym/Racquet Sports EX-2002, Library EX-2414, Marina EX-5270, Museum EX-2606, Rec Office EX-2002, Rifle/Pistol Club 640-6336, Stables EX-2288, Swimming EX-2973, Tennis EX-2003, Youth Center EX-2249. Lunga Park on base, year round, C-703-784-5270, D-312-278-5270, 13 camper spaces w/full hookups, six camper spaces w/W&E hookups, 12 tent spaces.

SPACE-A: None. See Andrews AFB, MD listing, C-301-981-1854/3526, D-312-858-1854, Fax 301-981-4241.

ATTRACTIONS: Borders Potomac River, near historic Fredericksburg, VA and Washington, DC.

VINT HILL FARMS STATION (VA03R1)
Warrenton, VA 22186-5010

Scheduled to close September 1997.

TELEPHONE NUMBER INFORMATION: Main installation numbers: C-703-349-6000, D-312-229-6000.

LOCATION: From Washington DC, area, take I-66 to VA-29/211 South, proceed four miles to VA-215 (Mitchell Road), left for two miles to Station main gate. USMRA: Page 47 (L-5). NMC: Washington, DC, 35 miles northeast.

GENERAL INFORMATION: CECOM Signal's Warfare Directorate, Intelligence Materiel Management Center.

TEMPORARY MILITARY LODGING: None. See Quantico Marine Corps Base listing, C-703-784-3148, D-312-278-3148.

LOGISTICAL SUPPORT: Limited support facilities available.

VIRGINIA
Vint Hill Farms Station, continued

CHAMPUS-349-5575	Chaplain-349-5176	Commissary-349-5231
Conv Store-349-1870	Family Services-349-5032	Legal-347-5259
Locator-349-5864	Medical-349-5170	NCO Club-349-5027
O'Club-349-5026	Police-349-6236	Shoppette-349-1870
Theater-349-6086		

HEALTH & WELFARE: US Army Health Clinic, Emergency C-703-349-5171, Appointments C-703-349-5171. Inpatient, see Walter Reed Army Medical Center, Washington, DC listing, C-800-433-3574. Chapel serving all faiths C-703-349-6632.

RECREATION: Auto Hobby EX-5883, Bowling EX-6584, Gym EX-5895, Library EX-5886, Multi-Craft EX-5925, Swimming EX-6793/6794, Tennis EX-6085, Youth Center EX-5920.

SPACE-A: None. See Andrews AFB, MD, listing, C-301-981-1854/3526, D-312-858-1854, Fax 301-981-4241.

ATTRACTIONS: Beautiful Northern Virginia horse farms, historic Middleburg and Warrenton nearby.

WALLOPS ISLAND
AEGIS COMBAT SYSTEMS CENTER (VA46R1)
Wallops Island, VA 23337-5000

TELEPHONE NUMBER INFORMATION: Main installation number: C-804-824-1979/1692.

LOCATION: From the south: Take Chesapeake Bay Bridge-Tunnel north, stay on US Rt 13, to Rt 175 (a right at T's Corner) for five miles, a left at Rt 798 (Ocean Deli). BQ facilities will be on right. From the north: Take Rt 13 south, five miles over MD/VA line to Rt 175, same directions as above. USMRA: Page 47 (P-7). NMC: Norfolk, VA 100 miles south.

GENERAL INFORMATION: Aegis Combat Systems Center is a tenant of NASA, Goddard Space Flight Center, Wallops Flight Facility.

TEMPORARY MILITARY LODGING: Lodging office, Bldg. R-20, Rt 798. 24 hours daily, BEQ C-804-824-2064, BOQ C-804-824-2355, Fax 804-824-1764. All ranks.

LOGISTICAL SUPPORT: Limited support facilities available.

CDO/OOD-824-2058	CHAMPUS-824-2130	Exchange-824-5434
Galley-824-1009	Locator-824-2079	Medical-824-2130
MWR-824-1836	Public Affairs-824-1692	Security-824-2037

HEALTH AND WELFARE: Peninsula General Hospital, Salisbury, MD, Emergency 301-546-6400. Inpatient, see National Naval Medical Center, MD listing, C-301-295-1400.

RECREATION: Morale and Recreation Officer 824-2549.

SPACE-A: None. See Dover AFB, DE listings, C-302-677-2854/4088, D-312-445-2854/4088, Fax 302-677-2953.

VIRGINIA
Wallops Island Aegis CSC, continued

ATTRACTIONS: NASA/Wallops Visitor Center. Close to beaches, boating, fishing. Assateague and Chincoteague Island, with wild horse populations.

YORKTOWN COAST GUARD RESERVE TRAINING CENTER (VA28R1)
Yorktown, VA 23690-5000

TELEPHONE NUMBER INFORMATION: Main installation numbers: C-804-898-3500, D-312-827-3500.

LOCATION: From I-64 exit 25D, follow signs to Highway 17. Left on Highway 17, then right at second light onto Cook Road. Follow this until road ends, then take a right. This will lead to the base. USMRA: Page 47 (N-8,9); Page 52 (D-1). NMC: Newport News, 15 miles southeast.

GENERAL INFORMATION: Coast Guard Training Schools.

TEMPORARY MILITARY LODGING: None. See Yorktown Naval Weapons Station listing, C-804-887-7621, D-312-953-7631, Fax 804-887-7631.

LOGISTICAL SUPPORT: Limited support facilities available.

CDO/OOD-898-2354
Exchange-898-2507
Locator-898-3500
Package Store-898-2156
Theater-898-2593

Chaplain-898-2245
Gas Station-898-2156
Medical-898-2245/30
Police-898-3500

EM Club-898-2141
Legal-898-2374
O'Club-898-2331
Snack Bar-898-2502

HEALTH & WELFARE: USCG Center Clinic, C-804-898-2230. Inpatient, see Fort Eustis listing, C-804-878-7675. Chaplain serving all faiths C-804-898-2245.

RECREATION: Auto Hobby EX-2279, Library EX-2396, Gym EX-2128, indoor pool, sauna, weight room, racquetball court. Campground on base, year round, C-804-898-2100, nine camper spaces w/W&E hookups, five tent spaces.

SPACE-A: None. See Langley AFB listing, C-804-764-4698/4311, D-312-574-4698/4311, Fax 804-764-5941.

ATTRACTIONS: Historic Yorktown, Jamestown, and Williamsburg nearby. Busch Gardens, Water Country USA.

YORKTOWN NAVAL WEAPONS STATION (VA14R1)
P.O. Drawer 160
Yorktown, VA 23691-0160

TELEPHONE NUMBER INFORMATION: Main installation numbers: C-804-887-4545, D-312-953-4545.

LOCATION: From I-64 exit 247, to US-143 West, Five miles to US-238 left, five miles to gate 3, Skiffes Creek. USMRA: Page 47 (N-8), page 52 (B,C-1). NMC: Newport News, 15 miles southeast.

VIRGINIA
Yorktown Naval Weapons Station, continued

GENERAL INFORMATION: Naval Ophthalmic Support and Training Activity, and support units.

TEMPORARY MILITARY LODGING: Lodging office, Bldg. 704, 0800-1530 Mon-Fri, BEQ/BOQ/DV/VIP C-804-887-7621, D-312-953-7631, Fax 804-887-4340. All ranks.

LOGISTICAL SUPPORT: Complete support facilities available.

CDO/OOD-887-4545	Chaplain-887-4711	Child Care-887-4734
Conv Store-887-2307	EM Club-887-4555	Exchange-887-2307
Family Services-887-4606	Fire Dept-887-7343	Golf Course-887-4323
ITT Office-887-4609	Legal-887-4358	Medical-887-7404
MWR-887-4234	O'Club-887-4272	Police-887-7103
Public Affairs-887-4444	Recreation-887-4233	SATO-887-1422

HEALTH & WELFARE: Naval Branch Medical Clinic, Emergency C-804-887-7404, Appointments C-804-887-7255. Inpatient, see Fort Eustis listing, C-804-878-7675. Chapels serving all faiths C-804-887-4711.

RECREATION: Auto Hobby EX-7294, Bowling EX-4207, Golf EX-4323, Gym EX-4918, Handball/Racquetball EX-4278, Library EX-4720/4726, Boats/Motors EX-4601, Picnic Area EX-4601, Swimming EX-460, Tickets EX-460, Youth Center EX-4824.

SPACE-A: None. See Langley AFB listing, C-804-764-4698/4311, D-312-574-4698/4311, Fax 804-764-5941.

ATTRACTIONS: Historic Yorktown, Jamestown and Williamsburg nearby, Busch Gardens, and Water Country USA.

Other Installations in Virginia

Chesapeake Coast Guard Exchange, 1430A Kristina Way, Chesapeake, VA 23326-1000.
USMRA: Page 52 (G-8). C-804-523-6002, Exchange-523-6002.
Chincoteague Coast Guard Group - Eastern Shore, 3823 S. Main Street, Chincoteague, VA 23336-1510.
USMRA: Page 47 (P-7), C-804-336-6511, CDO/OOD-336-2840, Exchange-336-2848.
Davison Aviation Command, 6970 Britten Drive, Fort Belvoir, VA 22060-5513.
USMRA: Page 47 (L,M-5). C-703-806-7225/7509, Space A-806-7246.

U.S. FORCES TRAVEL & TRANSFER GUIDE U.S.A. - 309

WASHINGTON

DOLLAR RENT A CAR Call 1-800-800-4000. Get a military rate by using your Military Living ID # ML3009. Retirees Active Duty Reserve Guard.

BANGOR NAVAL SUBMARINE BASE (WA08R4)
Silverdale, WA 98315-1199

TELEPHONE NUMBER INFORMATION: Main installation numbers: C-360-396-6111, D-312-744-6111.

LOCATION: Approximately 15 miles north of Bremerton, on WA-3, exits to base clearly marked. USMRA: Page 103(A-1,2). NMC: Tacoma, 40 miles southeast.

GENERAL INFORMATION: Ohio-class (TRIDENT) Submarines; Commander Submarine Group 9; Submarine Squadron 17; Trident Training Facility; Strategic Weapons Facility (Pacific); Trident Refit Facility; Marine Corps Security Force Company; Personnel Support Activity, Puget Sound.

TEMPORARY MILITARY LODGING: Lodging office, Bldg. 2300, Scorpion St, 24 hours daily, BEQ/BOQ/DV/VIP C-360-396-4046/6581, D-312-744-4046/6581, Fax 360-396-6032. Navy Lodge C-360779-9100.

LOGISTICAL SUPPORT: Complete support facilities available.

Cafeteria-779-3365
Chaplain-396-6005
Conv Store-697-8727
Exchange-697-8703
Fire Dept-396-4333
Legal-396-6157
MWR-396-4515
Police-396-4312
Retiree Services-396-4115
Snack Bar-779-9907

CDO/OOD-396-4800
Child Care-779-4066
CPO Club-697-8033
Family Hotline-396-6310
Gas Station-697-8711
Locator-396-5733
O'Club-697-8033
Post Office-396-6141
SATO-779-1458
Theater-779-3668

CHAMPUS-396-4391
Commissary-396-6025
EM Club-697-8039
Family Services-396-4115
ITT-396-4026
Medical-315-4391
Package Store-697-8727
Public Affairs-396-4843
SDO/NCO-396-4800
Visitor Center-396-4665

HEALTH & WELFARE: Naval Branch Medical Clinic, Emergency C-360-396-4222, Appointments C-360-396-4391. Inpatient, see Puget Sound Naval Shipyard listing, C-207-479-6600. Chapels serving all faiths C-360-396-6005/4864.

RECREATION: Arts/Crafts 779-3815, Auto Hobby 779-3596, Wood Hobby EX-2264, Bowling 779-2838, Golf 779-4852, Gym 779-4852, Library 779-9724, Swimming 779-4817, Rec Center 779-3815. Keyport Lagoon Rec Area (fishing & boating/no camping) C-206-396-2169, operated by Keyport Naval Underseas Water Energy Station. Also, see Puget Sound Naval Station listing for Pacific Beach Ocean Getaway.

SPACE-A: None. See McChord AFB listing, C-206-984-5327, D-312-984-2657, Fax 206-984-5659.

ATTRACTIONS: Kitsap and Olympic Peninsulas, Hood Canal, Puget Sound, Poulsbo, and the Seattle/Tacoma area.

WASHINGTON

EVERETT NAVAL STATION (WA10R4)
2000 West Marine View Drive
Everett, WA 98207-5001

TELEPHONE NUMBER INFORMATION: Main installation numbers: C-206-304-3000, D-312-737-3000.

LOCATION: Take I-5 north, exit 193 to Pacific Avenue. Turn right onto West Marine View Drive, base is on the left. USMRA: Page 101 (D-3), page 103 (C-2). NMC: Seattle, 25 miles south.

GENERAL INFORMATION: Support Activity for the Navy in the Seattle area.

TEMPORARY MILITARY LODGING: BOQ C-206-304-4860, BEQ C-206-304-3111/3112.

LOGISTICAL SUPPORT: Complete support facilities available.

CDO/OOD-304-3366
Commissary-304-3367
Fire Dept-911
Medical-304-4044
Police-304-3262
SATO-304-4001
CHAMPUS-304-3060
Exchange-304-4455
Legal-304-4551
MWR-304-3336
Public Affairs-304-3688
SDO/NCO-304-3366
Chaplain-304-3342
Family Services-304-3367
Locator-304-3000
Package Store-527-7858
Recreation-304-5967

HEALTH & WELFARE: Medical appointments C-206-304-4044/4045, Dental appointments C-206-304-4092. Chapel serving all faiths C-206-304-3342/3343/3344.

RECREATION: Rec Services EX-3336, Outdoor Rec EX-3167. Pacific Beach Resort & Conference Center, off base, year round, 1-800-626-4414, 43 camper spaces w/W&E hookups, 100 camper/tent spaces w/o hookups.

SPACE-A: None. See McChord AFB listing, C-206-984-5327, D-312-984-2657, Fax 206-984-5659.

ATTRACTIONS: Seattle and the Puget Sound area, hiking, camping, fishing and skiing.

FAIRCHILD AIR FORCE BASE (WA02R4)
1 East Bong Street
Suite 103
Fairchild Air Force Base, WA 99011-5000

TELEPHONE NUMBER INFORMATION: Main installation numbers: C-509-247-1212, D-312-657-1110.

LOCATION: Take US-2 exit from I-90 west of Spokane. Follow US-2 through Airway Heights, after two miles turn left to base main gate and visitors' control center. USMRA: Page 101 (I-4). NMC: Spokane, 12 miles east.

GENERAL INFORMATION: Air Mobility Command, 92nd Air Refueling Wing, 141st ANG Air Refueling Wing, USAF Survival School, and support units.

U.S. FORCES TRAVEL & TRANSFER GUIDE U.S.A. - 311

WASHINGTON
Fairchild Air Force Base, continued

TEMPORARY MILITARY LODGING: Lodging office, Bldg. 2392, Short St, 24 hours daily, C-509-247-5737, 509-244-2290, D-312-657-5737/5519. All ranks. Survival School, C-509-247-5127, 509-244-3028, D-312-657-5127.

LOGISTICAL SUPPORT: Complete support facilities available.

CHAMPUS-247-2672
Commissary-244-5591
Family Services-247-5154
Legal-247-2838
NCO Club-244-3622
Police-247-5493
Retiree Services-247-5359
Theater-244-5600

Chaplain-247-2264
Conv Store-244-5095
Fire Dept-247-2389
Locator-247-5875
O'Club-244-3622
Public Affairs-247-5704
RV/Camping-247-2511
Travel-247-5069

Child Care-247-2403/2408
Exchange-244-2832
Gas Station-244-5095
Medical-247-2361
Package Store-244-2601
Recreation-247-2511/2240
Snack Bar-244-2022
Visitor Center-247-5495

HEALTH & WELFARE: USAF Hospital, Emergency C-509-247-5661, Appointments C-509-247-2361, 45 beds. Chapels serving all faiths C-509-247-2264.

RECREATION: Arts/Crafts EX-2810/5189, Auto Hobby EX-2310, Bowling EX-2422, Gym EX-2791, Library EX-5556, Swimming EX-2242, Rec Center EX-5649, Youth Center EX-5601. Clear Lake Rec Area, off base, Apr-Oct, C-509-247-2511, 18 camper spaces w/W&E hookups, three cabins, 10 tent spaces.

SPACE-A: Pax Term/Lounge, Bldg. 1, 24 hours daily, C-509-247-5435, D-312-657-5435, Fax 509-247-4909, flights to CONUS and overseas.

ATTRACTIONS: Spokane, parks, EXPO site, theater, nightlife.

FORT LEWIS (WA09R4)
Building 5227 Spruce Avenue
Fort Lewis, WA 98433-5000

TELEPHONE NUMBER INFORMATION: Main installation numbers: C-206-967-1110, D-312-357-1110.

LOCATION: On I-5 in Puget Sound area, 14 miles north of Olympia. Exits clearly marked. USMRA: Page 101 (C-5), page 103 (A,B-7). NMC: Tacoma, 12 miles north.

GENERAL INFORMATION: I Corps Headquarters, and ROTC Region Headquarters.

TEMPORARY MILITARY LODGING: Lodging office, Bldg. 2111, between Utah and Pendelton Sts, 24 hours daily, C-206-967-2815, 206-964-0211, D-312-357-2815. All ranks.

LOGISTICAL SUPPORT: Complete support facilities available.

ACS-967-7166
Child Care-967-2494
CPO Club-967-5091
Family Services-967-7166
Golf Course-967-6522
Locator-967-6221
NCO Club-964-2555
Police-967-3107

CHAMPUS-968-2165
Commissary-967-5808
EM Club-964-0144
Fire Dept-967-4479
ITT Office-967-2050
Medical-800-404-4506
O'Club-967-4986
Public Affairs-967-0157

Chaplain-967-4849
Conv Store-964-2141
Exchange-964-3161
Gas Station-964-5459
Legal-967-0705
MWR-967-3171
Package Store-964-4128
Recreation-967-2539

WASHINGTON
Fort Lewis, continued

Retiree Services-967-4424   RV/Camping-967-7744   SDO/SNO-967-0015
Theater-976-4329   Visitor Center-967-4873

HEALTH & WELFARE: Madigan Army Medical Center, Emergency, C-206-968-1390, Appointments C-800-404-4506, 414 beds. Tri-Care Services Center, C-206-964-7136. Chapels serving all faiths C-206-967-3126.

RECREATION: Craft Shops EX-5001, Bowling EX-4661, Golf EX-6522, Gym EX-5869/4467/5975/7471, Rec Equip EX-5415, Stadium EX-2912, Handball EX-3694, Fitness Center EX-3508, Parachute Club EX-3906, Flying Club 964-4932, Riding Club 964-2318, Hunting/Fishing EX-6263, Marina EX-2401, Archery EX-6263, Library EX-5015/2824, Swimming EX-2490, Rec Center EX-2539/2802, Art/Theater EX-5636, Youth Center EX-6766/5776. Travel Camp on post, year round, C-206-967-7744, D-312-357-7744, 24 camper spaces w/full hookups, six camper spaces w/E hookups, five tent spaces. Also, Westport Rec Park, operated by USCG Station, Grays Harbor, Westport, Mar-Oct, C-360-268-0121, FTS-420-9307, 6 camper spaces w/W&E hookups, 6 tent spaces.

SPACE-A: Gray Army Airfield, Bldg. 3082, 0730-1700 Mon-Fri, C-206-967-6628/5998, D-312-357-6628/5998, OSA-206-967-2414, flights to West Coast and Midwest locations.

ATTRACTIONS: Military Museum, Tacoma, Olympia and Seattle nearby.

JIM CREEK NAVAL RADIO STATION (WA07R4)
21027 Jim Creek Road
Arlington, WA 98223-8599

TELEPHONE NUMBER INFORMATION: Main installation numbers: C-360-435-7335, 206-3004-5315, D-312-727-5315.

LOCATION: Take I-5 to Exit 208. Head toward Arlington. Approximately five miles after the town of Arlington, turn right on Jim Creek Road. Continue for eight miles to front gate. USMRA: Page 101 (D-3). NMC: Everett, 30 miles south.

TEMPORARY MILITARY LODGING: Completion date scheduled for Fall of 1996, C-360-304-5315.

LOGISTICAL SUPPORT: Limited support facilities available.

MWR-800-734-1123   Police-304-5314   Recreation-304-5315
Snack Bar-304-5315   Visitor Center*-304-5315

*Completion date scheduled for Fall of 1997.

HEALTH & WELFARE: None. See Everett NS listing, C-206-304-4044/4045.

RECREATION: Campground off base, year round, C-360-435-7335, D-312-727-5315 two camper spaces w/W&E.

SPACE-A: None. See McChord AFB listing, C-206-984-5327, D-312-984-2657, Fax 206-984-5659.

ATTRACTIONS: Beautiful mountains and wilderness, lakes for fishing and canoeing.

U.S. FORCES TRAVEL & TRANSFER GUIDE U.S.A. - 313

WASHINGTON

McCHORD AIR FORCE BASE (WA05R4)
100 Main Street
McChord Air Force Base, WA 98438-1109

TELEPHONE NUMBER INFORMATION: Main installation numbers: C-206-984-1910, D-312-984-1910.

LOCATION: From I-5 take exit 125. Clearly marked. USMRA: Page 101 (C-5); Page 103 (B-7). NMC: Tacoma, eight miles north.

GENERAL INFORMATION: Air Mobility Command Base. 62nd Airlift Wing, AFRES units, and other support activities.

TEMPORARY MILITARY LODGING: Lodging office, Bldg. 166, Main St, 24 hours daily, C-206-584-1471, D-312-984-5613. All ranks. DV/VIP C-208-584-2621.

LOGISTICAL SUPPORT: Complete support facilities available.

ACS-984-2813	CHAMPUS-984-2257	Chaplain-984-5556
Child Care-984-2958	Commissary-984-3285	EM Club-584-1371
Exchange-582-9451	Family Services-984-2813	Fire Dept-984-2603
Gas Station-584-8734	Golf Course-984-2053	Legal-984-5512
Locator-984-2474	Medical-984-5601	MWR-984-5836
NCO Club-584-1371	O'Club-584-5581	Package Store-588-2527
Police-984-5624	Public Affairs-984-5637	Recreation-984-2206
Retiree Services-984-5234	RV/Camping-984-5488	Shoppette-582-0788
Snack Bar-584-5145	Theater-984-5836	Travel-984-3521
Visitor Center-984-2119		

HEALTH & WELFARE: 62nd Medical Group Clinic, Emergency C-206-984-5601, Appointments C-206-984-3971. Inpatient, see Fort Lewis listing, C-800-404-4506. Chapels serving all faiths C-206-984-5556.

RECREATION: Arts/Crafts EX-2816, Auto Hobby EX-2407, Bowling EX-5954, Golf EX-2053, Gym EX-5666/2842, Rec Equip EX-2206, Library EX-3454, Swimming EX-2807, Rec Center EX-2068, Tickets EX-2216, Youth Center EX-2203. Holiday Park Fam-Camp on base, year round, C-206-984-5488, 18 camper spaces w/full hookups, 18 camper spaces w/W&E, 20 camper spaces w/o hookups, 20 tent spaces.

SPACE-A: Pax Term/Lounge, Bldg. 1179, 24 hours daily, C-206-984-2657/5327, D-312-984-2657, Fax 206-984-5659, flights to CONUS and foreign locations.

ATTRACTIONS: Tacoma and Puget Sound area.

PORT ANGELES COAST GUARD GROUP (WA19R4)
Port Angeles, WA 98362-0159

TELEPHONE NUMBER INFORMATION: Main installation numbers: C-360-457-2206, D-312-744-6431, FTS: 700-396-5206.

LOCATION: Take I-5 north to Tacoma, 16 north to Bremerton, 3 to Hood Canal Bridge, 104 to 101 west to Port Angeles. USMRA: Page 101 (B-3). NMC: Bremerton, 50 miles.

WASHINGTON
Port Angeles Coast Guard Group, continued

GENERAL INFORMATION: Coast Guard Air Station and Group.

TEMPORARY MILITARY LODGING: None. See Whidbey Island NAS listing, (BOQ), C-360-257-2529, D-312-820-2529, (BEQ), C-360-257-5513, D-312-820-5513.

LOGISTICAL SUPPORT: Limited support facilities available.

CHAMPUS-457-2275   Exchange-457-2285   Legal-457-2212
Locator-457-2226   Medical-457-2275   SDO/NCO-457-2226

HEALTH AND WELFARE: Emergency C-360-457-8513. Appointments C-360-457-2277.

RECREATION: None available on base.

SPACE-A: None. See McChord AFB listing, C-360-984-5327, D-312-984-2657, Fax 206-984-5659.

ATTRACTIONS: Olympic National Park, great hunting, fishing. hiking. Port Angeles only 18 miles south of Victoria, BC, and 87 miles west of Seattle (2 hour drive with ferry ride).

PUGET SOUND NAVAL SHIPYARD (WA11R4)
1400 Farragut Avenue
Bremerton, WA 98314-5001

TELEPHONE NUMBER INFORMATION: Main installation numbers: C-360-476-3711, D-312-439-3711.

LOCATION: Take I-5 north to highway 16 exit (Bremerton). The 24-hour gate is at Montgomery and Decatur Ave. Also, can be reached via a one hour ferry ride from Seattle. USMRA: Page 101 (C-4), page 103 (A-3). NMC: Bremerton, in city limits.

GENERAL INFORMATION: Homeport for ships undergoing repair and other ships.

TEMPORARY MILITARY LODGING: Lodging office, Bldg. 865, 24 hours daily, BEQ C-360-476-3251, D-312-439-2840. BOQ/DV/VIP C-360-476-7627, D-312-439-7627, Fax 360-476-6895.

LOGISTICAL SUPPORT: Complete support facilities available.

ACS-377-0602   CDO/OOD-476-3466   CHAMPUS-478-9386
Chaplain-476-2183   Child Care-476-1152   Commissary-405-1971
Conv Store-478-5527   CPO Club-476-3391   EM Club-476-2546
Exchange-478-5570   Family Services-476-5113 Fire Dept-911
ITT Office-476-7576   Legal-476-2156   Locator-476-3459
Medical-479-6600   MWR-476-8188   O'Club-373-5014
Package Store-377-8434   Police-476-2165   Public Affairs-476-7111
Recreation-476-2673   Retiree Services-476-5113 SATO-476-7576
Snack Bar-476-5756

HEALTH & WELFARE: Bremerton Naval Hospital, C-206-479-6600. Chapel serving all faiths C-206-476-2183.

WASHINGTON
Puget Sound Naval Shipyard, continued

RECREATION: Bowling, Hobby Shops, Swimming, Tennis, Picnic Area, Gym: call 476-2214. See Puget Sound Naval Station listing for Pacific Beach Ocean Getaway rec area.

SPACE-A: None. See McChord AFB listing, C-206-984-5327, D-312-984-2657, Fax 206-984-5659.

ATTRACTIONS: Puget Sound and Seattle/Tacoma area.

SEATTLE COAST GUARD SUPPORT CENTER (WA20R4)
1519 Alaskan Way South
Seattle, WA 98134-1192

TELEPHONE NUMBER INFORMATION: Main installation numbers: C-206-217-6400, FTS-396-6400.

LOCATION: Take I-5 to Spokane St (exit 163/163A), turn right on E. Marginal Way. Support Center is at Pier 36. USMRA: Page 103 (C-3). NMC: Seattle, in city limits.

GENERAL INFORMATION: Coast Guard Cutters: Bayberry, Mariposa, Mellon, Midgett, Polar Sea, and Polar Star. Units: Naval Engineering Support Unit Seattle, Electronic Support Unit Seattle, Marine Safety Office Puget Sound, Vessel Traffic Service Puget Sound, Group Seattle, Station Seattle.

TEMPORARY MILITARY LODGING: BEQ, 1519 Alaskan Way South, 0730-1600 daily, C-206-217-6410.

LOGISTICAL SUPPORT: Some support facilities available.

Cafeteria-217-6416
Exchange-587-0307
Medical-217-6430
SDO/NCO-217-6410
CHAMPUS-217-6510
Family Services-217-6999
Museum-217-9993
Chaplain-217-6995
Legal-220-7110
Package Store-587-0307

HEALTH AND WELFARE: Support Center Medical, Appointments: C-206-217-6430. Inpatient, see Fort Lewis listing, C-800-404-4506.

RECREATION: Camping Equip, Rec Equip, Gym, Physical Fitness Center call EX-6358. Rec Center EX-6410, Museum EX-6993. Point No Point Lighthouse Recreation Quarters EX-6400.

SPACE-A: None. See McChord Air Force Base listing, C-206-984-5327, D-312-984-2657, Fax 206-984-5659.

ATTRACTIONS: Space Needle, Seattle Zoo, Puget Sound, Olympic, Mt. Rainier National Parks, Seattle King Dome.

WHIDBEY ISLAND NAVAL AIR STATION (WA06R4)
3730 N. Charles Porter Avenue, B-385
Oak Harbor, WA 98278-5000

TELEPHONE NUMBER INFORMATION: Main installation numbers: C-360-257-2631, D-312-820-2631.

WASHINGTON
Whidbey Island Naval Air Station, continued

LOCATION: Take WA-20 to Whidbey Island, three miles west of WA-20 on Ault Field Road. USMRA: Page 101 (C-2,3). NMC: Seattle, 80 miles southeast.

GENERAL INFORMATION: Attack Wing Pacific Electronic Warfare Wing Pacific (COMATKWINGPAC), Tactical Electronic Warfare (COMVAQWINGPAC), Patrol Wing-10 (COMPATWINGPAC-10), Naval Facility, Marine Aviation Support Group, Naval Aviation Maintenance Training, and Naval Air Reserve Units.

TEMPORARY MILITARY LODGING: Lodging office: Bldgs. 973, 2527 (BOQ), C-360-257-2529, D-312-820-2529, Bldg. 11 (BEQ), C-360-257-5513, D-312-820-5513, DV/VIP C-360-259-2529, Fax 360-257-5962. All ranks.

LOGISTICAL SUPPORT: Complete support facilities available.

CDO/OOD-257-2631
Child Care-257-3302
EM Club-257-3308
Fire Dept-257-2533
Legal-257-2126
MWR-257-2432
Police-257-3108
SATO-257-4415

CHAMPUS-257-9542
Commissary-257-3318
Exchange-257-0600
Gas Station-257-2829
Locator-257-8787
O'Club-257-2521
Public Affairs-257-2286

Chaplain-257-2414
CPO Club-257-2892
Family Services-257-2902
Golf Course-257-2178
Medical-257-9500
Package Store-257-0574
Retiree Services-257-8054

HEALTH & WELFARE: Naval Hospital, clinics and depts, Emergency C-360-257-4354, Appointments C-360-257-4438 (AD), C-360-257-3131 (Dep), 25 beds. Chapels serving all faiths C-360-257-2414.

RECREATION: Arts/Crafts EX-2173, Auto Hobby EX-2295, Bowling EX-2074, Flying Club 679-4359, Intl Sports EX-2432, Golf EX-2178, Gym EX-2420, Rec Areas EX-2431, Sailing Club EX-2432, Rod/Gun Club EX-5539, Backpacking EX-2432, Archery Club EX-9723/0151, Library EX-2702. Cliffside RV Park on base, year round, C-360-257-2434, D-312-820-2434, 20 camper spaces w/W&E hookups. Rocky Point RV Park off base, year round, C-206-257-2434, D-312-820-2434, 23 camper spaces w/o hookups.

SPACE-A: Pax Term/Lounge, Bldg. 2734, 0730-1900 daily, C-360-257-2604, D-312-820-2604, Fax 360-257-1942, flights to CONUS locations.

ATTRACTIONS: Outdoor sports (mostly water), fishing, great seafood.

Other Installations in Washington

Fort Lawton 124th Regional Support Command, 4575 36th Ave West, Fort Lawton, WA 98199-5000, USMRA: Page 101 (C-4); Page 103 (B,C-2), C-800-347-2735, Family Services-800-677-3980/206-281-3131, Public Affairs-206-281-3026, Exchange-284-0450, Retiree Services-206-281-3131.
USAF Survival School, 811 W. Los Angeles Ave., Suite 101, Fairchild AFB, WA 99011-8628. USMRA: Page 101 (I,J-4) C-509-247-2691, Exchange-247-9615.
Vancouver Barracks, Bldg. 638, Hathaway Rd. Vancouver, WA 98661-3826. USMRA: Page 101 (C-8). C-360-694-7555, Exchange-694-8749.
Yakima Training Center, Bldg. T-157, Yakima, WA 98901-9399. USMRA: Page 101 (F-5,6). C-509-452-7356, Consol Club-454-8415, Medical-454-8251, Exchange-454-8416.

WEST VIRGINIA

DOLLAR RENT A CAR — Call 1-800-800-4000. Get a military rate by using your Military Living ID # ML3009. Retirees Active Duty Reserve Guard.

EASTERN WEST VIRGINIA REGIONAL AIRPORT (WV02R1)
Martinsburg, WV 25401-0204

TELEPHONE NUMBER INFORMATION: Main installation numbers: C-304-267-5100, D-312-242-3210.

LOCATION: From I-81, take exit 12 east, right to route 11, south for four miles, left to Paynes Ford Rd. Airport is approximately one mile on the right. USMRA: Page 47 (K-3,4). NMC: Hagerstown, MD, 15 miles north.

GENERAL INFORMATION: 167th Air National Guard Unit, C-130s.

TEMPORARY MILITARY LODGING: Very limited, C-304-267-5174.

LOGISTICAL SUPPORT: Limited support available.

Consol Club-267-5298   Exchange-267-5204   Medical-267-5244

HEALTH & WELFARE: Limited clinic services available, Appointments C-304-267-5244.

RECREATION: None.

SPACE-A: Bldg. 120, second floor, C-304-267-5250, D-312-249-9250, Fax 304-267-5144. Flights to CONUS and OCONUS locations.

ATTRACTIONS: Beautiful Shenandoah Valley 20 miles south.

SUGAR GROVE
NAVAL SECURITY GROUP ACTIVITY (WV04R1)
Sugar Grove, WV 26815-5000

TELEPHONE NUMBER INFORMATION: Main installation numbers: C-304-249-6304, D-312-564-7276.

LOCATION: From I-81 in VA take Rt 33 west from Harrisonburg VA, to Brandywine WV. Left on Sugar Grove Rd, approximately seven miles on the right. USMRA: Page 47 (I-6). NMC: Harrisonburg, VA, 36 miles east.

GENERAL INFORMATION: Naval Radio Station, Naval Security Group Detachment, Customer Service Desk, and branch medical clinic.

TEMPORARY MILITARY LODGING: Lodging office, Bldg. 63, 0730-1600 daily, C-304-249-6350, D-312-564-7276, Fax 304-249-6307.

LOGISTICAL SUPPORT: Most support facilities available.

WEST VIRGINIA
Sugar Grove Naval Security Group Activity, continued

CDO/OOD-249-6310	CHAMPUS-249-6380	Child Care-249-6309
Conv Store-249-6355	CPO Club-249-6362	EM Club-249-6362
Exchange-249-6355	Family Services-249-6354	Fire Dept-249-6390
ITT-249-6360	Medical-249-6380	MWR-249-6366
NCO Club-249-6362	O'Club-249-6362	Package Store-249-6355
Police-249-6310	Public Affairs-249-6304	Quarterdeck-249-6310
Recreation-249-6367	Retiree Services-249-6304	Theater-249-6362

HEALTH AND WELFARE: Medical Center Branch Clinic, 0800-1600 Mon-Fri, Emergency and Appointments, C-304-249-6360.

RECREATION: Arts/Crafts, Bowling, Camping Equip, Ceramics, Gym/Fitness Center, Library EX-6309, Rec Equip, and Swimming: call EX-6360. Special Services, Hobby Shop, Auto and Wood Hobby call EX-6363. Cabin on base, year round, C-304-249-6363.

SPACE-A: None. See Eastern West Virginia Regional Airport listing, C-304-267-5250, D-312-249-9250, Fax 304-267-5144.

ATTRACTIONS: Excellent hunting and fishing area.

YEAGER AIRPORT (WV05R1)
1679 Coonskin Drive
Charleston, WV 25311-1085

TELEPHONE NUMBER INFORMATION: Main installation numbers: C-304-341-6000, D-312-366-6100.

LOCATION: From I-77, take exit 102, follow signs to airport. USMRA: Page 46 (E-6). NMC: Charleston four miles southwest.

GENERAL INFORMATION: 130th AG, Air National Guard C-130H.

TEMPORARY MILITARY LODGING: None.

LOGISTICAL SUPPORT: Very limited support available.

Exchange-341-4957   Medical-341-6252

HEALTH & WELFARE: Limited clinic services available, Appointments C-304-341-6252.

SPACE-A: Hours 0730-1600 Mon-Fri, C-304-341-6185/6240, D-312-366-6185/6240, Fax 304-341-6142/6001. Unscheduled flights to CONUS and OCONUS locations.

ATTRACTIONS: Charleston, The State Capital, white water rafting.

Other Installations in West Virginia

Camp Dawson Army Training Site, 240 Army Rd., Kingwood, WV 26537-1077. USMRA: Page 46 (H-3). C-304-329-4337, Exchange-329-4469, TML-304-329-4420.
Charleston Armory, 1701 Coonskin Dr., Charleston, WV 25311-1085. USMRA: Page 46 (E-6). C-304-346-4957, Exchange-346-4957.

WISCONSIN

Call 1-800-800-4000. Get a military rate by using your Military Living ID # ML3009. Retirees/Active Duty/Reserve/Guard.
DOLLAR RENT A CAR

FORT McCOY(WI02R2)
100 E. Headquarters Road
Fort McCoy, WI 54656-5263

TELEPHONE NUMBER INFORMATION: Main installation numbers: C-608-388-2222, D-312-280-1110.

LOCATION: From I-90, to WI-21 northeast to fort. USMRA: Page 68 (C,D-7). NMC: La Crosse, 35 miles southwest.

GENERAL INFORMATION: Total Force Warfighting training.

TEMPORARY MILITARY LODGING: Lodging office, Bldg. 2168, 8th St, 24 hours daily, C-608-388-2107, D-312-280-2107, Fax C-608-388-3946. All ranks. DV/VIP C-608-388-3607, D-312-280-3607.

LOGISTICAL SUPPORT: Most support facilities available.

ACS-388-3505	CHAMPUS-388-2246	Chaplain-388-4203
Child Care-388-4124	Commissary-388-3542	Comm Club-388-2065
Conv Store-269-5364	Exchange-269-4860	Family Services-388-2919
Fire Dept-388-2508	Gas Station-388-5364	ITT Office-388-3505
Legal-388-2165	Locator-388-2225	Medical-388-2730
MWR-388-4375	Package Store-269-4860	Police-388-4116
Public Affairs-388-4209	Recreation-388-3360	Retiree Services-388-3716
RV/Camping-338-3517	SATO-388-2370	SDO/NCO-388-2266
Snack Bar-388-4968	Theater-388-4968	

HEALTH & WELFARE: Clinic C-608-388-3025. Inpatient, see Great Lakes Naval Training Center, IL, C-708-688-5600. Chapel serving all faiths C-608-388-4203.

RECREATION: Arts/Crafts EX-4353, Auto Hobby EX-3013, Gym EX-2290, Rec Equip EX-2619, Fishing/Hunting EX-3337, Library EX-2410, Swimming EX-2290, Rec Center EX-3213/2971, Tennis EX-2290. Pine View Recreation Area on post, 25 Apr-30 Nov, C-608-388-3517, D-312-280-3517, two duplexes, two cabins, 365 camper spaces w/full hookups, 70 camper spaces w/E hookups, 12 camper spaces w/o hookups.

SPACE-A: None. See Volk ANGB at Camp Douglas, Base Ops, Bldg. 508, 0800-1700 Mon-Fri, C-608-427-1210, D-312-798-3210, flights via transient ANG aircraft.

ATTRACTIONS: Historical Center, La Crosse, Sparta, and Tomah. Outdoor sports and recreation.

320 - U.S. FORCES TRAVEL & TRANSFER GUIDE U.S.A

WISCONSIN

GENERAL MITCHELL INTERNATIONAL AIRPORT/AIR RESERVE STATION (WI05R2)
300 East College Avenue
Milwaukee, WI 53207-6299

TELEPHONE NUMBER INFORMATION: Main installation numbers: C-414-482-5000 (AFRES), 414-747-4420 (ANG), D-312-950-5000 (AFRES), 312-550-8420 (ANG).

LOCATION: From I-94 take the 318 East exit to the airport. USMRA: Page 68 (G-9). NMC: Milwaukee, three miles north.

GENERAL INFORMATION: Units at General Mitchell IAP include the 128th Air Refueling Group (ANG) and the 440th Airlift Wing (AFRES).

TEMPORARY MILITARY LODGING: None. See Great Lakes Naval Training Center, IL listing, C-708-688-2170, D-312-792-2710.

LOGISTICAL SUPPORT: Limited support facilities available.

Consol Club-482-5711   Exchange-747-1207   Family Services-482-5424
Fire Dept-482-5000   Legal-482-5214   MWR-482-5706
Police-482-5375   Public Affairs-482-5481 SATO-482-5799

HEALTH & WELFARE: None. See Great Lakes Naval Training Center, IL, C-708-688-5600.

SPACE-A: Ops Hangar, 0800-1700 Mon-Fri, C-414-747-4132 (ANG), 414-482-5918-EX-222 (AFRES), D-312-580-8132 (ANG), 312-950-9110 (AFRES). Flights to CONUS, OCONUS, and foreign locations.

ATTRACTIONS: City of Milwaukee, Summerfest, Wisconsin State Fairgrounds, Lake Michigan.

MILWAUKEE COAST GUARD GROUP (WI06R2)
2420 South Lincoln Memorial Drive
Milwaukee, WI 53207-1997

TELEPHONE NUMBER INFORMATION: Main installation numbers: C-414-747-7181, FTS-8-362-7181.

LOCATION: Take I-94 west to Milwaukee to I-794 east. Proceed over Hoan Bridge on I-794 to stop sign. Turn left, office is one-quarter mile. USMRA: Page 68 (G-9). NMC: Milwaukee, in city limits.

GENERAL INFORMATION: USCG Group Base, Marine Safety Office, Station and Director of CG Auxiliary.

TEMPORARY MILITARY LODGING: None. See Fort McCoy listing, C-608-388-2107, D-312-280-2107.

LOGISTICAL SUPPORT: Very limited support facilities available.

Exchange-747-1466   SDO/NCO-747-7266

WISCONSIN
Milwaukee Coast Guard Group, continued

HEALTH & WELFARE: None. See Great Lakes Naval Training Center, IL, C-708-688-5600.

RECREATION: Sherwood Point Cottage off base, one cottage, Rawley Point Light Cottage off base, one cottage; both are available year round, C-414-747-7185.

SPACE-A: None. See General Mitchell IAP/ARB listing, C-414-747-4132 (ANG), 414-482-6400-EX-222, D-312-580-8132.

ATTRACTIONS: City of Milwaukee. Lake Michigan, lakefront festivals, recreational boating and charter fishing. Wisconsin farmland to the south, west, and north. All professional sports.

Other Installations in Wisconsin

Milwaukee Post Exchange, 4828 W. Silver Springs Dr., Milwaukee, WI 53218-5000.
USMRA: Page 68 (G-8). C-414-438-6219, Exchange-438-1466.
Truax Field, 3110 Mitchell St., Madison, WI 53704-2591.
USMRA: Page 68 (E-8). C-608-242-4200, D-312-273-8200, Exchange-249-5229, NCO Club-249-6201, Medical-242-4267.
Volk Field Air National Guard Base, 100 Independence Dr., Camp Douglas, WI 54618-5001. USMRA: Page 68 (D-7). C-608-427-1210, D-312-946-3210, Exchange-427-1274, Museum-427-1280.

WYOMING

DOLLAR RENT A CAR Call 1-800-800-4000. Get a military rate by using your Military Living ID # MIL3009. Retirees/Active Duty/Reserve/Guard.

FRANCIS E. WARREN AIR FORCE BASE (WY01R4)
5305 Randall Avenue
Francis E. Warren Air Force Base, WY 82005-2266

TELEPHONE NUMBER INFORMATION: Main installation numbers: C-307-775-1110, D-312-481-1110.

LOCATION: Off I-25, Exit # 11, two miles north of I-80. Clearly marked. USMRA: Page 102 (I-8). NMC: Cheyenne, adjacent to city.

GENERAL INFORMATION: Air Force Space Command base, Missile Wing, support units.

TEMPORARY MILITARY LODGING: Billeting Office, Bldg. 211, Randolph St, 24 hours daily, C-307-775-1844, D-312-481-1844. All ranks. DV/VIP C-307-775-3610/3750.

LOGISTICAL SUPPORT: Complete support facilities available.

CHAMPUS-775-2620
Commissary-775-2427
Exchange-634-1593
Gas Station-634-7432
Legal-775-2256
MWR-775-2858
Package Store-775-3008
Recreation-775-2988
SATO-634-2948
Visitor Center-775-3694
Chaplain-775-2451
Conv Store-634-7432
Family Services-775-2241
Golf Course-775-3556
Locator-775-1841
NCO CLub-775-3024
Police-775-3501
Retiree Services-775-2309
SDO/NCO-775-3921
Child Care-775-2639
EM Club-775-3024
Fire Dept-775-2931
ITT Office-775-2988
Medical-775-1847
O'Club-775-3048
Public Affairs-775-3381
RV/Camping-775-1844
Theater-775-2345

HEALTH & WELFARE: USAF Hospital, Emergency C-307-775-3461, Appointments C-307-775-1847, 25 beds. Chapels serving all faiths C-307-775-2451/3715.

RECREATION: Bowling EX-2210, Comm Center EX-2446, Golf EX-3556, Gym EX-2304, Library EX-3416, Rec Equip EX-2988, Youth Center EX-2564. Fam-Camp on base, year round, C-307-775-2988, D-312-481-2988, 25 camper spaces w/W&E hookups, 12 camper spaces w/W hookups, 15 camper spaces w/o hookups, 10 tent spaces.

SPACE-A: Limited. Base Ops C-307-775-1110, D-312-481-1110. Also, try Cheyenne Municipal Airport, Bldg. 115, 0730-1630 Mon-Fri, C-307-772-6347/6132, D-312-943-6347/6132, Fax C-307-772-6000, ANG flights to CONUS locations.

ATTRACTIONS: Cheyenne, historic Governor's Mansion, National First Day Cover Museum, State Capital.

WYOMING

Other Installations in Wyoming

Cheyenne Municipal Airport/ANGB, 217 Dell Range Blvd., Cheyenne, WY 82009-4799. USMRA: Page 102 (I-8). C-307-772-6201, D-312-943-6201, Space-A-772-6347.

Powell Air Force Station, 1300 Fort Drum Dr., Powell, WY 82435-5000. USMRA: Page 102 (D-1). C-307-754-5351, D-312-675-5273, Commissary-754-5351.

324 - U.S. FORCES TRAVEL & TRANSFER GUIDE U.S.A

UNITED STATES POSSESSIONS

GUAM

ANDERSEN AIR FORCE BASE (GU01R8)
Unit 14003, Box 25
APO AP 96543-4003

TELEPHONE NUMBER INFORMATION: Main installation numbers: C-671-366-1110, D-315-366-1110.

LOCATION: On the north end of the island, accessible from Marine Dr which extends the entire length of the island of Guam. USMRA: Page 130 (E,F-1,2). NMC: Agana, 15 miles south.

GENERAL INFORMATION: Pacific Air Forces. Air Base Wing, AMC Squadron and other support units.

TEMPORARY MILITARY LODGING: Lodging office, Bldg. 27006, 4th & Caroline Sts, 24 hours daily, C-671-366-8201/8144, D-315-366-8201/8144. All ranks. DV/VIP C-671-366-4228.

LOGISTICAL SUPPORT: Complete support facilities available.

Cafeteria-362-3247
Child Care-362-6280
Conv Store-366-3980
Fire Dept-911
Legal-366-2937
MWR-366-5107
Public Affairs-366-4202
RV/Camping-366-5197
Snack Bar-362-3149
CHAMPUS-366-6547
Commissary-366-5159
Exchange-362-1136
Gas Station-362-7244
Locator-113
Package Store-366-3980
Recreation-366-2209
SATO-653-8945
Theater-362-7440
Chaplain-366-6139
Cons Club-366-1201
Family Services-366-8136
Golf Course-362-4653
Medical-366-2978
Police-911
Retiree Services-366-4315
SDO/NCO-363-2981
Visitor Center-366-8005

HEALTH & WELFARE: USAF Health Clinic, Emergency C-671-366-4267, Appointments C-671-366-2978. Inpatient, see Guam Naval Activities listing, C-671-344-9340/9352. Chapels serving all faiths C-671-366-6139 (after hours C-671-363-2913).

RECREATION: Arts/Crafts 366-5214, Auto Hobby 362-1258, Bowling 362-2695, Golf 362-4653, Gym EX-8282, Rec Equip EX-5197, Library EX-4191/4294, Youth Center 366-3492. See Guam Naval Activities listing for Rec Area.

SPACE-A: Pax Term/Lounge, Bldg. 17002, 24 hours daily, C-011-671-366-2096/2097, D-315-366-209620/97, Fax 011-671-366-3984, flights to CONUS, OCONUS and foreign locations.

ATTRACTIONS: Great beaches, scuba diving, snorkeling, and many other popular water sports.

U.S. FORCES TRAVEL & TRANSFER GUIDE U.S.A. - 325

GUAM

GUAM NAVAL ACTIVITIES (GU02R8)
PSC 455, Box 169
FPO AP 96540-1099

TELEPHONE NUMBER INFORMATION: Main installation numbers: C-011-671-351-1110, D-315-355-1110.

LOCATION: South on Marine Drive. Clearly marked. USMRA: Page 130 (C-3). NMC: Agana, 10 miles north.

GENERAL INFORMATION: Headquarters Commander US Naval Forces Marianas; Naval Hospital; Camp Covington (Seabees); Naval Activities; Naval Pacific and Meterological Oceanography Center/Joint Typhoon Warning Center (NAVCMETOCCENT/JTWC); Marianas Section Coast Guard; Naval Computer & Telecommunications Area Master Station Western Pacific (NAVCAMS WESTPAC).

TEMPORARY MILITARY LODGING: Centralized lodging office, 24 hours daily, C-011-671-339-5259, D-315-339-5139, Fax 011-671-339-6250. All ranks.

LOGISTICAL SUPPORT: Complete support facilities available.

Cafeteria-564-3124
Conv Store-564-3285
Family Services-343-2981
Locator-355-1110
O'Club-472-4607
SDO-349-5235

Chaplain-339-2126
Consol Club-564-1834
Garage-564-3191
Medical-344-9202
Police-333-2989
Snack Bar-564-3124

Commissary-339-5177
Exchange-564-3177
Legal-333-2061
Navy Campus-339-8291
SATO-564-1636
Theater-564-1830

HEALTH & WELFARE: Naval Hospital, Emergency C-671-344-9314, Appointments C-671-344-9326/9327, 350 beds. Chapels serving all faiths C-671-339-2126.

RECREATION: Gym 564-18244, Golf 734-1124, Beach 564-1823, Swimming 564-1822, Hobby Complex 564-1826, Library 564-1836, Bowling 564-1828, Rec Center 564-1847. Camping allowed on some beaches, no hookups. Rec equipment available.

SPACE-A: None. See Andersen AFB listing, C-671-366-2095, D-315-366-2095, Fax 671-366-2079.

ATTRACTIONS: Great beaches, water sports, hiking, historical landmarks, miniature submarine tour, boat tours, Cocos Island.

326 - U.S. FORCES TRAVEL & TRANSFER GUIDE U.S.A

PUERTO RICO

DOLLAR RENT A CAR — Call 1-800-800-4000. Get a military rate by using your Military Living ID # ML3009. Retirees/Active Duty/Reserve/Guard.

BORINQUEN COAST GUARD AIR STATION (PR03R1)
Aguadilla, PR 00604-5000

TELEPHONE NUMBER INFORMATION: Main installation numbers: C-809-890-8400, D-312-831-3392-3399.

LOCATION: At the old Ramey AFB, north of Aguadilla. Take PR-2 west from San Juan or north from Mayaguez to PR-110 north to CGAS. USMRA: Page 130 (B,C-2). NMC: San Juan, 65 miles east.

GENERAL INFORMATION: Coast Guard Air Station for the Puerto Rico area.

TEMPORARY MILITARY LODGING: Lodging office, La Plaza, Room 26. 0800-1600 Mon-Fri, C-809-890-8492. All ranks. DV/VIP C-809-890-8400.

LOGISTICAL SUPPORT: Limited support facilities available.

Cafeteria-890-2581	CDO/OOD-890-2671	CHAMPUS-EX-1500
Chaplain-890-8486	Child Care-890-8494	Conv Store-890-8722/8723
CPO Club-890-8499	EM Club-890-8729	Exchange-890-3127/7272
Locator-882-8400	Medical-890-8485	MWR-890-8492/8493
OPS/ODO-890-8421	Package Store-890-8719	Police-890-8472
SATO-890-4722	SDO/NCO-890-8421	Theater-890-8495

HEALTH & WELFARE: Emergency C-809-890-8477. Inpatient, see Roosevelt Roads Naval Station listing, C-809-865-4133/7133. Chapel C-809-890-8486.

RECREATION: Gym, Racquetball, Tennis, Outdoor basketball/volleyball, Fitness trail, Pool, and Fitness center. Recreation Area off base, year round, C-809-890-8492, 16 cabins and two apartments.

SPACE-A: Pax Term/Lounge, CG Hangar, 0730-1530 Mon-Fri, C-809-890-8423, weekends, C-809-890-8421, unscheduled flights to Puerto Rico and CONUS.

ATTRACTIONS: Local beaches and restaurants, excellent surfing during winter months, 18-hole golf course available to military, excellent snorkeling and scuba diving, whale watching during migratory season.

CAMP SANTIAGO TRAINING SITE (PR07R1)
P.O. Box 1166
Salinas, PR 00751-1166

TELEPHONE NUMBER INFORMATION: Main installation numbers: C-809-824-2955/3110/4341, Fax 809-824-2022.

LOCATION: PR Route 52 (exit 68) from San Juan to Ponce and south area of Puerto Rico. Camp Santiago is at the town of Salinas, right of the exit of route 52. USMRA: Page 130 (D,E-3). NMC: Ponce, 25 miles.

PUERTO RICO
Camp Santiago Training Site, continued

GENERAL INFORMATION: Puerto Rico National Guard. 201st Evac Hospital, Troop E 192nd Cavalry, and other units.

TEMPORARY MILITARY LODGING: Currently under planning and development.

LOGISTICAL SUPPORT: Limited support facilities available.

Cafeteria-ext 210	EM Club-ext 210	Exchange-824-4270
NCO Club-ext 210	Officers Club-ext 210	Package Store-824-2562

HEALTH & WELFARE: None. See Roosevelt Roads Naval Station listing, C-809-865-4133/7133.

RECREATION: None available on base.

SPACE-A: None. See Roosevelt Roads Naval Station listing, C-809-865-4383, D-313-831-4383/3257, Fax 809-865-4208.

ATTRACTIONS: Sunny area, 85 degrees year round. Beaches, camping, fresh seafood. Museums in Ponce and Guayama.

FORT BUCHANAN (PR01R1)
Fort Buchanan, PR 00934-5026

TELEPHONE NUMBER INFORMATION: Main installation numbers: C-809-273-3400, D-313-740-3400.

LOCATION: From San Juan IAP toward San Juan, exit Caguas/Bayamon to PR-18, exit Bayamon right to PR-22, one-and-a-half miles to fort on left. USMRA: Page 130 (E-2). NMC: San Juan, six miles southwest.

GENERAL INFORMATION: The major US Army Post in Puerto Rico providing support to National Guard and Reserve units.

TEMPORARY MILITARY LODGING: Lodging office, Bldg. 556, 0700-1600 daily, C-809-273-3821, D-313-740-7289/3256. All ranks. DV/VIP C-809-273-3240.

LOGISTICAL SUPPORT: Complete support facilities available.

ACS-273-3292	CHAMPUS-273-3339	Chaplain-273-3336
Child Care-273-3280	Commissary-273-2078	Conv Store-273-8046
CPO/OOD-273-3773	Credit Union-273-1307	EM Club-273-3535
Exchange-273-2066	Family Services-273-3332	Fire Dept-273-3917
Gas Station-792-4297	Golf Course-273-3980	Legal-273-3345
Locator-273-2424	Medical-273-2043	MWR-273-3301
NCO Club-273-3535	O'Club 273-3535	Package Store-793-1984
Police-273-3913	Public Affairs-273-3205	Recreation-273-3301
Retiree Services-273-3877	Travel-273-3915	Visitor Center-273-3714

HEALTH & WELFARE: US Army Health Clinic/Emergency C-809-783-2424, Appointments C-809-783-2424. Inpatient, see Roosevelt Roads Naval Station listing, C-809-865-4133/7133. Chapel serving all faiths C-809-783-8251.

PUERTO RICO
Fort Buchanan, continued

RECREATION: Auto Hobby EX-8172, Ceramics EX-7172, Golf EX-7252, Health Club EX-7167, Library EX-3208, Rec Services EX-2101, Rec Equip EX-7134, Swimming EX-8182, Wood Hobby EX-8160, Youth Center EX-7187, Racquetball & Tennis Court EX-7134, Scuba EX-8280.

SPACE-A: None. See Roosevelt Roads Naval Station listing, C-809-865-4383, D-313-831-4383/3157, Fax 809-865-4208.

ATTRACTIONS: San Juan is the oldest city under the American flag. 16th-Century Spanish architecture, fortresses. Largest shopping center in the Caribbean. Rain forest. Beaches. Luxury hotels and casinos. Water sports, deep sea fishing. World's largest radio telescope.

ROOSEVELT ROADS NAVAL STATION (PR02R1)
FPO AA 34051-5000

TELEPHONE NUMBER INFORMATION: Main installation numbers: C-809-865-2000, D-313-831-2000/4311.

LOCATION: From Luis Munoz IAP, San Juan left (east) onto PR-3 for 45 miles, sign on right indicating exit to Naval Station. USMRA: Page 130 (F-2,3). NMC: San Juan, 50 miles northwest.

GENERAL INFORMATION: Fleet Air Caribbean, Atlantic Fleet Weapons Training Facility, Marine Corps Security Force Company, Naval Air Station, and support units.

TEMPORARY MILITARY LODGING: Navy Lodge C-809-865-8283. Lodging office, Bldg. 1708, FDR Dr, 0700-1530 Mon-Fri, C-809-865-5325/3058, D-313-831-5325/3058. Other times BOQ C-809-865-4334/3400, BEQ C-809-865-4145, Housing office C-809-865-4024. All ranks. DV/VIP C-809-865-3400. Navy Lodge C-809-865-8281/8283, Fax 809-865-1031/6000.

LOGISTICAL SUPPORT: Complete support facilities available.

CHAMPUS-865-7133	Chaplain-865-4326/4328	Child Care-865-4699
Commissary-865-4287	Conv Store-865-4868	CPO Club-865-5279
Deli-865-3509/4045	EM Club-865-5288	Exchange-865-3252
Family Services-865-4091	Gas Station-865-4609	ITT Office-865-4757
Legal-865-4315/4320	Locator-865-2000	Medical-865-4133/7133
O'Club-865-7200	Petty Ofc Club-865-4142	Package Store-865-7140
Police-865-4195	Red Cross-865-3428	Retiree Services-865-4091
SATO-865-1539/1570	CDO/JOOD-865-4311/4352	Theater-865-4380

HEALTH & WELFARE: US Naval Hospital, Ambulance C-809-865-4144/4123, Info C-809-865-4133/7133, 120 beds. Chapels serving all faiths C-809-865-4326.

RECREATION: Auto Hobby EX-4773, Bowling EX-4524, Comm Center EX-4854, Fitness Center EX-4033, Flying Club EX-3023, Golf EX-4751, Library EX-4353, Marina EX-3297, Stables EX-3345, Swimming EX-4033, Yacht Club EX-4537, Youth Center EX-3560/4926.

PUERTO RICO
Roosevelt Roads Naval Station, continued

SPACE-A: Pax Term/Lounge, Air Ops Bldg., STOP 23, 0700-1600 Mon-Sat, Sun for flights only, C-809-865-4383, D-313-831-4383/3257, Fax 809-865-4208, flights to CONUS, OCONUS and foreign locations.

ATTRACTIONS: El Yunque rain forest with waterfalls, hiking trails, and restaurants. Vieques Island with beaches, restaurants and guest houses.

SABANA SECA NAVAL SECURITY GROUP ACTIVITY (PR04R1)
FPO AA 34053-1000

TELEPHONE NUMBER INFORMATION: Main installation numbers: C-809-795-2255/2399, D-313-831-7202

LOCATION: From San Juan IAP, take Route 3 west to Bayamon exit to PR-22 west to PR-886 north (Las Arenas exit) to base. Or: take Interstate 22 west (toward Arecibo), get off exit La Arena. At the next intersection turn left, the base will be located on the left. USMRA: Page 130 (D,E-2). NMC: San Juan, 14 miles east.

GENERAL INFORMATION: Naval Security Group Activity for the Caribbean.

TEMPORARY MILITARY LODGING: None. See Fort Buchanan listing, C-809-273-3821, D-313-740-7289/3256.

LOGISTICAL SUPPORT: Limited support facilities available.

CDO/OOD-795-2255/2295	Chaplain-795-8386	Child Care-795-8451
Consol Club-795-8425	Exchange-795-8374	Fire Dept-795-8385
Gas Station-895-8405	ITT Office-795-8313	Legal-795-8398
Locator-795-2255/2399	Medical-795-8380	MWR-795-8363
Police-785-8310	Public Affairs-795-8307	Snack Bar-795-8429

HEALTH & WELFARE: US Naval Branch Medical Clinic, Emergency C-809-795-4165/795-2255-EX-290/291/292. Inpatient, see Roosevelt Roads Naval Station listing, C-809-865-4133/7133. Chapel serving all faiths C-809-795-2255-EX-300.

RECREATION: Auto Hobby EX-279, Bowling EX-372, Ceramics EX-278, Rec Center, Tennis, Sports Fields, Theater, Rec Services EX-270. Basketball, Swimming, Weight Room EX-371.

SPACE-A: None. See Roosevelt Roads Naval Station listing, C-809-865-4383, D-313-831-4383/3257, Fax 809-865-4208.

ATTRACTIONS: Great beaches, El Yunque Rain Forest, El Morro Fort and Casinos.

Other Installations in Puerto Rico

San Juan Coast Guard Base, Box S-2029, San Juan, PR 00903-2029. USMRA: Page 130 (E-2). C-809-721-3955, Exchange-721-3955.

VIRGIN ISLANDS

Installations in U. S. Virgin Islands

Virgin Islands National Guard Base, Alexander Hamilton Airport, Kingshill, St Croix, VI 00851-2270. USMRA: Page 130 (H-4). C-809-778-2200, Exchange-773-5000, SATO-772-7836, Space-A-778-2165/9261.

U.S. FORCES TRAVEL & TRANSFER GUIDE U.S.A. - 331

WAKE ISLAND

WAKE ISLAND AIR FORCE BASE (WK01R8)
APO AP 96518-5000

EDITORS NOTE: *This base is scheduled to close after clean-up work is completed.*

TELEPHONE NUMBER INFORMATION: Main installation numbers: C-Small Islands Operator in Honolulu (430-0111) can dial Wake extensions. D-315-424-2101, ask for Wake Island.

LOCATION: A U.S. Possession in the Pacific, 2100 miles west of Hawaii. Access by military aircraft only.

GENERAL INFORMATION: Host is Det 4, 15 ABW/PACAF. If not on official orders, a letter is required from the Commander of Det 4 authorizing visit.

TEMPORARY MILITARY LODGING: Very limited, usually filled by those on duty. Billeting D-315-424-2222.

LOGISTICAL SUPPORT: Limited support facilities available.

Exchange-424-2251   Food Bar-424-3100   Medical-424-2445
Post Office-424-2259

HEALTH & WELFARE: None.

RECREATION: Swimming, fishing, snorkeling, other water sports.

SPACE-A: Pax Term/Lounge, Base Ops, 0800-1700 Mon-Sat, C-808-424-2101/2320, D-313-424-2101, Fax 808-424-2165, flights to OCONUS and overseas.

ATTRACTIONS: Tropical climate, nice beaches.

332 - U.S. FORCES TRAVEL & TRANSFER GUIDE U.S.A

FOREIGN COUNTRIES

CANADA

DOLLAR RENT A CAR Call 1-800-800-4000. Get a military rate by using your Military Living ID # ML3009. Retirees/Active Duty/Reserve/Guard.

TRENTON CANADIAN FORCES BASE (CN04R1)
Astra, Ontario, CN KOK 1BO

TELEPHONE NUMBER INFORMATION: Main installation numbers: C-613-392-2811, D-312-827-7011.

LOCATION: Trenton is one-and-a-half hours east of Toronto, Ontario along Highway 401. Base is located one kilometer east of Trenton on Highway 2. NMC: Trenton, one mile.

GENERAL INFORMATION: CFB Trenton is home of Air Transport Group Hq, 3 Heavy Transport Squadrons, one Search and Rescue Squadron and one Air Transport Training Squadron. THIS IS NOT A U.S. BASE.

TEMPORARY MILITARY LODGING: Yukon Lodge, A.M.D.U. Road, 24 hours daily, C-613-965-3793, D-312-827-3793.

LOGISTICAL SUPPORT: Most support facilities available.

Chaplain-392-3665/2298
Exchange-392-1608
Golf Course-392-1544
NCO Club-392-3545
Public Affairs-392-2041
Snack Bar-392-5484

Child Care-392-2724
Family Services-392-3575
Legal-392-2574
O'Club-392-2205/2253
Recreation-392-3754

EM Club-392-3700/3409
Fire Dept-392-3511
Medical-392-8480
Police-392-3385
SDO/NCO-392-2811

HEALTH AND WELFARE: Base Hospital, C-613-965-3060. Inpatient, Trenton Memorial Hospital C-613-392-2541. Chapels: Prot C-613-965-3060, RC C-613-965-3059.

RECREATION: Bowling EX-2811/3305, Yacht club EX-8995

SPACE-A: None available.

ATTRACTIONS: Located on Bay of Quinte, excellent boating, camping and fishing area. Sand beaches nearby. Royal Canadian Air Force Museum on base.

U.S. FORCES TRAVEL & TRANSFER GUIDE U.S.A. - 333

CUBA

GUANTANAMO BAY NAVAL STATION (CU01R1)
FPO AE 09593-5000

TELEPHONE NUMBER INFORMATION: Main installation numbers: C-011-53-99-XXXX, D-313-723-3960/564-4063.

LOCATION: In the southeast corner of the Republic of Cuba. Accessible only by air. NMC: Miami, FL, 525 air miles northwest. Note: Access to Guantanamo is strictly controlled; only official travelers and relatives of base personnel (according to strict guidelines and when approved by the base commander) are permitted on base.

GENERAL INFORMATION: Navy Fleet Training Group. Ship repair facility, 100-bed hospital.

TEMPORARY MILITARY LODGING: Lodging office, Bldg. 1670, Deer Point Rd, 24 hours daily, C-011-53-99-2400/6350, D-313-723-3960. 24 hours daily, Navy Lodge. All ranks. DV/VIP C-011-53-99-3103.

LOGISTICAL SUPPORT: Complete support facilities available.

Cafeteria-EX-4815	Chaplain-EX-2323/2628	Child Care-EX-2205/2990
Commissary-EX-4134/2464	Conv Store-EX-2508	CPO Club-EX-2379
EM Club-EX-2304	Exchange-EX-4119/4346	Family Services-EX-4151/53
Fire Department-EX-4165	Gas Station-EX-4670	Golf Course-EX-2652
Legal-EX-4600	Locator-EX-4453	Medical-EX-2200
MWR-EX-2193	NCO Club-EX-2636/45	O'Club-EX-2531
Public Affairs-EX-4502	Police-EX-4105	SATO-EX-4517
SDO/NCO-EX-4366	Snack Bar-EX-3040	

HEALTH & WELFARE: Naval Hospital, C-011-53-99-7201, D-313-723-3960-EX-7201, 100 beds. Chaplains serving all faiths C-011-53-99-4550.

RECREATION: Special Services EX-2249, Boat and Fishing Rental, Swimming, Golf, Picnic Area, Bike Rental, Bowling, Auto Hobby, Gym, theater group, photo club, and corral.

SPACE-A: Pax Term/Lounge, C-011-53-99-4204/6408, D-313-723-564-4063, Fax 011-53-99-5092, flights to CONUS and foreign locations.

ATTRACTIONS: Beaches, fishing, boating, diving warm climate.

334 - U.S. FORCES TRAVEL & TRANSFER GUIDE U.S.A

DENMARK

DOLLAR RENT A CAR — Call 1-800-800-4000. Get a military rate by using your Military Living ID # ML3009. Retirees/Active Duty/Reserve/Guard.

THULE AIR BASE (DN02R7)
Unit 82501
APO AE 09704-5000

TELEPHONE NUMBER INFORMATION: Main installation numbers: C-011-299-50-646 (Ask for EX), D-314-268-1211-EX-2711.

LOCATION: Northwest coast of Greenland, 800 miles from the North Pole, 700 miles north of the Arctic Circle, 2500 miles from McGuire AFB, NJ. Closer to Seattle than New York City by five miles.

GENERAL INFORMATION: 12th Space Warning Squadron. Clearance from XO, 12th SWS, is required to enter Thule Defense Area; no dependents are allowed.

TEMPORARY MILITARY LODGING: Lodging office, Bldg. 97, 24 hours daily, EX-3276.

LOGISTICAL SUPPORT: Most support facilities available.

Barber-EX-3127
Exchange-EX-2103
Laundry-EX-2249
Police-EX-2335
Chaplain-EX-2209
Dining Hall-EX-2614
Medical-EX-2696
Recreation-EX-2242
Consol Club-EX-2418
Fire Dept-EX-3249
MWR-EX-2445
SDO/NCO-EX-2407

HEALTH & WELFARE: Hospital operated under contract by DAC personnel. Provides care and treatment to all assigned American and Danish military personnel EX-2696.

RECREATION: Rec Center (pool tables, TV lounge and recording center) EX-2242, Library EX-2539, Gymnasium EX-2519, Bowling EX-2435, Hobby Shops EX-2228, Golf, Skeet and Aero Club. Excellent sports facilities.

SPACE-A: Pax Term, Bldg. 623, 0800-1700 Mon-Fri, as needed on Sat, C-011-299-50-124 EX-2155, D-314-834-1211 EX-2155 Fax 011-299-50-636 EX-2556. Scheduled flights to and from McGuire AFB, NJ. Only Permanent Party military personnel returning from leave or personnel on TDY or PCS orders can travel to Thule.

ATTRACTIONS: Winter sports activities.

U.S. FORCES TRAVEL & TRANSFER GUIDE U.S.A. - 335

PANAMA

DOLLAR RENT A CAR — Call 1-800-800-4000. Get a military rate by using your Military Living ID # ML3009. Retirees/Active Duty/Reserve/Guard.

Note: Under the Panama Canal Treaty Implementation Plan, U.S. troops currently in Panama are scheduled to be withdrawn by the end of 1999.

ALBROOK AIR FORCE STATION (PN08R3)
APO AA 34002-5000

TELEPHONE NUMBER INFORMATION: Main installation numbers: D-313-285-6112.

LOCATION: Take PN-C-12 west to PN-C-11 south to the station on right. Or take PN-C-11 south to PN-C-11 north to the station.

GENERAL INFORMATION: Albrook is home to the 24th Air Postal Squadron, which is responsible for postal operations in Panama and Central South America.

TEMPORARY MILITARY LODGING: None. See Howard AFB listing, C-011-507-84-4914/5306.

LOGISTICAL SUPPORT: Very limited support facilities available.

Cafeteria-286-5226   Exchange-286-3136

HEALTH & WELFARE: Ambulance/Fire 119, Veterinary Emergency D-313-282-5222.

RECREATION: Auto Hobby 286-3613.

SPACE-A: See Howard Air Force Base listing, C-011-507-284-4306/5758, D-313-284-4306/5758, Fax 011-507-284-3848.

ATTRACTIONS: Panama Canal.

FORT CLAYTON (PN02R3)
APO AA 34004-5000

TELEPHONE NUMBER INFORMATION: Main installation numbers: C-507-287-6114, D-313-285-6110.

LOCATION: Near Pacific entrance to the Panama Canal. Take Galliard highway toward the Miraflores Locks, clearly marked. NMC: Panama City, eight miles southwest.

GENERAL INFORMATION: Headquarters: US Army South, 1st Battalion, 228th Aviation Brigade, MP Command, 5th/87th Infantry Batttlion, 106th US Army Signal Brigade, 536th Engineer Battlion.

TEMPORARY MILITARY LODGING: Billeting Office, Bldg. 518, Hospital Rd, 24 hours daily, reservations required C-011-507-287-4451/3251, DV/VIP C-011-507-287-5057/8.

336 - U.S. FORCES TRAVEL & TRANSFER GUIDE U.S.A

PANAMA
Fort Clayton, continued

LOGISTICAL SUPPORT: Complete support facilities available.

ACS-287-5426	Chaplain-287-33466	Child Care-287-6810
Commissary-285-5409	Exchange-285-4133	Family Services-282-5139
Gas Station-286-6280	Legal-287-6205	Locator-287-3139
Medical-282-5222	MWR-287-3903	NCO Club-287-3279
Police-287-4401	Public Affairs-287-3007	Recreation-287-5613
Snack Bar-287-4718	Theater-287-3279	

HEALTH & WELFARE: US Army Health Clinic C-507-287-4455, Medical Emergency C-507-282-5111.

RECREATION: Arts/Crafts, Boat Shop, Bowling, Ceramics, Gym, Library, Swimming, Scuba Rentals, Youth Center.

SPACE-A: None. See Howard Air Force Base listing, C-011-507-284-4306/5758, D-313-284-4306/5758, Fax 011-507-284-3848.

ATTRACTIONS: The Panama Canal, Panama City, 16th Century Cathedrals, Pacific and Atlantic beaches.

FORT KOBBE (PN07R3)
APO AA 34006-5000

TELEPHONE NUMBER INFORMATION: Main installation numbers: D-313-285-6112.

LOCATION: Located on the Pacific side of Panama near Howard Air Force Base. Take PN-K2 west past Howard to PN-K1A. The fort is on the left past the hospital.

GENERAL INFORMATION: Units at Fort Kobbe include the 2/187th Infantry Battalion, 536th Engineering Battalion, 15th Engineering Company, 210th Combat Aviation Battalion, 114th and 120th Aviation Companies, the 590th ACF Maintenance Company and the 214th Air Ambulance Detachment.

TEMPORARY MILITARY LODGING: None. See Howard Air Force Base listing.

LOGISTICAL SUPPORT: Complete support facilities available.

Chaplain-282-3610	Commissary-284-6156	Exchange-284-2395/3395
Legal-287-5401/5407	Police-110/287-4401	

HEALTH & WELFARE: Ambulance/Fire 119, ACS-D-313-284-5759, Family Advocacy D-313-285-4859, Veterinary Emergency D-313-282-5222.

RECREATION: Beach 284-5759, Outdoor Rec 287-3363, Teen Club 284-3323, Golf (Fort Amador) 282-4410.

SPACE-A: None. See Howard Air Force Base listing, C-011-507-284-4306/5758, D-313-284-4306/5758, Fax 011-507-284-3848.

ATTRACTIONS: Panama Canal, Miraflores Locks, 16th-century cathedrals.

U.S. FORCES TRAVEL & TRANSFER GUIDE U.S.A. - 337

PANAMA

FORT SHERMAN (PN06R3)
APO AA 34005-5000

TELEPHONE NUMBER INFORMATION: Main installation numbers: D-313-289-6113.

LOCATION: Located on the Caribbean/Atlantic side of Panama on the south entrance to Limon Bay. Accessible from PN-52 east which terminates at Fort Sherman. NMC: Colon.

GENERAL INFORMATION: The Jungle Operations Training Center is located at Fort Sherman.

TEMPORARY MILITARY LODGING: Gulick Guest House.

LOGISTICAL SUPPORT: Most support facilities available.

Chaplain-289-3319   Exchange-289-6331   Gas Station-289-6331
Library-289-6292   Legal-289-3886/3796   Rec Center-289-6402
Shoppette-289-6331   Theater-289-6251

HEALTH & WELFARE: Ambulance/Fire 119/D-313-289-6211/6233.

RECREATION: Library 289-6292, Outdoor Rec/Community Center 289-6402/6699, Arts/Crafts 289-6313, Beach 289-6190, Scuba/Rental Center 289-6104.

SPACE-A: None. See Howard Air Force Base listing, C-011-507-284-4306/5758, D-313-284-4306/5758, Fax 011-507-284-3848.

ATTRACTIONS: Panama Canal, Gatun Locks, Indian ruins.

HOWARD AIR FORCE BASE (PN01R3)
APO AA 34001-5000

TELEPHONE NUMBER INFORMATION: Main installation numbers: C-507-284-3010, D-313-284-3010. After duty hours: C-507-284-4556. Switch Operator: D-313-284-9805. Directory Assistance: D-313-285-6114.

LOCATION: Adjacent to Pan American Highway on Pacific side of Panama. 10 miles from Albrook AFS across the Bridge of the Americas. NMC: Panama City, 10 miles west.

GENERAL INFORMATION: Headquarters 24th Wing, Air Combat Command. 617th Airlift Support Squadron, 6933rd Electronic Security Squadron.

TEMPORARY MILITARY LODGING: Billeting Office, Bldg. 708, Carpenter Ave, C-507-84-5306. DV/VIP, Bldg. 119, reservations required 284-4601.

LOGISTICAL SUPPORT: Complete support facilities available.

Chaplain-284-3948   Child Care-284-6135   Commissary-284-3967
Exchange-284-5212   Family Services-284-5650   Fire Department-284-5305
Gas Station2-84-6001   Golf Course-284-6223   Legal-284-3499
Locator-284-3010   Medical-284-4649   MWR-284-6161
NCO Club-284-4107   O'Club-84-4260   Package Store-284-6001

PANAMA
Howard Air Force Base, continued

| Police-284-4711 | Public Affairs-284-5459 | Recreation 284-6107 |
| SATO-284-3071 | Theater-284-6225 | Visitor Center-284-4132 |

HEALTH & WELFARE: USAF Clinic C-507-84-3562, Dental Clinic C-507-84-4558. Gorgas Army Hospital, C-507-82-5400, operated by Canal Zone Government, provides all care for military personnel and dependents. Admission is arranged through the base clinic, except in emergencies C-507-82-5111. Chapel serving all faiths.

RECREATION: Off base: MWR offers a variety of tours and trips, 84-6109. On Base: Arts/Crafts 84-6361, Ceramics 84-6361, Fitness Center 84-3451, Library 84-6249, Stables 84-3770, Auto Hobby 84-3370, Rod/Gun Club 84-4858, Rec Center 84-6161, MWR Office 84-5907, Swimming 84-3569, Wood Hobby 84-3370, Youth Activities, Bowling 84-4190, Golf 87-6322, Camping/Rec Equip 84-6161. Kobbe Beach Complex on base. Rec Area at Gamboa, Republic of Panama, near buoy 46, C-507-284-6161. Activities include sunbathing, fishing and boating.

SPACE-A: AMC Pax Term, Bldg. 228, 0500-2100 daily. C-011-507-284-4306/5758/5702, D-313-284-4306/5758/5702, Fax 011-507-284-3848, flights to CONUS and overseas.

ATTRACTIONS: Panama City, 10 miles west. The Panama Canal, 16th-century cathedrals, Indian ruins, Atlantic and Pacific beaches.

PANAMA CANAL NAVAL STATION (PN09R3)
Unit 6249
FPO AA 34061-1000

Scheduled to close December 1999.

TELEPHONE NUMBER INFORMATION: Main installation numbers: C-507-283-4568, D-313-283-4568.

LOCATION: On the west bank of the Panama Canal, one mile west of the Bridge of the Americas.

GENERAL INFORMATION: Fleet support at the crossroads of the world.

TEMPORARY MILITARY LODGING: Lodging office, Bldg. 77, Rodman, C-507-283-4619, D-313-283-4619. All Ranks. Fax 011-507-283-4569.

LOGISTICAL SUPPORT: Complete support facilities available on board or on Howard Air Force Base.

All Hands Club-ext 4498	Chaplain-ext 4148	Conv Store-ext 4330
Exchange-ext 5338	Family Services-ext 5749	Legal-ext 3653
Medical-ext 4300	Package Store-ext 4075	Police-ext 5611/2
Public Affairs-ext 5644	Snack Bar-ext 6250	SDO/NCO-ext 4766

HEALTH & WELFARE: Medical/Dental Clinic, Bldg. 84, Rodman, C-507-83-4300. Chapel serving all faiths, Bldg. 88, C-507-83-4148.

RECREATION: Marina, Swimming Pools, Tennis, Golf (Horoko), Fishing, Gym, Softball Field, Soccer Field. For other recreation activities call Rec Services 83-3547. MWR Office 83-5103.

PANAMA
Panama Canal Naval Station, continued

SPACE-A: None. See Howard Air Force Base listing, C-011-507-284-3848, D-313-284-4306/5758, Fax 011-507-2844/3848.

ATTRACTIONS: Panama Canal, Perlas Islands and Panama City.

QUARRY HEIGHTS POST (PN03R3)
APO AA 34003-5000

TELEPHONE NUMBER INFORMATION: Main installation numbers: C-011-507-82-4666, D-313-282-4266.

LOCATION: On the Pacific side of Panama. Clearly marked. NMC: Panama City, in city limits.

GENERAL INFORMATION: USCINCSO, USSOUTHCOM.

TEMPORARY MILITARY LODGING: Billeting Office, Bldg. 518, Fort Clayton, 24 hours daily, D-313-287-4451/3251.

LOGISTICAL SUPPORT: Limited support facilities available.

Barber Shop-282-3517   O'Club-282-3439   Police-282-3054
Shoppette-282-3517

HEALTH & WELFARE: Gorgas Army Hospital D-313-282-5111.

RECREATION: None. See Howard Air Force Base listing, C-011-507-284-4306/5758, D-313-284-4306/5758, Fax 011-507-2844/3848.

SPACE-A: None. See Howard Air Force Base listing, C-011-507-284-3848, D-313-284-4306/5758, Fax 011-507-284-3848.

ATTRACTIONS: The Panama Canal, beaches, 16th-century cathedrals and ancient Indian ruins.

APPENDIX A

Country and State Abbreviations Used in this Book

COUNTRY

CN-Canada
CU-Cuba
DN-Denmark
GU-Guam*
VI-Virgin Islands

PN-Panama
PR-Puerto Rico*
US-United States
WK-Wake Island*

* US Possession or Territory

STATE

AK-Alaska
AL-Alabama
AR-Arkansas
AZ-Arizona
CA-California
CO-Colorado
CT-Connecticut
DC-District of Columbia
DE-Delaware
FL-Florida
GA-Georgia
HI-Hawaii
IA-Iowa
ID-Idaho
IL-Illinois
IN-Indiana
KS-Kansas
KY-Kentucky
LA-Louisiana
MA-Massachusetts
MD-Maryland
ME-Maine
MI-Michigan
MN-Minnesota
MO-Missouri
MS-Mississippi

MT-Montana
NE-Nebraska
NC-North Carolina
ND-North Dakota
NH-New Hampshire
NJ-New Jersey
NM-New Mexico
NY New York
NV-Nevada
OH-Ohio
OK-Oklahoma
OR-Oregon
PA-Pennsylvania
RI-Rhode Island
SC-South Carolina
SD-South Dakota
TN-Tennessee
TX-Texas
UT-Utah
VA-Virginia
VT-Vermont
WA-Washington
WI-Wisconsin
WV-West Virginia
WY-Wyoming

APPENDIX B

General Abbreviations Used in this Book

This appendix contains general abbreviations used in this book. Commonly understood abbreviations and standard abbreviations found in addresses have not been included in order to save space.

A
AAF-Army Airfield
AAFES-Army/Air Force Exchange Service
AB-Air Base
ACS-Army Community Services
AD-Active Duty
AF-Air Force
AFAF-Air Force Auxiliary Field
AFB-Air Force Base
AFRC-Air Force Reserve Center
AFRC-Armed Forces Recreation Center
AFRES-Air Force Reserve
AFS-Air Force Station
AMC-Army Medical Center
ANGB-Air National Guard Base
APG-Army Proving Ground
APO-Army Post Office
ARNG-Army National Guard
AS-Air Station
Ave-Avenue

B
BEQ-Bachelor Enlisted Quarters
BOQ-Bachelor Officers' Quarters
Bldg-Building
Blvd-Boulevard

C
C-Commercial Phone Number
CDO-Command Duty Officer
CG-Coast Guard
CGAS-Coast Guard Air Station
CGG-Coast Guard Group
CGSC-Coast Guard Support Center
CGTC-Coast Guard Training Center
CO-Commanding Officer
CONSOL-Consolidated
CONV-Convenience
CPO-Chief Petty Officer
CQ-Charge of Quarters
CSM-Command Sergeant Major

D
D-Defense Switched Network
DAVs-Disabled American Veterans
DO-Duty Officer
DoD-Department of Defense
Dr-Drive
DV-Distinguished Visitor
DVOQ-Distinguished Visitor Officers' Quarters
DVQ-Distinguished Visitor Quarters

E
EM Club-Enlisted Men's Club
ETS-Estimated Time of Separation
EX-Telephone Extension

F
FPO-Fleet Post Office
FTS-Federal Telephone System

G
GH-Guest House

H
HQ-Headquarters

I
IAP-International Airport
ITT-Information, Tickets & Tours
ITR-Information, Ticketing and Registration

J
JRB-Joint Reserve Base

M
MC-Marine Corps
MCAS-Marine Corps Air Station
MCB-Marine Corps Base
MCRC-Marine Corps Recruiting Station
MWR-Morale, Welfare and Recreation

N
NAB-Naval Amphibious Base
NAF-Non-appropriated Funds
NAS-Naval Air Station
NB-Naval Base
NCO-Noncommissioned Officer
NG-National Guard
NGX-National Guard Exchange
NMC-Nearest Major City
NMI-Nearest Military Installation
NS-Naval Station
NSB-Navy Submarine Base
NSO-Navy Security Office
NSWC-Naval Surface Weapons Center
NTC-Naval Training Center
NWC-Naval Weapons Center

O
O'Club-Officers' Club
OIC-Officer in Charge
OOD-Officer of the Day

P
PAO-Public Affairs Office
PCS-Permanent Change of Station
PERS-Personnel
PMO-Provost Marshall's Office

R
Rd-Road
REC-Recreation
RV-Recreational Vehicle

S
SC-Support Center
SDO-Staff Duty Officer
SDNCO-Senior Duty Non-Commissioned Officer
SNCO-Senior Non-Commissioned Officer
Space-A-Space Available
St-Saint
St-Street

T
TAD-Temporary Attached Duty
TDY-Temporary Duty
TEQ-Temporary Enlisted Quarters
TFL-Temporary Family Lodging
TLA-Temporary Lodging Allowance
TLF-Transient Lodging Facility
TLQ-Temporary Living Quarters
TML-Temporary Military Lodging
TOQ-Transient Officers' Quarters
TVEQ-Temporary Visiting Enlisted Quarters
TVOQ-Temporary Visiting Officers' Quarters
TQ-Temporary Quarters

U
USA-United States Army
USAF-United States Air Force
USCG-United States Coast Guard

U
USEUCOM-U.S. European Command
USMA-U.S. Military Academy
USMC-United States Marine Corps
USMRA-United States Military Road Atlas
USN-United States Navy

V
VA-Veterans Administration
VAQ-Visiting Airmen's Quarters
VEQ-Visiting Enlisted Quarters
VHA-Variable Housing Allowance
VOQ-Visiting Officers' Quarters
VQ-Visiting Quarters, all ranks

APPENDIX C

DEFENSE BASE CLOSURE AND REALIGNMENT STATUS

The first Department of Defense domestic (United States and Possessions) base closure actions since the 1960's was authorized in October 1988, when the Congress enacted Public Law 100-526 which created the Secretary of Defense Commission on Base Realignment and Closure (BRAC). In 1990 Congress created an independent five-year Defense Base Closure and Realignment Commission with the passage of Public Law (PL) 101-510 under Title XXIX. The amendment of PL 101-510 provides for the Defense Base Closure and Realignment Commission to meet in 1991, 1993 and 1995. The findings of the 1991, 1993 and 1995 commissions have been finalized in public law as reported to the DoD and the Congress. We have Listed below the bases which are remaining for closure and the scheduled dates of the closure. Bases which have been previously closed are not listed. We have only reported below on bases which have significant base support facilities and the related loss of support services for all military members and their families.

ALABAMA
Fort McClellan - No closure date has been established.

ALASKA
Adak Naval Air Facility - No closure date has been established.

ARKANSAS
Fort Chaffee - October 1997.

CALIFORNIA
Alameda Naval Air Station - March 1997.
El Toro MCAS - December 1999.
Long Beach Naval Shipyard - September 1997.
McClellan Air Force Base - No closure date has been established.
Moffett Federal Airfield NASA/AMES - No closure date has been established.
Novato-Department of Defense Housing Facility - No closure date has been established.
Oakland Army Base - No closure date has been established.

CALIFORNIA

Oakland Fleet & Industrial Supply Center - February 1998.
San Diego Naval Training Center - April 1997.
Stockton Naval Communications Station - No closure date has been established.
Treasure Island Naval Station - September 1997.
Tustin Marine Corps Air Station - December 1997.

COLORADO

Fitzsimons Army Medical Center - No closure date has been established.
La Junta Air Force Station - July 1996.
Pueblo Depot Activity - No closure date has been established.

FLORIDA

Cecil Field Naval Air Station - September 1998.
Orlando Naval Training Center - December 1998.

HAWAII

Barbers Point Naval Air Station - July 1999.

ILLINOIS

O'Hare Air Reserve Station - July 1997.

MARYLAND

Fort Ritchie - No closure date has been established.

MASSACHUSETTS

South Weymouth Naval Air Station - September 1996.

NEW JERSEY

Bayonne Military Ocean Terminal - Scheduled to close in 1998.

NEW YORK
Fort Totten - No closure date has been established.
Roslyn Air National Guard Station - No closure date has been established.
Seneca Army Depot - No closure date has been established.

OHIO
Newark Air Force Base - September 1996.

PENNSYLVANIA
Defense Personnel Support Center - June 1999.
Fort Indiantown Gap - October 1998.
Letterkenny Army Depot - No closure date has been established.
Warminster Naval Air Warfare Center - July 1996.

TEXAS
Dallas Naval Air Station - December 1996.
Reese Air Force Base - September 1997.

UTAH
Ogden Defense Depot - Scheduled to close in 1997.

VIRGINIA
Fort Pickett - September 1996.
Vint Hill Farms - Station September 1997.

WAKE ISLAND
Wake Island Air Force Base - Scheduled to close after the environmental clean up work is completed.

PANAMA
Panama Canal Naval Station - December 1999.

APPENDIX D

United Services Organization

The USO is a civilian, volunteer, nonprofit organization supported solely by private contributions. For 50 years, USO has exclusively served the human needs of military personnel and their families worldwide.

We have listed the USO's in the United States and U.S. Possessions. Uniformed Services can enjoy the following USO services provided at centers around the world.

Airport Centers: USO's 36 Airport Centers worldwide help military personnel and their families with travel connections, hotel arrangements, missing luggage and language difficulties. And they provide a place to relax between flights.

Fleet Centers: At 40 ports worldwide, USO assists Navy and Marine personnel and their visiting families with information on hotels and travel, currency exchange, telephones, local information and more.

Family and Community Centers: These centers provide access to information on day care, budgeting, housing, jobs and emergency assistance, as well as constructive recreational opportunities and a place to meet new friends.

Orientation and Intercultural Programs: USO provides education programs on language, history, tourism and culture to help military families adjust to new surroundings, and fosters interaction with host communities.

Celebrity Entertainment: USO tours entertain, uplift morale and reinforce ties to home and country—for those serving our country overseas. This long standing tradition continues today as top entertainers volunteer to perform for the U.S. military in remote locations around the world.

CALIFORNIA

Bob Hope USO of
Greater Los Angeles Area, Inc.
Fort MacArthur
2400 Pacific Ave., #403
San Pedro, CA 90731
(310) 514-3465
Fax: (310) 514-2709

USO-LAX Gen. James H.
"Jimmy" Doolittle Airport Lounge
Los Angeles IAP
400 World Way, Terminal #4
Los Angeles, CA 90045
(310) 642-0188
Fax: (310) 642-1903

Bob Hope Barstow USO
220 E. Buena Vista
Barstow, CA 92311
(619) 256-0102

Outreach Center
512 Barstow Road
Barstow, CA 92311
(619) 256-1735

USO of Northern. California, Inc.,
Naval Station
Treasure Island
San Francisco, CA 94130
(415) 391-1657
Fax: (415) 391-2610

USO of Orange County
23421 S. Pointe Drive
Suite 140
Laguna Hills, CA 92653
(714) 581-7807
Fax: (714) 588-9908

San Francisco International Airport USO
Mezzanine, South Terminal
San Francisco, CA 94128
(415) 761-4611
Fax: (415) 742-6747

San Jose International Airport USO
Terminal C
1661 Airport Blvd.
San Jose, CA 95110-1285
(408) 288-7603
Fax: (408) 288-7621

Travis Air Force Base USO
AMC Passenger Terminal
P.O. Box 1663
Travis AFB, CA 94535
(707) 424-3316
Fax: (707) 437-9430

USO San Diego
303 A Street
San Diego, CA 92101-1040
(619) 296-3192

USO Airport Center/
West Terminal
3707 N. Harbor Drive., #119
San Diego, CA 92101-1040
(619) 296-3192

COLORADO

USO of Pikes Peak Region, Inc.
The Downtown Center
201 N. Nevada Avenue
P.O. Box 1694
Colorado Springs, CO 80901
(719) 471-9790
Fax: (719) 471-1723

USO Airport Information Desk
Colorado Springs Municipal Airport
5750 E. Fountain Blvd.
Colorado Springs, CO 80916
(719) 574-9626

USO Outreach Center
The Meadow Park Community Center
1939 S. El Paso
Colorado Springs, CO 80906
(719) 471-9790

COLORADO

USO Outreach Center
Deerfield Hills Community Center
4290 Deerfield Hills Rd.
Colorado Springs, CO 80916
(719) 471-9790

DELAWARE

USO Delaware
500 Eagle Way, East Wing
Dover AFB, DE 19902-7507
(302) 677-2491 Administration
(302) 677-6905 Lounge
Fax: (302) 677-2982

DISTRICT OF COLUMBIA

USO World Headquarters
Washington Navy Yard
901 M Street, Bldg 198
Washington, DC 20374-5096
(202) 610-5700

National Airport
Interim Terminal
Washington, D.C. 20001
(703) 419-7705

National Airport
Main Terminal
Washington, D.C. 20001
(703) 419-3990

FLORIDA

USO Council of Dade County Inc.
Miami International Airport
Fourth Level, Concourse B
P.O. Box 900940
Miami, FL 33159

Homestead USO
(305) 248-5074 Administrationi
(305) 876-7585 Lounge
(305) 246 5072
Homestead, FL 33090-0940

Greater Jacksonville Area USO, Inc.
Building #1050
P.O. Box 108
NAS Jacksonville, FL 32212
(904) 778-2821
Fax: (904) 772-5214

USO Center of Jacksonville
2560 Mayport Rd.
Atlantic Beach, FL 32233
(904) 246-3481
Fax: (904) 241-0463

USO of Central Florida, Inc.
(Mailing address for all
USO Orlando locations)
P.O. Box 149472
Orlando, FL 32814
(407) 647-2241
Fax: (407) 647-2563

Brig. Emil B. Miller USO
Airport Lounge
Landside,"A" Third Level
Orlando International Airport
9263 Airport Blvd.
Orlando, FL 32827
(407) 855-7192

Mary Boutwell USO
Building #2008
Naval Training Center
Orlando, FL 32813
(407) 647-0407/2241

USO of Greater Pensacola Area, Inc.
Administrative Office
NAS Pensacola, Bldg 3813
P.O. Box 4321
Pensacola, FL 32507-0321
(904) 455-1064
Fax:(904)-455-1064

USO Airport Center
Penscola Regional Airport
Pensacola, FL 32504
(904) 433-2475

FLORIDA

USO of St. Augustine & St. Johns
Counties, Florida
Lightner Building
(City Building)
P.O. Box 4
St. Augustine, FL 32084
Fax: (904) 7728-5214
(Jacksonville office fax)

GEORGIA

USO Georgia, Inc., Admin Offices
P.O. Box 20963
Atlanta, GA 30320
(404) 761-8061
Fax: (404) 765-1794

USO Hartsfield International Airport
North Terminal, International Concourse
Atlanta, GA 30320
(404) 761-8061 Fax: (404) 765-1794

USO Warner Robins
Outreach
Robins AFB
Smith Recreation Center
Warner Robins, GA 31099
(912) 926-2105/2945

HAWAII

USO of Hawaii Inc.
Airport Center-Honolulu IAP
300 Rodgers Blvd., #48
Honolulu, HI 96819-1897
(808) 836-3351
Fax: (808) 833-2012

USO Hickam AMC Center
Hickam AFB
AMC Terminal, Second floor
Hickam AFB, HI 96853
(808) 449-2887

ILLINOIS

USO of Illinois, Inc.
332 N. Michigan Ave.
Chicago, IL 60601
(312) 781-0730
Fax: (312) 781-0740

O' Hare USO Center
O'Hare IAP
P.O. Box 66434
Chicago, IL 60666
(312) 686-7396

Midway USO Center
Midway Airport
5700 S. Cicero Ave.
Chicago, IL 60638
(312) 582-5852

Great Lakes USO
Great Lakes Naval Training Center
Building #27
P.O. Box 886935
Great Lakes, IL 60088
(708) 688-5591

INDIANA

USO Council of Indianapolis Inc.
Indianapolis IAP
N. Pennsylvania St., #600
Indianapolis, IN 46204
(317) 241-6070

KENTUCKY

USO of Kentucky Inc.
P.O. Box 34
Fort Knox, KY 40121
(502) 624-6800

USO Jerry Frost Airport Center
Louisville IAP
(502) 361-1888

MARYLAND

Indian Head Family Support Services
USO/Joint Services Support Center
Building #13, Riverview Village
Naval Surface Warfare Center
Indian Head, MD 20640
(301) 743-5180/753-5650

Andrews AFB
Air Terminal
(301) 981-2525

BWI Airport
Main Terminal
(410) 859-4425

MASSACHUSETTS

USO Council of New England
U.S. Coast Guard Support Center
427 Commercial Street
Bldg 8, Second deck
Boston, MA 02109-1027
(617) 720-4949
Fax: (617) 720-0982

Sgt. Maj. Frederick B. Douglass
USO Airport Center
Logan IAP
Boston, MA 02128
(Call USO Council of NE for
location and details)

USO of Pioneer Valley
1820 Seawolf Ave.
Westover ARB
Chicopee, MA 01022
(413) 593-6395
Fax: (413) 593-6397

MISSOURI

James S. McDonnell USO Inc.
P.O. Box 10367
Lambert St. Louis IAP
St. Louis, MO 63145
(314) 429-1234/7702
Fax: (314) 429-0506

NEW YORK

USO of Metropolitan New York Inc.
151 West 46th St., Ninth Floor
New York, NY 10036
(212) 719-5433
Fax: (212) 730-0870

USO General Douglas MacArthur
Memorial Center
151 West 46th St., Third Floor
New York, NY 10036
(212) 719-2364

NY USO Airport Centers
Delta Flight Center
TWA, Inc.
John F. Kennedy IAP
Domestic Arrivals Area
Bldg #58
Jamaica, NY 11430
(718) 995-5539

USO Fort Hamilton Center
Building #113
New York Area Command
Fort Hamilton
Brooklyn, NY 11252
(718) 630-4179

USO Council of Watertown
and Jefferson County
P.O. Box 912
Watertown, NY 13601
(315) 782-3082

NORTH CAROLINA

USO Council of Jacksonville
Camp Lejuene Area, Inc.
9 Tallman Street
Jacksonville, NC 28540-4846
(910) 455-3411
Fax: (910) 455-1341

OHIO

USO Council of Central
Ohio, Inc. - Lounge
Port Columbus IAP
4600 International Gateway
Columbus, OH 43219
(614) 231-7300

USO of Central Ohio
125 Fairway Blvd
Box 13268
Whitehall, OH 43213
(614) 759-8690
Fax: (614) 863-5348

MEPS USO Lounge
3333 Indianola Ave
Columbus, OH 43214
(614) 262-3044

USO of Northern Ohio
MEPS Center
1240 East Ninth Street,
Room 1503-B
Cleveland, OH 44199
(216) 621-4120
Fax: (216) 621-4316

USO Airport Center
Cleveland Hopkins IAP
Baggage Claim Level
Riverside Drive
Brook Park, OH 44135
(216) 433-7313

PENNSYLVANIA

USO of Philadelphia Airport
Center & Admin. Offices
Philadelphia IAP
Terminal D
Philadelphia, PA 19153
(215) 365-8889
Fax: (215) 365-0249

SOUTH CAROLINA

USO Charleston Airport Center
& Administrative Offices
Charleston IAP
5500 International Blvd., Suite 120
Charleston, SC 29418-6922
(803) 767-3963

TENNESSEE

USO of Metropolitan Memphis
and Shelby County
7918 Church Street
P.O. Box 907
Millington, TN 38083-0907
(901) 872-7722
Fax: (901) 872-7330

TEXAS

USO Greater Houston, Inc.
2700 Southwest Freeway
Houston, TX 77098
(713) 526-8300 ext 554
Fax: (713) 528-2422
Mailing Address
P.O. Box 397
Houston, TX 77001-0397

Houston Intercontinental Airport
Lt. Col. Robert L. Smith USO Center
Terminal C, North Concourse
(713) 443-2451

Houston Hobby Airport Center
Lower Level
Houston, TX
(713) 644-1131

USO Council of San Antonio
and Central Texas
420 East Commerce St.
San Antonio, TX 78205
(210) 227-9373
Fax: (210) 299-4435

TEXAS

USO of South Texas Inc.
Bldg 3 Naval Air Station
Corpus Christi, TX 78419
(512) 939-4165
Fax: (512) 939-2391

USO of South Texas,
Ingleside Center
USO Naval Station
Ingleside, TX 78362-5031
(512) 776-4778/79
Fax: (512) 776-4778/79

VIRGINIA

USO of Metro Washington
Bldg. #59, Post HQ
Room #B-9
Ft. Myer, VA 22211
(703) 696-2628/29
Fax: (703) 696-2550

Family Programs Office
Bldg. 59, Post HQ, Room B-12
Ft. Myer, VA 22211
(703) 696-3279/2552

Tencza Terrace
Family Support Center
Tencza Terrace Bldg. 501
Ft. Myer, VA 22211
(703) 696-3479

Woodbridge Run
Family Support Services
Community Center
1400 Eisenhower Circle
Woodbridge, VA 22191
(703) 494-5576

Fort Belvoir Family Support Services
Bldg. 200
SOSA Community Center
Ft. Belvoir, VA 22060
(703) 805-2464 ITR Office 2654

USO of Hampton Roads, Inc.
P.O. Box 7250
Hampton, VA 23666
Packages: Coliseum Mall,
Entrance A
1800 W. Mercury Blvd.
Hampton, VA 23666
(804) 827-1063
Fax: (804) 827-9020

NAS Norfolk, (AMC Terminal)
Building #LP-84
Norfolk, VA 23511-6691
(804) 440-0939

USO Fort Eustis
MWR Leisure Center
Bldg 671
Fort Eustis, VA 23604
(804) 878-2415/2407

Huntington Hall BEQ
Newport News Shipbuilding
3100 Huntington Ave.
Newport News, VA 23607
(804) 928-0801

Raymond B. Bottom USO
Newport News/
Williamsburg IAP
Newport News, VA 23602
(804) 988-0017

USOGRAM Norfolk
Bldg U115
West D Street
Norfolk Naval Air Station
Norfolk, VA 23511
(804) 440-2916

WASHINGTON

Admiral James S. Russell
USO Center
Main Terminal, Second floor
SeaTac IAP
Seattle, WA 98158
(206) 433-5438

WASHINGTON

McChord USO Center
Bldg 1183
McChord AFB
(206) 984-2400

USO Puget Sound Area
Administrative Office
Main Terminal, Second floor
Sea-Tac IAP
Seattle, WA 98158
(206) 246-1908
Fax: (206) 246-1914

WISCONSIN

USO Council of Wisconsin
South Eastern Region Inc.
War Memorial Center
Room 303
750 N. Lincoln Memorial Drive
Milwaukee, WI 53202
(414) 271-3133
Fax: (4140 273-1270

VIRGIN ISLANDS

St. Croix USO
114 Market Street,
P.O. Box 616
Frederiksted
St. Croix, VI 00841
(809) 772-0523

USO of St. Thomas
75 Veterans Drive
Charlotte Amalie
St. Thomas, VI 00802
(809) 774-8555

AT TIMES LIKE THIS.........

At times like this, when major changes are being made in the Uniformed Services, information on Space-A air travel, Temporary Military Lodging and Military RV, Camping and Recreation Areas can suddenly change.

If you want to be in the know before most everyone else, subscribe to **Military Living's R&R Space-A Report ®!** Breaking news will be carried in this six time yearly all ranks travel newsletter which is available by subscription only. To subscribe, see the coupons in this book or call **(703) 237-0203 for information or to order.**

CENTRAL ORDER COUPON
Military Living Publications
P.O. Box 2347, Falls Church, VA 22042-0347
TEL: (703) 237-0203 FAX: (703) 237-2233

Publications		QTY
R&R Space-A Report®. *The worldwide travel newsletter* Six issues per year. 1 yr/$15.00 - 2 yrs/$24.00 - 3 yrs/$33.00 - 5 yrs/$49.00		
Military Space-A Air Basic Training.	$13.95	
Military Space-A Air Opportunities Air Route Map.	(Folded) $13.95	
Military Space-A Air Opportunities Around the World.	$17.95	
Temporary Military Lodging Around the World.	$15.95	
Military RV, Camping & Rec Areas Around the World.	$13.95	
U.S. Forces Travel and Transfer Guide, USA and Caribbean Areas.	$13.95	
U.S. Military Museums, Historic Sites & Exhibits.	(Soft Cover) $17.95	
United States Military Road Atlas	$18.95	
U.S. Military Installation Road Map.	(Folded) $7.95	
United States Military Medical Facilities Map	(Folded) $7.95	
COLLECTOR'S ITEM! Desert Shield Commemorative Maps. (Two unfolded wall maps in a hard tube)	(Folded) $8.00 $18.00	
Assignment Washington Military Road Atlas.	$10.95	
California State Military Road Map - **Florida State Military Road Map -** **Mid-Atlantic States Military Road Map -** **Texas State Military Road Map -**	(Folded) $5.95 (Folded) $5.95 (Folded) $5.95 (Folded) $5.95	
Virginia Addresses add 4.5% sales tax (Books, Maps, & Atlases only)	**TOTAL $**	

Our America Online Address is: Mil LivRnR @ AOL.COM

*If you are an R&R Space-A Report® subscriber, you may deduct $1.00 per book. (No discount on the R&R Report itself or on the maps or atlas.) Mail Order Prices are for U.S. APO & FPO addresses. Please consult publisher for International Mail Price. Sorry, no billing.
We're as close as your telephone...by using our Telephone Ordering Service. We honor American Express, MasterCard, and VISA. Call us at **703-237-0203 (Voice Mail after hours)** or **FAX 703-237-2233** and order today! Sorry, no collect calls. Or...fill out and mail the order coupon below.

NAME:_____

STREET:_____

CITY/STATE/ZIP:_____

PHONE:_____ SIGNATURE:_____

RANK (or rank of sponsor):_____ Branch Of Service:_____

Active Duty:_ Retired:_ Widow/er:_ 100% Disabled Veteran:_ Guard:_ Reservist:_ Other:_

Card # _____ Card Expiration Date:_____

Mail check/money order to Military Living Publications, P.O. Box 2347, Falls Church, VA 22042-0347 - **Tel: 703-237-0203 - FAX: 703-237-2233.**

Save $$$s by purchasing any of our books, Maps, and Atlases at your military Exchange.

Prices subject to change. Please check here if we may ship and bill difference. ☐

U.S. FORCES TRAVEL & TRANSFER GUIDE U.S.A. - 357

MILITARY Living ™

Where the fun begins ™

HAVING A RETIREE DAY OR PRE-RETIREMENT BRIEFING?

Let **Military Living** ™ help make your big day a success!

Retirees are anxious to know more about flying Space-A on U.S. military aircraft. Military Living Publications is well-known as being a leading authority on military recreation and Space-A air travel.

Military Living ™ **will send your Retiree Activity Office complimentary sample copies of Military Living's *R&R Space-A Report* ® and door prizes to give away at the Retiree Day. We can also provide materials for your Pre-Retirement Briefings.**

To participate in Military Living's ™ **Retiree Day Program**, simply have your Retiree Activity Office to write or fax us on the office letterhead giving the date and time of the next retiree day. A name of the Retiree Office contact and phone number are also necessary. We must have a street address of the Retiree Activity office in order to send the publications by United Parcel Service. We also need to know how many people attended last year and the expected number for this year.

It would be greatly appreciated if you would include the participation of Military Living in advance publicity in order to let your retirees know that they should look for our publications at the Retiree Day.

As it is costly for our small business to supply the Retiree Day door prizes and copies of Military Living's *R&R Space-A Report* ®, we ask that if there are any leftovers of the newsletter, that you return them to your retiree activity office to give to visitors to your office. Please honor our copyright by **not** making copies of the *R&R Space-A Report* ®. We would appreciate your sending us a copy of your retiree newsletter if there is one being published.

Thanks to all of you who help military retirees so much!

Ann, Roy, and RJ Crawford
Publishers, Military Living Publications
PO Box 2347, Falls Church, VA 22042-0347
Phone (703) 237-0203; FAX (703) 237-2233

CENTRAL ORDER COUPON
Military Living Publications
P.O. Box 2347, Falls Church, VA 22042-0347
TEL: (703) 237-0203 FAX: (703) 237-2233

Publications		QTY
R&R Space-A Report®. *The worldwide travel newsletter* Six issues per year. 1 yr/$15.00 - 2 yrs/$24.00 - 3 yrs/$33.00 - 5 yrs/$49.00		
Military Space-A Air Basic Training.	$13.95	
Military Space-A Air Opportunities Air Route Map.	(Folded) $13.95	
Military Space-A Air Opportunities Around the World.	$17.95	
Temporary Military Lodging Around the World.	$15.95	
Military RV, Camping & Rec Areas Around the World.	$13.95	
U.S. Forces Travel and Transfer Guide, USA and Caribbean Areas.	$13.95	
U.S. Military Museums, Historic Sites & Exhibits.	(Soft Cover) $17.95	
United States Military Road Atlas	$18.95	
U.S. Military Installation Road Map.	(Folded) $7.95	
United States Military Medical Facilities Map	(Folded) $7.95	
COLLECTOR'S ITEM! Desert Shield Commemorative Maps. (Folded) $8.00 (Two unfolded wall maps in a hard tube) $18.00		
Assignment Washington Military Road Atlas.	$10.95	
California State Military Road Map - **Florida State Military Road Map -** **Mid-Atlantic States Military Road Map -** **Texas State Military Road Map -**	(Folded) $5.95 (Folded) $5.95 (Folded) $5.95 (Folded) $5.95	
Virginia Addresses add 4.5% sales tax (Books, Maps, & Atlases only) **TOTAL**		$

Our America Online Address is: Mil LivRnR @ AOL.COM

*If you are an R&R Space-A Report® subscriber, you may deduct $1.00 per book. (No discount on the R&R Report itself or on the maps or atlas.) Mail Order Prices are for U.S. APO & FPO addresses. Please consult publisher for International Mail Price. Sorry, no billing.

We're as close as your telephone...by using our Telephone Ordering Service. We honor American Express, MasterCard, and VISA. Call us at **703-237-0203 (Voice Mail after hours)** or **FAX 703-237-2233** and order today! Sorry, no collect calls. Or...fill out and mail the order coupon below.

NAME:_____

STREET:_____

CITY/STATE/ZIP:_____

PHONE:_____ SIGNATURE:_____

RANK (or rank of sponsor):_____ Branch Of Service:_____

Active Duty:_Retired:_Widow/er:_100% Disabled Veteran:_Guard:_Reservist:_Other:

Card # _____ Card Expiration Date:_____

Mail check/money order to Military Living Publications, P.O. Box 2347, Falls Church, VA 22042-0347 - **Tel: 703-237-0203 - FAX: 703-237-2233.**

Save $$$s by purchasing any of our books, Maps, and Atlases at your military Exchange.

Prices subject to change. Please check here if we may ship and bill difference. ☐

How Long Has It Been Since YOU Flew Space-A??

Whether the answer is NEVER or a year or so ago, you may find our book, Military Space-A Air Basic Training™ *to* be of great help. Numerous rules have changed in Space-A travel -in fact, this fringe benefit has gotten even better and more user-friendly than ever before! This is the **"HOW TO DO IT BOOK ON FLYING SPACE-A"**.

How to Go About Space-A Air Travel Step by Step

Our Space-A Basic Training book has:

• Helpful letters from military personnel, active, retired, Guard and Reserve.

• Detailed conversion and documentation charts.

• Latest Space-A rules, necessary forms and FAX numbers.

• Sample trips for active, retired, Guard and Reserve.

Look for Military Living's *Space-A Air Basic Training*™ at your military exchange, or order from Military Living Publications by phone with Visa, MasterCard or American Express. Phone **(703) 237-0203**. Mail orders - PO Box 2347, Falls Church, VA 22042-0347. The cost is $13.95 including our first class service.

360 - U.S. FORCES TRAVEL & TRANSFER GUIDE U.S.A

MILITARY Living's™

Brief Description of our money-saving Publications

MILITARY TRAVEL BOOKS

Military Space-A Air Opportunities Around the World™ - An in-depth and advanced book detailing more than 300 military air terminal of all services around the world. Departure installations & destinations are given complete with addresses, phone and fax numbers, flight schedules with routing frequency and MUCH more.

Military Space-A Air Basic Training & Reader Trip Reports™ - This is the first "How to do it" book on flying Space-A. The new edition will help those who have never flown Space-A air or those who have not flown recently and are not acquainted with the many new rules. Includes the new DoD Space-A regulations. This basic book is necessary for optimizing your Space-A air Travel.

Temporary Military Lodging Around The World™ (TML) - Our all-time best seller! Detailed information is given on more than 400 military installations offering transient lodging for all ranks. Includes all types of worldwide lodging such as guest houses, transient living quarters, Navy Lodges, BOQs, larger rec areas, etc. Has description of TML, key addresses & phone numbers so necessary for a successful trip.

Military RV, Camping & Rec Areas Around The World™ - You don't have to sleep in a pup tent to enjoy this book. Many rec areas listed have lodging in the form of cottages, A-frames, log cabins, etc. - plus the U.S. military recreation areas like the ones in Hawaii, Korea, Germany and on Walt Disney® World Resort, are included. Of course, the book has complete information on camping & RV areas.

U.S. Forces Travel & Transfer Guide USA & Caribbean Areas™ - This has all the information of all the items listed above - but not in as much detail. Golf courses and other recreational facilities are noted as well as medical facilities & other needed services on a military installation.

MILITARY TRAVEL ATLASES

United States Military Road Atlas™ - You see the military installations first! In fact, the almost jump off the page of each state and possession map. Also features 36 city maps with large military populations. Includes nearly 600 military installations. Addresses, phone numbers, special military travel appendices, mileage charts and more.

Assignment Washington Military Road Atlas™ - Maps & charts of greater Washington Area Military Installations. This Atlas helps make shopping at military facilities a breeze. Before you head out to the beltway, check out our atlas first!

MILITARY TRAVEL MAPS

Military Space-A Air Route Map™
U.S. Military Installation Road Map™
Mid-Atlantic U.S. Road Map™
Texas State Military Road Map™

U.S. Military Medical Facilities Map™
Desert Shield Commemorative Maps™
Florida State Military Road Map™
California State Military Road Map™

See order coupons on pages 356 & 358, or phone using the number on the back cover.